Mapping Goffman's Invisible College

Mapping Goffman's Invisible College

by
Wendy Leeds-Hurwitz

media
studies.
press

Mapping Goffman's Invisible College

by Wendy Leeds-Hurwitz

Published by:
mediastudies.press
414 W. Broad St.
Bethlehem, PA 18018, USA

Copy-editing: Emily Alexander

Cover design: Yan Qiu/Natascha Chtena

Landing page: mediastudies.press/mapping-goffman

Goffman in the Open series

isbn 978-1-951399-38-2 *(print)* | isbn 978-1-951399-34-4 *(pdf)*

isbn 978-1-951399-37-5 *(epub)* | isbn 978-1-951399-35-1 *(html)*

doi 10.64629/3f8575cb.dwb73w6d | lccn 2025939788

Edition 1 published in August 2025

Contents

Acknowledgments

My thanks to Yves Winkin for extended conversations about the content of this book, and not one but two helpful critical reviews. Other colleagues who answered questions about specific issues include Greg Smith, Philippe Vienne, Stuart Sigman, Jaime Duncan, Nancy Hornberger, Regna Darnell, Mary Hufford, Alice Kehoe, Fred Erickson, Harvey Sarles, and Phillip Guddemi. Robert Kleck graciously shared information about the conference he organized with Goffman's help in 1969 since there is virtually no documentation publicly available. Lorenza Mondada extended considerable effort in trying to help me locate further information about a grant proposal from the 1970s involving Goffman. Two blind reviewers helped provide an outside perspective, and useful suggestions, as did Dave Park, on behalf of mediastudies.press. And when it was all written, Emily Alex, the copyeditor for mediastudies.press, helped with a review of the writing and formatting, making the book stronger and more consistent; Jeff Pooley turned it from a manuscript into a book; Yan Qiu designed the front cover; and Natascha Chtena turned that into a front/back/spine final cover.

Thanks especially to Timothy Horning, but also Joseph-James Ahern at the University Archives and Records Center, as well as Alessandro Pezzati at the Penn Museum Archives, all at the University of Pennsylvania, for their substantial help in locating relevant materials; Tim went above and beyond to answer questions over the last several years. Thanks to Paul Sutherland at the American Philosophical Society, especially for letting me read files from the Hymes Papers still being catalogued and so not yet officially accessible on my first visit. Half a dozen others at APS helped me on several visits to access materials I needed; I did not get everyone's names but still appreciate their efforts. Mark Mahoney at Wenner-Gren Foundation; Alicia Gonzalez at New Mexico State University; Dean Smith at the Bancroft Library of the University of California, Berkeley; Aaron Lisec at the Southern Illinois

University Special Collections Research Center; Stephanie Krauss at the Center for the History of Medicine at Harvard University; Sarah Wharton for the Harvard Law School Library; Sydnie Martin, Alexa Tulk, and Christine Colburn at the Hanna Holborn Gray Special Collections Research Center at the University of Chicago Library; Barbara Truesdell and Maesa Ogas at the Indiana University Center for Documentary Research and Practice; Carrie Schwier at the Indiana University Archives; Julia Dudley and Coral Silver at the Special Collections Research Center at Syracuse University; and Joseph Diaz and Erika Castaño at the University of Arizona archives all helped me access additional archival collections relevant to this project and their help is also much appreciated. Dan Drollette Jr., Executive Editor of the *Bulletin of the Atomic Scientists*, located an early essay published in that journal. Hartmut Mokros helped me track down an elusive article in *Raritan Quarterly*; Julie Meidlinger supplied a copy.

An early version of what has turned into chapters 3 and 4 was presented as "Erving Goffman's 'Invisible College' at the University of Pennsylvania" to the Seminário Internacional "100 anos de Erving Goffman" [International seminar: 100 years of Erving Goffman] at the Universidade de Brasília, Brazil, on September 20, 2022, now published in Portuguese (Leeds-Hurwitz, 2024). My thanks to Édison Gastaldo, Gustavo Cunha, and Carlos Benedito Martins for the initial invitation and for giving me the rights to publish in English.

Abbreviations

I have consulted a wide variety of archival collections around the United States in preparing this book. The following abbreviations are used when these collections are cited in the text:

AD – Alan Dundes Papers, BANC MSS 2007/115, The Bancroft Library, University of California, Berkeley, CA.

ADG – Allen D. Grimshaw Papers, Collection C480, Indiana University Archives, Bloomington, IN.

AFCW – Anthony F. C. Wallace Papers 1920–2000, Mss.Ms.Coll.64a, Series I, Correspondence: Goffman, Erving, 1967, American Philosophical Society Library & Museum, Philadelphia, PA.

DS – David Schneider Papers [box 14, folder 6], Special Collections Research Center, University of Chicago Library, Chicago, IL.

ECH – Everett Cherrington Hughes Papers [box 28, folder 7–8], Special Collections Research Center, University of Chicago Library, Chicago, IL.

ETH – Edward Twitchell Hall papers (MS 196), Series I: Correspondence 1930–1979 [box 5 folder 19], Goffman, Erving, Special Collections, University of Arizona Libraries, Tucson, AZ.

HDD – Hugh Dalziel Duncan Papers, Special Collections Research Center, Morris Library, Southern Illinois University, Carbondale, IL.

HG – Henry Glassie, interview by Barbara Truesdell, March 13, April 4, April 24, April 30, May 7, May 10, May 29, June 6, 2007, Indiana University Center for Documentary Research and Practice, #07-001, Bloomington, IN.

HTP – Horowitz Transaction Publishers Archives, Editorial and scholarly correspondence (1958–), Pennsylvania State University Archives, University Park, PA.

JLM – Jacob L. Moreno Papers, B MS C66, Center for the History of Medicine at Harvard University, Cambridge, MA.

LLF – Lon L. Fuller Papers [box 3, folder 12], Historical and Special Collections, Harvard Law School Library, Boston, MA.

MK – Mike Keen Papers [box 7, folder 7], Special Collections Research Center, University of Chicago Library, Chicago, IL.

OP – Office of the President Records, Martin Meyerson Administration, UPA4, Faculty of Arts and Sciences, Departments, Folklore/Folklore Department, University Archives and Records Center, University of Pennsylvania, Philadelphia, PA.

RB – Richard Bauman Papers, Collection C342, Indiana University Archives, Bloomington, IN.

RED – Robert E. Davies Papers, UPT50 D255, Benjamin Franklin Professorships [box 3, folders 27–29], University Archives and Records Center, University of Pennsylvania, Philadelphia, PA.

SW – Sol Worth Papers, UPT50 W933, University Archives and Records Center, University of Pennsylvania, Philadelphia, PA.

TS – Thomas Sebeok Papers, Correspondence and subject files, 1940–2001, Goffman, Erving, 1970–1980, Indiana University Archives, Bloomington, IN.

TSz – Thomas Szasz Papers [box 24], Special Collections Research Center, Syracuse University Libraries, Syracuse, NY.

UCOP – University of Chicago Office of the President, Gray Administration Records [box 72, folder 31], Hanna Holborn Gray Special Collections Research Center, University of Chicago Library, Chicago, IL.

UR – University Relations, News and Public Affairs Records, Biographical Files, UPF 8.5B, University Archives and Records Center, University of Pennsylvania, Philadelphia, PA.

The single most important source has been the Hymes Papers at the American Philosophical Society, where there were so many relevant documents from various parts of that collection cited that longer citations are required if anyone else is ever to retrieve the same letters, so these appear in notes rather than in the text. The full citation to that collection is:

DHH – Dell H. Hymes Papers, Mss.Ms.Coll.55, American Philosophical Society Library & Museum, Philadelphia, PA.

Reading the same long names and titles over and over can become tedious. The following are abbreviations for organizations, projects, or institutions mentioned in the book:

AAA – American Anthropological Association

AACC – Association for the Aid of Crippled Children

AFS – American Folklore Society

ASA – American Sociological Association

ASB – Center for the Study of Art and Symbolic Behavior

ASC – Annenberg School of Communications (until 1990); Annenberg School for Communication (after 1990)

CAE – Council on Anthropology and Education

CC – Conduct and Communication

CCC – Codes in Context conference

CCCC – Cross-Cultural Communication Center

CFE – Center for Folklore and Ethnography

CUE – Center for Urban Ethnography

CUP – Cambridge University Press

EERF – Ethnography in Education Research Forum

ERG – Ethnographic Research Group

EPPI – Eastern Pennsylvania Psychiatric Institute

GSE – Graduate School of Education, University of Pennsylvania

IJSL – *International Journal of the Sociology of Language*

LCS – Interdisciplinary Program in Language, Culture, and Society

LII – Language and Interaction Institute

LiS – *Language in Society*

LSA – Linguistic Society of America

MAP – Multiple Analysis Project

NEH – National Endowment for the Humanities

NHI – *The Natural History of an Interview*

NICHD – National Institute for Child Health and Human Development

NIE – National Institute of Education

NIH – National Institutes of Health

NIMH – National Institute of Mental Health

NSF – National Science Foundation

SAA – Southwestern Anthropological Association

SAVICOM – *Studies in the Anthropology of Visual Communication*

SEDL – Southwest Educational Development Laboratory

SP – Semiotic Program

SSB – Interdisciplinary Program in the Science of Symbolic Behavior

SSRC – Social Science Research Council

List of Tables and Figures

CHAPTER ONE

Introduction

Erving Goffman (1922–1982), trained as a sociologist, was an important theorist of social interaction. My focus in this book, however, will not be on his ideas; those have already been the subject of a significant number of works,[1] and so I will take for granted that most readers are at least generally familiar with his ideas. Instead, this book will be about the *context* of his ideas: the groups where an overlapping set of ideas were discussed, the projects where they were worked out, and what turns out to be necessary to encourage the development of new ideas. My focus will be on multi- and interdisciplinary groups because Goffman spent far more time with those in other disciplines than his own original home of sociology. Ideas do not respect disciplinary boundaries, so those looking to create new ideas often ignore them as well. Since Goffman was part of a surprising number of projects with colleagues from multiple disciplines during his years at the University of Pennsylvania (1968–1982), and since very few of these have been examined to date, my focus will be on that time and that place. Thus, half of the chapters in this book will describe people and projects across his years at the University of Pennsylvania (always called Penn by those affiliated with it),[2] and the other half will describe an overlapping set of people and projects based elsewhere. Dell Hymes has pointed out that "the relevant past of our field is not a known terrain to which one can be given a packaged tour. Each scholar is a personal vantage point, and so the terrain must be explored afresh by each, who must make his or her own map, find his or her own way, inheritance and epiphanies" (1983a, xix). In keeping with this perspective, these pages document the map I have constructed for Goffman and his network of colleagues, on the assumption that it may serve as a useful starting point for others.

In his early work on theory groups, Mullins describes the significance of a *cluster*: "Clusters of students and colleagues form around the key figures in a group in one or a few institutions" and "A cluster generally includes three or more professionals (i.e., possessors of the PhD degree), who reinforce one another's interests, and several graduate students" (1973, 22–23). In his work building upon and expanding Mullins, Murray argues that "over the course of their careers, most scientists are never involved in groups advancing new theoretical perspectives" (1994, 486). So, it is noteworthy that Goffman was involved in not one, not a few, but almost a dozen projects intended to advance and/or share new theoretical perspectives just at Penn, and still more elsewhere. As such, Goffman serves as a good entry for studying the institutional context within which ideas are nurtured.

In the forty years since his death, Goffman frequently has been depicted as a "loner." To provide just a few examples, Smith says: "Goffman was a loner whose academic career consisted of a series of solo performances" (2022a, 128); Winkin says: "Goffman was a lone wolf who never built a research team" (2022a, 401); Jacobsen says: "Erving Goffman's role was that of a loner—he knew it, he pursued it and he embraced it" (2017, 225). Others agree.[3] However, the fact that he never built a research team does not mean he never participated in joint activities with colleagues, as will be demonstrated. Equally, the fact that "Goffman remained by choice an outsider to the sociology department at Penn" (Delaney 2014, 88) does not mean he was an outsider to other departments. In much the same way that Winkin (2022b) has examined the assumption that he rarely traveled and proved that to be incorrect, the myth of Goffman as loner must be subject to investigation. At least some of the explanation for this reputation is likely an artifact of researchers not having access to his papers, so his extensive correspondence with friends and colleagues has remained unread. Goffman is famous for having asked that his correspondence and other files not be made accessible, on the grounds that his work should stand on its own. This was his opinion consistently, not just at the end of his life. For example, when Irving Louis Horowitz (a sociologist at Rutgers University, and long-time friend)[4] wrote to say he had a student who wanted to write Goffman's biography, the response from Goffman was: "I feel that approaches are worth writing about but not people . . . biography strikes me as a way of reifying something that isn't worth that kind of candle. It is one thing to exploit one's social niche for all the material rewards one can draw from it. Biography strikes me by way of trying to make a virtue of that kind of opportunism, affecting piety where self-respect should dictate chagrin" (Jul 12, 1976, HTP). Clearly, other scholars have not held the same assumptions about biography, because, over the past few decades, multiple colleagues and friends have donated their papers, including considerable correspondence, to various archives. These now make it possible to recreate at least a reasonable depiction of Goffman's connections and to show him to have been far from a loner in fact, or, perhaps more carefully stated, both a loner and a colleague, just at different times and for different purposes. I agree with Murray that "more than in their publications, the 'natives' of those researching the history of social science speak for themselves in their correspondence" (1994, 499), and so have spent time reading through letters and other documentation preserved in various archives as related to Goffman's connections, most of these with a small number of particularly significant colleagues. Pooley and Park argue that "there is a great deal of untapped archival material, and as-yet unconducted oral history work, that should better inform histories of communication research" (2008, 6). I have now done some of that work for this topic, and the results are reported in the following pages. At one point I estimated that I had collected approximately two thousand letters and other unpublished documents. Clearly, these could have been supplemented by more interviews, but others have already gone that route. It has seemed more useful to take a different path and emphasize what was not yet widely known. As my focus is not Goffman's biography but the associations between scholars and their ideas that often lead to enhanced results, hopefully he would have approved. I am not looking to illuminate his personality, or major events in his life in these pages, but rather to explore at least some of the research-related collaborative efforts in which he participated. There is a distinction between biography (a genre which focuses on the events in an individual's life) and intellectual biography (a genre which focuses on an individual's work, and the context in which it was carried out). Emphasis on such topics as the institutions with which a scholar was affiliated, and the interactions with other people sharing overlapping interests, play an important role in an intellectual biography, even if they would be minor points in a more traditional, event-centered, individual biography. This book, then, is a contribution to Goffman's intellectual biography.

One important lesson made clear here is that most scholars are far more productive when they work with others rather than alone, sharing ideas prior to publication rather than only after, pushing one another to achieve new insights. "People develop ideas . . . so it is impossible to study ideas without also considering the people who invent them and elaborate upon them" (Leeds-Hurwitz 2021, 2). This is where the notion of an *invisible college* becomes relevant. An invisible college refers to connections between scholars whose ties are not evident to outsiders. The likely earliest use of the term referred to members of the Royal Society of London in the 1700s, who were close geographically, and shared scientific interests, but not an institutional affiliation (Lingwood 1969). De Sola Price (1963) expanded this to describe long-distance affiliations, and this version, as popularized by Crane (1972), is the one most often assumed by disciplinary historians today. An obvious example involves graduate students at one university who then move to new locations upon completing their degrees and taking academic positions in different locations, so that someone who does not know of their time as students together may be confused by their association— this is why it appears invisible. Lievrouw recommends a distance-neutral definition, "a set of informal communication relations among scientists or other scholars who share a specific common interest or goal," which will serve well here (1989, 622). The key element is thus multiple people who share interests without those commonalities being immediately evident to others. One way in which such connections become obvious is in citations, and so investigating who has been cited in various publications helps to make what is otherwise invisible visible. As Murray pointed out, "Patterns of acknowledgment and citation provide unobtrusive measures of connection, although only acknowledgments evidence social connection" (1998, 264). And so, some attention has been paid to who mentions who else in both acknowledgments and references, as well as the more obvious discussion of as yet unpublished drafts in correspondence.

Yet another element needs to be highlighted: the impact of collaboration on the creation of ideas. In her analysis of invisible colleges, Crane points out Coser's (1965) insight that "despite popular myth to the contrary, most intellectuals cannot produce their work in solitude but need the give and take of debate and discussion with their peers in order to develop their ideas. Not all intellectuals are gregarious, but most of them need to test their own ideas in exchange with those they deem their equals" (1972, 3–4). This is valuable for bringing ideas into the discussion and fits well both with what I experienced at Penn, and with what I have learned from reading correspondence and other documents housed in multiple archives. When scholars share interests but not disciplinary or departmental structures in common, new ideas frequently develop since diverse approaches to the same topic can be particularly fruitful. Joshua Fishman, well-known sociolinguist familiar with many of the scholars described in these pages, supports this, saying: "I did know that I did not want to continue to be without a community of like-minded scholars" (1997, 88). The question thus becomes: *Who did Goffman deem his own "community of like-minded scholars"?* This book provides multiple answers to that question.

By naming Goffman's connections (not only at Penn, but also at a few other universities) an invisible college, I intend to turn the concept on its side from how it has been most often used recently: He had multiple strong associations to scholars at the same university (instead of across campuses), but they were based in different disciplines and departments than his own, and thus they have often been overlooked. To those who assume affiliations within a discipline as the norm, those made across disciplinary boundaries are unexpected, unlooked for, thus invisible and ignored. Delaney says that: "[Philip] Rieff's campaign to bring Goffman to Penn, reaffirmed by Rieff himself, was met by adamant objections by several colleagues of senior rank in the sociology department" (2014, 89). But this does not mean others at Penn did not want him, or did not work hard to convince him to accept a position, as will be described in detail. The fact that Goffman spent little time with peers in sociology for most of his years at Penn (something Renée Fox changed, once she became chair of sociology), should not be taken to suggest that he did not spend time with colleagues in other departments. In fact, as will be demonstrated, he was involved in multiple specific, concrete projects with overlapping sets of scholars.

Of course it was not only Penn that matters here, and not only Goffman. There was a strong network of scholars, through the 1960s and 1970s, mostly based at the University of California, Berkeley and the University of Pennsylvania, but also Indiana University, and eventually the University of Texas, Austin (especially for the next generation), who kept in frequent touch, and who connected through a variety of conferences, research projects, and publications. The Social Science Research Council's Committee on Sociolinguistics, based in New York, was an important player due to helping to fund some of these activities, bringing together many of the relevant actors. Although Goffman never served on that Committee, he was part of not one but multiple projects they funded and facilitated.

A related point is that knowledge is not limited by disciplinary boundaries and that, in fact, it is often most productive to work with others sharing an interest in overlapping concepts, problems, or topics, but who approach these from divergent starting points. Of course, when group members do not share sufficient basic assumptions, definitions, or expectations in common, confusions can arise, but that does not mean it is not a worthy effort, or that there will be no useful results. Given that innovation often happens at the intersections of disciplines, rather than within the boundaries of only one, multi- and interdisciplinary collaborations frequently offer a particularly successful method of developing new perspectives, approaches, methods, etc.

The term "interdisciplinary" was only infrequently the focus of attention until the 1970s, but the basic idea was discussed much earlier. As Miller has explained:

> As early as the 1920s, the US Social Science Research Council (SSRC) recognized that, in only several decades after its invention, the departmental/disciplinary structure of the university was becoming an obstacle to effectively addressing comprehensive social problems. Especially in the 1930s, 1940s, and 1950s, the Rockefeller Foundation and then the Ford Foundation worked with the SSRC to fund interdisciplinary research and teaching in US higher education. (2010, 3900–1)

The essential idea for now is that the concept of interdisciplinary research existed and influenced Goffman, initially as a student, and certainly later as a faculty member. Klein tells us that "interdisciplinarity is a means of solving problems and answering questions that cannot be satisfactorily addressed using single methods or approaches" (1990, 196), and this is exactly what happened—mostly at Penn, but also at Berkeley, Indiana, and Texas, as will be portrayed in detail.

Interdisciplinarity is actually one of a set of multiple related terms. The concept of discipline comes first, obviously. As Eadie suggests, disciplines "are communities of inquiry organized around a particular topic" (2022, 4), and so the beginning point is recognizing that the communities of inquiry making up disciplines are socially constructed by scholars for their own use; that is, "academic disciplines are made, not found" (Leeds-Hurwitz 2012; see also Galanes and Leeds-Hurwitz 2009; Leeds-Hurwitz 2009). As a result, disciplinary boundaries are flexible, changing over time. Therefore, it would be unrealistic to assume that scholars will always respect disciplinary boundaries when conducting research; a new topic of interest often either crosses existing borders or flourishes in the spaces between them. In fact,

"Goffman studies" itself has become a good example of at least multidisciplinary, if not interdisciplinary, collaboration.

Now, to briefly sort out the several types of disciplinarity. *Multidisciplinary* (also sometimes named *cross-disciplinary*) research is the appropriate term for describing what happens when scholars who have been trained in, and thus self-identify as, members of separate disciplines collaborate, in order to bring their varying assumptions, theories, and/or methods to bear on a common topic. Typically, what such researchers learn is then brought back to their home disciplines. It is rare that new theories or methods are developed through multidisciplinary work, which more often means employing a series of different lenses to jointly examine a common phenomenon, just in a broader fashion. *Interdisciplinary* research typically describes a new topic being studied or created which previously had been overlooked as a worthwhile topic. Or it may be when an old topic is investigated in a significantly new and different way, applying a new method or theory. An example especially relevant to this book would be the ethnography of speaking, invented by Dell Hymes (1962), when he realized that anthropologists were using ethnography to study interaction, leaving speech to the linguists, while linguists were examining linguistic structure, and ignoring actual use of language, and so no one was analyzing real people holding conversations.[5] The key to interdisciplinarity is the element of *synthesis*, something usually missing from multidisciplinary work (Klein 1990). Given these definitions, what I am describing in these pages best meets the definition of multidisciplinarity some of the time, and interdisciplinarity most of the time; I will try to be deliberate about using these terms. *Transdisciplinary* research either involves an applied focus, or participation of a larger public interested in a topic, or both (Leeds-Hurwitz, forthcoming). An example would be when Hymes as dean of the Graduate School of Education established a program permitting K–12 principals to earn doctorates based on research conducted at their own schools. Projects in which Goffman became involved were most often either multi- or interdisciplinary, not transdisciplinary, but also not based solely within sociology. Camic (1995) is one of the few scholars to have already argued in favor of more often attending to interdisciplinary interactions when writing disciplinary history, a position that makes great sense to me. He also argues for attending to "local, interdisciplinary conditions" (1027), and by "local" he means specific universities. That is precisely what I will be doing for the majority of case studies described in these pages.

Writing Institutional History

Jansen tells us that "history matters" (2008, 98). I agree, which is why I have often written accounts of disciplinary history (or, more often, multi- or interdisciplinary history). Among the questions that have always interested me are why we study what we study, and why we study it in the ways we do; historical research supplies many of the answers. But there are multiple kinds of history, so it is worth explaining my emphasis here. Taylor (1972) and Murray (1991) both draw a distinction between being a historian of *ideas* and being a historian of *institutions*. In these pages, I clearly fall into the latter category, as my focus will be on the people and organizations supporting the ideas. Pooley and Park stress the need for "openness to institutional histories" (2008, 7), referring to what we might call the "activities of daily living" (to borrow a phrase from another context entirely, health care) that make up so much of an academic's time within a university. Institutions are the framework within which ideas are proposed and developed and, as such, merit investigation. I will be combining institutional history with interdisciplinary history.

Moore (1982) draws another useful distinction, that between *insider* and *outsider* histories. In this case, I am an insider, although standing at the far periphery of the action. My primary focus will be on Goffman's informal network at Penn, where I was a graduate student in residence from 1975 to 1979, thus during his time there (1968–1982). I came to know many of the scholars described in these pages as my professors and supervisors. I never took a course from Goffman: He offered only one course per year, which I did not manage to fit into my schedule. However, that did not mean I had no interactions with him. (Details are in chapter 3, along with the stories of other students.)

As a result of these connections, I am probably a good person to document what was happening around Goffman at Penn during his years there; I know something about the "intellectual furniture" as Smith (2022b, 90) has so gracefully referred to the given set of assumptions, ideas, and people active in a particular university at a particular moment in time. As "history is made of stories about people" (Nimura 2016), in these pages I will describe contexts I know from personal experience, substantially supplemented by what I have been able to learn from archival or published documents, and from correspondence and interviews with others who were in the right place at the right time. This book uses far more details documented by archival sources than any other; because there were so many, and they have so rarely been described, it seemed necessary to begin with them.[6] By the time I had written up what I had learned, I already had a lengthy book, so there simply was no room left to include interviews with everyone concerned. (Given that so many others have emphasized interviews, and ignored archival sources, the gap does not seem overly concerning.) The information contained in these pages is not only important for our understanding of Goffman as a scholar but should help us to understand more about the conditions under which intellectual creativity thrives, and how institutions can develop and support that creativity. After all, regardless of someone's areas of interest, knowing how to provide the context in which new ideas are most likely to thrive should always be of interest.

Organization of the Book

In keeping with the metaphor of mapping, this book is organized geographically, by the locations (mostly universities) where Goffman held affiliations. The initial answer to the question of "how did Goffman develop his own invisible college, becoming such a good colleague in interdisciplinary contexts?" is to be found by examining his experiences as a graduate student at the University of Chicago, where he studied with W. Lloyd Warner, Everett C. Hughes, Herbert Blumer, Anselm L. Strauss, and Louis Wirth. Chapter 2 thus begins with a brief review of his time there. Given that Chicago has always taken interdisciplinarity as a goal quite seriously, it becomes important in these pages as the place where Goffman was introduced to that idea. Then there is a summary of Goffman's time at the National Institute of Mental Health (NIMH), focusing on relationships he built with psychologists and psychiatrists, as well as resulting conferences and publications, a stage at which multidisciplinarity became more relevant. The story gathers speed at the University of California, Berkeley, where Goffman was first part of a solid interdisciplinary group as a faculty member. There the informal Saturday group established by linguist John Gumperz became most significant, and so, while the story starts at Chicago, Berkeley becomes the focus of attention in chapter 2. At the same time, while at Berkeley, Goffman worked with David Schneider in anthropology, and they made an attempt to conduct research across three departments; he was affiliated with the Center for the Integration of Social Science Theory while writing up his NIMH research, supported by a grant; he was part of an informal group with Aaron Cicourel based at the Center for the Study of Law and Society; he connected with Bateson and the Palo Alto group; and, finally, he helped to organize an interdisciplinary conference on "Strategic Interaction and Conflict," so those activities will also be summarized. His time at the Center for International Affairs of Harvard University merits only brief mention, for fewer activities and connections show up in available documentation for his time there (at least that have been uncovered at present).

The majority of the book will emphasize Goffman's years at Penn, where he was an active participant in not one but numerous multi- and interdisciplinary efforts, some with great success (mostly the interdisciplinary projects), although others saw either minimal success or were stillborn (mostly the multidisciplinary ones). Discussion of Penn has been divided into three chapters. Chapter 3 introduces the people at Penn: his closest connections (Dell Hymes,[7] William Labov, John Szwed, Ray Birdwhistell, and Sol Worth) in greatest detail, then the more peripheral group members more briefly. The goal is not to stop after introducing the initial narrow cast of characters, but rather to demonstrate the range of people who were part of his extended network at Penn. The faculty members described are only those whose who participated in one or more of the projects discussed in chapters 4 and 5; even so, introductions must be provided for an astonishing sixty-one colleagues, based in seventeen different departments across campus. It would have been far easier (and shorter) to stop with the core group of five. However, introducing everyone involved even in only one minor project allows far more variety: Instead of focusing on five White American men of approximately the same age, including this larger network means introducing women, as well as members of various minority groups, as well as an unexpected number of people born outside the US (as Goffman himself was). To make this more readable, a summary table is included in the chapter, with details relegated to the appendix, where they are available to anyone who wants to take the time to read them.

The last section of chapter 3 introduces two dozen students. As is well known, Goffman did not often take the role of dissertation advisor, but he did serve on dissertation committees, and obviously worked with even more students, mostly at the graduate level, but occasionally undergraduates. Students were only rarely part of the projects delineated in these pages, whether major or minor; they are important simply to demonstrate Goffman's interactions with and influence on the next academic generation. As with faculty peers, his connections with students routinely crossed over disciplinary borders.

Chapter 4 reviews the major projects at Penn: a small conference which Goffman helped to organize despite not yet being based on the east coast, Codes in Context; then four significant accomplishments: a large grant leading to the creation of a research center (the Center for Urban Ethnography, for which Goffman served as associate director); a book series, Conduct and Communication, for which Goffman was primary organizer and co-editor; and two journals, *Language in Society,* with Goffman a particularly active member of the editorial board, and *Studies in the Anthropology of Visual Communication,* where he first published *Gender Advertisements* (1976a, 1979a). For obvious reasons, the story of the successful projects makes up the bulk of the telling, not only because there is considerable documentation available for them, but also because they had the most impact, both at Penn and far beyond, both immediately and decades later. These were all primarily interdisciplinary; that is, they developed new approaches or topics rather than just reflecting different disciplinary assumptions about the same thing.

Chapter 5 describes the efforts to create a series of typically small and unsuccessful collaborative efforts across departments at Penn: the Semiotic Program, the Language and Interaction Institute, the Cross-Cultural Communication Center, the Interdisciplinary Program in the Science of Symbolic Behavior, the Center for the Study of Art and Symbolic Behavior, and the Interdisciplinary Program in Language, Culture, and Society. In addition, several minor activities in which Goffman participated due to his role as a Benjamin Franklin Professor will be described, including some relating to both campus and national politics, a library exhibit, and regular group meetings/dinners. Taken together these demonstrate that Goffman was part of an extensive network of colleagues at Penn, even though many of the organizational efforts were less successful, or just had less impact, than the major projects. And, despite the names, they were primarily multidisciplinary as they were more about sharing existing approaches than developing new ones. Despite these characteristics, they are still important: Sometimes we (both participants and historians) learn even more from unsuccessful ventures than from successful ones.

While at Penn, Goffman also pursued one major and several minor projects organized by people outside that university. The most substantial involved faculty based at Indiana University, and these serve as the focus of chapter 6, but several more were based at the University of Texas, Austin. Chapter 6 is titled "Penn Adjacent" because the projects involved others at Penn as well as Goffman, but were not led by Penn faculty, nor primarily managed by anyone there. These include an international conference Goffman co-organized on interaction ethology, held in Amsterdam in 1968, and the Multiple Analysis Project (MAP), designed in 1973, completed only in 1994. Given that the raison d'être of MAP was the development of sociolinguistics, even though it was not based at Penn, it is still important, for sociolinguistics was a frequent element in the collaborations at Penn (as at Berkeley, Indiana, and Texas). This project had much in common with the activities discussed in chapter 4, but was a failure in several ways, while those projects were all successful, so it should be instructive to look for the similarities and differences, using it as a negative case study. We do not spend enough time considering failures, but there is much we can learn from them, so as to avoid making the same mistakes repeatedly. The activities begun at Texas were smaller—conferences and a working papers series—but again, they demonstrate Goffman's involvement in additional projects, and especially the assumption by others that he would be an obvious participant. These can be considered either an expansion of Goffman's invisible college at Penn, or perhaps as additional, smaller, overlapping invisible colleges.

Chapter 7, titled "Beyond Penn," examines two activities having little to do with that campus except for Goffman's involvement in them. The first is yet another conference Goffman helped to organize, this one held in New York in 1969, Nonverbal Dimensions of Social Interaction. The second is the Committee for the Study of Incarceration, established in 1971, for which he was one of a group with various areas of expertise brought together in response to the uprising at Attica prison. There were many additional conferences in which Goffman participated—and these have been previously documented by others (especially Winkin 2022a, 2022e)—but there were only a few which he helped to organize; these are of greatest concern here since it can be assumed that any event which he took time to co-organize should point us to a topic he considered valuable, as well as involving people he respected, and with whom he wished to spend time. There has been virtually no discussion of his role in the Committee for the Study of Incarceration, so again, it seemed worth the time to sort out what can be learned at this point. The committee completes the circle, building as it did on Goffman's time at NIMH and the resulting work he published in the late 1950s/early 1960s. NIMH provided an interdisciplinary context, but the committee was better described as multidisciplinary. Again, as with chapter 6, people introduced in this chapter can either be considered additions to Goffman's invisible college or as members of additional, smaller invisible colleges.

Finally, chapter 8 provides the conclusion, summarizing what has been presented to that point, not only about Goffman, but also about multi- and interdisciplinarity, invisible colleges, and historical research more generally. An attempt will be made to draw together all the separate threads to suggest what lessons can be learned from these examples. The intent is not only to illuminate Goffman's role as multi- and interdisciplinary colleague—to make his invisible college visible and thus reveal more about him as a scholar—but also to make suggestions about what all of us can and should (or should not) do in order to coordinate our work with that of scholars across disciplinary borders, and finally, to provide a few general suggestions for what this research reveals about how new ideas can best be encouraged and supported. As explained earlier, the focus on this book will not be on Goffman's life or ideas but on the context of his life and ideas: how those ideas were generated, who he was talking with, and what projects he worked on. Conclusions here thus should have significance not only for those who study communication (the topic about which he most often wrote), or sociology (the discipline within which he was trained) but for scholars in any discipline. Ideas serve as the basic currency of academic life, and we all should want to know more about how to generate ideas, how to improve them, and how to share them effectively through collaborating with disciplinary others.

Endnotes

[1] A list of just some of the books would include: Burns 1992; Cefaï and Perreau 2012; Ditton 1980; Drew and Wootton 1988; Fine and Smith 2000; Jacobsen 2010, 2023; Jacobsen and Kristiansen 2015; Jacobsen and Smith 2022; Jaworski 2023; Joseph et al. 1989; Lenz and Hettlage 2022; Manning 1992; Martins and Gastaldo 2024; Maseda 2017; Mondada and Peräkylä 2024; Raab 2019; Riggins 1990; Scheff 2006; Shalin 2025; Smith 1999, 2006; Treviño 2003; Winkin 1988a, 2022a; Winkin and Leeds-Hurwitz 2013.

[2] I do know that current students tend to call it "UPenn," but that was not yet the term of choice during Goffman's tenure there, nor my own.

[3] Comparable comments are to be found in Elkind 1975 and Raab 2019.

[4] "Erving and I had close communication for the past 15 years—dating from a brief period when I was at the University of California. Although our work was in markedly different areas, utilizing different methodological techniques, our sense of mutual respect remained very high." Horowitz to Hymes, Nov 22, 1982, DHH, Subcollection 2, Series IV: Works by Hymes, Subseries D: Other Research, "On Erving Goffman," 1979–1984.

[5] Hymes changed the name of the topic to the ethnography of communication by 1964 (see Leeds-Hurwitz 1984 for a detailed analysis of the relationship of the two names).

[6] Also, of course, there is that wonderful comment by Goffman about the unreliability of interviews: "I find I cannot use the interview technique much. I do not believe people very much anyway, but in an interview I hardly believe them at all" (1957b, 181).

[7] While I certainly know that there has been a move to forego discussion of Dell Hymes due to inappropriate interactions with some students and colleagues, omitting him from discussion would be false history. I did not set out to highlight his role, but neither can I pretend he was not one of the central actors in much of the story told here. For another consideration of the relationship between Hymes and Goffman, see Meier zu Verl 2022.

CHAPTER TWO

Before Penn

G offman did not suddenly establish multi- and interdisciplinary connections with colleagues for the first time only after arriving at Penn.
Several prior contexts influenced him in this regard. The first of these was
the University of Chicago, the second was the National Institute of Mental
Health, but the most significant was the University of California, Berkeley.
Goffman was also briefly at Harvard University. Each of these contexts will
be described in this chapter.[1] Briefly, at Chicago Goffman was introduced
to a cohort of other students who shared some of his interests and learned
to take interdisciplinarity for granted as strong ties developed among both
faculty and students across multiple disciplines, but with a focus on sociology, anthropology, and psychology. At NIMH, the set of disciplines widened,
emphasizing not only psychology but also psychiatry, and he collaborated
with colleagues, having some of his work included both on conference
panels and in edited collections. At Berkeley, he more actively participated
in building multiple small collections of scholars interested in overlapping
topics, most significantly the Saturday group, a direct precursor to his later
invisible college at Penn.

University of Chicago

Goffman came by interdisciplinarity naturally, at least from his time as a
student at the University of Chicago, where he earned his MA (1949) and
PhD (1953). Applying Bourdieu's concept of "habitus" (1977), Winkin puts
it this way in describing Goffman's education at Chicago:

> His acquisition of a "scientific habitus"—that is his explicit professional train-
> ing—is easy enough to locate at the University of Chicago in the late 1940s. . . .
> Goffman, and the whole group of Chicago sociologists who graduated at the
> turn of the mid-century with PhDs, actually developed a certain disposition
> towards the world, a disposition which guided their perceptions, appreciations
> and actions throughout their later careers. This may be called the "Chicago
> habitus." (1999, 34)

Fine and Manning concur: "It was the social scene in Chicago's Hyde Park in
the years after the Second World War that had the most lasting and profound
impression. Erving Goffman was very much a product of this time and place"
(2003, 37). Like Penn, Chicago prides itself on interdisciplinarity, and always
has. In the 1930s, for example, Abbott suggests: "faculty offices in the [Social
Science Research] building were scattered with respect to discipline, precisely
to prevent departmental concentrations" (2010, 132–33n18). In the 1940s,
President Robert Maynard Hutchins specifically encouraged the development of committees crossing traditional disciplinary boundaries, such as the
Committee on Social Thought (Emmett 2010; see Wahl-Jorgensen 2004, on
the role played by these committees in the early days of communication as
a discipline). Partially as a result of these activities, by the 1940s and 1950s,
what is now widely known as "the Chicago School of Sociology"—among
the most progressive of the approaches taught at Chicago—first came into
being,[2] and it was nothing if not interdisciplinary (despite that term not being
in common use at the time). Camic describes the "pattern of open contact
across disciplines" as the standard in sociology at Chicago, particularly
including anthropology and psychology (1995, 1019), and this turns out to
have been true of other disciplines as well, as Deegan explains:

> Several University of Chicago departments also supported the work of Chicago
> ethnographers. For many decades, political scientists, such as Charles Merriam,
> social workers, such as Edith Abbott and Sophonisba Breckinridge, philosophers,
> such as George H. Mead, and geographers, such as Paul Goode, encouraged
> students and fostered the ideas associated today with 'Chicago sociology.' The
> massive interdisciplinary project at Chicago is at best only partially understood
> and documented today. (2001, 17)

Goffman's important models were professors like Herbert Blumer (Winkin
1999), Everett C. Hughes,[3] or W. Lloyd Warner,[4] who themselves served as
exemplars of interdisciplinarity.[5] However, other students were relevant
as well. Given the uncommonly low ratio of faculty to students at that
time (due mostly to high post-war enrollments while the GI Bill supported

veterans in earning college degrees), "graduate students banded together for social and intellectual support" (Fine and Manning 2003, 38). Winkin documents the details of what the department was like when Goffman arrived: "In Sociology, there were about 200 graduate students for about ten professors" (1999, 24). Platt tells us there was a specific "Canadian group" of students mentored by Hughes (himself Canadian) which included Goffman among its members (1995, 89). As Goffman has explained "My friends at Chicago and I formed a sort of solidarity group" (quoted in Winkin 1984a, 86;[6] see also Winkin 1988a; Verhoeven 1993). One of these others, Joseph Gusfield, tells of interactions among them: "The classroom spilled over onto the streets and, of course, into the living rooms and kitchens. My wife still remembers the night she thought I had met foul play when a search of the streets at 1:00 A.M. found me and Erving Goffman 'talking shop' under a lamp post.... The Social Science building had a daily interdisciplinary coffee hour. There were the frequent parties and, above all, the talk-talk-talk" (1995, xv). Winkin provides more detail, highlighting the significance of peers rather than faculty members:

> The four years Goffman spent at the University of Chicago certainly forged his intellectual dispositions, but not so much due to the courses he took, no matter how famous his professors were (from W. Lloyd Warner to Everett Hughes, from Herbert Blumer to Louis Wirth). Rather, it was thanks to the many conversations he had with his fellow students, and the many books he kept reading "voraciously," as Bott said (ibid), from philosophy to fiction, from detective stories to Marcel Proust. (2022c, 4)

This is supported by Herbert J. Gans, another of this group: "I also learned a great deal from my fellow students, who included Howie (Howard) Becker, Fred Davis, Eliot Friedson, Erving Goffman, and Joe (Joseph) Gusfield. The students really gave life to the Chicago School after the Second World War" (in Jaynes et al. 2009, 380). Gans points out an important and directly relevant assumption in place at Chicago then, that "social science was a unified field and the disciplines were somewhat arbitrary boundaries" (379). Kenneth Pike's book *Language in Relation to a Unified Theory of the Structure of Human Behavior* was already available at Chicago (published in 1967, the "preliminary edition" was printed in 1954 by the Summer Institute of Linguistics), and it summed up some of the assumptions in the air at the time.[7] Another relevant source was Grinker et al.'s *Toward a Unified Theory of Human Behavior* (1956), summarizing a series of conferences held 1950–1955, which included Jürgen Ruesch among other participants; Goffman and his peers were quite likely to have known about this as well. Both books were about the attempt to unify knowledge rather than make it manageable by dividing it into disciplines and also can be seen as another call for interdisciplinarity.

One of the other students contemporary with Goffman was Saul Mendlovitz, also studying sociology, who explains: "Erving and I used to go to parties and agree that we would exchange what we had seen. He especially was interested in what we had seen and then he would take copious notes on that. I have no idea of whether he ever used those notes or not, but he was very much into that observational stuff very early on" (2009). Speaking of Chicago just a few years later, David T. Apter echoes this: "Where I saw promise and intellectual opportunity was in the university's interdisciplinary tradition, which was particularly noteworthy at a time when most other academic institutions of merit were organized around departmental boundaries and tended to resist programs or centers that challenged or cut across disciplinary lines" (in Jaynes et al. 2009, 376–77).[8]

Returning to Goffman's cohort specifically, Dennis Wrong says, "All of us, including Erving, were most attracted by the cultural anthropology that strongly shaped the sociology we were taught" (1990, 10). As these quotes make abundantly clear, the context at Chicago was seriously interdisciplinary, and could not help but influence Goffman's assumptions.

Goffman occasionally mentioned individual professors by name, as here: "My teachers were [Robert E.] Park, [Ernest W.] Burgess, and Louis Wirth. And then later on Hughes. But the person I worked for initially, was Lloyd Warner. I was oriented to Social Anthropology at the time" (quoted in Verhoeven 1993, 321).[9] In sorting out some of his early influences in greater detail, Goffman went on to explain:

> There was the tradition of George Herbert Mead to provide the social psychological underpinnings of background for any study. From there one could go in all kinds of directions, one of which is the one [Everett] Hughes developed: a sort of occupational Sociology and basically Urban Ethnography. And what I did up to a few years ago before I got somewhat more interested in Sociolinguistics was a version of Urban Ethnography with Meadian Social Psychology.... If I had to be labeled at all, it would have been as a Hughesian urban ethnographer. (318)

Remember the terms *urban ethnography* and *sociolinguistics* as topics of interest to Goffman, for these will appear again and again as various projects are introduced.

A little later in the same interview, Goffman makes the implicit link to anthropology explicit: "Anthropology was close to sociology, people knew each other fairly well" (345). Thus, what anywhere else would have been treated as three distinct disciplines (psychology, anthropology, sociology) were interwoven strands at Chicago. Goffman broadens this even further: "When I was in Chicago in the 40s, one could still combine lots of different things: Ecology and social organization, class analysis with Warner, and the like . . . In the mid-40s, however, everybody did everything" (333). This should be more than sufficient to document the general context at Chicago for Goffman: Conversations across disciplinary boundaries were assumed as the norm by administrators, faculty, and graduate students, with particularly close relationships existing among sociology, anthropology, and psychology, and weaker links to additional departments.

In December 1979, Goffman was awarded an honorary degree by Chicago, Doctor of Humane Letters, recognizing that he "has transcended his teachers at Chicago while, at the same time, shared powerful parts of Chicago's intellectual tradition" and finding him to be "undoubtedly, one of the most creative social scientists alive."[10] This award was specifically given as a way to recognize "creative alumni."[11] What follows are just a few of the comments provided by multiple scholars around the country asked for their evaluations. Murray Davis (sociology, University of California, San Diego) argued that "in line with the synthetic approach of the Chicago Social Science Division, he has gone beyond the boundaries of sociology in the narrow sense to integrate anthropology (via Radcliffe-Brown), literary criticism (via Kenneth Burke), and philosophy (via George Herbert Mead) into his work";[12] Peter Blau (sociology, SUNY Albany) said that "his imaginative analyses of social life, subtle processes of communication, and total institutions cut across disciplinary boundaries";[13] Lewis Coser (sociology, SUNY Stony Brook) suggested that "by putting to excellent uses the older contributions of the Chicago School of Sociology and of Georg Simmel, he has created a body of work that has enduring significance and is considered a major landmark in Europe as well as in the United States";[14] and Alvin Boskoff (sociology, Emory University) argued that "Goffman has developed a unique place for himself in sociological analysis—and in relating sociological concerns to those of other disciplines and to the educated public at large."[15] Of course, they all pointed out his originality and contributions and influence as well—but what is noteworthy in this context is that they all highlighted his connections to, and expansions of, Chicago traditions, including interdisciplinarity. Goffman's acceptance and commitment to attend the ceremony was in keeping with these comments, also linking his achievements to what he learned there: "The University of Chicago is the institutional foundation of such life as I have, and there could be no award I feel more deeply."[16]

Goffman and Hughes

Jaworski (2000) and Vienne (2010, 2022) have already examined the work Goffman did at Chicago under Hughes, so that will not be repeated here. There is extensive documentation available specifically related to the interactions between Goffman and Hughes through letters they exchanged, which Hughes donated to the University of Chicago Library. Goffman, of course, did not deposit his correspondence anywhere, so any collection is at best woefully incomplete. But the Hughes papers give us some ideas about their interactions over the years. Both Hughes and Blumer were important influences, despite neither being consistently around during Goffman's years there. He has said: "Hughes was much more of an influence . . . but I found Blumer's [1969b] writings very congenial . . . And I was a colleague of his for a decade" (quoted in Verhoeven 1993, 320).[17] When Irving Horowitz asked if he wished to write a response to a review by Blumer of his book *Relations in Public* (1972), Goffman responded: "It's nice about the Blumer review, nice for you to encourage it and nice for you to do it. But no thanks about replying: Blumer has a special perspective with a logic of its own, and although I do not fully agree with it, I would not consider disputing it" (Mar 2, 1972, HTP). The following pages summarize the relationship with Hughes as part of the Chicago story, reserving Blumer for the next section, as part of the Berkeley story.

Goffman maintained a connection with Hughes long after leaving Chicago. Vienne has documented their "atmosphere of warm exchange" (2022, 113). As when he wrote to others, Goffman's sense of humor comes through in his letters. For example, while he was in Las Vegas doing research on casinos, he wrote Hughes that he had received a "police card" in order to be permitted to "go on the slots" and concludes "I'll save my card, collect one from Howie and members of all the other locals, and present them to you on a birthday: for by their union cards you shall know the participant observers" (Dec 13, 1960, ECH). To fully understand this, it is necessary to know that part of what Hughes taught Goffman and others was the sociology of institutions and occupations (Vienne 2010). Other times Goffman praises Hughes: "To have as one's teacher someone better than oneself, who reads what one writes and likes it, is rather a special experience, in part, I'm afraid, a family experience" (Nov 26, 1961, ECH).

In addition to demonstrating that they were regularly exchanging publications and drafts of manuscripts from 1955 on, the letters reveal that they regularly connected in person, and even more often tried to connect. For example, in 1961, Hughes thanks Goffman for a copy of his book *Encounters* (1961a), asking, "When may I have the opportunity of encountering you in person" (Aug 23, 1961, ECH). In response, Goffman turned the question around: "Any chance of you and Helen visiting California?" (Nov 26, 1961, ECH). In 1966, after discussing Goffman's book *Stigma* (1963a), Hughes wrote: "Perhaps you will sometime turn up where I can talk to you" (May 9, 1966, ECH). And in 1968, Hughes wrote Goffman: "Is a man really respectable if mail addressed to him is returned to the sender? Of course, nobility put a notice in the TIMES that no mail will be answered during an absence in Europe, but I saw no such notice. The letter simply wandered around and eventually came back" (Nov 20, 1968, ECH). In this way, Hughes demonstrates the same sort of humor in letters as Goffman. They reconnected in person in fall 1969, at a conference Goffman was involved in organizing at Penn, held in New York. Once they determined they would be able to see one another, Goffman responded, "I am glad indeed that you can come and visit with us in New York" (Oct 24, 1969, ECH). (Hughes was, at the time, based in New York for the year; Goffman was then based in Philadelphia, a few hours away by train.) Several months later, while still on the East Coast, Hughes wrote, "When Helen [his wife] was getting up a list of people to ask for dinner next week, I suggested she put you on the list. She reminded me that you don't live here. Well, it isn't far" (Feb 23, 1970, ECH). The answer from Goffman was: "Why can't we have dinner some time some place?" (Mar 24, 1970, ECH). Hughes offered: "We will be in New York for the Eastern Sociological [Association] meetings. Might we meet then?" (Mar 31, 1970, ECH). It's not clear whether they did connect at that event or not, but a few years later, Goffman wrote, "Will you be at the Colorado meetings?" (Mar 1, 1971, ECH). The point here is the frequency of attempts to meet, whether or not all worked out, because these demonstrate the strength of their connection.

Fairly often in these letters, each praised the other, and the other's work. Hughes wrote to Goffman discussing the article that *Time* magazine had published about him: That letter turned into a lengthy ramble, ending with a thank you for Goffman's contribution to the *Festschrift* prepared for Hughes

(Becker et al. 1968; Goffman's contribution was a reprint of "The Neglected Situation" 1964a). Hughes suggested: "Most of the people who wrote in it did really catch some facet of me. It must have been a matter of resonance. I certainly did not create anything in any of those people. You, for example, came down from Toronto already with your feelers out in all directions [illegible] . . . I am very grateful to all of you who had a share in that gift" (Feb 12, 1969, ECH). In response, Goffman argued that the most important thing Hughes had given him, and other students, was "a sense that sociological inquiry is real. Underneath it all, I think that is the task teachers are really involved in: to demonstrate that what they do is substantial and real. The point about yourself is that you did that job for so many of us—not because you had many students but because you had that effect on so many that you had. And you do it still. And that is the lesson of the master. Thanks" (Feb 26, 1969, ECH).

Both Hughes and Goffman maintained their interdisciplinary inclinations long after leaving Chicago, as was made clear in 1978 when Hughes told Goffman, "I become more and more grateful to colleagues and circumstances which prevented me from trying to separate social science into numerous departments unrelated to each other" (Feb 26, 1969, ECH). This is interesting for the reversal of standard assumptions: Most academics assume disciplines and/or departments are to be taken for granted, and that they must work to bring them together. My point here has not been to sort out what ideas Goffman might have learned from Hughes; others have already done that. Instead, what is relevant to this story is that they maintained friendly relations for decades, exchanging both publications and unpublished drafts, connecting in person as they could, despite mostly living in different parts of the US; equally, both maintained their assumptions of interdisciplinarity as practiced at Chicago as something both appropriate and valued.

While still a graduate student at Chicago, Goffman began publishing. In 1951, "Symbols of Class Status" was published in the *British Journal of Sociology*. In 1952, "On Cooling the Mark Out" first appeared in *Psychiatry*, and was later reprinted in *Advances in Psychiatry* (Goffman 1959a). Mabel Blake Cohen was at that point editor of *Psychiatry*, and explained in her introduction to the book that "the journal *Psychiatry* has always selected as its field of particular interest that zone where psychological, biological, and social sciences come together" (1959, 7), so all of the articles published in it can be assumed to be examples of at least multidisciplinary, if not interdisciplinary, work. She goes on to say: "This book represents a collection of some of the outstanding articles which have appeared in the journal *Psychiatry* in the last twenty years" (7). Reviewers of the collection apparently agreed because Solomon says Cohen "collected some leading papers" (1960, 476). These comments establish that Goffman's work was well received even in early days. Another reviewer praises Goffman's contribution in particular: "A most striking article, and one which beautifully exemplifies the kind of transdisciplinary approach to which *Psychiatry* is devoted. . . . At once an entirely successful tour de force and a highly creative synthesis based on sound application of theory, this work is a real joy to read, as well as a worthwhile scientific contribution" (Oken 1960, 133).

The use of "transdisciplinary" here is quite accurate; the goal was to not only synthesize sociology with psychology to study something new but to apply the results to a concrete context. Although it appeared in 1955, Goffman submitted another article, "On Face-Work," to *Psychiatry* before his time at NIMH ("This paper was written at the University of Chicago," 1955a, 213). That one was reprinted as the lead chapter of *Interaction Ritual* (Goffman 1967).

National Institute of Mental Health (NIMH)

Goffman completed his PhD at Chicago in 1953. That year, sociologist John Clausen, director of the new Laboratory of Socio-Environmental Studies at the National Institute of Mental Health (NIMH), hired him. His new, rather long and complicated title was Visiting Scientist, Section on Social Studies in Therapeutic Settings, Laboratory of Socio-Environmental Studies; that Section was part of NIMH (Walter Reed Army Institute of Research 1958, v). As a result, Goffman spent 1954–1957 based in Bethesda, Maryland, a suburb of Washington, DC. As part of his job, in 1955–1956 Goffman conducted a year's fieldwork in St. Elizabeths, a large psychiatric hospital in DC, leading to his books *Asylums* (1961b) and *Stigma* (1963a). The story has been told in Smith (2022d), Winkin (1922d), and Winkin and Leeds-Hurwitz (2013), and so will not be repeated here. However, the context, working primarily with psychologists and psychiatrists, merits attention.

Harry Stack Sullivan was affiliated with St. Elizabeths and the journal *Psychiatry*, both of which became relevant to Goffman's story. Sullivan also was affiliated with Chestnut Lodge, important because psychiatrist Frieda Fromm-Reichmann worked there, and she likely played a small role in the story as well. Sullivan had connected in important ways with linguist Edward

Sapir in Chicago in the 1920s, long before Goffman got there. As Darnell explains: "The interdisciplinary triumvirate of Sapir, Sullivan, and political scientist Harold D. Lasswell persuaded others to participate in the construction of a yet unnamed multidiscipline emerging around the study of the individual in culture, the very problem that had worried Sapir as theoretician of culture at least since 1917" (2001a, 127). So, just as at Chicago and later at Penn, at NIMH Goffman was placed into a context where disregarding disciplinary boundaries in inventive ways was deemed appropriate. In addition, it seems likely that the connection to Sullivan's sphere of influence, and Goffman's own publications (1952, 1955a, as already noted; then 1957a, 1959b) in *Psychiatry* (a journal founded by Sullivan in 1938, where Sapir also published), would have brought national attention to Goffman (because the journal became so well-known, and then because his work was included in the "best of" volume) and later would have become a topic of conversation at Penn with J. David Sapir, Edward Sapir's son. Peters points out that *Psychiatry* "was one of the leading outlets for thinking about communication for the next three decades" (2008, 153), and Bazerman refers to it as a "remarkable interdisciplinary nexus" (2005, 16). Details on that period can be found in Stewart Perry (1966), as he was at NIMH at the same time as Goffman, and Goffman thanks both Helen and Stewart Perry for their help in writing of "The Insanity of Place" (Goffman 1969). Helen Perry was editor of *Psychiatry* from 1946 to 1951 and thus worked with Goffman on his first article in that journal (Saxton 2002). Stewart Perry examined "the *micro*sociology of science. I am concerned what goes on within the small interacting group of researchers in a single research program" (1966, 6; emphasis in original). Microsociology was, of course, of substantial interest to Goffman as well.

Like academics today, Goffman did not just conduct research in the years when he was affiliated with NIMH, he also presented at conferences and published articles and books. Because it will become relevant later, notes about additional publications and conferences related to his work at NIMH follow. This is not the place to summarize what he wrote about in these early publications—that has already been done by others (e.g., Gronfein 1999). Instead, the focus will be to demonstrate his connections with disciplines beyond sociology, primarily with psychology and psychiatry, thus putting into practice what he had learned at Chicago about the value of crossing disciplinary boundaries (or, perhaps more accurately, ignoring them entirely). The intent is to briefly summarize what he did, thus documenting his participation in both a regional and a national network of scholars.

In 1955, Goffman reviewed the books *Children's Humor: A Psychological Analysis* (1955b) and *Tobatí: Paraguayan Town* (1955c) for *American Journal of Sociology*. These are interesting only because they demonstrate that he was participating in the standard ritual of a new PhD reviewing books for major journals. He wrote a few more reviews, noted below, but soon stopped as he became too busy with his own original work. In addition, it was his opinion that, as he wrote to Hughes:

> There is that commitment to the jointly lived life of one's discipline that leads you to write book reviews and letters in the first place. No one insists on it; you don't put the pieces in a bibliography. They are something extra, something that won't get paid for, something to show that even When an official occasion is not in progress, a man should be involving himself in the life that exists between himself and others. (Feb 28, 1969, ECH)

So it makes sense that he did not write a lot of book reviews in his career: They were "something extra," not something essential. Even so, those he did write are relevant because they demonstrate his attention to and connections to other scholars.

In 1956, Goffman participated in one of the Group Processes conferences held by the Josiah Macy Jr. Foundation, and his presentation appeared in the resulting volume, including the discussion with Gregory Bateson and Margaret Mead (Goffman 1957b). Ray Birdwhistell (one of Goffman's professors from his undergraduate days at the University of Toronto, an earlier Chicago alum, and a later colleague at Penn) was a regular participant in that series and arranged for Goffman to be invited. When it was his turn to present, Goffman discussed his observations at St. Elizabeths. In the Macy Conferences, presenters were constantly interrupted by questions, and then the entirety was transcribed and published, permitting a wide circle of others to gain a clear sense of what occurred. The fact that Margaret Mead argued with Goffman about his use of specific vocabulary choices has been previously well documented.[18] Overall, Goffman comes off as young and untested, which makes sense at that early point in his career. The research he presented at that event was later published in several versions (Goffman 1958, 1961c) and he specifically thanks Bateson for a helpful comment, saying: "The binary character of total institutions was pointed out to me by Gregory Bateson" (1958, 46n2; the same quote appears in 1961c, 18). The relevant binary here is the division into inmates and staff. Goffman got along far better with Bateson than Mead and connected with him again on several occasions.[19]

Also in 1956, Goffman published "The Nature of Deference and Demeanor" (1956a) and "Embarrassment and Social Organization" (1956b), both similarly based on his time at St. Elizabeths and both reprinted in *Interaction Ritual* (1967). Finally, he participated in the Research Conference on Socio-Environmental Aspects of Patient Care in Mental Hospitals, presenting "The Patient as a 'Normal Deviant': Problems of Stigma and Isolation," later included as a chapter in the resulting book (1957c). Interestingly, this book was reviewed by Belknap (1958), a book of whose Goffman had just reviewed (1957d). The web of connections with sociologists, psychologists, and psychiatrists was already growing.

In 1957, Goffman reviewed *Human Problems of a State Mental Hospital*, bemoaning the fact that "no new concepts are added to our means for understanding social organization" (1957d, 120). That tells us what he valued, and what he later supplied in his turn. That same year, he presented the "Natural History of the Patient" at the American Sociological Association (ASA) meeting in Washington, DC, as part of a panel entitled "The Sociology of Mental Health: Treatment Services and Processes" chaired by Clausen (his boss at NIMH) and jointly sponsored by the Society for Study of Social Problems.[20] Note that the phrase "natural history" was being used at that point by Birdwhistell, Bateson, and others as part of *The Natural History of an Interview* project (McQuown 1971; Leeds-Hurwitz and Kendon 2021), something Goffman certainly would have known. Goffman's ASA paper was first published under the slightly revised title "The Moral Career of the Mental Patient" (1959b) in *Psychiatry*, and later republished as a chapter in *Asylums* (1961b). Clearly, his primary audience at that stage was not sociologists, although he did publish "Alienation from Interaction" in *Human Relations* (1957e), a journal more likely to be read by sociologists (also reprinting that article as a chapter in *Interaction Ritual* in 1967).

Still in 1957, again in Washington, DC, Goffman participated in the Symposium on Preventive and Social Psychiatry, organized by the Walter Reed Army Institute of Research. That event was sponsored jointly by the Institute, the Walter Reed Army Medical Center, and the National Research Council, resulting in a book (Walter Reed Army Institute of Research 1958). At that event, Goffman presented as part of the first panel, "Communication, Values, Influence and Group Structure"; the other panelists were psychologists or psychiatrists.[21] Goffman's presentation, "Characteristics of Total Institutions," was based on his Macy Conference presentation (as acknowledged in Goffman 1958, 44n1). Luckily, as at the Macy Conference, the group's discussions after each panel have been included in the proceedings, so it is possible to learn that Goffman's presentation sparked numerous questions, both immediately after his panel (when his answer to a single question takes up a substantial amount of the discussion session), as well as during comments on later panels. The point here is not to dissect those comments in detail, but rather to point out that his work was being taken seriously and referred to multiple times throughout the symposium by others, mostly people he likely had not known before the event. As everyone who has ever participated in a conference knows, whether others respond to what you have presented makes a huge difference. So, comments from later sessions such as "This would relate to some of the things that Dr. Goffman was talking about this morning" (Walter Reed Army Institute of Research 1958, 184), or "I just can't resist referring back to Dr. Goffman's paper of Monday" (529) are significant, showing that his ideas were striking home and being taken seriously. Goffman first turned his presentation at that conference into two longer book chapters (1961c, 1961d), and then integrated much of what he said into *Asylums* (1961b). In a review of the symposium proceedings, Wilson says: "Goffman in a brilliant discussion of 'total' institutions limns the encapsulating properties of organizations such as the army or the hospital. The eternal dialectic of organizational goals and individual needs continues to plague the social psychiatrist as it has long riven the democratic philosopher" (1959, 433). It is a minor detail, but these chapters were published as part of a volume edited by Cressey, *The Prison: Studies in Institutional Organization and Change* (1961). This is noteworthy because Goffman had previously published a review of a very different book by Cressey, on embezzlement (1957f). That volume is irrelevant to this discussion, except that it was by Cressey and so indicates that they were at least aware of one another, again demonstrating the network Goffman was already building. In addition, it presages (and was probably one of the publications that led to) his later involvement in The Committee for the Study of Incarceration, documented in chapter 7.

Finally, in 1957, Goffman published "A Sociologist's View (On Some Convergences of Sociology and Psychiatry)" (1957a), important not least for an early use of the word "microsociology" (201). Even then he was thinking about interdisciplinarity, for example, using the phrase "interdisciplinarian encroachment" to refer to sociologists stepping onto ground generally ceded to psychiatrists (201). This essay is particularly noteworthy for the fact that he was one of two people (the other being a psychiatrist) invited to comment on six articles in a special issue of a journal, rather an early honor for such a junior scholar, indicating that at least some scholars found his opinions already worthy.

Supporting this move to being considered more senior than perhaps already merited is the fact that in 1960, he chaired the panel "Social Psychology: Information, Commitment and Identity" for ASA. Participants were Albert D. Biderman (Bureau of Social Science Research in DC), Harold Garfinkel, Robert J. Stoller, and Alexander Rosen (all at the University of California, Los Angeles), Evelyn Hooker (also at UCLA), Dorothy Hillyer (Psychopathic Hospital, State University of Iowa), and Thomas C. Schelling (Center for International Affairs at Harvard).[22] One interesting follow-up activity to this conference was that Goffman and Biderman both served as discussants for the workshop "Issues in Research: Covert Research Funding" at the American Sociological Association's convention in 1978. The organizer was Richard M. Stephenson (Rutgers University), and the panelists were Bradford H. Gray (National Academy of Science), Myron Glazer (Smith College), William Bates (Berkeley), and Jay Schulman (National Jury Project).[23] Goffman connected again with Bates at Berkeley, and with Schelling in 1964 at the Strategic Interaction and Conflict conference held at Berkeley, and was invited to spend a year at Harvard by Schelling as a result.

In 1962, Goffman presented "Mental Symptoms and Public Order" at the Association for Research in Nervous and Mental Disease, first published in the volume resulting from that conference, *Disorders of Communication* (1964b), and then republished as part of *Interaction Ritual* (1967). Finally, in 1969, he published "The Insanity of Place," the last relevant piece, later included as part of *Relations in Public* (1971). Again, we see him crossing over the border of sociology to connect with psychologists and psychiatrists.

Goffman and Duncan

While developing new connections in psychology and psychiatry, Goffman also maintained connections, or developed new ones, to at least some sociologists, so he absolutely was not leaving one field for another, merely applying what he had learned in the one to study contexts or topics common to the other. A specific example of this was in 1957, when Hugh Duncan, another former Chicago student, wrote to him. Apparently, they did not know one another before this exchange of letters, because Goffman responded: "As an ex-Chicago student with a sometime interest in the sociology of knowledge, of course I know and own your book on the sociology of literature" (Feb

19, 1957, HDD), something he presumably would not have said to someone he had known as a peer. A few weeks later, Goffman suggests: "It would be very nice to have a conference in Chicago with Burke and others" (Feb 26, 1957, HDD). Kenneth Burke taught at the University of Chicago from 1949 to 1950, so it is likely they both would have known him. Collins describes the attraction: "Goffman's old classmates tell me that he was very much impressed with the literary critic Kenneth Burke, who wrote about the social stances of rhetoric and espoused the notion of everyday life as a kind of theatre" (1986, 110).

Apparently, Goffman and Duncan agreed that Goffman would critique the draft of a book by Duncan. Based on the comments, this seems likely to have been *Communication and Social Order* (Duncan 1960). Goffman said: "We have indeed hit upon the same things to talk about and the same point of view to take in regard to them. . . . On the critical side, it seems to me you have tried to do it the hard way by talking about everything in the world. Burke certainly does this and certainly gets away with it, but Burke is Burke. . . . All this bitching is probably due to jealousy" (Mar 25, 1957, HDD). A few months later, there is a lengthy (five-page, single-spaced) letter from Duncan to Goffman critiquing a book manuscript of Goffman's in return.

> First off let me say I like your book very much. I sent a copy to Kenneth. He thinks highly of your work. In his reply to me he devotes a full page to it. He sums up by saying: "It's a highly intelligent book. I'm glad he let me in . . . I'd vote it a highly reputable job. Its observations on the nature of social finagling are excellent." He does not agree with your theoretical frame for reasons which you might better get directly from him. Write him. If you do not hear from him within a reasonable time I will send you a copy of what he said. In talking to him on the phone about another matter I mentioned your work and he was pleased (as I am) to know that you are alive and daring to do such original work. (May 1, 1957, HDD)

What follows are detailed comments on Goffman's manuscript of what must have been *The Presentation of Self in Everyday Life* (1959c). These are very small critiques: For example, Duncan questions the choice of the term "sign-equipment," asking: "How does this relate to a dramatistic model?" or "Mystification as Burke's pontification, transcendence, etc. might round this out more." But there is also high praise: "And my delight in your thinking soars again." Or: "Here begins the kind of sensitive observation and writing which I find very exciting." And: "As they say in book reviews, I couldn't put it down till I had read it through. It is full of excellent concrete propositions and wonderful illustrative material." The major critique is that "I think you suffer as I do from lack of decision about whom you write for." And the major praise: "I would like to have written these pages. They are so good I feel sure I will be stealing them for something I will write. I am a bare faced but merry burglar. I do not have to dislike the man I rob. So, if you should ever read anything of mine wherein I do not credit you for the backstage statement curse me into the night" (May 1, 1957, HDD). Duncan's letter ends with an offer: "I do not mean to intrude on your privacy but if there is anything very practical I can do let me know. It would help if you would tell me enough about yourself so I think of how I might help you to get in the kind of spot you need to go on with the kind of rare writing you can do." In his immediate response Goffman asked, "When can we have a meeting? In the Fall I may go to Berkeley and Blumer to become a temporary paper-grader, with palm, second class" (May 6, 1957, HDD). His lovely closing: "It's nice to share meanings."

In fall of the same year, Goffman thanks Duncan for comments on the total institutions paper (presumably the one published as Goffman 1958), hopes for a connection at the anthropology meetings in Chicago that year, and again asks about connecting with Burke (Sep 17, 1957, HDD). Over the course of the few months covered in these letters, Goffman progressed from "Mr. Duncan" to "Hugh Duncan" to "Hugh," so presumably this really was their first contact, despite common history at Chicago. While Goffman did not specifically acknowledge the detailed comments by Duncan when he published *Presentation of Self* in 1959, he did thank "fellow students of oc-cupations at the University of Chicago" (x), which presumably would have included Duncan.

Progress in Psychotherapy

In addition to these stories of his professional activities, there were times Goffman turned down an opportunity. One specific example follows. In 1958, he was invited to submit a chapter to *Progress in Psychotherapy*, an annual review, edited by psychiatrists Jules Masserman and Jacob Moreno. A few years earlier, the 1956 volume had been co-edited by Moreno with Frieda Fromm-Reichmann, someone well known to Birdwhistell (she was the per-son whose questions eventually led to *The Natural History of an Interview*, as documented in Leeds-Hurwitz 1989a), so the suggestion to involve Goffman may have originated with her.[24] It is unclear whether Goffman met her, but it is certainly feasible; after all, he cited her work as early as his dissertation

(1953), so he certainly knew about her, and their networks overlapped. In any case, the invitation letter from both Masserman and Moreno explained that they edited an annual "in which outstanding authorities throughout the world contribute chapters on their specialty in the field." As the next volume would be on social psychiatry, Goffman was invited to contribute the topic "Social Influences in Psychotherapy, or a related title of your own choice." They explained that "a summary or modification of some of your recent writings in this field would serve the purpose admirably" (Jun 19, 1958, JLM), so presumably they had read some of his work. Oddly, Moreno's secretary had difficulty in locating the correct Goffman; the letter in the file is addressed to "Mr. Irwin W. Goffman" at the University of Michigan, and there is a separate letter from Ann Manzoeillo, Moreno's secretary, to Masserman, saying that letter was returned, marked "unknown," and requesting further information. She realized he had mentioned "Erving" as the person's name, but "the one we found as a member of the American Psychological Society was Irwin" (Jun 30, 1958, JLM). The correct name and address were obviously supplied, because the next month Goffman answered: "Some day I would like to do a paper on the specific subject you mention, but for the next half year or so I'm afraid other commitments prevent me from doing so." Goffman enclosed a prepublication copy of "The Moral Career of the Mental Patient," to show "the sort of thing I do" and suggesting that "You are of course welcome, if *Psychiatry* is willing, to use it or any other of my published pieces" (Jul 28, 1958, JLM). They were not interested in that option but did leave open the possibility of Goffman making "a contribution in the future" (Aug 4, 1958, JLM). This example of a missed opportunity was presumably only one of multiples, but it is one for which documentation is available. It demonstrates at the very least that Goffman's name was being circulated and his reputation built (through just the sort of invisible college he later more actively participated in building) if people he did not yet know were writing to offer opportunities. It is important especially because these were not sociologists offering the invitation, but psychiatrists, also demonstrating the sort of disciplinary boundary-crossing that was becoming a taken-for-granted by Goffman.

University of California, Berkeley

Goffman taught at Berkeley from 1958 to 1968, moving with uncommon speed from a Visiting Assistant Professor in 1958 to Professor in 1962 due to completing an astonishing five books in his first years there (1959c, 1961a, 1961b, 1963a, 1963b). He obtained the position as the result of an invitation from Herbert Blumer, another of his professors in sociology at Chicago (see Winkin 1999 for details). Blumer had begun his position in sociology at Berkeley in 1952, and six years later invited Goffman to join that department (Fine and Manning 2003). Marx tells us that "Berkeley in 1960 represented the best of the Chicago, Columbia, and Harvard socio-logical traditions" (1984, 650), so it was a wonderful place for him to be. Goffman's first important connection outside of sociology at Berkeley was with anthropology.

Schneider and Anthropology

David M. Schneider took a position in anthropology at Berkeley before Goffman arrived, leaving before him as well, in 1960.[25] They already knew one another—correspondence dating back to 1952 has been preserved—al-though not at Chicago because Schneider earned his doctorate from Harvard. They were quite comfortable early, as Goffman teased often in these letters, especially playing with forms of address: "Boy" in 1954,[26] "Sweatpea" in 1956 (a letter which made clear he hoped they would share a hotel room for the ASA meeting that year) (Nov 4, 1956, DS), and "Hero of the People" in 1957 in a letter asking, again in teasing fashion, what Schneider thought about Berkeley (Feb 5, 1957, DS).[27] Importantly, Schneider wrote an extremely positive recommendation for Goffman to Reinhard Bendix of the depart-ment of sociology at Berkeley, concluding:

> The particular problem—the structure of social interaction—which Erving Goffman has devoted himself to—is not popular because it is so very tough. I know of a few people who have tried to work at it, but I do not know of a living person either in the United States or in Europe who even approach Goffman in either the quality or the quantity of published output, or who even approaches him in intellectual structure. (Nov 6, 1958, DS)

In fact, Goffman did begin teaching at Berkeley in 1958. There is documen-tation from 1959 that together Goffman and Schneider were

> exploring the feasibility of applying on behalf of the two departments to the National Institute of Mental Health for a five-year grant. This grant would be designed to set up a training program in the social aspects of mental health. It would provide the funds necessary for the faculty member principally responsible for the program, for secretarial assistance, and for a number of relatively generous graduate fellowships for students electing to work in this field.[28]

The two of them wanted to work with Merton Gill, a psychoanalyst in private practice in Berkeley, who had taught in the psychology department.[29] The quote just provided comes from a letter arguing that Gill should be hired in sociology to facilitate this three-way collaboration. However, Gill was not hired, and the next year Schneider left Berkeley for Chicago,[30] and so that project never happened. (In fact, Goffman argued for Schneider to return to Berkeley,[31] simultaneously with trying to get Berkeley to hire Gill,[32] simultaneously with Schneider trying to get Chicago to hire Goffman.[33]) In any case, this connection between scholars in sociology, anthropology, and psychology is a good example of an early multidisciplinary collaboration at Berkeley (and presages Goffman's assistance in preparing the proposal for the Center for Urban Ethnography at Penn a few years later).

Despite this instance, neither multi- nor interdisciplinary connections were taken for granted at Berkeley in the same way they had been at Chicago. For example, Neil Smelser (2009), a colleague of Goffman's in sociology at Berkeley starting in 1958, describes the group of regular poker players of which they were both part, and everyone listed is a sociologist, which sounds quite different from the diverse group of graduate students with whom Goffman had spent time at Chicago. But there was one particularly significant successful interdisciplinary group at Berkeley that included Goffman.

The Saturday Group

Fine and Manning argue that the sociolinguists William Labov and Dell Hymes were "perhaps most significant in terms of his [Goffman's] social and intellectual development" (2003, 40), but they are talking about when all three of these scholars were based at Penn. However, their connection began earlier, for Goffman connected with Hymes, as well as with others, at Berkeley, and that is the heart of the story to be told here. This was an interdisciplinary group rather than a multidisciplinary one because they were jointly inventing a new way to study interaction.

Table 2.1: Saturday Group at Berkeley, by Department

Anthropology: Dell Hymes, Ethel Albert
Sociology: Erving Goffman, Aaron Cicourel
Linguistics: John Gumperz (also South Asian studies), Wallace Chafe (later: Sidney Lamb, Julian Boyd)
Speech/Psychology: Susan Ervin-Tripp (later: Josephine Miles)
Psychology: Dan Slobin
Philosophy: John Searle, David Schroeder
Folklore: Alan Dundes
(From **Stanford University, in Anthropology**: Charles Frake, Roy D'Andrade [later: Duane Metzger, Kimball Romney])
(Occasionally, from **UCLA, in Sociology**: Harold Garfinkel)

Hymes taught at Berkeley from 1960 to 1965, with a joint appointment in linguistics and anthropology, so he overlapped with Goffman for five years. He and Goffman were both part of the informal gathering sometimes called the "Saturday group" (Murray 1998, 149), starting about 1960, which also included John Gumperz and Wallace Chafe in linguistics; John Searle and David Schroeder in philosophy; Ethel Albert in anthropology (but not David Schneider, as he had already left for Chicago); Dan Slobin in psychology; Alan Dundes in folklore; Aaron Cicourel, then at the Center for the Study of Law and Society[34] and later in sociology; and Susan Ervin-Tripp (officially based in psychology, then speech, then psychology again, but often counted as a linguist).[35] For details on the Saturday group, see Murray (1998, 2013) and Winkin and Leeds-Hurwitz (2013). Meyer says that Harold Garfinkel "sometimes participated in these meetings" as well (2024, 33). Hymes has portrayed the Saturday group as "a loose confederation at Berkeley in the early 1960s, one that became the basis of a continuing network of 'socio-linguistic' activity until this day" (1984, 621), and pointed out in a 1994 interview with Murray that members "were not the established figures in their various departments" (300). Hymes later expanded on this, crediting Gumperz as primary organizer.[36]

John Gumperz was of great importance in reaching out and bringing together people at Berkeley and elsewhere. Marginality again was the probable part of the motivation. He was teaching Hindi in a South Asian program, innovatively indeed, but without much recognition for his linguistics. John organized a local production of Saturday papers with John Searle, Erving Goffman, Sue Tripp, myself, and some others, which led to a session at the AAA [American Anthropological Association] meetings in San Francisco in 1963, and the *Ethnography of Communication* special publication of the AAA in 1964. (1997, 126) [37]

Silverstein characterizes the Saturday group as "a lively crowd of trans-departmentally located age cohorts" (2010, 935), adding in Sydney Lamb, in linguistics at Berkeley, as well as Charles Frake and Roy D'Andrade, in anthropology at nearby Stanford University. All three of Silverstein's phrases are relevant: They were the lively crowd, they were close in age, and they were not yet central in terms of specializations within their home departments. In an interview, Gumperz added in Julian Boyd, in linguistics, and Josephine Miles, in English, both at Berkeley, as well as Duane Metzger and Kimball Romney, in anthropology at Stanford (Murray 2013). Asked if the meetings involved formal papers, Gumperz responded, "Oh, no, no, no. We just had luncheons and talked, we talked very freely" and whoever was available on a particular day got together at someone's home (6). Gumperz has written about how important the group was to him personally: "Another major influence in my own development were the associations I formed in the nineteen sixties at the University of California in Berkeley with Dell Hymes, Erving Goffman, Susan Ervin-Tripp, and with Charles Frake and others at Stanford" (1997, 115). He mentions the major publications resulting from the group's "informal discussions" (115) as being a journal special issue (Gumperz and Hymes 1964a) and the expanded book version (Gumperz and Hymes 1972).

As Gumperz and Hymes explain in their preface to the special issue of *American Anthropologist*, "The good fortune of co-presence in the same area over several years has enabled many of the contributors to have frequent discussions and to discover the common interests that link their work; travels, meetings, and letters have brought one or more of them into more than casual personal contact and discussion with the others" (1964b, v). But participants did not just gather informally in a sort of faculty seminar; multiple members of this group first participated in two regional conferences: a joint meeting of the Kroeber Anthropological Society and the Southwestern Anthropological Association (SAA) in 1962. Panelists at SAA were Goffman, Hymes, Frake, and Gumperz (Murray 2013).[38] Although there is no record of what Goffman presented, most likely it was an early version of the paper selected for the resulting Gumperz and Hymes volume. Then they presented a symposium at the AAA in 1963 (Gumperz and Hymes 1964b). It was these presentations which lead everyone to write up their ideas for either or both the journal special issue and later book. Participants included not only the two editors, but also Goffman, Albert, Ervin-Tripp, and Frake from the Saturday group, as well as William Labov, later part of the Penn group. Ray Birdwhistell only joined in the 1972 collection, but Labov connected earlier, and so was included in both volumes (Labov 1964, 1972a).[39] In his introduction, Hymes highlighted Goffman's contribution "The Neglected Situation" (Goffman 1964a) as one that "strikes to the heart of the matter" (1964a, 4), so Goffman was clearly identified as a relevant and valued participant even in those early days. Later, in 1984, Hymes expanded on the matter: "In this paper, as in his conversation at the time, Erving welcomed the emerging attention to the social dimension of language" (621). As one of the major participants, Ervin-Tripp felt that the departure of Hymes from Berkeley and the Saturday group "severely damaged this network" of sociolinguists (1997, 75).[40] She also valued Goffman's presence on campus: He participated in her 1968 summer workshops, a project sponsored by the SSRC Committee on Sociolinguistics, along with others, including Gumperz, Hymes, Charles Ferguson, Harvey Sacks, Emanuel Schegloff, Aaron Cicourel, Roger Shuy, Vera John and Courtney Cazden (see Ervin-Tripp [1969] for the report; doctoral students, including Ben Blount, Brian Stross, and others who do not otherwise appear in these pages, filmed interaction during participant observations around the world in order to study children's communicative competence). In addition to these others, Ervin-Tripp writes, "Erving Goffman joined the group to analyze filmed interaction" (23n2), an activity for which he is certainly not much known. Once Goffman had left Berkeley, the others in the group lost their connection to sociology, as Gumperz explained to Murray: "I kept getting the last of his [Goffman's] students for two or three years, but we've had no relationships with sociology" (2013, 8), whereas ties between anthropology, linguistics, psychology, and philosophy endured, although Gumperz did say the remaining group members did not meet as often in later years.

The point here is that Goffman was an active member of a productive interdisciplinary group (interdisciplinary rather than multidisciplinary because they were creating sociolinguistics, a new topic) which met informally and collaborated on multiple joint products: conference panels, a journal special issue, and a book. He was putting into practice what he had learned at Chicago, refined at NIMH, and would go on to develop much further at Penn—that is, not only coordinating with people having common interests but turning those interests into significant publications, whether sole-authored or edited collections. As Gumperz was the instigator of that group, it is worth spending a little more time on his connection to Goffman.

Gumperz and Goffman

Gumperz was the same age as Goffman, but had started at Berkeley two years earlier, in 1956, so it makes sense that he was the organizer of the Saturday group. His comments about that group have already been quoted, but in several places Gumperz also has been quite explicit about what he learned from Goffman through their connection. For example, in Blom and Gumperz (1972), Goffman is one of those (along with Edmund Leach and Fredrik Barth) credited for the conceptual framework used. In an interview in 1992, Gumperz said: "But now I realize what Goffman has contributed. He's the first one who's given us a language really to study interaction, a set of concepts: situation, encounter, focused interaction and things of that sort and involvement in particular which have been really basic to conversational analysis, even though conversational analysts never mention these notions" (Murray 2013, 20). In a 1995 interview, he provided a slightly different explanation of where his work and Goffman's overlapped: "To look at talk as it occurs in speech events is to look at communicative practices. Along with others, I claim that such practices constitute an intermediate and in many ways analytically distinct level of organization. A sociological equivalent here is Erving Goffman's 'interaction order,' a level of organization which bridges the linguistic and the social" (Prevignano and Di Luzio 2003, 8). Gumperz provided an even more detailed evaluation of what he considered most valuable about Goffman's work. The crucial part is this:

> Goffman has given us the outline of a communicative perspective on the social world. In his earlier work he sets aside traditional analytical categories such as role, status, identity, and the like to concentrate on the phenomenal bases of interactive processes ... Interaction, he goes on to claim, should be seen as a separate level of communicative organization: thus the interaction order, which bridges the verbal and the social, must be analyzed in terms of its own analytical units both at the level of language and in interaction. His arguments thus foreshadow current thinking on communicative practice. (2001, 217)

The use of the phrase "a communicative perspective on the social world" here is key. But even the fact that Gumperz was still talking about the influence of Goffman's ideas on him and others decades after Goffman died serves to demonstrate the significance of his role both at Berkeley and as a leading scholar. Although Gumperz did not continue as an important member of Goffman's invisible college after the move to Penn, he demonstrated how to create an invisible college while they were both at Berkeley and had a connection to the Multiple Analysis Project based at Indiana.

Minor Projects at Berkeley

The Saturday group was Goffman's most significant interdisciplinary association at Berkeley, but it was not the only one. Clearly, none of the following was as influential (on Goffman or on others) over the long term, but all merit at least brief mention. First, he was affiliated with the Center for the Integration of Social Science Theory. Second, he participated in an informal group at the Center for the Study of Law and Society with Aaron Cicourel and others. Third, he connected with Bateson and the Palo Alto Group. And finally, he was one of the organizers of a conference, Strategic Interaction and Conflict.

Center for the Integration of Social Science Theory

Goffman was affiliated with the Center for the Integration of Social Science Theory while he had a grant from NIMH to write up the books *Asylums* (see the preface to that book, 1961b) and *Encounters* (see that preface, 1961a). In this case, there is no evidence that he had much to do with others at the center, so it's an exceedingly minor affiliation, although it is possible that further research will uncover more details.

Center for the Study of Law and Society

Aaron Cicourel (part of the Saturday group) has written (in 2009) about another informal group at Berkeley that included Goffman.

> I frequently saw Erving from the summer of 1961 to the summer of 1965 and during the academic year 1965–66, I was affiliated with the Law and Society Center at the Boalt Law SŒchool in Berkeley. Phil Selznick had organized a kind of on-going seminar. Erving, Shelly Messinger, David Matza, Ed Lemert, Ruth Kornhauser, Carl Werthman, Jerry Skolnick, and a few others were also participants in the regular meetings of the Center. We spent a lot of time together

during [the] 1965–66 academic year in Berkeley when I was a visiting professor in sociology and at Phil Selznick's Center. In the spring of 1966, Erving attended my graduate seminar regularly.

Selznick was based in sociology with Goffman and Cicourel, and started the Center for the Study of Law and Society at Berkeley.[41] Sheldon Messenger was vice chair at the center, also based in sociology,[42] as were all the others named here. As will be evident in chapter 3, Goffman apparently enjoyed this sort of gathering of colleagues, for he participated in comparable informal seminars at Columbia University with Labov, and occasionally attended other people's graduate seminars as well once he moved to Penn.

Palo Alto Group

Fred Erickson mentions an intriguing possibility about Goffman's connections in his early days at Berkeley, in this case not with anyone on campus, but with several people based nearby: Gregory Bateson, Jürgen Ruesch, and Weldon Kees, all well known for their work in communication. He writes: "As sound recording became easier after World War II, Bateson, in collaboration with Jürgen Reusch [*sic*] and Weldon Keys [*sic*], made sound cinema films of family therapy interviews using a 16-mm camera (Reusch [*sic*] & Keys [*sic*] 1956). Erving Goffman became involved with Reusch [*sic*], Keys [*sic*], and Bateson, and their family therapy efforts when he arrived at the University of California, Berkeley, after the mid-1950s" (Erickson 2011, 180). When asked for details, Erickson clarified that "Ron [Scollon] said that while Goffman was at UC Berkeley he visited with the people at the family therapy research group at the VA hospital in Palo Alto" (email to the author, Apr 28, 2024). Bateson was one of the people then working with that research group, now typically referred to as the Palo Alto Group (Wilder 1979; Winkin 1988b). Goffman cited Bateson in his dissertation (1953) and had met him in person at least by the 1956 Macy Conference as mentioned earlier; he also cited Ruesch and Bateson (1951) on communication and psychiatry in his dissertation and had met Ruesch at least by 1957 when they participated in the same panel for the Symposium on Preventive and Social Psychiatry, previously mentioned.

In addition, Burns briefly refers to "the working relationship he [Goffman] came to establish at Berkeley with Gregory Bateson's group" (1992, 17). Thus, despite the lack of documentation seen to date, Goffman may well have joined Bateson and Ruesch to participate in some of their film analysis; he is known to have done that on several other occasions, even though film analysis was not a frequent activity for him. Clearly, both Bateson and Goffman worked with psychologists and psychiatrists and framed at least some of their work as having special interest for that audience. And Bateson began working with Ruesch, a psychiatrist, at the Langley Porter Clinic in San Francisco by the late 1940s, preparing several films for analysis with Kees.[43] The fact that Goffman required students to read Ruesch and Bateson in a course at least by 1960 (Winkin 2022f) may only show the significance of their ideas, or may be another hint that they were talking in person at that point.

Overall, these three affiliations to two UC Berkeley groups and one off-campus group demonstrate that Goffman was beginning to forge connections with not one but several multi- and/or interdisciplinary research groups, finding a surprising variety of scholars sharing at least some research interests with him, and joining them for various periods of time and at various levels. These increased in level of involvement over time: First, he was affiliated with the Center for the Integration of Social Science Theory as an administrative home while he held an NIMH grant to complete not one but two books—basically a solitary activity, although there may well have been connections with others there that have not yet been documented. Second, he was part of an informal group meeting through the auspices of the Center for the Study of Law and Society, a group which met to talk (rather than conduct research). While there may have been some concrete results (perhaps a conference panel organized?), no evidence has yet been located. Third, and most enticing, he met informally with Bateson's group at Palo Alto and was apparently a participant in at least a few of their research discussions analyzing filmed interaction. As with these other activities, there is very little documentation available, so it is difficult to be certain how active Goffman was, but at the very least all three demonstrate his participation in multidisciplinary conversations, setting him up for a fourth, more productive activity relating to still another group on campus.

Strategic Interaction and Conflict Conference

Goffman was one of the members of the Conference Planning Committee for Strategic Interaction and Conflict, an event sponsored by the Institute of International Studies in 1964, working with Seymour Martin Lipset, who directed the institute (Jaworski 2019, 2023). Lipset was based in Berkeley's sociology department 1956–1966; he had previously been a lecturer at the

University of Toronto (1946–1948), which he and Goffman would have noticed, though their time there did not coincide; afterwards Lipset moved to Harvard (1966–1975),[44] overlapping with Goffman's year there.

Table 2.2: Strategic Interaction and
Conflict Conference, by Department

Sociology: Erving Goffman (Berkeley), Seymour Martin Lipset (Berkeley), William Gamson (University of Michigan), Jessie Bernard (Pennsylvania State University)
Psychology: Morton Deutsch (Columbia University), Alex Bavelas (Stanford)
Economics: Thomas C. Schelling (Harvard), John C. Harsanyi (Berkeley), Martin Shubik (Yale), Daniel Ellsberg (US State Department), Frederick Balderston (Berkeley)
Math: Anatol Rapoport (Michigan)
Political Science: Albert Wohlstetter (Rand Corporation)
Institute of International Studies: Kathleen Archibald (Berkeley)
Results: *Strategic Interaction and Conflict: Original Papers and Discussion* (Archibald 1966)

A few others beyond Lipset are notable: Kathleen Archibald served as coordinator at the institute rather than being primarily affiliated with any department; earlier she had earned a master's in social work and later a PhD in sociology (Archibald 1968); she was one of the organizers of the conference, editing the resulting volume (1966). Before Rapoport was at Berkeley, he was at Chicago, something he and Goffman were likely to have discovered. Gamson had already read Goffman's work, used it in his own teaching, and later invited Goffman to the University of Michigan to give the Katz-Newcomb lecture, hosting him for a several-day visit (Gamson 2009; Gamson also reviewed Goffman's book *Frame Analysis* in 1975). Jaworski reports that "Goffman's central contribution was in the second part of the conference. . . . Goffman introduced the discussion of 'Communication and Enforcement Systems' . . . Goffman had prepared what amounted to a full paper" (2023, 85–6). Jaworski summarizes Goffman's comments, but the point here is not what he said so much as that he was involved both in organizing a multidisciplinary event while at Berkeley, and in helping participants to synthesize the ideas discussed, roles which he went on to reprise in later activities.

In fact, Goffman's role as discussant at conference panels continued across multiple organizations over the years, e.g., the American Sociological Association in 1971, where he was a discussant for "The Sociology of Sex Roles";[45] ASA 1978, for "Issues in Research: Covert Research Funding";[46] twice at the American Anthropological Association in 1976, for "The Mental Hospital as a Small Culture: The Anthropology of a Total Institution and for Approaches to the Analysis of Face-to-Face Interaction," with Adam Kendon, Madeleine Mathiot, Ray McDermott, Emanuel Schegloff, and Ervin-Tripp;[47] and AAA in 1978, for "Discourse: Speech Acts and Contextualization," with presentations by Bambi Schieffelin, Judith Irvine, Joel Sherzer, and Gumperz, and with Hymes as a second discussant.[48] Uncommonly, Goffman was the keynote speaker at the Chicago Linguistic Society, along with Michael Silverstein, in April 1979, followed by what has been described as "a quite spirited and engaging debate between the two" (Mokros 2010, 299).

All told, while at Berkeley Goffman connected with multiple informal groups as well as more established research centers, and helped to organize at least one conference, most of these activities leading to further connections in later years. Clearly, the Saturday group was the most substantial of these affiliations. The major (documented) result of the several minor activities was an invitation to Harvard.

Harvard University

Goffman apparently was in a visiting position at Harvard twice, once in 1959 (Jaworski 2023; Meyer 2024; Smith 2006), and again in 1966–1967. Certainly, Goffman was citing Garfinkel's work around that time, as in his 1959 article, "The Moral Career of the Mental Patient," and Rawls (2023) has documented the details of their drafting a book together, though it was never completed. The second visit was when Schelling invited Goffman to be a research fellow at the Center for International Affairs in 1966–1967 while on sabbatical from Berkeley (Jaworski 2019; Winkin 2022b). Schelling was at Harvard from 1958 to 1990 in economics and co-founded the Center for International Affairs in 1958.[49] According to the official history, "In 1958, Schelling, along with Robert R. Bowie, Henry A. Kissinger and Edward S. Mason, cofounded the Center for International Affairs at Harvard as a home for basic research in international relations, at a time when academia did not recognize the legitimacy of this discipline" (Nicholasen 2016).

Goffman and Schelling did not meet for the first time at Berkeley but had known each other during Goffman's time at NIMH in the 1950s. As Schelling (2015) has explained:

> I met him when he was at the Institutes of Health in Washington. He approached me, I visited him and we talked, and I think he gave me reprints of "Facework" and "Cooling the Mark Out," which I've always loved. Sometime in the middle 60's I invited him to Harvard's Center for International Affairs, at which I had some Ford Foundation money for bringing scholars to Harvard, and he spent a year, finishing one of his books; I don't remember which one. . . . When he was my guest at Harvard we didn't become close friends. He was very distant.

A few clarifications: by "Institutes of Health" Schelling presumably means the National Institute of Mental Health, an easy error to make because NIMH is but one of the National Institutes of Health, all based on a single campus in Bethesda, Maryland. Also, the book Goffman prepared while at Harvard was *Strategic Interaction* (1970). Preda (2022) points out that he actually wrote one chapter while at Berkeley, and the other while at Harvard. In fact, in the first chapter, "Expression Games," Goffman first points out that he had published "a preliminary statement" in Archibald (1966) and then credits Archibald with "having made a great number of suggestions which I have incorporated freely into the text without acknowledgment" (1970, 3n1).

Although there is not much documentation available, we know Goffman participated in at least one semi-formal gathering at Harvard, a "discussion club," because Lon Fuller, who was Carter Professor of Jurisprudence at Harvard Law School at the time, wrote a letter to Goffman in 1966, following up on a conversation they had. As attachments, Fuller sent three articles. "The third piece, on adjudication, is the one I discussed with you briefly the night of the meeting of our discussion club." He asks Goffman to read them. "I hope I might coax out of you some help and criticism. I am in the quandary of dealing with what seem to me to be sociological problems, but at the same time problems that appear not to be dealt with in the existing literature of sociology. These problems have to do with social roles, and particularly with the responsibility that attach to the discharge of a particular role" (Oct 26, 1966, LFF). There is no response in the file, but presumably they met and continued the conversation. So, Goffman made at least one new connection while at Harvard.

At the same time, for the larger story being told here, what is most relevant about Goffman's time at Harvard is that he apparently did not make the same sort of long-term connections with multiple colleagues from a range of departments there as he had made previously at Berkeley, and would go on to make at Penn. And this was despite the several scholars he knew at Harvard; not only did he know Schelling and Lipset before he arrived, but Hymes had been based in the Department of Social Relations at Harvard prior to Berkeley, which he explained as a combination of "social anthropology, social psychology, sociology, maybe developmental psychology" (Scollon 2004, 52), so Goffman may have had an introduction to one or two people in that department as a result, despite the fact that Hymes did not leave on the best of terms. Gamson (2009) mentions that Harvard had a "department of social relations which also had this interest in the interdisciplinary bridging," but it is unclear whether Goffman connected with that group, just as it is unclear whether he connected again with Lipset. He did know George A. Miller, since they served on a panel together in 1957, as well as Ozzie G. Simmons (a student of Clyde Kluckhohn and Talcott Parsons, and faculty in anthropology at Harvard)[50] and Howard E. Freeman (a research associate at the School of Public Health)[51] from another panel the same year, as mentioned in the section on NIMH. It seems likely he would have connected with one or more of them, and/or various colleagues and friends while he was there. Goffman did at least get a lot written while at Harvard: He wrote a chapter and prepared the manuscript for *Strategic Interaction* (1970). In addition, he credits the Center for the Study of Law and Society as one of the sources of funds supporting his writing of "Where the Action Is," published as a chapter of *Interaction Ritual* (1967).

Conclusion

Chicago is where Goffman first developed a solid understanding of interdisciplinarity, made friends with peers across disciplinary boundaries (especially in anthropology and psychology, among the closest disciplines to sociology in that place at that time), and connected strongly enough with several of his professors that he was invited to apply to Berkeley by one (Blumer), and maintained a long-term friendship with another (Hughes). He joined fully in the "community of scholars" that Chicago deliberately fostered.[52] That was the beginning of his invisible college, although it is one that many others have described. NIMH is where he connected with notable numbers

of psychologists and psychiatrists, published in relevant journals such as
Psychiatry, and conducted the observations that led to major publications
such as *Asylums* (1961b). In the process, he expanded his invisible college
considerably, adding psychiatry to the mix of disciplines.

Even in his first teaching role at Berkeley, Goffman displayed a willingness to cross disciplinary borders. This is clear not only from his incomplete
efforts to work with Schneider and Gill on a grant proposal, his participation
in the Saturday group and resulting conferences and publications, as well as
his work on the Strategic Interaction and Conflict conference and the other
small projects there, but in memories of students. For example, Emanuel
Schegloff has said in an interview with Cmejrkova and Prevignano that
Goffman made him read the "literature of all the fields that were contiguous
to what I was working on"—and that included nine fields! While he did not
appreciate it at the time, he did later (2003, 21).

While at Berkeley, Goffman not only met Hymes, with whom he worked
frequently on multiple projects large and small until his death, but also
Gumperz, Cicourel, Garfinkel, Schegloff, Sacks, and others, many of whom
he maintained contact with after leaving California, and most of whom became part of one or another later project. Goffman had Gumperz available
as a model for how to develop and coordinate multi- and interdisciplinary
efforts, and he was included in a publication resulting from those early
efforts (Goffman 1964a). And it was while he was at Berkeley that he first
became involved with the development of sociolinguistics, a topic which
remained an interest for the rest of his life, and formed a larger scholarly
community that was quite different from the community of psychologists
and psychiatrists previously developed during his years at NIMH, including
now scholars based mostly in linguistics, philosophy, and folklore. In addition, the conference which he helped to organize at Berkeley led not only to
further connections with people in additional disciplines (economics, math,
political science) but also led directly to his year at Harvard, the addition of
at least one more discipline (international relations), and the completion of
another book. Until and unless someone else who was his contemporary at
Harvard supplies additional information (or deposits letters into an archive),
we must rely on Schelling's report that Goffman did not develop the same
sort of informal network at Harvard that he did earlier at Chicago, NIMH,
and Berkeley, and later at Penn, Indiana, and Texas, unlikely as that seems.

Given that sociology at Berkeley was a more prestigious department
than the one at Penn, one might ask why Goffman was willing to leave at

all. There is correspondence explaining this as a move to permit a lighter teaching load and granting more time for research and publications, so that is at least one obvious answer. A letter from UCLA demonstrates that Goffman was considering leaving Berkeley for that university as early as 1965 in exchange for a particularly light teaching load.[53] There is another letter from Schneider telling Goffman he was wanted at Chicago and could get the same light teaching load (Jun 6, 1965, DS). The Chicago position would have been a joint affiliation between anthropology and sociology, just what he ended up with at Penn (Schneider to Goffman, Jun 11, 1965, DS). There is not a lot of documentation explaining why Penn won this competition, but it may well have had to do with the strong push from Hymes and others there, as well as the additional reward of becoming a Benjamin Franklin Professor and the resulting higher salary. In addition, Murray describes a few negatives about the context at Berkeley, based on interviews with Hymes and Gumperz, which led Hymes to consider leaving, and which probably were relevant to Goffman's move as well. Briefly, there was some "mutual unease between the generations" (according to Gumperz), and junior faculty felt they "didn't have any weight in decisions" (according to Hymes) (Murray 2010, 98). In any case, the invisible college that Goffman had been developing while at Chicago, NIMH, and Berkeley was not lost when he moved to Penn; rather it was expanded considerably. Some of the connections he made involved strong personal relationships that lasted decades (as demonstrated by his correspondence with Hughes and Schneider); some led to publications (as with the Saturday group); and others led to an invitation to the next stage (both Harvard and Penn).

Endnotes

[1] I am not describing the years between enrolling at Chicago and completing the dissertation as that period has been more than adequately covered; see especially Winkin 2000; also Winkin 1988a, 1999, 2010, 2022c, 2022d, 2022e; Winkin and Leeds-Hurwitz, 2013. For Goffman's dissertation research in the Shetland Islands (in Scotland), across 1949–51, see Smith 2022a; Winkin 2000, 2022c. On Goffman's undergraduate days in Canada, see Bott-Spillius 2010; Smith 2003; Winkin 1984a, 1988a, 2022c, 2022f; Wrong 1990. For further details about Goffman's graduate days at Chicago, see Smith and Winkin 2013; Winkin 2022a.

[2] There were actually two Chicago Schools of sociology (Fine 1995), but distinguishing between them is not the issue in this context.

[3] See Jaworski 2000; Vienne 2010, 2022; Winkin 1988a. And Shalin suggests that Hughes is important for his "doubts about disciplinary boundaries" (2023, 769).

[4] See Chapoulie 1996; Smith 2022a; Smith and Winkin, 2012, 2013.

[5] See Winkin 1999 for discussion of the problematic term "influences" (31–33).

[6] Winkin published this in French: "Mes amis de Chicago et moi, nous avons formé une sorte de groupe solidaire" (1984a, 86), although he has pointed out that Goffman spoke to him in English and so suggested that the quote should appear here in English.

[7] I remember Birdwhistell talking about it and encouraging us to read it.

[8] Even into the early 1960s, William Kornblum explains: "Chicago is the most exciting intellectual community that I have ever been part of. . . . One of the best things about sociology at the University of Chicago was its proximity to anthropology. . . . The interdisciplinary tradition that Robert Redfield and Robert Park started was of inestimable importance for me" (Jaynes et al. 2009, 381).

[9] Interestingly, he did not mention either Edward Shils or Edward Banfield, as those are the professors for whom he actually served as research assistant in different years (Goffman CV, n.d., UCOP).

[10] Committee on Honorary Degrees to unnamed administrator, Jun 12, 1979, UCOP.

[11] Alvin Boskoff to Wilson, Feb 14, 1979, UCOP.

[12] Murray S. Davis to William Julius Wilson (Chair of Sociology at Chicago), Feb 27, 1979, UCOP.

[13] Peter M. Blau to Wilson, Mar 6, 1979, UCOP.

[14] Lewis A. Coser to Wilson, Feb 16, 1979, UCOP.

[15] Alvin Boskoff to Wilson, Feb 14, 1979, UCOP.

[16] Goffman to D. Gale Johnson (Provost), Aug 1, 1979, UCOP.

[17] The reference to Blumer 1969b is part of the quote from Verhoeven, so it is Blumer 1969 in the references section.

[18] Specifically, see Leeds-Hurwitz 1994, 2022; Winkin 2022d; Winkin and Leeds-Hurwitz 2013.

[19] For more on Goffman's relationship with Bateson, see Leeds-Hurwitz 2022.

[20] Other participants were Ozzie G. Simmons and Howard E. Freeman at Harvard University; Henry J. Meyer and Edgar F. Borgatta at New York University; and John H. Mabry, E. L. Siegal, W. A. Mann, S. Furman, and A. McLaughlin, jointly authoring one paper, and coming from New York State College of Medicine or Syracuse Veterans Administration Hospital (https://www.asanet.org/wp-content/uploads/1957_am_final_program_complete_o.pdf).

[21] The panel chair was Lawrence C. Kolb (director of the New York State Psychiatric Institute); other participants were George A. Miller (psychology, Harvard University), Solomon E. Asch (psychology, Swarthmore College), and Jürgen Ruesch (psychiatry, University of California School of Medicine, known for his work with Bateson).

[22] https://www.asanet.org/wp-content/uploads/1960_am_final_program_complete_with_cover.pdf.

[23] https://www.asanet.org/wp-content/uploads/1978_annual_meeting_program.pdf.

[24] Fromm-Reichmann died in 1957, so either she made the suggestion about Goffman's inclusion in this particular volume before the letter of invitation was written in 1958, or she was not the one who recommended him.

[25] https://www.lib.uchicago.edu/e/scrc/findingaids/view.php?eadid=ICU.SPCL.SCHNEIDERD.

[26] Undated letter with the handwritten note "1954?" from Goffman to Schneider, DS.

[27] Goffman is not listed in the ASA program that year (https://www.asanet.org/wp-content/uploads/1960_am_final_program_complete_with_cover.pdf), but it was held in New York, so he may just have gone without presenting; New York is only a few hours from Washington, DC by train.

[28] Letter from Reinhard Bendix, chair of sociology, to Lincoln Constance, Dean of the College of Arts and Letters at Berkeley, Feb 16, 1959, DS.

[29] https://www.nytimes.com/1994/11/19/obituaries/merton-m-gill-psychoanalyst-is-dead-at-80.html.

[30] https://www.lib.uchicago.edu/e/scrc/findingaids/view.php?eadid=ICU.SPCL.SCHNEIDERD#idp3351112.

[31] Goffman to Schneider, n.d. [May 1965, based on internal evidence], DS.

[32] This three-way collaboration was still being discussed a few years later, as Goffman wrote to Schneider: "Marty's [Merton Gill] away in S. America; when he comes back I'll talk to him again about us all forming a social science research institute (that would be one way he could stay), but that's a very long shot" (Goffman to Schneider, n.d. [May/June 1965, based on internal evidence], DS).

[33] Schneider to Goffman, Jun 11, 1965, DS.

[34] The Center for the Study of Law and Society provided funding for doctoral projects, including those of Harvey Sacks, Emanuel Schegloff, David Sudnow, and Roy Turner, as well as a postdoc for Cicourel (Meyer 2024). Cicourel and Goffman obviously stayed in touch, because Goffman was included on a panel Cicourel organized and chaired, "The Problem of Integrating Macro and Micro Sociological Theory" for the American Sociological Association in 1977. Other panelists were Randall Collins (UC San Diego) and A. W. Gouldner (Washington University) (https://www.asanet.org/wp-content/uploads/1977_annual_meeting_program.pdf).

[35] https://oac.cdlib.org/search?style=oac4;Institution=UC%20Berkeley::Bancroft%20Library;idT=991077445029706532.

[36] Heller also reiterates Gumperz's influence in bringing others together "into an interdisciplinary network" (2013, 398), although her focus is on the time after Goffman had left Berkeley.

[37] The publication he mentions is Gumperz and Hymes (1964a). To highlight the connection between the 1964 Committee on Sociolinguistics conference held at Indiana and Gumperz and Hymes's 1972 volume, *Directions in Sociolinguistics*, which grew out of their 1964 special issue, it is worth noting that Ferguson's report on the former event was titled "Directions in Sociolinguistics" (Ferguson 1965). A related title was used by Grimshaw for an article, "Directions for Research in Sociolinguistics" (1966).

[38] The SAA panel was probably part of the spring meeting of 1962, held at Berkeley (Dixon 1983).

[39] Hymes first wrote to Labov at Uriel Weinreich's recommendation when he was looking for people interested in contributing to the Gumperz and Hymes special issue "The Ethnography of Communication" (Hymes to Labov, Jan 9, 1963). Labov responded that he had already read Hymes's 1962 work on the ethnography of speaking (Labov to Hymes, Jan 24, 1963, DHH); he was included in the 1964 collection (Labov 1964). They quickly found areas of shared interest, as when Labov wrote, "Your letter demonstrated to me that we are looking at the world through the same pair of spectacles, or binoculars, or whatever they may be" (Oct 4, 1965, DHH). Labov and Hymes's full exchange can be found in DHH, Subcollection 1, Series I: Correspondence 1951–1987, Labov, William, folder 1, 1963–1972.

[40] Although Levinson documents that many of the same connections remained available, at least to students of Gumperz, through the 1970s: "In Berkeley at that time there was a rare and wonderful confluence of ideas from different disciplines concerning the study of meaning" (2003, 32).

[41] http://news.berkeley.edu/2010/06/16/selznick/.

[42] https://newsarchive.berkeley.edu/news/media/releases/2003/03/13_messinger.shtml.

[43] Ruesch and Bateson 1951; Ruesch and Kees 1956; see Leeds-Hurwitz 1922 for further discussion of the connections between Goffman and Bateson.

[44] The finding aid to his papers does not have an entry for Goffman, so it is unlikely they corresponded: https://findingaids.loc.gov/exist_collections/ead3pdf/mss/2018/ms018030.pdf.

[45] https://www.asanet.org/wp-content/uploads/1971_annual_meeting_program_c.pdf.

[46] https://www.asanet.org/wp-content/uploads/1978_annual_meeting_program.pdf.

[47] https://openanthroresearch.org/index.php/oarr/preprint/view/38/70.

[48] https://openanthroresearch.org/index.php/oarr/preprint/view/40/74.

[49] https://news.harvard.edu/gazette/story/2016/12/thomas-schelling-game-theory-pioneer-95/; https://news.harvard.edu/gazette/story/2021/03/thomas-crombie-schelling-95/.

[50] https://sirismm.si.edu/EADpdfs/NAA.1997-10.pdf.

[51] https://oac.cdlib.org/view?docId=hb5g50061q&chunk.id=div00037&brand=oac4&doc.view=entire_text.

[52] https://provost.uchicago.edu/sites/default/files/documents/reports/KalvenRprt_0.pdf.

[53] Richard Morris, acting chair of sociology at UCLA, to Goffman, May 27, 1965, DS.

CHAPTER THREE

People at Penn

Goffman left Berkeley for the University of Pennsylvania in 1968, staying until his death in 1982. First at Chicago, then at NIMH, and then Berkeley, and to a limited extent at Harvard, he had connected informally with scholars across disciplines, developing a nascent invisible college. Once he moved to Penn, he developed the full-blown version, creating particularly strong ties with colleagues based in several other departments, despite having uncommonly weak ties with peers in his own specialization of sociology for much of his time there. My focus in the last chapter was on Goffman's early experiences, up to and including his first academic position at Berkeley and his short-term position at Harvard. In this and the following two chapters, my focus will be on Goffman's connections and activities at Penn. The story begins with how relationships built at Berkeley helped convince Goffman to move to Penn. Then will come brief descriptions of the peers with whom Goffman worked at Penn on the various projects yet to be examined in chapters 4 and 5. Even though other faculty members on campus are noteworthy for a wide variety of reasons, only those relevant to the stories told here will be mentioned, but that includes a surprisingly large number. First, the core group of those involved in a set of major projects will be introduced, then the peripheral group members who were either minor players in major projects or only involved in minor projects. Finally, there will be a section about students who worked with Goffman at Penn. The focus will be on doctoral students who studied directly with him, but there will also be a few stories of other student interactions with him. In all cases, emphasis in that section will be on student interactions with and/or statements about Goffman and/or interdisciplinarity at Penn.

In all three chapters about Penn, the focus will be on the widening circle of those who interacted with Goffman on topics related to research, although the focus is less on conducting research and more on deciding upon and then sharing what had been learned (so, establishing journals and a book series to permit publication and share knowledge take center stage rather than a focus on joint research resulting in published articles or books). Clearly, not all members of Goffman's invisible college were equally important or received equal amounts of his time and attention. Even so, they were all part of an elaborate set of interconnected networks that seem well worth exploring. It would be interesting to document whether most scholars also either participate in or develop their own comparable interconnected networks; although that stands far beyond what this book can examine, it does seem likely, for it becomes clear that additional connections between others—even without Goffman—developed over time.

Getting Goffman to Penn

Dell Hymes moved from Berkeley to Penn in 1965. He wrote to Goffman in early 1968, suggesting that together they could build an interdisciplinary group at Penn comparable to the Saturday group at Berkeley.

> I believe that we are gradually building up an informal constellation of people with related interests and affinities that is approaching a sort of critical mass, where there just would be a large enough group who understand the point, of what you are doing, and of what the rest of us are doing. . . . The place isn't perfect but it has great possibilities and I believe you would find it a good place for yourself. And I want very much for you to come...The thought is that for you to work as you wish with a few students will both lead to some good work being done being done by them, and indirectly act as a very desirable stimulus to other students.[1]

Specific colleagues Hymes mentioned as part of the potential group were Ward Goodenough and William Davenport in anthropology, Kenneth Goldstein in folklore, Sol Worth in communications, and William Labov (then at Columbia University in New York; he joined Penn shortly after). Ray Birdwhistell (Goffman's professor at Toronto) arrived after Goffman, and so was not mentioned as enticement, though he was already based in the same city (Philadelphia) while teaching at Temple University a short distance away, a fact that Goffman certainly knew. Even from the very beginning, the goal was to bring together a group of people sharing common research interests, despite belonging administratively to different departments. At the time, "the department of sociology was a Parsonian stronghold not too happy about his coming to Penn" (Winkin 2022c, 10), so his initial appointment was as Benjamin Franklin Professor of Anthropology and Sociology, and his office was always in the Penn Museum, with anthropologists.[2] In 1977, all Franklin Professors were granted an even more prestigious title, so he became the Benjamin Franklin *University* Professor of Anthropology and Sociology.[3] Hymes once inadvertently referred to Goffman in print as Professor of Anthropology and Psychology, a statement which has been widely reprinted, but the university personnel records should have the final word, and they list the title as anthropology and sociology. Presumably, the confusion came about because Goffman later was granted a secondary appointment in psychology.

Numerous faculty members in other departments were delighted to have Goffman around, just as Hymes had promised. Looking back in 1997, Hymes reflected on the shift from Berkeley to Penn:

> A little later in Pennsylvania (ca. 1965) a cross-department network emerged that was important. It had diverse roots—personal drives, the earlier "communication" interest of Mead, Bateson, and others, Chicago symbolic interaction, etc. For a while there were the late Sol Worth (whose work was with film, but who interacted with all the rest), Ray Birdwhistell, Erving Goffman, myself, then Bill Labov. Again, for a certain time, affinities, not a common discipline. (126)

Here are named most of the key actors included below; presumably, John Szwed was not mentioned because he arrived a bit later, but he too will be integral to the story.

There was some small confusion about the initial invitation to Goffman. In April 1967, Provost David R. Goddard acknowledged a letter from Hymes about Goffman, in which Hymes said he would be having lunch with Goffman and "I hope that we are going to succeed in persuading him to join the University of Pennsylvania."[4] Then there is a gap until a letter in October 1967, from Goddard to Philip Rieff and Marvin Wolfgang (both in sociology; Wolfgang was acting department chair and graduate group chair at the time),[5] and Anthony Wallace (in anthropology), which says: "I must apologize for having failed to send the invitation to Dr. Erving Goffman as Benjamin Franklin Professor of Sociology last spring. I have now corrected this. He has been invited to come as Benjamin Franklin Professor of Sociology, or of Sociology and Anthropology, leaving the preference to him" (Oct 4, 1967, AFCW). A few days later, Wallace sent a letter directly to Goffman, urging him to accept, since "I have admired your work for many years and feel that you would make a great contribution to the development of the social sciences in Philadelphia" (Oct 9, 1967, AFCW). And Delaney (2014) mentions Rieff's campaign to get Goffman to Penn, as previously noted.[6] Clearly, it was not just Hymes trying to convince his former colleague Goffman to take the position.

A few months later, just after the Codes in Context conference held in December 1967 at Annenberg School of Communications[7] (described in chapter 4), Dean George Gerbner wrote to Goddard, with copies to Rieff and Worth, saying that he understood that Goffman had now been offered a Benjamin Franklin professorship. He was writing because he had been told that while at the conference Goffman had expressed interest in "some special relationship or affiliation with the [Annenberg] School" and that he was in favor of that, so long as such affiliation led to actual connections. "An occasional exposure in the Proseminar and advice in the selection and guidance of some of the graduate students who would come to communications because of Professor Goffman's presence on the list of affiliated faculty were examples I cited of the concrete forms of such participation."[8] Gerbner did not identify those who had reported their conversations with Goffman to him, but Hymes and/or Worth seem likely choices. In any event, Goffman began teaching at Penn in fall 1968, without an affiliation to ASC, as a Benjamin Franklin Professor only required to teach one course per year. (Chapter 5 examines his role as one of the small set of Benjamin Franklin Professors.)

There is extensive documentation for the fact that Hymes and others made multiple attempts to bring in likely colleagues to their group (elaborated upon shortly). In addition, there is at least some evidence that Goffman did the same for a few others. For example, Cicourel has written that "he [Goffman] was part of a small group at Penn that asked me if I wanted to move there" (2009). They had known each other well at Berkeley, as previously mentioned, and were both part of the Multiple Analysis Project (described in chapter 6). The "small group" mentioned here is exactly Goffman's core group at Penn.

Colleagues

The core group of colleagues who worked with Goffman on a set of major projects were involved in many of the same minor projects; in addition, they frequently shared students because, unlike many universities, at Penn even graduate students were (and presumably still are) encouraged to enroll in courses across multiple departments. Goffman's core group was made up of Hymes, Labov, Birdwhistell, Szwed, and Worth.[9] Since these five were so important, they will be described first and at greatest length, to set the stage.

Primary Peer Group

First in order is a review of the major scholars at Penn with whom Goffman worked on a variety of projects. As Huber suggests, "One thing that Erving took seriously was quality of scholarship" (2009). Evidently, what he did at Penn was to look for those who not only had overlapping research interests, but who were also especially good scholars, because they all either were already well-known and frequently recognized for their contributions or became so later.[10] Penn has always highlighted the interdisciplinary nature of the campus and faculty, and secondary appointments are one way to demonstrate this. Nearly all of the scholars at Penn relevant to this story held secondary appointments across departments, representing their diverse interests.[11] This included Goffman, who was on occasion considered a significant member of the anthropology department,[12] and was granted a secondary appointment in psychology as of 1977,[13] in Annenberg in 1978,[14] as well as in nursing in 1979.[15] Since his primary appointment already included two disciplines, this made five for him. Part of the impetus for both secondary appointments, and the creation of a network of scholars based in different departments was the same: "The impulse to band together depended on a sense of marginality in a home discipline" (Hymes 1980, x). According to Penn's official explanation of secondary appointments:

> When a professor's knowledge or expertise was considered to be beneficial to students outside of the department they were already affiliated with the second department would invite the professor to teach in their department also. If you were given the second appointment with voting rights that meant you had full standing in that department and could vote on issues at meetings called by the chair. (email from Tim Horning, May 5, 2023)

Members of this group supported one another's research interests and, in the process, created strong ties. For example, they shared early versions of their work with one another. Goffman had copies of unpublished papers, and prepublication versions of at least some published work of all the central actors in this circle, and many of those with peripheral involvement. We know this because Goffman kept a set of files accessible to students. "It happens that Goffman systematically archived the many papers, published and unpublished, which he received over the years from his colleagues. In June 1998, I made a complete listing of the content of the file cabinet which ended up in the Social Sciences Library in the McNeil Building at the University of Pennsylvania" (Winkin 2022b, 169). That list makes evident that Goffman had unpublished work by Dell Hymes, Labov, Szwed, Birdwhistell, and Worth, as well as by Virginia Hymes, Barbara Kirshenblatt-Gimblett, Dan Rose, Gillian Sankoff, Joel Sherzer, and W. John Smith (and many, many others outside of Penn).[16] This is quite standard in academia among colleagues working on related problems; as such, it documents Goffman's willingness to work with others, to provide his feedback, and to both solicit and listen to theirs. The only surprise here is that such connections have so rarely been documented for Goffman. Among those few examples are Vienne (2022), who mentions that Goffman sent Hughes draft papers on total institutions for critique before publishing *Asylums*, and Rawls (2023), who documents correspondence about a book Goffman and Harold Garfinkel planned to write. Other chapters in this book document that Goffman exchanged drafts with Hugh Duncan, David Schneider, and Allen Grimshaw,[17] so the list of people with whom he exchanged manuscripts was certainly not limited to colleagues at Penn.

Table 3.1 summarizes the half dozen scholars in Goffman's primary peer group, with information provided on the years they were based at Penn, as well as their primary and secondary appointments.

What follows are longer descriptions of these peers.

Dell H. Hymes (1927–2009)

Dell Hymes and Goffman connected through the Saturday group at Berkeley, all five of the major projects in chapter 4, all six of the minor projects in chapter 5, as well as several of those in chapter 6, so this was probably the strongest and most productive connection of those Goffman had at Penn. (At the same time, it must be acknowledged that my view may be biased by the considerable documentation Hymes made available by donating his papers; perhaps others had more connections than we yet know.) Hymes earned a PhD in linguistic anthropology at Indiana University in 1955, where he formally studied linguistics, anthropology, and folklore (Scollon 2004); he first took a position at Harvard (1955–1960), and then Berkeley (1960–1965), where he had a dual appointment in anthropology and linguistics (Sherzer et al. 2010), moving to anthropology at Penn in 1965.[18] Ward Goodenough called him in fall 1963 about the possibility of moving. At the time, the anthropology department had not yet spoken with the dean about a new hire, but Irving Hallowell had just retired and they had high enrollments, so clearly needed more staff. Goodenough followed up the call with a letter: "But I should say that our interest is not in getting someone to teach particular courses so much as it is in getting you as the kind of person we very much want as our colleague."[19] His use of "we" here refers to Goodenough and Anthony Wallace as the senior faculty members in the department; Loren Eiseley was also senior, but part-time, with a primary appointment in the Museum. The response from Hymes: "It's very flattering to have you think of me for the position at Penn."[20]

Table 3.1: Goffman's Primary Peer Group, by
Department, Showing Years at Penn

Erving Goffman (1968–1982)
Primary appointments: anthropology and sociology
Secondary appointments: psychology, communications, nursing
Dell Hymes (1965–1987)
Primary appointments: anthropology, then folklore, then education
Secondary appointments: linguistics, sociology, communications, history and sociology of science, comparative literature and literary theory
John Szwed (1969–1982)
Primary appointment: folklore
Secondary appointment: education
William Labov (1971–2015)
Primary appointment: linguistics
Secondary appointments: psychology, education, communications
Ray Birdwhistell (1969–1988)
Primary appointment: communications
Secondary appointment: none (but strong informal affiliation with folklore)
Sol Worth (1960–1977)
Primary appointment: communications
Secondary appointment: education

Wallace followed this up with a letter saying that, with the vita and bibliography Hymes had sent in, they could now request a formal offer be made. They were especially interested in "The particular combination of interests which you represent—linguistics, the history of anthropology and formal analysis" to fill in gaps in their program.[21] Obviously, either Wallace and/or Goodenough had told Henry Hoenigswald, then chair of linguistics, that they were negotiating with Hymes, because he also wrote Hymes to say: "Yesterday I heard what I consider the greatest piece of academic news in a long time. All of us hope and trust that it will soon be topped by an even better piece of news, and that we shall see you and your family settle down here."[22] By spring 1964, Wallace sent a formal letter of offer with a starting date of fall 1965.[23] Hymes accepted a few days later and immediately got down to details, including which courses he would teach.[24] By fall, Hoenigswald invited Hymes to become a member of the graduate group in linguistics once he was at Penn, and started the conversation about specific courses to put into the linguistics schedule.[25] Hymes immediately accepted the position.[26] All of this is relevant to the larger story told here because this is exactly the process Hymes used in approaching Goffman (and then others) about moving to Penn: informally, often before there was a position officially available, and with support of colleagues both in the same department and beyond.

Nearly twenty years later, when asked for a history of the anthropology department at Berkeley to elaborate on his reasons for leaving, Hymes emphasized that his move was based on personal choices; it was specifically "not part of a stance toward the department or the University." He provided several explanations: Having been invited to apply to both Columbia and Penn, the offer from Penn was most attractive, including a promotion to professor (which Berkeley tried to match, but it turned out there were two levels there, and they only offered the lower one, which "rankled a bit"). Also, his wife, Virginia, was interested in moving east. Also, he recalled that "Penn's reputation at that time for linguistic work in anthropology, because of the presence of Wallace and Ward Goodenough, and the recent presence of Paul Friedrich and Robbins Burling, must have been a factor as well."[27] When discussing the matter with Worth a few years after joining Penn, Hymes specifically named the interdisciplinarity of the campus as "the major reason" he chose to move.[28] This was important to him, as he explained to Vartan Gregorian in the 1970s, because: "I was trained at a broad-gauged liberal arts college (Reed), and in a graduate school program (Indiana) in which the earlier unity of anthropology, folklore, and linguistics, centered around study of the American Indians, still obtained. To me it seems that I work within a coherent, if broad, tradition, from which the fragmentation of academic life has departed, and to which hopefully it may begin to return."[29]

Hymes was formally based in multiple departments at Penn over the years: Becoming unhappy with anthropology colleagues when J. David Sapir was not granted tenure (Mills 2011),[30] he was offered a home in sociology by Rieff,[31] but instead chose to move his primary affiliation to folklore in 1972, where he had already been a member of the Interdisciplinary Committee since 1965.[32] In addition, he held formal affiliations with the graduate groups in linguistics (from 1965),[33] communications (from 1967), history and sociology of science (from 1971), and comparative literature and literary theory (from 1980); and formal secondary appointments to sociology (from 1973)[34] and communications (from 1978).[35] In fact, with the departure from anthropology came a new, joint title to Professor of Folklore and Linguistics. "Admittedly the proposal for the title came from Erv Goffman, who felt it would give a better public impression to my leaving anthropology if linguistics were associated with the new location."[36] Goffman had apparently been almost as upset about the denial of tenure for Sapir, for Hymes wrote to Wallace in spring 1971: "Erving Goffman and I, while believing that it is too late this spring for further consideration of the matter, wish to raise it again with the department, and the University subsequently, in the fall. We are not prepared to accept the decision as final."[37] But it was Hymes who resigned from the department over Sapir, not Goffman.

As if all these affiliations were not enough in the way of multidisciplinary connections for Hymes, he also took on the role of dean (and professor) of the Graduate School of Education in 1975, a position for which Szwed had first recommended him (Hymes 1999).[38] Provost Eliot Stellar's official announcement of that appointment said: "Dell Hymes will bring to the post of dean of the Graduate School of Education a distinguished record of accomplishment in anthropology, folklore, and linguistics, and will doubtless provide an intellectual bridge among these disciplines and the Graduate School of Education."[39] Hymes wrote to Stellar a year later, saying: "I accepted the Deanship last August with two things foremost in mind: that the immediate need was to listen and care and help build a cooperative ethos; that the long-range need was to build University ties and national distinction in areas in which the University was already strong."[40] He was perhaps blunter in a letter to Goffman: "I have a chance to affect the environment for linguistics at this university."[41] As dean, Hymes did indeed provide a bridge across departments and schools, documented extensively in chapters 4 and

5. He also had other reasons, such as when he told local teachers it was due to "my own desire to make a difference in the real world."[42] He stayed in that position until fall 1987, when he moved to the University of Virginia, following Sapir there (Scollon 2004).[43] Hymes once explained the logic of his movement from place to place thus: "The trouble is, I'm not really any of these things (folklorist, anthropologist, linguist, you name it), and have reached a point of understanding that one shouldn't be—social scientist is about as low-level and specific a commitment as seems to me justifiable and all the rest womb-hunting and jurisdictional dispute that serves the wrong interests, not the interests of mankind."[44] Hymes was basically against formal institutional structures, departments among them, as he made clear on several occasions. Here is how he explained his view to Labov in 1973:

> (My sour attitude toward institutionalized, departmentalized, compartmentalized disciplines is evident in the introduction to REINVENTING ANTHROPOL-OGY . . . I more and more move over toward the anti-institutionalized academy attitude you expressed when you came to Penn.) . . . I take it for granted that any ongoing discipline leaves out of account things that are important and that any institutionalized discipline in this society is going to beg questions that are essential to radical critique and change. . . . my recent and academic history has had one good effect: I can no longer care a damn about named disciplines.[45]

A year later, Hymes told then Dean Vartan Gregorian he had "a clear commitment to the relative irrelevance of departmental and disciplinary boundaries" because "all the things I most want to find out seem to be impeded by such labels, and the boundary maintenance they inspire."[46] Remember this focus on the insignificance of disciplines, as this attitude is central to understanding the goals of the group surrounding Goffman at Penn. Yet, whether because of or despite this dislike of departments, Hymes seemed always to become deeply involved in thinking about broad programmatic matters, whether as a member of anthropology, folklore, linguistics, or then, most significantly, as dean of education.[47]

There is particularly strong documentation for Hymes's high level of involvement with the folklore department: He wrote exam questions and discussed the spread of courses to be offered, budget issues, and not least, what he thought it would take to make folklore a success.[48] He prepared a lengthy argument for understanding the ways in which folklore had always been interdisciplinary,[49] should work to reinforce that,[50] and was already and should continue to focus on cross-disciplinary concerns.[51] He taught courses within the department through the 1970s and 1980s, even after he took on the role of dean of GSE.

In 1971, at the point when Hymes was most unhappy with his colleagues in anthropology, he wrote a letter to Goffman saying that, while he was considering leaving Penn for a new position elsewhere, "there are many reasons for staying in Philadelphia. In particular, you and Bill [Labov] . . . I don't want to desert you and Bill, and if there is a way or a necessity of sticking it out, okay."[52] The letter is marked "NOT sent" in Hymes's writing, so presumably Goffman never saw it, although in some cases a letter not sent turns out to indicate that the content had been conveyed by telephone instead, making a written version redundant rather than unshared. In any case, Hymes did not leave Penn then.

Hymes acknowledged Goffman in multiple publications, including the introduction to the 1964 special issue of *American Anthropologist*, "for pointed argument as to the notion of communication" (1964a, 28n1). In the introduction to *Foundations in Sociolinguistics,* he says, "I owe a special debt to Erving Goffman: sociolinguistics is discovering that at its core lie concerns that have long been his, and this book would not exist without his intervention" (1974, x). In specific chapters he provides additional acknowledgments, such as "I owe this idea to the stimulation of conversations with Erving Goffman, but he is not responsible for it" (192n3); and in "Breakthrough into Performance," he thanks Goffman (along with Gumperz, Labov, and Garfinkel) "for discussions over the years that have helped shape the perspective of this paper" (1975, 12n1). A few years later, he referred specifically to Goffman's concepts of deference and demeanor (1983a, 199). In turn, Goffman thanks Hymes for discussion of the concept of performance (1974, 124), and for pointing him to Roman Jakobson's work (211); and later used Hymes's terms "speech events" (1981, 139, 166) and competence (202), acknowledged Hymes for pointing out problems of assuming a speaker-hearer dyad (144), and generally acknowledged Hymes for help with references (161, 202). He sent draft manuscripts to Hymes for critique, claiming, "This material is as much yours as mine (I only have monopoly of ownership), and I need your comments worse than do your most needful students."[53] Elsewhere he writes: "Thank you for the prolonged and useful comments on my paper on the lecture."[54]

Hymes quite literally brought everyone in the core group together. By 1967 he was already in regular correspondence with George Gerbner, who had become dean at ASC in 1964, describing the ways in which their interests overlapped. He concluded a lengthy letter: "We have at Penn the possibility, I think, of a unique and exciting development centered in the Annenberg School, and I shall be delighted to be of any help I can."[55] In response, Gerbner said, "I envisage an important role for your area of interest in our PhD program and hope you will agree to serve on the committee when it is formed."[56] When the doctorate was approved in December 1967, Hymes was in fact on the list of faculty members at Penn outside ASC who served on the graduate group supervising that program.[57] Hymes (along with Renée Fox, Peggy Sanday, and Ken Goldstein) later served also on the Committee of the Undergraduate Major in Communications, once that had been established, and which Worth chaired.[58]

Not long after, Hymes mentioned the faculty at Annenberg as being "to me the most congenial group on the campus."[59] ASC issued a press release in 1978 describing a change in structure, and the graduate group in communications was replaced by a set of associated faculty, including Goffman, Hymes, Labov, Fox, Dan Ben-Amos, and Brian Sutton-Smith, all relevant to the story told here, as well as over a dozen others.[60] If any further evidence of his multidisciplinarity is required, Hymes served as president of four distinct national associations: American Anthropological Association (1983),[61] American Folklore Society (1973–1974),[62] American Association for Applied Linguistics (1985–1986),[63] and Linguistic Society of America (1982).[64] In fact, at the same time that Hymes learned he had been elected LSA president, he heard that Goffman had been elected president of the American Sociological Association. He immediately wrote Goffman: "I am delighted at word that you have been elected president of ASA. As you know from Gillian [Sankoff], the analogous thing has happened to me with the LSA. What is the world coming to? Maybe we could integrate sociolinguistics by going to each other's meetings in place of each other?"[65]

Hymes was not only essential to gathering most of the core group at Penn, but he also tried to bring others he knew and respected to campus as well. Just as Goodenough had encouraged Hymes to apply to Penn while he was still happy at Berkeley, so Hymes encouraged others. As early as fall 1965, when Alan Dundes (who Hymes knew well from Berkeley) wrote to say that Ken Goldstein was considering leaving Penn for a position at UCLA and there was a concern that the folklore department at Penn would be without a strong leader,[66] Hymes wrote a letter to Dean Otto Springer supporting the potential appointment of Dundes in Goldstein's place, praising him and concluding, "If we get Dundes, we will get the man who is recognized as *the* comer in the field"[67] (emphasis in original). Hymes also worked to convince

Dundes to move, telling him all about what he had found once he moved to Penn. Perhaps the major argument was that he felt like "a somewhat bigger frog because the puddle is somewhat smaller" at Penn than at Berkeley.[68] At the same time, Hymes mentioned that he was working on getting David Sapir to Penn as well. In the end, Sapir did take a position at Penn, while Dundes did not (partly out of concern by his Berkeley colleagues that the folklore program there would fold if he left).[69] A few years later, Hymes helped his former student Bob Scholte get a job at Annenberg,[70] partly by involving Worth,[71] and even Wallace in anthropology.[72] Hymes also tried to interest Susan Philips, a Penn PhD, in a job at Penn in anthropology; that effort was unsuccessful.[73] Also unsuccessful was his bid to get Michael Silverstein hired by anthropology, as a way to ensure that linguistic anthropology would be adequately represented in that department after his departure from it.[74] Hymes had better success encouraging Fred Erickson apply for a position in education.[75]

In addition to bringing together a group of like-minded colleagues interested in a common set of ideas, Hymes was also good at self-promotion, ensuring those in power were kept up to date on what was happening. For example, in 1971 he wrote to President Martin Meyerson (who had only begun that position in 1970 and was still fairly new to campus), documenting that the AAA had passed a resolution acknowledging the importance of studying American society (traditionally, anthropologists had studied other societies, not their own) and stressing the importance of "language and symbolic forms in culture," another major emphasis in the field at the time.[76] He wanted to make it clear that:

> With John Szwed, Erving Goffman, Bill Labov, Dan Ben-Amos, Ken Goldstein, John Fought, Ray Birdwhistell, Sol Worth, Pennsylvania has one of the strongest constellations of people in these areas in the country. Some people have begun to remark that it is perhaps the strongest.... we have good working relationships across the various department and school lines, and can hope to make quite a mark for the University in these areas in the years ahead.[77]

The combination of these faculty members would not have been at all obvious to someone new to campus, given that they were based in five different departments. Meyerson wrote back: "You know my enthusiasm for cross-disciplinary work. I am delighted to know about the good working relationships that exist at Penn among those studying contemporary American Society and language and other symbolic forms of culture, and I look forward, as do you, to many productive results of that interrelationship."[78]

So Hymes helped facilitate the creation of the core group, and he made sure the university administration knew about them; Meyerson made clear that the emphasis should be on "productive results." Those did in fact come about and are detailed primarily in chapter 4. (The projects in chapter 5 were less successful, leading to few of the sort of productive results Meyerson—and presumably everyone else involved—preferred.) But even when no obvious publications resulted, Hymes was also right that his "constellation of people" would be noticed. One example is a letter from well-known anthropologist Edmund Leach, of the University of Cambridge, in 1970, expressing interest in the graduate program at Annenberg that listed Birdwhistell, Goffman, and Hymes as affiliates because one of his best undergraduates was potentially interested in applying.[79]

John F. Szwed (1936–)

Szwed was hired into folklore at Penn in 1969, the year after Goffman arrived, and given a secondary appointment in education as of 1976. He earned an MA in communications in 1960,[80] and a PhD in sociology/anthropology in 1965 at Ohio State University, where he also studied linguistics and folklore (Szwed 2005), so by training his interests were nearly as multidisciplinary as those of Hymes, and across some of the same topics. His dissertation research was conducted in Newfoundland, so he also shared a connection to Canada with Goffman.[81] After initially teaching language and culture at the University of Cincinnati, and then taking a position at Lehigh University in social relations (1965–1967), he moved to anthropology at Temple University (1967–1969);[82] when he left Penn for Yale University in 1982, it was for anthropology and African American studies as his primary affiliations, with secondary appointments in American studies, music, film studies, and additional teaching in literature (Szwed 2005, 9). When he later left Yale for Columbia, he became director of the Center for Jazz Studies.[83] Szwed explained his multiple affiliations this way:

> My model for all this was Dell Hymes, who escaped his own department at the University of Pennsylvania by joining the Program in Folklore and Folklife and the Department of Linguistics, and later by becoming Dean of the Graduate School of Education. (Erving Goffman, himself a self-proclaimed academic cowboy, once admonished Hymes for his academic restlessness and suggested that he pick, say, six good departments and settle down for good.) (9)

Given this comment, it's ironic that Szwed and his wife, Marilyn Sue Szwed, then based in education (she earned her MS in education in 1976),[84] were the reason for Hymes's final move to GSE. Hymes says they "asked did I mind if they put in my name [as a candidate for dean]. I said 'No,' and forgot all about it" (Scollon 2004, 56).

Szwed first contacted Hymes in 1965, asking him to serve as advisor if an application to the National Science Foundation for a postdoctoral fellowship were approved.[85] Hymes agreed, but the proposal was denied.[86] Szwed was already citing Goffman before either of them moved to Penn (e.g., Szwed 1966) and he acknowledged Goffman's influence on his writing after they both arrived (see Szwed 1972, 153). He experienced inner city urban culture primarily through music, to the point of becoming a jazz musician himself (long before he became an anthropologist), which influenced how the Center for Urban Ethnography ended up with the focus it had. He was writing Hymes and meeting with Goffman extensively by 1968 while negotiating both the grant from the NIMH and a position at Penn in exchange for housing the grant there, asking their advice as he made decisions.[87] His story is central to only one major project, CUE, but that was an important resource for all of the core group.

As Hymes and Szwed corresponded, they occasionally compared their own research to that of Goffman, discussing overlaps or gaps. For example, Szwed wrote to Hymes in 1972 about Hymes's then unpublished manuscript on performance, saying he had some ideas about how to expand it if Hymes would be interested in a co-author.[88] Hymes responded: "This ties in with Erv's Georgetown paper,[89] except that where he seems to see the problem at a very general theoretical level (to show the continuity and congruity between everyday life and what is writ large on the stage) we would also want to pin it down, 'here, now, this Philadelphia,' to adapt Eliot's quartet."[90] In the end, Hymes completed that paper alone (1975).

William D. Labov (1927–2024)

William Labov, best known for his study of linguistic variation, earned a BA in English and philosophy at Harvard (Labov and Sankoff 2023) and an MA and PhD at Columbia University, where he then taught from 1964 to 1970.[91] He had connected with both Hymes and Goffman when they were at Berkeley, through the recommendation of his teacher and mentor, Uriel Weinreich. At least Hymes and Labov routinely corresponded as a result of that connection, so we know that by 1966 Labov was reading work by Ken Goldstein (in folklore at Penn) on narratives.[92] In spring 1967, Labov invited Hymes to participate in a seminar at Columbia, The Use of Language, which included Uriel Weinreich, Emanuel Schegloff, John Gumperz, and Marvin Herzog.[93] The seminar seems to have been composed of faculty discussing issues across disciplinary lines over dinner, rather than being a course intended for students, so it can be thought of as one more iteration of Berkeley's Saturday group. This serves as a good reminder not to assume people stay in the same place all the time: We think of Gumperz as being at Berkeley, but in 1967 he was readily available to participate in a seminar in New York.

In January 1968, while trying to convince Goffman to take a position at Penn, Hymes told him: "Bill said that if you were to come to Penn, that would be a strong pull for him . . . I think he things [*sic*] there is much he could learn from you, and that there are things he could contribute to the kind of work you want to develop."[94] In fall 1968, after Goffman moved to Penn but before Labov did, another Columbia faculty seminar was organized, this time with Goffman's participation, which apparently worked quite well, for Labov reported to Hymes: "Goffman is a pleasure to have around."[95] By the end of the semester, Labov's opinion of Goffman was even higher.

> The seminar wound up very well. It was certainly worthwhile for me, and I think Joel [Sherzer] handled it nicely. Goffman was himself worth the price of admission. He came up to my class to give a lecture once, and I drove him back down, so we had a good chance to talk. I think that Erving is one of the top people in whatever we're doing, and he's getting better all the time. You're very fortunate to have him at Penn.[96]

Joel Sherzer, first graduate student and then faculty member at Penn, will be introduced shortly. Notice that phrase: "whatever we're doing. " Even for the major participants, there was a sense that what they were doing was so new they were making it up as they went along. Equally important, their interest in analyzing social interaction was not based solely in any of their disciplines, standing rather at the confluence of linguistics, sociology, and anthropology.

In fall 1968, Henry Hoenigswald, then chair of linguistics at Penn, invited Labov to teach a course during spring 1969. For Labov, still based at Columbia, this course proved to be part of what convinced him to move to Penn.[97] In a lengthy explanation to Hymes of what he thought he might include that would be useful, Labov wrote: "In the last four weeks, I'll bring everybody together to worry about the limitations of rules. When you're busy breaking rules, are you really engaging in rule-governed behavior? Goffman likes to say that you are engaged in 'interpretable' behavior."[98] This demonstrates clearly how the research interests of Goffman, Labov, and Hymes overlapped, and also shows the attention each paid to what the others were saying and/ or writing. After starting the course at Penn (Hymes was in England that year, and so could not participate), Labov reported:

> Goffman is a tremendous asset.... He never comes to any topic without leaving something with it in the way of new and striking insight. For example, I was talking about codas in narratives, and their function in cutting off any further "What happened then?" questions. Erving stuck up his hand and pointed out that maybe a coda gave a second evaluation, a new point of view to add to the first. And that *is* the case with a number of codas of the best type that I have on hand [emphasis in original].

> Goffman and I are conferring regularly on some of these rules for speech events. At the moment, we're debating the question of Type I rules—whether they are plainly and simply the set of invariant behaviors, or whether the rules of interest are those of a special sort that are close to the interactional heart of things.[99]

This sort of detailed discussion of sociolinguistic analysis is not typically thought of as being what Goffman did, but it was typical of the conversations in letters between Hymes, Goffman, and Labov.

Labov wrote Hymes in December 1968 that "we ought to think about the advantages of being at the same place, with Goffman, and the other good people that you have collected at Penn."[100] In January 1969, Hymes wrote Worth that "Bill Labov, incidentally, has inquired about the possibility of coming to Penn. God, if we can only swing that. We could turn out students that would transform the subject."[101] And indeed they did. In response to a request from Hymes to think about what kind of a situation he would prefer, Labov admitted that he would consider an interdisciplinary appointment.[102] It helped considerably that he was then teaching a course at Penn, because he was impressed by the students—and enjoyed having Goffman actively participating in his course. Hymes told Labov that he had immediately written to Hoenigswald in linguistics, Wallace in anthropology, and Worth at ASC to explore possibilities.

> The fact is that there are so many depts and schools at Penn that would be interested that it ought to be a small convention if they all get together. Linguistics, anthropology, folklore (Goldstein), psychology, Annenberg, to my certain knowledge . . . I wish I was on hand in Philadelphia to stir the pot personally, but am doing it to some extent long-distance by letter, and Goffman and Hoenigswald are actively concerned there.[103]

So Goffman as well as Hymes and Worth worked to bring Labov to Penn. In his letter to Worth, Hymes explained that Labov

> is already a luminary and will become more and more brilliant a one. . . . From the standpoint of Annenberg, the attraction, besides getting a first-rate man, who has really no peer, would be a guaranteed link with linguistics, folklore, and Goffman (to name three distinct subjects). Goff is enamored of Bill and learns from him; Goldstein et al envy him his narrative work; linguistics sees him as the white hope for social (as distinct but not opposed to formal) approach; his work on sound change will be classic. . . . I'm not sure how good a case I can make in the anthropology dept. . . . The main pitch for Bill would be urban ethnography, about which the anthro dept. is already a bit apprehensive (of becoming a dog wagged by a large-grant-tail). . . . If you think there is some prospect of Annenberg interest, could you let Hoenigswald know? and Goffman? Maybe there ought to be a lunch meeting of all you cats to plot (Hoenigswald, psychology dept. head [Burton S. Rosner], Tony [Anthony Wallace], Goff, you and George [Gerbner] and Perce [Percy H. Tannenbaum, at Annenberg] perhaps, [Kenneth] Goldstein).[104]

As a reminder, Hymes himself could not join the others at the proposed lunch because he was still in England. And the "dog wagged by a large-grant tail" refers to the Center for Urban Ethnography. But this was far from the end of the story; over the next few months Hymes continued to discuss multiple potential placements for Labov. In May, he made it quite clear to Labov how important this was to him: "If all this about the job gets to the point where you feel it's necessary to talk with me, I'll find someway [sic] of getting back, if you can't come here. This is too important, to me, and to Penn, and to the future of the subject, to let anything interfere with getting it right."[105] As this offer to fly across the Atlantic was made at a point in time when such travel was not undertaken lightly, it was a big deal. In a letter to George Gerbner a few days later, Hymes discussed how Labov might fit into psychology, linguistics, anthropology, or ASC, and then goes on to say "Erf [sic] Goffman, John Szwed, and I would use the visiting appointment in our urban ethnography grant to secure him an equivalent for the year's sabbatical he would lose" by leaving Columbia that year.[106] Hymes was quite excited about Labov, especially in connection with Goffman, for he told Worth at the same time that:

> If there is any one person in the country, besides Goffman, who is a natural—and one would think a must—for the future of communicative research, it is Labov. At least from the standpoint of my own perspective and interests—the linguistic, anthropological, interaction aspects—they're the two key men for what can develop at Penn, and in the country. . . . it just seems inevitable that Bill, Erv, flanked by

> Dave Sapir and myself in anthropology, Goldstein and Ben-Amos in folklore,
> and with cooperation in linguistics, would build something multidisciplinary and
> worthwhile, or die in the attempt. The key thing is that the effort is in important
> part trans-disciplinary.... Erv has made the jump almost completely, following
> his work rather than his label, where it leads him.[107]

So it was not just Hymes and occasionally Goffman who had become multidisciplinary, casually discussing what department might make a good fit,
but also Labov—despite the fact that multidisciplinarity is not something
he's known for emphasizing today. Also notice that Hymes was counting
on having Sapir as a member of the group, one part of why he was so upset
with the tenure decision.

In June, while continuing negotiations with Gerbner on Labov's behalf,
Hymes explained how Labov's work overlapped with his own and that of
Birdwhistell: "He is the only linguist I know to work closely with videotape,
and to analyze nonverbal behavior as integral to, and essential to, explanation
of linguistic facts. He is the most successful linguist I know in working in
urban ethnography—indeed, he may be said to have created the possibility of a meaningful urban linguistics in American life."[108] At the same time,
Hymes told Worth that Labov would provide "a fantastic center of attraction for anyone interested in field study of behavior, focused on speech."[109]
As matters were getting clearer in late June, Goffman wrote Hymes, still in
England, with an update: "My word on Labov is that psychology is going to
bring him here. The Center for Urban Ethnology [*sic*] offered to give him his
first year for pure research, or part-time for five years, in a decision made
in your physical but not spiritual absence; but it turns out this help will not
be necessary."[110] So Szwed and Goffman were working to do their part to
make a move to Penn sufficiently attractive. Psychology was faster than
linguistics, and did in fact make Labov an offer,[111] and there was confusion
all around about where he could/should/would end up in terms of a home
department. Meanwhile, Labov wrote that Columbia was asking him to
commit to becoming department chair in linguistics for three years (apparently thinking he would like that offer, which he did not), and concluding
that he hoped instead for an interdisciplinary appointment at Penn.[112] By
January 1970, matters still had not been settled, and Hymes (now back in
the US) was still exchanging detailed letters with Labov over what would
make the most sense.

> I realized that, as I said, I'd never asked myself why I wanted you to come. I knew
> I did, I never had to reason about it. But of course it must make a difference to

you to know what the reason would be. One, of course, as with Erv, is just that the interaction in and out of courses would be exciting, would make this so clearly the best possible world to be in. And it would help to crystallize in some ways, perhaps to cap, the cross-departmental sector of interest that we've built up over the years here—and for which in the several departments we have strong Administration support. (Incidentally, the probable new president of Penn is a friend of Erv's, which can't hurt) . . . try to imagine the place with you part of it, with all of us responding to you and your work, cooperating across dept. lines as we do actively now, drawing students who want the kind of continuation of ethnography, social interaction and linguistic analysis we can offer, with the chief journal in the field edited here, with people who think you what is not an interesting adjunct but the heart of what things should be.[113]

A few clarifications: The new president of Penn in 1970 was to be Martin Meyerson, who had taught at the University of Chicago 1948–1952, thus while Goffman was a graduate student there, and had been both faculty member and administrator at Berkeley 1963–1966, thus while Goffman was faculty there. In addition, he was both faculty and administrator at Harvard 1957–1953, so before Goffman spent his sabbatical year there in 1966–1967, but perhaps a small part of the reason for that choice of sabbatical.[114] So it makes sense that Hymes went on to refer to him as "someone whose ear Erv has."[115] By the "chief journal in the field," Hymes was alluding to the not yet published but already approved *Language in Society*, the first issue of which appeared in 1972. Notice that Hymes thought a university that held him, Goffman, and Labov would be "the best possible world to be in." And notice that he highlights the cross-departmental connections already built up at Penn in the few years since he and Goffman had arrived. (He went on to mention especially good students at Penn, naming Joel Sherzer and Regna Darnell as immediate examples, and then adding Elinor Ochs, Susan Philips, Judith Irvine, and Richard Bauman.) He also put the work into context:

> And I think that the analysis of discourse, st[y]le, speech acts, where grammatical structures and situational/social structures mesh, is the right place to focus now. And I want very much—I think is vital to the future of anthropology—as I said at the conference in New York in November (Szwed, Goffman, et al.)—for anthropology to work in US society effectively, to show that ethnography is a method that applies here, can apply here, as well.[116]

The Center for Urban Ethnography sponsored that conference in New York. Presumably, Labov agreed with at least some if not all of these arguments, for he did end up moving from Columbia to Penn, accepting a position in linguistics in February 1970.[117]

Labov first served as research professor at the Center for Urban Ethnography for a year[118]—a position which entailed no teaching responsibilities (though he did offer to give a series of public lectures on his research, and mentioned that he hoped to participate in a seminar with Goffman and Hymes both on "the interactional basis of discourse rules")—before beginning a full-time position in linguistics in fall 1971, signing himself at that point, "With best regards and great expectations."[119] However, since Labov then received a Guggenheim fellowship applied for earlier, he actually spent the academic year 1970–1971 writing, moving his arrival at Penn back a year.[120] As explained to Allen Grimshaw in early 1970, he would be associated with Penn during this time, but would be writing rather than teaching, and participating in seminars with Goffman and Hymes (Mar 9, 1970, ADG). Later, he provided details for what happened when he began his stint as a CUE fellow:

> During the year 1971–72, I served as Research Professor with the Center for Urban Ethnography, and I am deeply indebted to the Center for the support which made it possible to assemble this volume [*Sociolinguistic Patterns* 1972a], along with *Language in the Inner City* [1972b]. The original impetus to put these studies together into a single volume and organize them into a single coherent framework came from Erving Goffman, whose help and encouragement is acknowledged with many thanks. (1972b, xvii–xviii)[121]

As part of the negotiations with Labov, there was extensive discussion as to whether he should take a position either fully or partially within anthropology. So it is relevant that when discussions continued in that department about whether and who they needed in the area of sociolinguistics, Hymes became outraged at Goffman's exclusion from the conversation. In January 1971, he wrote Labov:

> Some points that must be kept in mind in assessing a possible appointment in sociolinguistics in the anthropology department.
>
> First and foremost, it is shocking that Erv was not informed and not made a member of the committee. Of the committee appointed to evaluate candidates, Wallace and Goodenough are reasonable, and having Wallace as co-ordinator may be a diplomatic gesture. But the third member [name deleted] is the guy in the dept. who hates my guts; who violently has opposed urban ethnography, and wanted to [*sic*] dept. to publicly disassociate itself from same; who argued that fellowships for black students should not be given, etc. (Ask John Szwed). And none of them is competent to evaluate present training or work in sociolinguis-

tics.... I could not in good conscience encourage anyone to take an appointment in the anthropology dept. at this time, esp. in this area.[122]

Two things are important here: Hymes wanted Labov to understand the situation at Penn even before setting foot on site, and he staunchly defended Goffman's knowledge of sociolinguistics, despite his (former) peers in anthropology not thinking Goffman would be an obvious source of knowledge in that area. The gap in linguistic training within anthropology (the discipline where linguistics got its start, and where it is often still today administratively located across universities in the US) becomes relevant to this story of Goffman and various colleagues again when considering the proposal for an Interdisciplinary Program in Language, Culture, and Society in chapter 5. Hymes continued:

> Someone who is good and who cares about training will necessarily recognize the need to work with linguistics and related fields; will recognize that the center of "sociolinguistics" at Penn is at Eisenlohr Hall [where linguistics was based]. Presumably will subscribe to *Language in Society*, and presumably will be attracted to Penn in important part because you are here....
>
> If an appointment were made that added to our strength, complementing it, well and good. Erv is entirely right, I believe, in saying that a good person will necessarily join us.... The crux, I think, is Erv. Any candidate should be acceptable, and more than acceptable, positively attractive, to him. The primary role such a person could play would be to help bring along a few good students in anthropology itself who would work with Erv. If such a person can help in that respect, work with Erv and in that way, then I would suppress any either reservations or feelings about the matter. On the other hand, if this person hired undercuts Erv, cannot relate to his work, then my reservations and feelings will be foremost in my mind. The situation would appear to be of the same kind as that involving Dave Sapir.
>
> So, if you have the chance in meeting with [illegible] and Goodenough, the most important first response to this situation might well be incredulity and shock that Goffman is not the primary person involved in the appointment, let alone not even on the committee....
>
> In sum, concern for me and my position can be entirely tacit; but concern for Erv and his position ought to be forcefully explicit.[123]

This letter was copied to Goffman. There is no response from either him or Labov in the file. But we learn several things: that Hymes looked out for Goffman's interests in anthropology; that he relied upon Labov, who was not yet even full-time at Penn, to play a supporting role; and that Hymes and Goffman both assumed any new hire would quickly discover and join the group they were building around the study of language and culture, and which they hoped to expand by the addition of Labov. Of course, the recent history of the anthropology department (namely, Sapir being denied tenure and Hymes leaving the department over that decision) has great relevance to his anger and unhappiness with the decisions made. As he told Goodenough, much of his negative response was due to his feeling that "you have played a central role in destroying what I came here to build up, and did build up for some years."[124] But clearly, he was nearly as angry about the way Goffman was being treated as he was about the way Sapir had been treated (attributed to antisemitism in this same letter).

Labov was formally appointed as professor in linguistics as of fall 1971 (despite not beginning to teach until fall 1972), and given secondary appointments in psychology and education starting in 1976,[125] as well as in communications in 1978.[126] Notice that it took considerable effort from not only Goffman and Hymes but also Worth and Szwed to make this happen, mostly because Labov expressed an interest in moving to Penn before the university advertised an available position for which he could apply. Also worth noting: Even letters ostensibly about getting Labov to Penn were filled with detailed discussions of draft manuscripts being exchanged, of publications by people they knew in common, and what they thought of them, as well as national associations, and also politics, especially but not exclusively in letters between Hymes and Labov.[127]

To summarize Labov's connection with Goffman and others before even getting to Penn: in addition to having been a late and peripheral member of the Berkeley Saturday group (mostly, when it came to publications, Labov 1964, 1972a), he involved both Hymes and Goffman in faculty seminars at Columbia and taught a course at Penn before his formal appointment there, which included Goffman not only sitting in but actively participating. Once he arrived on campus, Labov started in-house linguistics colloquia with faculty members presenting their own research to one another, as a way to keep up to date on who was doing what—but Goffman, not being in the department, was not included in the list of presenters, while both Dell and Virginia Hymes, John Fought, Leila Gleitman, Ellen Prince, Nessa Wolfson, and others were.[128] In terms of publications, Goffman thanks Labov for suggestions in several (1976b, 257; 1978, 787; 1983, 1), and is acknowledged in return for helpful comments in some of Labov's.[129] It comes as no surprise that Labov's year as a fellow with the Center for Urban Ethnography resulted in no fewer than thirteen of his publications being listed in the final record of publications sponsored (Center for Urban Ethnography 1978).

In addition to all these activities, Labov was partially attracted to Penn by the possibility of co-teaching, as Hymes mentioned to Worth early in their discussions: Labov "would want to give a regular research seminar, involving probably Goffman and myself as well."[130] Labov and Goffman actually co-taught several courses: Conversational Analysis in 1973, 1975,[131] and 1976: "I have been teaching a course with Erving on error correction" (May 19, 1976, ADG; Tagliamonte [2015] adds that Gillian Sankoff was the third instructor for the course), and then teaching jointly with Goffman again in 1980–1981, this time Linguistics 560: The Study of Speech Community (Labov et al. 2013, 33), again apparently with Sankoff co-teaching.[132] Goffman also mentioned co-teaching with Labov in 1973 to Hymes: In his review of a manuscript by Gail Jefferson for *Language in Society* (the published version is Jefferson 1974), he talks about possibly reorienting the paper, saying if that happens, "Gail should make mention of the appreciable body of work on malapropisms, slips of tongue, and other anomalous utterances—which indeed she and I and Labov and others looked at a little in a review of recorded bloopers."[133]

Raymond L. Birdwhistell (1918–1994)

Ray Birdwhistell, like Goffman, earned his PhD at the University of Chicago, but in anthropology, and a few years earlier, in 1951. He taught Goffman at the University of Toronto (1944–1946)[134] despite being only four years older and still a graduate student himself. Goffman said of him "He taught us a lot. . . . It is very difficult today to see how ground-breaking Birdwhistell was at the time" (Winkin 2022f, 153).[135] As Winkin goes on to explain: "Birdwhistell trained his students to observe micro-behavior, as fieldworkers do, with the naked eye" (154) and, of course, this is what Goffman did in the majority of his research. They stayed in touch despite Birdwhistell's later moves to the University of Louisville (1946–1956), University of Buffalo (1956–1959), and Temple University (1959–1969), where he was based in both anthropology and psychiatry while simultaneously serving as Senior Research Scientist at Eastern Pennsylvania Psychiatric Institute (EPPI).[136] In addition, Birdwhistell was a participant in the Macy Conferences on Group Processes and arranged for Goffman to participate in the 1956 event, as previously noted.

Birdwhistell attended the panel at the 1963 AAA which resulted in the publication of a special issue of *American Anthropologist* on the ethnography of speaking (Gumperz and Hymes 1964a), and wrote Hymes after it appeared, congratulating him on the project.[137] That got an immediate response, including discussion of common interests, a statement that Hymes had been aware of Birdwhistell's work since the early 1950s, and notice that Hymes would shortly be based in Philadelphia, near Birdwhistell.[138] Their correspondence quickly drew in Bob Scholte (a former student of Hymes then still at Berkeley), who Hymes recommended Birdwhistell meet,[139] and Albert Scheflen, then working with Birdwhistell at EPPI, who Birdwhistell recommended Hymes meet. Scheflen invited Hymes to join their research project, at least as a consultant, telling him that they were studying communication patterns in American subcultures, and making film recordings across generations, with Margaret Mead and Norman McQuown both involved in the project.[140] Hymes agreed to serve as consultant but did not think he would have time for more.[141] There are no letters documenting whether that did in fact happen, but the relevant point is that Hymes and Birdwhistell had made substantive contact, and had then drawn in others in their individual circles across several disciplines, before either of them even got to Penn. There was an additional relevant connection between them: In 1967, when the Gumperz and Hymes journal special issue (1964a) was being turned into a book (Gumperz and Hymes 1972), Hymes invited Birdwhistell to contribute a chapter, to be drawn from *The Natural History of an Interview* project: "We are very eager to have such a piece, and from you."[142] That offer was accepted (Birdwhistell 1972).

Also in 1967, Birdwhistell was one of those invited to the Codes in Context conference at Penn. Although unable to attend, he and Worth exchanged several letters as a result of the invitation. Worth was very disappointed to hear Birdwhistell would be unable to participate. "I had been looking forward to your coming because for the past three years I have been thinking of some way in which I could involve you in the kind of work that I was doing and that we were doing here at Penn."[143] However, Worth also noted that Birdwhistell was scheduled to present a colloquium at Penn in December that year (no mention of who invited him, but presumably the talk was to be at ASC), and said he looked forward to having more time to connect then.

Once Hymes was based at Penn, he and Worth both worked behind the scenes to invite Birdwhistell to transfer from Temple to Penn.[144] Hymes was explicitly asked by Dean Gerbner for his opinion about Birdwhistell ("I am asking your opinion of his scholarly accomplishments, of his ability to guide student research, and of his other qualifications for a senior position on a small graduate faculty").[145] Hymes recommended him enthusiastically: "On balance I would be in favor of offering Ray Birdwhistell a position as Professor of Communication. He is a distinguished scholar in the field, internationally known for his work; and he is an enthusiastic lecturer and teacher, who, I think, would take great interest in guiding student research. He would also serve as a link to some of the other sectors of the university with interests in communication."[146] Those with common interests most notably included Goffman.

Birdwhistell was not immediately appointed, and Hymes expressed his dismay to Gerbner, for "Ray would have provided a personal and close link with Goffman, and others. In retrospect that seems almost enough reason to have appointed him, especially if not appointing him should mean that someone like him is not appointed at all."[147] More directly, Hymes told Worth "the school desperately needs someone like him, someone with his interests and orientations."[148] A week later, Gerbner told Hymes that a visiting appointment for the next year might be possible,[149] and that is in fact what happened. Goffman helped convince Birdwhistell to move from Temple to Annenberg in fall 1969,[150] even though it was only for an initial one-year appointment; he was converted to tenure-track the next year, at the rank of professor.[151] He taught at Penn until his retirement in 1988.

Goffman only occasionally mentioned Birdwhistell in print, but when he did, he gave substantial credit: "Persons like Ray Birdwhistell and Edward Hall[152] have built a bridge from speaking to social conduct, and once you cross the bridge, you become too busy to turn back" (1964a, 134; for further discussion, see Winkin and Leeds-Hurwitz 2013). When Smith suggests that "Goffman placed greater store by what he could observe rather than by what people told him about whatever they were doing or thinking" (2022c, 17), that is a very Birdwhistellian assumption.

Hymes tried to include Birdwhistell, even before he moved to Penn, in *Functions of Language in the Classroom*, a collection he co-edited with Courtney Cazden and Vera John, both at Harvard (published as Cazden, John, and Hymes 1972).[153] Cazden formally invited Birdwhistell to prepare a chapter,[154] and he accepted,[155] but four months later she wrote again, asking whether he would be able to complete a chapter on time. At that point she was able to describe the others scheduled to provide chapters for the nonverbal communication section: Edward Hall, Paul Byers, and Aaron Cicourel.[156] As Birdwhistell has no chapter in the book, it can be assumed that he did not in the end submit one.

One example of Birdwhistell's willingness to cross disciplinary boundaries is found in the fact that he presented colloquia in other parts of the university, as for folklore in 1981.[157] A second is the assumption that "no serious doctoral student at the University of Pennsylvania who was interested in culture and human conduct could avoid Birdwhistell's teachings" (Kendon and Sigman 1996, 249). A third is that he periodically served on dissertation committees for students in other departments, as with Diane Sidener-Young in folklore.[158] A fourth is that, unexpectedly, when looking for a home for his collection of films, books, articles, and conference presentations (often by others as well as his own), he chose the Folklore Archive, rather than ASC.[159] Finally, when he retired, the folklore department threw him a party,[160] demonstrating that they considered him a relevant peripheral member despite the fact that he never held an official secondary appointment there. He also taught students from education, frequently sent by Hymes.[161]

Birdwhistell's early influence on Goffman shows itself in such details as Goffman's casual understanding of the amount of work required to transcribe paralinguistic elements of a recording, revealed when he reviewed one submission to *Language in Society* by saying, "I was particularly touched by the statement . . . that all paralinguistic sounds 'are noted'—a modesty not likely to be found in anyone who really tried to make a full transcription from a tape,"[162] or another saying: "In the linguistic tradition we would want to see something of the data base, and this might take many pages of verbatim transcription to provide. Processes lasting a half-hour or so might need to be illustrated by more data than we would have pages to print."[163] Through such statements, Goffman clearly demonstrated his familiarity with the exceedingly detailed transcription of recorded interaction that Birdwhistell pioneered, even though it was not quite what he did himself (see Winkin 2022f for details of their connection). And, as is fairly well known, Goffman convinced Birdwhistell to publish a book in the Conduct and Communication series.

While Birdwhistell did not publish in *Language in Society*, he did publish a book review (1978) in *Studies in the Anthropology of Visual Communication*, and a memorial essay about Mead in the later iteration, *Studies in Visual Communication* (1980). He did not play a role in the Center for Urban Ethnography and was the only core group member to never lead any of the projects, major or minor. He was part of two minor projects, one successful and one not. Kendon and Sigman have explained: "Above all, Birdwhistell's strength and his passion lay in his pedagogy" (1996, 248), which may be part of the explanation for why he did not play a more substantial role in the various faculty projects. Even so, he did embody interdisciplinarity for his students, and presumably his colleagues, easily combining anthropology, linguistics, and communication into a single cohesive approach to interaction.

Sol Worth (1922–1977)

Sol Worth was a professional photographer and filmmaker who never earned a graduate degree (although awarded an honorary MA from Penn in 1971). He did take graduate courses in film production, film animation, and film editing at the New School for Social Research (1948–1950), and Margaret Mead worked with him analyzing his ethnographic films for a year (1967–1968).[164] From his description (published posthumously as Worth 1980), he essentially received a year of tutoring from Mead in anthropological analysis of patterns, which presumably is where he learned the anthropological approach. He served as a consultant in the early days of Annenberg, then visiting lecturer, both while commuting from New York. In 1960 he accepted a part-time position and was shortly named director of the Documentary Film Laboratory and supervisor of Media Laboratories at ASC. By 1964 he was promoted to assistant professor and moved to Philadelphia, becoming professor by 1973. Worth was Birdwhistell's colleague in communications (he was hired before Birdwhistell, remaining until his untimely death in 1977), and father-in-law to one of Hymes's children.[165] Like Hymes, Labov, Goffman, and Szwed, Worth held a secondary appointment in another program—in his case, education.[166] He worked with Mead and others to establish the Society for the Anthropology of Visual Communication (Worth 1980), serving as the first president, 1972–1974, and also on the board of directors, and he was founding editor of the affiliated journal, *Studies in the Anthropology of Visual Communication* (Chalfen 1979), a major project. He participated in one of the Center for Urban Ethnography conferences and was published in the resulting volume (Worth 1972a). He was also a member of the editorial supervisory board of the University of Pennsylvania Press, and thus loosely connected with the Conduct and Communication book series ("Sol Worth" 1977). In addition, Worth appeared in that series posthumously (Worth 1981), a stronger connection. And it seems likely that, at some point, Worth surely would have discovered that Goffman (as an undergraduate) had worked for the National Film Board in Canada where, as Winkin puts it, he "absorbed a cinematographic culture" (2022c, 3), so they shared some assumptions about the value of visual records.

Shortly after Hymes's arrival at Penn in fall 1965, Worth began exchanging papers with him and discussing common interests.

> I have read your piece on Ethnographic Communication [either Hymes 1962 or 1964a]. At the risk of sounding ridiculous I'd like to say that it's the most meaningful and beautifully organized piece about the "field" of communication that I have seen.
>
> I would like very much for us to spend some time talking about 1) The implications of the piece for the Annenberg school and for me and my work personally. 2) Hearing your comments about the papers of mine you have read. 3) Telling you about current work I'm doing and asking you some specific questions about direction. 4) Listening to what you've been doing. . . . How about lunch . . . or dinner . . . or you suggest a date.[167]

The response is not in the file, but presumably they connected, leading to further interactions at Penn.

In fall 1967, Worth organized the Codes in Context conference and, even though Goffman was still at Berkeley, Hymes got him involved. In spring 1968, still before Goffman's arrival at Penn, Hymes sent Worth a draft manuscript of Goffman's for critique. He does not provide the title, but given the timing it may well have been part or all of *Strategic Interaction* (Goffman 1970). Worth says: "The body of the paper is an incredibly good description but but [sic] really doesn't seem to tie up with the theoretical underpinnings at the beginning of the paper. . . . The problem seems to me to have not only a theory which is pretty if not elegant, but a theory which implies a direction and organization and description of the codes in context that one is talking about."[168] Note the reference to the conference they had all attended. Worth obviously listened closely to what Goffman said at the conference as well as reading his publications, for a month later in a letter to Hymes he casually mentioned "Goffman's notion of a team performing a 'performance,'" obviously assuming Hymes would know what he was talking about.[169]

In spring 1969, after Goffman was settled at Penn, Worth wrote to him about a dinner that included Ray Birdwhistell, and apparently multiple others.

> Ray called me on Tuesday, and we spent a long time talking about his putting together the book of papers. I suspect that you may be right about his not doing it, but I guess I am willing to appear more romantic and hopeful than you, and I believe that he may. Of course you know him longer and better than I do. I definitely feel that we should have him here. I think that the objections I

had are outweighed by the great many positive qualities that he can add to the university faculty.[170]

Of course, the book being discussed here turned into *Kinesics and Context* (Birdwhistell 1970), published in the series that Goffman and Hymes edited. And, of course, Birdwhistell did end up at Penn, with the support of Goffman, Hymes, and Worth. Worth included several drafts of his own papers with the letter, telling Goffman: "I appreciate your agreeing to read them and to talk with me about them."[171]

Worth and Goffman corresponded regularly. For example, Goffman sent Worth the draft of a letter he had prepared for Herbert Blau (then at Oberlin College) for review as part of an effort to recommend Worth for the position of artistic director of the Center of Communication Arts and Sciences. Worth approved the letter with only one minor spelling correction, explaining with delight, "I took the liberty of correcting the spelling which—considering I am correcting a writer second only to Kafka in our time—is no mean feat."[172] In early 1973, Herbert F. Ostrach, then teaching film studies at Boston College, wrote to Goffman, and Goffman forwarded the letter on to Worth, as being more directly relevant to his interests. Ostrach was looking for someone who shared some of his research areas, and presumably Goffman thought Worth was a likely candidate.[173] When Worth was promoted to professor later that year, Goffman sent the following teasing congratulatory note: "Dear Sol Baby, I hear you're a professor. Big deal."[174] (He then mentioned a meal they would have to celebrate.)

At one point, Worth explicitly stated what others only assumed: Talking specifically about the relationship of folklore to communication, he wrote Hymes: "I don't care where these people are, as long as they're around for me to be with."[175] That basic sentiment seems to have been common to nearly everyone discussed in these pages, even if they did not make it as explicit as Worth does here. As part of that same letter (written before Goffman was at Penn), Worth added a paragraph distinguishing between his ideas and those of Goffman:

> One thing that I haven't said, and that I think I should make clear about my own interests, is where they differ from someone like Erv Goffman. It seems to me that he is interested in human behavior as an entity much larger and quite separate from the kind of communicative-expressive behavior that I am interested in. Where he is interested in film he is interested in it as a record which he can study to find out something about the way people behave in what might be called a physical sense. That is, he is not interested in the behavior as it is portrayed in a

visual mode by the man who is portraying it on film, but rather in the way the person himself portrays it that is caught on film. Erv himself in a conversation with me put it this way, "You're interested in film film, I guess I'm interested in people film." It's hard to make a real division between his interest and mine, and it's hard to be clear about what that division is. But I feel quite strongly that at the moment, although each is related, they are two quite different tracks.[176]

This makes clear that it is not the case that everyone in the inner circle shared all their assumptions. But the important point is that they shared enough that they could easily work together and usefully review one another's manuscripts. And the fact that they were formally affiliated with different departments made very little difference; ideas counted far more than administrative homes.

Peripheral Colleagues

In addition to the set of major players in Goffman's circle at Penn, a surprising number of faculty members show up playing a role in at least one project relating to Goffman. These are organized in the following table showing their primary affiliations by department, for each discipline contributed something different to the network of people and projects. A few people played exceedingly minor roles, or were part of only a minor project, or joined quite late, but they are still part of the story and so are included. Further research will likely uncover even more connections, with these same individuals or with others, as Goffman was affiliated with Penn for fourteen years. The important point to remember is that there is substantial evidence that Goffman developed ties to a large number of colleagues at Penn, and that these were often productive connections in terms of leading to research results. Their involvement in various projects will be explained in either chapter 4 (the major projects) or chapter 5 (the minor projects). Together they considerably enlarged Goffman's invisible college at Penn. This is absolutely not a complete list of all those who were in each of these departments at the time Goffman was at Penn—just a list of those who were part of a project at some point. Of course, the implication is that the list of peripheral colleagues actually included even more people than just those described in this book.[177]

Table 3.2: Goffman's Peripheral Colleagues at Penn, by Department

Anthropology: Anthony Wallace, Ward Goodenough, William Davenport, J. David Sapir, Peggy Reeves Sanday, Arjun Appadurai
Sociology: Philip Rieff, Renée Fox, Elijah Anderson, Teresa Labov
Linguistics: John Fought, Gillian Sankoff, Henry Hiz, Ellen Prince, Anthony Kroch
Folklore: Kenneth Goldstein, Dan Ben-Amos, Barbara Kirshenblatt-Gimblett, Roger Abrahams, Virginia Hymes, Henry Glassie
Communications: Steven Feld, Larry Gross, Perry Tannenbaum, Paul Messaris, Amos Vogel
Education: Brian Sutton-Smith, Leila Gleitman, Morton Botel, David Smith, Fred Erickson, Nancy Hornberger, Michael Long, Nessa Wolfson, Shirley Brice Heath, Bambi Schieffelin
Psychology: Rochel Gelman, Leo Hurvich, Dorothea Jameson Hurvich, David Premack, Dan Osherson, Burton S. Rosner
Landscape architecture: Dan Rose
Biology: W. John Smith
English: Barbara Herrnstein Smith, Houston Baker Jr.
Romance languages: Gerald Prince, Jean Alter, Lucienne Frappier-Mazur, Michèle H. Richman
Slavic languages: Gary Saul Morson, Peter Steiner
History of art: Leo Steinberg, Irene Winter
Music: Leonard B. Meyer
American civilization: Janice Radway
Electrical engineering: Aravind Joshi
Oriental studies: Ahmet Evin, Peter Gaeffke, William L. Hanaway Jr., Barbara Ruch

Given that this list includes sixty-one faculty members, details about each of them, their roles at Penn, and how each connected to Goffman, have been relegated to the appendix. However, general comments about Goffman's links to each department fit here.

The central departments are anthropology, sociology, linguistics, folklore, and communication, for these were either where Goffman himself was officially based (anthropology and sociology) or the homes of the core faculty with whom he had the closest ties (thus adding in linguistics, folklore, and communication). What is most surprising is the range of disciplines and substantial number of colleagues involved in the various projects. They include not only education (where Hymes was based for about half of Goffman's years at Penn) and psychology (where Goffman himself held a secondary appointment), but landscape architecture, biology, English, Romance languages, Slavic languages, history of art, music, American civilization, electrical engineering, and Oriental studies. (This list is organized by the strength of the connection to Goffman.) As will become obvious, Goffman certainly did not know all these people well, and in a few cases may not even have had direct contact with them, but his name and theirs appear on common proposals for projects, and so it is important to understand at least a few basics of who they were. Again, details are in the appendix; what appears here are overviews for each of the most significant departments in terms of Goffman's connections to faculty based within them.

Anthropology

Hymes, Szwed, and Birdwhistell all had formal training in anthropology as graduate students; Worth named his area "the anthropology of visual communications" (Gross 1980, 4) and, prior to his arrival at Penn, had worked closely with Mead, the personification of anthropology. Although Goffman trained in sociology at Chicago, the use of ethnography as a method joined anthropology to sociology there, and most students took courses in both departments. That meant these members of the core group all shared some theoretical and methodological assumptions, which likely facilitated their ability to understand one another. Significantly, it was through the efforts of senior faculty in anthropology (Anthony Wallace, Ward Goodenough, William Davenport), that Goffman was even invited to join Penn, that department providing the initial welcome when sociology proved unwilling. Once at Penn, Goffman was given an office in the Penn Museum on campus, which is where all the anthropology faculty had their offices at that point, so he was in closest proximity to them, thus more likely to run into them than people organizationally based in other departments. Joel Sherzer was both student and faculty member at Penn (he taught Hymes's courses while Hymes was in England on sabbatical 1968–1969).[178] As he was a student far longer, and most of his interactions were in that capacity, he will be introduced in the section on Penn students. After graduating from Penn, Sherzer began teaching at the University of Texas, Austin, and so, although he was a small part of one major project at Penn, he plays a far larger role in several minor activities once he was based at Texas. Others in anthropology with links to Goffman were J. David Sapir, Peggy Reeves Sanday, and Arjun Appadurai.

Sociology

The study of social interaction should find an obvious home in sociology, even for a department with other concerns as their primary focus, yet in the beginning the senior sociologists at Penn had little to no interest in Goffman or his publications (despite comments to the contrary about Philip Rieff). Those who came later, especially Renée Fox, understood the value of his work, and took the time to better integrate him into the department, finally giving him voting rights. It is noteworthy that one of Goffman's roles under Fox as department chair was to meet with potential new hires, implying that he was seen as someone likely to attract high quality junior faculty to the program, such as Elijah Anderson. One other person with links to Goffman was Teresa Labov, who was married to William Labov, and later shows up as a minor part of MAP.

Linguistics

William Labov, John Fought, Gillian Sankoff, Henry Hiz, Ellen Prince, and Anthony Kroch had primary appointments in linguistics, and both Dell and Virginia Hymes were given secondary appointments in linguistics. The specific focus that brought most of these scholars together was the mutual influence of language and society, and these are the scholars who represented the linguists' point of view in that conversation. Grimshaw mentions "Labov's claim that there is no sociolinguistics, but only a better informed, socially-based linguistics" (1978, 168). As Hymes wrote to the department in 1974, speaking of potential overlaps between other departments and linguistics: "Our commonality of interest, as Bill Labov states, is partly a function of institutional circumstances; but perhaps institutional circumstances function as they do because there is an important intellectual commonality, an exploratory interest that ranges beyond conventional compartments."[179] The use of language in the inner city was one of the major concerns of the Center for Urban Ethnography; indeed, Shuy credits Penn with "a burst of training and research" (1990, 200) leading to the development of socio-linguistics, made possible by funding from NIMH through CUE. Beyond Labov, who was part of both major and minor projects, others in linguistics mostly played a small role in one or more minor projects.

Folklore

Ken Goldstein and Dan Ben-Amos offered a home for Szwed in folklore, and later for Hymes (once he left anthropology). Folklore was also the primary organizational home for multiple peripheral members of the network including Virginia Hymes, Henry Glassie, Barbara Kirshenblatt-Gimblett, and Roger Abrahams. Dell Hymes was surprisingly active in the administration of folklore degrees. At least some of the time his ideas were taken seriously and implemented, as when Ben-Amos prepared the undergraduate major proposal in 1974, incorporating specific phrases taken from Hymes's draft.[180] The immediate reason for establishing an undergraduate program was that noticeable numbers (45 to 66 percent depending on the semester) of undergraduates were enrolling in graduate courses, frustrating faculty and graduate students alike. The proposal stressed the interdisciplinarity of the program, with students encouraged to take courses across multiple departments (including American civilization, anthropology, linguistics, and more).[181] That proposal was approved, and Virginia Hymes was given the role of undergraduate chair.

That folklore served as the first institutional home of both the Center for Urban Ethnography and *Language in Society* may seem odd to those unfamiliar with either that discipline or with the history of Penn. But looking back from a moment when this was no longer the case, Hufford tells us that "in the 1970s, Penn magnificently supported folklore's interdisciplinarity" (2020, 111). In keeping with that, in addition to department faculty, "folklore graduate students studied with Erving Goffman, Anthony Wallace, Arjun Appadurai, Ray Birdwhistell, William Labov, Barbara Herrnstein Smith, and other transdisciplinary luminaries" (111; see also Leeds-Hurwitz and Sigman [2010] for an overlapping list of brilliant faculty members with whom we were all encouraged to study, regardless of anyone's home disciplines). So, it made sense at that time and in that place that folklore should serve as an obvious nexus, and a natural home for this network of scholars.

Henry Glassie served as department chair in the mid-1970s, and describes the context this way:

It was just an amazing gathering of people, and it was at a time when the University of Pennsylvania was radically committed to interdisciplinary work, and particularly interdisciplinary work based upon anthropology. . . . And there was a gathering of people at Penn. Bill Labov was there. Erving Goffman was there. Saul [sic] Worth was there. Steve Feld was there. And then the folklore department itself was just a gathering of stars. . . . I was just a little individual of minor importance, but I was in an amazing crowd of people. (116, HG)

As a result of that amazing crowd of people, the folklore department was particularly well respected nationally through the 1970s. Hymes viewed his move from anthropology to the folklore department as a positive thing:

I want in years to come my presence in folklore dept to be understood, and seen, at least by those who are open to seeing it not as a purely historical accident which has to be explained by going back some years to a set of circumstances no longer visible, but as an obvious appropriateness, as the place one would of course expect to find someone like me, given the obvious differences between what is going on in anthropology and in folklore, or, given the obvious role of folklore in the active, exciting things that are going in [sic] with regard to communication and semiotics.[182]

The department's significance can be demonstrated by the fact that multiple members were officers of the American Folklore Society. In addition to Hymes being elected president in 1973, Goldstein was elected president in 1975, and at the same time Kirshenblatt-Gimblett was elected second vice president (she later served as president, as did Glassie and Abrahams).[183] In fact, as Goldstein made clear in a letter to then Dean Gregorian, "For the 1975/'76 period, every officer of the Society is either a faculty member or a graduate of the Folklore Department of the University of Pennsylvania. . . . in addition, six of the nine members of the Executive Board of the Society are faculty members or graduates of our department" (Feb 19, 1975, OP; his emphasis). In that same letter, Goldstein concluded that although Penn was neither the oldest nor the largest folklore department in the US, these facts should be understood to mean that "we are regarded by our academic peers as the best department of its kind."

Despite this level of national recognition, not everyone at Penn was always cooperative, as Goldstein complained to Hymes in 1969, when he was being asked to help get both Szwed and Labov to Penn, for while Hymes, Goodenough, Sapir, and Goffman were all in favor of cooperation between anthropology and folklore, the same could not be said of everyone in anthropology.[184] By the mid-1980s, Goffman had died, D. Hymes had moved to GSE, Szwed had left for Yale, and Kirshenblatt-Gimblett had left for New York University. The folklore department never recovered the same significance and never again played the same central role (either at Penn or nationally), despite the valiant efforts of Ben-Amos, Abrahams, Hufford herself, and others.

It may seem that folklore had little to do with Goffman, but his work was read across multiple courses, so even those who did not take one of his rare courses encountered his ideas. For example, in 1984, when Hymes prepared a list of doctoral exam questions, one of them was "Assess the relevance of the work of the late Erving Goffman to folklore and folklife. Cite specific works and concepts."[185] Interestingly, Hymes preserved a letter of his evaluating a student's answer to that specific question, not being entirely happy with the result.[186] That evaluation is several pages long, far more extensive that would be expected in this context, including not only discussion of Goffman's work, but clarifying the relationship between Goffman and ethnomethodology.

Communications

Both Birdwhistell and Worth had their primary homes within the Annenberg School of Communications, as did Steve Feld, Larry Gross, Perry Tannenbaum, Paul Messaris, and Amos Vogel; Dell Hymes and Goffman had secondary affiliations. Hymes's activities included being respondent to a talk at ASC by Marshall McLuhan,[187] and he regularly corresponded with Dean George Gerbner, even before he was a dean himself. Goffman was invited to present a colloquium at ASC shortly after his arrival but turned down the opportunity. (Worth complained to Hymes that Goffman was not yet getting involved with programs at Annenberg as "he even refused to give a colloquium.")[188] Labov did present a colloquium at ASC shortly after his arrival.[189] Just as the role of language in social life was essential to multiple projects, so was the extension of relevant behavior to include the nonverbal (Birdwhistell) and the visual (Worth). The fact that both Birdwhistell and Worth grounded their respective research agendas in anthropology meant that they shared assumptions of theory and method with the other central players in this story, despite having their academic home in a different part of the university. Just as folklore initially housed one of the relevant journals (*Language in Society*, under the auspices of the Center for Urban Ethnography), ASC housed the other (*Studies in the Anthropology of Visual Communication*). While Goffman facilitated the publication of Birdwhistell's

Kinesics and Context (1970), Worth facilitated the publication of Goffman's *Gender Advertisements* (1976a). And then, when Worth died suddenly, Hymes and Goffman facilitated the publication of his collected works, *Studying Visual Communication* (1981) in their series. When Gerbner became editor of the *Journal of Communication* in November 1973, he put Worth on the editorial board, while Birdwhistell, Goffman, and Hymes appear on a long list of consulting and contributing editors.[190] For his part, Hymes viewed communication as an obvious home for the core peer group's interests, telling Worth as early as 1969 that he saw it as "the general frame of reference within which it all makes sense" and had "a vision of it being the answer to all the world's problems in regard to symbolic forms in communication."[191] Worth echoed that language a few years later when he was quoted as saying, "I think Penn is the strongest center in the world in dealing with symbolic events, language, and non-verbal communication. Our faculty is delving into the sociology of communication, the psychology of art, the meaning of communication itself."[192]

Interestingly, despite the connections to both Worth and Birdwhistell, and reports to Gerbner about potential interest to the contrary, and his official standing once granted a secondary appointment, Goffman never become formally involved with activities at ASC (although he did connect with other scholars in communication through several of the minor projects). However, he did participate in activities with communication faculty at Temple, a few miles from Penn. For example, Ruby reports that "Erving attended many of the Conferences on Visual Anthropology I organized at Temple" (2015, 1968–80), and provides details for two of the events: Goffman was one of several discussants for "The Anthropological Relevance of Fiction Film: A Screening of Ramparts of Clay" in 1971, and organizer of a session ("A Critical Approach to the Use of Videotape for Social Science Research: Frankenstein Meets his Monster") in 1972.

Education

In addition to Dell Hymes becoming dean of GSE in 1975, Brian Sutton-Smith, Leila Gleitman, Morton Botel, David Smith, Fred Erickson, Nancy Hornberger, Michael Long, Nessa Wolfson, Shirley Brice Heath, and Bambi Schieffelin all had their primary appointments there, although most of them only connected to Goffman via minor projects, and in small ways. Once Hymes moved into education as his primary home, he gave secondary appointments to Labov, Szwed, Worth, Fought, and Sanday, all at once in 1976,[193] thus more firmly establishing their connections with GSE. In addition, he shifted focus a bit by highlighting the use of language in the classroom as an important topic, along with outreach to K–12 students in Philadelphia, their teachers, and principals. Hymes also used his new position to host various campus colleagues and present them to faculty and students based in GSE. For example, in 1975, there was a one-day seminar, "Language in the Classroom: The Positive Implications of Cultural and Linguistic Diversity," with Hymes presenting on "The Ethnography of Speaking," and Labov on "Language Learning as a Social Process";[194] in 1977, Hymes, Labov, and Szwed all presented on "Ethnography as Educational Methodology";[195] and during the 1979–1980 Language in Education Colloquium series, invited speakers included Szwed,[196] Sankoff,[197] Kirshenblatt-Gimblett,[198] and Ben-Amos.[199] Goffman does not seem to have presented colloquia in education any more than he did in communications, however he did serve on at least one search committee, in 1976.[200] In addition, Heath (2011) mentions multiple faculty members across multiple departments at Penn who attracted education students into their courses, thus documenting boundary crossing: Anderson, Birdwhistell, Goffman, Goodenough, Labov, Sanday, and Szwed. All of these were just the sort of connections several of the minor projects were designed to facilitate.

Psychology

Labov was initially offered a job in psychology, both Labov and Goffman were given secondary appointments, several minor projects involved various psychology faculty (Rochel Gelman, Leo Hurvich, Dorothea Jameson Hurvich, David Premack, Dan Osherson, and Burton S. Rosner), and Dorothea Hurvich connected to Goffman as a University Professor. In the early days (specifically, in 1969), Hymes expressed his delight that psychology was "moving toward an ethnographic sort of orientation."[201] Of course, Goffman's work often overlapped with psychiatric contexts (e.g., Goffman 1959b, 1961a, 1961c, 1961d, 1963a), which meant he had spent a lot of time interacting with psychologists and psychiatrists prior to his arrival at Penn, mostly while based at NIMH. In addition, Birdwhistell's work at EPPI continued past his arrival at Penn, and he likely had connections with faculty in psychology, although available documentation does not reflect this; also, at least some of his earlier work had taken a psychiatric interview as the primary context (Birdwhistell 1972; McQuown 1971). Yet again there were overlapping interests across core group members in one more discipline.

Other departments (landscape architecture, biology, English, Romance languages, Slavic languages, history of art, music, American civilization, electrical engineering, and Oriental studies) were not ones where Goffman had any significant connections to the program. Only a few colleagues based in this set of departments connected with Goffman through major projects; most were minor parts of minor projects. For details, see the appendix.

Students

People included to this point were Goffman's faculty colleagues at Penn, but an invisible college must include students, or it cannot continue beyond the first generation. The evidence as to Goffman's interactions with students is somewhat contradictory. However, while it is frequently assumed that Goffman "did not seek to build a coterie, and also did not interact socially with students" (Murray 1998, 45), that does not mean he did not interact with students at least on matters relating to academic content. In fact, he taught students based in most of the central departments mentioned to this point (certainly anthropology, sociology, linguistics, folklore, and communications), and sporadically served on dissertation committees jointly with Hymes, Labov, Birdwhistell, Worth, Fox, and Fought, to my certain knowledge, and probably others not yet discovered. The following section thus provides brief introductions to relevant students, arranged by decade. The obvious year to mention is that of a terminal degree, even though someone would have been a student some years earlier, even occasionally considerably earlier. Most of the following descriptions are of students who completed their doctorates at Penn, as that is the most significant student group he influenced. But a few were MA students, or those in residence at Penn at one point whose degrees were completed elsewhere. Clearly, these are not the only students to have ever worked with Goffman; they are just ones for whom I have already found documentation, especially discussions of how Goffman influenced them and their research.

These descriptions of students document another dimension of the invisible college surrounding and supporting Goffman at Penn. The larger point to remember is the significance of theory groups: In order to ensure one's ideas are shared with future scholars and further developed, establishing individual connections with others is essential; publications alone are not enough (Leeds-Hurwitz 2021; Murray 1994). While Goffman is frequently said to have not done this, the following section demonstrates that assumption to be incorrect. Even though Goffman did not build a "school" or "followers" in the traditional sense, he did influence not one but several academic generations of students, across multiple disciplines, not only through his writing but through his interactions with them, at least at Penn.

Table 3.3: Students Who Interacted with Goffman at
Penn, by Decade of Degree and Department

1960s degrees	
Anthropology	Joel Sherzer, Regna Darnell
American Civilization	Richard Bauman
1970s degrees	
Anthropology	William O. Beeman, Judith Irvine, Susan U. Philips, Elinor Ochs, Marjorie Harness Goodwin, Lee Ann Draud
Sociology	Gary Alan Fine, Samuel Heilman, Eviatar Zerubavel, Michael Delaney
Communications	Charles Goodwin, Yves Winkin, John Thomas Carey
Linguistics	Marilyn Merritt, John Baugh
Folklore	Michael J. Bell
1980s degrees	
Sociology	Carol Brooks Gardner
Communications	Stuart J. Sigman, Barbara Ann Lynch
Linguistics	Deborah Schiffrin
Folklore	Amy Shuman, Wendy Leeds-Hurwitz

Now, to tell their stories.

1960s degrees

Joel Sherzer earned a PhD in anthropology at Penn in 1968 (preceding Goffman's arrival, working under Hymes). Discussing his training at Penn in 2014, Sherzer wrote: "I was fortunate to study and interact with a creative, dynamic, and pioneering group of people in various departments. The work of my Penn teachers has remained with me all of my scholarly life. Along with others, I frequently crossed the street between the anthropology and linguistic departments." He named Hymes, Sapir, Goffman, and Labov as particularly influential faculty members with whom he took courses. Although Labov was not yet at Penn when he was a student, Sherzer participated in Labov's 1968 seminar at Columbia along with Goffman.

Sherzer was the rare person to experience being both student and faculty member while at Penn: He taught linguistic anthropology as a lecturer in 1968–1969, substituting for Hymes, who was on leave in England that year ("For the moment, I'm swimming not walking in your shoes"[202]). As a result, Sherzer wrote detailed letters to Hymes about what was happening in his absence. "Both Goffman and Fought have been coming to the seminars—makes things kind of lively. We've worked in a little on a film of a psychiatric interview—with the help of some Annenberg students in the seminar. We'll be trying to write rules for both the verbal and non-verbal aspects of communication in the film."[203] Birdwhistell may have been the source of that film, due to his connections with EPPI, but he apparently was not invited to the seminar. A month later, apparently Labov had joined Sherzer's course as well: "The seminar continues to be interesting. Goffman and Labov are good to have along."[204] Then he updated Hymes on difficulties between Goffman and Worth:

> The misunderstanding between Goffman and Sol Worth is unfortunate. I get along very well with Erv simply by realizing that his surface structure is quite different from his deep structure which is quite serious and quite brilliant (to use a metaphor I learned somewhere). His surface structure is also quite interesting, but can be irritating if one expects consistency. All you have to do to understand all this is to read his works, of course. His contribution to the seminar has been quite good since he acts as everybody's devil's advocate (including his own) and makes you sharpen your thinking.[205]

Presumably the metaphor he learned "somewhere" was in fact learned from Hymes. A few weeks later, the group visiting Sherzer's seminar had expanded again. "John Gumperz happened to be in town to speak to the South Asia dept. He and Goffman and I had dinner and then all went to seminar. Labov presented his video tape and got very good discussion in response. He seems to appreciate very much having Goffman as a sounding board and thus continues to show up every other week."[206] And then a final report, describing plans for the spring seminar he would teach:

Next semester Bill Labov gives his course down here—it's certain now. Should
be pretty lively. He'll probably stay overnite and we'll have the seminar the next
day. Hope to have presentations by Goffman, J. Szwed, Bill Stewart, as well as a
couple of things by me. I'm going to try and orient the thing a little away from
interaction analysis after Goffman's presentations. I think the kids have forgotten
a little just how vast an area "language and culture" is.[207]

Language and Culture was the title of the course. Hymes responded with
extensive discussion of Labov's interest in Penn and the possibility of his
time being split between departments, including anthropology, due to concern as to whether such a move would complicate the possibility of Sherzer
himself getting an appointment in anthropology.[208] Sherzer responded immediately that he had already interviewed at the University of Texas, Austin,
and thought it would make the most sense to take that position. Part of the
logic was "spreading the word": "I think it's important that I am in such a
place where I can communicate the type of thing we've been doing here to
other scholars."[209] And, of course, that is exactly what happened. Later that
spring, Sherzer was able to update Hymes on some departmental politics
within anthropology: There was some resentment by those not typically
included in more recent activities. Among the issues specifically named were:

Goffman's arrival furthering the interdisciplinary approach to scholarship which
they fight tooth and nail; the Szwed grant (which in a sense culminates all—focus
on urban problems, especially black; liberal-radical point of view; interdisciplinary point of view with a focus on sociolinguistics; involvement of people like
you, Goffman, and Szwed). I write this to keep you in touch with dept. splits....
Goffman presented his point of view very undogmatically in dept. meetings.[210]

Sherzer was mainly concerned in this letter about the potential unintended
impact of faculty disagreements on students, especially on evaluations of
student doctoral exams. In the next letter, he had talked with Sapir, who had
been around longer, and had more experience with departmental politics.
By the end, Sherzer passed on a comment he had made to Goffman about a
potential way to keep things calm between faculty factions in the anthropology department: "My suggestion to Goffman was that you people somehow
try to coordinate the urban ethnography program with [faculty member
name]'s field work course, at least to some degree, so that both factions will
have at least this link between them. He (Goffman) seemed amenable."[211]
That never happened, and things blew up within anthropology when Sapir
was denied tenure.

Sherzer was connected to both major and minor projects and so returns in several later chapters. He attended and then wrote up Goffman's conference in Amsterdam in 1970 (Sherzer 1971); he submitted his dissertation to Conduct and Communication for publication as a book. He expressed gratitude for Goffman's critique of his article "On Linguistic Semantics and Linguistic Subdisciplines," published in *Language in Society* (1973a, 127n8), and mentioned Goffman as one of several people who had reviewed an unpublished manuscript of his in 1980 that was later published in 1983 as *Kuna Ways of Speaking: An Ethnographic Perspective.*[212] In a review essay published in that same journal, Sherzer (1973b) referenced an as yet unpublished version of Goffman's 1974 book, *Frame Analysis*. Later, he served on the editorial board of *Language in Society*. Goffman, in his turn, acknowledged Sherzer in his own publications (e.g., Goffman 1981, 78n1).

Sherzer did end up going to Texas, where he was a primary organizer of several activities sponsored by the SSRC's Committee on Sociolinguistics: the publication *Working Papers in Sociolinguistics*, the conference on The Ethnography of Speaking in 1972, and another on Comparative Ethnographic Analysis in 1975. His activities are particularly important since, just as he had said to Hymes, he used them to share with others what he had learned at Penn. Like Sankoff, he was one of the younger generation tapped for membership in the Committee on Sociolinguistics, and he worked hard to prepare one of their major grant proposals to NSF (unfortunately, at a point when funds were no longer being distributed liberally, and it was denied). All these stories are told in chapter 6.

At one point, Sherzer tried to follow up an idea that he credited to Hymes for combining programs, one that would have involved Goffman.

> Do you remember a few years ago you had the idea that students could get their degrees in anthropology but not at a particular institution, sort of moving around and getting the benefit of working with various people. Of course the field and individual departments are much too rigid now for that sort of thing. But I would like to suggest an experiment on a mini scale that I think we could pull off as a sort of model as how things OUGHT to be done. This year we've got a couple of damn interesting students, just beginning as grad students in linguistic anthropology. They like it here but they are excited by the work of you, Bill, and Erv at Penn. I think we here at least are flexible enough to let them spend a semester or two in lovely Phila. taking courses with you people, then come back here and get their degrees here but also getting credit (and person benefit) from their work at Penn. (And vice versa if you've got someone say, who wants some Latin American contact.) What do you think? They'd probably be

better off to enroll in folklore at Penn if we try this than in anthropology, which would probably be against the idea anyway.[213]

This sounds a bit like a small version of the ERASMUS scheme put into place in the European Union much later.[214] Hymes liked the suggestion: "Your cooperative idea is very much to my own liking . . . Folklore, or, if it can be arranged, the group in 'semiotics' (reaching into Annenberg) that Ken [Goldstein] is working on, would be good. Of course, students could use folklore/semiotics as a base and take work in linguistics. Enrolled in anthropology, there would be so far as known not anyone to guide them. Labov would welcome this sort of thing too."[215] This was another idea that did not come to fruition, but the important point is the variety of ways in which Sherzer and others in the second generation attempted to expand upon what they had been taught about studying interaction, as well as maintaining the multi- and interdisciplinary approaches they had been taught. A few years later, Sherzer wrote to Hymes: "Your other postcard says that Penn is doing its best to keep pace with Texas. I never had any doubts or worries about Penn. . . . We don't have the clout at Texas that you, Bill, Erving, etc. have at Penn."[216]

Sherzer obviously interacted with other faculty members at Penn beyond Hymes, Labov and Goffman; for example, in 1978 he reviewed a book by W. John Smith (1977) in *Language in Society*, arguing for Smith's relevance to sociolinguistics, because his book "is about communication and stresses the importance of both contextual and interactional approaches to this area" (437). He concluded that "Smith is to be praised for having organized the vast and disparate research on animal communication in semiotic and interactional terms, pointing to the potential relevance of this research for the study of human communication, including language" (437–38). Also, Sherzer and Smith designed a book together, though it seems not to have been published.

Regna Darnell was a peer of Sherzer's who completed her PhD in anthropology at Penn in 1969. Even so, she managed to take a course with Goffman (Darnell 2022), and remembers him clearly:

> The addition to the Penn faculty of Erving Goffman in a cross-appointment between anthropology and sociology and of Bill Labov in linguistics, with Dan Ben-Amos and Kenneth Goldstein already in Folklore and Folklife and Sol Worth at the Annenberg School of Communication, heralded a new interdisciplinary synthesis. For me at least, this synthesis was grounded in anthropology and discussed endlessly in the University Museum coffee shop. The Center for

> Urban Ethnography coalesced just after I left Philadelphia, but its commitment
> to test theory against data from fieldwork was already central to Dell Hymes's
> ethnography of speaking/communication throughout the sixties. (2001a, xx)

Darnell returns to the topic later in that book, adding further details, specifically that: "Erving Goffman used to hang around with anthropologists, haranguing the graduate students in ethnography of communication at Penn that we could not, on the basis of cross-cultural fieldwork, produce insights as sophisticated as those he derived from studying his own society by member intuition" (315). She names other graduate students studying the ethnography of communication at the time in a different publication (2011), listing Michael Foster, Helen Hogan, Judith Irvine, Elinor Ochs Keenan, Susan Philips, Sheila Dauer Seitel, and K. M. Tiwari, and points out that Virginia Hymes was also part of the research cluster at the time (193; see Murray 1994 and Leeds-Hurwitz and Sigman 2010 for further details about which students were at Penn and in which department when). This makes sense, because Virginia Hymes would have been enrolled as a doctoral student in linguistics at that point. In a separate discussion, Darnell tells a story about the ethnography of speaking students trying to convince Goffman of the importance of documentation from other cultures.

> Goffman argued repeatedly that anthropologists could not, on the basis of their
> fieldwork, produce insights nearly as sophisticated as those Goffman himself
> derived by supposed native intuition from studying his own society. In some very
> interesting sense, the whole fieldwork ethos of the first generation of ethnography
> of speaking people from the University of Pennsylvania, beginning in the late
> 1960s, derives from proving Goffman wrong, by assuming that it is possible to
> acquire native-like intuitions in a society in which one has not been socialized
> as a child. Various of us presented Goffman with evidence as detailed as his own
> for "other" cultures. . . . We also challenged Goffman on the claim that he was
> in fact studying his own society. He was not, to any public knowledge, either
> homosexual or mentally ill, yet his descriptions of these subgroups of "our society"
> are appropriately acknowledged in several disciplines as foundational. (1991, 8)

In a summary statement about what it was like to be at Penn in the 1960s, Darnell emphasizes that "ideas were important" (2001a, xx). This was taken for granted by everyone at Penn, student or faculty member, and held true across the 1970s and 1980s as well as the 1960s. Darnell was included in the 1972 Ethnography of Speaking conference in Texas, and published in the resulting volume (Darnell 1974), making clear that, even after her move to Canada, she remained part of the invisible college.

Richard Bauman earned an MA in folklore at Indiana in 1962, then enrolled at Penn, where he earned a simultaneous MS in anthropology and PhD in American civilization in 1968.[217] Like Sherzer, he took a position at the University of Texas, Austin, where he worked until 1986, returning then to Indiana as a faculty member. Bauman is important to this story for his connection with the Conduct and Communication book series (both for his own volume and his evaluation of one of Goffman's), as well as for his role in co-organizing the Ethnography of Speaking conference in 1972, and co-editing the *Working Papers in Sociolinguistics*, both with Sherzer. He cites Goffman, especially when discussing performance (e.g., Bauman 1975; Bauman and Briggs 1990). In an early letter to Hymes in 1968, just before completing his degrees, but after moving to Texas, Bauman began: "Dear Professor Hymes (Dell?—I can't no-name you in writing)."[218] No-naming refers to avoiding direct address and is especially common when there is a status differential between the people interacting, so that it might be awkward to use any of the available choices; one avoids the issue by not using any of them. Hymes replied "Dear Dick, First names are fine, titles from people one knows are disconcerting."[219]

1970s degrees

The first few students listed below completed their degrees in the 1970s, but were part of the same cohort as Darnell, Sherzer, and Bauman; recall that Darnell names Irvine, Philips, and Ochs as among those who hung out at the museum talking informally with Goffman.

Judith Irvine earned her PhD in 1973 in anthropology, with a focus on linguistic anthropology. She was a participant in the 1972 Ethnography of Speaking conference and published in the resulting volume (1974). With Schieffelin, she was a panelist on "Discourse: Speech Acts and Contextualization" at the AAA in 1978 for which Goffman and Hymes served as discussants.[220] She cites Goffman in her work (e.g., 1979) and served on the editorial board of *Language in Society*.

Susan U. Philips completed her PhD in anthropology in 1974; Hymes chaired her dissertation committee, with Goffman and Goodenough the other members. In the published version, she thanks Goffman, for "useful criticisms of an earlier version of the book" (1983, vii). While still a graduate student, she participated in the 1972 Ethnography of Speaking conference and was published in the resulting volume (1974). In spring 1974, Hymes asked Fox to consider hiring Philips for a position in sociology. As part of his efforts to expand sociolinguistics on campus, he wanted to ensure they hired appropriate people, and he considered her a likely choice; apparently so did Goffman.[221] Hymes sent Philips's dissertation to Fox, with an explanation of the idea, letting Philips know.[222] Fox read it, and reported she had "found it a very fine piece of work, indeed," promising to have a phone conversation with Philips.[223] A few months later, Hymes was still hopeful, telling Labov: "In terms of sociological problems and aspects of language, we do have possibly an immediate opportunity, in the sociology department. There is at least initial interest in considering a junior appointment in this area. I have suggested Susan Philips as a possibility to Rene [sic] Fox." A little later in the same letter, now speaking more generally of potential hires in sociology, he continued: "Like Erv, I would welcome someone interested in 'pragmatics' and such, if same was not dogmatic about relying on introspection but rather open to ethnographically based work." [224] The effort to hire Philips obviously failed as she never joined Penn's faculty.

Elinor Ochs earned a PhD in anthropology at Penn in 1974, first taking a position at the University of Cambridge for a year (1973–1974) and then moving to linguistics at the University of Southern California in 1974. She explained herself in 2022 thus: "I am, simply, disciplinarily errant," going on to explain how that came about. Much of that explanation centers on Penn faculty and the connections she found there.

> In 1966, I entered The University of Pennsylvania PhD program in anthropology, joining the second generation of ethnographers of communication under Dell Hymes and David Sapir. I also assisted Ward Goodenough in his kinship studies. Linguistic anthropology was an inventive program, with contributions from Sol Worth (in the Annenberg School of Communication) and Erving Goffman (from the Department of Sociology). (2)

Her inclusion of Worth here is significant, given that so few other students name him as part of the group of faculty members they worked with and/ or saw working together.

Marjorie Harness Goodwin received a PhD in anthropology at Penn in 1978 under Goffman. She was awarded a Center for Urban Ethnography grant for her dissertation research, and acknowledges comments from Goffman, Labov, and Gail Jefferson (another CUE grant recipient) on at least her 1980 paper on gossip, a topic that Szwed had previously written about (Szwed 1966), and she cites his work. In a later paper (1982), she again acknowledges the CUE grant, mentions comments from Goffman, Labov, and Jefferson, and cites Goffman, Hymes, Labov, and Szwed. Several later papers also credit CUE funding and acknowledge or cite overlapping members of the group. In her 1999 article on participation, she cites Goffman multiple times, highlighting the ways his insights "have been useful for linguistic anthropologists" (179). Corsaro's review of a book that grew out of that research (Goodwin 1990) specifically compares her to Goffman: "Goodwin's careful and insightful scholarship is one of many scholarly traits that display the influence of one of her mentors, Erving Goffman" (Corsaro 1992, 1182). Goodwin also acknowledged CUE funding for a second book (Goodwin and Goodwin 1987). As described in chapter 6, she was one of those named in a grant proposal that was to also include Goffman, but which was not funded.

William O. Beeman, who went on to get a PhD in anthropology and linguistics from Chicago in 1974, describes what it was like to be a student at Penn in 1970.

> I would like to mark a debt in this book to an intellectual community of great strength. Although my former graduate studies were completed at the University of Chicago, the formal cast for this work was conceived at the University of Pennsylvania, where I was resident in 1970. At that time I was thrown into one of the most vital groups of scholars I have ever encountered, consisting of Ray Birdwhistell, John Fought, Erving Goffman, Dell Hymes, William Labov, David Sapir, Bob Scholte, John Szwed, and the late Sol Worth. These individuals would likely deny that they ever met all together as a group. Nonetheless, the atmosphere at Penn was electric at the time I was there. Communication passed through students these men had in common and through other informal means. The community broke up shortly thereafter through death and a sad set of shortsighted personnel decisions, but even a decade later, I am still sustained by the energy that was generated there at that time. (1986, xv)

In fact, those he named connected—in smaller groups at least—far more often than any of us realized at the time, as documented in the next two chapters.

Lee Ann Draud was a student in anthropology who earned an MA and then worked as Goffman's secretary and/or research assistant through the 1970s. She is thanked in several publications for specific comments, not just the general acknowledgment typically given. For example, Goffman writes: "Note, self-induced misalignment is likely to involve mainly perception, not action, for the latter must soon face corrective action from others" and then, in a footnote: "An argument recommended by Lee Ann Draud" (1974,

112n46; see also 1976a, vi, 30; 1976b, 257; 1978, 787), and finally: "For all of which, and for much other help, I am grateful to Lee Ann Draud" (1979a, 18).

Gary Alan Fine earned a BA in sociology at Penn in 1971 but did not stay for graduate school. However, he took two courses with Goffman as an undergraduate, and Goffman wrote letters of recommendation for him when it was time to go to graduate school. In addition, Fine has written that Goffman would "on occasion . . . invite me to his home on Society Hill, a very elegant area in Philadelphia. We would sit together and talk about my career, the kind of things professors and undergraduates would do. Not talk about his career so much, although I might have asked him questions about particular things we were reading; not that I would ask about his life" (2009). Even though he was an undergraduate taking graduate courses, Fine says: "I was ready for this; it connected with some other classes I was taking. I took classes with Dell Hymes, David Sapir, and later with Ray Birdwhistell, so there was a group of men at Penn at that point interested in similar kinds of issues." Fine further mentions that several faculty members sat in on the course, including Labov. Fine became "an unpaid research assistant," helping Goffman to categorize bloopers in radio shows as part of the research for *Forms of Talk* (Goffman 1981), splicing together reels of those most useful (Fine 2009). A paper of his was cited by Goffman (1974), and he was invited by Goffman to participate in a panel at the American Sociological Association in 1982, the year Goffman was president but was too ill to attend (Fine 2009). Given that he was an undergraduate while at Penn, Fine played no role in any of the projects described in these pages.

Samuel Heilman earned his PhD in sociology at Penn in 1973. Unlike Fine, Darnell, Sherzer, and others, he did not participate in casual conversations over coffee with Goffman. In fact, he says about Goffman: "He worked from his home, he was seldom seen around the campus, he didn't really present himself as a member of the University of Pennsylvania community" (Heilman 2009), so obviously they had very different experiences. Heilman's dissertation research was funded through the Center for Urban Ethnography. As he tells the story,

> at some point I was hanging around the center, with Szwed and Goffman there. They were talking about religious institutions or something like that. I remember Goffman said it would be a "gas" if somebody did a study on synagogue. I said, "Well, I could do that." I was very much involved with the synagogue where I was living. So I said, "If I had a grant, I could do that." They agreed to give me a grant, a dissertation grant from the center. I was still taking courses, but now

> I wanted to take some more courses from Goffman. But Goffman said I wasn't
> ready to take his courses, I had to do a lot of reading. So I started reading. He
> gave me a massive reading list. We reviewed it in the form of a tutorial held at
> his house, just the two of us. It was not on a regular basis—I would meet him
> every few weeks. That is in itself a story. (2009)

CUE also funded several papers that Heilman delivered at SAA and AAA,
both in 1974 (Center for Urban Ethnography 1974), and mentions one of
these (Heilman 1975), as well as his dissertation about to be published as
a book (Heilman 1976), as resulting from their funding (Center for Urban
Ethnography 1975). In the first paper, CUE is acknowledged, along with
Fox and Goffman: "who at every stage of the project helped in the deciphering of the field data and the formulation of ideas" (1975, 371). In the book,
Heilman thanks Goffman and mentions him frequently. "To Erving Goffman go thanks, not only for stimulating the project, but for his continued
advice through all stages of the work" (1976, xxvii). Heilman also attended
the CUE-sponsored conference in 1969 on urban ethnography.

Eviatar Zerubavel's PhD in sociology was completed in 1976, under the joint
direction of Goffman and Fox (Sabetta and Zerubavel 2019, 58), and both
are acknowledged in the published version: "Erving Goffman has certainly
influenced my thinking more than any other sociologist I have met, and I
consider myself most fortunate to have studied with him" (1979, xxiii). He
reports having entered Penn in 1972 specifically to study with Goffman:

> What attracted me was not in the sociology department, since it was a depart-
> ment with strengths in demography and criminology. Instead, I was attracted
> by three specific individuals, three figures: William Labov (in the Department
> of linguistics), Dell Hymes (in the Department of folklore), and Erving Goffman
> (in the Department of anthropology). So, I ended up taking courses with all of
> them, but it was the encounter with Goffman [that was] the most fruitful from
> an intellectual point of view. (Sabetta and Zerubavel 2019, 58)

He was happy with his decision, for "as I had hoped, the highlight of my
first semester at Penn was indeed Goffman's 'Social Interaction' seminar,
the most intellectually transformative course I have ever taken" (2024, 525).

After Goffman's death, Zerubavel participated in an ASA panel by Goffman's students about what they had learned from him, as he relates here:

> You know, two years after he died, some of us (Goffman's former students like
> Sam Heilman, Gary Alan Fine, Sherri Cavan—this last one, the "only one real
> student" that Goffman once said to [have] ever had) had a session at the ASA

annual meeting on what we learned from Goffman. What was amazing was that all of us mentioned the same thing, without preparing it in advance: the fact that we learned how to look, something that we would have never guessed from his writings only. Moreover, he never explicitly taught us anything about analytical gaze, sociological eye and similar stuff. We acquired this skill only by watching him in action: how to look at the most micro-micro-microscopic situations and visualize invisible dimensions which you couldn't have seen otherwise. (Sabetta and Zerubavel 2019, 69)

Cavan was a student of Goffman's at Berkeley (he chaired her dissertation committee in 1965 [Cavan 2013]), and so won't be discussed here.[225] Gary Marx, John Lofland, Harvey Sacks, David Sudnow, and Emanuel Schegloff were other Goffman students at Berkeley rather than Penn, and so their biographies and comments are also not included here, although Sacks and Schegloff become relevant to the story of MAP in chapter 6.

Michael Delaney enrolled in graduate studies at Penn due to Goffman's presence there. He earned a PhD in sociology in 1979, taking two courses with Goffman in the early 1970s, and then "in 1973, partly owing to my continued fascination with frame analysis, Goffman invited me to provide a critical reading of the draft of the resulting book" (2014, 87). He mentions that Goffman "mostly consorted with a select, ethnographically oriented circle at Penn, including those associated with urban anthropology and ethnography, folklore, communication studies, and sociolinguistics—Dell Hymes, John Szwed, Ray Birdwhistell, among others" and highlights one connection as particularly important: "Birdwhistell and Goffman seemed to get on famously, demonstrating that Goffman was eminently capable of generous collegial solidarity with intellectually like-minded others" (90). Hopefully the details provided in this chapter and the rest of this book document that Birdwhistell was hardly the only one to benefit from that generosity.

Charles Goodwin received a PhD in communications at Penn in 1977, officially under Klaus Krippendorff's direction, but also unofficially worked with Goffman. He describes how Gail Jefferson got to Penn, and how he and his wife, Marjorie Harness Goodwin, worked with her:

When SACKS asked GOFFMAN to give Gail JEFFERSON a post-doc at the Center for Urban Ethnography he happily accepted and that is how she came to Philadelphia. . . . after she arrived there was an extraordinary series of seminars at the Center for Urban Ethnography with GOFFMAN, LABOV, Gail JEFFERSON and other students. We didn't realize at the time just how extraordinary the education we were getting was. (Goodwin and Salomon 2019, 4; emphasis in original)

He further writes, "We were kind of his [Goffman's] students, though I wasn't officially, but we were working with him" (4). This was not as uncommon at Penn as it might have been at some other universities: Shared interests frequently trumped official roles. I suspect that most of us never realized how extraordinary our education was until later, when we discovered that other students at other universities had very different experiences. As described in chapter 6, both Goodwins were named in a grant proposal that was to also include Goffman, Jefferson, and Sacks.

Yves Winkin earned an MA in communications at Penn in 1979 (with Birdwhistell as his advisor and Hymes as a second reader), returning home to the University of Liège in Belgium to earn his PhD there in 1982. He first contacted Goffman because the sociologist Pierre Bourdieu, who he knew from Paris, had suggested he do so.

> To make a long story short, Goffman invited me to come to his place. Either that visit or the next, I asked him what courses to take, and I remember him telling me bluntly: "take linguistics; it is so boring that you will never want to take such courses again later." He also suggested that I take John Smith's course in human ethology. So I went to the zoo and asked John Smith to "sit" in his class. Since I was sent by Goffman, he accepted. . . . As far as linguistics was concerned, I went to Labov's first class, at Goffman's suggestion. Bill Labov asked us to take a sheet of paper and to write in the phonetic international alphabet a few words he said. We were to hand him the sheet, or to leave the room if we hadn't been able to write the words in phonetic alphabet. I had to leave the room. (email to the author, Feb 25, 2024)

Clearly, Goffman did not just collaborate with Labov and Smith as colleagues; he sent students their way as well.

Winkin has shared the reading list of Goffman's course Social Interaction from 1976. In this context, what is most relevant, beyond the incredible breadth of what it includes (not to mention the length, at seventeen pages, which is long even for a graduate seminar at Penn in the 1970s), is that every one of the primary peer group (Hymes, Labov, Birdwhistell, Szwed, and Worth) is represented in it, some having multiple entries. As well, some peripheral group members are also included: Goodenough, W. J. Smith, and Rose.

After returning to Belgium, Winkin also spent considerable time in France where he served as liaison between Bourdieu and Goffman. Expanding that role, he went on to publish multiple works on Goffman, first publishing an interview with Goffman in 1984, then translating some of his work into French and framing it with a portrait of the sociologist as a young man (1988a). These early publications were supplemented by a wide variety of others examining Goffman's life, work, and influence. Winkin has frequently translated Goffman's ideas for the French context,[226] sometimes emphasizing his connections with other scholars, as with Birdwhistell (2022c) or Bourdieu (1993b, 2022f). Given that several of his books have been translated into other languages (so that his initial translations of Goffman's writings into French for 1988a then served to also introduce Goffman in Spanish, Portuguese, and Japanese), he gets credit not only for his biographical research but for spreading the word around the world. For obvious reasons, he was the one chosen to prepare the introduction to Goffman's 1953 dissertation when that was finally published (2022e).

John Thomas Carey completed a PhD at Penn in 1976, supervised by Birdwhistell. Goffman cites him several times: for working with Draud to prepare the slides Goffman used in *Gender Advertisements* (1979a, vi), and elsewhere in that book: "For this latter point, and for other suggestions incorporated without further acknowledgment, I am very grateful to John Carey" (19).

Marilyn Merritt completed her PhD in linguistics in 1976, with Henry Hoenigswald as chair and Goffman, Hymes, Labov, and Fought as committee members (1976a).[227] In the published version of one chapter in *Language in Society*, she thanks Goffman, as well as Hymes, Fought, and Labov for their comments (1976b, 315; see also Merritt 1979), and she uses Goffman's publications extensively. Decades later she wrote about Goffman as "interdisciplinary anthropologist," emphasizing "Goffman's twin legacies of (1) model work in uncharted waters of the type that builds collaborative interdisciplinary knowledge and (2) useful concepts for studying face-to-face social interaction, derived from his analytical paradigm for studying the institutionalization of social order" (2018, 1). She has explained that "at Penn, Goffman served as faculty member for the Graduate Group of several university departments, including Anthropology, Sociology, Linguistics, Psychology, Folklore, and Communication, and encouraged numerous students and colleagues" (2). By this she does not mean that he was an official member of all these departments; he clearly was not. Rather he worked with students in all these programs, something which was far more important to all of us as students.

Merritt highlights Goffman's role with *Language in Society* in the detailed description she has provided for her first submission to that journal. She first "dared to informally query Erving Goffman," who she describes as "co-editor," presumably in practice though not in name, as to how to get published. By following his advice at several stages of the process, she succeeded in getting her article accepted (Johnstone 2010, 311).

John Baugh earned a PhD in linguistics in 1979, supervised by Labov, with Goffman, Hymes, and Fought as the other committee members.[228] He uses Goffman's ideas throughout his work (e.g., 1983). His CV makes clear that he perfectly demonstrates the multi- and interdisciplinarity we all learned at Penn, for he describes himself as "Professor of Psychological and Brain Sciences, Anthropology, Linguistics, Education, English, African & African American Studies, American Culture Studies, Philosophy-Neuroscience-Psychology, and Urban Studies" (a list supported by the various positions he held after leaving Penn). In addition, he was principal investigator and project director for the Ford Foundation's "Linguistic Profiling in Interdisciplinary Perspective."[229]

Together with Sherzer, Baugh prepared a reader synthesizing what had been produced at Penn and elsewhere in sociolinguistics during the 1970s (Baugh and Sherzer 1984). They wanted to include Goffman's "Replies and Responses," initially published in *Language in Society* in 1976, but discovered it was already slated for reprinting in Goffman's *Forms of Talk* (1981).[230] When first told of their idea for a book, Hymes responded with lengthy suggestions about the potential approaches they might take (summarizing new work versus providing an introductory textbook).[231]

Michael J. Bell was awarded a grant from 1971 to 1973 from the Center for Urban Ethnography to conduct the fieldwork which led to his dissertation in folklore (1975), titled "Running Rabbits and Talking Shit: Folkloric Communication in an Urban Black Bar" (Center for Urban Ethnography 1978). John Szwed was his chair, with Ken Goldstein on his committee. He thanks Goffman, along with Szwed and Hymes, for criticizing his initial research proposal, which likely served the dual purpose of being the CUE grant proposal and his dissertation proposal. In both the dissertation and the published version (1982), he thanks Szwed, Goldstein, Abrahams, Hymes, Birdwhistell, and Goffman, and cites multiple Goffman books as relevant. In both, as well as in some of his articles, he expands upon some of Goffman's terms (e.g., Bell 1979, which applies impression management and remedial exchanges).

1980s degrees

Students included below earned their degrees in the 1980s, but that means they were mostly Goffman's students in the 1970s, when Goffman was a fairly recent arrival on campus, and perhaps more open to interactions with graduate students, given that he had not yet developed all of his later connections with faculty members across campus.

Carol Brooks Gardner earned a PhD in sociology with Goffman as her dissertation advisor in 1983. She acknowledges Goffman, as well as Hymes, Anderson, and others, citing Goffman frequently in the substantially revised and published version (1995). In an earlier paper on the same topic, she thanks him again: "Erving Goffman provided a detailed critique of an earlier draft" (1980, 329). She had actually first seen Goffman at Berkeley in 1968 while a student of Ervin-Tripp's, as part of "a summer institute on sociolinguistics, psycholinguistics, and anthropological linguistics for faculty and grad students, although I was an undergraduate" (2008; in addition to Goffman, Hymes, Gumperz, and Basil Bernstein were among the others present). That institute was sponsored by SSRC's Committee on Sociolinguistics. Once Goffman arranged for her to be accepted as a graduate student at Penn, she spent little time in the sociology department "because Goffman made it clear from the start that he required me to take or audit a long list of courses in other fields, principally folklore, Urban Studies, linguistics, and anthropology" (2008). She describes him as "both an able and an incredibly quick respondent when he received work—he read and critiqued one 80-page paper I wrote overnight, and another in the same span" (2008).

Stuart J. Sigman earned his PhD in 1982 at Annenberg with Birdwhistell as his chair. Goffman was originally included as a dissertation committee member, but as his illness worsened, he did not complete that service (email to the author, May 4, 2024). Sigman explains that "class with Goffman was to some degree an exposure to the redacted notes that had formed the basis of his previously published works, or the display of notes, pictures, newspaper clippings, and so forth, that were laying the groundwork for his next book" (Leeds-Hurwitz and Sigman 2010, 247). He goes on to describe more of what it was like taking a course with him.

> After class one day, and then through a series of discussions in his home and at
> his office in the Penn Anthropology Museum, Goffman and I talked about my
> emerging views. First, he rejected the idea that I floated at one point, that it made
> any sense to correlate communication behavior with particular social structural
> "variables." I'm paraphrasing here, of course, but I remember his response as
> something like, "There are too many variables. Eyebrows and gender. Eyebrows
> and rank. That's not going to get us to the structure of interaction. Or to the
> structure of society." (247–48)

In his May 4, 2024 email to the author, Sigman explained that "Goffman
was strongly influenced both by the structural-functional sociology that
was part of his own doctoral work and the interdisciplinary environment
at Penn that owed much to structural linguistics. He was not interested in
correlational studies, but rather in the deeper structures that give rise to the
interaction order and social organization" (see also Sigman 1987).

Sigman was one of the organizers of the Ethnographic Research Group,
a collection of graduate students from multiple departments who got together from spring 1978 to spring 1979 in order to practice what we were
learning about in our courses, and specifically to videotape our own group's
conversation and then analyze it (see the description in Leeds-Hurwitz and
Sigman 2010). I was a member, along with Yves Winkin, Barbara Lynch,
Mary Moore Goodlett, and Bob Aibel. Aside from encouraging us to attempt microanalysis of filmed interaction, Sigman organized a panel at the
International Communication Association's convention in Philadelphia in
1979, providing the first major conference experience for most of us and the
debut of what we called the "Penn Tradition" (Leeds-Hurwitz and Sigman
2010). In addition, the videotape developed by ERG figured in a report that
Sigman presented to Goffman and subsequently published (1981).

Barbara Ann Lynch completed a PhD in 1984 in communications with
Birdwhistell as her supervisor; Goffman served on her committee, along
with Don Yoder in folklore, Gail Zivin (who started in education but soon
moved to ASC), and Charles Wright and Paul Messaris at ASC. She reports
that Goffman's "late night reviews of early drafts (over milk and homemade
cookies) helped anchor both the data analysis and researcher in a real-world
larger context" (1984, vi). Since he died before she finished, she dedicates
her dissertation to his memory and that of two others, saying he "helped
me to see what I was observing" (iv). She quotes him extensively throughout
her analysis of the religious use of space, citing more than a dozen of his

publications. She was also the senior member and primary organizer of ERG in 1978–1979.

Deborah Schiffrin completed her PhD in linguistics in 1982, supervised by Labov, with Goffman and Sankoff serving on her committee, and thanks Goffman for all he taught her and for helpful comments, both then (1982, iii) and earlier (1977, 679; 1980, 199). She has explained the transition from discovering Goffman to working with him in some detail.

> In my senior year of college at Temple University, I read Erving Goffman's *Presentation of Self in Everyday Life* during a course in sociological theory.... I was so excited by his work that I went on to read everything else he had written and then decided to continue studying face-to-face interaction in a PhD program in sociology at Temple.... While still at Temple, I wrote an article on the semiotics of the handshake, which I boldly sent to Goffman. What followed was an invitation to a personal meeting and then his permission to audit a course with him.... When my advisor at Temple decided to leave for another position, I had already decided to try to work with Goffman. Ironically, it was Goffman himself who first turned my thoughts toward a PhD in linguistics: during our first meeting, he proclaimed his belief that linguistics could add rigor and respectability to the analysis of face-to-face interaction.
>
> Once I was enrolled in the PhD program in linguistics at the University of Pennsylvania, I quickly learned that, although linguists knew that understanding social interaction was important, the *study* of social interaction itself had a somewhat peripheral role in the linguistics curriculum. What I found instead was Labov's sociolinguistics: an energizing mix of fieldwork, urban ethnography, variation analysis, and narrative analysis.... As it became time for me to write my dissertation, I decided that I wanted to use what I had learned as a linguist to study social interaction. I remember my sense of confusion, though, when I tried to use what I had learned about the systematicity of language, as well as to follow the advice of both Labov and Goffman. Labov presented me with one mission: solve an old problem with a new method. But Goffman presented me with another: describe something that had not yet been described. After spending some time trying to apply these directives to the study of everyday arguments, I ended up focusing on discourse markers. (Schiffrin, Tannen, and Hamilton 2015, 3–4)

Elsewhere, she expressed a common sentiment among students described here, saying that Goffman "has been a major figure in my intellectual life" (2009).

Amy Shuman completed a PhD in folklore in 1981 under Szwed; she also mentions Goffman, Hymes, Labov, Ben-Amos, and Kirshenblatt-Gimblett as strong influences. She says: "They have influenced my work as much through personal help as through their printed works" (1986, ix). She thanks

Goffman in some of her publications (e.g., Shuman 1981), credits his work as central to her own in others (Shuman 2006; Shuman and Bohmer 2012), and has published an overview of his work (Shuman 2013). Like Merritt and other students in this section, she specifically discusses the invisible college at Penn, in her case during an interview:

> I was very fortunate to be at Penn during (what I regard as) its heyday. I studied with not only great faculty but also, and as importantly if not more, an amazing group of students. Of my teachers, Barbara Kirshenblatt-Gimblett was particularly influential, but John Szwed, Erving Goffman, Dell Hymes, Dan Ben-Amos, and Henry Glassie were hugely important. I would be surprised if any of the students who were at Penn at the same time as I was would say that influence ended in the classroom. We all read as much out of class as in it. (Kunze 2011, 8–9)

Since I was in her cohort (we both entered Penn in 1975), I can confirm her comments.

Wendy Leeds-Hurwitz: My own story of connections to Goffman follows. These examples show the intellectual generosity from faculty to students typical at Penn, at least during the 1970s when I was there, as well as the cross-over between departments. The first story: Dell Hymes liked a paper I wrote for one of his courses (The Ethnography of Speaking in fall 1975), well enough that he sent it to Goffman, who responded with a lengthy critique. (The full letter is reproduced in Winkin and Leeds-Hurwitz 2013, 31–2.) It goes without saying that I was delighted to have my work passed on to such an eminent scholar, and I was impressed with Goffman's playfulness in using multiple forms of address to discuss a paper on forms of address. (Of course, I did not yet know that Goffman frequently played with forms of address in his own letters, so this was a topic bound to attract his attention, and likely much of the reason why Hymes sent it on.) More importantly, I was astonished that a professor I had never met, not to mention one so well known, would take the time to write up two pages of comments on a student paper for someone who was not even *his* student, taking a course in another department! I put these comments to use in revising the paper for my master's thesis, which was then published (Leeds-Hurwitz 1980, 1989b).

A second story about Goffman's generosity to other people's students: A year later, someone suggested that Eviatar Zerubavel's dissertation (completed in 1976, published in 1979) would be helpful as I was preparing another course paper. It was not yet available even at the campus library, but when

I left a message with Lee Ann Draud, Goffman agreed to loan his copy to me. Again, I was delighted.

And finally: Goffman opened his considerable files of articles (both published and unpublished) to his students so that they would have access to a wide range of materials otherwise inaccessible. Of course, he was not the only faculty member at Penn who was so generous to students, even those not his own. For a different project, William Labov generously opened his closet of research audiotapes to me; although I was taking a course with him at the time, the paper I was working on was for Dan Ben-Amos. In a similar vein of general collegiality, Gillian Sankoff, who I had never met, walked by the linguistics department office one day as I was explaining to another student what I was writing about for yet another course paper; she stopped to suggest a source which proved to be fantastically helpful. And, parallel to Goffman opening his files to students, Labov and Sankoff later created the Linguistics Lab library.[232] Less formally, Ray Birdwhistell kept copies of all his own papers and publications at EPPI, encouraging students to drop by and take copies for themselves.[233] (Birdwhistell only published two books, but wrote an enormous number of articles, chapters, and conference presentations, all of which he made available to his students.)

In addition to Goffman, I had multiple connections to many of those mentioned in these pages. I took courses with Ray Birdwhistell, both Dell and Virginia Hymes, William Labov, John Szwed, John Fought, Ken Goldstein, Dan Ben-Amos, Barbara Kirshenblatt-Gimblett, Henry Glassie, Brian Sutton-Smith, Shirley Brice Heath, and Arjun Appadurai (as well as others who are not relevant to the larger narrative). I was teaching assistant to Dell Hymes twice, and worked on his first NIE grant (which included both Peggy Sanday and Elijah Anderson as peripheral members), serving as research assistant to Virginia Hymes, Szwed, and Ben-Amos at various times during my years at Penn. Szwed was my first dissertation committee chair, but moved to Yale before I finished, so Ben-Amos graciously took over; Dell Hymes and Fought were the other members of my committee. I also prepared the index to Hymes and Fought (1981), and Fought asked me to work on a grant in summer 1976 (which, in the end, he did not receive). The only one of the central actors here with whom I had no contact was Sol Worth, who died before I had the chance to study with him, although I did attend a showing of the Navajo films documented in Worth (1972b) at Annenberg. All this demonstrates that it was very easy for any student at

Penn to interact with faculty members across campus, beyond just enrolling in courses in multiple departments.

Beyond links to specific faculty members, I had a strong connection to one of the major projects to be examined in detail, and a weak connection to two others. Specifically, I served as research assistant to the Center for Urban Ethnography under Szwed's supervision in 1978–1979 (the grant support had ended, but the university paid for an assistantship on the grounds that they were pursuing additional funding). I published two book reviews in *Language in Society* (2000a, 2000b), although that was after all the parts of the story told here occurred. And, of course, I read all the books in the Conduct and Communication series published either before or during my time as a graduate student, either as course assignments or just because I ran across them in the campus bookstore.

Conclusion

The intent of this chapter has been to introduce three groups of people at Penn: first, Goffman's primary peer group, the small set of faculty members with whom he worked on various projects repeatedly, all of whom were part of multiple major projects, as well as minor projects. Second, a far larger group of faculty members who have been labeled peripheral because they were either only involved in one major project, or were involved in a minor way, or were affiliated with only one or more minor projects. Third, students, with a small selection included here because they are ones I know about, often ones who overlapped with my own time at Penn, or because they have chosen to write about Goffman's influence on them. Everyone shared the common assumptions that ideas matter, that multi- and interdisciplinarity were to be taken for granted, and that disciplines be understood as social constructions having permeable rather than rigid boundaries. At least on this campus, at least in the decades relevant here, ideas were to be followed where they led, not only to the edge of a discipline. Even though Goffman did not supervise many dissertations and so did not create a traditional school of followers, he had huge influence on both faculty members and students, many of us in many ways, and could be far more generous and collegial than he appears to be in some stories told by some others. People are complex; Goffman was no exception.

Obviously, Goffman had his most significant interactions with his primary peer group: They collaborated on a series of projects that were both major and successful, and many people on campus at the time knew about them even if they were not involved in them. In addition, because most of those projects were so successful, they influenced both faculty members and graduate students on other campuses as well. But even the lesser projects involving mostly what have been termed peripheral group members (lesser because they were not often successful, and even the successful ones had little influence beyond the campus) are significant; at the very least, they demonstrate the continuing interest in sharing information across campus and beyond departmental boundaries. And some lucky peripheral group members were included in the major projects, thus exposed to what it takes to develop something larger and more significant. In terms of students, those listed here had at least one or a few interactions with Goffman, whether with or without other members of his invisible college participating, thus being exposed to both his ideas and his willingness to take us seriously as scholars (something unfortunately not true of all faculty members, especially famous ones), whether that meant critiquing our work or sharing relevant resources. In any case, he served as a model for what we might want to develop for ourselves. The creation of the Ethnographic Research Group serves as one example of how graduate students saw their faculty members coordinating their research interests, and we did the same ourselves, although on a far smaller and less influential level. As to what Goffman got from peers and students, that is more open to conjecture. At the very least, it is clear that he was exposed to a wider variety of ideas and approaches than he would have been if he had stayed within disciplinary boundaries, as so many other scholars, before and after, have done.

Endnotes

[1] Hymes to Goffman, Jan 9, 1968, DHH, Subcollection 1, Series I: Correspondence 1951–1987, Goffman, Erving, 1967–1982.

[2] https://almanac.upenn.edu/archive/v14pdf/n06/031668.pdf.

[3] https://almanac.upenn.edu/archive/v24pdf/n01/071577.pdf.

[4] Goddard to Hymes, Apr 27, 1967, DHH, Subcollection 1, Series I: Correspondence 1951–1987, Goffman, Erving, 1967–1982.

[5] According to the Staff & Faculty Directory (UPM 95.1, vol. 1967–68, UR).

[6] When Worth was organizing the Codes in Context conference in fall 1967, he wrote to Rieff asking whether he wanted some time to check in with Goffman while he would be on campus, saying that Hymes had already written to Goffman, and he had agreed to participate (Worth to Rieff, Oct 31, 1967, SW, Codes in Context Meeting 1967, box 8, folder 19).

[7] The official name is now Annenberg School *for Communication*, but it was the Annenberg School *of Communications* until 1990, so the word communication will be shown as either singular or plural, depending on the year and the context: I understand the singular form to be the standard name for the discipline.

[8] Gerbner to Goddard, copied to Rieff and Worth, Dec 21, 1967, SW, Codes in Context Meeting 1967, box 8, folder 19.

[9] It will shortly become obvious that there are in fact two scholars named Hymes who are relevant in these pages (Dell and Virginia), as well as two Labovs (William and Teresa), two Hurvichs (Leo and Dorothea), two Goodwins (Marjorie Harness and Charles), two Princes (Ellen and Gerald), and three Smiths (W. John, David, and Barbara Herrnstein). When multiple actors with the same name are relevant in the same discussion, initials will be used; but given that V. Hymes and T. Labov are peripheral actors, unless clearly identified otherwise, "Hymes" will mean D. Hymes, and "Labov" will mean W. Labov. All the Smiths and both Hurvichs are peripheral actors who become relevant at different times, so it should be clear which is intended at any point.

[10] Initially, I kept a list of all the major awards, honors, and grants received by these scholars at Penn, but there simply were too many. Suffice it to say that they were each recognized many times over by organizations such as the Guggenheim Memorial Foundation, Rockefeller Foundation, the American Academy of Arts and Sciences, American Council of Learned Societies, Center for Advanced Study in the Behavioral Sciences, National Science Foundation, National Endowment for the Humanities, National Institute of Mental Health, National Institute of Education, etc.

[11] Secondary appointments led to occasional teaching in the new department. (For example, I took one course from Hymes offered by folklore, and another from him offered by linguistics.) It also led to participation in special events, as when Hymes invited those he granted secondary appointments at GSE to give presentations.

[12] As, for example, this comment: "The recent and tragic death of Erving Goffman reduces our strength to 9 cultural anthropologists in the primary faculty" (Arjun Appadurai to unknown recipients, apparently most if not all members of the anthropology department, Nov 30, 1982, DHH, Subcollection 1, Series I: Correspondence 1951–1987, Subseries E: Other Committees, Interdisciplinary Committee for a Program in Language, Culture and Society, 1979–1986).

[13] https://almanac.upenn.edu/archive/v24pdf/n01/071577.pdf. It's unclear who nominated him for this, but it was granted in the same year (1977) that Labov and Leila Gleitman were also given secondary appointments in psychology.

[14] "Communications #35: The Annenberg School of Communications, University of Pennsylvania," 1978, DHH, Subcollection 1, Series I: Correspondence, 1951–1987, University of Pennsylvania, Annenberg School of Communication, 1978–1984.

[15] https://almanac.upenn.edu/archive/v25pdf/n18/012379.pdf.

[16] I attempted to locate that file cabinet in 2023 but had no success.

[17] Grimshaw was a sociologist at Indiana University with a Penn PhD, who knew all the key players well, including Goffman, and who stands at the heart of chapter 6, as the organizer and leader of a major project outside Penn involving Goffman.

[18] UPF 1.9AR: Office of Alumni, Alumni Record Files, Hymes, Dell, UR.

[19] Goodenough to Hymes, Oct 1, 1963, DHH, Subcollection 2, Series I: Correspondence, University of Pennsylvania, 1963–2006.

[20] Hymes to Goodenough, DHH, Sep 27, 1963, Subcollection 2, Series I: Correspondence, Goodenough, Ward H., 1968–2001.

[21] Wallace to Hymes, DHH, Oct 16, 1963, Subcollection 2, Series I: Correspondence, University of Pennsylvania, 1963–2006.

[22] Hoenigswald to Hymes, Nov 27, 1963, DHH, Subcollection 2, Series I: Correspondence, University of Pennsylvania, 1963–2006.

[23] Wallace to Hymes, Mar 16, 1964, DHH, Subcollection 2, Series I: Correspondence, Wallace, Anthony F. C., 1964–1965. The year's delay was because Hymes was on sabbatical 1963–64 and would have had to repay the cost if he did not return to teach at Berkeley in 1964–65.

[24] Hymes to Wallace, Mar 19, 1964, DHH, Subcollection 2, Series I: Correspondence, Wallace, Anthony F. C., 1964–1965.

[25] Hoenigswald to Hymes, Oct 28, 1964, DHH, Subcollection 2, Series I: Correspondence, University of Pennsylvania, 1963–2006.

[26] Hymes to Hoenigswald, Nov 4, 1964, DHH, Subcollection 2, Series I: Correspondence, University of Pennsylvania, 1963–2006.

[27] Hymes to Grace Buzaljko, Sep 10, 1986, DHH, Subcollection 1, Series I: Correspondence 1951–1987, University of California-Berkeley, Dept. of Anthropology.

[28] Hymes to Worth, Jun 10, 1969, DHH, Subcollection 1, Series I: Correspondence 1951–1987, Worth, Sol, 1966–1977.

[29] Hymes to Gregorian, Jul 8, 1974, DHH, Subcollection 1, Series I: Correspondence 1951–1987, Gregorian, Vartan, 1974–1981.

[30] Hymes summarized the situation for Gregorian a few years later: "The facts are these: the department voted unanimously for tenure; the faculty review committee voted in favor by a majority. . . . the Dean of the College wrote a letter of transmittal to the Provost's staff conference such that the latter felt it had no alternative but to deny tenure. No explanation was ever offered" (Hymes to Gregorian, Jul 8, 1974, DHH, Subcollection 1, Series I: Correspondence 1951–1987, Gregorian, Vartan, 1974–1981).

[31] "I am distressed to learn that the Department of Anthropology has not been an altogether congenial home for you. How great it would be for me, and for the Department of Sociology, if your affiliations were, in whatever way you please, with this department" (Rieff to Hymes, Sep 27, 1971, DHH, Subcollection 1, Series I: Correspondence 1951–1987, Rieff, Philip, 1967–1972).

[32] Hymes's curriculum vitae, n.d., ca. 1987, DHH, Subcollection 2, Series III: Research Files, Subseries D: Other Research.

[33] Hymes joined the graduate group in linguistics while being primarily based in anthropology when he arrived at Penn. As he later put it, "I had always been counted in Linguistics, from when I first came to Penn. And I didn't leave it when I found a place in Folklore and Folklife, and beyond that, the Graduate School of Education" (email to the author, Feb 20, 2005).

[34] William Owen to Hymes, Feb 13, 1973, DHH, Subcollection 1, Series I: Correspondence 1951–1987, University of Pennsylvania, Department of Sociology.

[35] Hymes's curriculum vitae, n.d., ca. 1987, DHH, Subcollection 2, Series III: Research Files, Subseries D: Other Research, Curriculum vitae, ca. 1987.

[36] Hymes to Gregorian, Jul 8, 1974, DHH Subcollection 1, Series I: Correspondence 1951–1987, Gregorian, Vartan, 1974–1981.

[37] Hymes to Wallace, copied to Goffman, Apr 28, 1971, DHH, Subcollection 1, Series I: Correspondence 1951–1987, Wallace, Anthony F. C., 1961–1971, 1980, 1986.

[38] This was not Hymes's first connection with education. He had called Neal Gross, dean in 1969, expressing interest in learning what was happening there with regard to either psycholinguistics or sociolinguistics. He got a lengthy response, suggesting he talk to Morton Botel, as the obvious person for conversations about linguistics within GSE faculty, was invited to attend a colloquium on psycho- and sociolinguistics, and further, was invited to present his own colloquium on sociolinguistics (Gross to Hymes, Nov 26, 1969, DHH, Subcollection 1, Series I: Correspondence 1951–1987, University of Pennsylvania, Graduate School of Education, 1969–1986).

[39] "GSE Gets New Dean," *Pennsylvania Gazette*, Nov 1975, UPF 1.9AR, Office of Alumni, Alumni Record Files, Hymes, Dell, UR.

[40] Hymes to Stellar, Mar 3, 1976, DHH, Subcollection 1, Series I: Correspondence 1951–1987, University of Pennsylvania, Graduate School of Education, 1969–1986. (This was part of a fifteen-page letter about GSE.)

[41] Hymes to Goffman, Sep 28, 1975, DHH, Subcollection 1, Series I: Correspondence 1951–1987, Goodenough, Ward H., 1958, 1960, 1970–1986. (It may be misfiled, but it is indeed in the Goodenough file.)

[42] "Remarks on the Ethnography of Speaking," 1975, DHH, Subcollection 2, Series IV: Works by Hymes.

[43] At Virginia, Hymes added yet one more disciplinary affiliation to his list, given that he received a dual appointment in anthropology and English (https://almanac.upenn.edu/archive/v33pdf/n23/021787.pdf). This made sense because at that point he was working on establishing more faithful translations of verse from Sahaptin to English.

[44] Hymes to Fox, Nov 27, 1972, DHH, Subcollection 1, Series I: Correspondence 1951–1987, Renée Fox, 1972–1977.

[45] Hymes to Labov, Jan 25, 1973, DHH, Subcollection 1, Series V: Language in Society, Subseries A: Early Correspondence, Labov, William 1970–1973.

[46] Hymes to Gregorian, Aug 7, 1974, DHH, Subcollection 1, Series I: Correspondence 1951–1987, Gregorian, Vartan, 1974–1981.

[47] As, for example, evidenced by his detailed comments responding to a memo from Goodenough on revisions to the anthropology program (Hymes to Goodenough, n.d. [prior to 1970], DHH, Subcollection 1, Series I: Correspondence 1951–1987, University of Pennsylvania, Department of Anthropology, 1964–1986).

[48] "I say this to folklorists and think Ken [Goldstein] and Ben-Amos somewhat agree—the way to success for folklore is for it to make itself now the place in which study of on-going performances of verbal art is developed—that is a key, relatively neglected area" (Hymes to Worth, Jun 10, 1969, DHH, Subcollection 1, Series I: Correspondence 1951–1987, Worth, Sol, 1966–1977). For further documentation of Hymes's involvement in the folklore department, see DHH, Subcollection 1, Series I: Correspondence 1951–1987, University of Pennsylvania, Department of Folklore & Folklife.

[49] "Boas was folklorist, linguist, anthropologist, all in one, as to varying degrees were his great students, Kroeber, Sapir, Lowie, Radin" ("Only the name has been kept to protect the innocent: A new traditional saying," Feb 26, 1972, DHH, Subcollection 1, Series I: Correspondence 1951–1987, Ben-Amos, Dan, 1973–1974).

[50] "We are reviving a unity that did once exist, and that is missing now because of fragmentation and growth in the past generation or two of academic disciplines" ("Only the name has been kept to protect the innocent: A new traditional saying," Feb 26, 1972, DHH, Subcollection 1, Series I: Correspondence 1951–1987, Ben-Amos, Dan, 1973–1974).

[51] Specifically: "a) analysis of structure and functions of traditional genres, particularly

in performance; b) identification and interpretation of the traditional as reintegrated in novel forms; c) method and theory pertaining to the above, in terms of a general (universal) understanding of the role of the traditional, esp. the verbal, in human life" ("Only the name has been kept to protect the innocent: A new traditional saying," Feb 26, 1972, DHH, Subcollection 1, Series I: Correspondence 1951–1987, Ben-Amos, Dan, 1973–1974).

[52] Hymes to Goffman, Aug 19, 1971, DHH, Subcollection 1, Series I: Correspondence 1951–1987, Goffman, Erving, 1967–1982.

[53] Goffman to Hymes, Nov 24, 1970, DHH, Subcollection 1, Series I: Correspondence 1951–1987, Goffman, Erving, 1967–1982. It is likely this manuscript was part or all of Goffman (1971). Or, when he said, "I've also been working on the enclosed, but it's a long way from justifying the use of paper" (Goffman to Hymes, Jan 21, 1981, same collection).

[54] Goffman to Hymes, Nov 16, 1979, DHH, Subcollection 1, Series I: Correspondence 1951–1987, Goffman, Erving, 1967–1982. Apparently Hymes had offered to publish "The Lecture" in *Language in Society*, because Goffman goes on to say: "Before you decide you'd best look at other things I am working on." (That paper was not published in LiS but as part of *Forms of Talk* [Goffman 1981]).

[55] Hymes to Gerbner, Jan 11, 1967, DHH, Subcollection 1, Series II: Conferences and Committees, 1955–1987, Subseries E: Other Committees, University of Pennsylvania, Annenberg School of Communication, Graduate Group in Communications, 1967–1975.

[56] Gerbner to Hymes, Jan 16, 1967, DHH, Subcollection 1, Series II: Conferences and Committees, 1955–1987, Subseries E: Other Committees, University of Pennsylvania, Annenberg School of Communication, Graduate Group in Communications, 1967–1975.

[57] "PhD in Communication, University of Pennsylvania," December 1967, DHH, Subcollection 1, Series II: Conferences and Committees, 1955–1987, Subseries E: Other Committees, University of Pennsylvania, Annenberg School of Communication, Graduate Group in Communications, 1967–1975.

[58] Worth to Gregorian and Gerbner, Apr 9, 1975, DHH, Subcollection 1, Series I: Correspondence 1951–1987, Worth, Sol, 1966–1977.

[59] Hymes to Dean George Gerbner, Jun 10, 1969, DHH, Subcollection 1, Series II: Conferences and Committees, 1955–1987, Subseries E: Other Committees, University of Pennsylvania, Annenberg School of Communication, Graduate Group in Communications, 1967–1975.

[60] "Communications #35: The Annenberg School of Communications, University of Pennsylvania," 1978, DHH, Subcollection 1, Series I: Correspondence, 1951–1987, University of Pennsylvania, Annenberg School of Communication, 1978–1984.

[61] https://americananthro.org/about/leadership/presidents/.

[62] https://americanfolkloresociety.org/about/board/past-afs-presidents/.

[63] https://archives.upenn.edu/wp-content/uploads/2018/04/commencement-program-1985.pdf.

[64] https://www.linguisticsociety.org/content/memoriam-archive.

[65] Hymes to Goffman, Sep 4, 1980, DHH, Subcollection 2, Series IV: Works by Hymes, Subseries D: Other Research, "On Erving Goffman," 1979–1984.

[66] Dundes to Hymes, Oct 25, 1965, DHH, Subcollection 1, Series I: Correspondence 1951–1987, Dundes, Alan, 1965–1975, 1977.

[67] Hymes to Springer, Nov 30, 1965, DHH, Subcollection 1, Series I: Correspondence 1951–1987, Dundes, Alan, 1965–1975, 1977.

⁶⁸ Hymes to Dundes, Dec 26, 1965, DHH, Subcollection 1, Series I: Correspondence 1951–1987, Dundes, Alan, 1965–1975, 1977.

⁶⁹ Dundes to Hymes, Feb 27, 1966, DHH, Subcollection 1, Series I: Correspondence 1951–1987, Dundes, Alan, 1965–1975, 1977.

⁷⁰ Dundes to Hymes, Jan 23, 1968, DHH, Subcollection 1, Series I: Correspondence 1951–1987, Dundes, Alan, 1965–1975, 1977. Scholte completed his PhD in anthropology at Berkeley in 1969, under Dundes, and was hired as assistant professor of communications for three years, effective fall 1969 (https://archives.upenn.edu/wp-content/uploads/2017/04/19690613fac.pdf). Hymes had exchanged letters with him about a possible position at ASC several years earlier (Scholte to Hymes, Oct 6, 1965, DHH, Subcollection 1, Series I: Correspondence 1951–1987, Scholte, Bob, 1963–1979; Scholte to Worth, copied to Hymes, Oct 16, 1965, DHH, Subcollection 1, Series I: Correspondence 1951–1987, Scholte, Bob, 1963–1979). The connection between Worth and Scholte was an easy one: Worth had worked with Margaret Mead, and Scholte had studied with Gregory Bateson, and both Worth and Scholte were interested in the Balinese films Bateson and Mead had made together (1942). In fact, when Scholte was scheduled to give a presentation at ASC in spring 1968, apparently Mead was preceding him as guest lecturer, and he must have asked whether she would be able to stay for his talk, because Worth said he would ask her (Worth to Scholte, copied to Gerbner, Michael Studdert-Kennedy [a faculty member at ASC], and Hymes, Jan 31, 1967, DHH, Subcollection 1, Series I: Correspondence 1951–1987, Scholte, Bob, 1963–1979).

⁷¹ Scholte to Worth, May 3, 1968, DHH, Subcollection 2, Series I: Correspondence, Scholte, Bob, 1965–1995.

⁷² Wallace to Scholte, Jan 2, 1969, DHH, Subcollection 1, Series I: Correspondence 1951–1987, Scholte, Bob, 1963–1979.

⁷³ Hymes to Philips, Mar 19, 1974, DHH, Subcollection 1, Series I: Correspondence 1951–1987, Philips, Susan, 1967–1984.

⁷⁴ Documented in Hymes to Fought, Apr 7, 1977, DHH, Subcollection 1, Series I: Correspondence 1951–1987, Fought, John, 1973, 1977–1986; Hymes to Goodenough, Oct 25, 1976, DHH, Subcollection 1, Series I: Correspondence 1951–1987, Goodenough, Ward H., 1958, 1960, 1970–1986; Hymes to Goodenough, Apr 20, 1977, DHH, Subcollection 1, Series I: Correspondence 1951–1987, Goodenough, Ward H., 1958, 1960, 1970–1986.

⁷⁵ Erickson to Hymes, Feb 12, 1999, DHH, Subcollection 2, Series I: Correspondence, Erickson, Frederick, 1999.

⁷⁶ Hymes to Meyerson, Nov 17, 1971, DHH, Subcollection 1, Series I: Correspondence 1951–1987, Meyerson, Martin, 1971, 1979.

⁷⁷ Hymes to Meyerson, Nov 17, 1971, DHH, Subcollection 1, Series I: Correspondence 1951–1987, Meyerson, Martin, 1971, 1979.

⁷⁸ Myerson to Hymes, Dec 14, 1971, DHH, Subcollection 1, Series I: Correspondence 1951–1987, Meyerson, Martin, 1971, 1979.

⁷⁹ Leach to Hymes, Feb 11, 1970, DHH, Subcollection 1, Series I: Correspondence 1951–1987, Leach, Edmund, 1965, 1970. There is no response in the file, but there is a handwritten note in Hymes's writing saying "suggest write to Sol."

⁸⁰ Szwed to Hymes, Nov 10, 1965, DHH, Subcollection 1, Series I: Correspondence 1951–1987, Szwed, John F., 1965–1981.

⁸¹ Szwed to Hymes, Nov 10, 1965, DHH, Subcollection 1, Series I: Correspondence 1951–1987, Szwed, John F., 1965–1981.

⁸² Biographical Files, Szwed, John, box 159, folder 17, UR.

[83] https://music.columbia.edu/bios/john-szwed.

[84] https://archives.upenn.edu/wp-content/uploads/2018/04/commencement-program-1977.pdf.

[85] Szwed to Hymes, Nov 10, 1965, DHH, Subcollection 1, Series I: Correspondence 1951–1987, Szwed, John F., 1965–1981.

[86] Szwed to Hymes, Mar 13, 1966, DHH, Subcollection 1, Series I: Correspondence 1951–1987, Szwed, John F., 1965–1981.

[87] Szwed to Hymes, Dec 17, 1968, DHH, Subcollection 1, Series I: Correspondence 1951–1987, University of Pennsylvania, Center for Urban Ethnography, 1968–1971.

[88] Szwed to Hymes, Jul 24, 1972, DHH, Subcollection 1, Series I: Correspondence 1951–1987, University of Pennsylvania, Center for Urban Ethnography, 1968–1971.

[89] This most likely refers to the 1972 Georgetown University Round Table (GURT) conference on sociolinguistics, which Goffman attended. His presentation was not included in the resulting book (Shuy 1973a).

[90] Hymes to Szwed, Jul 29, 1972, DHH, Subcollection 1, Series I: Correspondence 1951–1987, University of Pennsylvania, Center for Urban Ethnography, 1968–1971.

[91] Biographical Information: William Labov, 1973, UPF 8.5B: University Relations, News and Public Affairs Records, Biographical Files, Labov, William, box 81, folder 17, UR.

[92] Labov to Hymes, Mar 26, 1966, DHH, Subcollection 1, Series I: Correspondence 1951–1987, Labov, William, folder 1, 1963–1972.

[93] Labov to Hymes, Oct 24, 1966, DHH, Subcollection 1, Series I: Correspondence 1951–1987, Labov, William, folder 1, 1963–1972.

[94] Hymes to Goffman, Jan 9, 1968, DHH, Subcollection 1, Series I: Correspondence 1951–1987, Goffman, Erving, 1967–1982.

[95] Labov to Hymes, Oct 24, 1968, DHH, Subcollection 1, Series I: Correspondence 1951–1987, Labov, William, folder 1, 1963–1972.

[96] Labov to Hymes, Dec 16, 1968, DHH, Subcollection 1, Series I: Correspondence 1951–1987, Labov, William, folder 1, 1963–1972.

[97] In a May 3, 1970 letter, Hymes mentioned to Grimshaw that "Bill [Labov] and Erv Goffman were very much concerned with that [social interactional universals] during Bill's course last spring" (DHH, Subcollection 1, Series I: Correspondence 1951–1987, Grimshaw, Allen, 1966–1986).

[98] Labov to Hymes, Dec 16, 1968, DHH, Subcollection 1, Series I: Correspondence 1951–1987, Labov, William, folder 1, 1963–1972.

[99] Labov to Hymes, Feb 15, 1969, DHH, Subcollection 1, Series I.:Correspondence 1951–1987, Labov, William, folder 1, 1963–1972.

[100] Labov to Hymes, Dec 16, 1968, DHH, Subcollection 1, Series I: Correspondence 1951–1987, Labov, William, folder 1, 1963–1972.

[101] Hymes to Worth, Jan 14, 1969, DHH, Subcollection 1, Series I: Correspondence 1951–1987, Worth, Sol, 1966–1977.

[102] Labov to Hymes, Feb 15, 1969, DHH, Subcollection 1, Series I: Correspondence 1951–1987, Labov, William, folder 1, 1963–1972.

[103] Hymes to Labov, Feb 21, 1969, DHH, Subcollection 1, Series I: Correspondence 1951–1987, Labov, William, folder 1, 1963–1972.

[104] Hymes to Worth, Feb 21, 1969, DHH, Subcollection 1, Series I: Correspondence 1951–1987, Worth, Sol, 1966–1977.

[105] Hymes to Labov, May 20, 1969, DHH, Subcollection 1, Series I: Correspondence 1951–1987, Labov, William, folder 1, 1963–1972.

[106] Hymes to Gerbner, May 23, 1969, DHH, Subcollection 1, Series I: Correspondence 1951–1987, University of Pennsylvania, Annenberg School of Communication, Graduate Group in Communications, 1967–1975.

[107] Hymes to Worth, May 25, 1969, DHH, Subcollection 1, Series I: Correspondence 1951–1987, Worth, Sol, 1966–1977.

[108] Hymes to Gerbner, Jun 10, 1969, DHH, Subcollection 1, Series II: Conferences and Committees, 1955–1987, Subseries E: Other Committees, University of Pennsylvania, Annenberg School of Communication, Graduate Group in Communications, 1967–1975.

[109] Hymes to Worth, Jun 10, 1969, DHH, Subcollection 1, Series I: Correspondence 1951–1987, Worth, Sol, 1966–1977.

[110] Goffman to Hymes, Jun 23, 1969, DHH, Subcollection 1, Series I: Correspondence 1951–1987, Goffman, Erving, 1967–1982.

[111] Hymes to Worth, Jun 20, 1969, DHH, Subcollection 1, Series I: Correspondence 1951–1987, Worth, Sol, 1966–1977.

[112] Labov to Hymes, Dec 9, 1969, DHH, Subcollection 1, Series I: Correspondence 1951–1987, Labov, William, folder 1, 1963–1972.

[113] Hymes to Labov, Jan 21, 1970, DHH, Subcollection 1, Series I: Correspondence 1951–1987, Labov, William, folder 1, 1963–1972.

[114] https://president.upenn.edu/university-leadership/history/martin-meyerson.

[115] Hymes to Labov, Jan 21, 1970, DHH, Subcollection 1, Series I, Correspondence 1951–1987, Labov, William, folder 1, 1963–1972.

[116] Hymes to Labov, Jan 21, 1970, DHH, Subcollection 1, Series I: Correspondence 1951–1987, Labov, William, folder 1, 1963–1972.

[117] Labov to Hoenigswald, copied to Hymes, Goffman, Rosner, Feb 3, 1970, DHH, Subcollection 1, Series I: Correspondence 1951–1987, Labov, William, folder 1, 1963–1972.

[118] Biographical Information: William Labov, 1973, UPF 8.5B: University Relations, News and Public Affairs Records, Biographical Files, Labov, William, box 81, folder 17, UR. This required agreement between Goffman, Szwed, and Hymes (Hymes to Hoenigswald, May 20, 1969, DHH, Subcollection 1, Series I: Correspondence 1951–1987, Hoenigswald, Henry, 1967–1983).

[119] Labov to Hoenigswald, Feb 3, 1970, DHH, Subcollection 1, Series I: Correspondence 1951–1987, Labov, William, folder 1, 1963–1972.

[120] Biographical Information: William Labov, 1973, UPF 8.5B: University Relations, News and Public Affairs Records, Biographical Files, Labov, William, box 81, folder 17, UR.

[121] Essentially the same acknowledgment is made in *Language in the Inner City* (Labov 1972c, xxiv).

[122] Hymes to Labov, Jan 6, 1971, DHH, Subcollection 1, Series I: Correspondence 1951–1987, Labov, William, folder 1, 1963–1972.

[123] Hymes to Labov, Jan 6, 1971, DHH, Subcollection 1, Series I: Correspondence 1951–1987, Labov, William, folder 1, 1963–1972.

[124] Hymes to Goodenough, Nov 27, 1971, DHH, Subcollection 1, Series I: Correspondence

1951–1987, Goodenough, Ward H., 1970–1986.

[125] https://almanac.upenn.edu/archive/v24pdf/n19/020778.pdf.

[126] "Communications #35: The Annenberg School of Communications, University of Pennsylvania," 1978, DHH, Subcollection 1, Series I: Correspondence, 1951–1987, University of Pennsylvania, Annenberg School of Communication, 1978–1984.

[127] See for example, Labov to Hymes, Aug 4, 1969, DHH, Subcollection 1, Series I: Correspondence 1951–1987, Labov, William, folder 1, 1963–1972.

[128] Labov to linguistics department, Feb 2 and Feb 23, 1977, DHH, Subcollection 1, Series I, Correspondence 1951–1987, University of Pennsylvania, Department of Linguistics, folder 2, 1977–1980.

[129] In addition to the quote in 1972b above, he's also mentioned in 1972d (817). See also Labov and Fanshell 1977 for frequent mention of Goffman's work.

[130] Hymes to Worth, Feb 21, 1969, DHH, Subcollection 1, Series I: Correspondence 1951–1987, Worth, Sol, 1966–1977.

[131] Labov mentions that such a course occurred in 1973 and was planned for 1975 ("A Proposal to the University of Pennsylvania for an Institute of Language and Interaction," 1974, DHH, Subcollection 1, Series II: Conferences and Committees, 1955–1987, Subseries E: Other Committees, Language and Interaction Institute, 1974–1977).

[132] Hymes to Goffman, Sep 4, 1980, DHH, Subcollection 2, Series IV: Works by Hymes, Subseries D: Other Research, "On Erving Goffman," 1979–1984.

[133] Goffman to Hymes, Jun 26, 1973, DHH, Subcollection 2, Series I: Correspondence, Goffman, Erving, 1968–1982.

[134] For discussion of Goffman's time at Toronto, see Bott-Spillius 2010; Smith 2003; Winkin 1984a, 1988a, 2022c, 2022f; Wrong 1990.

[135] Paterno (2022) provides a current re-evaluation of Birdwhistell.

[136] Birdwhistell CV, 1975, UPF 8.5B, University Relations, News and Public Affairs Records, Biographical Files, Birdwhistell, Ray, box 12, folder 25, UR.

[137] Birdwhistell to Hymes, Feb 11, 1965, DHH, Subcollection 1, Series I: Correspondence 1951–1987, Birdwhistell, Ray, 1965, 1967, 1981.

[138] Hymes to Birdwhistell, Feb 21, 1965, DHH, Subcollection 1, Series I: Correspondence 1951–1987, Birdwhistell, Ray, 1965, 1967, 1981.

[139] Birdwhistell to Hymes, Mar 3, 1965, DHH, Subcollection 1, Series I: Correspondence 1951–1987, Birdwhistell, Ray, 1965, 1967, 1981.

[140] Scheflen to Hymes, Jun 2, 1965, DHH, Subcollection 1, Series I: Correspondence 1951–1987, Birdwhistell, Ray, 1965, 1967, 1981. McQuown was a linguist and anthropologist based at the University of Chicago from 1946 until retirement who was closely involved with Birdwhistell in *The Natural History of an Interview* project, editing the final analyses (McQuown 1971; for discussion see Leeds-Hurwitz 1987; Leeds-Hurwitz and Kendon 2021).

[141] Hymes to Scheflen, Jun 4, 1965, DHH, Subcollection 1, Series I: Correspondence 1951–1987, Birdwhistell, Ray, 1965, 1967, 1981.

[142] Hymes to Birdwhistell, Feb 21, 1967, DHH, Subcollection 1, Series I: Correspondence 1951–1987, Birdwhistell, Ray, 1965, 1967, 1981. However, a few weeks later, he reported to Gumperz, "I fear we got over-enthusiastic and over-extended," so Goffman (and several others) did not have their 1964 chapters reprinted in the 1972 volume (Hymes to Gumperz, Feb 22, 1967, DHH, Subcollection 1, Series I: Correspondence 1951–1987,

Gumperz, John J., 1966–1986).

[143] Worth to Birdwhistell, Nov 14, 1967, SW, box 8, folder 19, Codes in Context Meeting 1967.

[144] Worth to Hymes, May 7, 1968, DHH, Subcollection 1, Series I: Correspondence 1951–1987, Worth, Sol, 1966–1977.

[145] Gerbner to Hymes, Apr 18, 1969, DHH, Subcollection 1, Series II: Conferences and Committees, 1955–1987, Subseries E: Other Committees, University of Pennsylvania, Annenberg School of Communication, Graduate Group in Communications, 1967–1975.

[146] Hymes to Gerbner, Apr 23, 1969, DHH, Subcollection 1, Series II: Conferences and Committees, 1955–1987, Subseries E: Other Committees. University of Pennsylvania, Annenberg School of Communication, Graduate Group in Communications, 1967–1975.

[147] Hymes to Gerbner, May 23, 1969, DHH, Subcollection 1, Series II: Conferences and Committees, 1955–1987, Subseries E: Other Committees, University of Pennsylvania, Annenberg School of Communication, Graduate Group in Communications, 1967–1975.

[148] Hymes to Worth, May 25, 1969, DHH, Subcollection 1, Series II: Conferences and Committees, 1955–1987, Subseries E: Other Committees. University of Pennsylvania, Annenberg School of Communication, Graduate Group in Communications, 1967–1975.

[149] Gerbner to Hymes, Jun 2, 1969, DHH, Subcollection 1, Series II: Conferences and Committees, 1955–1987, Subseries E: Other Committees, University of Pennsylvania, Annenberg School of Communication, Graduate Group in Communications, 1967–1975.

[150] Email from Harvey Sarles to the author, Jan 9, 2013.

[151] Press release, Jun 23, 1970, UPF 1.9AR, Office of Alumni, Alumni Record Files, Birdwhistell, Ray, box 191, UR.

[152] Goffman and Hall connected by mail in 1957, finally meeting in person in 1962. In the early 1960s they corresponded regularly, exchanged drafts and publications, and met periodically at conferences, including presenting together on a panel at AAA organized by Hymes (ETH).

[153] Cazden to John and Hymes, Nov 17, 1967, DHH, Subcollection 1, Series I: Correspondence 1951–1987, Cazden, Courtney, 1965–1972. Hymes has added a handwritten note to the section on nonverbal communication which says "Birdwhistell?"

[154] Cazden to Birdwhistell, Oct 30, 1968, DHH, Subcollection 1, Series I: Correspondence 1951–1987, Cazden, Courtney, 1965–1972.

[155] Birdwhistell to Cazden, Nov 11, 1968, DHH, Subcollection 1, Series I: Correspondence 1951–1987, Cazden, Courtney, 1965–1972.

[156] Cazden to Birdwhistell, Mar 18, 1969, DHH, Subcollection 1, Series I: Correspondence 1951–1987, Cazden, Courtney, 1965–1972.

[157] "Updated schedule of speakers," n.d. [internal evidence reveals it was 1981], DHH, Subcollection 1, Series I: Correspondence 1951–1987, University of Pennsylvania, Department of Folklore & Folklife, folder 2, 1979–1981. After his presentation, the department hosted an "official department thank-you reception."

[158] I know about this one in particular because Birdwhistell became ill and was unable to remain on the dissertation committee, and I was asked to take his place, which I did. The completed dissertation is Sidener-Young (1994).

[159] His collection was moved to the Penn Museum Archives when the folklore department was downgraded to a graduate group.

[160] Flyer, n.d. [Birdwhistell retired in 1988, so this must be dated that year], DHH, Subcol-

lection 1, Series I: Correspondence 1951–1987, University of Pennsylvania, Department of Folklore & Folklife, folder 3, 1982–1985.

[161] Birdwhistell to Hymes, Apr 13, 1981, DHH, Subcollection 1, Series I: Correspondence, 1951–1987, Birdwhistell, Ray, 1965, 1967, 1981.

[162] Goffman to Hymes, Feb 25, 1974, DHH, Subcollection 2, Series I: Correspondence, Goffman, Erving, 1968–1982.

[163] Goffman to Hymes, Mar 25, 1975, DHH, Subcollection 2, Series I: Correspondence, Goffman, Erving, 1968–1982.

[164] All details about Worth's life come from the biographical note in https://archives. upenn.edu/wp-content/uploads/2017/03/upt50w933.pdf, except the comment about working with Mead for a year on analyzing his Navajo films, which comes from Worth's essay about her (1980).

[165] Hymes described Worth to Labov as "my son Bobby's girlfriend Debby's father" (Hymes to Labov, May 20, 1969, DHH, Subcollection 1, Series I: Correspondence 1951–1987, Labov, William, folder 1, 1963–1972). Another time, he called Worth his "machantenister (I may misspell)" (email from Hymes to the author, Feb 21, 2005). This is a reference to the Yiddish word "machitin," a term for your child's in-law.

[166] https://almanac.upenn.edu/archive/v24pdf/n01/071577.pdf.

[167] Worth to Hymes, n.d. [from internal evidence, written October 1965], DHH, Subcollection 1, Series I: Correspondence 1951–1987, Worth, Sol, 1966–1977.

[168] Worth to Hymes, May 7, 1968, DHH, Subcollection 1, Series I: Correspondence 1951–1987, Worth, Sol, 1966–1977.

[169] Worth to Hymes, Nov 28, 1967, DHH, Subcollection 1, Series I: Correspondence 1951–1987, Worth, Sol, 1966–1977.

[170] Worth to Goffman, Feb 5, 1969, SW, General Name Files, Ga–Go, box 2, folder 27, UR.

[171] Worth to Goffman, Feb 5, 1969, SW, General Name Files, Ga–Go, box 2, folder 27, UR.

[172] Goffman to Blau, with handwritten note on it from Worth to Goffman, Jan 10, 1974, SW, General Name Files, Ga–Go, box 2, folder 27, UR. (The word he changed is "loath" to "loathe," but the original was in fact correct, as a separate note attached by Worth's secretary pointed out.)

[173] Ostrach to Goffman, Jan 9, 1973, SW, General Name Files, Ga–Go, box 2, folder 27, UR.

[174] Goffman to Worth, Aug 31, 1973, SW, General Name Files, Ga–Go, box 2, folder 27, UR.

[175] Worth to Hymes, Jan 7, 1968, DHH, Subcollection 1, Series I: Correspondence 1951–1987, Worth, Sol, 1966–1977.

[176] Worth to Hymes, Jan 7, 1968, DHH, Subcollection 1, Series I: Correspondence 1951–1987, Worth, Sol, 1966–1977.

[177] For example, Magali Sarfatti-Larson taught in sociology at Penn from 1975 to 1978, and has described several interactions with Goffman (Sarfatti-Larson 2009).

[178] Hymes to Scholte, Jan 27, 1969, DHH, Subcollection 1, Series I: Correspondence 1951–1987, Scholte, Bob, 1963–1979.

[179] Hymes to linguistics department, May 15, 1974, DHH, Subcollection 1, Series I: Correspondence 1951–1987, University of Pennsylvania, Department of Linguistics, 1970–1980.

[180] Ben-Amos to all faculty members in folklore, Mar 1, 1974, DHH, Subcollection 1, Series I: Correspondence 1951–1987, Ben-Amos, Dan, 1973–1974, 1980–1986.

[181] Ben-Amos to all faculty members in folklore, Mar 1, 1974, DHH, Subcollection 1, Series I: Correspondence 1951–1987, Ben-Amos, Dan, 1973–1974, 1980–1986.

[182] Hymes to Worth, Feb 12, 1973, DHH, Subcollection 1, Series I: Correspondence 1951–1987, Worth, Sol, 1966–1977.

[183] https://americanfolkloresociety.org/about/board/past-afs-presidents/.

[184] Goldstein to Hymes, Mar 20, 1969, DHH, Subcollection 1, Series I: Correspondence 1951–1987, Goldstein, Kenneth S., 1969–1987.

[185] Hymes to Goldstein, "Questions for examinations in Folklore and Folklife," Feb 16, 1984, DHH, Subcollection 1, Series I: Correspondence 1951–1987, Goldstein, Kenneth, S., 1969–1987.

[186] Hymes to Goldstein, Apr 17, 1984, DHH, Subcollection 1, Series I: Correspondence 1951–1987, Goldstein, Kenneth, S., 1969–1987.

[187] https://web.asc.upenn.edu/gerbner/Asset.aspx?assetID=2460.

[188] Worth to Hymes, Jun 14, 1969, DHH, Subcollection 1, Series I: Correspondence 1951–1987, Worth, Sol, 1966–1977.

[189] It was titled "Communication Between Therapist and Patient: An Analysis of Therapeutic Discourse" and presented November 6, 1972. (Press release, Oct 4, 1972, UPF 8.5B, University Relations, News and Public Affairs Records, Biographical Files, Labov, William, box 81, folder 17, UR.)

[190] Goffman and Worth are listed until the issue after each of their deaths, so vol. 33, no. 1 (1983) for the former, and vol. 28, no. 1 (1978) for the latter; Birdwhistell continues to be listed until vol. 26, no. 3 (1976), and never reappears. D. Hymes stayed on the list even after he moved to the University of Virginia, with a change of affiliation, until the new editor, Mark Levy, took over in vol. 42, no. 1 (1992). Neither Labov nor Szwed was ever listed.

[191] Hymes to Worth, Jun 10, 1969, DHH, Subcollection 1, Series I: Correspondence 1951–1987, Worth, Sol, 1966–1977.

[192] W.K. Mandel, "Getting Serious About Flicks," *Pennsylvania Gazette*, May 1972, UPF 1.9AR, Office of Alumni, Alumni Record Files, Worth, Sol, box 3051, UR.

[193] https://almanac.upenn.edu/archive/v24pdf/n01/071577.pdf.

[194] https://almanac.upenn.edu/archive/v22pdf/n11/110475.pdf.

[195] https://almanac.upenn.edu/archive/v23pdf/n24/030877.pdf.

[196] https://almanac.upenn.edu/archive/v26pdf/n09/101179.pdf.

[197] https://almanac.upenn.edu/archive/v26pdf/n12/110179.pdf.

[198] https://almanac.upenn.edu/archive/v26pdf/n19/011780.pdf.

[199] https://almanac.upenn.edu/archive/v26pdf/n26/030680.pdf.

[200] Hymes to Gregorian, Aug 8, 1976, DHH, Subcollection 1, Series I: Correspondence 1951–1987, Gregorian, Vartan, 1974–1981.

[201] Hymes to Worth, Jun 10, 1969, DHH, Subcollection 1, Series I: Correspondence 1951–1987, Worth, Sol, 1966–1977.

[202] Sherzer to Hymes, Sep 24, 1968, DHH, Subcollection 1, Series I: Correspondence 1951–1987, Sherzer, Joel, 1968–87.

[203] Sherzer to Hymes, Sep 24, 1968, DHH, Subcollection 1, Series I: Correspondence 1951–1987, Sherzer, Joel, 1968–87.

[204] Sherzer to Hymes, Oct 23, 1968, DHH, Subcollection 1, Series I: Correspondence 1951–1987, Sherzer, Joel, 1968–87.

[205] Sherzer to Hymes, Oct 23, 1968, DHH, Subcollection 1, Series I: Correspondence 1951–1987, Sherzer, Joel, 1968–87.

[206] Sherzer to Hymes, Nov 8, 1968, DHH, Subcollection 1, Series I: Correspondence 1951–1987, Sherzer, Joel, 1968–87.

[207] Sherzer to Hymes, Dec 19, 1968, DHH, Subcollection 1, Series I: Correspondence 1951–1987, Sherzer, Joel, 1968–87.

[208] Hymes to Sherzer, Feb 21, 1969, DHH, Subcollection 1, Series I: Correspondence 1951–1987, Sherzer, Joel, 1968–87.

[209] Sherzer to Hymes, Feb 28, 1969, DHH, Subcollection 1, Series I: Correspondence 1951–1987, Sherzer, Joel, 1968–87.

[210] Sherzer to Hymes, Apr 29, 1969, DHH, Subcollection 1, Series I: Correspondence 1951–1987, Sherzer, Joel, 1968–87.

[211] Sherzer to Hymes, May 10, 1969, DHH, Subcollection 1, Series I: Correspondence 1951–1987, Sherzer, Joel, 1968–87.

[212] Sherzer to Hymes, Feb 14, 1980, DHH, Subcollection 1, Series I: Correspondence 1951–1987, Sherzer, Joel, 1968–87.

[213] Sherzer to Hymes, Oct 28, 1971, DHH, Subcollection 1, Series I: Correspondence 1951–1987, Sherzer, Joel, 1968–87.

[214] Thanks to Yves Winkin for the suggestion.

[215] Hymes to Sherzer, Nov 2, 1971, DHH, Subcollection 1, Series I: Correspondence 1951–1987, Sherzer, Joel, 1968–87.

[216] Sherzer to Hymes, Aug 31, 1980, DHH, Subcollection 1, Series I: Correspondence 1951–1987, Sherzer, Joel, 1968–87.

[217] https://folklore.indiana.edu/images/profiles/profiles-768x768/Bauman,-Richard-CV-Oct-2022.pdf.

[218] Bauman to Hymes, May 27, 1968, DHH, Subcollection 1, Series I: Correspondence 1951–1987, Bauman, Richard, 1968, 1971–1982, 1987.

[219] Jun 3, 1968, DHH, Subcollection 1, Series I: Correspondence 1951–1987, Bauman, Richard, 1968, 1971–1982, 1987.

[220] https://openanthroresearch.org/index.php/oarr/preprint/view/40/74.

[221] Hymes to Labov, Mar 11, 1974, DHH, Subcollection 1, Series I: Correspondence 1951–1987, Labov, William, folder 2, 1974–1987.

[222] Hymes to Philips, Mar 19, 1974, DHH, Subcollection 1, Series I: Correspondence 1951–1987, Philips, Susan, 1967–1984.

[223] Fox to Hymes, Mar 26, 1974, DHH, Subcollection 1, Series I: Correspondence 1951–1987, Renée Fox, 1972–77.

[224] Hymes to Labov, May 15, 1974, DHH, Subcollection 1, Subseries A: Early Correspondence, Labov, William, folder 2, 1974–1987.

[225] Some of Goffman's students at Berkeley are discussed in Bergmann and Peräkylä (2022). Others have either been interviewed or have written up their memories for Sha-

lin's project *Bios Sociologicus: The Erving Goffman Archives* (https://digitalscholarship.unlv.edu/goffman_archives/).

226 To name only some of them: Winkin 1983, 1989, 1990, 1993a, 1999, 2000, 2002, 2010, 2015, 2020, 2022a, 2022b, 2022c, 2022d, 2023; Leeds-Hurwitz and Winkin 2022; Smith and Winkin 2012, 2013; Winkin and Leeds-Hurwitz 2013.

227 https://gwu.academia.edu/MarilynMerritt/CurriculumVitae; https://www.dignitymemorial.com/obituaries/falls-church-va/marilyn-merritt-10041421.

228 https://web.stanford.edu/~jbaugh/vita.

229 https://sites.wustl.edu/baugh/cv-contact/.

230 Prospectus for *Social Orientations Toward Language Study*, sent by Sherzer to Hymes, n.d., ca. 1981, DHH, Subcollection 1, Series I: Correspondence 1951–1987, Sherzer, Joel, 1968–87. Relevant others included at that point were Gumperz, Labov, Ervin-Tripp, Schegloff, Sacks, Irvine, Hymes, Basso, Sankoff, Heath, Merritt, and Bauman. Hymes wrote a note saying "in his new book" next to the entry for Goffman.

231 Hymes to Sherzer, Sep 15, 1980, DHH, Subcollection 1, Subseries A: Early correspondence, Sherzer, Joel, 1972–74, 1980.

232 "Bill Labov and Gillian Sankoff have an extensive, noncirculating collection of books, journals, dissertations, and photocopied papers available in the Linguistics Lab" (https://www.ling.upenn.edu/advice/libuse.html).

233 Birdwhistell maintained his affiliation with EPPI for some years after moving from Temple to Penn.

CHAPTER FOUR

Major Projects
at Penn

Clearly, as Hymes had promised, he and Goffman were able to develop a viable community of peers, evident not only from the comments about connections made to this point, but especially through the joint projects examined in this chapter: the Codes in Context conference (CCC), the Center for Urban Ethnography (CUE), the book series Conduct and Communication (CC), and the journals *Language in Society* (LiS), and *Studies in the Anthropology of Visual Communication* (SAVICOM). All of these were about research: a conference to share ideas; the center, which provided funding to support training a new generation of researchers and influence research conducted by already accredited scholars, as well as sponsoring conferences; the two journals and the book series providing publication outlets. None of these projects was primarily about socializing or making friends, but obviously pre-existing relationships were drawn upon and strengthened, and new relationships created. In each case, the focus will be on the various roles played by Goffman, but additional content regarding the project as a whole and other participants seems useful to fully understand what happened and why and with what result.

In the following table, the organizers of each project are shown in bold. As a reminder, all these individuals already have been named in chapter 3 (with peripheral group members described in detail in the appendix).

Table 4.1: Goffman's Penn Colleagues by Major Project

CCC	CUE	CC	LiS	SAVICOM
Sol Worth	**John Szwed**	**Erving Goffman**	**Dell Hymes**	**Sol Worth**
Dell Hymes	**Erving Goffman**	**Dell Hymes**	**William Labov**	Erving Goffman
Erving Goffman	**Dell Hymes**	Ray Birdwhistell	Erving Goffman	Dell Hymes
William Labov	William Labov	William Labov	John Fought	Ray Birdwhistell
Ray Birdwhistell	Ken Goldstein	Henry Glassie	Teresa Labov	William Davenport
Ken Goldstein	Dan Ben-Amos	Gillian Sankoff		Henry Glassie
David Sapir	Sol Worth	Joel Sherzer		Steve Feld
Percy Tannenbaum	Fred Erickson	Barbara Kirshenblatt-Gimblett		Larry Gross
	Roger Abrahams	Brian Sutton-Smith		
	Nancy Hornberger	Sol Worth		
	David Smith	Steve Feld		
		J. David Sapir		

Codes in Context Conference (CCC)

Although small and brief, this conference is important because it was an early successful effort, and because it was Goffman's first interdisciplinary collaboration at Penn, made even more noteworthy for the fact that he was still based at Berkeley at the time.

Table 4.2: Codes in Context Conference,
December 15– 16, 1967, at ASC

Primary organizers: Sol Worth (communications), Dell Hymes (anthropology)
Secondary organizer: Erving Goffman (sociology at Berkeley)
Penn participants: Percy Tannenbaum (communications), Ken Goldstein (folklore), David Sapir (anthropology)
Not-yet-at-Penn participants: Erving Goffman (sociology at Berkeley), William Labov (linguistics at Columbia)
Beyond Penn participants: Jay Haley (psychology)
Results: The phrase was used later, and it helped cement the core group; publications were discussed but never created.

Of the central people in what was to become Goffman's Penn primary network, Worth, Hymes, and Labov were all part of this event; Birdwhistell was invited but had a prior commitment; Szwed was still at Temple at the time and not yet part of the group. Goffman helped to plan it, and participated, although still based across the country at Berkeley. In October 1967, Worth invited an unknown number of colleagues to a conference that he said he and Hymes had spent the prior year discussing. Those selected were chosen because they were "all working around a set of similar problems that we have tentatively titled 'Codes in Context.'"[1] The letter continued: "We feel that a school of communication is the appropriate framework for this kind of research" and mentioned that ASC had agreed to sponsor "a small two-day work session conference" for about ten people to "meet and talk about their specific research in this area, and will try to formulate plans for an ongoing teaching and research program revolving around the study of a variety of codes in a variety of contexts." And, further on: "Erv Goffman, who will join us for this meeting, has suggested that each of us plan to present a short 'concentrated excerpt' of his work in this area, and that the rest of the time be spent exploring the possibilities of actual collaboration and interdisciplinary research among the participants and their students."[2] In addition to his organizational suggestions, Goffman not only came in from California (writing to Hymes, "Providing you are there and Labov, I would be willing to come"[3]) but also made concrete suggestions of others who might be both interested and appropriate: Paul Ekman, Gregory Bateson, Edward Hall, Ralph V. Exline, Robert Sommer,[4] Emanuel Schegloff, David Sudnow, Norman McQuown, Ray Birdwhistell, and Harold Garfinkel.[5] Ekman, Hall, Exline, and Sommer all participated in the 1969 conference in New York which Goffman helped to put together, and Bateson, Ekman, Argyle, and Sommer were at the Amsterdam conference in 1970 which Goffman co-organized, so these were people he knew and thought of as potentially making relevant contributions on more than one occasion.

In the end, in addition to Goffman, those invited to participate were Tannenbaum, Goldstein, Sapir, Birdwhistell (still at Temple and EPPI), Labov (still at Columbia), Jay Haley (known for his collaborations related to family therapy with Bateson at the Mental Research Institute in Palo Alto; based at that point at the Philadelphia Child Guidance Clinic), Salvador Minuchin (Director of the Philadelphia Child Guidance Clinic),[6] Schegloff (then at Columbia), and Garfinkel (UCLA).[7] The final list of who was able to actually attend is shown in table 4.2. As there was no funding available to cover transportation, it makes sense that most participants were either local or only a short train ride away. Goffman was the primary exception to this rule.

The event was held all day, December 15 and 16, 1967. Hymes called it "our great working seminar" and said "there is here an emerging focus that we all will pursue."[8] Worth commented just after the event about how important it would be "to come to some commonly agreed upon set of definitions and criteria for work in the area that we have loosely called Codes in Context."[9] Important here is both the inclusion of Goffman while he was still based at Berkeley, and the influence this conference had on him, for "it was at the little seminar a year ago December that Goffman and Labov first got to know each other's work and person well."[10] At about the same time, Hymes was trying to convince colleagues in anthropology of the importance of the topic of codes in context generally, and specifically of the relevance of folklore to that topic, saying, "Some of us have talked about a seminar in which such subjects might be regularly discussed."[11] The list of recipients of that letter includes faculty members in folklore, linguistics, and communications, in addition to anthropology, as Hymes was trying to involve all of them in the same conversation.

Several of those invited to the Codes in Context conference were unable to participate and sent regrets. Birdwhistell responded to Worth that it "sounds very exciting" but he was already committed to participate in a conference in Salt Lake City across those dates. "I cannot tell you how sorry

I am because the entire group is one which I respect and I am eager to know what they are doing." He asked if it could be postponed; if not, maybe he and Worth could at least get together for dinner afterwards to talk about what he had missed.[12] Worth said he was particularly sorry, but he couldn't postpone the event because "it depends on Irv [*sic*] Goffman who I think can only make it on that date." But he immediately offered to connect for dinner after the meeting, to "give you a rundown of what we did and accomplished, and also what we are planning and doing here at The Annenberg School."[13] Birdwhistell then wrote expressing his regrets again about missing "what looks like it will be a very fine get together" and asked: "By the way, when you see the Goffman [*sic*] tell him I'm going to be at the Center for Advanced Study in Palo Alto for the year 1968–69 and we can get together then. Kenneth Pike and Kai Ericson will be there at the same time—so we might be able to work on middle-sized stuff."[14] The center's full name is Center for Advanced Study in the Behavioral Sciences. Birdwhistell was conducting fieldwork in Alaska at the time, which must be why he asked that word be passed to Goffman rather than writing to him directly; there were winter storms and he was having issues with mail.[15] It's unclear whether his reference to "the Goffman" is a tease or a typo. Of course, by 1968–1969 Goffman was on the east coast, not conveniently nearby Birdwhistell, who left Pennsylvania for California that year. Minuchin also had to send regrets, saying he had been away from his clinic too often to justify one more absence.[16]

Goffman was not only happy to participate but told Worth, "I am going to try to come a day early for the conference so as to get a better chance to talk to you and Dell and to look around."[17] After the conference was over, Goffman thanked Worth "for the conference, the party, the reprints, the extra day of hospitality, and for being so open about the possibility of my occasional use of Annenberg equipment."[18] It is intriguing to consider what use of Annenberg's video equipment he anticipated, and whether he ever followed up on that possibility.

A few weeks before this conference, Hymes circulated to all participants a report from the Conference on Folklore and Social Science, which he had just attended (November 10–11, 1967), on the grounds that "the conference was vigorous and full of promise for the area of concern with communication, with codes in contexts." He wanted to "stimulate feedback with regard to the importance of folklore in our concern for the development of the area of 'codes in contexts' at Penn."[19] That event was funded by Wenner-Gren Foundation for Anthropological Research, sponsored by the Social Science

Research Council, and held at the Wenner-Gren Foundation's offices in New York (Wenner-Gren 1967).[20] In addition to Hymes, who was one of the organizers, other participants relevant to the story told in these pages were Alan Dundes, as well as Roger Abrahams and Ken Goldstein; Ward Goodenough and Anthony Wallace were discussed as potential participants. Hymes explained that the goal was explicitly to bring social scientists, who had "an analytic bent," together with folklorists, who had "primarily literary interests." [21] Worth responded with a lengthy letter talking about how important it would be "to delineate the place of other disciplines in the general area of study which we might call Communication and Culture, or The Ethnography of Communication, or whatever. What I see you doing here is setting out a rationale for the study of Folklore within the context of Ethnography, Communication, and Codes in Context."[22] Worth used the phrase "codes in context" again in an article published a few years later: "We are not ready to propose a theory of codes in context that would be integral to a complete analysis of our data" (Worth and Adair 1970, 22). And Hymes used it in a letter to Glassie, where he said, "We have growing up through personal ties and community of interest, across departments and schools, perhaps the strongest concentration of talent for the study of—well, no one name serves, but the study of communicative conduct, of 'codes in context' (Sol Worth), 'ethnolinguistics' in some of its aspects, 'sociolinguistics' in other, verbal behavior from an ethnographic standpoint."[23] The take-away here is that the topic of codes in context was obviously timely, and useful to participants as a way of referencing shared interests across disciplines, even if there were no formal presentations, and even if no major publication resulted.

Worth had hopes of turning the conference into a book series, tentatively to be sponsored by Annenberg, and provisionally titled Codes in Context Monograph Series, but that never happened. He saw the potential series as a steppingstone, telling Hymes: "I agree with you that ultimately we went to establish Penn as a center for this kind of work." [24] A year later, in 1969, Hymes was still discussing the possibility of establishing some sort of interdisciplinary center where they could all collaborate on the ideas brought up at the conference. Interestingly, at that point he was assuming that it might also serve as the primary home for the faculty involved, for "if the university set up a new institute or department where we could do our work and get the cooperation we need in training, we might all jump."[25] Obviously, that never happened, but having different administrative homes proved no barrier to collaborations. At the same time, their discussion should be noticed as an early precursor to the repeated efforts to create some sort of either multi- or interdisciplinary framework for an overlapping group of faculty members sharing interests in the minor projects. And it is important that, for at least several members of the group, Worth's phrase "codes in context" was comparable to Hymes's phrase "ethnography of communication."[26] As Worth put it, "Both Dell and I feel that the area which I call 'codes in context,' and which Dell calls the ethnography of communication, is an area that we want to develop on this campus and for which we don't have either enough of the right people."[27] Of course, they shortly would add "the right people": Goffman, Labov, Birdwhistell, and Szwed. It is perhaps worth mentioning that Gumperz at least once, in a letter to Hymes, referred to "a Goffman-ethnography of communication framework."[28] The point to be made is that there was no final agreement on what to call what they were doing, yet they had no difficulty in thinking the different approaches they were taking should be viewed as having substantial overlaps.

Center for Urban Ethnography (CUE)

The Center for Urban Ethnography was established in 1969 through a grant from the National Institute of Mental Health (NIMH) titled "A Program for Metropolitan Culture Studies" (Center for Urban Ethnography 1975, 1).[29] The center's name was likely a tribute to Hughes, given that Goffman, who helped write the proposal, had studied with Hughes at the University of Chicago, and once said that Hughes "developed . . . Urban Ethnography" and "what I did . . . was a version of Urban Ethnography," concluding, "If I had to be labeled at all, it would have been as a Hughesian urban ethnographer" (in Verhoeven 1993, 318).[30] In any case, the initial grant in 1969 was made to Szwed, Goffman, and Hymes; Szwed served as director, with Goffman and Hymes as associate directors, until 1974, when the funding ran out.[31] Szwed tells the story:

> Some of our writings and talks had been seen by a few people at the National Institute of Mental Health, and I was invited to apply for a sizeable grant to develop an anthropological approach to urban life in America. . . . at least some people at NIMH saw a void in our knowledge of our cities, and thought anthropological methods applied to urban culture were worth supporting. . . .
> I was offered a million dollar, five-year grant to create a research center that could itself sponsor research for projects that avoided the judgmental negativity and punitive research inspired by the current crisis, and also help fund minor-

ity graduate students who wished to focus on the cultures of urban life. I was then a member of the Department of Anthropology at Temple University, and they wanted no part of what they called "tramp scholars" in their midst. Erving Goffman, then new to the University of Pennsylvania, and Dell Hymes of Penn's Department of Anthropology encouraged me to locate the grant in their institution. But the Penn anthropologists were also against the idea, some of whom objected because it involved racial issues and controversies. Only the Program in Folklore at Penn was willing to take it on. So I quit my job at Temple, made formal application to NIMH through the University of Pennsylvania, located the new Center for Urban Ethnography within Folklore, and by default became a folklorist. (2015, 426–27)

A million dollars in 1969 would be equivalent to $8,547,384 in 2025,[32] so this really was an astonishingly large amount of money. Szwed provides a few more details about Goffman's role:

Erving Goffman had just arrived in town from Berkeley to assume a chair in anthropology and sociology at the University of Pennsylvania, and told me that he was looking for "something to do." We met over corned beef in a South Philadelphia deli and in a few minutes had worked out a plan to form the Center for Urban Ethnography at Penn. Within a week the administration of the University of Pennsylvania bought the idea. The Department of Anthropology chose not to get involved, however, with at least one of its faculty members accusing us of discriminating against white students. It was instead the Program in Folklore and Folklife that welcomed the Center to Penn, and asked me to teach in their unit; and with Goffman, Dell Hymes, and myself as co-directors, we recruited a talented group of young researchers and opened an office in the fall. (2005, 10–11)

Goffman supports this description in a letter to Hymes, then in England, saying: "The grant looks like it is almost in, and that is because John and I have worked so hard. Tomorrow morning when you shave, look at yourself and try to feel guilty."[33]

The center followed directly in the tradition of the Chicago School, designed to take "the best-trained pre-doctoral students ready to undertake dissertation research we could find, and to help guide and focus their interests and to put them into the urban field following the ethnographic approach" (Center for Urban Ethnography 1975, 1). Specifically, as Szwed explained to Hymes while they were waiting for final approval, there would be "7 student researchers per year, 3 (black) tuition stipends, and one faculty research assistantship for visiting scholars. . . . there'll be plenty funds for travel and seminars too."[34] In keeping with this, fellowships were advertised in places like *Anthropology News*. Here are the essentials, from one of the ads:

"In order to increase the recruitment of members of minority groups into ethnography, fellowships are available to members of ethnic groups who wish to do graduate study in the Departments of Anthropology, Folklore and Linguistics at the University of Pennsylvania. These students would continue to be supported through their doctoral research" (*Anthropology News* 1970, 7). As Szwed explains, "Incredible as it now seems, African Americans were not of that much concern to social scientists in the early 1960s" (2005, 8), and he wanted to change that by creating "a major research center that would make its focus urban ethnography—basic research on the lives of people in American cities—with African Americans and other ethnic groups at its core" (10).[35] One goal in establishing the center was finding a home for "the cluster of colleagues from anthropology, sociology, linguistics, folklore, and elsewhere, all interested in urban ethnography" (Hymes, in Hornberger 2002, 1), and among others drawn in were not only Labov, but Goldstein, Worth, and Ben-Amos (Darnell 2001b, 2011).[36] This language nicely echoes Mullins (1973), in his discussions of clusters of people making up a theory group.

Such an enormous grant made a huge difference in encouraging people to study a new topic. The center distributed numerous small grants from the funding obtained from NIMH in order to shift focus and attention to subjects typically overlooked. In addition to studies of racial and ethnic groups, there were studies of those who came into contact with these groups (such as the police) and, more generally, of public places and the "public order" (Center for Urban Ethnography 1975, 2). In the beginning, Szwed suggested it might take as much as a year before they saw substantial numbers of applications, but he was convinced they would get noticed.[37] He was right, and by 1975 it was possible to write: "To date this research has produced 23 completed dissertations (with 9 others in progress), 63 papers or chapters in books published or in press, 24 books or monographs, and nearly 100 papers delivered at conferences, meetings, etc." (Center for Urban Ethnography 1975, 3). Best known of the publications are major works by Goffman (1971, 1974), Hymes (1972a, 1972b, 1974), Labov (1972b, 1972c), and Szwed (1970; Szwed and Abrahams 1978; Szwed and Witten 1970), as well as shorter pieces by Gail Jefferson (1973, 1974; Sacks et al. 1974), John and Angela Rickford (1976), and Dennis and Barbara Tedlock (D. Tedlock 1976; Tedlock and Tedlock 1975). Some of the dissertations supported were those of Michael J. Bell, Marjorie Harness Goodwin, Gregory Gizelis, Samuel Heilman, Elizabeth Mathias, Dan Rose, and Clarence Robins. In addition, by 1975 Szwed was able to write: "We have placed 13 of our researchers in academic departments where they are pursuing the subject of urban ethnography" and "we now have on hand and pending a body of materials that demonstrates the importance of what has loosely been called 'ethnicity' for the everyday lives of a great number of people" (Center for Urban Ethnography 1975, 3).

By 1970 CUE was getting international requests for student support. An example is a request for information from Mervin C. Alleyne (a member of the editorial board of *Language in Society*), based at the University of the West Indies. Hymes responded:

> On the funds at Penn: our "Center for Urban Ethnography" cannot enroll students, or admit them. That can only be done through established departments and schools. What we can do is provide financial support to students considered members of "minority groups," if a dept. or school wishes to accept it. . . . I can't promise financial aid sight unseen. If they are admitted by the Linguistics dept (and this would be a good place to come—Labov is joining us next year), then I'm pretty confident we will be able to provide the financial support. Such money is included in our grant. The only criteria would be an interest in urban problems (which I would take dialectology to imply) and minority group status—I apologize that this sounds like "racism in reverse," but if they're black, that will suffice, despite being from the majority in their own country. "Minority" operationally means non-white.[38]

Elsewhere Hymes reported on the actual functioning of the center, this time to Courtney Cazden, at Harvard.

> The Center for Urban Ethnography, John Szwed, Director, Erving Goffman and Dell Hymes, fellow conspirators to disburse the government's millions, operates by telephone and casual conversations, gives money only for other people to do their own individual work, and doesn't insist on the work being done in Philadelphia. I have to say that Erv Goffman is more anthropological than the anthropologist, and might be unhappy about work not involving direct participation.[39]

In fact, CUE did more than just distribute research grants in the effort to "disburse the government's millions"; another activity was to organize several of what were variously termed meetings or conferences. There is documentation available for two of these.

Table 4.3: Urban Ethnography Conference, November 14–15, 1969, New York

Primary organizers: John Szwed, Dell Hymes, Erving Goffman
Penn participants: Ken Goldstein (in addition to Szwed, Hymes, and Goffman)
CUE supported student participants: Marjorie Harness, Emma Lapsansky, Dan Rose, Jonathan Rubenstein
Not-yet-at-Penn participants: William Labov, Fred Erickson, Roger Abrahams
Beyond Penn participants: David Amidon (history, Lehigh University), Mr./Mrs. Stephen Baratz (Washington, DC), R. S. Bryce-Laporte (sociology, Yale), Joan Katcher (anthropology, Beaver College), J. L. Dillard (educational psychology, Yeshiva University), Steven Dodd (sociology, Berkeley), Edwin Eames (anthropology, Temple), W. H. Ferry (California), Herbert Gans (urban studies at MIT/Harvard), Blanche Geer (sociology/anthropology, Northeastern University), Judith Goode (anthropology, Temple), Joan Howard (anthropology, Syracuse University), Everett Hughes (sociology, Boston University), Charles Keil (American studies, SUNY Buffalo), Thomas Kochman (linguistics, Northeastern Illinois State College), Bruce Lee (Washington, DC), Elliot Liebow (NIMH), Walter Miller (urban studies, MIT/Harvard), Laura Nader (anthropology, Berkeley), Stanley Newman (anthropology, Northeastern Illinois State College), Esther Newton (anthropology, Queens College), Lee Rainwater (social relations, Harvard), Harvey Sarles (anthropology, University of Minnesota), Ethel Sawyer (sociology, Temple), David M. Schneider (anthropology, University of Chicago), A. Sivanandan (Institute of Race Relations, London), Raymond T. Smith (anthropology, University of Chicago), William Stewart (Washington, DC), Dr./Mrs. Charles A. Valentine (anthropology, Washington University), David T. Wellman (sociology, Berkeley), Carl Werthman (sociology, Berkeley), William L. Yancy (sociology, Vanderbilt University)
Results: Coordination and discussion of major ideas, no publications, but some overlaps with the second conference, which resulted in a book

The first event was held at the Statler Hilton Hotel in New York, November 14–15, 1969,[40] with Labov, Lee Rainwater, and Laura Nader giving presentations, among others. This was "a two-day meeting of most of the urban ethnographers in this United States, with papers and seminars" (Center for Urban Ethnography 1974, 3). Goffman discussed it in a letter to Hughes: "I am glad indeed that you can come and visit with us in New York. The meeting is on urban ethnography in general and race in particular. A letter from John Szwed ought to have reached you by now with the details." (Oct

24, 1969, ECH). That letter from Szwed explained that all expenses would be paid by CUE and included the list of participants.

Table 4.4: Reinventing Anthropology Conference,
May 7, 1971, Philadelphia

Primary organizers: Dell Hymes (anthropology), John Szwed (folklore)
Penn participants: Bob Scholte,[41] Sol Worth (both in communications)
Not-yet-at-Penn participants: Dan Rose (anthropology, University of Wisconsin-Madison)
Beyond Penn participants: George N. Appell (anthropology, Brandeis University), Stanley Diamond (anthropology, New School for Social Research), A. Norman Klein (anthropology, California Institute of the Arts), Alfonso Ortiz (anthropology, Princeton University), Trent Schroyer (anthropology, New School for Social Research), William Willis (anthropology, Southern Methodist University)
Results: Publication of *Reinventing Anthropology* (Hymes 1972a)

A second major event was held May 7, 1971,[42] intended to provide the opportunity for participants to talk through the issues and then publish in a book Hymes had agreed to edit, which he originally described as "the book on radical anthropology"[43] but eventually titled *Reinventing Anthropology* (1972a). Goffman was not part of this event, as it was more specifically aimed at those identifying as anthropologists, particularly those concerned with the direction of the field. Of those participating, Hymes wrote the introduction, and Szwed had a chapter (1972) as did Worth (1972a), and Scholte (1972). Diamond, Klein, and Willis were also at this meeting, as well as several others (including Eric Wolf and Laura Nader, who had participated in the earlier CUE-sponsored conference). So, in some ways it may be accurate to consider the second conference to have been a smaller, more focused event resulting from the first conference.

The transformation of the second conference into a book has an interesting back story; in fact, uncommonly, the offer to publish a book came first. Hymes wrote a review essay of *The Dissenting Academy* (the book is Roszak 1968, the review is Hymes 1968). That book's publisher, Pantheon, immediately invited Hymes to contribute to the series of their "anti-textbooks." As editor Andre Schiffrin explained: "During the last year we have tried very hard to find someone who might undertake to edit a collection of dissenting essays in anthropology."[44] The idea intrigued Hymes, but he was over-committed and could not agree to doing anything at that point.[45] Despite that, the conversation continued based on the fact that "we have obviously found the perfect editor" and a contract was immediately offered.[46] Hymes had no time until after returning to the US, but they continued the conversation, which eventually led to the conference in spring 1971 (with a representative of Pantheon in attendance),[47] and the publication of the book in 1972. Given that Hymes's departure from anthropology happened as he was working on the manuscript, in this context he explained that move (and delays it caused) by saying, "The official dept is resolutely determined that anthropology shall not be reinvented. They like it the way it 'always was.'"[48]

Of the resulting volume, Szwed pointed out:

> We had high hopes for the book, and for the possibility of transforming the goals of anthropology: we talked of introducing reflexivity into the discourse and practice of the field, and of confronting what we saw as the arrogance with which anthropologists had limited their field to the exotic while at the same time assuming that they knew all that they needed to know about their own societies to do comparative studies. But the book was quickly disposed of in the few reviews it got. . . . Years later, however, we learned that we had struck a chord, at least among graduate students. (2005, 11)

Shirley Brice Heath later labeled the book "one of the most radicalizing texts in the history of anthropology" (2011, 402), so it was not only participants who thought it well worth the time and effort. Then, in 1999, nearly thirty years after its publication, Hymes received a request to reprint the book in paperback;[49] perhaps it was just ahead of its time.

Continuing the story of general CUE activities, in January 1973, Hymes wrote to Szwed first with a suggestion that CUE invite Martin Silverman, in anthropology at Princeton, who was doing related work on trends in social theory to campus for a talk, then turned that into a larger suggestion in a letter to Szwed.

> Maybe the Center next year could undertake a small series of talks or working meetings on aspects of the notion of performance. The key dimensions might be: performance as aesthetically tinged conduct, or behavior; performance as having emergent properties, not reducible to expressions of personal competence (knowledge); performance as having a moral dimension in the particular sense of the acceptance of responsibility, not only for knowing, but also for doing (as a performer). . . . Erv ought to be willing to join in. Marty Silverman. Who else?[50]

There is no response in the file, and it is unlikely that event happened, but this is interesting both because it was a proposal to connect what the center was doing regarding urban ethnography to Hymes's work at the time on performance, and because of the assumption that Goffman would be an obvious participant.

The variety of additional activities documented as having been supported by CUE include, among others:

- "a meeting of scholars on problems of confidentiality and ethics in field research"
- "a meeting on the problems of writing ethnography for both professional and popular purposes"
- "a meeting of scholars of Afro-American studies" (eventually leading to two books: Abrahams and Szwed 1975; Szwed and Abrahams 1978)
- partial sponsorship of the Conference on Marginal Religious Movements in America Today at Princeton in 1971
- sponsorship of "panels and symposia . . . on urban ethnography and Afro-American studies at meetings of the American Psychological Association, the American Folklore Society, the American Anthropological Association, and the American Association for the Advancement of Science" (Center for Urban Ethnography 1974, 3)
- *Urban Poetry*, a collection of poems and fiction, circulated at least once[51]

In addition to supporting research, publications, conferences, and presentations, the center occasionally appointed fellows. Labov was a research fellow; Gail Jefferson was a postdoctoral fellow,[52] accepted at Harvey Sacks's request (according to Goodwin and Salomon 2019); and Abrahams was a fellow "whenever his job at Texas allowed it" (Szwed 2016, 427). And there was at least one series of seminars sponsored by the center, with Goffman, Labov, Jefferson, Charles and Marjorie Goodwin, and other students, which has been characterized as "extraordinary" (Goodwin and Salomon 2019, 4).

The center was funded for five years only. In 1974, Hymes wrote Labov that "John [Szwed] has some hopes still that new funds will come into the center."[53] But they did not.[54] By 1977, Hymes wrote to Goffman, "Maybe the Center for Urban Ethnography could rise again, phoenix-like."[55] Hymes talked with Glassie about the same thing, how to revitalize the center, in 1979.[56] And then the phoenix did rise, more or less, although with substantial differences. First, when the Ethnography in Education Research Forum

(EERF) was started by Hymes in 1980, it operated under the auspices of CUE, which at that point had moved to the Graduate School of Education (GSE), where he was dean.[57] Surprisingly, the center is still today credited as a co-sponsor of that event,[58] despite the lack of outside funding, despite the fact that none of the original participants are now involved, and despite the fact that the topic changed to a focus solely on education. After a few years, both CUE and EERF were passed on to colleagues in GSE; later directors have included David Smith, 1980–1985; Frederick Erickson, 1986–1999; and Nancy Hornberger, 2000–2015 (Hornberger 2003, 2011; Smith 2002). This second iteration of the center was also home to several large research grants from a different funding source, the National Institute of Education (NIE), emphasizing the use of ethnography to study inner city schools, from 1979–1983, two with Hymes as PI ("Ethnographic Monitoring of Children's Acquisition of Reading/language Arts Skills In and Out of School" [Hymes 1981a] and "Ethnolinguistic Study of Classroom Discourse" [Hymes 1982]), and one with Smith as PI ("Using Literacy Outside of School: An Ethno-graphic Investigation" [see Smith 1982, 2002]). At least the first of these was clearly conceived as a CUE-related grant, as Hymes put it to Szwed: "The Center for Urban Ethnography could be and ought to be the vehicle for this, should it not?"[59]

Second, in 1999, what might best be described as a tribute version of the center was designed by Abrahams, the Center for Folklore and Ethnography (CFE), which still maintained a connection to Goffman. As a reminder, Szwed has been quoted as saying that Abrahams participated in discussions creating the original version, so he was well aware of the goals. CFE was part of a compromise made in 1999 to avoid completely closing the Department of Folklore and Folklife; instead, the Penn administration returned the department to the status of a graduate program (how it had begun) and a research center (see Hufford 2020 for the story). As founding director of CFE, Abrahams established the mission, maintaining some overlap with the original center's mandate, saying the new mission was "to create practical fieldwork programs for students, to co-ordinate conferences and seminars of regional, national and international significance, and to collaborate with local folklore institutions on ethnographic projects reflecting regional cultural diversity."[60]

In the announcement of CFE's inaugural conference in 2000, Goffman was specifically mentioned, along with Hymes and Birdwhistell:

> In the 1960s and 70s there was an unusually rich conversation that took place, centered at the University of Pennsylvania, arising from the work of Dell Hymes and his colleagues and very gifted students in the Ethnography of Communication; Erving Goffman, through his analyses of the cultural constructions of everyday life, explored through the metaphors of theatrical play, game play, ritual practice, and aesthetic framing; and Ray Birdwhistell, whose discussions of the microbehavioral dimension of cultural practice enlivened the intellectual environment here and elsewhere. Between them, they deeply affected the way in which ethnographic observation is now carried out.
>
> Now twenty-some years later it seems useful to bring together many of those involved in this discussion, not to lament its passing, nor to celebrate its accomplishment, but to bring back some of the questions that arose then that remain unanswered.[61]

Participants at the event included Hymes, Szwed, Glassie, Ben-Amos, and Kirshenblatt-Gimblett, among many others. In 2001, Abrahams retired, and Mary Hufford, a Penn folklore PhD student from the late 1970s, returned to teach in folklore at Penn, taking over as director until it closed in 2008 (Hufford 2020). In her capacity as director, she organized additional conferences, including a symposium to honor Abrahams when he retired,[62] as well as workshops and a visiting fellows program,[63] and taught courses, including a field practicum (Hufford 2020; email to the author, June 19, 2022).

It is uncommon for a research center funded for only five years to end up lasting decades, and to have not one but two reincarnations, but then this center was uncommon in multiple ways: the amount of initial funding, the goal of bringing ethnography back to the US (when traditionally anthropologists studied other cultures and countries than their own), the focus on urban culture and minorities, and the support of mostly junior rather than senior scholars. Goffman played a role from start to finish during the first five years, from helping Szwed with the initial proposal, to serving as associate director, to participating in some of the events, although clearly not all of them. He was not around to be part of the later incarnations yet was still acknowledged for his early contributions.

Conduct and Communication (CC)

Goffman and Hymes co-edited the book series Conduct and Communication (CC) for the University of Pennsylvania Press (frequently abbreviated to just "Penn Press").[64] This series was particularly important because Goffman was the one who first suggested it, at least as early as 1968: Worth wrote to Hymes, "In regard to Goffman's suggestion about a publication series, I think it is a superb idea, and one that is very, very needed."[65] Worth went on to talk about whether it might work out better to produce the series through ASC, since Gerbner was potentially interested in publishing monographs in communications. Worth offered to edit the series if someone else would manage the money, linking it to the conference he and Hymes had organized in 1967, suggesting they call it Codes in Context Monograph Series. That never happened, although even the suggestion makes clear the connection between these two otherwise quite different projects.

Table 4.5: Conduct and Communication, University of Pennsylvania Press, 1970–1982

Year	Author	Title	Citations*
1970	Goffman	*Strategic Interaction*	3,587
1970	Birdwhistell	*Kinesics and Context*	6,798
1972	Labov	*Language in the Inner City*	13,681
1972	Labov	*Sociolinguistic Patterns*	19,267
1974	Hymes	*Foundations in Sociolinguistics*	11,133
1976	Kirshenblatt-Gimblett	*Speech Play*	155
1980	Sankoff	*The Social Life of Language*	675
1981	Goffman	*Forms of Talk*	16,918
1981	Worth (edited by Gross)	Studying Visual Communication	563
1981	Hymes	*In Vain I Tried to Tell You*	1,726
1981	Rose	*Energy Transition and the Local Community*	43
1981	Sutton-Smith	*The Folkstories of Children*	302
1981	Sutton-Smith	*A History of Children's Play*	171
1982	Feld	*Sound and Sentiment*	3,326

* citations in Google Scholar as of March 2025

Two years after their initial discussion of the series, Hymes told Worth, "Erv has persuaded Penn Press to have a series, on trial basis, in conduct and communication, that he and I will run,"[66] and the first books appeared remarkably quickly, in 1970. The name is likely a subtle reference to Goffman's dissertation, "Communication Conduct in an Island Community" (1953). The series continued even after Goffman's death because Sankoff and Glassie stepped in to serve as co-editors with Hymes from 1983 to 1990. The entire series has been called "distinguished and provocative" by Weigle (1988), in her review of Basso (1985), one of the volumes published in it, and indeed it was. The list of only those books published between 1970 and 1982, and thus under Goffman's supervision, is in table 4.5. They were all carefully chosen, and nearly all of them have been frequently purchased, and cited, and have influenced later work in significant ways.[67]

When the press made a formal report to the campus about recent activities in 1973, all three authors published in this series by that point (Goffman, Birdwhistell, and Labov) were highlighted.[68] A new director, Robert Erwin, began service in fall 1974 and, in the "President's Letter to the Faculty" on that occasion, Meyerson highlighted work by all the authors in this series by that time (now including Hymes).[69]

The first book to appear was Goffman's *Strategic Interaction.* There is very little documentation concerning its publication, but what has survived is a very odd example of marketing. Whether of their own volition or at Goffman's request is unclear, but Marilyn Sale, an editor at the press, sent a copy to J. Edgar Hoover, in his role as Director of the FBI, before it was even published. "We are sending to you, under separate cover, a copy of Erving Goffman's *Strategic Interaction,* which we will publish shortly and which we believe might be of interest to you and your staff. In this book, Professor Goffman uses espionage and police literature to show how men elicit, cover, and reveal information in game-like interaction" (Sale to Hoover, Jan 15, 1970, MK). A few weeks later, there was a response from Hoover, saying, "I have not yet received this book but I am looking forward to doing so. I certainly appreciate your sending it to me" (Hoover to Sale, Jan 23, 1970, MK). There is no letter, at least none in the same archival collection, showing whether Hoover read it when it did arrive, or what he thought of it.

The second book in the series, *Kinesics and Context,* was by Birdwhistell; today that is the work for which he is best known. He has explained that it "would not have appeared if it had not been envisaged by Erving Goffman" (1970, xiv). Others also acknowledged Goffman's achievement in making this book appear, as when Robert Sommer sent Goffman congratulations on getting Birdwhistell to prepare the book, which he felt was long overdue,[70] Birdwhistell's only other book having been published in 1952.[71] Obviously, they were working on *Kinesics and Context* during Birdwhistell's first year at Penn, given that it was published in 1970. The book was neither written as a single piece, nor simply a collection of previously published papers; it consists of conference papers, unpublished manuscripts, and prior publications edited into a single narrative by a Penn graduate student. "Barton Jones[72] has tried to make a coherent whole from an assemblage of very diverse pieces" (Kendon 1972, 452). In his review of the book, Kendon not only calls attention to Jones's unusual role as a student editing the work of a professor, but also mentions Goffman, saying, "Had it not been for the insistence of Erving Goffman (the coeditor of the series in which this book is published) and the work done by Barton Jones, we might never have had these papers in print" (453). Kendon includes Goffman in the list of "others who share this perspective and who have been influenced by Birdwhistell" (453n1); he earlier defines "this perspective" as "the 'structural' approach to communicational behavior" (441). The important point to remember is that Birdwhistell's signature work likely would never have appeared if Goffman had not ensured its publication.

The third and fourth books were by Labov, who credits "the urging of Dell Hymes and Erving Goffman" for their completion.[73] Hymes similarly credits Goffman with initiating what turned out to be the fifth book in the series, *Foundations in Sociolinguistics,* telling Fought it was "through agency of Erv Goffman" that the book came to be.[74]

Goffman took quite seriously the mandate he and Hymes established that, to be included, books must address both language and society, rather than either one or the other. Hymes shares that "in the two years before his death, he [Goffman] worried that the series might have exhausted its purpose, because the manuscripts coming to attention were strongest in attention to speech genres and text, and were not balanced by manuscripts strong in social structure" (1984, 627). At the same time, Hymes reports that when the press suggested that his own work, *In Vain I Tried to Tell You* (1981b), be published within the series, a book which falls nearly entirely in the language category, with virtually nothing about society, "the logic of scholarly categories was replaced by the logic of academic kinship" (1984, 627).

At least some of the time, Goffman took the lead on corresponding with the press on whether manuscripts should be accepted,[75] and he clearly did at least some of the administrative work of the series, including writing the hard letters rejecting proposals. Joel Sherzer submitted a manuscript in 1974 for the series to which Goffman responded:

> On behalf of Dell and myself, I inquired of Erwin, the editor of the University of Pennsylvania Press, about the possibility of the Indian language book ... apparently the costs would run about $7000 and Erwin feels that if $5000 could be raised, there might be a possibility. We buried scholarship, praised the wage that the laboring man was getting these days, and I said goodbye. I think it's a good idea to give general courses to undergraduates, but dissertation writers ought to be trained in something practical, like screenplays, TV scripts, and grant proposal writing.[76]

The book in question was most likely Sherzer's dissertation (published as Sherzer 1976). They knew each other long before this exchange, as documented in the story told previously about Labov's hiring. Their connection was reaffirmed by the way Goffman's letter closes: "You are boobs, party poopers, etc. for not going to Mexico City. Love to the great French chef," presumably a way to ensure that the friendship would continue beyond this rejection.[77] The reference to Mexico City is mostly likely to the American Anthropological Association meeting held there in fall 1974.[78]

Another dissertation under consideration for the series was Philips's *The Invisible Culture*,[79] but that eventually was published elsewhere as well (1983). And Hymes was to have had another volume of his own in the series, a collection of essays entitled *Language as Culture*, but that never appeared (apparently because it was never submitted).[80] He was still working on it in 1980, when he explained that he couldn't agree to an invitation because he already had too many commitments, including "to Penn Press, a collection of essays, promised 5 years ago."[81] But he did manage to complete a different book for them on which he apparently was working simultaneously, *In Vain I Tried to Tell You* (1981b); he had been working on that one also at least since 1975.[82]

And there was at least an exchange between Hymes and Ray McDermott (at Rockefeller University), after the latter gave a presentation at Penn, about the possibility of publishing his dissertation from Stanford, "Kids Make Sense" (1976), as a book in the series. Hymes outlined the process they followed:

> If the manuscript came to us for the series, both Erv and I would read it, and both would make careful analytic comments. ... Erv writes marvelously cogent accounts of papers for the journal and no doubt would do likewise for the book ms. ... The main question Erv would raise, as you know from your talk at Penn,

is the relation between what goes on in the classroom and what the participants, esp. the children, bring to the classroom.[83]

Indeed, Goffman's comments for the series also proved to be "marvelously cogent." In the end, that book was also not published.

A few years later there was a flurry of activity relating to Sapir's book, *The Social Use of Metaphor* (eventually published as Sapir and Crocker 1977). One problem was that Sapir was interested in submitting it to other publishers first;[84] another was that Goffman did not particularly view it as appropriate for their series. Erwin sent a letter to Goffman saying that he and Hymes were "more or less inclined" to accept Sapir's manuscript in the series, and that "Dell asks: are you disposed to go along with us on this one, so far as including the book in the Conduct and Communication Series is concerned?"[85] Apparently the answer was no, because Erwin wrote Hymes, "Erv prefers not to include the volume in the Conduct and Communication Series. . . . for him, it lacks the experimental aspect and breadth of concern that he covets for the series. He also continues to be dubious about books of papers for the series. I assume that, like the UN Security council, you and Erv extend mutual veto powers to each other."[86] Hymes responded that he would vote for publishing in the series, but that "if Erving feels definitely that the book should be separate from the conduct and communication series, I would of course defer." He then proposed that if not in their series, perhaps the book could be published in Ken Goldstein's series with the press (more on that below).[87] A month later matters still had not been resolved, because Erwin wrote, "I am reluctant to step into the line of fire between you and Goffman, but I hope we can include the book in the Conduct and Communication series. In any case, we will promote the book to the same audience."[88] Finally, there is a note from Hymes to Goffman saying, "Erwin reports that the Sapir book is approved. I don't want to make an issue of its inclusion in the Conduct and Communication series. If Dave [Sapir] comes with Penn (rather than Indiana), I would be happy to have it, because it will carry a dedication to KB [Kenneth Burke]. But not enough to make you unhappy."[89] In the end, the book was published by Penn Press, just not in their series (or Goldstein's).

A few years after that (1978), when faced with a submission to the series of which he said it "doesn't strike me as very interesting," Hymes concluded a detailed report to the press by saying, "If Erving should like it, I wouldn't object to its being published; just so long as it isn't called 'ethnography.' If others should like it, I wouldn't insist on its not being published."[90] The point here is that Hymes and Goffman did not always agree on the value or appropriateness of submissions to their series but worked hard to resolve their differences cordially and, as Erwin suggested, did give one another veto power.

A more successful proposal was one by Sankoff for *The Social Life of Language* (1980). This one was first encouraged by Labov,[91] and put forward by Goffman to Erwin, with the comment "Sankoff won't be long in these parts, and I hope we can tie the thing down with a decision quickly."[92] (Of course, Sankoff did in fact stay both in the city and at Penn.) Hymes also wrote Erwin supporting it, saying he had had a chance to talk with Goffman about it, and "I agreed with him that such a volume is an excellent idea."[93] By the next month, Erwin offered Sankoff a contract, telling her, "Messrs. Hymes, Labov, and Goffman supplied such glowing endorsements that I believe I could have got you canonized."[94] The manuscript was submitted in early 1979, and Erwin told Hymes, "Erv Goffman told me before Christmas that he would bring you the good news. Gillian Sankoff has finished her book, and it includes the 'assertive' Introduction you counseled long ago. Erv also said that he would urge you to write a Foreword, a suggestion that I heartily second."[95] He asked whether Hymes needed a copy of the manuscript and imposed a six-week deadline. Hymes responded, "Erv and Gillian brought by her manuscript and I shall do my darndest to provide the foreword in time. . . . I very much want to help the book along."[96] He did in fact complete the foreword (Hymes 1980).

In addition to *Strategic Interaction* (1970), Goffman published a second book in the series, *Forms of Talk* (1981), and there is more documentation available for that one. Goffman sent the manuscript to John McGuigan, acquisitions editor for Penn Press in January 1980. "Betimes we have spoken of a set of papers I was preparing in my capacity as amateur sociolinguist, and these I now submit for possible publication in the Conduct and Communication Series" (Goffman to McGuigan, Jan 3, 1980, RB). He admitted to having some concern about the marketability of the book, given that "the focus is too narrow for the sociologists who might be attracted because of what I usually write about, and I have a doubtful claim on the attention of the linguistically trained." McGuigan sent the manuscript to Richard Bauman for review, with the comment that obviously they would publish it, but that he did still need a review for the editorial committee (Jan 14, 1980, RB). Unfortunately, it is not clear at this point who exactly was on that committee. Bauman responded with a Goffman-level detailed evaluation (three single-spaced pages), saying that, while "it is always a stimulating experience to read his work," "this is some of his very best" and "certainly a case in which the whole adds up to more than the sum of its parts," concluding that the book "will have a very significant impact on the burgeoning field of conversational analysis" (Jan 28, 1980, RB). He named "The Lecture" his favorite of all the chapters he had previously read, for "the thread of reflexive and shape-shifting play that runs through it," but considered the one that was new to him, "Radio Talk," to be "superb—I've never enjoyed or profited from a Goffman paper as much as this one." Obviously, he recommended publication.

John McGuigan first brought the manuscript and this review (and possibly others) to the editorial committee, and then wrote to Hymes saying:

> As you know, the editorial committee [of Penn Press] formally approved for publication Erving's FORMS OF TALK. Erving requested that I send the manuscript to you—*sans* introduction, which is still being written—for your critical eye. He very much wants the manuscript carefully scrutinized. Also, Erving is letting the formal decision of whether or not his book appears in the Conduct and Communication series rest in your hands. Of course it ought to be included, but Erving wants to avoid the appearance of any overt conflict of interest.[97]

Goffman was not copied on that letter. Within a few days, Hymes wrote back four single-spaced pages of comments, far too much to quote in its entirety here, but the following are some of the highlights.

> As you know, I had seen all but the last long piece, "Radio Talk" before.
>
> I quite agree with the decision of the Editorial Committee to publish the book. I also believe that the book should appear in the Conduct and Communication Series. (Recognizing in saying that, that the precise status of the Series is presently uncertain). Certainly the book should appear in paperback simultaneously with hardcover.
>
> Some comments in the order of the chapters, which Erving may or may not want to take into account.
>
> Ch. 1. [Replies and Responses] Obviously I think this is good, having published it in LANGUAGE IN SOCIETY. . . . As the later chapters of this book show, conversational constraints may be complex but are not non-existent. . . . The fact that participants can be sanctioned by others for departing from expected constraints shows them to exist. . . . What Erving goes on to say about footing is far more valuable to the work that needs to be done to come to understand just what different people make of the means of communication available to them. But somewhere the ugly notion of norms, expectations, "rules," patterns, whatever, raises its head, often invoked by the participants we observe themselves.

Ch. 2. [Response Cries] A very nice paper and a delight to have appear in LAN-GUAGE.

Ch. 3. [Footing] A very good paper. The Nixon instance is offensive (I hope) but maybe thereby holds the attention. It is good of Erv to describe the first sixteen pages as a lengthy gloss on Hymes. . . .

Ch. 5 "Radio Talk" is very interesting. It would be helpful to advertise at the outset more clearly where the long discussion of radio talk will end. The end opens up, using radio talk as a way of defining something not radio talk. That's important to people who may or may not be interested in radio talk itself. . . . Erv is perhaps too uncritical of the notion of "literacy" here. . . .

The ending is very important but not, I fear, all that it could be. The basic contrast is powerful and worth waiting for. But why not pursue it a little farther? . . . Something very important might be opened up here for research. And a glancing comment on Habermas and ideal communicative competence would seem very much in order! Indeed, it seems strange to discuss linguistics and competencies without a mention of CHOMSKY. No need to mention me. In writing TOWARD LINGUISTIC COMPETENCE I drew on Erv for support in extending the notion. But now that Habermas has made ideal communicative competence a notion much discussed in some sociological and philosophical circles; and given that linguists still treat it seriously in something like Chomsky's sense—some do anyway, it would seem very strange to pass by oblivious.

To say this is not to fault the manuscript for lacking a reference and a bibliographical nod. What Erv has to say about competency is important to that general discussion. I should very much like to see him address it, if only in a paragraph or a page.

What Erv says about informal talk sounds rather like what Habermas says about "discourse"—as distinct from ordinary talk. . . .

If Erv wants to insist on a two-way contrast between the freedom of "informal talk" and the restraint of "formal talk," as in radio announcing, then he ought to mention at least where that puts him in relation to the Habermas idea and discussions of it. My own guess is that Erv could develop the two-way contrast into a scale. . . .

Anyway a paragraph or a page, please![98]

A few notes. First, of course Hymes wanted Goffman's book to be published, and in the series; that was likely a given. Second, Hymes's comments are comparable in content, volume, and style to those Goffman typically wrote for submissions, displaying clear understanding of what was said, and frequently attempting to put it into the larger context of what others were also saying. For example, even after noting that chapter 1 had already been published in *Language in Society* (meaning he had already had an opportunity to critique it ahead of time), Hymes wrote half a page of discussion of it. Third, chapter 3 sparks a detailed response that is not at all critique but more a meditation on how the content fits with prior work by Ethel Albert, Hymes himself, Keith Basso, and Charles Goodwin. Chapter 4, The Lecture, has no comments at all, which seems surprising, but then Hymes had had the opportunity to provide critique ahead of time, and presumably did. The comments on chapter 5 mostly consider Goffman's ideas in relation to those of Habermas. Fourth, what surprises me most is that it seems Goffman did not take any of these suggestions into account in preparing the book for publication: Albert, Basso, Chomsky, Habermas—none of them have been added to the final version. However, Goffman did acknowledge and cite many others, including those mentioned elsewhere in these pages: both Dell and Virginia Hymes, both Teresa and William Labov, as well as Jefferson, Philips, Sankoff, and Sherzer. A few others only got acknowledgments for specific suggestions, but this makes evident at least a few of those with whom he was exchanging drafts: Lee Ann Draud, John Fought, Rochel Gelman, Anthony Kroch, W. John Smith, and Allen Grimshaw. Finally, the status of the series was at that time uncertain for two reasons: There was always an issue of funding, but also Goffman was concerned about the lack of appropriately balanced submissions (that is, ones considering both language and society). More on that shortly.

Worth had one book published in the series (posthumously, in 1981), but his classic, *Through Navajo Eyes* (1972b), was rejected. Hymes wrote a letter to the press saying he had not had a chance to review the manuscript and asking that it be considered for the series.

> I would consider it a crime and a shame not to publish the book here. What can be the point of having people here strong in research in those areas of communication, and of launching a series to benefit from one of the University's distinctive strengths, if a book that represents both is not published by our Press? . . . I further understood when the series was initially launched, that it would have a trial period in which Erv and I would be able to select the books (monographs). I understand from Erv that he did not in fact take a clear position on Sol's ms., leaving you more or less on your own to judge it. I've told Erv my view of it, and his reservations apparently have to do with commitment to the future of the series itself, rather than with the ms. With all this in mind, I wonder if it would not be a good thing for us to get together to discuss both?[99]

As the book did not in fact appear in the series, but with Indiana University Press instead, it seems obvious that this argument was unsuccessful.

In 1979, at a point when several years had gone by with no books at all published in the series, Grimshaw wrote to both Goffman and Hymes saying he recently had been asked whether he was going to publish a collection of his sociolinguistic papers, so he wanted to explore the possibility. "It occurred to me that such a volume *might* be an appropriate for the conduct and communication series at the Penn press," he wrote (emphasis in original), and included a CV and prospectus. "If the series is defunct, or if you're not interested, just tell me. If you think the idea is a disastrous one and that I shouldn't pursue the possibility with any press, I'd consider it a personal favor if you'd tell me that. If you think the notion is a sound one and if you think that you might be interested in such a volume for your series, let me know that and I'll be delighted to send copies of whatever papers you don't already have."[100] Notice that he could assume they would both already have unpublished versions of most of his sociolinguistic papers. The response from Goffman has not been preserved. Hymes's response was:

> The idea of a book of your papers seems a good one. I can't speak with definiteness about our series. It has lagged although not disappeared. Erv and I are to have a meeting soon with the newly appointed director of the Press to talk about the series. A month from now we will know better what its prospects will be.... In your own interest, given the present uncertainty here, I'd suggest being in touch with Anwar S. Dil and the Stanford series.... We'll let you know once we have meet with the Press director what our situation is.[101]

In fact, Grimshaw did publish with Stanford (1981), rather than with Penn.

There was a connection between the Center for Urban Ethnography and the book series in addition to the fact that Hymes and Goffman were essential to both, which is that researchers or research projects funded by the former were frequently published within the latter. To give a few specific examples (taken from Center for Urban Ethnography 1978):

- Both books published by Hymes (1974, 1981b), and both books published by Goffman (1970, 1981) in their book series were listed as having been supported by CUE.
- Labov was a fellow at CUE, first receiving funding for time spent writing, and then receiving two book contracts with the series (1972a, 1972b).[102]

- Dennis Tedlock had a CUE grant for one project, resulting in two publications, neither of which was part of the series (1976; Tedlock and Tedlock 1975), and then a book contract with the series for another project (1983).
- Dan Rose received funding from CUE first for fieldwork and then for writing up his dissertation (1973; as detailed in 1987, 223), which was later published in the book series (1987). That book details Goffman's influence on his choice of research methods. In addition, Rose published a different book in the series as well (1981).

What might not be immediately obvious from the list of authors is that the series was primarily, certainly in the years considered here, a way for Penn faculty (and occasionally students, or those affiliated with CUE) to get their work published. As Hymes explained to a non-Penn author (whose work was eventually published elsewhere): "Erv and I have been intending to discuss the scope and future of the series which so far has been essentially a Penn faculty (or former student) series. Your book will provide a welcome concrete focus for this."[103] (In fact, the series did later accept work by those without Penn affiliations, but not often and not many.) Goffman was part of the larger discussion with the press of what should be accepted, and the obvious acceptance of work by faculty at Penn. As he wrote Hymes, "My position on our series is that we can insist on a couple of books that won't sell, but that for the rest the Press depends on being able to get most of its investment back. So quality and some salability would ordinarily be required. But both have accepted tacitly and tactfully a basic exception: books by full time members of the faculty when the book falls in the area covered by the series. Thus Worth and Feld."[104] (The books by Worth and Feld were in fact published in the series and are included in table 4.5.)

It is unclear whether the press knew about, or agreed with, the de facto limit to Penn-affiliated authors. Although it does seem they should have noticed, at least some of the correspondence indicates not. For example, six months later, McGuigan, the acquisitions editor, wrote to Hymes that the press should "be more than a passive receptor for manuscripts." He asked for names of those Hymes and Goffman considered potentially appropriate authors for the series, so the press could pitch the series to them.[105] There is no list of potential authors in the file, so it is unclear whether one was sent or not. The issue may have been dropped, because two weeks later Hymes wrote McGuigan an angry letter, saying, "I am outraged that the University of Pennsylvania Press will sponsor a party at the AFS meetings for a book by someone not at Penn, while ignoring Brian and myself. If I am to be insulted in this way, I simply will withdraw from any further connection with the Press. . . . A helluva reward for years of loyalty."[106] AFS is the American Folklore Society, of which Hymes then served as president; Brian is Sutton-Smith, who had just published not one but two books in the series. The matter turned out to be a misunderstanding, triggering apologies by Malcolm Call (associate director of the press) immediately, and from McGuigan as soon as he returned from a conference, explaining that the event was a Penn party at AFS and, with Hymes not attending that event, they simply thought they might sell a few of another author's books. Hymes apologized.[107]

When a new director was being hired for the press in 1979, Hymes wrote to Provost Gregorian on Goffman's behalf as well as his own, saying:

> I should just like to express concern that the new director will be someone academically oriented, having experience with university presses and their particular problems. And I very much hope that the new director will be someone interested in maintaining the special strengths of the Press in the areas of sociolinguistics, folklore, and symbolic anthropology. It has been rewarding to see these strengths develop, and to be able to contribute something to that development. There would be a great sense of loss if these strengths were to be abandoned.
>
> Erv Goffman joins me in this concern.[108]

In fact, the crisis was averted: The next director was just as happy with their book series, so there was no difficulty.

At the same time, Goffman was unhappy with the press for another reason, as Hymes told Philips: "Erv is miffed with the Press because the late director said it could not put books out in paperback, as well as hardback, unless they were sure to sell well on the basis of established reputations."[109] And then later: "Erv is adamant that the continuation of the series depends upon the Press bringing out the books in paper as well as hard cover. I agree with him." As there had just been a change of director at the press (Erwin had left for another job, and Morris English had just been hired), they could not get a quick answer.[110] In fact, over a year later, at least for *Forms of Talk*, the press agreed to publish both cloth and paperback editions at the same time.[111]

As compared to Goffman's reviews for *Language in Society*, which frequently provided not just detailed but extensive critique, his reviews for the book series, where they have survived, are less detailed. He explained the distinction he was making to Hymes: "I felt my complaints would not be taken as those of a critic, to be attended to or not as the writer sees fit, but as an editor who might not accept a ms if displeased by it. You might be in the same position. Let's have a chat about it."[112] It seems surprising that Goffman was so careful not to come across as heavy-handed, even when he had considerable notes that might have been useful to an author. Perhaps especially so because Hymes did not seem to share the same qualms, as evident in a letter he sent Goffman with nine single-spaced pages of notes about how he thought a collection for the series was good but might be completely reconceptualized to make it even stronger.[113]

This book series was actually one of a set having overlapping editorial responsibilities. In 1967, the Haney Foundation agreed to sponsor The Haney Foundation Series in the Humanities and Social Sciences through Penn Press, and Hymes served on the editorial committee (along with Goldstein, and several others from Penn not otherwise mentioned in these pages). Basically, it was a way to be able to publish "works of scholarly value and interest which might not otherwise easily find their way into print without financial assistance."[114] Hymes chaired the Haney Foundation Committee for much of the time,[115] meaning that he would already have known the relevant staff at Penn Press and understood the general processes they followed before *Conduct and Communication* even began. In that capacity, he asked Goffman for help in locating reviewers for at least one submitted manuscript.[116]

And there were other relevant series. Just before *Conduct and Communication* was established, in 1968, Goldstein founded Monographs in Folklore and Folklife at Penn Press, with the first one published being a book by Glassie (1968). Associate editors for that series included Ben-Amos, Hymes, and Szwed, as well as Tristram Coffin and Don Yoder, senior colleagues in the folklore department.[117] Kirshenblatt-Gimblett's book was accepted into the *Conduct and Communication* series, but not before being the subject of a small tug of war. Hymes mentioned to Sherzer that "Ken Goldstein likes it for the folklore series here, and Erv is sympathetic for our series. . . . He thinks very highly of Barbara."[118] After reading the manuscript, Goffman had "reservations," mostly due to it being the first edited volume considered for the series.[119] In the end, it was accepted, but a question remained about the title. Kirshenblatt-Gimblett wrote, "I'd like to approach Erving Goffman on the title question as he has a flare for good titles."[120] In fact, the final title was slightly revised (1976), but there is no documentation showing whether that was Goffman's suggestion or not. Another example is Fought's book *Chorti Mayan Texts* (1972a), which was accepted into Goldstein's series, with the support of the Haney Foundation, as well as reviews by Goldstein and Ben-Amos.[121]

Then, in 1980, Labov and Sankoff began co-editing a new series, Quantitative Analyses of Linguistic Structure, for Academic Press, publishing a collection edited by Labov (1980) as the first volume. Hymes and Goffman had an exchange about whether that new series should be viewed as a competitor to their own. Goffman argued that it absolutely should not. Apparently, they were both startled that Labov had not mentioned it ahead of time, given how well they knew him and how often they talked. Goffman concluded that if he were to be upset, it would be for proposing the series with Academic Books rather than Penn Press.[122] Here Hymes was the outraged party, while Goffman was the one arguing for reason and calm. Perhaps for that reason, it was signed "love, Erv," which was not the way his letters were usually signed, at least not to Hymes.

The next year, 1981, in writing about the press and its financial difficulties (there was a good chance of significant funding decreases), Labov mentioned that he and Sankoff had proposed a new series on Language Change and Variation, which would have supplemented Conduct and Communication.[123] He pointed out that if funding were withdrawn from the press, they could easily move the series to another academic press, since they had received significant interest. It seems that series never appeared (although a journal of the same title did).

Earlier, in 1974, there was discussion of a multidisciplinary research project on Native American use of language (and likely also narratives) that was to involve Fought and Goldstein as well as both Dell and Virginia Hymes, but that also never appeared in print.[124] A few years later, yet another series under consideration (or perhaps the 1974 series reconfigured?) would have involved Dell Hymes, Wallace, Fought, and John Gerard Witthoft.[125] Erwin told Hymes:

> The notion of a Native American series suits me right down to the ground. An editorial board consisting of you, Wallace, Witthoft, and Fought would be perfect, and I would ask the Editorial Committee [of the press] to delegate power of approval, so as to give you a freer hand and save time and paperwork.... The only thing is, books on Navajo ritual and such are not likely to be lucrative. It would be ghastly to start up and then fizzle out after a couple of books. I suggest that a sound foundation would be $10,000 and a salable book for the first offering. This base could become a revolving fund that kept us going indefinitely. Any ideas on where to see the $10,000 start-up fund?[126]

Hymes was deeply offended by the suggestion that books on Native Americans might not sell well, arguing that of all the groups, the Navajo were particularly well recognized nationally. He concluded with the beautiful phrase: "I thought I was offering you a strawberry amidst a snow."[127] After a further exchange of letters, Hymes wrote that "John Fought is enthusiastic about a series of publications in this area and will try to think about possibilities for funding,"[128] so apparently he himself had given up the fight. Without obvious funding, that series also never appeared.

A final proposal for a series at the press was made in 1978 by Sapir (years after he had left Penn), jointly with Chris Crocker and Peter Metcalf, for a series tentatively to be called Studies in the Ethnography of Symbolic Forms, adapting the title of a course Hymes originally developed at Penn, and then turned over to Sapir. "I am taking the liberty of sending a copy of this letter to Dell who would be interested in making sure the series, if it ever comes to pass, would fit in and complement his and Erving's."[129] Given that notice, Erwin immediately wrote to Hymes saying, "I would appreciate your confidential advice."[130] Hymes responded fairly quickly, and was generally positive.[131] Oddly, no one seems to have copied Goffman on the issue, but presumably he was told about it in person. That series also did not appear.

The original Conduct and Communication series had a crisis in the last six months of Goffman's life. The concern he had expressed in 1980 had only grown: He apparently wanted either to expand beyond Penn affiliates, and/or to halt publication until more sociologically oriented manuscripts were submitted. In April 1982, McGuigan told Hymes, "I've gotten some strange words from Erving, concerning the series. We need to talk about this."[132] Hymes responded the next day: "I haven't heard anything from Erv about the series, but will be glad to talk to you about it," mentioning that he did know about Goffman's "general complaint about sociologically oriented work being lacking."[133] After some discussion of two volumes then under consideration for the series, Hymes went on to say:

> In regard to Erv's missing sociologically strong work, I can only agree, and wish that he could recommend some to us. That absence doesn't seem a reason for failing to publish work with other kinds of strength. I don't know whether or not he would think that William Corsaro at Indiana, or Aaron Cicourel at San Diego, or any other particular person would be likely to provide a book of the sort he would like to see. I would be glad to help encourage anyone that he thought we should encourage.[134]

It does not seem unreasonable to expect that, of the two editors, the sociologist would be the one to locate relevant submissions emphasizing society over language. An undated letter in the file from Hymes to McGuigan seems to come next, implying that they have had a conversation in person (otherwise there are missing letters):

> A few thoughts about the conduct and communication series.
>
> In terms of interest and range, Gillian Sankoff would be an obvious choice to replace Erving. And I would be willing to ask her the embarrassing question. Possibly even he would see that as a diplomatic outcome. . . .
>
> Seeking for balance on the anthropological side, I think of John Szwed, but don't know how consistently he would respond. John might be less of an overlap with the folklore series? I think Henry would be very good, but with Henry my tendency is to think we need a third person not identified with folklore to maintain the "conduct and communication" balance, even without and despite Erving. Although he is junior, Steven Feld is a possibility? Though I don't know anything about him in an editorial capacity. Larry Gross might be better, more experienced. And of sufficient standing not to make Erving think he had been traded in for a tenderfoot.
>
> On balance, my thoughts run to a trio, to make it seem less inviting to copare [*sic*] new single person with Erving: Gillian, if possible, and one or two out of the set of Szwed, Glassie, Gross, keeping in mind a need to maintain distinction from folklore . . .[135]

McGuigan responded that "with luck, the business with Erving and the Series will be resolved one way or the other."[136] Then Hymes talked with Goffman and wrote McGuigan a lengthy explanation of what was going on.

> Erv Goffman called me yesterday morning (Thursday) to tell me his views on the series and the two manuscripts now being considered for it (Bauman, Tedlock). He said he was going to call you later that morning. . . .
>
> I understand some of Erv's view but not all of it. At the heart appears to be a dissatisfaction, indeed a change of heart, about the network of personal ties and relationships that has been involved in the series. Essentially it has been a Penn-based series, bringing out collections and work by people here—Birdwhistell, Erv himself, L[a]bov, myself, Gillian, Erv and me again. That has seemed to me a virtue. There is an increasing amount of publication, almost a flood, in the areas touched upon by the series. Academic Press, Cambridge, Routledge Kegan Paul and others bringing out a great deal. The advantage to the University and to the Press, I think, is the presentation of scholarship from our own matrix, or connected closely with its strengths. It is hard to imagine a different conception,

one that would not become diffuse, eclectic and difficult to differentiate from any other collection. . . .

[Details about Bauman's manuscript under consideration] . . . The fact that we know Dick, that he was at Penn, that Texas has various personal links with us, seems to trouble Erv, almost as if incestuous; but it is hard for me to conceive of the series on another basis than one of a network, which is indeed the basis it has had. I don't feel any embarrassment, unlike Erv, about having published Worth's book. I continue to feel that it was something that should be done.

[Details about Tedlock's manuscript under consideration] . . . The essential thing, I believe, is that publishing it will strengthen the Press and the University in one of its areas of scholarly strength, verbal art, folklore, ethnopoetics, and the like, and the interaction between it on the list of the Press, my book, Henry Glassie's books, will be good for all concerned.

If it would resolve Erv's concerns to reserve final judgment on the Bauman book until we see the final manuscript, and to introduce Tedlock's book in the other series, I would be happy to agree with him this far in the interests of maintaining a longstanding partnership.

What I can't accept is that the series should become dormant or that in principle we ought not to look to our friends, colleagues, and former students for contributions. We ought to be judicious, of course. And in regard to strength from the sociological side, I would be eager to have any manuscripts that could be suggested of that kind.[137]

In response, a month later McGuigan wrote about a particular book under consideration, then said: "Erving returns on Monday. It's time, I think, for a final session with Erving—and for a final determination of Erving's status as series editor."[138] Hymes returned to Goffman's concerns:

My memory of Erv's telephone conversation with me, before he left, is that he thought of putting the series as such on hold for a while, on the ground of a lack of suitable books.

This seems to me the fundamental question. I should not like to see the series suspended, let alone ended, and do not share the view that there will not be a chance of suitable books in the near future. That seems to me to be the general question, separable from a judgment of a particular book's appropriateness for inclusion.

If Erving sees the possibility of continuing the series actively on a case-by-case basis, I should not want to prevent his doing so by insisting on including [a particular] book in the series. It is a good book, worth publishing, but I am not so enthusiastic about it as to rupture a long-standing relationship with Erving over it. . . .

> If, however, Erv does not think that [this] book is the issue in and of itself, but the series as such, then I feel that we should try to see what might be done to keep the series going.[139]

The question here is why Hymes was not simply meeting with Goffman to sort things out. Apparently, Goffman was out of town part of the time, but surely not across all these months. And Hymes was in Oregon in summers, but only for the few summer months. This issue extended far longer.

Then there is a large gap in the file, with no further relevant correspondence until Goffman's death in November 1982, when McGuigan writes to Hymes, saying he has just heard about Goffman from Grimshaw. "Damn, I still can't accept the fact—Erving was too much a fighter."[140] In his response, Hymes focused on the implications for the series.

> Erving's death poses the question of the Conduct and Communication Series acutely, as you realize. My immediate thought is that we should proceed to invite Henry Glassie to be an editor of the series, as we have discussed with each other and with Henry. And that it would be desirable to have a third person as an editor—I believe we discussed that as well. Earlier I mentioned Brian Sutton-Smith and Larry Gross as people whose interests might reinforce the "communication" and social science aspects of the series. Now I think it would be a good idea to invite Gillian Sankoff to be the third editor. Gillian is rooted in the linguistic side of the field, as a member of the Dept. of Linguistics full time; she has a wide network of friends in linguistics and anthropology; she knows the sociolinguistic work of Bill Labov's sort first hand, including quantitative analyses of linguistic variation.
>
> With such a set of three, I think we could responsibly cover quite a range of prospective materials, from the kind of work that might involve considerable technical linguistics (like Bill Labov's two volumes in the series) to work whose focus was more cultural and theoretical (as my first book might be said to be). Henry has a familiarity with linguistics and the ethnography of communication, as does Gillian and as of course do I, yet extends our range considerably through his knowledge of material culture and ethnography in western societies. The three together ought to be able to provide good judgment and prospects.[141]

Hymes went on to suggest that Tedlock's book should be the first item on the agenda for the new editors. It was in fact accepted and published (1983). A week later McGuigan agreed that "Henry is of course a logical successor. And your suggestion of Gillian is a marvelous idea, and would represent both a touching and appropriate gesture of continuity."[142] Sankoff did agree, as did Glassie.[143] His answer has been preserved: "It humbles me and honors me to be asked to serve with Gillian and Dell as co-editor of the Conduct and Communication series. I accept and will do what I can."[144] Summary notes from a meeting of John McGuigan of the press, Hymes, Sankoff, and Glassie in April 1983, indicate the following agreements:

1. In public announcements (e.g., catalog and/or advertising), the Press shall announce the name of the series, the names of the new editorial board, the list of series titles, and a brief statement that will include a) our deep regrets over the loss of Erving; b) a sentence affirming the continuous existence of the Series, "devoted to well grounded work in communicative conduct and all its aspects"; c) and a concluding sentence to the effect that the Press is pleased to announce that Gillian Sankoff and Henry Glassie have agreed to join Dell Hymes as co-editors.

2. All Series books after Tedlock will carry with the series title the names of Erving and Dell as "Founding Editors," followed by the names of the present general editors.

3. Dennis Tedlock's THE SPOKEN WORD AND THE WORK OF INTER-PRETATION will be included in the Series, under the editorship of Dell and Erving.[145]

This is interesting precisely because Goffman withheld his decision about the Tedlock book until he could see the revisions, but then ran out of time before that was possible.[146] Books published in the series after Goffman's death include: Tedlock (1983), Basso (1985), Moerman (1987), Rose (1987), Briggs (1988), Errington (1988), Kuipers (1990), and Trix (1993).

There is one final part to the story of the series and the press related to Goffman. The university decided it had an interest in "recognizing Erving's contribution to its distinction in sociolinguistics and related fields—to give some practical sign of its appreciation" and so Maurice English, then director of the press, reported to Mary Ann Meyers (then secretary of the board of directors)[147] and Provost Thomas Ehrlich that he had met with Sankoff and offered that the university (not the press) would cover all reasonable costs related to preparing Goffman's unpublished papers as a book. This was to include copyediting, research, collation etc.; the time of Lee Ann Draud (who had moved from working for Goffman to being copy editor for the press); and course release for Sankoff so she would have time available to work on the project. What they wanted in exchange was an estimate of costs.[148] Obviously, such a volume was never published, in the Conduct and Communication series or elsewhere.

Language in Society (*LiS*)

In addition to the book series with Goffman, Hymes established a new journal, *Language in Society* (LiS). There was discussion of the need for a journal
focusing on sociolinguistics at the SSRC Committee on Sociolinguistics in
1968, led by Hymes, supported by Charles Ferguson (then committee chair),
who followed up by writing a memorandum explaining why this might be
needed, for use by anyone on the committee who wanted to pursue the possibility. In that memo, Ferguson referenced comments that he, Hymes, and
Paul Friedrich had been mentioned as examples of scholars who might be
appropriate as editors.[149] Apparently, Hymes mentioned the possibility of a
new journal to Thomas Sebeok at a conference in Urbana, Italy that summer,
who then urged all haste in establishing something.[150] Hymes told Ferguson
that Sebeok had offered to publish the new journal through the Language
Research Center at Indiana. They had also discussed potential editorial
board members, with Sebeok suggesting Grimshaw, of whom Hymes said,
"I would think of him as quite possible [*sic*] a key member of the editorial
committee." At the same time, he clarified: "I would like to have it always
clear that in proposing such a jornal [*sic*], and arguing for the need for it, I
did not envisage myself as editor, though I did have in mind being an active
participant." Instead, he thought Ferguson the obvious choice, with Joshua
Fishman as a possible second choice. He also thought an existing journal,
such as *Word*, might agree to be "responsible for sociolinguistics" as part
of a broader mandate in linguistics. He proposed potential advisory board
members, including Goffman, arguing that "Goffman might take an active
part on an editorial board."[151]

In early 1969, Frances Welch at Cambridge University Press wrote to
John Pride at the University of Leeds about starting a new journal in sociolinguistics. She asked whether he could talk about it with Hymes who
would be visiting England, and to write up their ideas for the journal, so
presumably this was in response to an effort by Hymes to talk with Pride (or
Welch) about whether Cambridge would be an appropriate publisher.[152] At
that point, Hymes still hesitated to become editor. He wrote Elbridge Sibley
(staff at SSRC), "I am ambivalent. No one is eager to undertake the work,
and to add yet another title to the many that exist. At the same time it is a
great weakness to the subject not to have any central place of publication,
and even more, review and regular coverage. No one journal interested
students can be advised to get and read."[153] Grimshaw was the committee

member delegated to look into possible publishers, so he organized meetings with University of New Mexico Press, Indiana University Press, Academic, Sage, and Cambridge University Press to gauge their interest.[154] The draft document (presumably to use in those meetings) attached to the letter says there were already "over 500 scholars on the mailing list for the Sociolinguistics Committee," so there should be an established audience available for a new journal. In response, Hymes said, "I was surprised to learn that the committee had come to the decision to launch a journal. As before, I believe it desirable, but am ambivalent about the energy required." If this were to happen, he said he would "urge giving CUP serious consideration" because it would be international, but with a New York office for convenience, and he stressed the importance of this being an international effort.[155] Ferguson told Hymes: "My chief concern in all this at the moment is that you be personally committed to a key role in the publication of the journal, preferably as its responsible editor."[156] The meeting between Hymes, Pride, and Michael Black (chief editor at CUP) occurred in June 1969, with Black agreeing to work with Grimshaw on technical details. Given a choice, Hymes clearly preferred Cambridge over other options, even Sebeok's, for the prestige and international connections. Black also asked Hymes to become the editor, but he was still hesitating. As he told Grimshaw: "All this has gone a bit further faster than I had quite prepared myself for." Hymes asked if the committee could meet with Black that fall in New York.[157] Simultaneously, he wrote much the same letter to Ferguson, to keep him in the loop.[158] Cambridge clearly was interested, as Black followed up immediately with a long letter providing details.[159] Grimshaw forwarded that on to all committee members, pointing out that they were unlikely to get a better offer, and arguing that they should ask Hymes to be editor, put together an editorial board, and immediately start commissioning manuscripts for the first two issues.[160] The committee met with Elizabeth Case representing Cambridge (and based in their New York office) in the fall,[161] asked Hymes to be editor, and the project moved forward quickly. Hymes asked Provost Goddard for support (that Penn would formally be signatory to the letter, given that the committee could not play that role, and that he be provided funding for a half-time assistant to work on the journal); both requests were granted. Basically, Hymes argued that this would put Penn "at the communicative center of the field; it would be good for our interested faculty and students, and would give Penn the reputation of being not only a center, but perhaps the center for the subject in many countries."[162] Hymes copied the chairs of anthropology, linguistics, psychology, and sociology on his letter, because "I would expect to associate Professor Hoenigswald and Professor Goffman with me closely in the planning of the journal and one or more interested colleagues in other departments."

Six months later, in spring 1970, the committee was running out of funds and considering whether to ask SSRC to close them down. Hymes used the not-yet-started journal as part of the argument for why he did not want them to disband at that point, characterizing himself as "the editor of the yet to be born journal, who felt rather as if he had been cast out of the crib before his time."[163] He also suggested that an obvious solution for those who felt "what we need most is not a committee meeting, but time for our work" was to recommend that they bring in younger members who might have more energy (this is how Sherzer and Sankoff came to be invited to join the committee).[164] The group agreed, and decided to hold another meeting shortly to sort things out. At that meeting, Ferguson strongly suggested that they also should organize a conference to evaluate the state of sociolinguistics,[165] which led to the Georgetown University Round Table Conference on Sociolinguistics: Current Trends and Prospects, held in 1972, organized primarily by committee member Roger Shuy (published as Shuy 1973a).[166] (This is another conference in which Goffman participated, in this case as one of a set of plenary speakers, although one of the first things Shuy says in his published introduction is "It is regrettable that the presentation by Erving Goffman will not be included at the author's request" (1973b, v). The issue was likely that Goffman had arranged to publish his presentation elsewhere. All of this is relevant context for understanding the difficulties of establishing a new journal, deciding who to choose as publisher and editor, and all of that happening at just the moment the committee was running out of funds as well as energy on the part of long-serving members. In the end, instead of folding, they took reasonable steps to stay active: They did start the journal, they did hold a major conference to gauge the current state of sociolinguistics, and they did apply for, and receive, additional grant funding to keep a surprising number of widely divergent projects going across the country (especially involving Gumperz and Ervin-Tripp at Berkeley, Grimshaw at Indiana, as well Sherzer at Texas). And, perhaps most importantly, the funded projects did result in multiple conferences and publications, positively influencing the growth of sociolinguistics.

The idea of a sociolinguistics journal apparently had been on many people's minds, not just those of committee members. Both Mouton[167] and the University of Hawaii[168] were considering starting overlapping journals; both said they would not want to compete if Hymes went ahead with the journal they had heard he was considering. After an exchange of letters, Kenneth Jackson at Hawaii offered to divide up topics so both journals could move forward.[169] Hymes declined, finding that idea "not really possible."[170] It does seem reasonable that he did not want to divide up the territory of such a new topic too quickly, thereby limiting what could be accepted by his own journal before he even got it started, especially given that a major goal was to develop a single journal for sociolinguistics as a single topic.

Hymes wrote to Gumperz (and a dozen others) in 1970, saying, "Cambridge University Press has invited me to serve as editor of a journal in the field of sociolinguistic research. I should like to invite you to be a member of the editorial board."[171] As he was getting things organized, he explained the logic: "The time for a truly 'sociolinguistic' communicative approach to speech is almost upon us. As something that will not be a principle, but a growing practice. Right now there seems a real possibility of a new journal, perhaps published by Cambridge University Press (who want to do it) that could shape this field."[172] Their first task was to choose a good name: "Suggestions so far include: Journal of Sociolinguistics; Journal of Sociolinguistic Studies; Language in Society (perhaps with the sub-title, A journal of sociolinguistic (and ethnolinguistic?) research)."[173] The first issue of what the group decided to name *Language in Society* appeared in 1972. Hymes served as editor for twenty years, until 1992. Labov and Grimshaw served as associate editors. Goffman served on the editorial board from 1974 until his death. Labov and Grimshaw began as members of the editorial board, like all the others, but after the first year, Hymes realized he was calling on their areas of expertise far more often than on others, and he decided they needed to be formally recognized.[174] In response to the invitation to become an associate editor, Labov responded by saying, "You are the activist editor a great journal needs."[175] This comment was followed by four single-spaced pages of detailed discussion of who was doing good, or not so good, work in sociolinguistics at the time. Labov concluded with the importance of having direction from a single editor who could set the tone.

Goffman never served as an official associate editor, but he reviewed an absolutely astonishing number of submissions—far more than most others in that role, so far as I have seen, and his reviews often provided far more detailed analysis. In addition to his editorial role, Goffman also published in *LiS*—specifically, "Replies and Responses" (1976b, later reprinted in *Forms of Talk* (1981). He also submitted "Felicity's Condition" for consideration. Hymes reluctantly pointed out that, while he appreciated "your willingness to think about contributing to the journal," and it "has some neat points," it was "long for the journal, I'm afraid," both in terms of number of pages but also as "a fairly leisurely presentation,"[176] so instead Goffman published it in the *American Journal of Sociology* (1983). As well, Hymes wrote editorials and an enormous number of book reviews; Labov wrote several articles (1972e, 1973); and Fought wrote a review of a book of Goffman's (1972b), as well as many others. *LiS* was obviously a multidisciplinary journal (given that Hymes was then in anthropology, Labov in linguistics, and Grimshaw in sociology), providing an outlet for the new interdisciplinary subject of sociolinguistics, just as the Committee on Sociolinguistics had envisioned.

Hymes's "ambitious vision" in establishing the journal was characterized recently by Ehrlich and Milani as "the publication of empirically-grounded analyses that push linguistic and social theory in new and exciting directions" (2021, 1). Michael Silverstein puts it particularly well, explaining that "Hymes's editorial style at *Language in Society* was to lead, in the slow motion of a print journal, a virtual seminar in which his contributing authors spoke to and through him to their readership" (2010, 937). Similarly, Christina Bratt Paulston has said, "Submitting an article to Language in Society when Dell Hymes was editor became a tutorial in sociolinguistics" (in Johnstone 2010, 312).

Hymes documented some of Goffman's reviews of *LiS* submissions in a paper for the memorial session honoring both Goffman and Hughes at the American Sociological Association in fall 1983 (published as Hymes 1984). As he explained to Sankoff when requesting permission to quote from what Goffman wrote, "One resource I want to use are the analytic comments Erving included in evaluation [*sic*] mss. for Language in Society. Some of them show nicely his concern for certain kinds of standards, and yet also for encouraging younger people. . . . Of course I would protect the innocent (and guilty alike), not identifying individuals."[177] Goffman's comments were incisive, blunt, occasionally even cutting. But they were always carefully worded, as when he argued against the use of only minimal text for analysis: "After all, to ask us to focus on such a small strip when there is no way for us to know the *biography of the occasion* and its participants is to imply that magical unpacking is going to occur. But it doesn't." (Goffman, quoted in Hymes 1984, 624; emphasis added). So far as I can determine that wonderful phrase, "the biography of the occasion," does not even show up in Goffman's publications, but it is perfectly clear and seems quintessential Goffman. As Hymes goes on to explain, "The controlling consideration, for Erving as editor, was rather a finely tuned sense of what would and would not suffice, given the state of the art and the advancing edge of understanding in the field" (623). Hymes emphasizes Goffman's "insistence on the situation as a whole, on doing what is required to learn about the relevant local world as well as a detail" (624), and the quotes from reviews make clear his unhappiness with "worrying a small piece of data to death" (625).

In addition to the selections from reviews made available by Hymes, entire letters with either those or other reviews are now available as part of the Hymes Papers at the American Philosophical Society, making clear that Goffman wrote exceedingly long and detailed responses to submissions. Interestingly, many of his comments were not necessarily appropriate to pass on to authors. As when he concluded three pages of notes by saying: "Dell, I don't know what, if anything, of this can be conveyed to the authors. For me the lesson is that in inviting all the new perspectives, we should be careful not to allow shiny appearances to blind us to the absence of any substance."[178] Goffman was both funny and good at stepping back to look at the larger picture, as when he said, after reading a paper he suggested be rejected, "Perhaps there ought to be some sort of sifting process by someone not yourself or me to weed out these particular flowers of academia."[179] A week later, he apologized for that "ill-tempered" response, explaining that "I was seeking for a way, an objective correlate, to express my feeling about our having to deal with persons who have grade school intelligence and university connections."[180] Yet he continued to be just as critical, if not more so, in later reviews. A few examples of how he could be both cutting and funny follow:

- "As analysis this stuff is merely poor; as journalism, it is hopeless."[181]
- "I think this paper is more of a college try than a university success."[182]
- "The paper is entirely without merit . . . not a drop of data gets through. (I wish I could seal off my tile deck from the rain that well)."[183]
- "The paper is incomplete, unimaginative, but certainly half-worthwhile— indeed, worth publishing somewhere but not quite in LANGUAGE IN SOCIETY."[184]
- "A textbook example of trained incompetence. I'm glad he's one of theirs (psychology), not ours. I wonder how God feels about graduate schools doing this to students' heads: how sad and resigned S/He must be."[185]

Goffman was not always negative. Examples of exceedingly positive comments include:

- "a fresh and lively paper. I have learned considerably from it and I wish I had had access to it months ago."[186]
- "I think this paper deals with a significant topic and brings some significant order to it."[187]

But typically, he provided sharp critiques, worded in such a way as to be amusing, clearly intended for Hymes rather than the author of a paper he was reviewing, as made particularly obvious when he writes, "Do let me know your response to my response, so I can let you know mine to yours." And signs himself in that letter "Entanglingly yours."[188] Hymes concluded at one point, "I wish the papers we get for the journal were as much fun and worth reading as the letters you write to reject them."[189] It is revealing to see how Hymes handled Goffman's critiques in his role as journal editor: He obviously understood them as part of an extended conversation between Goffman and himself rather than automatically being intended for those submitting the manuscripts. Typically, he did not pass on Goffman's lengthy comments (often two or three single-spaced pages), but rather a gentler version of the conclusion. He did explicitly tell Goffman that "I always want your judgment . . . and value your analyses highly. . . . I don't recall offhand ever deciding to publish something you were set against."[190] At least once Hymes referred to Goffman in a letter to an author as "a very esteemed colleague" when passing on a specific positive comment.[191] Goffman was fine with not having his entire review passed on to authors, as he made clear by saying, "In any case, your job is to treat my view as merely another one and decide for yourself."[192]

Both Goffman and Hymes were well aware of the extensive relevant literature being published elsewhere, leading to casual comments about where else a submission might be published if rejected by *LiS*, or comments about already having read a prior publication by an author. As a result, when Goffman recommended rejecting a submission, he often then made suggestions for where it might better fit, as when he said: "Perhaps you might recommend Gerbner's journal *Communication* or *Public Opinion Quarterly*,"[193] neither of which was a journal most sociologists could be assumed to be reading.

Goffman was substantially involved in discussions of the direction and impact of *LiS*, not only as a reviewer or author. For example, in 1974, as part of a long letter to Labov about the difficulties in maintaining adequate funding (since, at two years since creation, the journal was not yet fully subscribed to a sufficient level that all costs were covered), Hymes mentioned: "In talking to Erv, I found that he sees the fundamental issue, as far as he is concerned, as that of making visible our interests and activities, so that Penn will have a distinctive image that will attract good students. This makes great sense to me. Erv seems to think that the journal contributes to this image—certainly it should do so, and I hope that it does."[194] Having just documented that Goffman wanted their book series to move beyond the Penn network, it may seem surprising that he was happy to limit *LiS* to that same network. The difference is likely one of timing – what made sense in 1974 (when he considered a Penn emphasis appropriate for the journal) may no longer have seemed as reasonable in 1980–1982 (when he expressed concern about publishing only authors affiliated with Penn in the book series), given the considerable expansion in numbers of those who might write appropriate submissions over that time.

In 1976, there was an exchange of letters about whether to move *LiS* from Cambridge because the purchase price for subscribers was too high. The initial letter Hymes wrote about this has not been preserved, but Goffman's answer has; he offers to help make connections with other publishers. He begins by emphasizing the significance of *LiS*: "About the journal: I think it is crucial for us all and for the University" and ends: "We do so need continuation of what LANGUAGE IN SOCIETY does."[195] In response, Hymes explained: "I have to apologize. I flew into a fit without reading far enough." It turned out that the high purchase price was for libraries, not individuals, so the crisis was averted.[196] Even so, what we learn here is both how much Goffman valued *LiS*, and how he took on the role of being the voice of reason: stepping back to reiterate the importance of their endeavor, and providing helpful, concrete suggestions, rather than fanning the flames of anger.

In 1979, Grimshaw and Hymes corresponded about a paper that Grimshaw had submitted to *LiS*, and which was not as well received as he might have hoped (remember, he had strongly supported the establishment of this new journal and helped to find an appropriate publisher a decade earlier). Grimshaw wrote that he was "deeply distressed" by Hymes's reaction and also that "I suspect, on the basis of Erving's reactions to some earlier papers of mine, that he won't much care for this one either."[197] Hymes responded, "I asked Erv to look at the paper."[198] The next letter in the file is from Grimshaw to Hymes, thanking him for a letter not preserved, but which apparently included "your reasons for nonenthusiasm about my paper. I withdraw it from consideration (a superfluous action under the circumstances) and will publish it elsewhere. I will publish it in spite of the fact that you and Erv think it is seriously defective because I don't, in this instance, share your view. . . . Warm personal regards, as always."[199] Presumably the closing meant that he would not let disagreement about the value of his manuscript come between friends. Indeed, two months later, he invited Hymes to submit a paper to a special issue on sociolinguistics he was organizing for the journal *Society*.[200] Hymes turned the opportunity down due to having too many other commitments, but he did so in a friendly way that makes clear he also assumed the friendship had survived.[201] It is important that for all three of them—Goffman, Hymes, Grimshaw—friendship came first, and was strong enough that it could withstand occasional disagreements, as documented in multiple places throughout this book.

In his remembrance of Goffman published in *LiS*, Grimshaw specifically points out his "valuable service to this journal" (1983, 147). The essentials about Goffman's time on the *LiS* editorial board are that he frequently reviewed submissions, that he took the time to write quite lengthy and considered responses complete with incisive comments that read like some of his publications, and that Hymes as editor nearly always trusted his judgment, even turning down manuscripts he personally found to have potential value. To extend Silverstein's evaluation, it was not only Hymes who used the journal to lead a virtual seminar in slow motion, but Goffman also, through his comments.

Service to *LiS* overlapped with that to the Center for Urban Ethnography for both Goffman and Hymes. From the start, submissions to the journal were to be sent to Hymes in care of CUE;[202] this continued until 1977, when the address changed slightly to Hymes at GSE (as a reminder, Hymes moved to GSE in 1975, and CUE ran out of funding in 1974, so this seems a reasonable and obvious move). Also, the journal was included in the list of official Center-sponsored activities: "The principal investigators, in addition to their publications, also undertook a number of activities of relevance to the grant: Dell Hymes founded and edits the journal *Language in Society . . .*" (Center for Urban Ethnography 1974, 4). In the brief notice marking the end of his time as editor of *LiS* after twenty years, Hymes thanks "all who have contributed to the journal and to its work" including "John Szwed and Erving Goffman, who, through the Center for Urban Ethnography at the University of Pennsylvania, gave it its first home" (1992, 711; see also

Center for Urban Ethnography 1974). Specifically, what the center did for the journal was to cover mailing costs (for correspondence, not mailing the journal to subscribers).[203]

In addition, there was an overlap between the journal, *LiS*, and the book series, Conduct and Communication. In 1975, Hymes wrote to Goffman:

> Bill reports to me that you mentioned to him (as you had before to me) the notion of a volume collecting articles from Language in Society. It wasn't clear to me whether or not you thought we would be able to publish such a collection with the Press here. Cambridge has copyright; whether or not they would want to release copyright to another publisher, I don't know. They haven't broken even on the journal yet (because of rising costs); if there were to be a possibility of recouping from a collection, they might want themselves to be the beneficiary.
>
> Anyway, it is worth thinking about. My own thought is that it might be possible to choose a worthwhile set from the first five years (through 1976), to find papers that could be represented as representative of something. It's not completely certain. I'd appreciate very much your own suggestions. With them in hand, I could raise the matter with Cambridge sometime soon. . . .
>
> One principle of selection might be to put modalities, devices, ways of speaking to the fore; perhaps the journal title, LANGUAGE IN SOCIETY, ought to be the title of a volume, suitably accompanied; and/or perhaps some other title would be best, but I'd hope we could use the journal title, explaining any focus in selection of contents by subtitle or preface.[204]

The remainder of the letter provides several possible arrangements of topics and articles to place in each section. He includes a plea, "Please don't go on acting as [*sic*] I had gone awol," a likely reference to the fact that Goffman was talking about this with Labov rather than with him directly (the presumed cause being that Hymes had literally just assumed the position of dean of GSE at that point, which undoubtedly kept him busier than he had been as a faculty member, and moved him physically and administratively out of the College of Arts and Sciences). The idea of a collection came up again in 1976, when Goffman wrote Hymes: "You might want to give some more consideration to bringing out a book of papers from the Journal."[205] Apparently there was at least some further discussion, because in 1977 an editor at Cambridge wrote to Hymes, "I am hoping to hear further from you, also, about a book derived from previous issues of *Language in Society*. Don't let's drop that idea."[206] In any case, such a collection was never published. Hymes explained part of the difficulty in a letter a few years later, when mentioning the idea to Sherzer and John Baugh, who had written him about a reader they were then preparing (Baugh and Sherzer 1984). "Erv a few years ago suggested an anthology from Language in Society, and Cambridge expressed interest. Of the editors, only David Crystal replied, very much opposed, to an inquiry about the idea. There are quite a few good pieces in the 9 years, I think, but I can't find time in the foreseeable future to construct an anthology, or rather, to see one through (I did work up a table of contents)."[207] The reference to "editors" here is to "editorial board members," and so it was a combination of insufficient interest on the part of those most involved with the journal (who might have been assumed to be the most likely to want to order copies and use them in their own teaching, thus serving as a good indication of potential audience), and lack of time on Hymes's part that doomed the project.

Just as Goffman had to be replaced after his death for the book series, he had to be replaced on the editorial board of *LiS*. Barbara Colson, journals manager at CUP, sent a note in October 1983 reminding Hymes that "I don't believe an appointment has been submitted replacing Erving Goffman."[208] The immediate answer from Hymes was that "it is almost impossible to think of someone to replace Erving Goffman."[209] He asked Grimshaw who he thought would have a chance of taking Goffman's place. "A difficult question, though, is the loss of Erving. No one can write the kind of commentary he wrote, but are there people you would suggest in somewhat the same sphere? We do have Hugh Mehan on the board, as well as yourself (and Bill [Labov]). Is Fred Ericson [*sic*], now at Michigan State, an appropriate person? Or is my sense of a gap about a person, not a category?"[210] In addition to being associate editor for *LiS*, a sociologist, and a long-time friend of Goffman, Grimshaw had directly relevant experience as editor of *American Sociologist*. In answer, he sent extensive evaluation both of Goffman's past performance, and discussion of the scholars he thought might conceivably replace him on the board. Only a few segments can be quoted here.

> You remark that no one can write the kind of commentary Erving did; that is certainly true. What you don't mention is something that you may have come to take for granted in dealing with Erving as an editorial associate, i.e., his very high degree of professional responsibleness. You found, as did editors of at least several sociological journals, that Erving not only provided some very useful (and sometimes quotable) reviews, but that he also provided them with dispatch. He did an extraordinary amount of editorial reading (even more impressive in amount when his own high productivity is considered); he did it quickly and usually without complaint. Not only are there few people who can read so many

kinds of things with such insight and intelligence, even fewer work as efficiently as he apparently did. . . .

Erving's ability to simultaneously get his own work done and nonetheless accept and fulfill responsibilities for commentary on the work of others was unusual, if not unique. On a second dimension he may quite well have been unique. There are a number of sociologists who shared his interest in interaction and not a few who have interesting and insightful observations to make about what goes on in, e.g., focused and unfocused encounters. There are other sociologists who know quite a bit about talk, and even something about social accomplishment in talk.[211]

In the rest of the letter, Grimshaw reviews potential candidates for the position, searching for the perfect choice, what he called "a 'Goffman type' for your board" (mostly finding them inappropriate, often because they were so over-committed that they would not be able to make time for the necessary work). At the same time, Grimshaw describes his own future projects, ironically inviting Hymes to participate in one. In the process of the latter, he returns to his evaluation of Goffman's strengths, including the comment "I am a heavy user of Goffman" because, he explains, "Talk with him was always instructive; his writing influences most of what I did in the monograph and influences can be found scattered throughout my work."[212] The point here is not who they found to replace Goffman, but the shared high estimation of his abilities, despite the periodic times they all disagreed, and argued, and became angry with one another.

Just as there were other book series at Penn Press having overlapping editors, other journals were begun around the same time as *LiS*. There was a major complication the year after *LiS* began publishing: Joshua Fishman decided to establish the *International Journal of the Sociology of Language* (IJSL) and asked some of the same people to serve on his editorial board. In May 1973, when *LiS* had been operating for a year, Hymes told Grimshaw:

I have learned that Josh asked Erv Goffman, Courtney Cazden, Carl Voegelin, to be members. That sure doesn't appear to be a complementary approach. Erv thought it a bit thick and declined, and Cortney [*sic*] did also. I don't feel I can tell anyone what to do in such a case, and that I must make the best of it. Someone among middle-aged sociolinguists ought to try to rise above personal ambition and glory. It does take some edge of the pleasure of the work of the journal (for which I get nothing, and which takes much time). There has been the satisfaction of thinking oneself to be performing a unique service, bringing something into being not otherwise available. . . .

[Einar] Haugen apparently raised questions about the propriety or suitability of a second journal, and Fergie [Charles Ferguson] that he has not yet responded to an invitation, although probably he eventually will accept, but wishing it had not been launched at this time. Maybe in this case there is such a thing as a public opinion concerned with the best interests of the field. I do worry about financial success, viability. (May 8, 1973, ADG)

Hymes said much the same to Ferguson directly.

I have been troubled myself that Josh is going ahead with the Mouton journal, more so when I learned that he was asking so many people to be on the board that would seem to me to be more naturally involved with the emphases of LinS (more linguistic and ethnographic) than the other (presumably more sociological and institutional). He even invited Erv Goffman, which seemed a little thick (to Erving as well as to me).[213]

Oddly, especially given Hymes's frequent shows of temper in letters to people with whom he was angry, he maintained a cordial connection with Fishman. Fishman notified Hymes as soon as his new journal was approved, saying, "I have agreed (after initially refusing to do so for more than two years so that Dell Hyme's [sic] journal could become well established) to edit for Mouton an *International Journal of the Sociology of Language*." He then invited Hymes to join the editorial board himself, and to edit a special issue.[214] Given the way he has phrased this, it seems likely Mouton had mentioned their earlier exchange with Hymes, and that they probably did not expect a warm response. However, the response was remarkably cordial (again, especially for Hymes, who regularly shows anger in letters and, in this case, even more surprising given his comments to others as just quoted above): "I think it is a good policy to have 'interlocking directorates' in these matters."[215] So, unlike Goffman, Hymes immediately accepted a role on Fishman's editorial board, although he did decline the offer to edit a special issue. In any case, for the larger story told here, what is most noteworthy is that Goffman was immediately asked to serve on the editorial board of not just one but also a second sociolinguistics journal. Perhaps even more noteworthy is that he immediately refused out of loyalty. Grimshaw's response to *IJSL* was also interesting; in a letter to Hymes and David Jenness, staff to the Committee on Sociolinguistics, he wrote: "I see no reason why we should abandon the sociological side of language in society to him [Fishman]."[216] Therefore, he offered to spend more time encouraging more sociologists to submit to *Language in Society*. This was likely to be productive, since Grimshaw was a sociologist, having far more connections to other sociologists than did most linguists. A year later, Hymes expressed continuing concern that perceived duplication might lead to the destruction of both journals. "I don't see much comparison between first issues of the two journals, but the second might make just enough difference to prevent either from being solvent, and so lose both."²¹⁷ Perhaps surprisingly, both journals are still regularly publishing today, some fifty years later, a testament to the size and strength of the group of sociolinguists which developed.

Studies in the Anthropology of Visual Communication (*SAVICOM*)

Language in Society was not the only journal started at Penn in which Goffman was involved. *Studies in the Anthropology of Visual Communication* (SAVICOM) was established in 1974, under the auspices of the Society for the Study of Visual Communication, which developed out of the American Anthropological Association's Program in Ethnographic Film (for details of the founding of both the organization and the journal, see Takaragawa 2020; Worth 1980). Worth served both as president of the society and founding editor of the journal (Gross 1980). In his introduction to the first volume, Worth suggests: "The old disciplines are finally beginning to break down. People in Sociology, in Art History, in Psychology, as well as in Communication and Anthropology, are addressing themselves to similar problems" (1974, 1–2). He was referring specifically to visual communication, but it seems likely this comment was at least in part a result of the peer group at Penn in which both he and Goffman participated (so it is not unrelated to note that Birdwhistell and Hymes both served on the advisory committee of the Society for the Anthropology of Visual Communication). Just as Birdwhistell had earlier argued for the expansion of the study of communication to include nonverbal elements, Worth argued for it to include visual elements.

Goffman's involvement with this journal was shorter term than with *LiS*, but nonetheless significant, for one of his books, *Gender Advertisements* (1979a, was first published as a monograph in *SAVICOM* (1976a). As Fine and Manning point out, "*Gender Advertisements* could only have been developed in an intellectual context in which the content analysis of media sources was intellectually central and academically legitimate" (2003, 41). Annenberg at Penn was just such a place. Jay Ruby, who should know, reports that Goffman asked Worth to publish it there (2015). Worth's (1976) introduction does a nice job of setting the context, clearly demonstrating his familiarity with Goffman's ideas. In the acknowledgments for the version published as a book, Goffman writes: "I am very grateful for its [SAVICOM's] then editor, the late Sol Worth, for support in working out the original edition and for permission to use its plates and glossies" (1979a, vi) and goes on to quote him (12). When Worth died suddenly in 1977, Larry Gross (at Penn) and Jay Ruby (at Temple) took over as editors of the journal through 1979. A few years later, Gross and Ruby arranged for ASC to take over the publication, and it was renamed *Studies in Visual Communication* (Gross and Ruby 1980). At that point, Goffman joined as a consulting editor from 1980 to 1982; Glassie and Davenport were also consulting editors; Feld served on the editorial board).[218] In addition to Goffman, Feld also published in the journal while Worth was editor (1974; Feld and Williams 1975). While *SAVICOM* did not last decades as *LiS* did, it still marked an important shift, leading to an entirely new topic of study (Ruby 2005).

Birdwhistell was also involved in *SAVICOM*, but only after Worth had died. He published a book review (1978), and he wrote a eulogy honoring Mead upon her death, included in the 1980 special issue of the successor journal, *Studies in Visual Communication*. As a reminder, Mead was one of the anthropologists who originally helped to found both the organization and the journal and served as an important mentor to Worth. Unlike Worth, Birdwhistell never really worked directly with Mead, but he knew her (and Bateson) for decades and considered her a good enough friend that she was godmother to his daughter (Birdwhistell 1980). That issue also included a paper Worth had presented at a conference honoring Mead at her seventy-fifth birthday the year before his death, in 1976 (Worth 1980).

Conclusion

The five projects included in this chapter demonstrate the conditions under which intellectual creativity thrives, and how Penn developed and supported that creativity. As President Meyerson at one point made explicit to Hymes, the goal was never just for faculty members to enjoy talking with colleagues, it was to have "productive results" of some concrete sort.[219] This chapter has documented exactly the sort of results that were explicitly the goal at Penn, and likely (either explicitly or implicitly) at most other universities as well. These projects are all important because they demonstrate that the small circle of colleagues around Goffman at Penn did not just find areas in common to discuss but that together they were enormously consequential. They did not just sit around and talk about new ideas and approaches. Although that is often a good beginning point, they moved far beyond that: They held a conference on one new topic, bringing together relevant people to discuss what needed to happen next; they obtained a particularly substantial grant to start a research center on another topic, funding mostly students and some faculty fellowships, research projects, and conferences, and leading to many, many publications; and they began a book series on a third related topic and established two journals on additional, overlapping topics.

Goffman was the primary leader of one project, proposing the book series Conduct and Communication, and served as an equal partner with Hymes in deciding what to publish. He helped Worth and Hymes design the Codes in Context conference even before arriving at Penn, suggesting participants and an organizational structure for the event. He helped Szwed write the grant proposal to NIMH for funds to establish the Center for Urban Ethnography, and then served as its associate director, with Hymes in an equal role, for five years, resulting in multiple conferences and other events, as well as supporting both research and publications, with some of his own books supported by the NIMH funding given to CUE. He was an unusually active editorial board member for *Language in Society*; and extensive documentation exists demonstrating that, even though he was neither the editor, as Hymes was, nor an associate editor, as Labov and Grimshaw were, he still took considerable time to respond to significant numbers of submissions, helping to determine the direction the journal would take, and what work would be published. He was less involved with Worth's new journal, *Studies in the Anthropology of Visual Communication*, but publishing the first edition of one of his books in that venue was no small contribution. Although Goffman was the leader in only one of these projects, he clearly was an essential, involved participant in all five. The ideas he and the others proposed were significantly taken up: The conference may not have had huge impact on anyone outside the participants, but it served as a vehicle for developing vocabulary needed to discuss common interests. Certainly, the center, the book series, and the two journals were noticed, and all had substantial impact not only contemporaneously but still today. These projects provide clear evidence that Goffman was a central, active member of a steadily expanding invisible college.

Henry Glassie describes the moment in time when these major projects were being established in an interview:

> I got to be a part of that amazing moment at the University of Pennsylvania, which is now much passed. But it was a moment. It was a moment when it was, probably ought to be known as the "Hymes-Goffman era." They were co-editors

of a magnificent series called Conduct in Communication on the, sort of the anthropology of communication. And they were the two superstars around which this larger group was gathered, and it was just exhilarating to be in their company. So that was very fortunate. (119, HG)

All of us who were present in that place at that time were equally impressed.

What can other scholars and other universities learn from these projects? Often the goal of research is assumed to be constructing a theory group to conduct original investigations, then write up and publish results for dissemination to a wider audience. Often the obvious group for this is assumed to be one or a few faculty members surrounded by a cluster of advanced graduate students, all of whom co-author articles and occasionally books. But doing team-based research is not the only goal and was not the focus of what happened at Penn during Goffman's time there. Organizing conferences, obtaining major grants, starting a book series or a journal or two—these are all obvious next steps. None of them require that colleagues conduct research jointly, yet all of these vehicles advance the research of any and all members of a group. In addition, they all involved far more scholars than just the core set of peers described in detail in this chapter and so demonstrate the influence a small group such as this can have on a far larger audience. The fact that all of the core group members were senior faculty members is relevant: They had already taken the first steps of conducting original research and publishing results. They had already argued for a set of novel ideas, whether these were called codes in context, ethnography of speaking, sociolinguistics, linguistics, interaction, urban ethnography, or communication. What they did once they came together at Penn was to take the next step: bringing their ideas to a wider group and helping that expanding group come together for discussions (as with a conference), expanding their numbers through grants for degrees as well as further research (as with CUE), and disseminating their ideas nationally and internationally (as with the book series and the two journals).

What could other institutions do to follow Penn's example in supporting intellectual creativity while also encouraging concrete results? Annenberg supported the conference, and other universities could certainly support conferences on innovative topics. Penn Press supported the book series, and other university presses could certainly support book series on novel topics. When the anthropology department at Temple was uninterested in the major grant establishing CUE, the folklore department at Penn stepped in and gladly accepted it. Presumably, in later years at least some of those at

Temple regretted their decision, so the lesson is to support such innovation. SSRC's Committee on Sociolinguistics helped get *Language in Society* off the ground, providing initial support (GSE helped as well), while the Society for the Study of Visual Communication supported the establishment of *SAVICOM* (and ASC helped there); other academic organizations, funding agencies, and schools could certainly follow suit more often. Clearly, administrative support from various parts of Penn was required for these projects to get off the ground and succeed, and so comparable support for other projects, by other faculty members, at other universities, should be just as useful. Of course, having the "right people"[220] as core group members is also important, so hiring decisions that take into account overlapping interests and concerns across not just members of a single department but also spanning departments should be useful as well. No one person at Penn did everything; it was a set of colleagues sharing overlapping interests that proved particularly effective. It would be fascinating to apply the sort of analysis proposed by Farrell, who has examined what he terms "collaborative circles," that is, peers "who, through long periods of dialogue and collaboration, negotiate a common vision that guides their work" (2001, 11). However, that effort would require considerably more—and far more detailed—documentation than I have yet found for the projects at Penn described in these pages.

Endnotes

[1] Worth to Kuno Beller at Temple, Oct 31, 1967, SW, University of Pennsylvania, Codes in Context Meeting 1967, box 8, folder 19. This is one of a series of letters that were identical except for addressee.

[2] Worth to Kuno Beller at Temple, Oct 31, 1967, SW, University of Pennsylvania, Codes in Context Meeting 1967, box 8, folder 19.

[3] Goffman to Hymes, Oct 26, 1967, DHH, Subcollection 1, Series I: Correspondence 1951–1987, Goffman, Erving, 1967–1982.

[4] Goffman was citing Sommer's work at least as early as 1961 (Goffman 1961c, 23).

[5] Goffman to Hymes, Oct 26, 1967, DHH, Subcollection 1, Series I: Correspondence 1951–1987, Goffman, Erving, 1967–1982. For more on the relationship between Goffman and Garfinkel, see Meyer (2022).

[6] https://minuchincenter.org.

[7] Worth to Kuno Beller at Temple, Oct 31, 1967, SW, University of Pennsylvania, Codes in Context Meeting 1967, box 8, folder 19.

[8] Hymes to Worth, May 25, 1969, DHH, Subcollection 1, Series I: Correspondence 1951–1987, Worth, Sol, 1966–1977.

[9] Worth to Hymes, Nov 28, 1967, DHH, Subcollection 1, Series I: Correspondence

1951–1987, Worth, Sol, 1966–1977.

[10] Hymes to Gerbner, Jun 10, 1969, DHH, Subcollection 1, Series II: Conferences and Committees, 1955–1987, Subseries E: Other Committees, University of Pennsylvania, Annenberg School of Communication, Graduate Group in Communications, 1967–1975.

[11] Hymes to Ben-Amos, Davenport, Fought, Gerbner, Goldstein, Goodenough, Sapir, Sherzer, Tannenbaum, Wallace, Worth, Michael Studdert-Kennedy, and Harvey Winson, Nov 20, 1967, DHH, Subcollection 1, Series I: Correspondence 1951–1987, University of Pennsylvania, Department of Anthropology, 1964–1986.

[12] Birdwhistell to Worth, Nov 7, 1067, SW, University of Pennsylvania, Codes in Context Meeting 1967, box 8, folder 19.

[13] Worth to Birdwhistell, Nov 14, 1967, SW, University of Pennsylvania, Codes in Context Meeting 1967, box 8, folder 19.

[14] Birdwhistell to Worth, Nov 23, 1967, SW, University of Pennsylvania, Codes in Context Meeting 1967, box 8, folder 19.

[15] Birdwhistell's fieldwork in Alaska was never published, so it may be useful to share a summary of what he was doing. "This is my second trip to Cordova—part of my preparation for a seven week tour next fall to Antarctica to look at the men isolated for 7 weeks on the Pole Station" (Birdwhistell to Worth, Nov 23, 1967, SW, University of Pennsylvania, Codes in Context Meeting 1967, box 8, folder 19).

[16] Minuchin to Worth, Dec 5, 1967, SW, University of Pennsylvania, Codes in Context Meeting 1967, box 8, folder 19.

[17] Goffman to Worth, Nov 16, 1967, SW, University of Pennsylvania, Codes in Context Meeting 1967, box 8, folder 19.

[18] Goffman to Worth, Dec 18, 1967, SW, University of Pennsylvania, Codes in Context Meeting 1967, box 8, folder 19.

[19] Hymes to Ben-Amos, Davenport, Fought, Gerbner, Goldstein, Goodenough, Sapir, Sherzer, Michael Studdert-Kennedy, Percy Tannenbaum, Wallace, Harvey Winston, and Worth, Nov 20, 1967 DHH, Subcollection 1, Series I: Correspondence 1951–1987, University of Pennsylvania, Department of Anthropology, 1964–1986.

[20] Lita Osmundsen, Director of Research at Wenner-Gren, to participants, including a complete list, n.d., DHH, Subcollection 1, Series II: Conferences and Committees, Subseries E: Other Committees, University of Pennsylvania, Conference on Folklore and Social Science, 1967.

[21] Hymes to Dundes, Dec 26, 1965, DHH, Subcollection 1, Series I: Correspondence 1951–1987, Dundes, Alan, 1965–1975, 1977.

[22] Worth to Hymes, Nov 28, 1967, SW, University of Pennsylvania, Codes in Context Meeting 1967, box 8, folder 19.

[23] Hymes to Glassie, Feb 7, 1970, DHH, Subcollection 1, Series I: Correspondence 1951–1987, Glassie, Henry, 1970–82.

[24] Worth to Hymes, May 7, 1968, DHH, Subcollection 1, Series I: Correspondence 1951–1987, Worth, Sol, 1966–1977.

[25] Hymes to Worth, May 25, 1969, DHH, Subcollection 1, Series I: Correspondence 1951–1987, Worth, Sol, 1966–1977.

[26] Originally the "ethnography of speaking"; these two terms were and are often used interchangeably. See Leeds-Hurwitz (1984) for the history of the relationship.

[27] Worth to John Roberts, May 16, 1967, DHH, Subcollection 1, Series I: Correspondence

1951–1987, Worth, Sol, 1966–1977. (Hymes had introduced the two, which presumably explains why a copy of the letter is in his files.)

²⁸ Gumperz to Hymes, Mar 11, 1969, DHH, Subcollection 1, Series I: Correspondence 1951–1987, Gumperz, John J., 1966–1986.

²⁹ The Center for Urban Ethnography documents cited in these pages are in my possession because I was research assistant to Szwed for CUE in 1978–1979. They are most likely to have been prepared either by or for John Szwed but have no attribution. The dates are written on them in my own writing; Szwed handed me the first two, which I dated as 1974 and 1975 at the time, and I prepared the documentation supporting the third, dated 1978. These are final reports of activity (the grant having run 1969–1974). As I remember it, Szwed showed me into an office where every surface was covered with stacks of papers and books, and told me to prepare a bibliography, as these had all been supported by the NIMH grant to the center. The issue is that, while supported research leads to publications, they typically appear several years after the support was provided, thus the need for reports long after a grant has ended if publications resulting from funding are to be documented. The reports have not been made publicly available, so far as I am aware, although they were prepared for NIMH, and are presumably accessible in their grant files.

³⁰ Hymes also knew Hughes (1967, 632n1), and of course, Birdwhistell did, as he had been a Chicago student before Goffman. I remember reading an unpublished manuscript (book-length, not an article) by Hughes on fieldwork for a Birdwhistell course, which he supplied.

³¹ Some documents list all three as co-directors, some just list Szwed; however, it is clear that Szwed was the one originally invited to apply for funding, and that he did so with Goffman's help in preparing the proposal, and Hymes's support from afar (he was in England that year). Rose says Szwed was director, with Goffman and Hymes serving as associate directors (1987, 17), and letters typed on CUE letterhead support that (e.g., Szwed to unnamed colleagues, Oct 29, 1969, DHH, Subcollection 1, Series I: Correspondence 1951–1987, University of Pennsylvania, Center for Urban Ethnography, 1968–1971).

³² https://www.usinflationcalculator.com.

³³ Goffman to Hymes, Dec 9, 1968, DHH, Subcollection 1, Series I: Correspondence 1951–1987, Goffman, Erving, 1967–1982.

³⁴ Szwed to Hymes, Dec 17, 1968, DHH, Subcollection 1, Series I: Correspondence 1951–1987, University of Pennsylvania, Center for Urban Ethnography, 1968–1971.

³⁵ "The 55 people associated with the Center for Urban Ethnography had interests in ethnicity distributed as follows: 24 researched topics concerning Black Americans, 4 with Puerto-Ricans on mainland U.S., 1 with Cape Verdeans in Rhode Island, 1 with Mexican-Americans, 2 with Italian-Americans, 4 with Native Americans, 1 with Molokans (Russian Protestants) in the U.S., 2 with Greek-Americans, 2 with Jewish-Americans, 1 with French Canadian-Americans, 1 with East Indian-Americans, 1 with Poles temporarily resident in the U.S., and 11 others carried out research among multi-ethnic populations" (Center for Urban Ethnography 1975, 2).

³⁶ I have no independent documentation for how Ben-Amos was connected to the Center for Urban Ethnography, but Darnell was there and should know. Worth attended at least one of the conferences, as explained below.

³⁷ Szwed to Hymes, May 6, 1969, DHH, Subcollection 1, Series I: Correspondence 1951–1987, University of Pennsylvania, Center for Urban Ethnography, 1968–1971. To help spread the word, Hymes mentioned it at a meeting of the Committee on Sociolinguistics. "He urged members of the committee to bring this to the attention of potential claimants for grants or fellowships" (Minutes, Committee on Sociolinguistics, October 24–25, 1969,

DHH, Subcollection 1, Series II: Conferences and Committees, Subseries D: Social Science Research Council, Committee on Sociolinguistics, 1969).

[38] Hymes to Mervyn C. Alleyne at the University of the West Indies, Apr 30, 1970, DHH, Subcollection 1, Series V: Language in Society, Subseries A: Early Correspondence, Editorial Board, folder 1, 1969–1970.

[39] Hymes to Courtney Cazden, Nov 27, 1969, DHH, Subcollection 1, Series I: Correspondence 1951–1987, Cazden, Courtney, 1965–1972.

[40] Szwed to unnamed colleagues, Oct 20, 1969, DHH, Subcollection 1, Series I: Correspondence 1951–1987, University of Pennsylvania, Center for Urban Ethnography, 1968–1971.

[41] Scholte was a former Hymes student (2/21/65, Hymes to Birdwhistell, DHH, Subcollection 1, Series I. Correspondence 1951-1987. Birdwhistell, Ray, 1965, 1967, 1981) who Hymes helped to get a position at Annenberg (1/23/68, Dundes to Hymes, DHH, Subcollection 1, Series I. Correspondence 1951-1987. Dundes, Alan, 1965-1975, 1977).

[42] Hymes and Szwed to unnamed colleagues, Apr 13, 1971, DHH, Subcollection 1, Series I: Correspondence 1951–1987, University of Pennsylvania, Center for Urban Ethnography, 1968–1971.

[43] Hymes to Szwed, Feb 15, 1970, DHH, Subcollection 1, Series I: Correspondence 1951–1987, University of Pennsylvania, Center for Urban Ethnography, 1968–1971.

[44] Andre Schiffrin to Hymes, Nov 15, 1968, DHH, Subcollection 1, Series I: Correspondence, 1951–1987, Pantheon Books, 1968–1974, 1980–1982.

[45] Hymes to Schiffrin, Jan 21, 1969, DHH, Subcollection 1, Series I: Correspondence, 1951–1987, Pantheon Books, 1968–1974, 1980–1982.

[46] Schiffrin to Hymes, Feb 5, 1969, DHH, Subcollection 1, Series I: Correspondence, 1951–1987, Pantheon Books, 1968–1974, 1980–1982.

[47] Paula McGuire of Pantheon to Hymes, May 26, 1971, DHH, Subcollection 1, Series I: Correspondence, 1951–1987, Pantheon Books, 1968–1974, 1980–1982.

[48] Hymes to McGuire, Dec 8, 1971, DHH, Subcollection 1, Series I: Correspondence, 1951–1987, Pantheon Books, 1968–1974, 1980–1982.

[49] Michael Kehoe of University of Michigan Press to Hymes, Apr 3, 1999, DHH, Subcollection 2, Series I: Correspondence, Reprint Permissions, folder 4, "Reinventing Anthropology," 1998–1999.

[50] Hymes to Szwed, Jan 5, 1973, DHH, Subcollection 1, Series I: Correspondence 1951–1987, Szwed, John F., 1965–1981.

[51] Issue of *Urban Poetry*, n.d., DHH, Subcollection 1, Series I: Correspondence 1951–1987, University of Pennsylvania, Center for Urban Ethnography, 1968–1971. This includes poems by Hymes and Szwed, a piece of short fiction by Rose, and several poems by others. It is filed after a letter dated December 1971, so it is most likely from the winter 1971–72.

[52] Jefferson (1974) lists the Center for Urban Ethography as her primary affiliation, and of course that article is published in *Language in Society*.

[53] Hymes to Labov, May 15, 1974, DHH, Subcollection 1, Series I: Correspondence 1951–1987, Labov, William, folder 2, 1974–1987.

[54] Szwed submitted a request for renewed funding which was denied; in a letter Hymes complains about not being able to get to a conference in Mexico as a result: "Had the Center been refunded, I might have had money to go. . . . But no refunding, and no travel money" (Hymes to Sherzer, Sep 13, 1974, DHH, Subcollection 1, Series I: Correspondence

1951–1987, Sherzer, Joel, 1968–87).

[55] Hymes to Goffman, Jul 5, 1977, DHH, Subcollection 1, Series I: Correspondence 1951–1987, Goffman, Erving, 1967–1982.

[56] Glassie to Hymes, n.d. [received Apr 4, 1979], DHH, Subcollection 1, Series I: Correspondence 1951–1987, Glassie, Henry, 1970–82.

[57] https://www.gse.upenn.edu/academics/research/center-urban-ethnography-education-forum.

[58] https://2021forum.dryfta.com.

[59] Hymes to Szwed, Jan 4, 1979, DHH, Subcollection 1, Series : Correspondence 1951–1987, Szwed, John F., 1965–1981.

[60] https://www.sas.upenn.edu/folklore/center/PastDirectors.html.

[61] https://www.sas.upenn.edu/folklore/center/ConferenceArchive/secondnature.html.

[62] https://www.sas.upenn.edu/folklore/center/ConferenceArchive/voiceover/voiceover.html.

[63] https://www.sas.upenn.edu/folklore/events/index.html.

[64] Goffman had previously worked hard to help others get their books published, as with Harold Garfinkel 1962–66 (documented in Rawls 2023). Members of the network described in these pages periodically served on the Faculty Editorial Committee of the Press, as when both Fox and Glassie were on it in 1984 (https://almanac.upenn.edu/archive/v30pdf/n21/020784.pdf).

[65] Worth to Hymes, May 7, 1968, DHH, Subcollection 1, Series I: Correspondence 1951–1987, Worth, Sol, 1966–1977.

[66] Hymes to Worth, May 25, 1969, DHH, Subcollection 1, Series I: Correspondence 1951–1987, Worth, Sol, 1966–1977.

[67] Looking just at Goffman, Shalin (2023) examines different sorts of citation figures, including sorting citations to Goffman's publications by discipline.

[68] https://almanac.upenn.edu/archive/v19pdf/n17/010973.pdf.

[69] https://almanac.upenn.edu/archive/v21pdf/n03/091074.pdf.

[70] Sommer to Goffman, Apr 24, 1970, TS. (The letter is in the Sebeok papers because Sommer wrote to Goffman mostly in response to an invitation to the conference Goffman was organizing with Sebeok; Goffman then forwarded that letter to Sebeok.)

[71] Birdwhistell (1952) was published by Foreign Service Institute of the US Department of State, with limited circulation. See Leeds-Hurwitz (1990) for the explanation of that unlikely pairing.

[72] I have not been able to discover anything about Barton Jones or how he ended up being the one to organize Birdwhistell's papers.

[73] Labov to President Sheldon Hackney, copied to Hymes, Apr 24, 1981, DHH, Subcollection 1, Subseries A: Early Correspondence, Labov, William, 1974–1987.

[74] Hymes to Fought, Jul 6, 1973, DHH, Subcollection 2, Series I: Correspondence, Fought, John G., 1972–2004.

[75] For example, Erwin to Goffman, Sep 27, 1974, DHH, Subcollection 1, Series I: Correspondence 1951–1987, University of Pennsylvania Press, folder 1, 1969–1981.

[76] Goffman to Sherzer, copied to Hymes, Nov 15, 1974, DHH, Subcollection 1, Series I: Correspondence 1951–1987, Goffman, Erving, 1967–1982.

[77] This sort of humor is also evident in earlier letters by Goffman to Garfinkel, as documented in Rawls (2023).

[78] https://annualmeeting.americananthro.org/general-info/future-past/.

[79] Erwin to Hymes, Jan 6, 1976, DHH, Subcollection 1, Series I: Correspondence 1951–1987, University of Pennsylvania Press, folder 1, 1969–1981.

[80] Erwin to Hymes, Jan 6, 1976 and Apr 6, 1976, DHH, Subcollection 1, Series I: Correspondence 1951–1987, University of Pennsylvania Press, folder 1, 1969–1981.

[81] Hymes to Grimshaw, Apr 10, 1980, DHH, Subcollection 1, Series I: Correspondence 1951–1987, Grimshaw, Allen, 1966–1986.

[82] Hymes to Goodenough, Sep 28, 1975, DHH, Subcollection 1, Series I: Correspondence 1951–1987, Goodenough, Ward H., 1958, 1960, 1970–1986.

[83] Hymes to McDermott, Jul 5, 1977, DHH, Subcollection 1, Series I: Correspondence 1951–1987, McDermott, Ray, 1977–1986.

[84] Erwin to Hymes, Apr 15, 1976, DHH, Subcollection 1, Series I: Correspondence, 1951–1987, University of Pennsylvania Press, folder 1, 1969–1981.

[85] Erwin to Goffman, copied to Hymes, May 17, 1976, DHH, Subcollection 1, Series I: Correspondence, 1951–1987, Goffman, Erving, 1967–1982.

[86] Erwin to Hymes, May 24, 1976, DHH, Subcollection 2, Series I: Correspondence, University of Pennsylvania Press, 1966–1999.

[87] Hymes to Erwin, May 26, 1976, DHH, Subcollection 2, Series I: Correspondence, University of Pennsylvania Press, 1966–1999.

[88] Erwin to Hymes, Jun 14, 1976, DHH, Subcollection 1, Series I: Correspondence, 1951–1987, University of Pennsylvania Press, folder 1, 1969–1981.

[89] Hymes to Goffman, Jun 25, 1976, DHH, Subcollection 1, Series V: Language in Society, Subseries A: Early Correspondence, Goffman, Erving, 1973, 1976, 1979.

[90] Hymes to John McGuigan, Feb 3, 1978, DHH, Subcollection 1, Series I: Correspondence 1951–1987, University of Pennsylvania Press, folder 1, 1969–1981.

[91] Labov to Hymes, Nov 4, 1976, DHH, Subcollection 1, Series V: Language in Society, 1968–1992, Subseries A: Early Correspondence, Labov, William, 1970–1973.

[92] Goffman to Erwin, copied to Hymes, Dec 6, 1976, DHH, Subcollection 1, Series I: Correspondence, 1951–1987, Goffman, Erving, 1967–1982.

[93] Hymes to Erwin, Dec 9, 1976, DHH, Subcollection 2, Series I: Correspondence, University of Pennsylvania Press, 1966–1999.

[94] Erwin to Sankoff, copied to Hymes and Goffman, Jan 31, 1977, DHH, Subcollection 1, Series I: Correspondence 1951–1987, University of Pennsylvania Press, folder 1, 1969–1981.

[95] Erwin to Hymes, copied to Goffman, Jan 4, 1979, DHH, Subcollection 1, Series I: Correspondence 1951–1987, University of Pennsylvania Press, folder 1, 1969–1981.

[96] Hymes to Erwin, Jan 9, 1979, DHH, Subcollection 1, Series I: Correspondence 1951–1987, University of Pennsylvania Press, folder 1, 1969–1981.

[97] McGuigan to Hymes, Feb 14, 1980, DHH, Subcollection 1, Series I: Correspondence 1951–1987, University of Pennsylvania Press, folder 1, 1969–1981.

[98] Hymes to McGuigan, Feb 18, 1980, DHH, Subcollection 1, Series I: Correspondence 1951–1987, University of Pennsylvania Press, folder 1, 1969–1981.

99 Hymes to Fred Wieck, Director of the Press, May 25, 1970, DHH, Subcollection 1, Series I: Correspondence 1951–1987, University of Pennsylvania Press, folder 1, 1969–1981.

100 Grimshaw to Goffman and Hymes, Nov 26, 1979, DHH, Subcollection 1, Series I: Correspondence 1951–1987, Grimshaw, Allen, 1966–1986.

101 Hymes to Grimshaw, Dec 21, 1979, DHH, Subcollection 1, Series I: Correspondence 1951–1987, Grimshaw, Allen, 1966–1986.

102 Hymes actually offered to include one or more of Labov's books in the series as early as 1969, saying, "If you want your piece out quickly, you know Erv and I would be delighted at Penn," presumably meaning in their series at the Penn Press (Hymes to Labov, Aug 10, 1969, DHH, Subcollection 1, Series I: Correspondence 1951–1987, Labov, William, folder 1, 1963–1972).

103 Hymes to Jaber Gubrium, copied to Goffman and to McGuigan, Kuriloff, and Bosk at the Press, Apr 29, 1981, DHH, Subcollection 1, Series I: Correspondence 1951–1987, University of Pennsylvania Press, folder 1, 1969–1981.

104 Goffman to Hymes, May 22, 1981, DHH, Subcollection 2, Series I: Correspondence, Goffman, Erving, 1968–1982.

105 McGuigan to Hymes, Oct 2, 1981, DHH, Subcollection 1, Series I: Correspondence 1951–1987, University of Pennsylvania Press, folder 1, 1969–1981.

106 Hymes to McGuigan, Oct 16, 1981, DHH, Subcollection 1, Series I: Correspondence 1951–1987, University of Pennsylvania Press, folder 1, 1969–1981.

107 Call to Hymes, Oct 23, 1981; McGuigan to Hymes, Oct 30, 1981; and Hymes to Call, Nov 5, 1981; all in DHH, Subcollection 1, Series I: Correspondence 1951–1987, University of Pennsylvania Press, folder 1, 1969–1981.

108 Hymes to Gregorian, copied to Goffman, Oct 1, 1979, DHH, Subcollection 1, Series I: Correspondence 1951–1987, Gregorian, Vartan, 1974–1981.

109 Hymes to Philips, Oct 23, 1979, DHH, Subcollection 1, Series I: Correspondence 1951–1987, Philips, Susan, 1967–1984.

110 Hymes to Philips, n.d. [Feb 6, 1979?], DHH, Subcollection 1, Series I: Correspondence 1951–1987, Philips, Susan, 1967–1984.

111 Maurice English to Goffman, copied to Hymes and McGuigan, Mar 11, 1980, DHH, Subcollection 1, Series I: Correspondence 1951–1987, Goffman, Erving, 1967--1982.

112 Goffman to Hymes, Nov 7, 1979, DHH, Subcollection 1, Series I: Correspondence 1951–1987, Goffman, Erving, 1967–1982.

113 Hymes to Goffman, Aug 19, 1971, DHH, Subcollection 1, Series I: Correspondence 1951–1987, Goffman, Erving, 1967–1982.

114 The Haney Foundation Editorial Committee press release, May 15, 1967, DHH, Subcollection 1, Series II: Conferences and Committees, Subseries E: Other Committees, University of Pennsylvania, University of Pennsylvania Press—Haney Foundation Editorial Committee, 1967–1976.

115 Goldstein to Hymes, Jan 23, 1971, DHH, Subcollection 1, Series II: Conferences and Committees, Subseries E: Other Committees, University of Pennsylvania, University of Pennsylvania Press—Haney Foundation Editorial Committee, 1967–1976.

116 Hymes to Goffman, Mar 11, 1971, DHH, Subcollection 1, Series II: Conferences and Committees, Subseries E: Other Committees, University of Pennsylvania, University of Pennsylvania Press—Haney Foundation Editorial Committee, 1967–1976.

117 https://almanac.upenn.edu/archive/v15pdf/n08/041669.pdf.

[118] Hymes to Sherzer, Sep 13, 1974, DHH, Subcollection 1, Series I: Correspondence 1951–1987, Sherzer, Joel, 1968–87.

[119] Hymes to Kirshenblatt-Gimblett, Oct 5, 1974, DHH, Subcollection 1, Series I: Correspondence 1951–1987, Kirshenblatt-Gimblett, Barbara, 1974, 1985.

[120] Kirshenblatt-Gimblett to Robert Erwin, copied to Hymes, Oct 5, 1974, DHH, Subcollection 1, Series I: Correspondence 1951–1987, Kirshenblatt-Gimblett, Barbara, 1974, 1985.

[121] For the request to publish it with Haney Foundation funding, see Goldstein to Hymes, Jan 28, 1971, DHH, Subcollection 1, Series II: Conferences and Committees, Subseries E: Other Committees, University of Pennsylvania, University of Pennsylvania Press—Haney Foundation Editorial Committee, 1967–1976. For a formal review, see Ben-Amos to Goldstein (Jan 18, 1971, same collection) and Ben-Amos to Fought (Jan 18, 1971, same collection): "First, let me tell you that I am really jealous! It is a magnificent work of which you should be proud."

[122] Goffman to Hymes, May 22, 1981, DHH, Subcollection 2, Series I: Correspondence, Goffman, Erving, 1968–1982.

[123] Labov to President Sheldon Hackney, copied to Hymes, Apr 24, 1981, DHH, Subcollection 1, Subseries A: Early Correspondence, Labov, William, folder 2, 1974–1987.

[124] Hymes to Labov, DHH, Subcollection 1, Series I: Correspondence 1951–1987, Labov, William, folder 2, 1974–1987.

[125] Witthoft was a faculty member in anthropology at Penn from 1966 to 1986 (https://www.museum.upenn.edu/collections/archives/findingaid/552900).

[126] Erwin to Hymes, Jan 5, 1977, DHH, Subcollection 1, Series I: Correspondence 1951–1987, University of Pennsylvania Press, folder 1, 1969–1981.

[127] Hymes to Erwin, Jan 10, 1977, DHH, Subcollection 2, Series I: Correspondence, University of Pennsylvania Press, 1966–1999.

[128] Hymes to Erwin, Feb 2, 1977, DHH, Subcollection 1, Series I: Correspondence 1951–1987, University of Pennsylvania Press, folder 1, 1969–1981.

[129] Sapir to Erwin, Mar 17, 1978, DHH, Subcollection 1, Series I: Correspondence 1951–1987, University of Pennsylvania Press, folder 1, 1969–1981.

[130] Erwin to Hymes, Mar 28, 1978, DHH, Subcollection 1, Series I: Correspondence 1951–1987, University of Pennsylvania Press, folder 1, 1969–1981.

[131] Hymes to Erwin, Apr 7, 1978, DHH, Subcollection 1, Series I: Correspondence 1951–1987, University of Pennsylvania Press, folder 1, 1969–1981.

[132] McGuigan to Hymes, Apr 5, 1982, DHH, Subcollection 1, Series I: Correspondence 1951–1987, University of Pennsylvania Press, folder 2, 1982.

[133] Hymes to McGuigan, Apr 6, 1982, DHH, Subcollection 1, Series I: Correspondence 1951–1987, University of Pennsylvania Press, folder 2, 1982.

[134] Hymes to McGuigan, Apr 6, 1982, DHH, Subcollection 1, Series I: Correspondence 1951–1987, University of Pennsylvania Press, folder 2, 1982.

[135] Hymes to McGuigan, n.d. [filed after the letter from Apr 6, 1982], DHH, Subcollection 1, Series I: Correspondence 1951–1987, University of Pennsylvania Press, folder 2, 1982.

[136] McGuigan to Hymes, Apr 19, 1982, DHH, Subcollection 1, Series I: Correspondence 1951–1987, University of Pennsylvania Press, folder 2, 1982.

[137] Hymes to McGuigan, Apr 30, 1982, DHH, Subcollection 1, Series I: Correspondence

1951–1987, University of Pennsylvania Press, folder 2, 1982.

[138] McGuigan to Hymes, Jun 9, 1982, DHH, Subcollection 1, Series I: Correspondence 1951–1987, University of Pennsylvania Press, folder 2, 1982.

[139] Hymes to McGuigan, Jun 9, 1982, DHH, Subcollection 1, Series I: Correspondence 1951–1987, University of Pennsylvania Press, folder 2, 1982.

[140] McGuigan to Hymes, Nov 23, 1982, DHH, Subcollection 1, Series I: Correspondence 1951–1987, University of Pennsylvania Press, folder 2, 1982.

[141] Hymes to McGuigan, Nov 23, 1982, DHH, Subcollection 1, Series I: Correspondence 1951–1987, University of Pennsylvania Press, folder 2, 1982.

[142] McGuigan to Hymes, Nov 30, 1982, DHH, Subcollection 1, Series I: Correspondence 1951–1987, University of Pennsylvania Press, folder 2, 1982.

[143] Maurice English, Director of the Press, to Sankoff, Dec 17, 1982, DHH, Subcollection 1, Series I: Correspondence 1951–1987, University of Pennsylvania Press, folder 2, 1982. English mentions that he understands Sankoff has agreed but wants a written acceptance; a copy is not in the files.

[144] Glassie to English, copied to Hymes and Sankoff, Feb 9, 1983, DHH, Subcollection 1, Series I: Correspondence 1951–1987, University of Pennsylvania Press, folder 3, 1983.

[145] John McGuigan to Hymes, Sankoff, and Glassie, Apr 8, 1983, DHH, Subcollection 1, Series I: Correspondence 1951–1987, University of Pennsylvania Press, folder 3, 1983.

[146] McGuigan to Hymes, Sankoff, and Glassie, Feb 14, 1983, DHH, Subcollection 1, Series I: Correspondence 1951–1987, University of Pennsylvania Press, folder 3, 1983.

[147] https://archives.upenn.edu/collections/finding-aid/upa8/.

[148] English to Meyers and Ehrlich, copied to Sankoff, Dec 14, 1982, DHH, Subcollection 1, Series I: Correspondence 1951–1987, University of Pennsylvania Press, folder 2, 1982.

[149] Minutes, Committee on Sociolinguistics, Social Science Research Council, July 12–13, 1968, DHH, Subcollection 1, Series I: Correspondence 1951–1987, Language in Society, 1968–1971.

[150] Sebeok to Hymes, Aug 5, 1968, DHH, Subcollection 1, Series I: Correspondence 1951–1987, Language in Society, 1968–1971.

[151] Hymes to Ferguson, Aug 14, 1968, DHH, Subcollection 1, Series I: Correspondence 1951–1987, Language in Society, 1968–1971.

[152] Frances Welch to John Pride, Feb 18, 1969, DHH, Subcollection 1, Series I: Correspondence 1951–1987, Language in Society, 1968–1971.

[153] Hymes to Sibley, Feb 26, 1969, DHH, Subcollection 1, Series II: Conferences and Committees, Subseries D: Social Science Research Council, Committee on Sociolinguistics, 1969.

[154] Grimshaw to Ferguson, copied to Hymes, Mar 25, 1969, DHH, Subcollection 1, Series I: Correspondence 1951–1987, Language in Society, 1968–1971.

[155] Hymes to Grimshaw, Mar 29, 1969, DHH, Subcollection 1, Series I: Correspondence 1951–1987, Language in Society, 1968–1971.

[156] Ferguson to Hymes, Jun 12, 1969, DHH, Subcollection 1, Series I: Correspondence 1951–1987, Language in Society, 1968–1971.

[157] Hymes to Grimshaw, Jun 22, 1969, DHH, Subcollection 1, Series I: Correspondence 1951–1987, Language in Society, 1968–1971.

[158] Hymes to Ferguson, Jun 22, 1969, DHH, Subcollection 1, Series I: Correspondence 1951–1987, Language in Society, 1968–1971.

[159] Black to Grimshaw, Jun 26, 1969, DHH, Subcollection 1, Series I: Correspondence 1951–1987, Language in Society, 1968–1971.

[160] Grimshaw to Committee on Sociolinguistics, Jul 1, 1969, DHH, Subcollection 1, Series I: Correspondence 1951–1987, Language in Society, 1968–1971.

[161] Minutes, Committee on Sociolinguistics, October 24–25, 1969, DHH, Subcollection 1, Series II: Conferences and Committees, Subseries D: Social Science Research Council, Committee on Sociolinguistics, 1969.

[162] Hymes to Goddard, copied to Anthony Wallace (chair of anthropology), Henry Hoenigswald (chair of linguistics), Burton Rosner (chair of psychology), Wolfgang (chair of sociology), O. P. Williams (chair of political science), and Neal Gross (dean of education), Oct 31, 1969, DHH, Subcollection 1, Series I: Correspondence 1951–1987, Language in Society, 1968–1971. The formal decision was delayed due to Goddard being ill, but eventually the vice-provost, John Hobstetter, wrote Hymes, saying the requests had been approved, concluding, "I am really delighted at the prospect of this new journal and wish you the best of luck in launching it" (Hobstetter to Hymes, Jan 6, 1970, DHH, Subcollection 1, Series I: Correspondence 1951–1987, Language in Society, 1968–1971).

[163] Memorandum on Committee on Sociolinguistics by Hymes to Committee, Apr 11, 1970, DHH, Subcollection 1, Series II: Conferences and Committees, Subseries D: Social Science Research Council, Committee on Sociolinguistics, 1970.

[164] Memorandum on Committee on Sociolinguistics by Hymes to Committee, Apr 11, 1970, DHH, Subcollection 1, Series II: Conferences and Committees, Subseries D: Social Science Research Council, Committee on Sociolinguistics, 1970.

[165] Minutes, Committee on Sociolinguistics, June 13, 1970, DHH, Subcollection 1, Series II: Conferences and Committees, Subseries D: Social Science Research Council, Committee on Sociolinguistics, 1970.

[166] Minutes, Committee on Sociolinguistics, March 18–19, 1971, DHH, Subcollection 1, Series II: Conferences and Committees, Subseries D: Social Science Research Council. Committee on Sociolinguistics, 1970.

[167] Peter de Ridder of Mouton to Hymes, Dec 18, 1970, DHH, Subcollection 1, Series I: Correspondence 1951–1987, Language in Society, 1968–1971.

[168] Kenneth Jackson to Hymes, Feb 11, 1971, DHH, Subcollection 1, Series I: Correspondence 1951–1987, Language in Society, 1968–1971.

[169] Jackson to Hymes, Apr 5, 1971, DHH, Subcollection 1, Series I: Correspondence 1951–1987, Language in Society, 1968–1971.

[170] Hymes to Jackson, Apr 16, 1971, DHH, Subcollection 1, Series I: Correspondence 1951–1987, Language in Society, 1968–1971.

[171] Hymes to Gumperz, Jan 9, 1970, DHH, Subcollection 1, Series V: Language in Society, Editorial Board, folder 1, 1969–1970.

[172] Hymes to Worth, Jun 10, 1969, DHH, Subcollection 1, Series I: Correspondence 1951–1987, Worth, Sol, 1966–1977.

[173] Hymes to Gumperz, Jan 9, 1970, DHH, Subcollection 1, Series V: Language in Society, Editorial Board, folder 1, 1969–1970.

[174] Hymes to Grimshaw, Nov 13, 1972, DHH, Subcollection 1, Series II: Conferences and Committees, 1955–1987, Subseries E: Other Committees, Language and Interaction Institute, 1974–1977; and Hymes to Labov, Nov 13, 1972, DHH, Subcollection 1, Series V:

Language in Society, Subseries A: Early Correspondence, Labov, William, 1970–1973.

[175] Labov to Hymes, Jan 17, 1973, DHH, Subcollection 1, Series V: Language in Society, Subseries A: Early Correspondence, Labov, William, 1970–1973.

[176] Hymes to Goffman, Jan 22, 1981, DHH, Subcollection 2, Series IV: Works by Hymes, Subseries D: Other Research, "On Erving Goffman," 1979–1984.

[177] Hymes to Sankoff, Jul 7, 1983, DHH, Subcollection 1, Series I: Correspondence 1951–1987, Gillian Sankoff, 1969–1985.

[178] Goffman to Hymes, Feb 12, 1975, DHH, Subcollection 2, Series I: Correspondence, Goffman, Erving, 1968–1982.

[179] Goffman to Hymes, Mar 25, 1975, DHH, Subcollection 2, Series I: Correspondence, Goffman, Erving, 1968–1982.

[180] Goffman to Hymes, Apr 2, 1975, DHH, Subcollection 2, Series I: Correspondence, Goffman, Erving, 1968–1982.

[181] Goffman to Hymes, Sep 16, 1975, DHH, Subcollection 2, Series I: Correspondence, Goffman, Erving, 1968–1982.

[182] Goffman to Hymes, Apr 14, 1977, DHH, Subcollection 2, Series I: Correspondence, Goffman, Erving, 1968–1982.

[183] Goffman to Hymes, Oct 18, 1978, DHH, Subcollection 2, Series I, Correspondence, Goffman, Erving, 1968–1982.

[184] Goffman to Hymes, Nov 22, 1978, DHH, Subcollection 2, Series I: Correspondence, Goffman, Erving, 1968–1982.

[185] Goffman to Hymes, Apr 8, 1982, DHH, Subcollection 2, Series I: Correspondence, Goffman, Erving, 1968–1982.

[186] Goffman to Hymes, Oct 6, 1980, DHH, Subcollection 2, Series I: Correspondence, Goffman, Erving, 1968–1982.

[187] Goffman to Hymes, Apr 13, 1981, DHH, Subcollection 2, Series I: Correspondence, Goffman, Erving, 1968–1982.

[188] Goffman to Hymes, Apr 13, 1981, DHH, Subcollection 2, Series I: Correspondence, Goffman, Erving, 1968–1982.

[189] Hymes to Goffman, Jun 25, 1976, DHH, Subcollection 1, Series V: Language in Society, Subseries A: Early Correspondence, Goffman, Erving, 1973, 1976, 1979. Overall, Hymes appreciated Goffman's writing, in his publications as well as in letters. For example: "At least you have the comfort of being able to write in an inimitable way! Others can get the words, but not the tune!" (Hymes to Goffman, Dec 24, 1981, same collection).

[190] Hymes to Goffman, Apr 17, 1979, DHH, Subcollection 1, Series V: Language in Society, Subseries A: Early Correspondence, Goffman, Erving, 1973, 1976, 1979.

[191] Hymes to Klatzky, Feb 20, 1977, DHH, Subcollection 2, Series I: Correspondence, Goffman, Erving, 1968–1982. (As a specific sentence from Goffman's review is quoted, and that review is also available, there is no question but that he is the esteemed colleague in question.)

[192] Goffman to Hymes, Jan 21, 1981, DHH, Subcollection 2, Series I: Correspondence, Goffman, Erving, 1968–1982.

[193] Goffman to Hymes, Mar 31, 1982, DHH, Subcollection 2, Series I: Correspondence, Goffman, Erving, 1968–1982.

[194] Hymes to Labov, May 15, 1974, DHH, Subcollection 1, Series I: Correspondence

1951–1987, Labov, William, folder 2, 1974–1987.

[195] Goffman to Hymes, Jun 10, 1876, DHH, Subcollection 1, Series V: Language in Society, Subseries A: Early Correspondence, Goffman, Erving, 1973, 1976, 1979.

[196] Hymes to Goffman, Jun 25, 1976, DHH, Subcollection 1, Series V: Language in Society, Subseries A: Early Correspondence, Goffman, Erving, 1973, 1976, 1979.

[197] Grimshaw to Hymes, Dec 21, 1979, DHH, Subcollection 1, Series I: Correspondence 1951–1987, Grimshaw, Allen, folder 2, 1978–1980.

[198] Hymes to Grimshaw, Dec 21, 1979, DHH, Subcollection 1, Series I: Correspondence 1951–1987, Grimshaw, Allen, folder 2, 1978–1980.

[199] Grimshaw to Hymes, Jan 8, 1980, DHH, Subcollection 1, Series I: Correspondence 1951–1987, Grimshaw, Allen, folder 2, 1978–1980; Grimshaw to Hymes, Dec 21, 1979, same collection.

[200] Grimshaw to Hymes, Mar 25, 1980, DHH, Subcollection 1, Series I: Correspondence 1951–1987, Grimshaw, Allen, folder 2, 1978–1980.

[201] Hymes to Grimshaw, Apr 10, 1980, DHH, Subcollection 1, Series I: Correspondence 1951–1987, Grimshaw, Allen, folder 2, 1978–1980.

[202] See the "Note for Contributors" in the front matter of the first issue.

[203] Hymes to Dean Vartan Gregorian, Jul 8, 1974, DHH, Subcollection 1, Series I: Correspondence 1951–1987, Gregorian, Vartan, 1974–1981.

[204] Hymes to Goffman, Sep 28, 1975, DHH, Subcollection 1, Series I: Correspondence 1951–1987, Goodenough, Ward H., 1958, 1960, 1970–1986. (This letter seems to have been misfiled.)

[205] Goffman to Hymes, Jun 10, 1976, DHH, Subcollection 1, Series V: Language in Society, Subseries A: Early Correspondence, Goffman, Erving, 1973, 1976, 1979.

[206] Jeremy Mynott at Cambridge University Press to Hymes, Dec 22, 1977, DHH, Subcollection 1, Series I: Correspondence, 1951–1987, Cambridge University Press, folder 2, 1977–1983.

[207] Hymes to Sherzer and John Baugh, Sep 15, 1980, DHH, Subcollection 1, Series V: Language in Society, Subseries A: Early Correspondence, Sherzer, Joel, 1972–1974, 1980.

[208] Colson to Hymes, Oct 14, 1983, DHH, Subcollection 2, Series I: Correspondence, University of Pennsylvania Press, folder 3, 1983. (This letter may have been misfiled.)

[209] Hymes to Colson, Oct 18, 1983, DHH, Subcollection 2, Series I: Correspondence, University of Pennsylvania Press, folder 3, 1983.

[210] Hymes to Grimshaw, Oct 18, 1983, DHH, Subcollection 1, Series I: Correspondence, 1951–1987, Grimshaw, Allen, 1966–1986, folder 3.

[211] Grimshaw to Hymes, Mar 5, 1984, DHH, Subcollection 1, Series I: Correspondence, 1951–1987, Grimshaw, Allen, 1966–1986, folder 3.

[212] Grimshaw to Hymes, Mar 5, 1984, DHH, Subcollection 1, Series I: Correspondence, 1951–1987, Grimshaw, Allen, 1966–1986, folder 3.

[213] Hymes to Ferguson, May 7, 1973, DHH, Subcollection 1, Series V: Language in Society, Subseries A: Early correspondence, Ferguson, Charles, 1970–1978.

[214] Fishman to Hymes, Feb 9, 1973, DHH, Subcollection 1, Series I: Correspondence 1951–1987, Fishman, Joshua, 1968–1975.

[215] Hymes to Fishman, Mar 3, 1973, DHH, Subcollection 1, Series I: Correspondence

1951–1987, Fishman, Joshua, 1968–1975.

[216] Grimshaw to Hymes and David Jenness, May 5, 1973, DHH, Subcollection 1, Series II: Conferences and Committees, Subseries D: Social Science Research Council, Committee on Sociolinguistics, May–December 1973.

[217] Hymes to Sherzer, Sep 13, 1974, DHH, Subcollection 1, Series I: Correspondence 1951–1987, Sherzer, Joel, 1968–1987.

[218] https://repository.upenn.edu/handle/20.500.14332/48338.

[219] Myerson to Hymes, Dec 14, 1971, DHH, Subcollection 1, Series I: Correspondence 1951–1987, Meyerson, Martin, 1971, 1979.

[220] Worth to John Roberts, May 16, 1967, DHH, Subcollection 1, Series I: Correspondence 1951–1987, Worth, Sol, 1966–1977.

CHAPTER FIVE

Minor Projects at Penn

The projects in the last chapter are those many of us knew about at the time; they were mostly large, successful, and most either were publications or resulted in publications, so they influenced others, both at Penn and beyond. Even the smallest, the Codes in Context conference, was successful, in that it was organized, held, and as demonstrated, at least some participants used the phrase later. (Students who were at Penn in the 1970s remember hearing the phrase, and one of the core topics in the doctoral program at Annenberg at the time was named "Communication Codes and Modes."[1]) However, in addition to these, there were multiple less significant and/or unsuccessful collaborations at Penn involving Goffman. Mostly these efforts were intended to coordinate activities across departments at Penn; their story forms the majority of this chapter.

These activities are justifiably called minor primarily because they either had fewer substantial results (especially in terms of funding and/or publication, thus influence both across and beyond Penn) or because they were attempted but failed, yet all of them are part of the larger story to be told of Goffman's invisible college at Penn. There are also significant differences between the two types of projects in terms of timing, involvement, and commitment. In terms of timing, most of the major projects were begun in the late 1960s and early 1970s, while most of these minor projects were begun in the late 1970s. In terms of involvement, nearly everyone in the primary peer group was involved in all the major projects in some capacity, but only some were involved in the minor projects. In terms of commitment, all the major projects were managed by primary peer group members, and each of them except Birdwhistell took charge of at least one. But it is a different story with the minor projects: While Hymes and Labov each took charge of two, none of the others oversaw any of them. Thus, these projects can appropriately be characterized as minor in all these ways, as well as for not being either as ambitious or as successful. In addition, they were typically multidisciplinary rather than interdisciplinary; that is, they involved bringing together people from different disciplines, but did not develop new theories, approaches, methods, or ideas that would not have fit within any of the participating disciplines.

Although the names changed for several of them (typically as they were being developed, but in a few cases, even after they were formally established), the names used most often were these: the Semiotic Program (SP), the Language and Interaction Institute (LII), the Cross-Cultural Communication Center (CCCC), the Interdisciplinary Program in the Science of Symbolic Behavior (SSB), the Center for the Study of Art and Symbolic Behavior (ASB), and the Interdisciplinary Program in Language, Culture, and Society (LCS). Given that these names are so long, abbreviations will be used in the table below.

In addition to these specific projects, Goffman was a Benjamin Franklin Professor, and there were a few activities organized by or on behalf of the group of Benjamin Franklin Professors. These were by nature multidisciplinary, since such professors were scattered across departments at Penn, and so several activities specifically involving Goffman are included. There were other such efforts, presumably, but the documentation located thus far is limited. Even so, what has been learned establishes yet another context in which Goffman collaborated with peers at Penn. The Benjamin Franklin Professors were a small, elite group, having between six and twenty members in any given year, so it is not terribly surprising that there were only three overlaps between that list and those in either the lists of primary or peripheral group members. (Those three were Philip Rieff in sociology, Leo Steinberg in history of art, and Leonard Meyer in music, all of whom are described in the appendix.)

Multidisciplinary Coordination Efforts

Together the six endeavors below establish that Goffman was a valued and integral part of a network at Penn extending far beyond the primary peer

Table 5.1: Goffman's Penn Colleagues by Minor Project

SP	LII	CCCC	SSB	ASB	LCS
D. Hymes	**Labov**	**Labov**	**Goodenough**	**B.H. Smith**	**Goodenough**
Ben-Amos	Botel	**Gelman**	Birdwhistell	**Ben-Amos**	**D. Hymes**
Fought	Fought	Fought	Fought	**Gross**	Birdwhistell
Goffman	Gelman	Gleitman	Gleitman	**Meyer**	Feld
Goldstein	Gleitman	Goffman	Goffman	**G. Prince**	Fought
Labov	Goffman	Goodenough	D. Hymes	Appadurai	Glassie
Sapir	Goodenough	D. Hymes	Labov	Baker	Goffman
Szwed	D. Hymes	Joshi	W. J. Smith	Botel	Heath
Worth	Joshi	Osherson		Davenport	V. Hymes
	Osherson	Premack		Evin	Kroch
	Premack	E. Prince		Fought	Labov
	Rosner	W. J. Smith		Frappier-Mazur	Long
	W. J. Smith	Szwed		Gaeffke	Sankoff
	Szwed			Glassie	Schieffelin
				Goffman	D. Smith
				Goodenough	Szwed
				Hanaway	Wolfson
				Hiz	
				D. Hurvich	
				L. Hurvich	
				D. Hymes	
				Joshi	
				Kirshenblatt-Gimblett	
				Messaris	
				Meyer	
				Morson	
				Premack	
				E. Prince	
				Radway	
				Richman	
				Rosner	
				Ruch	
				Steinberg	

Table 5.1: Goffman's Penn Colleagues by Minor Project (cont'd)

SP	LII	CCCC	SSB	ASB	LCS
				Steiner	
				Sutton-Smith	
				Szwed	
				Vogel	
				Winter	

group responsible for the more significant and successful projects. That means he was part of a large number of informal conversations, letters, meetings, and meals, not to mention the occasional conference or other event, with overlapping groups of colleagues across numerous departments and schools at Penn. In the table below, leaders of each group are shown first, and in bold; everyone else is listed alphabetically so it becomes possible to quickly see who was involved in which. Goffman was involved in all of them, since that is how they were chosen for inclusion here. And his small circle of primary peers was involved in most of them: Hymes led two and was part of all the others;[2] Labov led two and was involved in three others; Szwed was part of five; Birdwhistell was part of two; and Worth was only part of one. (The fact that Worth died in 1977 is likely a reason for his limited involvement.)

Why Was Multidisciplinary Coordination Needed?

The first question to be addressed for this set of projects is why the coordination efforts they represented were even necessary. The short answer is that overlaps between members of each group occasionally conflicted or were not adequately accounted for. A single example will make the problem abundantly clear. Labov wrote to Hymes in 1976: "We (I) slipped up badly on one point. Nobody told John Szwed about Gillian's course on Pidgins and Creoles. So instead of teaching his course on Creole literature in the spring, when it would have had a big enrollment, he held it this fall and had to cancel it with only 3 students. This was bad coordination and we have to do better."[3] Hymes responded: "I'm very sorry to hear about the situation affecting John's course. It is indeed hard to keep everyone informed of everything. Maybe we could benefit from a conscious decision to get together once a semester to share teaching plans, etc.?"[4] Several attempts, mostly unsuccessful, to address this issue of coordination across departments and colleges were made by overlapping sets of people. Each of these will be briefly outlined below.

Semiotic Program (SP)

As early as 1969, when Hymes was a member of the folklore graduate group but not yet based full-time in the folklore department, he argued that the department needed to expand in ways that would better tie it to other programs on campus. One specific direction he saw as obvious was a move into semiotics. His position was that "the present program of the department is not at all 'folklore' in the sense given the term by so many. It emphasizes communication, performance, structure, style, interdisciplinary relations; the fundamental premise is that folklore is an aspect of social science. It is distinguished within social science by its specific substantive concerns, not by its general goals."[5] Later in the same letter, he proposed a new name: "Terms such as 'semiotics,' 'symbolic forms' suggest themselves."

In 1971, Hymes reported to Sebeok: "Today Ken Goldstein, Dan Ben-Amos, and John Szwed and I spoke with our graduate dean to explore the possibility of a graduate group that might call itself 'semiotics.' Sol Worth and Erving Goffman might join in with us." He went on to explain that if the anthropology department would not fight to keep Sapir, he would work with linguistics instead of anthropology, and "try to get the interdisciplinary semiotics program going."[6] A few weeks later, Hymes wrote to Goldstein with more detailed ideas.

> Here are some thoughts on the prospective "semiotic" program, a general observation or two, and a suggestion of the form that the actual graduate course of study might take. . . . we are trying to reconstruct the unity between folklore, linguistics and cultural anthropology that obtained when these disciplines flourished a half-century or more ago, and made some of their greatest contributions, had some of their greatest figures . . . [Franz] Boas, [Alfred] Kroeber, [Edward] Sapir, [Robert] Lowie, etc. . . .
>
> Our possibly "historic" opportunity is to reconstruct such a unity on a new basis. . . . Whereas the earlier period realized its best work in study of independent symbolic forms—language, folktale, cultural pattern in abstraction, the challenge now is to discover the integration of symbolic forms, and the emergent structure of symbolic forms, in everyday life. . . . In folklore, the study of performance is the prime example. . . . We have the chance to put the interest in symbolic forms on a new footing. . . .

> This focus has various labels: ethnography of communication, language in context, in part sociolinguistics, etc. "Semiotics" can serve, as concise and of appropriate scope, so long as we can make clear that our focus is not study of texts or formal structures per se, but has a specific thrust. "Dynamic semiotics" as it were . . .[7]

He then listed specific courses in anthropology, folklore, and linguistics that he was proposing be part of the program, with details about what happened in each. In addition to Ken Goldstein and Dan Ben-Amos in folklore, he named Ward Goodenough and Dave Sapir in anthropology, Labov and John Fought in linguistics, Goffman and himself as those teaching the relevant courses. For Goffman, he had no specific course listed, but only "Goffman course or seminar." He argued that verbal art and other symbolic forms were "universal" and that "such study requires training and understanding cutting across quadrant boundaries, linking 'humanistic' and 'social science' fields."[8] That proposal was copied to Fought, Goffman, Goodenough, Labov, Sapir, and Worth, as likely group members who might be interested in the plan. There is no response preserved in the file from any of those concerned. This proposal seems to have died nearly as soon as it was put forward, so is primarily noteworthy for demonstrating that Hymes thought of Goffman as linked to semiotic theory, not the obvious assumption by most others, and as a precursor to later attempts. The fact that both Hymes and Goffman organized conferences jointly with Thomas Sebeok, well-known for his role in institutionalizing semiotics, provides useful background information, but was not made explicit in this proposal. (Those conferences form part of chapter 6, given that Sebeok taught at Indiana rather than Penn.)

Language and Interaction Institute (LII)

Labov, Hymes, and Goffman tried to build on the Codes in Context conference and simultaneously expand upon *Language in Society*, Conduct and Communication, and the Center for Urban Ethnography, developing something new, variously named the "Institute of Language Behavior," the "Institute on Language and Interaction," and, finally, used here to refer to all the iterations, "Language and Interaction Institute" (LII). These were all different names for the same basic structure. This provides a fascinating demonstration of the way this group saw their efforts to be interrelated and overlapping, as well as providing documentation for how they succeeded in getting what they wanted—for, unlike the Semiotic Program, this one was approved. And Goffman was in the center of it, made evident when Hymes defined it as "the Institute about which Eliot Stellar talked to Erv Goffman."[9]

Hymes saw a way to link this institute to a conference he was already planning, through the Committee on Sociolinguistics, to be held January 1975 on Comparative Ethnographic Analysis of Patterns of Speech in the United States, and wrote to David Jenness, staff to that committee, saying, "I learned from our Provost (Eliot Stellar) that he had suggested to Erv Goffman the possibility of some sort of Institute at Penn, involving the links among the work of Erv, Bill Labov, myself and others. I don't know if this has gone further, or where it will go, but if something concrete results, it could help to develop a larger activity beyond this conference."[10] The idea for the LII apparently originated with Labov, who discussed a potential new institute in conversation with several of the top administrators at Penn at the time: Martin Meyerson (president), Eliot Stellar (provost), and John Hobstetter (associate provost); Stellar mentions this, and then explains, "I have since discussed it informally with Erv Goffman, Leila Gleitman, and Rochel Gelman, and they reacted positively. Dell Hymes is also positive, as you can see from his letter of June 14 [described below], and so is John Szwed." This quote comes from a proposal Stellar made for a meeting of all in this group once everyone was back on campus that fall. "The purpose of the meeting will be to discuss goals and scope of the 'institute,' its organization and relation to cognate departments, and the most important question of its leadership, administrative and intellectual."[11] A note at the end of the copy in the APS, in Hymes's writing, says, "Call Erv." So, what did Hymes say in the referenced letter to Stellar? He began with an apology: "I am very sorry that I shall be gone for the summer before there is a chance to meet with you and Erving Goffman. As it happened, there was a chance to talk with Erv that evening about the general idea of an institute or the like. We are in general agreement, but let me set down a few further thoughts as to my own particular perspective."[12] Hymes then outlined the idea in detail (over five single-spaced pages). He first summarized the topic of common interest as "the problematic nature of the organization and use of linguistic means," arguing that "this perspective . . . is one that could be uniquely developed here at Penn." After a quick evaluation of the relative strengths of programs at MIT, Berkeley, and Chicago, he concluded, "Nowhere is there the solid basis for empirical work, work with hard data from the speech community, as there is now at Penn, through the dynamism of Bill Labov (aided and abetted by some of the rest of us)." Then he highlighted weaknesses of Berkeley, Chicago, and Texas, concluding that the already existing connections at Penn between folklore, linguistics, sociology, education, and psychology might easily be developed into a future strength.

> The great gap which now exists in knowledge of our own society with regard to language is largely due to the absence of successful efforts by linguists and social scientists. . . . Those of us who are concerned with such a program have diverse primary foci. Bill Labov will probably continue to be primarily influenced by problems of linguistic change, and formal linguistic theory. Erv Goffman will probably continue to be primarily concerned with the development of basic method and knowledge in the observation of interaction. I will probably continue to be primarily interested in personal and cultural patterning of speech. But all of us can work together, and hopefully, through an adequate institutional arrangement, our efforts can reinforce each other and multiply fruitfully."[13]

After that lengthy explanation as to the logic of his proposal, he made a series of points: First, he highlighted the significance of *Language in Society*, the roles he, Goffman, and Labov had in making it a success, and its potential role in making Penn "a major center of sociolinguistic work." Then he talked about the Center for Urban Ethnography and the way in which it brought people together, saying that the major grant funding was about to run out, and hoping that Szwed's report of activities would demonstrate its value both for the subject and the university. He recommended Szwed for "an active part in the proposed institute," praising his past activities as director of CUE and his "deep knowledge of cultural and social history," and requested that any meetings held over the summer in his absence about the institute with Goffman and Labov might also include Szwed. He wrote:

> I'm very excited about the initiative you've taken and at the prospect of an organized way to pool our efforts here. . . . We have unique resources here—not as many people as crowd the halls of Berkeley but fundamental people—no one rivals Bill, or Erv, in their own spheres. I think we could do a better job of training people, and producing significant research, than anywhere else, given the opportunity. . . . We could have here at Penn the first place in the country to seriously take as its object of study what the life of language is like in the United States. Not that we ourselves could tackle more than a fraction of the whole. But we could make a decisive difference, that would radiate very far."[14]

This letter was copied to Goffman, Labov, and Szwed, to keep them in the loop.

Hymes spent that summer, as he did every summer, conducting research with the Warm Springs Sahaptin in Oregon; returning to campus in the fall, he found Stellar's previously mentioned letter waiting. He responded with delight that the idea was under consideration, only asking that John Fought be added to the group.[15] Stellar invited everyone plus Fought to a meeting in October.[16] As a result of that meeting, and presumably after additional conversations with the others in the group, Labov drafted a formal proposal to the university for what was then being called the Institute for Language and Interaction, circulating it to the others (which he now named "initiating members") for comments.[17] In it, he names as the central group members Fought, Gelman, Gleitman, Goffman, Hymes, Labov, and Szwed, and adds W. John Smith. Together they represented anthropology, biology, education, folklore, linguistics, and psychology. In addition, he said they had support from sociology, communications, English, and Romance languages. Labov explained the logic behind the request for establishing the institute thus:

> Over the course of the last ten years, our university has brought to Philadelphia a sizeable group of scholars whose major interest centers on language and linguistic means of communication. In our efforts to understand language and the abilities that lie behind it, a number of us have individually come to the conclusion that we cannot make much further progress by studying it in isolation: that the act of speaking must be examined in its social context as the most typical form of human interaction.[18]

Using the figure of ten years makes clear that Labov calculated the relevant period of time spent gathering the group from the start of Hymes's tenure at Penn, rather than his own. Labov further explained that: "The activities proposed for the Institute fall under three headings: promotion of interdisciplinary training; joint research; and publications." He proposed a new publication, *Pennsylvania Working Papers on Language and Interaction*, and wanted to house the two existing publications (the journal *Language in Society* and the book series Conduct and Communication) with which group members were already involved under the auspices of the new institute.[19] The group also wanted to offer an interdisciplinary program for graduate training and gave examples of how specific departments could take advantage of such training for their students (for example, "sociolinguistic research in the department of linguistics which requires experimental techniques developed in psychology and ethnographic methods developed in anthropology").[20] Members of the institute would co-teach seminars, following the example of Labov and Goffman teaching Conversational Analysis in 1973 and 1975. Interdisciplinary research projects and grants would be housed within the institute, following CUE's example.

They requested of the university:

1. Space within Eisenlohr Hall, where *LiS*, CUE, an NSF grant to Labov, as well as seminars by Labov, were already located.
2. An initial budget to start the new *Working Papers* series.
3. A small budget to support printing brochures for new and future students to learn about the institute.
4. Continuing support for *LiS*.[21]

Although currently housed in a separate folder,[22] it seems likely that a series of three diagrams documenting how the initial group members overlapped belongs with the proposal for the institute.[23] However, these seem to have been intended for a later version of a proposal than the one preserved, given that they all include a few additional people. All three are undated, so it is difficult to be sure when they were created. With those caveats in mind, figure 5.2 shows departmental affiliations for members of the institute.

Figure 5.2: Language and Interaction Institute: Departmental Affiliations

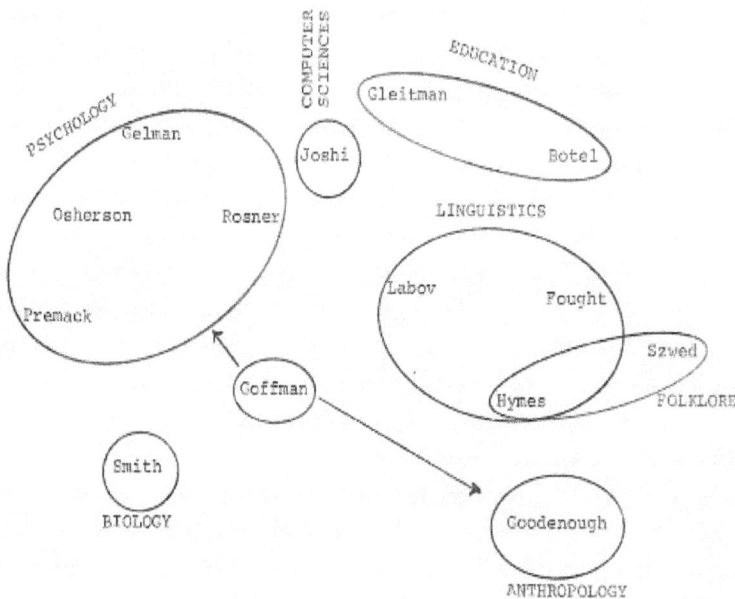

Most of the names here will be familiar. The new people mentioned are those in psychology, education, and computer sciences. One noteworthy oddity is the choice to link Goffman to anthropology and psychology rather than to anthropology and sociology, given that the image was likely prepared after his re-integration into that department by Fox. However, it was also likely after his secondary appointment to psychology, so that may have seemed more relevant in this context.

The next figure includes the same people, but this time, secondary affiliations are added.

Figure 5.3: Language and Interaction Institute: Departmental Affiliations, with Secondary Affiliations

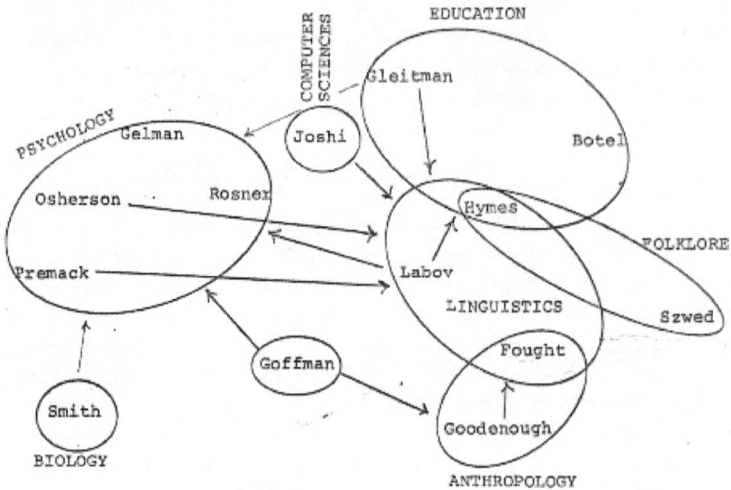

This figure is confusing to look at, due to all the information, but it should be interpretable after a little study. What is useful is that, by showing secondary affiliations, it becomes clear that no one was an island at Penn; the majority of these people had secondary affiliations. However, given Goffman's primary affiliation with sociology as well as anthropology, it is jarring to see sociology still missing entirely. This has to have been created in the late 1970s, which was after the point when Renée Fox had convinced Goffman to participate more actively in sociology. 'Tis a puzzlement.

Figure 5.4: Language and Interaction Institute: Interdisciplinary Activities and Research Projects and Proposals

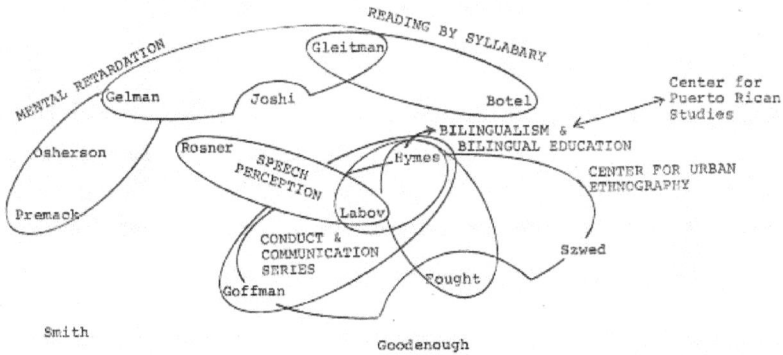

This final figure introduces a great deal of new information, documenting who was working on what, and with whom. The most directly relevant part is the inclusion of both the Conduct and Communication series (Hymes and Goffman), and the Center for Urban Ethnography (Szwed, Hymes, and Goffman). As with the omission of sociology, given the inclusion of both the book series and the center, it seems surprising that *Language in Society* was omitted.

In support of the proposal, Fought prepared three versions of a potential budget just for the new working papers series.[24] For some reason this documentation seems to have been submitted independently of the complete project; perhaps it was not ready at the same time, or perhaps as the discussion became serious, it was requested later. As a result, Dean Gregorian responded to Fought that there was insufficient funding available within the school for any, even the cheapest, option.[25] However, apparently some level of support was eventually granted to at least some other parts of the proposal for, at least by November 1976, Labov was signing himself as Director of the Language and Interaction Institute.[26] Unfortunately, there is little further documentation available, so it is unclear what impact the institute had. CUE and *LiS* stayed in Eisenlohr for a few years, so at least some space must have been granted. Labov edited a later publication, *Working Papers in Linguistics*; however, this was not a variation of the series initially proposed for the institute, but rather a later iteration of the series used as a model in this proposal which Labov was already editing, *Working Papers on Linguistic*

*Change and Variation.*²⁷ Most important is probably that the institute put forth a proposal for a Cross-Cultural Communication Center, explained below.

In May 1975, before the institute proposal had been resolved, Hymes sent a lengthy plan (five single-spaced pages) to Szwed for a new project intended to simultaneously re-invigorate the Center for Urban Ethnography and link it to the Language and Interaction Institute, ideally supported by obtaining funding through the SSRC Committee on Sociolinguistics (which Hymes was co-chairing at that point). Much of the logic was to take advantage of the solid cohort available at Penn. "We really have a very strong set of people already at Penn who could contribute, were they willing; hard to think of any place else with such a group, given our insistence on an ethnographic basis for the work." The topic would be "domestic ethnography" with a focus on "cross-cultural differences in speaking." He highlighted relevant work by "ERV obviously, not only for mode of work but for analytic contributions" (emphasis in original), Szwed, Labov, Worth, Fought, as well as Peggy Sanday (anthropology), Renée Fox (sociology), Barbara Kirshenblatt-Gimblett (folklore), Ellen Prince (linguistics), Virginia Hymes (folklore), and George Gerbner (communications). He saw the plan as involving the design of a guide (by spring 1977), hosting a summer institute at Penn, sponsored by CUE (during summer 1977), field research by core participants (fall 1977 through 1978), and a small conference "to compare experience and work, suggest revisions in guide."²⁸ Hymes asked Szwed to make copies for the others named, given that at that point he and Virginia Hymes were traveling out to Oregon for the summer.

So, what happened to his meticulous plan? The very last sentence of this letter tells us. "The Provost's office tried to reach me by phone. I'll call on Monday. Don't know what about." In fact, the provost asked Hymes to return to Penn to interview for the role as dean of the Graduate School of Education. He did, but was neither certain he would be offered the position nor whether he would accept it, so when they got to Oregon, he wrote David Jenness at SSRC about the idea he had earlier outlined for Szwed, this time more succinctly: He wanted to study "the linguistic ethnography/sociolinguistic description of situations in the United States."²⁹ In that same letter he mentioned that the call was about interviewing for the position of dean, which led to a question: "I trust there's no rule against Deans as members of committees." The provost did offer Hymes the position of dean, and he did accept, and that role absorbed much of his time, energy, and creativity for years. The project on linguistic ethnography/domestic ethnography was, as a result, reconfigured into two major grants from the National Institute of Education having a clear focus on education.[30]

Overlapping with the proposal for the Language and Interaction Institute, in fall 1974, Fought tried establishing a Native American Languages and Verbal Arts Program, which would have involved him and Dell and Virginia Hymes most directly, but others indirectly (not including Goffman, however). Fought was especially concerned to provide financial support for summer fieldwork by students.[31] A few months later, in support of this effort, Fought proposed that he and Hymes meet with the person responsible for grants for Indian education at the US Office of Education; they needed only minimal funding to cover a train ticket.[32] However, there is no documentation suggesting such a program was ever created.

Cross-Cultural Communication Center (CCCC)

Once the Language and Interaction Institute was established, there was a secondary move to create a new center within it, the Cross-Cultural Communication Center. Note the overlap of some of the goals of this new center with the goals of the earlier Center for Urban Ethnography. CCCC was proposed in 1976, two years after funding for CUE had run out. The proposal, signed by Rochel Gelman (in psychology) and Labov, begins:

> Over the past ten years, the University of Pennsylvania has assembled a group of scholars with a wide range of competence in the study of language and social interaction, with the demonstrated ability to work together on interdisciplinary problems. Such a group has recently concluded discussions on the formation of an institute for studying language and social interaction, combining joint competences in the investigation of cognitive processes, linguistic structure, and social interaction.
>
> Our common interests have come to a focus on the problem of failures in cross-cultural communication, as it affects children in many levels of our society.[33]

The focus was to be on "Black, Hispanic, and Amerindian cultures." It would include two phases: One would emphasize "the mapping of differences in the communicative systems that can lead to misunderstanding," and the other "an effort to locate the factors that make individuals sensitive to the existence of such conflicts, and to design programs that build on this capacity."[34] Those initiating the proposal came from various departments across campus: biology, psychology, linguistics, folklore, anthropology, education, and computer sciences. They explained that "each of us has directed research projects which demand interdisciplinary cooperation; a description of our past and current research indicates how the needs of our subject have brought each of us to the areas where joint thinking and scientific cooperation are required." Group members would be the existing LII members (Fought, Gelman, Gleitman, Goffman, Hymes, Labov, J. Smith, and Szwed), supplemented by the addition of Ward Goodenough (anthropology), David Premack (psychology), Dan Osherson (psychology), and Aravind Joshi (computer sciences). They emphasized the well-established links between group members, using as an example Goffman and Smith, who had "joined forces in conferences on the ethological study of human behavior and provided joint supervision of students working in this area." (The reference is to Goffman and Sebeok's conference on interaction ethology, described in chapter 6.) The proposal concludes: "A primary mission of the proposed center is interdisciplinary research and training of graduate students and postdoctoral fellows. Joint planning and investigation will be undertaken at all stages; colloquia and conferences will be directed to the fundamental issue of how an understanding of several aspects of human communicative competence will bear on the problems of cross-cultural communication outlined above."[35] In this, the group showed themselves to be far ahead of most others who would later argue the need to study cross-cultural (or, more often, intercultural) communication.[36] Obviously, there was no one at ASC studying the topic at the time, or they would have been included. (His students knew that Birdwhistell was interested in the influence of culture on interaction, especially given his training in anthropology, but that is not what most of his colleagues considered to be one of his research topics.)

In January 1977, Hymes forwarded that proposal to several colleagues within education: Allan Glatthorn, Mary Hoover, James Larkin, and Nessa Wolfson. His cover letter explains that the proposal was "intended simply to register an interest with the Administration so that it could so inform the Sloan Foundation, which is understood to be considering a grant in the general area of language." He did not invite these GSE faculty members to participate, but only wanted to let them know what was going on ("I thought you would like to see it").[37] Later that month, Provost Stellar, who also worked with Sloan to award research fellowships,[38] formally responded to Gelman and Labov by detailing a response from Ken Klivington at Sloan to the draft proposal. Klivington felt it was "too applied," and so Stellar sent formal guidelines for them to follow in an actual application. If they did that, Stellar felt that Penn had a good chance at being given a grant: "We are multidisciplinary. We do have strengths in the areas he is concerned with: development of language in the child, linguistics, acquisition of native languages, brain mechanism in language, use of symbols by Chimpanzees, etc. We also have an excellent record in graduate education."[39] At the same time, he warned that:

> We are, indeed, further ahead than his proposal guesses and are much closer than he thinks to being an interdisciplinary center of excellence already. Knowing Ken and the Sloan Foundation, however, we must follow their time schedule. Therefore, we should talk first about workshops, visiting professorships; then training; then a center of excellence. Each step should lead to the other so that we could have our "center" after a year or two.[40]

He asked that Gelman and Labov talk with the others and let him know if the group wanted to pursue the option. He attached the formal guidelines from Sloan for the new area of cognitive science, having highlighted the following (among other elements): that Sloan was interested in transdisciplinary research involving both graduate students and faculty, and that they had "identified language as a central focus in the cognitive sciences." He highlighted those parts of the document emphasizing language, especially one sentence: "Evidently no one institution now possesses the full range of linguistic competence suggested here."[41] Presumably, his assumption was that Penn did in fact possess such a range, which would serve as a compelling argument for awarding them the grant.

In response, in February 1977, Labov sent a note to everyone in the group bringing them up to date, passing on the documentation from Stellar as well as his letter. He outlined two opportunities: One would be to follow up with Sloan, while the other would be to apply to the National Institute for Child Health and Human Development (NICHD, one of the National Institutes of Health), through a program focusing on the health of American children. While this appears to be a quite different topic from either the initial proposal or Sloan's focus on cognitive science, he argued that the initial proposal could be recast and submitted for that instead. He had already spoken with someone at NICHD, who "strongly suggested that we are an ideal group to make such a proposal" given that they were looking for "some initiative from the behavioral sciences, which is now missing."[42] Apparently, one or more meetings and discussions were held that spring, with individual group members submitting specific drafts of parts of a proposal, for Labov wrote the group in June 1977 soliciting further input. He circulated a draft requesting funding for two workshops (so they had followed Stellar's guidelines).

One was to be organized by Joshi and Ivan Sag (a not-yet-mentioned faculty member in linguistics), and another by Gelman, Premack, Leila Gleitman, and another new name, her husband, Henry Gleitman (also in psychology). Labov acknowledged that a third workshop, on cross-cultural aspects of cognitive behavior, might be appropriate, but said they currently had no one who could offer that. He then asked that everyone think of someone not at Penn who could be brought in to work with them on joint research fellowships in the future, funded by a Sloan grant if one were obtained.[43]

In response to that draft, Hymes suggested that the new faculty member in education, Dan Wagner, might be added to the group to manage the third workshop.[44] And then he immediately wrote to Wagner, sending the proposal, and asking if he would be interested. Although Labov was by then using the title of Director of the Institute, Hymes first referred to it as "a proposed Institute" and then said it "has been more of a nominal intention for some time than anything else."[45] So it existed but was not terribly active.

In the end, not one but three proposals were accepted and substantial funding awarded. Penn received a small initial grant (in 1977), a second, larger one ($500,000 across the early 1980s), [46] and then a third one (again $500,000, across the mid-1980s),[47] all from Sloan, intended to establish a program in cognitive science. However, despite the success in obtaining funding, that support was not for cross-cultural communication; cognitive science is not an overlapping topic but an entirely different one. The project directors for the cognitive science grants were Leila Gleitman and Aravind Joshi. While Rochel Gelman and David Premack (both in psychology) of the original group participated, it appears that none of the others who were part of the institute and in the initial group proposing this center were included once the focus shifted to cognitive science.[48] (In their place, other faculty members, and graduate students, in each of their departments were brought into the project; most relevant in these pages would be Ellen Prince and Gillian Sankoff.[49]) These Sloan grants led to the later Institute for Research in Cognitive Science established at Penn in 1990, with still further funding from Sloan as well as some from NSF,[50] and involving a broader group of faculty across linguistics, math, philosophy, psychology, computer science, and neuroscience, [51] so they were absolutely a positive result, just not the result Labov and others had originally intended, no longer involving either cross-cultural communication or Goffman. Finally, it is worth noting that at least one of the goals of the original proposal—that of introducing courses on cross-cultural communication into the curriculum—was finally met in

1985, when Kathryn Woolard offered a new course in education, Seminar in Intercultural Communication and Miscommunication.[52]

Interdisciplinary Program in the Science of Symbolic Behavior (SSB)

We need to take a step back in time a few years for the next project because the history of these overlapped considerably. Despite the potential for confusion, the important lesson is that multiple people at Penn were thinking about creative ways to bring together people having organizational homes in different departments, and that they always included Goffman in the mix (at least for all of the ideas outlined here). In fall 1975, Ward Goodenough (anthropology) wrote to Dean Gregorian about the possibility of creating an Interdisciplinary Program in the Science of Symbolic Behavior, because "symbolic behavior is obviously the medium through which social life is maintained, human emotions and values are expressed, culture is created and shared, and individual human beings learn to perceive themselves and their world and also learn to be functioning members of their community."[53] The relevance was that it would be "central to problems in linguistics, cultural anthropology, psychology, philosophy, and sociology" and what was learned by scholars in these areas would have "direct application to problems in education, business management, and public administration (including public health)." He further pointed out that while "organized research and training programs are virtually nonexistent" because they require cooperation across disciplines, Penn already had "a group of people who can put together an integrated program" at the graduate level, and perhaps at the undergraduate level as well. He concluded, "I see this as not just another interdisciplinary program, but as an effort at building a science."[54] So he had found a gap and thought Penn had the resources to productively fill it.

The letter was copied to Birdwhistell, Fought, Gleitman, Goffman, Hymes, Labov, and W. J. Smith, by now a familiar cast of characters. The copy to Hymes included a handwritten note, "Do you have any thoughts about this?" Hymes initially responded positively: "I certainly think that this could be a valuable things [*sic*] today. It might provide a way of bringing together interests in anthropology, linguistics, sociology, folklore, and other fields here at Penn. It is my sense of the situation that there are a number of people in these different programs with interests in common which are not entirely at home together in any existing arrangement."[55] But then Hymes went on to bring up an alternative, his original idea from 1969 of establishing a semiotic program, "the semiotic seminar, if it were to be developed . . . the central thrust would not be to address all the many and vast problems associated with symbolism, but to develop a cadre of people able to describe and analyze symbolic activity wherever found. This might be initially a less glamorous thing to do but also might be ultimately the most important and rewarding."[56] Neither of these interdisciplinary proposals seems to have been put into place. However, they most likely prepared the ground for the next such efforts of overlapping groups of faculty and other interdisciplinary programs on campus over the next few years, including one in East Asian studies,[57] and another in ethnohistory,[58] as well as a general campus-wide "commitment to interdisciplinary study" advertised in 1978, involving the establishment of three new administrative structures: the Institute for Social Sciences, Institute for Humanities, and Institute for Mathematical Sciences.[59] Those stories will not be told here, as none of them (so far as I have seen) involved Goffman, nor most of the others.

Center for the Study of Art and Symbolic Behavior (ASB)

In early 1979, Penn announced the establishment of a Center for the Study of Art and Symbolic Behavior. Barbara Herrnstein Smith (English) was director, with Dan Ben-Amos (folklore), Larry Gross (communications), Leonard B. Meyer (music), and Gerald Prince (Romance languages) serving as the governing board. It was funded by a grant from the National Endowment for the Humanities, so we know that, unlike some of the other minor projects, this one was definitely established and financed. The goals were to "focus on the interdisciplinary study of the arts, language, literature and other forms of symbolic behavior" and to "encourage the exchange of ideas between the humanistic and social-scientific disciplines." Faculty were drawn from anthropology, art history, communications, folklore, linguistics, music, sociology, and psychology. Activities would include "a residence program for both junior fellows and senior scholars, seminars and lectures by visiting scholars, research projects and workshops for non-academic participants interested in applying such research to their own fields, colloquia, conferences and publications."[60]

In a letter sent out by the governing committee members to the thirty-two campus faculty members invited to become "Regular Members" of the center, in addition to Goffman, Hymes, and Szwed, are many names mentioned for their connections to previous efforts, either major or minor: Davenport, Fought, Glassie, Goodenough, Joshi, Kirshenblatt-Gimblett, Premack, Rosner, and Sutton-Smith. But there are also a surprising number of new names: Jean Alter (Romance languages), Arjun Appadurai (anthropology), Houston Baker, Jr. (English/Afro-American studies), Ahmet Evin (Oriental studies), Lucienne Frappier-Mazur (Romance languages), Peter Gaeffke (Oriental studies), William L. Hanaway, Jr. (Oriental studies), Henry Hiz (linguistics), Dorothea Jameson Hurvich and Leo Hurvich (both in psychology), Paul Messaris (communications), Gary Saul Morson (Slavic languages), Ellen Prince (linguistics), Janice Radway (American civilization), Michèle H. Richman (Romance languages), Barbara Ruch (Oriental studies), Leo Steinberg (history of art), Peter Steiner (Slavic languages), Amos Vogel (communications), and Irene Winter (history of art).[61] Accompanying the letter was a lengthy report explaining why the center should be established. Most importantly, the argument was not just for recognition of "a blurring or even dissolving of boundary lines between traditional disciplines" but for "a comprehensive and radical reorganization of the whole intellectual map, closer to a geological upheaval in the contours of a continent than a mere re-allocation of national territories." And there was a secondary argument that Penn "is eminently, perhaps uniquely, suited to sponsor" such a center, given "the university's unusual strength in almost all of the individual disciplines that relate to the study of art and symbolic behavior (e.g., anthropology, sociology, psychology, folklore, linguistics, communications)."[62]

The *University of Pennsylvania Almanac* chronicles numerous important and well-known names as guest lecturers over the next few years sponsored by this center: Among them were Mihaly Csikszentmihalyi,[63] Ruth Finnegan,[64] and James Fernandez[65] in 1981; Gayatri Chakravorty Spivak in 1982;[66] and Michel de Certeau in 1983.[67] In addition, the center sponsored a conference on Literature and Psychoanalysis, in 1986.[68] But activities had slowed down by 1986, when the center was reorganized and renamed the Center for Cultural Study, with Gerald Prince taking over as co-director. In 1987, the Mellon Foundation provided a major grant,[69] and, as a result, the name changed again to Program for Assessing and Revitalizing the Social Sciences (PARSS),[70] with additional lectures and conferences.[71] PARSS continued until 1998, when it was consolidated with several other campus programs into the new Penn Humanities Forum.[72] Clearly, the effort to bring impressive guest lectures and conferences on topics of broad interest across campus was successful, although how much the initial group members were involved in each of these activities is difficult to discern at this point. Unfortunately, there is no record of whether Goffman's role was more than just being one of the thirty-two scholars invited to participate.

Interdisciplinary Program in Language, Culture, and Society (LCS)

The recognized need for information sharing led to a final effort to create a new interdisciplinary program at Penn sparked by Goodenough, involving both Dell and Virginia Hymes, Goffman, Labov, and Sankoff, to have a focus on what was originally named "language, behavior, and society." First, it may help document the overlaps in content being taught by faculty based in different departments, with relevant courses overlooked by students who presumably would have wanted to know about them. In fall 1979, Hymes asked anthropology graduate students Linda May and Ako Imamura to prepare a list of "graduate courses on Language and Culture" being offered at Penn in spring and fall 1980, with information about course numbers and readings, as well as which departments they were offered by and any they were cross-listed with.[73]

This list demonstrates the breadth of the problem: The group of people having overlapping interests was significantly larger in the late 1970s than it had been in the late 1960s, so if students were to discover relevant courses across campus, they would need help learning of them. (Incidentally, the move to begin with this list is not mine but Hymes's; it was filed in the folder for the Interdisciplinary Program in Language, Culture, and Society.)

In February 1980, Hymes answered a letter from Goodenough that is missing; he said he was responding to "your initiative in planning interdepartmental work in language and culture," describing what he considered a related conversation he had been having with Sankoff about "the need for a curriculum in 'ethnolinguistics.'"[74] Shortly after, Dell and Virginia Hymes, Goffman, Labov, Sankoff, and Goodenough all met and agreed it was time to attempt something new. Goodenough represented the group in writing to Dean Robert H. Dyson Jr. because "the lack of such a program was commented on adversely by the External Review Committee for Anthropology last year."[75] The group recommended that the committee to run the program should include, in addition to Goodenough and Hymes: Fought, Labov, Sankoff, and Kroch (all in linguistics); Wolfson, Heath, and Schieffelin (in education); Glassie (folklore); Birdwhistell (communications); and Goffman (anthropology and sociology). The program would not award degrees but instead play a role in coordinating existing graduate groups across campus

Table 5.5: Graduate Courses on Language and Culture at Penn, Spring/Fall 1980

Department	Faculty Members and Courses
Spring 1980	
Anthropology	Erving Goffman (Social Interaction) Virginia Hymes (Language and Culture)
Linguistics	Dell Hymes (Ethnography of Speaking; Problems in Ethnography of Speaking) Anthony Kroch (Research Seminar on Language in Context) Gillian Sankoff (Languages in Contact; Study of Speech Community) Virginia Hymes (Native American Languages)
Education	Sue Fiering (Classroom Discourse and Interaction) Nessa Wolfson (Languages of Inequality; Sociolinguistics in Education; Selected Topics in Educational Linguistics)
Folklore	Dan Ben-Amos (Problems in Folk Narrative Research; Structural Analysis) Brian Sutton-Smith (Play and Games; Research Seminar on Games)
Communications	Ray Birdwhistell (Interpersonal Communication Codes; Interpersonal Communication Seminar) Larry Gross (Aesthetic Communications)
Fall 1980	
Anthropology	Ward Goodenough (Formal Analysis of Ethnographic Data)
Linguistics	Gillian Sankoff (Introduction to Ethno- and Socio-linguistics; Pidgins and Creoles)
Education	David Smith (Anthropology and Education) Nessa Wolfson (Educational Linguistics; Selected Topics in Educational Linguistics) Leila Gleitman (The Psychology of Language) Shirley Brice Heath (Language Planning and Public Policy; Ethnographic Methodology: Community to Classroom)
Folklore	John Szwed (Creole Literatures) Dan Ben-Amos (Theoretical Aspects of Myth; Prose Narrative; The Folktale) Kenneth Goldstein (Folklore of Britain and Ireland)
Communications	Ray Birdwhistell (Advanced Seminar)

by minimizing overlap and filling in gaps. A few weeks later, Hymes wrote a note to Goodenough with suggestions for how to improve their chances of getting the program approved.[76] A few weeks after that, Hymes told Goodenough that he'd heard from Dyson that there was an issue with the term "behavior" in the name of the group, because that implied psychology should be involved, and perhaps using the term "ethnolinguistics" would solve the matter.[77] In the end, Dyson wrote a letter in May 1980 inviting all the group members who had been named initially to be members of a new Committee on Language, Culture, and Society, with Goodenough serving as chair. (This final name was likely a nod to Hymes's (1964b) and Goodenough's (1971) books, which both used the same words, just in different order.) Dyson mentioned that, in fact, not just one but two external review committees had encouraged this (those would have been for anthropology and, presumably, linguistics). The goal would be to "try to strengthen the available offerings in this interdisciplinary study area and to maximize the use of our existing resources through the elimination of overlapping course content, the strengthening of existing courses, the addition of new courses where needed, and the identification of core courses and reading lists fundamental to all students of the subject regardless of their specialized interests."[78] It only took a single day before Hymes wrote a letter to Goodenough about a coordination issue (the need for someone to teach ethnolinguistics, since there was a group of students wanting to study the topic, and pass a PhD exam question on the topic, but no one regularly teaching it, given that Hymes, who usually took responsibility for it, was too busy as dean of GSE).[79] Two days after that, Hymes notified Dyson that Heath needed to be replaced on the committee because she had just accepted a position at Stanford, recommending David Smith (also in education) as her replacement. Glassie also needed to be replaced because he would be on leave for the year; Hymes recommended Szwed for that vacancy.[80] That fall, while organizing his spring courses, Hymes decided that "those of us explicitly concerned with students in linguistics, education, and folklore" should meet and sort out logistical concerns; that meant V. Hymes, Sankoff, Schieffelin, and Wolfson. He said he wanted "a group small enough to arrive at specific proposals" by "those in 'ethnolinguistics' and 'educational linguistics.'"[81]

By November 1980, Feld (in communications, first in addition to, and later as a replacement for, Birdwhistell) and Long (in education) had been added to the group, and the substitutions of D. Smith and Szwed had been accepted, when Goodenough called a first meeting.[82] But apparently something happened over the next year, because Hymes sent a note in fall 1981 to a reduced group (Birdwhistell, Glassie, Goffman, Kroch, Labov, Sankoff, Schieffelin, Wolfson) saying that Dyson had made him chair when Goodenough stepped down.[83] Then, in January 1982, Hymes sent a very unhappy note to an even smaller subset of the committee (Fought, Schieffelin, and Wolfson) saying that he had only gotten one reply to his fall request for details of course offerings so they could coordinate, and asking if this group thought it would be possible to get things moving again (and if so, he would recommend adding V. Hymes to represent folklore), or if he should ask Dyson to disband it. "I mentioned this to Bob Dyson Friday and he said that he had appointed the committee because asked to do so, but would of course dissolve it if there were in fact nothing to do. Which would be only appropriate."[84] Schieffelin responded with an equally unhappy message about how she had not gotten much cross-departmental enrollment in a course that she had advertised in anthropology, folklore, and linguistics.[85] Apparently, Hymes considered that more a personal note than a formal response because he wrote to Fought a few months later, saying, "There's been still no response from anyone on my memo regarding a last-ditch effort to breathe some life into the language and culture sequence." He asked for a meeting with Fought, Wolfson, and V. Hymes to sort things out, then they would bring in Sankoff and Schieffelin. Apparently, at that point all the other committee members were dropped from consideration.[86] There is no documentation of what happened next, but apparently the committee somehow kept on going because in May 1982, Dean Dyson asked Hymes to serve a further two years as committee chair, and to review the list of members. Hymes approved Goodenough, Sankoff, Labov, Kroch, Glassie, Goffman, Wolfson and Schieffelin, pointed out that Fought had been inappropriately omitted, and requested (again) that Feld serve in lieu of Birdwhistell.[87] Goffman died in November 1982; presumably, he was irreplaceable, as no one proposed a substitute. In spring 1983, a formal report by Hymes on behalf of the committee to Acting Dean Donald D. Fitts sounds as if they were at that point again a functional committee. Group members copied on that report were Birdwhistell, Feld, Fought, Goodenough, Glassie, V. Hymes, Kroch, Labov, Sankoff, Schieffelin, D. Smith, Wolfson, and Kathryn Woolard (a new name in this group, based in education).[88] In fall 1983, Hymes was reappointed chair, with the members now being Feld, Fought, Glassie, Goodenough, Kroch, Labov, Sankoff, Schieffelin, Wolfson, and Woolard.[89] By fall 1984, Goodenough resumed the position of chair, with Hymes remaining as a committee member; Glassie did not sign up for another term, although the others all did. By that point the group was more a name than an active body; Hymes was sorry to report "that it does not seem to be able to do much, not even to exchange course descriptions regularly," and so it was "a potential that isn't realized."[90] In spring 1985, Goodenough requested a group meeting to discuss its future.[91] Apparently, the group was by then somehow re-energized, for the minutes of that meeting sent around by Goodenough include ten major points involving future activities. These were mostly concerned with coordination and information sharing, but also the establishment of a faculty seminar and a possible new undergraduate major.[92] However, most of these goals were never realized. Over the next few years, members of the group dropped out, and were replaced by others, but that was long after Goffman had died, and almost none of the new members had documented contact with him.[93]

One interesting note: In Penn's five-year plan for 1988–1992, this committee was specifically mentioned. At one point the plan says, "The School of Arts and Sciences has a tradition of interdisciplinary innovation" and folklore is listed as a department which is "interdisciplinary by nature." After listing other noteworthy programs, the paragraph concludes: "SAS faculty from across departments also work together on academic Committees—for example . . . language, culture and society—through which they share mutual research interests and work toward the development of pertinent courses."[94]

To summarize this committee's activities: It involved both central and peripheral actors in Goffman's invisible college, and he was a member until his death. The group was established to facilitate coordinating activities and offerings across multiple departments and schools, and to ensure that the topic of language and culture (or ethnolinguistics, depending on year) continued as an area of strength, despite the distribution of group members across campus. It was a final (partially successful) effort (in terms of having been approved and come into existence) to coordinate across disciplinary boundaries, so that activities of interest (especially courses) beyond a single department might be shared ahead of time, which would have the added benefit of increasing enrollments. The group faced substantial difficulty in keeping everyone consistently involved but became re-energized after several years of minimal participation. This was a successful group in terms of having been approved, and holding periodic meetings, but remarkably unsuccessful if judged by consistent effort or producing any notable results. It is unclear what role Goffman played beyond attending at least some meetings and being listed as a member for the first two years.

Center to Study Marketing to Children

There is one other minor interdisciplinary project meriting brief mention, although it was not begun by anyone at Penn and, in the end, turned out to be more thought experiment than actuality, so it has not been added to table 5.1. However, it did involve Goffman, at least tangentially, and in an unusual way. Here is the story. In spring 1972, Penn started something new, the College of Thematic Studies, established by Vice Provost for Undergraduate Education Humphrey Tonkin. The goal was to "provide undergraduate education with coherence and structure" by placing "top professors and non-academic 'experts' in small undergraduate seminars" open only to freshmen and sophomores (Silver 1972, 1). In spring 1973, the experiment was repeated, and Robert B. Choate Jr., then chair of the Council on Children, Media and Merchandising and nationally known as a consumer advocate, was invited to campus as one of fifteen speakers; his topic was "Children and Television Advertising" (Murphy 1973). Choate mentioned to a student reporter that he wanted to start a Center to Study Marketing to Children, and was asking for leadership rather than funding from Penn because he had already requested major funding from several foundations for "an initial multi-million dollar, five-year program"; the student wrote that he "hopes to receive a commitment from the Ford Foundation, among others, as early as next week" (Biddle 1973, 1). This center is relevant because not only had faculty across Wharton (business), Annenberg (communications), and the Law School expressed interest in the "inter-departmental and inter-institutional center," but Goffman was specifically named, along with Dean Gerbner, Larry Gross, and President Meyerson as "having expressed 'enthusiasm' about the project" (7). Goffman presumably became involved because Choate was the brother of his first wife, Angelica Schuyler Choate, who had died in 1964.[95] Despite the relationship, it is unlikely Goffman was responsible for Choate's campus visits because the family had a long prior history of involvement with Penn.[96]

However, when Choate returned to present a colloquium at ASC six months later, this one on "Television Broadcasting: An Attractive Nuisance to the Child," he was interviewed by another student reporter. This time he explained that the plans for the center were "sort of on a back burner" and he had not carried out negotiations with Penn since spring because "Penn didn't seem any more eager to have it than any other institution, so I'm not sure it'll come here" (Berger 1973, 2). So far as I have been able to discover, the center was never established, and certainly not at Penn. Thus, as mentioned earlier, this becomes a minor footnote in the story of Goffman's multidisciplinary collaborations—one that was conceived, greeted initially with enthusiasm by Goffman among others, but never put into practice.

Benjamin Franklin Professors

When Goffman was hired, it was as a Benjamin Franklin Professor. "Benjamin Franklin Professorships (which don't exist anymore) were very prestigious appointments for especially distinguished scholars" (Fox 2009). They were invented so "the University can attract to its faculty other scholars of outstanding achievement and promise in academic areas of particular importance to the intellectual concerns of the era."[97] Further, there was an understanding that anyone nominated "should possess three qualities, international reputation, a strong interdisciplinary dimension and a bold innovative approach,"[98] for they were "the greatest honor that the University of Pennsylvania can bestow on anyone."[99] The Haas Community Fund provided a gift to Penn to supplement the salary of such professors.[100] As Louis Schwartz, chair of the Benjamin Franklin Professors in 1971, explained: "The whole idea was to make a batch of impressive appointments that would command attention in academia and the public press, and possibly start a flow of high talent in the direction of Pennsylvania."[101] The press release announcing Goffman's hire mentions that, at the same time, two existing faculty members were being promoted to Benjamin Franklin Professors: Zellig Harris (in linguistics) and Robert Duncan Luce (in psychology). In addition, the press release reports that another five faculty members at Penn having the title "University Professor," a separate honor,[102] were simultaneously promoted to "Benjamin Franklin Professors." That group included Loren Eiseley (anthropology), Lawrence Klein (economics), Charles Price (chemistry), Philip Rieff (sociology), and Louis B. Schwartz (law).[103] (Rumor suggests that these others were angry someone new would be brought in at the highest possible level and demanded to be given improved titles as well, but this is difficult to confirm so many years after the fact.) In 1977, all Benjamin Franklin Professors were converted to Benjamin Franklin University Professors, in recognition that these positions "cut across disciplinary or professional lines."[104] This change included Goffman.

By 1970, there were nine in the group: those already named (Eiseley, Goffman, Harris, Klein, Price, Rieff, and Schwartz), as well as Thomas C. Cochran (history) and Robert E. Davies (molecular biology); in addition, there were three former members who had either left the university (Robert Duncan Luce, psychology), died (Ephraim A. Speiser, Oriental studies) or resigned (Kenneth Setton, history).[105] The group met several times each year, most often to discuss additional candidates for membership in the group, drawn either from existing faculty at Penn, or potential new hires when departments wanted to increase the prestige of their offer. For the few meetings where minutes or letters sent to group members after a meeting have been preserved, Goffman was always one of those listed as having attended.[106] In addition, there were periodic dinners with President Martin Meyerson, often as an opportunity to meet with prospective new honorees, or to celebrate a current group member who was retiring.[107] Hymes mentions that he was nominated in 1972, although he was not accepted.[108] The longer story is fascinating: On the occasion of the republication of *Reinventing Anthropology*, Hymes chose to explain several controversial decisions taken by various anthropology departments with which he had been associated. One of these was at Harvard, where he was not granted tenure (despite being recommended by his department), likely for political reasons; another was at Penn, where he said he had been proposed as a Benjamin Franklin Professor (by no less a person than Penn's then-president, Meyerson), yet "the proposal was blackballed by one incumbent, an anthropologist known, it turned out, for hostility to linguistics" (1999, x). The only possible person this describes is Loren Eiseley, given that he was the sole anthropologist granted the title. Ward Goodenough and Anthony Wallace, also in anthropology, were also apparently proposed as potential members (their curriculum vitaes are in the file[109]), but if so, they also were not accepted.

A consistent theme was whether group members should take on a more active role on campus. In 1970, Davies proposed regular dinners with particularly good students drawn from different parts of the university discussing "major topics of current or universal interest," a series of seminars "on fundamental problems and progress in areas of general interest in our respective fields of scholarship," as well as proposing that they "supply members for a committee created to adjudicate in disputes over cases such as those involving tenure and promotion."[110] And in 1974, Price wrote to President Meyerson and Stellar: "We have discussed our possible roles, from a purely 'honorific' title to a major functional activity in the intellectual life of the University."[111] It is not clear which, if any, of these activities were implemented, but there is a record of the following three group activities, one passive, the other two active.

Group Library Exhibit

What all Benjamin Franklin Professors had in common was status: They were the best of the best being recognized for their achievements. In keeping with that understanding, it makes sense that in 1972 the Van Pelt Library at Penn organized an exhibition titled "Works by Benjamin Franklin Professors" to highlight their publications, accompanied by biographies and photographs. In addition to Goffman, those included in the exhibit were Cochran, Davies, Eiseley, Harris, Klein, Price, Rieff, Schwartz, Setton, and Speiser.[112] No further information is available, including what books of Goffman's would have been included in the display, but it seems reasonable to assume it would have been most if not all books he had published by 1972.[113]

National Politics

At least a subset of the Benjamin Franklin Professors was substantially involved in the Moratorium in 1969. This was a national event in response to the Vietnam War and the resulting anti-war sentiment evident across the US. Goffman has been said to have been indifferent to the anti-war protests while at Berkeley, but in 1969 he was one of "five Benjamin Franklin Professors who were signatories to the petition requesting dismissal of classes" (the five were Cochran, Goffman, Klein, Price, and Rieff), on what was designated a national Moratorium Day, October 15, 1969, as a form of opposition to the Vietnam War. (At that point, Price was chairing the university's Committee on Open Expression [Riley 1969], which may have been what led to the petition.) Provost David R. Goddard turned them down, on the grounds that "it is University custom not to close classes during occasions which involve matters of conscience or belief." Instead, he asked the petitioners "to plan and convene a campus-wide assembly for that day" (*Pennsylvania Gazette* 1969). The goal was to "have an opportunity to discuss a report entitled 'The Causes of Student Unrest and the Proper Response of the Universities to that Unrest,'" which had been submitted by the Committee on the Goals of Higher Education at Penn.[114] The provost agreed to make classes that day optional and allowed for two hours of campus-wide discussions. The campus student newspaper, *The Daily Pennsylvanian*, reported that nearly three thousand students, faculty, and staff attended (while bemoaning the fact that more did not). The assembly passed multiple resolutions (condemning the war, calling for withdrawal of troops, urging amnesty for those who chose jail or exile rather than military service), but a proposed resolution recommending that Penn no longer accept contracts and grants from the Department of Defense failed to pass. Several faculty members were photographed for the paper; given his known distaste for being photographed, it comes as no surprise that Goffman was not among them.

There is a related story. In 1970, Hymes mentioned to Labov that "Cambodia has even Erv signing petitions."[115] Here is what he was referring to: In the continuing effort to show opposition to the Vietnam War, students called for a strike across final exams in spring 1970, but there was a concern about how many students would feel free to participate, given the impact on their grades. As a result, Sol Worth prepared a "petition supporting the student strike and agreeing to provide alternative solutions for students who cannot take their exams as scheduled." Goffman signed, as did Cochran and Klein (Price and Rieff did not), along with Ben-Amos, Gleitman, Goldstein, Gross, Hymes, Scholte, and Szwed (of those involved in any of the other projects in these pages), and many, many dozens more not otherwise mentioned here (Faculty statement 1970).

Campus Politics

While Goffman and Rieff signed a petition in common for the Moratorium, in the next example, they came down on different sides. In 1980, choice of the next president of Penn became contentious. The search committee recommended Sheldon Hackney instead of then Provost Vartan Gregorian, who was quite popular and had been widely expected to be promoted. As a result, six Benjamin Franklin Professors signed the following statement: "We urge that Provost Vartan Gregorian's name put before a meeting of the Trustees to be voted on for President of the University of Pennsylvania." The six signatories were: Goffman, Davies, Klein, Schwartz, Meyer, and Steinberg—by then Price had retired.[116] They were not the only ones writing in to the *Almanac* with opinions on the matter, of course. However, the seventh Benjamin Franklin Professor at that time, Rieff, wanted it noted "as a matter of record that he was asked to sign and refused, and that he opposes the resolution."[117] Rieff had served on the search committee that made the decision of who to recommend to the trustees, and he stood by that decision.[118] Partly as a result of the position taken by the six Benjamin Franklin Professors, a special session of the Faculty Senate was held, and Gregorian was formally approved (although it turned out that this was not a legal maneuver, thus having no effect on the formal process). Shortly after, Gregorian called for one more special session of the Senate, explicitly inviting those six Benjamin Franklin Professors, as well as his deans, and a few others who had been publicly supporting him, to thank everyone who had made the motion to place his name in nomination. At the same time, he respectfully declined the honor.[119] Gregorian really had no choice, as the legal process simply did not permit a group outside the search committee to play a role in the decision. Hackney became the next university president, and Gregorian stepped down as provost.[120] This story, like the last few, is interesting for the fact that Goffman, often said to have been apolitical, several times joined others in this group in political activities.

Controversy

In 1979, there was substantial unhappiness among some faculty over Benjamin Franklin Professors—not with any individual having that title, but with the system itself. Briefly, the Senate Committee on the Faculty (a subcommittee of the Faculty Senate) prepared a report discussing the issues and making recommendations. They argued that "the Benjamin Franklin Professorships are defined by the trustees as 'the most distinguished professorships the University has to bestow.' We find this offensive to the holders of various named chairs and unseemly." There were specific objections to the fact that only those already in the group could nominate new members, which was felt to be "inherently unwise" based on the "concentration of power" in a small number of incumbents. What they found to be even more objectionable was that "the nominal purpose of the Benjamin Franklin Professorships was to honor 'interdisciplinary scholarship.' Thus the University proclaims that its highest academic honor is reserved for interdisciplinary scholars, and the two Nobel Laureates at the University are thereby disbarred!"[121] Faculty Senate held a meeting to discuss the matter on April 29, 1979, and the report was adopted.[122] That meant there could be no further Benjamin Franklin Professors appointed after that date, so Goffman remained one of a tiny minority of faculty members ever granted that prestigious title.

In 1980, after the Benjamin Franklin Professorships had been terminated, they were replaced by Distinguished Professorships. Ellen Prince wrote a dissenting statement to the *Almanac* arguing that at least some of these should be "reserved for individuals whose work has an interdisciplinary nature." She was willing to say that not all should be, as the Benjamin Franklin Professorships had been, but strongly felt that at least some needed to be.[123] It is not clear whether she won or lost that argument. By August 1981, since there could be no more new Benjamin Franklin Professors appointed, that group was combined with University Professors for most purposes. That meant that Goffman was routinely connecting with not only with the few other remaining Benjamin Franklin Professors (Davies, Klein, Meyer, Rieff, Schwartz, and Steinberg) but also with a set of University Professors that included Ward Goodenough, Dorothea Hurvich, and Barbara Herrnstein Smith, as part of the expanded Benjamin Franklin Professors and University Professors group. Of course, Goodenough, Hurvich, and Smith are all relevant because they overlapped with him on various minor projects. (There were at that point twenty combined members, including President Meyerson, Provost Gregorian, and the prior provost, Elliot Stellar—all of whom by then had been granted the additional title of University Professor—plus several who have no other role in these pages.)[124]

Conclusion

Goffman was part of a series of minor projects intended mostly to expand coordination across disciplinary boundaries on Penn's campus. These were largely unsuccessful, although not all in the same way. The Language and Interaction Institute proposed and directed by Labov was holding organizational meetings in 1974, and was established by 1976, yet has left remarkably little evidence of its activities. The Interdisciplinary Program in Language, Culture, and Society was organized by Goodenough and established in 1980, and directed either by him or Hymes depending on the year, but membership changed frequently, and it is unclear whether even the basic goal of coordinating course offerings across departments was ever met; certainly Hymes complained of a depressing lack of responses in the years he chaired that group. Efforts to create a Semiotic Program, proposed by Hymes, and the Interdisciplinary Program in the Science of Symbolic Behavior, proposed by Goodenough, as well as the smaller Native American Languages and Verbal Arts program proposed by Fought (that one not including Goffman), all seem to have been stillborn. The Center for the Study of Art and Symbolic Behavior was funded and did host a series of guest lectures by notables from outside Penn, as well as several conferences, and lasted surprisingly long (although undergoing not one but two name changes); however, activities seem to have been largely limited to these special events, and their impact remains unclear. The most successful effort out of the entire set, the Cross-Cultural Communication Center, initially designed by the Language and Interaction Institute, made a significant shift away from cross-cultural communication (the topic intended to bring together the network of members in the institute) toward cognitive science (a topic relevant to only a few institute members). As a result of this shift, the center received substantial funding, eventually becoming the Institute for Research in Cognitive Science. However, it was no longer a project involving Goffman—nor most of the others initially listed as potentially interested.

Despite the lack of any notable success for the majority of these efforts, they are all still worthy of attention given that they demonstrate the frequent conversations about multi- or interdisciplinary connections across campus, and the larger group (or rather, the set of overlapping groups) within which Goffman was situated at Penn. Goffman was part of all these efforts, although he does not seem to have been an organizer or key player for any of them. In addition, they are worth including since they highlight the effort to name the topic in which these scholars shared an interest: semiotics, symbolic behavior, language and interaction, cross-cultural communication, as well as language, culture and society. All of these terms and phrases are still in use today, although no one term is yet accepted as including them all.

The few activities of the Benjamin Franklin Professors for which there is available documentation are quite different, both in membership and focus, but demonstrate that Goffman was part of yet one more multidisciplinary cluster of faculty members on campus—in this case, all scholars whose research was explicitly interdisciplinary, and all of whom were being honored by their peers. In the process, the specific activities described reveal a Goffman who was more political than his reputation, both in terms of campus and national politics.

Just as the major projects showed what universities can do to develop and support creativity on the part of their faculty members, these minor projects expand what we understand. Despite being organized into disciplines for administrative purposes, universities can encourage and facilitate productive conversations across disciplinary boundaries, and reward interdisciplinarity (as with the Benjamin Franklin Professors). At the same time, the histories related in this chapter demonstrate just how difficult it can be for such connections to succeed, even when everyone is interested: Despite goodwill and the best of intentions, in fact, participants often become sidetracked by the administrative requirements of their own departments, and even when they have argued for the need to share information across departmental borders, doing so takes time and effort, which can be in short supply. So even with good intent, the results do not always live up to expectations.

Despite this, demonstrating the way in which Goffman was clearly connected to dozens of faculty members across so many parts of Penn during
his time there, in so many ways, reveals a complexity that has until now
been hidden, and often remains unacknowledged even when it is known.
Goffman should be considered to have been enmeshed in over a dozen different collectives and now can more clearly be seen to have been a valued
partner not only in the few successful major projects described in the last
chapter, but also multiple overlapping, less successful endeavors. He clearly
knew far more people, and was part of far more networks, than has generally
been acknowledged. Thus, although his publications were all sole authored,
they were conceived and written within a context of multiple conversations
with disciplinary others.

Endnotes

[1] https://www.asc.upenn.edu/about/mission-and-history/gerbner-years-1964-1989.

[2] To some extent, this may be an artifact of the archives consulted, as the Hymes Papers
proved the most useful source; obviously Hymes would not have had documentation for
projects in which he was not a participant.

[3] Labov to Hymes, Oct 7, 1976, DHH, Subcollection 1, Series I: Correspondence, 1951–
1987, Labov, William, folder 2, 1974–1987.

[4] Hymes to Labov, Oct 13, 1976, DHH, Subcollection 1, Subseries A: Early Correspondence, Labov, William, 1974–1987.

[5] Hymes to Ben-Amos, Feb 26, 1972, DHH, Subcollection 2, Series I: Correspondence,
Ben-Amos, Dan, 1970–2004.

[6] Hymes to Sebeok, May 4, 1971, DHH, Subcollection 1, Series I: Correspondence
1951–1987, Sebeok, Thomas, 1955–1982.

[7] Hymes to Goldstein, copied to Goffman, Labov, Sapir, Fought, and Worth, May 15, 1971,
DHH, Subcollection 1, Series I: Correspondence 1951–1987, Goldstein, Kenneth, S.,
1969–1987.

[8] Hymes to Goldstein, copied to Goffman, Labov, Sapir, Fought, and Worth, May 15, 1971,
DHH, Subcollection 1, Series I: Correspondence 1951–1987, Goldstein, Kenneth, S.,
1969–1987.

[9] Hymes to Gregorian, Jul 8, 1974, DHH, Subcollection 1, Series I: Correspondence
1951–1987, Gregorian, Vartan, 1974–1981.

[10] Hymes to Jenness, Jul 18, 1974, DHH, Subcollection 1, Series II: Conferences and Committees, Subseries D: Social Science Research Council, Committee on Sociolinguistics,
July–December 1974.

[11] Stellar to Donald N. Langenberg (Vice Provost), Vartan Gregorian (then Dean of Arts
and Sciences), and Hobstetter (Associate Provost), Aug 13, 1974, DHH, Subcollection 1,
Series II: Conferences and Committees, 1955–1987, Subseries E: Other Committees,
Language and Interaction Institute, 1974–1977.

[12] Hymes to Stellar, Jun 11, 1974, DHH, Subcollection 1, Series II: Conferences and Com-

mittees, 1955–1987, Subseries E: Other Committees, Language and Interaction Institute, 1974–1977.

[13] Hymes to Stellar, Jun 11, 1974, DHH, Subcollection 1, Series II: Conferences and Committees, 1955–1987, Subseries E: Other Committees, Language and Interaction Institute, 1974–1977.

[14] Hymes to Stellar, copied to Labov, Goffman, Szwed, Jun 11, 1974, DHH, Subcollection 1, Series II: Conferences and Committees, 1955–1987, Subseries E: Other Committees, Language and Interaction Institute, 1974–1977.

[15] Hymes to Stellar, Sep 3, 1974, DHH, Subcollection 1, Series II: Conferences and Committees, 1955–1987, Subseries E: Other Committees, Language and Interaction Institute, 1974–1977.

[16] Stellar to Fought, Gelman, Gleitman, Goffman, Gregorian, Hobstetter, Hymes, Labov, Langenberg, J. Smith, Szwed, Sep 24, 1974, DHH, Subcollection 1, Series II: Conferences and Committees, 1955–1987, Subseries E: Other Committees, Language and Interaction Institute, 1974–1977.

[17] "A Proposal to the University of Pennsylvania for an Institute of Language and Interaction," n.d. [1974], DHH, Subcollection 1, Series I: Correspondence 1951–1987, Labov, William, folder 2, 1974–1987.

[18] "A Proposal to the University of Pennsylvania for an Institute of Language and Interaction," n.d. [1974], DHH, Subcollection 1, Series I: Correspondence 1951–1987, Labov, William, folder 2, 1974–1987.

[19] "A Proposal to the University of Pennsylvania for an Institute of Language and Interaction," n.d. [1974], DHH, Subcollection 1, Series I: Correspondence 1951–1987, Labov, William, folder 2, 1974–1987.

[20] "A Proposal to the University of Pennsylvania for an Institute of Language and Interaction," n.d. [1974], DHH, Subcollection 1, Series I: Correspondence 1951–1987, Labov, William, folder 2, 1974–1987.

[21] "A Proposal to the University of Pennsylvania for an Institute of Language and Interaction," n.d. [1974], DHH, Subcollection 1, Series I: Correspondence 1951–1987, Labov, William, folder 2, 1974–1987.

[22] While Labov's proposal was found in the folder for his correspondence, the diagrams were found in the folder for the Language and Interaction Institute. (See next footnote for details.)

[23] These are filed after the letter and attachments from Stellar discussed in the next section, so they seem likely to have been created in 1977 (Stellar to Gelman and Labov, Jan 17, 1977, DHH, Subcollection 1, Series II: Conferences and Committees, 1955–1987, Subseries E: Other Committees, Language and Interaction Institute, 1974–1977).

[24] Fought to Gregorian, Jan 8, 1975, DHH, Subcollection 1, Series II: Conferences and Committees, 1955–1987, Subseries E: Other Committees, Language and Interaction Institute, 1974–1977.

[25] Gregorian to Fought, Feb 6, 1975, DHH, Subcollection 1, Series II: Conferences and Committees, 1955–1987, Subseries E: Other Committees, Language and Interaction Institute, 1974–1977. Fought forwarded that letter on to Hymes with the handwritten note "Any ideas?" There is no copy of a response.

[26] "A proposal for a research program on cross-cultural communication from the members of the Language and Interaction Institute," Nov 18, 1976, DHH, Subcollection 1, Series II: Conferences and Committees, 1955–1987, Subseries E: Other Committees, Language and Interaction Institute, 1974–1977. (So far, no additional documentation for the Language

and Interaction Institute has been located beyond the few pieces of the story found at APS; there is nothing in Penn's archives. Despite having been a student at Penn across 1975–1979, working with Hymes, Labov, and Fought among others, I have no memory of hearing about LII.)

[27] Interestingly, in 2004, the 27th Annual Penn Linguistics Colloquium held a special session in honor of Goffman, and several papers were published from that event in this series (e.g., Toye 2004).

[28] Hymes to Szwed, Jun 15, 1975, DHH, Subcollection 1, Series II: Conferences and Committees, Subseries D: Social Science Research Council, Committee on Sociolinguistics, May 1975.

[29] Hymes to Jenness, Jun 30, 1975, DHH, Subcollection 1, Series II: Conferences and Committees, Subseries D: Social Science Research Council, Committee on Sociolinguistics, May 1975.

[30] These grants would more accurately be described as transdisciplinary than interdisciplinary, given that the focus was on both of the assumptions required of transdisciplinary work: practical application and involvement of practitioners. However, since Goffman had no part in them, it is relevant only as a side note to this discussion.

[31] Fought to Gregorian, copied to Lisker (linguistics), Hymes, and John Witthoft (anthropology), Nov 4, 1974, DHH, Subcollection 2, Series I: Correspondence, Fought, John G., 1972–2004.

[32] Fought to Gregorian, copied to Lisker and Hymes, Apr 18, 1975, DHH, Subcollection 2, Series I: Correspondence, Fought, John G., 1972–2004.

[33] "A proposal for a research program on cross-cultural communication from the members of the Language and Interaction Institute," Nov 18, 1976, DHH, Subcollection 1, Series II: Conferences and Committees, 1955–1987, Subseries E: Other Committees, Language and Interaction Institute, 1974–1977.

[34] "A proposal for a research program on cross-cultural communication from the members of the Language and Interaction Institute," Nov 18, 1976, DHH, Subcollection 1, Series II: Conferences and Committees, 1955–1987, Subseries E: Other Committees, Language and Interaction Institute, 1974–1977.

[35] "A proposal for a research program on cross-cultural communication from the members of the Language and Interaction Institute," Nov 18, 1976, DHH, Subcollection 1, Series II: Conferences and Committees, 1955–1987, Subseries E: Other Committees, Language and Interaction Institute, 1974–1977.

[36] The topic existed, of course, mostly within communication programs, but it was not yet a standard option in communication departments across the US, as it is today.

[37] Hymes to Allan Glatthorn, Mary Hoover, James Larkin, and Nessa Wolfson, Jan 12, 1977, DHH, Subcollection 1, Series II: Conferences and Committees, 1955–1987, Subseries E: Other Committees, Language and Interaction Institute, 1974–1977.

[38] https://sloan.org/storage/app/media/files/annual_reports/1974-1978_annual_reports.pdf.

[39] Stellar to Gelman and Labov, Jan 17, 1977, DHH, Subcollection 1, Series II: Conferences and Committees, 1955–1987, Subseries E: Other Committees, Language and Interaction Institute, 1974–1977.

[40] Stellar to Gelman and Labov, Jan 17, 1977, DHH, Subcollection 1, Series II: Conferences and Committees, 1955–1987, Subseries E: Other Committees, Language and Interaction Institute, 1974–1977.

[41] "Proposed particular program in cognitive sciences" Sloan Foundation document, attached to Stellar to Gelman and Labov, Jan 17, 1977, DHH, Subcollection 1, Series II: Conferences and Committees, 1955–1987, Subseries E: Other Committees, Language and Interaction Institute, 1974–1977.

[42] Labov to Language and Interaction group, Feb 4, 1977, DHH, Subcollection 1, Series II: Conferences and Committees, 1955–1987, Subseries E: Other Committees, Language and Interaction Institute, 1974–1977.

[43] Labov to Language and Interaction group, Jun 17, 1977, DHH, Subcollection 1, Series II: Conferences and Committees, 1955–1987, Subseries E: Other Committees, Language and Interaction Institute, 1974–1977.

[44] Hymes to Labov, Jul 18, 1977, DHH, Subcollection 1, Series II: Conferences and Committees, 1955–1987, Subseries E: Other Committees, Language and Interaction Institute, 1974–1977.

[45] Hymes to Wagner, Jul 18, 1977, DHH, Subcollection 1, Series II: Conferences and Committees, 1955–1987, Subseries E: Other Committees, Language and Interaction Institute, 1974–1977.

[46] Both the first and second grants are documented in the Sloan Foundation's Annual Report for 1979 (https://sloan.org/storage/app/media/files/annual_reports/1979-1982_annual_reports.pdf).

[47] https://sloan.org/storage/app/media/files/annual_reports/1983-1986_annual_reports.pdf.

[48] https://almanac.upenn.edu/archive/v26pdf/n16/120679-insert.pdf.

[49] https://almanac.upenn.edu/archive/v34pdf/n21/020988-insert.pdf; https://almanac.upenn.edu/archive/v26pdf/n16/120679-insert.pdf.

[50] https://www.psych.upenn.edu/history/history.htm.

[51] https://repository.upenn.edu/exhibits/orgunit/ircs.

[52] Course flyer for spring 1985, included in DHH, Subcollection 1, Series II: Conferences and Committees, 1955–1987, Subseries E: Other Committees, Interdisciplinary Committee for a Program in Language, Culture and Society, 1979–1986.

[53] Goodenough to Dean Vartan Gregorian and Dean Richard Lambert, copied to Birdwhistell, Fought, Gleitman, Goffman, Hymes, Labov, and J. Smith, Oct 20, 1975, DHH, Subcollection 1, Series I: Correspondence 1951–1987, Goodenough, Ward H., 1958, 1960, 1970–1986.

[54] Goodenough to Dean Vartan Gregorian and Dean Richard Lambert, copied to Birdwhistell, Fought, Gleitman, Goffman, Hymes, Labov, and J. Smith, Oct 20, 1975, DHH, Subcollection 1, Series I: Correspondence 1951–1987, Goodenough, Ward H., 1958, 1960, 1970–1986.

[55] Hymes to Goodenough, Dec 1, 1975, DHH, Subcollection 1, Series I: Correspondence 1951–1987, Goodenough, Ward H., 1958, 1960, 1970–1986.

[56] Hymes to Goodenough, Dec 1, 1975, DHH, Subcollection 1, Series I: Correspondence 1951–1987, Goodenough, Ward H., 1958, 1960, 1970–1986.

[57] https://almanac.upenn.edu/archive/v25pdf/n05/092678-insert.pdf (South Asia Regional Studies had been established much earlier, at least by 1954: https://almanac.upenn.edu/archive/v01pdf/n01/110154.pdf).

[58] https://almanac.upenn.edu/archive/v24pdf/n32/052378-insert.pdf.

[59] https://almanac.upenn.edu/archive/v24pdf/n32/052378-insert.pdf.

⁶⁰ https://almanac.upenn.edu/archive/v25pdf/n27/040379.pdf.

⁶¹ Ben-Amos, Gross, Meyer, G. Prince, Herrnstein Smith to Regular Members, copied to Meyerson and Gregorian, Dec 13, 1978, DHH, Subcollection 1, Series II: Conferences and Committees, 1955–1987, Subseries E: Other Committees, Center for the Study of Art and Symbolic Behavior, 1978, 1986.

⁶² Ben-Amos, Gross, Meyer, G. Prince, Herrnstein Smith to Regular Members, copied to Meyerson and Gregorian, Dec 13, 1978, DHH, Subcollection 1, Series II: Conferences and Committees, 1955–1987, Subseries E: Other Committees, Center for the Study of Art and Symbolic Behavior, 1978, 1986.

⁶³ https://almanac.upenn.edu/archive/v27pdf/n19/012781.pdf.

⁶⁴ https://almanac.upenn.edu/archive/v27pdf/n26/032481.pdf.

⁶⁵ https://almanac.upenn.edu/archive/v28pdf/n11/111781.pdf.

⁶⁶ https://almanac.upenn.edu/archive/v28pdf/n24/032382.pdf.

⁶⁷ https://almanac.upenn.edu/archive/v29pdf/n26/032983.pdf.

⁶⁸ https://almanac.upenn.edu/archive/v32pdf/n24/022586.pdf.

⁶⁹ https://almanac.upenn.edu/archive/v35pdf/n08/101188.pdf.

⁷⁰ https://french.sas.upenn.edu/sites/default/files/2019%20cv%20prince.pdf.

⁷¹ One conference was on Jean Genet, co-sponsored with the French Institute for Culture and Technology and the Romance languages department, held in 1993 (https://almanac.upenn.edu/archive/v39pdf/n29/041393.pdf); a second was Code Black: Constructing Race in Early Modern England and France, held in 1994 (https://almanac.upenn.edu/archive/v41pdf/n09/102594.pdf). Examples of additional guest lectures were: "Historical Data and Theories of Rational Choice" (https://almanac.upenn.edu/archive/v34pdf/n27/032988.pdf) in 1988; "Seminar on Afro-American Intellectual History: Cultural Studies and Black Liberation" with bell hooks in 1991 (https://almanac.upenn.edu/archive/v38pdf/n04/091791.pdf); "Black America and the Urban Scene" with Andrew Ross in 1992 (https://almanac.upenn.edu/archive/v39pdf/n08/102092.pdf); and "The Environmental Situation in the Former Soviet Union" with Nikolai N. Vorontsov of the Russian Parliament in 1993 (https://almanac.upenn.edu/archive/v39pdf/n32/050493.pdf).

⁷² https://almanac.upenn.edu/archive/v45pdf/980929/092998.pdf.

⁷³ "Graduate courses on language and culture," 1980, DHH, Subcollection 1, Series II: Conferences and Committees, 1955–1987, Subseries E: Other Committees, Interdisciplinary Committee for a Program in Language, Culture and Society, folder 1, 1979–1981.

⁷⁴ Hymes to Goffman, copied to Sankoff and Glassie, Feb 14, 1980, DHH, Subcollection 1, Series II: Conferences and Committees, 1955–1987, Subseries E: Other Committees, Interdisciplinary Committee for a Program in Language, Culture and Society, folder 1, 1979–1981.

⁷⁵ Goodenough to Dyson, Mar 7, 1980, DHH, Subcollection 1, Series II: Conferences and Committees, 1955–1987, Subseries E: Other Committees, Interdisciplinary Committee for a Program in Language, Culture and Society, folder 1, 1979–1981.

⁷⁶ Hymes to Goodenough, Mar 27, 1980, DHH, Subcollection 1, Series II: Conferences and Committees, 1955–1987, Subseries E: Other Committees, Interdisciplinary Committee for a Program in Language, Culture and Society, folder 1, 1979–1981.

⁷⁷ Hymes to Goodenough, Apr 17, 1980, DHH, Subcollection 1, Series II: Conferences and Committees, 1955–1987, Subseries E: Other Committees, Interdisciplinary Committee for a Program in Language, Culture and Society, folder 1, 1979–1981.

[78] Dyson to Hymes, Sankoff, Labov, Fought, Kroch, Glassie, Goodenough, Goffman, Birdwhistell, Wolfson, Heath, Schieffelin, May 27, 1980, DHH, Subcollection 1, Series II: Conferences and Committees, 1955–1987, Subseries E: Other Committees, Interdisciplinary Committee for a Program in Language, Culture and Society, folder 1, 1979–1981.

[79] Hymes to Goodenough, May 28, 1980, DHH, Subcollection 1, Series II: Conferences and Committees, 1955–1987, Subseries E: Other Committees, Interdisciplinary Committee for a Program in Language, Culture and Society, folder 1, 1979–1981.

[80] Hymes to Dyson, May 30, 1980, DHH, Subcollection 1, Series II: Conferences and Committees, 1955–1987, Subseries E: Other Committees, Interdisciplinary Committee for a Program in Language, Culture and Society, folder 1, 1979–1981.

[81] D. Hymes to V. Hymes, Sankoff, Schieffelin, Wolfson, Nov 1, 1980, DHH, Subcollection 1, Series II: Conferences and Committees, 1955–1987, Subseries E: Other Committees, Interdisciplinary Committee for a Program in Language, Culture and Society, folder 1, 1979–1981.

[82] Goodenough to Hymes, Szwed, Feld, Wolfson, Schieffelin, Smith, Sankoff, Labov, Fought, Kroch, Goffman, Birdwhistell, Long, Nov 21, 1980, DHH, Subcollection 1, Series II: Conferences and Committees, 1955–1987, Subseries E: Other Committees, Interdisciplinary Committee for a Program in Language, Culture and Society, folder 1, 1979–1981.

[83] Memo from Hymes to Birdwhistell, Glassie, Goffman, Kroch, Labov, Sankoff, Schieffelin, Wolfson, n.d. [1981], DHH, Subcollection 1, Series II: Conferences and Committees, 1955–1987, Subseries E: Other Committees, Interdisciplinary Committee for a Program in Language, Culture and Society, folder 1, 1979–1981. Given that spring 1982 courses are discussed, it must be from fall 1981. In fact, another letter makes clear he had agreed to the position in spring 1981 but only found out about the appointment when he saw the official list of who was on what committees (Hymes to Dyson, Sep 30, 1981, DHH, Subcollection 1, Series II: Conferences and Committees, 1955–1987, Subseries E: Other Committees, Interdisciplinary Committee for a Program in Language, Culture and Society, folder 1, 1979–1981)! Apparently, Goodenough intended to stay on the committee, just not as chair (Hymes to Dyson, Oct 15, 1981, DHH, Subcollection 1, Series II: Conferences and Committees, 1955–1987, Subseries E: Other Committees, Interdisciplinary Committee for a Program in Language, Culture and Society, folder 1, 1979–1981).

[84] Hymes to Fought, Schieffelin, Wolfson, Jan 10, 1982, DHH, Subcollection 1, Series II: Conferences and Committees, 1955–1987, Subseries E: Other Committees, Interdisciplinary Committee for a Program in Language, Culture and Society, folder 2, 1982–1986.

[85] Schieffelin to Hymes, Jan 13, 1982, DHH, Subcollection 1, Series II: Conferences and Committees, 1955–1987, Subseries E: Other Committees, Interdisciplinary Committee for a Program in Language, Culture and Society, folder 2, 1982–1986.

[86] Hymes to Fought, Apr 3, 1982, DHH, Subcollection 1, Series II: Conferences and Committees, 1955–1987, Subseries E: Other Committees, Interdisciplinary Committee for a Program in Language, Culture and Society, folder 2, 1982–1986.

[87] Dyson to Hymes, May 20, 1982, DHH, Subcollection 1, Series II: Conferences and Committees, 1955–1987, Subseries E: Other Committees, Interdisciplinary Committee for a Program in Language, Culture and Society, folder 2, 1982–1986.

[88] Hymes to Fitts, Apr 29, 1983, DHH, Subcollection 1, Series II: Conferences and Committees, 1955–1987, Subseries E: Other Committees, Interdisciplinary Committee for a Program in Language, Culture and Society, folder 2, 1982–1986.

[89] Hymes to committee, Sep 30, 1983, DHH, Subcollection 1, Series II: Conferences and Committees, 1955–1987, Subseries E: Other Committees, Interdisciplinary Committee for a Program in Language, Culture and Society, folder 2, 1982–1986.

[90] Hymes to Frank Johnston (chair of anthropology), n.d., DHH, Subcollection 1, Series II: Conferences and Committees, 1955–1987, Subseries E: Other Committees, Interdisciplinary Committee for a Program in Language, Culture and Society, folder 2, 1982–1986.

[91] Goodenough to Feld, Fought, Hymes, Kroch, Labov, Sankoff, Schieffelin, Wolfson, Woolard, Mar 15, 1985, DHH, Subcollection 1, Series II: Conferences and Committees, 1955–1987, Subseries E: Other Committees, Interdisciplinary Committee for a Program in Language, Culture and Society, folder 2, 1982–1986.

[92] Goodenough to Feld, Fought, Hymes, Kroch, Labov, Sankoff, Schieffelin, Wolfson, Woolard, Mar 25, 1985, DHH, Subcollection 1, Series II: Conferences and Committees, 1955–1987, Subseries E: Other Committees, Interdisciplinary Committee for a Program in Language, Culture and Society, folder 2, 1982–1986.

[93] Exceptions were Ben-Amos, Anderson, Abrahams, and Sutton-Smith, but their membership in this group in the late 1980s as substitutes for members who left does not merit much attention in this context.

[94] https://almanac.upenn.edu/archive/v33pdf/n32/042887-insert.pdf.

[95] https://ancestors.familysearch.org/en/LRZS-BGF/angelica-schuyler-choate-1928-1964.

[96] For example, in 1908 Joseph H. Choate, former Ambassador to Great Britain, spoke at the annual alumni banquet, and was awarded an honorary degree (*Daily Pennsylvanian* 1908).

[97] University of Pennsylvania press release, Jan 24, 1968, UR, Biographical Files, Goffman, Erving, box 53, folder 10.

[98] Thomas Cochran to Lawrence Klein, Feb 27, 1973, RED.

[99] Robert Davies to Hugh Huxley, Oct 30, 1970, RED.

[100] Originally the Phoebe Waterman Foundation (1945–1970), then the Haas Community Fund (1970–1974), then the William Penn Foundation (1974–) (https://fconline.foundationcenter.org/fdo-grantmaker-profile?key=PENN001; https://williampennfoundation.org/history-and-heritage).

[101] Louis Schwartz to Provost Curtis Reitz, Apr 15, 1971, RED.

[102] "University professorships were established in 1961 to honor those faculty members who are particularly distinguished in scholarship and whose contributions to knowledge have been made in more than one discipline, rather than in a narrow field of specialization" (https://almanac.upenn.edu/archive/v14pdf/n04/011668.pdf). Eiseley had been appointed the first University Professor in 1961 (https://almanac.upenn.edu/archive/volumes/v54/n10/eiseley.html).

[103] University of Pennsylvania press release, Jan 24, 1968, UR, Biographical Files, Goffman, Erving, box 53, folder 10.

[104] https://almanac.upenn.edu/archive/v24pdf/n01/071577.pdf.

[105] "Benjamin Franklin Professors at the University of Pennsylvania to date," Dec 1, 1970, RED.

[106] Charles Price to Benjamin Franklin Professors, shows Davies, Eiseley, Goffman, Klein, Rieff, and himself in attendance, Sep 23, 1974, RED; Price to Benjamin Franklin Professors, shows Davies, Goffman, Harris, Rieff, and himself in attendance, Oct 22, 1974, RED; Price to Goffman and Rieff appoints them as a subcommittee to evaluate one of the potential candidates, Sep 23, 1974, RED.

[107] Lawrence Klein to Benjamin Franklin Professors, invited them to a dinner with President Meyerson honoring Cochran on his retirement, Jan 22, 1973, RED.

[108] "If my nomination for a Franklin Professorship had gone through two years ago" (Hymes to Dean Vartan Gregorian, Jul 8, 1974, DHH, Subcollection 1, Series I: Correspondence 1951–1987, Gregorian, Vartan, 1974–1981).

[109] Their CVs appear after a letter dated 1972, but no minutes discussing them as candidates have been preserved (RED).

[110] Robert Davies to Lawrence Klein, Nov 4, 1970, RED.

[111] Charles Price to President Meyerson and Provost Stellar, copied to Benjamin Franklin Professors, May 8, 1974, RED.

[112] "Notice of a campus event," Feb 18, 1972, UR, Biographical Files, Goffman, Erving, box 53, folder 10.

[113] By this time, these publications included Goffman 1959c, 1961a, 1961b, 1963a, 1963b, 1970, 1971.

[114] Press release, Sep 26, 1969, UR, Biographical Files, Goffman, Erving, box 53, folder 10.

[115] Hymes to Labov, May 11, 1970, DHH, Subcollection 1, Series I: Correspondence 1951–1987, Labov, William, folder 1, 1963–1972.

[116] https://almanac.upenn.edu/archive/v25pdf/n24/030679.pdf.

[117] https://almanac.upenn.edu/archive/v27pdf/n07/100780.pdf.

[118] https://almanac.upenn.edu/archive/v25pdf/n03/091278.pdf.

[119] https://almanac.upenn.edu/archive/v27pdf/n09/102180.pdf.

[120] https://almanac.upenn.edu/archive/v27pdf/n10/102880.pdf.

[121] https://almanac.upenn.edu/archive/v25pdf/n28/041079.pdf.

[122] https://almanac.upenn.edu/archive/v25pdf/n30/042479.pdf.

[123] https://almanac.upenn.edu/archive/v26pdf/n25/022880.pdf.

[124] "University Professors, August 1981," RED.

CHAPTER SIX

Penn Adjacent

There was, of course, a world outside of Penn, and Goffman participated in a variety of multi- and interdisciplinary projects that were neither begun at, nor closely affiliated with, his role at that university. Two of these were organized by scholars at Indiana University, and three by scholars at the University of Texas, Austin; given that all involved other participants from Penn as well, it seems reasonable to label them "Penn adjacent." All but one of these projects were based in the US. All of them expanded his invisible college, although perhaps thinking of these as a set of overlapping invisible colleges would be more accurate.

Indiana University

The earliest activity was a conference on interaction ethology, which Goffman co-organized with Thomas Sebeok at Indiana University, and which was held in Amsterdam in 1968. The second was the Multiple Analysis Project, known as MAP, organized by Allen Grimshaw, also at Indiana. (The project name was changed while still in the process of being organized: "Partly for acronymic reasons, this title has replaced the earlier 'Joint Analysis Project.'")[1] The conference is interesting for several reasons: It is one of the few that Goffman was involved in organizing; it provided the occasion for his invention of the phrase "interaction ethology"; and it demonstrates his own efforts to bring together scholars across disciplines, and thus his emphasis on ideas over disciplinary training and affiliation. MAP is interesting partly because it involved most of the central players among Goffman's colleagues at Penn, despite being organized elsewhere; partly because of the way it demonstrated how Goffman at the time was clearly aligned with Harvey Sacks and Emanuel Schegloff in terms of assumptions about how to conduct research on interaction, despite the common knowledge they did not always agree, and frequent statements in print that they took divergent approaches and were not on good terms; and partly because it was a failure—it was (finally, after several decades) completed, yet despite the enormous time and effort (and some money), the resulting publications had little influence, and the original goals were unfulfilled. We can learn at least as much from failures as from successes, especially those as well documented as this one.[2] There is an enormous amount of detail available for this project, yet almost nothing has been written about it, so it seems worth the time to sort out what happened, and especially why it was not successful.

Interaction Ethology Conference

Hymes, Worth, and Goffman all organized and attended Wenner-Gren sponsored conferences. The Wenner-Gren Foundation for Anthropological Research has supported anthropologists through multiple types of grants as well as conferences and symposia since 1941 (see Douglas 1986; Lindee and Radin 2016 on that organization). Events are interdisciplinary by design: "Wenner-Gren International symposia recognise no boundaries—intellectual, national, or subdisciplinary."[3] In the 1950s, when funding from a variety of national organizations, such as NIH, NSF, and NEH, became available to anthropologists, the foundation decided to emphasize "'very good mavericks,' scholars who fell between the existing categories as fashionably defined" (Douglas 1986, 523). Burg Wartenstein, Wenner-Gren's eleventh-century castle in Austria, was deliberately established as an ideal location from which to host small, international, interdisciplinary summer conferences (Douglas 1986).

Worth organized a conference with John Adair through Wenner-Gren (The Navajo as Filmmaker: Some Recent Investigations in Visual Communication), which was held in 1967 (Wenner-Gren 1967). Hymes organized two events (The Use of Computers in Anthropology in 1962[4] and Revolution vs. Continuity in the Study of Language in 1964[5]) and participated in at least one other (Folklore and Social Science in 1967). Goffman participated in at least two others: (Ethnic Identity: Cultural Continuity and Change in 1970, and Secular Rituals in 1974), both at Burg Wartenstein, and co-organized a third (see Winkin 2022a on these as well as discussion of Goffman's participation in the NATO Advanced Study Institute on Nonverbal Behavior Research

Methods in London in 1979, which overlaps with the Interaction Ethology conference in terms of topic and participants); the one he co-organized is the focus here. Interaction Ethology was held in Amsterdam from August 31 to September 4, 1970 (Sherzer 1971; Wenner-Gren 1970). Goffman co-organized it with Thomas Sebeok (who had previously co-organized the conference on computers with Hymes in 1962). Sebeok himself had organized a prior Wenner-Gren conference in 1965, Animal Communication, attended by Gregory Bateson, Charles Hockett, and W. John Smith, among many others, setting the stage for this one.[6] (Participants may not always attend to connections and overlaps between conferences, but intellectual historians must notice them.)

Goffman and Sebeok knew one another at least as early as 1962, since Goffman was a participant in an event organized by Sebeok, the Conference on Paralinguistics and Kinesics, held at Indiana University May 17–19, 1962. This was a deliberately interdisciplinary event, with "Five 'state of the art' papers . . . written by a specialist in one of the five principal disciplines represented (cultural anthropology, education, linguistics, psychiatry, and psychology)" (Sebeok et al. 1964, 7). As with the Macy conferences, the goal was to encourage debate, and so transcripts of discussion were included in the resulting book. Birdwhistell was also a participant, as were Margaret Mead, Charles Ferguson, Edward Hall, Norman McQuown, George Mahl, Robert Rosenthal, and Harvey Shands, along with dozens of others not mentioned in these pages. Birdwhistell and Mead spoke often during the discussions, and at length; Goffman spoke at several sessions, although a lot less. As at the Macy conference he attended in 1956, Goffman got into a bit of an argument with Mead again, although this time he seems to have placated her quickly through clarifying what he meant (139–40). Most interesting is that, in the session on cultural anthropology, presented by Weston La Barre, during discussion, Goffman says, "I have been asked to present my version of the frames of reference within which the material we have discussed might be placed" (232; it is unclear who asked him, but presumably Sebeok as the organizer) and goes on at great length—three pages—essentially serving as respondent to that session. Oddly, unlike at other conferences, almost no one picks up on what he says, and the conversation moved to other topics. However, Mead herself finally does pick up on something Goffman said in a later discussion, saying:

It would be very nice if we could go away from here with at least a preliminary agreement on the use of some phrase that we could apply to this whole field. Kinesics and paralinguistics, after all, are two.

We have been challenged by Dr. Goffman to say what we are doing and we are, I think, conceivably working in a field which in time will include the study of all patterned communication in all modalities, of which linguistics is the most technically advanced. If we had a word for patterned communications in all modalities, it would be useful. I am not enough of a specialist in this field to know what word to use, but many people here, who have looked as if they were on opposite sides of the fence, have used the word "semiotics." It seems to me the one word, in some form or other, that has been used by people who are arguing from quite different positions. (275)

Sebeok responds by pointing out that the word semiotics is already in use to mean something else entirely, and proposes "the non-linguistic aspect of communication," which no one likes, as it is not a single word such as she has requested. Finally, Birdwhistell proposes: "There is an old-fashioned word which we have been using and that is 'communication.' The word 'communication' relates to a series of special derived systems. I see no reason why the word 'communication' cannot be elevated to meet this need" (275–76). In fact, that is the term Birdwhistell used ever after for the broad study of social interaction, including both verbal and nonverbal behavior. Both "semiotics" (defined as "patterned communications in all modalities" (5) and "multimodal" (with no definition provided, either on page 7, or during Mead's presentation, on 286) are used in the preface as cover terms for the topic discussed at the conference, but with a clear preference for semiotics as the more obvious choice (see Mondada 2016 for a good introduction to multimodality). The question of a name for what they were studying recurs across numerous contexts.

To return to the Amsterdam conference. Sherzer was a participant: He apparently "helped Goffman and Sebeok" in some ways as they were organizing it,[7] and published a lengthy description, although there was no proceedings volume (one was never intended: the formal invitation says, "No published report is envisaged; accordingly, no tape or stenographic recordings will be made"[8]). Sherzer reports that "the conference was a natural extension or rather a formal recognition of the unity of the varied interdisciplinary research currently being carried out by the participants" (1971, 19). The names and disciplinary affiliations in table 6.1 come from Sherzer.

Table 6.1: Interaction Ethology Conference, by Discipline

Anthropology/Sociology: Gregory Bateson, Erving Goffman, Suzanne Ripley, Harvey Sacks, O. Michael Watson
Linguistics: Kenneth L. Pike, Thomas Sebeok, Joel Sherzer
Nonverbal communication: Paul Ekman, Adam Kendon
Psychiatry: Harvey C. Shands
Psychology: Michael Argyle, John H. Crook, Robert Sommer
Zoology: Stuart A. Altmann, Michael Chance, Irenäus Eibl-Eibesfeldt, Heini Hediger, Hans Kummer, Glen McBride, Desmond Morris, W. John Smith, J. A. R. A. M. van Hooff

While Hymes was invited by Goffman, and fully intended to participate, he had a conflict with the date.[9] Susan Ervin-Tripp and William Labov were also invited but were also unable to join.[10] Goffman did not know all of the scholars who did attend, but he definitely knew Ervin-Tripp, Sebeok, Sacks, Bateson, Ripley,[11] Sommer,[12] Smith, and Sherzer, and at least some were citing his work long before this event (e.g., Sommer and Osmond 1960). Presumably, he knew Chance, Morris, and Crook as well, for he provided their addresses, along with that of Ripley, to Sebeok for the invitation to participate (Jan 21, 1970, TS).

Goffman recommended the following substitutions in case not everyone invited responded positively: Emanuel Schegloff for Sacks; Ralph Exline or Ekman for Argyle; Joel Schaeffer (who worked with Albert Scheflen) for Adam Kendon;[13] Birdwhistell for Bateson; some of their students in lieu of Chance and Crook, and the same for Smith. He also suggested that they had enough linguists without McQuown (Jan 21, 1970, TS). Sebeok agreed to most of these ideas (though he balked at paying overseas travel for a Smith student) and said this about Birdwhistell: "If Bateson can't come, I will write to Birdwhistell next—sigh, sigh! (I think that between the two of us we should be able to handle him)" (Feb 4, 1970, TS), so apparently he was not a fan. Overall, Goffman was more worried about the balance of research specializations. "My only concern is that we might end up with too many ethologists who haven't yet begun to look systematically at humans. One or two we can and should stand; but too many will thin things down a bit in terms of current work being presented."[14] This is especially significant because it became one of the concerns he voiced after the conference as well, and it clearly shows his ability to step back and consider general questions such as balance in theoretical approaches. Further along in the correspondence, Goffman wrote: "Our minds are so much alike in these matters that when you have doubt and wonder what I think, and there is no easy time to find out, please assume that I think what you think." (That letter begins: "Dear Tom: I love you" [Feb 9, 1970, TS].) Goffman was thrilled that they had received the grant to hold the event, and at one point during the organizing discussions said, "I am seeing Lita tomorrow. I will kiss her for you after I kiss her for me" (Feb 26, 1970, TS; Lita Osmundsen was president of Wenner-Gren). The correspondence showed that they had a pretty easy time organizing everything. One of the other concerns Goffman expressed was "to make sure that enough participants are ready without long preamble to present a densely-packed example of actual, ongoing work." And once the letters of invitation went out, as Goffman felicitously phrased it: "People seem not to be declining" (Feb 16, 1970, TS). In fact, nearly everyone who was invited was able to arrange their schedule to attend—with the notable exceptions of Hymes, Labov, and Ervin-Tripp, as mentioned, three of those Goffman knew best. Goffman acknowledged Sebeok's organizational skills, saying, "If you run for president, I will become an American citizen and vote for you" (Feb 18, 1970, TS).

Goffman was particularly involved in organizing the event's structure. "I think evening discussion should emerge as a reaction to and compensation for what occurs formally; and I think this can only happen when those who want to leave or are not wanted have a chance to move off" (Mar 24, 1970, TS). And he drafted the description of what they were trying to accomplish, and the program. His draft says:

> The conference is designed to focus on the formal patterns of behavior overtly manifest during face-to-face interaction among humans. The emphasis will be on description as opposed to final explanation, and the approach that of the fine-grain contextual analysis of sociolinguistics and ethology.
>
> It is hoped that the participants will assume that they are in an audience of like-minded peers and will spend no time presenting arguments concerning the significance of the area or the fruitfulness of particular methodologies. The participants will be assumed to have reasonable familiarity with all the published material in the field, and it is to be hoped that we can move directly to a consideration of current finds and hypotheses. (May 6, 1970, TS)

The major topics people were asked to choose between were conversational mechanics, contact phenomena, dominance behavior, spacing and territoriality, facial displays, on differences between animal troops and human gatherings (May 6, 1970, TS). The plan was to meet from 9:30 a.m. to 12:00 p.m., then break for lunch, resuming discussion from 2:00 to 5:00 p.m., with evenings free. (Or, as explained, free for those who wished, while the others would meet to discuss what happened during the day's sessions.) Goffman put the goal of the conference especially clearly in a letter to Sebeok: "Our focus is on observable patterns of objective behavior occurring in natural settings where the context involves two or more people. That excludes the big things like institutions and the internal things like souls. What is involved is the discipline modesty that sends individuals out to look at small behavior" (Apr 29, 1970, TS). Goffman also could be quite explicit about what he did not want people to talk about, once they submitted their proposals. For example, as he wrote to Robert Sommer:

> Honestly, the last thing in the world I want to see you do is to elaborate on dramaturgical terms from my retired books. . . . What we are trying to cultivate is what you illustrated beautifully in your small group papers. It is that sort of thing that we built this conference for. My stricture was that you tell us about patterns you haven't published on yet, and tell this to an audience whom you can assume starts with your interests. You don't have to sell us on the work you've done, but just provide additions to the shelf. Of course you can generalize on your findings, that would be lovely, too. But for God's sake, pick the terms that are naturalistically the most convenient for you and not things that I've done. (Apr 30, 1970, TS)

Goffman prepared a revised program and sent it to Sebeok along with an offer to coordinate any further changes since he would be based in the US during the summer. At that point, the major topics were down to three: behavior in gatherings, conversational encounters, and contact phenomena (May 12, 1970, TS).

During the conference, it was Goffman's role to summarize what they had learned, and on the last day he outlined "the subareas of interaction ethology" as follows: traffic systems, states of talk, territoriality, supportive rituals, turn-systems, remedial work done by individuals in interactions, social occasions, and tie signs (Sherzer 1971). Particularly interesting is the way Goffman gracefully combined what he and others, but especially Sacks, had come to understand about the structure of interaction. For example, Winkin (2022a) points out how close this list is to the major topics in *Relations in Public* (Goffman 1971). It is worth mentioning that Sebeok reports Bateson "took a leading part in our Amsterdam get-together" (1991, 22), which supports Erickson's suggestion that Goffman had worked with Bateson while at Berkeley. Sherzer's review of the event concludes: "The success of the conference on interaction ethology was its delineation of a new field pulling together the resources of recent research in a number of disciplines. The potential weaknesses of such a field were also present at the conference—the misunderstandings and oversimplifications endemic to broad interdisciplinary work" (1971, 21). Although no book resulted from the conference, its influence is evident in books that followed from W. John Smith (1977) and Adam Kendon (1990).

Long after the fact, Sebeok wrote about the event, specifically explaining how they arrived at the title.

> Goffman and I together once amicably organized and ran an international conference, in total concord on the venue (Amsterdam), the participants, and topics to be discussed (Sherzer 1971). Yet we could not agree on the title. I wanted this title to reflect the identifying trademark, "Semiotics." After all, it was aspects of that which we were in the Netherlands to discuss. Goffman, who years before had published what I considered his most insightful contribution to semiotics, *Stigma* (1963 . . .), and who later cheerfully offered his "Footing" to be first published in *Semiotica* (1979[b]), kept insisting that he didn't wish his work pinned down by that term, indeed by any one term. Hence we compromised on the *ad hoc* weasel phrase "Interaction Ethology," which scarcely anyone, save a participant or two in that conference (e.g., Drew and Wootton 1988, 91), has used before or since (although "interaction order" does appear in the subtitle of this collection of essays on Goffman [ibid]). (1991, 21)

Sebeok at one point used the two titles as synonyms, referring to "the holistic field of interaction ethology (alias semiotics)" (1975, 10).

In fact, Sebeok turned out to be wrong that scarcely anyone would use the phrase "interaction ethology"—for it was noticed and is still in use more than fifty years later (although sporadically, no question). For example, Ciolek, Elzinga, and McHoul say:

> We have been inspired by Goffman's call for an "interaction ethology" in which what he as termed the "ultimate behavioral materials" of interaction—the glances and stances, the gestures and utterances of participants—are examined, not for what they reveal about the participants as individuals, but for what they reveal about how people organize their behavior so that they can become participants in interactional events. (1979, 2)

More recently, Pallante et al. argue that Goffman was "an influential figure within micro-sociology, who suggests that this subfield should be practiced as an 'interaction ethology.' His realization was that it was ethologists that had developed the most detailed methodological skillset and procedures for systematically observing behavior in situ, and this should be taken as a methodological model for how micro-sociology should be conducted" (2022, 2). Knapp also mentions the phrase; although he argues against using it (because "human ethology is incompatible with the structuralist approach"), he still feels Goffman's books "are on a 'must read' list for anyone interested in learning about the ways human beings organize their encounters" (2013, 19). Kendon mentions that the phrase interaction ethology is to be found in *Relations in Public* (1971, x), proposing that: "By this he [Goffman] intended recognition of the fact that in the study of interaction from the viewpoint of how occasions of it are organized, there is much in the method of observation and analysis used that resembles the methods of the ethologists" (1979, 21n50). After running through the arguments for the need of a new name to describe studying face-to-face interaction (and citing Goffman 1967 there), Kendon considers multiple potential names various scholars were proposing in the 1970s: his own "the study of the organization of behavior in face-to-face interaction," Scheflen's "the communication systems approach," or Duncan's "the structural approach," the ever-popular "nonverbal communication," of which Kendon said, "Even if it were the case that we could somehow study how people interact with one another *vis-à-vis* apart from the words they use, it is inelegant and hopelessly vague to label a field by saying what it is not" (21n50). He also brings up semiotics, correctly attributing that suggestion to Mead, but he argues quite reasonably that "we cannot use a term which is now well established as the name for a broad field of study as a name for one of this field's subfields" (21n50). That is what gets him to the phrase interaction ethology. Finally, Streeck and Mehus argue: "Goffman pleaded for a framework of 'interaction ethology,' combining Durkheimian categories of norms of conduct with ethological perspectives in the study of ordinary human conduct in face-to-face interaction" (2005, 384). Despite all these comments showing Sebeok to be wrong that no one would ever use the phrase again, he was also essentially correct for, although the term clearly has been used by some scholars, interaction ethology is not currently in widespread use as the phrase describing the approach Goffman and/or others developed.

Once the conference was over, Goffman sent Sebeok a detailed analysis, and proposal for follow-up events. Briefly, he was delighted with how it had gone, but thought they now could do more, especially to bring more sociolinguists to a future conference, since this one had been heavily weighted toward ethologists. Of course, if Hymes, Labov, and Ervin-Tripp had attended as planned, they would have significantly improved the balance. Goffman highlighted the importance of bringing together ethology and linguistics as "the most promising naturalistic disciplines" of the last twenty years and saying that they "have induced a small core of anthropologists, sociologists, and psychologists to engage in naturalistic observations of minute strips of social interaction and to try to employ sophisticated techniques of analysis of a nonstatistical kind" (Oct 7, 1970, TS). He mentioned that the Amsterdam event was the third conference in three years on related topics (presumably, one was the conference on nonverbal communication he worked on with Kleck, explored in chapter 7), "and was incidentally the best." He argued for holding two more meetings: one emphasizing sociolinguistics, and the other ethology. The former was needed for "edging socio-linguists over into a full-fledged look at social interaction in which speech occurs." The latter was needed because ethologists "must develop a sense of how extraordinarily difficult it is to make any sound statement of a function in regard to human behavioral practices" (Oct 7, 1970, TS). It was not explicitly stated but implied that he was offering to help organize these events. He proposed a specific structure, at least for the sociolinguistic conference, thus presaging MAP.

Follow-up Activities

Goffman returned to the idea of one or more future conferences a week later in a letter to Sebeok, saying that he would be in San Diego (AAA met there in November 1970, so that is likely what he was referring to),[15] and hoped to see Sebeok there to talk further. He also wanted to share the news that "a group at Texas is attempting to fund a conference on sociolinguistics in the interactional sense," which would mean that one of the two follow-up events he had earlier proposed would happen (Oct 23, 1970, TS). Goffman was referring to the conference organized by Bauman and Sherzer on the ethnography of speaking, held in Austin, Texas, in 1972 (summarized in the section on Texas, below). The younger generation was taking responsibility for the next obvious step, so neither Goffman nor Sebeok needed to spend time organizing a sociolinguistic follow-up event. In fact, Goffman may well have discussed the need he saw for such an event with Sherzer, given that Sherzer had been at the Amsterdam conference.

There was eventually a second conference related to Goffman's suggestion for a follow-up among ethologists as well, although it had been under discussion by Sebeok and others previously and so was not a direct result of the Amsterdam conference. In any case, this was one at which Goffman was a participant despite not being represented in the resulting publication, which is something of a story. Briefly, Sebeok organized the Conference on the Clever Hans Phenomenon: Communication with Horses, Whales, Apes, and People, held by the New York Academy of Sciences, May 6–7, 1980 (published as Sebeok and Rosenthal 1981). There was some overlap with Amsterdam: Hediger and Ekman participated, as well as Goffman. In addition, Starkey Duncan Jr., who was peripherally involved with the MAP project, also participated. Sebeok must have written Goffman with the idea for the event in February 1979, for there is an answer in which Goffman says it is "a wonderful idea for a conference," but unfortunately, he has conflicting plans (Feb 19, 1979, TS). Sebeok clarifies that the event is scheduled for 1980 not 1979, saying, "Do come, if at all possible; the Conference wouldn't be the same without you!" (Feb 19, 1979, TS).[16] Goffman could participate in 1980, but he said, "I still don't see what I can write a paper on. Do let me come merely as a carper" (Feb 26, 1979, TS). Sebeok was fine with that, but warned Goffman that the Academy would only cover expenses if he played some formal role: "I suppose this means being a discussant, or 'carper,' or something of the sort" and proposed a role as discussant on the final day, although he would have to check in with the Academy about whether that would be approved (Mar 5, 1979, TS). So that was what happened: The Academy accepted Goffman as a discussion leader, so he would not present a paper. He was listed in the program as discussion leader for the morning session, with Sebeok and Rosenthal serving the same role for the afternoon session, on the final day.[17]

But a problem arose when it came to the published results of the event. In August 1980, Goffman wrote to Sebeok:

> Just got back from vacation to find some 70 pages of type-script and a request for its edited return in a week. The jibberish I would have to reconstitute into orderly talk would require at least a month to do so, and I have returned to some more duties even more pressing. So I don't see how I can get anything to you. I

guess you'd best drop me from the proceedings, which I understand was a right. Sorry about all this. The thing comes at just the wrong time. (Aug 7, 1980, TS)

Sebeok was "very sympathetic to your position" and hated to divert him from "more important writing commitments," but he did not want to go ahead without Goffman, and he explained the logic. It was not only that "the volume will be a much diminished piece of work without your masterful summary statement and interventions." It was also that: "You made numerous interventions to which many of us severally reacted. Now many of the 'reactants' have already returned their 'cleaned up' texts, which make specific reference to one statement of yours or another. I just don't see how I can impose on our colleagues and now ask them to again reshape their texts, on the assumption that you were 'not there'" (Aug 11, 1980, TS). Sebeok offered a compromise: that Goffman could take a month to sort things out. Unfortunately, no response has been preserved. What we do know is that Goffman was not included in the final volume, so he must have said he simply did not have time to do what was needed. In the published volume, only Duncan (1981) refers to Goffman, mentioning at the same time Kendon, McQuown, and Schegloff. All comments by Goffman (or anyone else) have been removed; the volume reads as if participants had simply submitted their written papers. There is no mention anywhere of Goffman's participation, and no synthesis provided at the end of the volume, as there was at the event in person.

Even so, we know that the discussions apparently were quite impassioned. Goffman mentioned to Sebeok having received a letter from the Academy, "asking if I was concerned about the heatedness of the conference, and I wrote back and told them that they should be ashamed of having such concern, for the history of natural science has been periodically vented and needfully so, by exactly that sort of commotion" (Aug 7, 1980, TS). Susan Fowler (editor of the journal *Lab Animal*) attended but did not present. Her published description of the event makes clear that she was unimpressed with Sebeok and most of the others, saying it had been "an unprofessional, unpleasant attempt of the part of a semiotics professor to discredit the whole area of ape/human communication research" (1980, 356), only serving "as a showplace for its organizers' prejudices" (359). Perhaps Goffman got off easy by not being included in the published results. In any case, this event was clearly not a good example of positive connections across disciplinary boundaries. Even so, it is noteworthy that at both the Amsterdam conference in 1970, and Clever Hans in New York in 1980, Goffman was the one who provided the summary and synthesis, as he had earlier for the conference at Berkeley; he was particularly suited to that role, as he was well able to sort out what had been learned and to highlight what work remained.

OTHER RELATED CONFERENCES

In addition to these two conferences, there were at least three other events on related topics, far less central to this story, but they probably merit a brief mention. First, Goffman was a panelist on "Ethology and Sociology" at the American Sociological Association meeting in 1972 in New Orleans, sponsored jointly with the Rural Sociological Society. The panel chair was Neil H. Cheek (Georgia State University), and the other two panelists were John Baldwin (University of California, Santa Barbara), and Robin Fox (Rutgers University). No title for Goffman's paper (or that of any other participant) is listed in the program.[18] Second, Kendon, a participant in the Amsterdam conference, went on to organize the Symposium on Human Ethology for the Australian and New Zealand Association for the Advancement of Science meeting held in Canberra in 1975.[19] It seems reasonable to assume that both of these were influenced by the Amsterdam conference. The third event, Colloquium on Human Ethology, was held in October 1977, sponsored by the Werner-Reimers-Stiftung [Werner Reimers Foundation] in Bad Homburg, Germany (the proceedings volume is von Cranach et al. 1979).[20] The Reimers Foundation, established in 1963, is "dedicated to the fostering of science and research that concerns itself with the studies of mankind, its nature and environment."[21] Goffman presented "Response Cries," and it is included in the von Cranach et al. volume (1979c); it was also published separately (1978, and as a chapter in 1981). Other presenters at the 1977 event who had previously participated in the Amsterdam conference were Eibl-Eibesfeldt, Ekman, and Kummer; Jürgen Habermas commented on Goffman's paper (Habermas 1979). There are other connections between Goffman and ethology as well (see Jerolmack et al. 2024), but those are less obviously linked to the projects, topics, and people mentioned in these pages.

As well, in addition to these conferences, at least one publication was planned as a result of the Amsterdam conference, although it seems not to have been carried through. Sherzer spent time with W. John Smith in Amsterdam (they likely had met earlier at Penn), and they shared enough common interests that a year later they outlined a potential book, involving Goffman and several others, which Sherzer summarized for Hymes.

244 | Chapter Six

When in Panama City, I spent quite a bit of time with John Smith, an ethologist in the biology dept. at Penn who I think you have never met. He has been quite excited about what I have to say about Cuna pointed lips (which he originally heard me present in Amsterdam last year) and made use of some of my approach in a series of papers he's been working on tongue gestures (in humans, with insights from some animals). He thought it might be interesting to put together in a book his stuff on the tongue and mine on Cuna gestures and maybe some other things. . . . I talked briefly with Erv in Phila. And he sounds like he would contribute a piece on greetings. John plans to write to Paul Ekman and Adam Kendon (both participants of the Amsterdam conference) to see if they would like to contribute papers focusing on the inter-relation of gesture and speaking, pretty much the theme of the book in a way. John has seen your long letter to me about the pointed lip gesture and we both wonder if you would like to contribute a piece along the lines you developed there, i.e., of the importance of studying communicative activities as such rather than studying gesture, lg, etc., each in their separate boxes. We envisioned such a piece not as an introduction to the book—there would be no introduction (unless it comes out that it is needed) but rather as one of the contributions, a contribution which provides a theoretical perspective greatly needed in this kind of work. John has written to Tom Sebeok who would like such a book for Studies in Semiotics. What do you think about the project? The possibility of your contributing?[22]

A few months later, it became obvious that at least Hymes would be too busy, and Sherzer wrote: "About book that John Smith and I are planning: of course I hope you can talk to Erv and John about it sometime in Phila. But I suppose the AAA election (and I'm betting on you for winning [the presidency] . . . and other commitments have you with your back to the wall."[23] The book clearly moved ahead, for two years later Sherzer wrote Hymes about it again: He wanted to include a revised version of his own just published article in *Language in Society* (1973b), and asked about permissions. At that point, he said, "The book is to be published in the Approaches to Semiotics series and will go to press in about a month (if the others get their papers done)."[24] Perhaps the others (Smith and Kendon) did not complete their chapters, because, unfortunately, it seems the book was never published.

The Multiple Analysis Project (MAP)

MAP was organized by Allen Grimshaw, a sociologist at Indiana University, but it involved nearly all the major and some of the minor players in Goffman's invisible college at Penn, and the conference at the end occurred on Penn's campus, so it seems worthy of inclusion even though it is a long and complicated story. Yet even failed projects, sometimes especially failed projects, are worth attending to for what they can teach us.

Initial discussions leading to MAP occurred at the SSRC Committee on Sociolinguistics in 1973, which Hymes was chairing at the time, when Grimshaw, who also served on the committee, brought up the possibility of that group sponsoring a new project. As the minutes record:

> Mr. Grimshaw introduced his proposed project on verbal strategies, which would involve the close analysis from several different points of view of a common "text" (e.g., videotape of natural conversation or another form of interaction). Discussion centered around the potential impracticability of asking different investigators, with diverse methods and conceptual interests, to work on the same material, which might not be of great salience to them or suitable for their approaches; the question of the interaction domain from which the material might be selected, and the desirability that this be a socially relevant one, if possible; the danger of creating a kind of contest among the participants, with the mistaken implication that one method would prove superior to the others; and, in general, the technical complexity and great costs of the project. The committee regarded the basic idea of the project as very worthwhile.[25]

Thus, the key elements were present from the very beginning: it was to involve videorecording live interaction and then comparing different forms of analysis of that video. At the same time, group members were already able to point out some of the difficulties that might, and in fact did, occur due to the complex design.

MAP was intended to develop the new topic of sociolinguistics by getting sociologists and linguists to talk to one another through working on a collaborative research project. As Grimshaw later explained to Fred Erickson, at that point a potential participant, MAP "developed out of a concern of the SSRC Committee on Sociolinguistics about the proliferation of methods and theoretical orientations in the analysis of conversational interaction and the ethnography of speaking, which began to develop towards the end of the sixties" (Jan 11, 1979, ADG). He wrote that the goal was to "permit at least a rough test of the relative strengths and weaknesses of some of the many contemporary perspectives, permitting analysts to learn from both the successes and failures of their colleagues and to share what they learned with others" (1981, 360). More formally, he explained:

> The Committee on Sociolinguistics (CSL) had three identifying characteristics: (a) interdisciplinary membership and constituencies; (b) a strong comparative interest, and; (c) a unifying intellectual concern with talk in social contexts. In

the early 1970s it seemed to CSL members that the first and second of these characteristics were often contradictory to the third, with the result that socio-linguistic research was simultaneously growing exponentially, and becoming increasingly diffuse and noncumulative. (1989, xiii)

In an effort to resolve this issue, Grimshaw "was charged to seek support for the collection of an extensive data base on a naturally-occurring conversational event and to locate and recruit a group of analysts" (xiv). The result was MAP.

MAP began in 1973, with major publications finally appearing nearly twenty years later (Grimshaw 1989; Grimshaw et al. 1994a), so long after the initiation of the project that they were barely noticed and had little impact on other researchers, then or now. (Even other participants only mention it briefly, if at all, in their later publications [see Erickson 2006]). Over several years, funding for MAP was provided by SSRC, the William T. Grant Foundation, and the National Science Foundation (Grimshaw 1987a).[26] It was "a collaborative project in which thirteen investigators, representing a range of theoretical and methodological perspectives in anthropology, linguistics, psychology, and sociology are individually examining the same data record" (Grimshaw 1982a, 38n2). Initially, Grimshaw was concerned that scholars would miss work in unrelated research strands, but later he realized that even "people studying the *same* sociolinguistic topics are often unaware of relevant work being done by colleagues in different disciplines and even in different 'traditions' within disciplines" (Grimshaw 1991, 844; emphasis in original). In the end, the diversity of theoretical and methodological approaches that had been intended as the project's strength proved to be its undoing, and the project outlasted even the Committee on Sociolinguistics that brought it into being (the committee was disbanded in 1979; Heller 2018 provides details).

MAP's leader and guiding force was Allen D. Grimshaw, a sociologist at Indiana University, who served on the SSRC's Committee on Sociolinguistics starting in 1967, much of the time with Hymes, Labov, Charles Ferguson, John Gumperz, and Susan Ervin-Tripp as other members, part of the time as chair or co-chair. Grimshaw also served as associate editor of *Language in Society*, as described in chapter 4. Becoming convinced that the joint study of language and society was essential, he wanted to draw together the various research strands. He credited Hymes with at least part of the logic, since: "[a]ccording to Hymes (1967) there is a sense in which *the study of language is inseparable from the study of society*" (Grimshaw 1969a, 313; emphasis in original). Grimshaw had met Labov and Gumperz at least as early as 1964 at the SSRC/LSA Summer Institute on Sociolinguistics, held at Indiana University (Grimshaw 1981, 14, 358), and that seminar developed into the Committee on Sociolinguistics;[27] he had met Hymes in the early 1960s. From that point forward he typically acknowledged Gumperz, Labov, and Hymes for their help in publications (e.g., saying that they "have given time beyond the proper demands of colleagueship in instructing a neophyte in radically new 'thoughtways'" [1973a, 49]). Fairly quickly he added Goffman as well, writing at one point, "I fear that sometimes I have absorbed their ideas without realizing where I've learned them" (1981, 99; this is a revision of a paper presented in 1972, originally published as Grimshaw 1973b, so the influence dates to at least a decade earlier). At the same time, he was quite open about the fact that "I am a sociologist, not a linguist. My interest in discourse is less in how it is put together structurally than in what its producer-users manage to socially accomplish with it—and how" (1987a, 213).

Grimshaw and Goffman

In addition to Grimshaw's central role in MAP, he was an important member of Goffman's invisible college, so it is worth taking a detour to understand a little about who he was, and how they connected, before returning to MAP itself. Grimshaw's BA was in anthropology and sociology from the University of Missouri, and his PhD was in sociology, from Penn in 1959;[28] that was on the topic of race riots,[29] so he fit in well not only with the group of sociologists and linguists inventing sociolinguistics, but also with the major concerns of the Center for Urban Ethnography once it was established in 1969. He was in regular correspondence with Goffman, Hymes, and Labov on issues related to sociolinguistics from the 1960s, routinely met with them at a wide range of conferences (the American Sociological Association, the Linguistics Society of America, and/or the American Anthropological Association), and exchanged drafts of papers. For example, Goffman at one point wrote Grimshaw: "Won't be seeing you in Canada, so we might have to wait for Mexico, as I will be in France, although over the next month here in Philly" (Jun 21, 1974, ADG). And at another point, Grimshaw wrote Goffman: "The Temple meetings are March 13–15; I'm committed for the 15th. Per your suggestion, I hope we can all get together—maybe the same crew as last time (Labovs and Hymeses (?) too). I'll look forward to seeing you" (Feb 27, 1975, ADG). This makes it clear that Goffman, both Grimshaws, both

Labovs, and both Hymeses were in the habit of connecting at conferences, local and national, across multiple disciplinary associations.

In fall 1969, Grimshaw invited Goffman to Indiana University, to give a public lecture, teach a seminar, and have a social evening because "a growing number of people in the university community are becoming aware of the exciting things that are being done in sociolinguistics generally and interaction studies more specifically; they would like to have details from you as someone intimately involved in the most exciting work in the area" (Dec 4, 1969, ADG). Goffman answered by return mail: "I'm afraid I just can't. It would be terrific to talk about sequencing in conversation to people who know about it, but I have overcommitted myself for the rest of the year and just can't make it" (Dec 11, 1969, ADG). At the same time, however, he sent back comments on a draft manuscript Grimshaw had included. In response, Grimshaw asked about moving the date to fall 1970 (Dec 17, 1969, ADG). Goffman's answer has not been preserved, but it was apparently several years before he was able to make time to visit Indiana and give presentations. Of course, the fact that he did manage to make time for that visit at all is significant; as demonstrated in chapters 4 and 5, he had an awful lot of commitments in those years (even so, only one part of the story has been told; he also had significant numbers of conference presentations, nationally and internationally, as well as guest lectures at various universities, on his schedule, and these have not been detailed).

The fact that Goffman and Grimshaw wrote letters of recommendation for one another is one measure of their mutual esteem. In early 1973, for example, Grimshaw wrote: "Thanks very much for your good letter. If I don't get support I certainly can't blame you" (Jan 17, 1973, ADG). In spring 1974, Grimshaw was asked to review a proposal by Goffman to the National Endowment for the Humanities, which he did at great length. It was to involve Sacks, both Goodwins, and Jefferson, requiring a 20 percent time commitment from Goffman. In his evaluation, Grimshaw suggested that the proposal was part of a move bringing together students of speech in interaction (such as Charles Fillmore, Michael Halliday, John Gumperz, and Aaron Cicourel), and he said: "It is difficult for me to imagine a more auspicious beginning for the long-range activity than the work here proposed. If successfully carried off this project will have implications of major magnitude for research and theory-building in the range of disciplines within the social sciences and the humanities."[30] At the same time, however, he concluded:

It is difficult to comment on the research design or plan of work for the project—the investigators have not spelled it out. Neither Goffman nor his student
Sacks have been much concerned about the preoccupation with research design
which has characterized many of their colleagues in sociology. Goffman's own
style has been to keep his eyes and ears open and to find data either where it
occurs naturally.... In this he has been extremely successful.[31]

Grimshaw went on to mention that the intended technique was to "record
and film everyday ceremonials, commercial encounters, or whatever." He
did wish they had done more to link their intentions explicitly to theory, but
even so, "I don't see how given their past work it can fail to be interesting
and valuable.... I don't think many people can do the kind of work he [Goff-
man] does." He hoped that Goffman would do the writing up, as "Goffman's
work has been widely read and understood by scholars (and lay persons) in
a large number of fields," whereas he had found Sacks's and Jefferson's work
"obscure and difficult to read." He said the budget was minimal but assumed
they would collect data and then analyze it, so perhaps it would be enough.
"In summary, I think this is potentially a project which could be counted as
an important coup for the NEH and I urge its support."[32] Unfortunately, the
grant proposal is not in Grimshaw's files, nor is official notice of whether
or not it was funded, but it seems not to have been.

Then in 1976, Grimshaw wrote Goffman: "I have given your name as
someone who could be contacted (not as a letter writer); I hope you don't
mind." This was apparently for an NEH grant of his own, because the letter
mentions "Enc: NEH materials" (Jun 25, 1976, ADG). There is a handwritten
note on the original letter, returned by Goffman without a new date: "Will
do anything I can, with pleasure. A worthy venture." And in 1980, Grimshaw wrote Goffman that he was applying for a Guggenheim to write up
his analysis of MAP, adding, "I have been told that I should list as references
'top people' who know my work. May I list your name? ... My thanks if
you feel you can write a reference—I'll certainly understand if you feel you
can't (I know you think I am wrong-headed in some of my thinking)" (Sep
5, 1980, ADG). Apparently, this time Goffman turned him down, because
there is a follow-up letter that begins, "Thanks for your prompt response,
I've asked someone else to serve as a reference" (Sep 15, 1980, ADG). But
they continued friendly correspondence for the next few years, with lots of
stories about trips, and they clearly continued to connect at conferences, so
this refusal did not threaten their friendship any more than did the problems
that developed with MAP.

In addition, Goffman and Grimshaw frequently exchanged drafts. For example, Grimshaw mentioned in a letter to Hymes in 1973 that he had received a draft of a Goffman manuscript: "It's dense (in the positive sense) and will need a lot of thinking—but I think he is going in a very interesting direction—as he has been right along."[33] And a few years later, Grimshaw told Hymes, "When we were at Sugarloaf, Erving said something about all of us getting together for dinner sometime during the meetings—I hope that will be possible. . . . I hope it will be possible to see you two, the Labovs, and Goffman (I gather it's likely I'll see Sol [Worth] at the Temple meetings)."[34] Sugarloaf was the name of the conference center for the event held in January 1975. So Grimshaw knew not only Hymes, Goffman, and Labov, but also Worth—and knew them well enough to connect repeatedly with them at both large and small conferences, and his papers provide evidence that he was in frequent correspondence with them all.

In addition, Grimshaw was editor of *American Sociologist* from 1976 to 1979 (Grimshaw 1981, xiii) and used Goffman as a reviewer for submissions to that journal.[35] Some of Goffman's reviews are fairly brief, or only part has been retained in the file, but they seem to be roughly comparable to the ones written for *Language in Society*: good detail at least some of the time, and sporadically amusing. One of the notable exchanges is for a manuscript Grimshaw sent to Goffman for a specific reason: "Since your work is the inspiration of the enclosed, I thought you might be interested" (Mar 6, 1979, ADG).

Grimshaw cites Goffman repeatedly, not just for the chapter "The Neglected Situation" (Goffman 1964a), but also several of Goffman's books (e.g., in Grimshaw 1966), all at considerable length, clearly indicating that Goffman was to be numbered among the group of important early sociolinguists. A few years later, Grimshaw (1969a) discusses several of Goffman's ideas in detail, including times when speech behavior defines social structure, stage management, and the manipulation of encounters. In one review essay, Grimshaw specifically mentions that he will not be reviewing "Goffman's seminal work" (1973c, 575), and in another he several times mentions work by Goffman as being an example of "some of the most important activity going on in this area" (1974a, 10). In several reviews he points out that one author or another does not mention Goffman when, as he puts it, "a reading of Goffman would be helpful" (1974b, 317; see also 1974a). A decade later, neither he nor anyone else would have expected him to include Goffman, and a decade after that, even the mention of Goffman's name as part of discussing sociolinguistics had become infrequent. Much later, Grimshaw provides a particularly clear definition of sociolinguistics: "how talk gets used to accomplish social ends in (primarily) face-to-face interaction" (1998, 444). That definition makes obvious why Goffman would have been interested in sociolinguistics as it was developing.

Grimshaw at Penn

In 1970, Grimshaw talked with NEH about the possibility of a two-year retraining grant to learn more linguistics, in order to develop a better version of sociolinguistics; he hoped to spend the time at Penn with Hymes, Labov, and Goffman (his documentation for this does not mention Worth, whose major research area was substantially different, focusing on visual communication).[36] Hymes was quite responsive, writing about which topic out of the three that Grimshaw had mentioned was already of interest to both Goffman and Labov (social interactional universals), which overlapped with Fought's interests (semantic description), and providing the requested information about courses which Grimshaw might audit. He specifically recommended Goffman's course, although he did not provide a title or subject. (As a reminder, Goffman only taught one course per year, so if you wanted to take a course with him in a given year, you took whatever he offered.) Hymes also recommended that Grimshaw put his plans on hold for a year, given that Labov would not yet be teaching regular courses in 1970–1971.[37] Thus, in 1972 Grimshaw applied for an SSRC grant to visit Penn for two years to work with all three in order to improve his understanding of linguistics. He sent a draft to them all, explaining that he wanted "to study sociolinguistics in a setting in which the relevance of language to sociological and linguistics issues is accepted and sociolinguistic research is encouraged. Such a setting exists at the University of Pennsylvania with Erving Goffman, Dell Hymes, and William Labov gathered on the same campus and engaged in joint research and training activity."[38]He proposed working with Hymes on semantics, Labov on rule derivation and formal linguistics, and "with Goffman on rules for social interaction."[39] All three supported him; even so, he was not awarded the grant and so did not spend the year at Penn. In 1972, once it was clear Grimshaw had not been awarded the retraining grant, Goffman wrote up comments about a paper Grimshaw had sent and said: "I wish even more that we were to have you here for a year" (Feb 9, 1972, ADG). In 1973–1974, Grimshaw had a sabbatical, and again there was discussion of his spending time at Penn. Goffman evidently

252 | Chapter Six

tried to arrange for him to teach there, for Grimshaw replied, "I have thought over your kind offer to see about some teaching at Penn next year, and have decided I had better take a rain check. I will be taking courses this summer at the Linguistics Institute which will mean two months away from here. . . . Depending on how things go this summer, I will plan on spending some time in Philadelphia during the fall semester."[40] He added that Frank Furstenberg in sociology had offered to arrange for library privileges, office space, and possible teaching. Goffman responded: "We'll take whatever of your time you want to give us," and "See you at the Institute," so, apparently, he also intended to participate. His closing was typically cute: "Regards to she who married down to you" (Apr 27, 1973, ADG).

That Summer Institute involved more of those relevant to this story. Grimshaw described it in some detail in a letter to Schegloff much later, in 1996:

> I remember with great pleasure the Ann Arbor summer with courses from Harvey [Sacks], Michael Halliday, and Bill Labov and Gillian Sankoff and the workshop/tutorial you and Harvey did on CA matters. I like to tell people about the day when Halliday sat in Harvey's adjacency pairs class and came up with an extensive alternative reading which really got Harvey's attention. The entire summer was an intellectual feast.[41]

In this context, it is relevant to note that one of the reviews (by Murray, a sociologist) of a book by Grimshaw lauded him for "publicizing the work of Bernstein, [Penelope] Brown, Goffman, Gumperz, Hymes, and Labov to his inattentive sociology colleagues," further praising him for his "attempt to carry the message of sociolinguistics to sociologists," explained as "a missionary endeavor" (1982, 743–44).

Grimshaw not only knew Hymes, Labov, Goffman, and Worth, and corresponded with them all, but he also knew at least some of their younger students and colleagues because Bambi Schieffelin, Steve Feld, and Joel Sherzer are all mentioned as part of a conference panel he was organizing in 1977. Goffman was to be discussant, talking about "The Analysis of Ritual Idiom" (the same phrase is used in Goffman 1971). Other panelists were to be Charles Ferguson, Shirley Brice Heath, William Corsaro, and Karl Reisman. Schieffelin was being proposed as a replacement for Steve Feld, who could not participate, and Sherzer was apparently one of the organizers. In the end, Grimshaw was not on the panel, but Goffman did serve as discussant, joined by Hymes. The chair was Ben Blount (Texas), with other panelists being Bambi Schieffelin (Columbia), Judith Irvine (Brandeis), Joel Sherzer

(Texas), and Gumperz (Berkeley). The title was "Discourse: Speech Acts and Contextualization."[42]

MAP and Berkeley

Berkeley and Gumperz also both played a role in the origin story of the MAP project. MAP was mostly funded by grants to the SSRC Committee on Sociolinguistics, which included substantial representation from Berkeley (Ervin-Tripp was a member from the start, with Gumperz, Hymes, and Grimshaw, who was mostly at Indiana but also based at Berkeley for a year), as well as Charles Ferguson (a Penn PhD, mostly based at Stanford, who served as the first committee chair when it began in 1963 and for many years after that), later adding Labov, Sankoff, and Sherzer at different times (all affiliated with Penn).

But there is another, quite specific, way in which Gumperz played a significant role in MAP. In a 1973 letter to Hymes, at the very start of the project, Grimshaw explained that the "the major project that I had outlined for the CSL [Committee on Sociolinguistics] could be an important intellectual contribution and that at the same time it did have a substantial research component. . . . I would like to go ahead with the project." One thing stopping him, however, was that Gumperz felt he had had the same idea, earlier.

> It simply is not clear to me precisely if John thought that I was somehow "ripping off" an idea that he had had. I gather that he and the Lakoffs and one or two others in the Bay area had been getting together informally to jointly examine data. I did not have the impression that he had in mind any idea about asking a somewhat diverse group to independently examine common data. Yet at the end of our Sunday session he seemed to imply that he would see the activity I had outlined as competitive to his interests and that he might take an active role in persuading some of his friends and colleagues to not cooperate in a CSL sponsored and supported activity. (Apr 2, 1973, ADG)

The story goes on at great length: Grimshaw and Gumperz met the next day to try to sort things out, and Gumperz apologized for being "obstreperous," saying that he only wanted "to insure [*sic*] the success of the project." Grimshaw made it clear that he wanted Gumperz not only to support the project, but also to participate, and was asking Hymes to help ensure things would work out (Apr 2, 1973, ADG). By the end of the letter, Grimshaw decided "maybe I should stop trying to get more training and get down to doing research," which ties together his unsuccessful efforts to get a post-doctoral training grant to study with Hymes, Goffman, and Labov at Penn, with his efforts to manage MAP, also tying in Gumperz and colleagues at Berkeley. The letter demonstrates that Grimshaw knew this might be a difficult project from the very beginning, especially given the "'Primadonnaesque' nature of some of the proposed participants" (Apr 2 1973, ADG). As matters turned out, he was right to be concerned.

MAP Timeline and Participants

With this background in mind, it is time to return to MAP. Basically, MAP took a scientific approach to theory building: The plan was to bring all the research traditions then developing together, have everyone analyze the same data, and compare the resulting analyses. It was one of a surprisingly large number of efforts supported by the SSRC Committee on Sociolinguistics. As Heller (2018) explains,

> The idea was that bringing these different analytical angles to the same piece of data would allow for the emergence of a truly interdisciplinary understanding of language as social action . . . but the project seems to have foundered over major disagreement about the meaning and value of the experiment. . . . One result, then, may well have been the end of the interdisciplinarity that characterized the early years of the committee, and a retreat into silos.

In other words, the result was the exact opposite of the goal of the project.

What follows is a table showing the major participants at three different points in time when the group came together: a meeting in 1975 in Santa Fe to get things started, a conference in 1982 at Penn to discuss what had been learned, and a joint book (finally) published in 1994 (Grimshaw et al. 1994a). These are not the only people or dates that matter to understanding MAP, but they are the most essential points of information necessary to an understanding of the toll taken on this project by changing personnel over time.

This demonstrates that only four out of twenty analysts were present for all three key moments, which is indicative of the problems this project faced. It will be worth examining in some detail who was involved with the project at not just these three moments, but at multiple stages, what the goals were, and what led to the project foundering. In this way it can serve as a cautionary tale. Everyone agreed on at least one thing: as Grimshaw put it to Ferguson, "the idea of common data is, I think, critical to the whole idea" (May 16, 1973, ADG). Yet, as the friendliest reviewer of the resulting book pointed out: "What indeed the corpus would be, and then how it would be recorded, rendered, and distributed, in the company of what other case

Table 6.2: MAP Personnel Over Time

Analysts			
	1975	*1982*	*1994*
Charles Bird	x	x	
Peter Burke		x	x
Aaron Cicourel	x	x	x
Jenny Cook-Gumperz		x	x
William Corsaro		x	x
Fred Erickson		x	
Charles Fillmore	x	x	x
Erving Goffman	x		
Allen Grimshaw	x	x	x
John Gumperz		x	x
Michael Halliday		x	x
Ruqaiya Hasan		x	x
Dell Hymes		x	x
Elinor Keenan		x	
Adam Kendon	x		
Teresa Labov		x	x
Harvey Sacks	x		
Emanuel Schegloff	x		
Lily Wong Fillmore	x	x	x
Laurence Wylie		x	

Table 6.2: MAP Personnel Over Time (cont'd)

Filmmakers			
	1975	*1982*	*1994*
Steve Feld	x	x	x
Carroll Williams	x		
Joan Williams	x		
SSRC Staff			
David Jenness	x		x
NSF Staff			
Alan Bell	x		

relevant information, seems to have been the single most serious cause of friction, and even schism" (Macbeth 1995, 706). That was a major problem. (See Grimshaw et al. [1994b] for a far longer and more detailed explanation of what happened than can be provided here.)

Perhaps the best starting point in this context is the story of how Goffman became involved with the project. Goffman already knew Grimshaw from his days at Berkeley, and so was one of those invited to participate when the project was first conceived.[43] Grimshaw and Goffman were thus friends before MAP started—but more than friends, Grimshaw clearly respected Goffman's publications, and found them useful: "I have also found the work of Erving Goffman to be a highly valuable source of new ways of looking at patterned social behavior" (1973d, 106). And the reverse was true: Goffman clearly found Grimshaw's comments useful, as when he wrote: "Thanks very much for the critical comments on my two papers; I have been able to use almost all of them" (Aug 10, 1977, ADG). And so, in return, Goffman sent detailed comments on Grimshaw's own drafts. A good example is provided by the detailed comments he sent in response to a draft of what was eventually published as Grimshaw (1980).

Re your monograph on verbs of manipulation. Your command of the literature is masterful. Your effort to get from what linguists do into the sociologist's grasp of social life, however, raises questions which I think I could only get to through discussion with you. By the way, your sense of cajol doesn't fit with mine. (Nor do I take a dictionary's definition as necessarily very sensitive, nor the easy out of saying "in my dialect." For surely we should not in this count ourselves as each merely one voice.) I think cajol essentially refers to A's attempt to get B to do something that is easily within B's power but which he declines to do because of being hostile to something or somebody that would be involved in the doing. To cajol is to employ lightly toned, semi-humorous means of showing B that there is a way of defining the situation that would allow him to take the action A is encouraging. Sometimes A himself can be the target of the initial hostility and the cajoling therefore requires a splitting of the self, but ordinarily the target would be a third person. And I don't think deceit has anything to do with it. But, of course, even if we could agree on an explication, a question would be where in sociological space we could go with it. Certainly linguists and now yourself have shown how systematically responsive sentences are to social meaning; but this, it seems to me, is still of primary concern to sociolinguists, not sociology. (Aug 10, 1977, ADG)

This is especially relevant because it fits so well with what Goffman wrote in 1975 in response to Grimshaw's cajoling of him to fit in more activities in his visit to Indiana than he felt appropriate (see below for that part of the story). As early as April 1973, after MAP was conceived but before it was funded, Grimshaw reminded Goffman of his initial expression of interest, saying: "If we do the project, I certainly hope you will be involved" (Apr 17, 1973, ADG). There is no immediate response in the file, although there is an enthusiastic response a year later. At the same time, Grimshaw wrote to Sacks and Schegloff as well.[44] Schegloff responded that his interest would depend on both the data collected and other commitments (May 3, 1973, ADG). And at the same time Grimshaw wrote to Paul Byers because he had attended sessions that Byers and Alan Lomax had organized at the American Anthropological Association convention in 1970, held in San Diego, on film analysis of culture and communication. He mostly asked for advice in terms of equipment that would be required. "We anticipate that there will be between 8 and 12 teams working on the data," so they needed to determine what would be economical but also functional to write up a grant proposal. His letter contains a particularly clear explanation of the thinking behind the project.

> Let me start off by telling you something about a project which may be undertaken by the Committee on Sociolinguistics of the Social Science Research

Council. We have been impressed by the variety of perspectives which have been developing over recent years for the investigation and analysis of extended verbal social interaction. Some sociologists with diverse kinds of perspectives ranging from those of Harvey Sacks and Manny Schegloff and their notions of conversational analysis to people like Erving Goffman with his ideas of frame analysis to Robert F. Bales with his work on interaction analysis have long been engaged in work in this general area. In addition, John Gumperz and Dell Hymes and other ethnographers of communication have been developing various perspectives for such analysis. These two groups of investigators are now being joined by linguists like Charles Fillmore and Robin Lakoff who want to extend semantic interpretation to include more social dimensions and other linguists who are interested in moving beyond the confines of the sentence. Our committee is contemplating a project in which some set of people representative of the several kinds of perspectives mentioned will all take a common piece of data and analyze it using the theoretical frames which they have been developing. (Apr 13, 1973, ADG)

Byers was delighted with the project, saying:

Once in a very great while a letter arrives that signals, to me, an important event or possibility. Your letter of April 13 is such a letter.

Your plan to have people representative of several perspectives analyze the same piece of film-data is, in the view of many of us, the only conceivable way to bring some order to an important but much disordered and confused area of concern. I have sat with several groups hoping to bring off such a project. None has succeeded. If your committee can bring this off, I think it may represent a critical turning point in behavioral research. I believe, incidentally, that such a project will cross many disciplinary lines and do for us what no amount of talk or writing can do. (Apr 18, 1973, ADG)

Byers then responded to all the specific questions. The presentation in San Diego had been by William Condon, and Kendon had used similar machinery for a similar analysis. He provided extensive details about what equipment they used for what purposes, warning Grimshaw about multiple technical issues that might arise. In addition, he explained something that Grimshaw should perhaps have taken more seriously: "In discussions I have had in the past concerning such a project, it has been difficult to find a single data-film idea that would suit everyone" (Apr 18, 1973, ADG). That did, in fact, become a huge issue with MAP. Byers also warned that very few people were skilled at film recording, and recommended Jacques Van Vlack at EPPI (who worked with Birdwhistell). "This aspect of the project is certainly the most critical since a poor record cannot be repaired whereas analyses can be done over and over." Again, his warning was prescient.

Grimshaw replied a few weeks later that he had found the comments "overwhelming" for while "I knew that I didn't know anything about film and their analysis—I didn't realize just how naive I was. My linguist colleague characterized your letter as suggesting that I was trying to do astronomy with binoculars. The more I think about it the more I think I may have been trying to do astronomy with a child's magnifying glass" (May 4, 1973, ADG). He admitted that his project was not likely to need such sophisticated apparatus since most of the group "are rank amateurs in this kind of activity." He thought they should include "a small meeting prior to the period in which analysis will be done at which we can all learn something about the use of film." He concluded, "The purpose of our activity is to bring together analysis at different levels and see what we can learn about the rule governed nature of social interaction, including verbal interaction" (May 4, 1973, ADG).

In early May, Grimshaw wrote Hymes and David Jenness, staff to the Committee on Sociolinguistics: "To this date I have had confirmation of interest only from Goffman (though I have, as you know, written Sacks-Schegloff, Fillmore, Halliday, and Robin Lakoff [I am assuming that Joel will still want to participate])."[45] So Goffman not only participated but was the first to agree to join in. By late May, Grimshaw wrote to Ferguson mentioning that Fillmore, Goffman, Charles S. Bird (his colleague at Indiana), Sherzer, and he were all likely participants, while Robin Lakoff, Michael Halliday, Joseph Grimes, Sacks, and Schegloff were further possibilities (May 16, 1973, ADG). Despite (or perhaps because of) the early stage of the project, Grimshaw also said, "*Damnit,* I hope we can do this—it would be extraordinarily exciting and could make a really important contribution!"[46] (emphasis in original).

At that stage Hymes thought the project important, but difficult and time-consuming, to the point that most of those who would have the most to contribute would not be able to make the necessary time (including himself).

> It is marvelous that you elicited such a constructive response from Byers. It brings home to me the great gap between linguistics as commonly practiced, and the world of those who have attempted to move ahead with direct observation with the aid of visual means. If we could accomplish some interaction and lay a base for further cooperation, as between these worlds, as well as within them, we would accomplish a great deal. The kinesics, paralinguistics, communicative behavior work goes on rather bereft of linguistics or associated with older styles of linguistics. The generative semantics, and indeed ethnomethodology, doesn't seem to require much attention to observation, replicability, hard data. Wouldn't

> it be quite a coup to gain ground on this score? A successful meeting on this basis
> might reveal a group willing to tackle your full project. That is, hang gotten to
> know each other, to discover personal affinities, and intellectual adjacencies,
> some might want to push further. (May 8, 1973, ADG)

Hymes's proposal was to first hold a meeting, and assume that people would decide the project was interesting and want to participate, and maybe those who needed more linguistics would acquire that, and those who needed more observation of actual behavior, would decide to add that in. And, in the end, they would have the kind of project Grimshaw wanted. Grimshaw did not answer this directly but simply acknowledged to Hymes that the project was "both complicated and expensive" (May 16, 1973, ADG).

In August 1973, David Jenness of SSRC responded to a progress report that Grimshaw had submitted to the Committee on Sociolinguistics: "I'm happy to hear that people like Goffman and Halliday, and others, are so enthusiastic." Understanding that it would take some travel to consult with relevant experts (Byers and Worth were mentioned by name), "we should allocate up to $1,000 from committee funds for this project during the coming academic year. Dell Hymes agrees with that, so let us consider it done" (Aug 17, 1973, ADG). Thus, the first stage of sorting out who would be involved and what needed to be filmed, by whom, and where, was settled and funded. The first few steps had been taken.

In September 1973, Byers wrote Grimshaw with details about organizing a meeting with interested parties while Grimshaw would be in New York. Adam Kendon and Albert Scheflen were both scheduled to be involved, and Byers said he would try to also involve Margaret Mead. He also recommended that Grimshaw go to Boston to see Condon and Erickson, as well as to Philadelphia, to connect with Worth, Birdwhistell, and maybe Van Vlack. Byers pointed out that he had only included anthropologists because he did not know many sociologists or linguists (Sep 11, 1973, ADG). There is no answer in the file, but a follow-up letter from Grimshaw thanks Byers for his time at their meeting (other documentation shows that it was in fact held in fall 1973),[47] letting him know that the project was going ahead, and that "I am assuming that you will participate in some way" (Jun 14, 1974, ADG). In fact, Byers did not participate in MAP (nor did Scheflen, nor Mead). However, both Kendon and Erickson ended up part of the group at least for some activities, and since they were both later affiliated with Penn, it may be worth explaining a little more about them and how they became involved. First, Kendon. In a letter of recommendation for Kendon, Grimshaw wrote:

I first met Kendon when the Social Science Research Council Committee on Sociolinguistics was engaged in initial planning for the MAP project; I was introduced to him by Paul Byers who spoke highly of the work that Kendon was doing—at that time at Bronx State Hospital. I spent a day at Bronx with Kendon and others and he demonstrated the work he was then doing. . . . I was positively impressed with both the intrinsic significance of the work he was doing and the comfortable way in which he talked about [it] to me—clearly a neophyte. I subsequently read several of his papers, talked to others about his work, and engaged in some correspondence with him—as I looked for a skilled film analyst to participate in the MAP. As you know, we ultimately settled on Kendon as a participant and have invited him to involve himself in the project. Such involvement, we were aware, would necessitate bringing him from Australia twice—as well as provision of ancillary equipment—we felt that there was no one better qualified here and insisted on inviting him.[48]

A decade later, in a different recommendation letter for Kendon, written to Starkey Duncan, Grimshaw includes the tantalizing comment that he felt that "he [Kendon] has become more sensitive to interactional dimensions (in part because of his long association with and interest in Goffman) over the years" (May 20, 1987, ADG).

As for Erickson, he was the only one originally considered as a potential group member who was untenured when the project began, so initially he was not invited to participate. Grimshaw explained the logic to Laurence Wylie (a late addition to the project): "The feeling was that participants were being asked to make a very major commitment of time and energies for which payoff in terms of publication would be substantially delayed (and subsequent events have certainly proven the correctness of this concern)" (Jan 11, 1979, ADG). But by 1979, it was felt Erickson was in a more secure position, and so he was invited to join. Grimshaw explained MAP to him this way: As sociolinguistics developed in the 1960s, there had been a "proliferation of methods and theoretical orientations" and "little communication among scholars" and "little comparability across investigations and their reported findings." The original group had been "chosen on the basis of representation of different analytic and theoretical perspectives in anthropology, linguistics, psychology and sociology" (Jan 11, 1979, ADG). Erickson agreed to join the group.

Returning to 1974, and the effort to organize MAP, Grimshaw reported to Jenness that he had spent time in Philadelphia meeting with Goffman, Worth, and Hymes (as well as others unnamed), and that:

> Goffman spent two hours telling me why MAP couldn't be done—and ended up by insisting that he be included *in*. . . . Both Sol and Erving seem to believe that it will be *very* difficult to get our participants to actually write papers which permit rigorous comparisons of their interpretations—in part because of the difficulty of writing about what you see in film (Goffman); in part because the participants are really artists and not scientists willing to specify their concepts (Worth); in part because several of the participants are highly defensive and protective and somewhat unlikely to take the risk of exposure to hard criticism (both). (Jun 11, 1974, ADG; emphasis in original)

Unfortunately, they both proved correct in most of these warnings. Grimshaw had met with them separately, something he said he regretted after the fact in a letter to Goffman:

> I much enjoyed our session last Wednesday—and that following with Sol. Sol raised still other problems but seems to feel that the risk is well worth taking—he agrees with you, of course, about the difficulties of writing about what is seen on film. He's not optimistic about "scientific" comparisons—but wants to see analyses juxtaposed and an attempt made at synthesis. He's also very critical of the notion of "naturally occurring." I wish the three of us had met together—we would all have enjoyed it. (Jun 12, 1974, ADG)

Grimshaw went on to explain that he also had met with Carroll Williams, who had recommended Feld, who had expressed interest, and said, "I think you're quite right, Erving, about the 'protectiveness' of some of our colleagues about their work. Should the occasion arise, I hope you'll encourage Harvey [Sacks] and Manny [Schegloff] to take part" (Jun 12, 1974, ADG).

Worth followed up on the meeting with Grimshaw by sending a letter strongly recommending Carroll Williams: "He runs a school called The Anthropological Film Center in Santa Fe in which he takes social scientists for a period of four months and teaches them what they have to know about technology in order to do what they want to do." He also recommended Steve Feld, then a doctoral student at Indiana. "He was a student of mine at a summer institute in visual anthropology that Jay Ruby and I held two summers ago at Carroll Williams' place in Santa Fe. He knows more about linguistics than most people in linguistics." In fact, he thought they should both be involved: "I believe that the combination of Steve Feld and Carroll Williams are about the finest combination for the kind of work that you want done, that you can find in the world. And I mean that without reservation" (Jun 17, 1974, ADG). It's important to note that Worth felt particularly strongly that there was a need for people with appropriate training to both create and analyze films of interaction. Only shortly before, he had written, *"The only group of professionals involved in the making and use of anthropological films who have no training AT ALL in the making, analysis, or use of film are anthropologists.* One can count on the fingers of both hands the anthropologists who are trained to study films, not as a record of some datum of culture, but as a datum of culture in its own right" (1972a, 359; emphasis in original). One of the problems may have been that, despite this warning, Grimshaw did not end up with people trained to both create and analyze filmed interaction. After a formal invitation through which Grimshaw asked potential participants to confirm their involvement, Goffman wrote back, "I commit myself to you" (Jun 21, 1974, ADG). Finally, Grimshaw announced in June 1974 that the Committee on Sociolinguistics was now ready to receive a full proposal, which he would write, and they would submit for grant support.

Goffman was not to be the only Penn faculty member Grimshaw wanted to involve: Hymes, Labov, and Worth also were asked to contribute in various capacities. Hymes was on the board of directors of the SSRC (1969–1972), and chair (or co-chair) of the Committee on Sociolinguistics at various points (1970–1979).[49] In that administrative role, he talked through some of the major issues with Grimshaw in the early days (e.g., May 16, 1973, ADG), and, as already shown, approved initial funding to help Grimshaw organize the project. Although he played a part in the initial planning, as early as 1973 Hymes wrote to Grimshaw that he would have to turn down any more direct involvement: "I would not be able to even consider for a moment such a commitment of time" (May 8, 1973, ADG). Despite this, he remained active in the role of overseer and so was copied on much of the relevant correspondence, eventually becoming involved in the later stages.

Like Hymes, Labov was invited to actively join the project rather than remain in only an administrative role. (He also served on the committee in some years, as in 1972.) Like Hymes, he declined to participate even before things really got underway.[50] And, while Worth was neither on the committee nor formally part of MAP, he became peripherally involved given that he helped Grimshaw locate appropriate filmmakers for the project, as explained. In exchange for his efforts, some years later Grimshaw categorized him to MAP participants as "a friend of our project since its inception" (Feb 1, 1977, ADG). He said the same to Labov the next year, when requesting comments on a draft proposal for additional funding: "I consider you a 'friend' of the project" (Dec 18, 1978, ADG).

Grimshaw wrote a detailed letter to Sacks and Schegloff in June 1974, stating that the committee "has instructed me to move ahead in preparing a proposal for the Multiple Analysis Project," so it was time to confirm who could commit to the project, and what equipment they already had or would need. Carroll Williams, "the top anthropological film producer according to Sol Worth," was working with him on what they would do for data collection and would likely do the filming and recording. It was necessary to sort out equipment needs first, to know how much to request from the NSF in terms of grant funds. If NSF did not award a grant, he would try elsewhere. His estimate was that they would be funded in fall 1974 and distribute data in spring 1975: "We've waited this long—it will be worth waiting a little longer to do things properly." He made a distinction between "principals" and "associates," asking to be told of any associates who should be listed, but warning that only principals would be funded for attendance at a meeting to discuss their results (Jun 12, 1974, ADG). Apparently Grimshaw had met with Schegloff and Sacks in January 1974 for an initial discussion of their involvement in MAP, and they had agreed to participate.

At the same time, Grimshaw wrote to Kendon, thanking him for their meeting in fall 1973, and similarly checking in whether he could commit to becoming involved in MAP. In that letter, he says that the committee had met in early June "for long talks with potential participants (e.g., Goffman) and friends of MAP (e.g., Sol Worth)." While he said, "I would still very much like to involve you, in some way, in MAP," he fully acknowledged that the focus would be on verbal rather than nonverbal behaviors ("We are also constrained by our goal of keeping the size of the final working conference to a manageable size" despite "the full acknowledgment of the importance of kinesic accompaniment, proxemic management, social contexts, etc.") (Jun 14, 1974, ADG). It is interesting that this makes clear his understanding of *The Natural History of an Interview* project—both its existence and the difficulties it involved, especially that it was never formally published (see Leeds-Hurwitz and Kendon [2021] for analysis of that project). It is a pity that he did not take the lessons learned from that project more to heart.

In July 1974, Halliday wrote Grimshaw responding to one proposed context, academics conversing over dinner, which he considered not terribly interesting. Instead, he preferred that they record something "socially significant" with at least some "goal-directed activity." But he also expressed delight that they would have the services of "a top anthropological film maker" concluding, "I look forward very much to taking part" (July 10, 1974, ADG).

A few days later, Grimshaw wrote Hymes and Jenness saying, "I now have confirmation on MAP participation from Fillmore, Goffman, Gumperz, Halliday and Schegloff and I think from Cicourel. I think, in brief, that we're OK on that dimension." (Jul 12, 1974, ADG). As they were preparing the proposal, Jenness told Grimshaw: "Fortunately, we could hardly have a more impressive set of participants; right there is a testimonial to the basic worth of the project from the scientific point of view."[51] He was correct, which is why it caused such difficulties when these impressive people began leaving the project.

Jenness and Grimshaw were the co-PIs for the NSF grant received by SSRC and used to fund MAP. The proposal was submitted in December 1974. However, the application process was not straightforward, and there were several stumbles. First, they formally amended it in February 1975, requesting the timetable be moved up, with an initial grant of funds for three months so they could begin immediately.

> We do this in the understanding that a progress report and further proposal for continued support for the project will be prepared shortly after the end of the initial period. . . . The initial three-month period will include shooting the film footage, its rough processing and editing, and preparing for and the pre-analysis technical seminar, at the Anthropology Film Center in Santa Fe, where the participant-analysts will agree on what analyses are to be undertaken and what procedures will be used.[52]

Grimshaw was worried about not receiving funds until the end of the academic year, which would mean that the selected context (meetings at Indiana) would no longer be available; in addition, Cicourel was about to begin a year abroad, and they did not want to lose his expertise. Jenness and Grimshaw thus submitted a revised budget, including technical costs, project working costs, and personnel costs (small amounts for Grimshaw and Jenness; nothing for the analysts). Their request was honored, and the grant was partially funded in 1975 for that year only (SOC75-10933). Funds were "earmarked" for continuation, although not guaranteed, which turned out to make a huge difference.[53] The proposal title was "Linguistics and Social Analysis of an Extended Interaction: Converging Methodological and Theoretical Perspectives."[54] In retrospect, this move to divide the grant to permit earlier filming was to prove a strategic error.

In February 1975, Grimshaw wrote Goffman with the informal results:

> The news looks good! (How does news *look* anything?) As of yesterday, it appears very likely that NSF will fund MAP. . . . As things now stand, it appears

that we will be funded by three NSF programs (linguistics, sociology, and social psychology) and that the grant will be spread over two fiscal years—but that we will probably get most of what we need for the project . . . we should be able to do the filming in mid-April and have our technical conference (for discussion of the exact data to be used and to familiarize all of you with the equipment we hope to provide) in late June. I'm hopeful that all of you will be able to work on your analysis through much of the next academic year and the summer of 1976 and that we can point toward an analysis-comparing meeting sometime during the late fall of 1976. (Feb 27, 1975, ADG; emphasis in original)

Grimshaw tentatively scheduled a meeting in Santa Fe for three days during June 15–22, and wrote a letter to everyone: "We do need to have the meeting in June because the NSF is asking for a brief report on that meeting before they release the second part of the grant." The budget included funding for copying and circulating about one hundred pages from each participant or team to the entire group, intended to either explain "your analytic mode" or for "clarifying your theoretical position" (Feb 27, 1975, ADG). Goffman wrote back: "Congratulations and hurrahs on the warm prospect of funding" (Mar 3, 1975, ADG). June would be difficult, as he expected to be in Germany at a meeting with Cicourel, but the first week was possible.[55] However, he hated the idea of circulating materials ahead of time, as he explained:

About circulated, printed materials. I seem always to be bitching, and here is another bitch. The people in this field have followers and writings. I understood the purpose of the experiment was to get these leaders to really look at one anothers' doings. A face to face presentation, therefore, which falls back on, demands, and presupposes, a hundred pages of text is quite precisely the disease that the conference is meant to cure. If we could each sympathetically read 100 pages of the others' writings, there would be no need for the conference in the first place. So please, Allen, don't neutralize the undertaking. What we want is confrontation, not perusings. (Mar 3, 1975, ADG)

Well, they did get confrontation. In April 1975, Grimshaw was finally able to write to all of what he was by then calling "participant-analysts": "Official word from the NSF came this week. We are to have the funds for making and processing the film and for the technical seminar in Santa Fe." They would film what they had initially agreed on: "Graduate Affairs Committee; Graduate Students Association; a dissertation defense," as well as a secondary context "(e.g., a nursery school board, etc.)" (Apr 28, 1975, ADG).

Two months later, Grimshaw wrote Jenness a five-page letter detailing progress to that point. Carroll and Joan Williams and Feld had arrived at Indiana, and, after logistical issues involving fleas and miscommunications, they had filmed the graduate student group, but it proved not to be very useful: "They weren't good on the criterion of getting much of anything socially accomplished with talk." So, they tried again, filming another meeting, but the filmmakers weren't impressed with that session either. (Grimshaw doesn't mention who that meeting involved, but likely the Graduate Affairs Committee, as planned.) Then they filmed a third session, a dissertation defense, but they had further issues with location: This time the room was too noisy to film, so Marge Zabor[56] located an available sound studio, though there was an issue with getting permission to use it.[57] Eventually they were able to film, and this time, finally, all went well. Grimshaw told MAP participants: "The candidate was relaxed and forceful without being aggressive; the faculty participants all behaved exactly as they had on other occasions." (Grimshaw himself was a participant, so he was speaking from experience.) Filming lasted for three hours, and the filmmakers were happy with what they got; however, Grimshaw was less happy, worrying "about possible contamination of the analysis by my participation." However, it might still work:

> Bird and I are interested in identifying elements in on-going interaction that are being used; Sacks and Schegloss [sic] are interested in adjacency pairs; Kendon is interested in movement accompaniments to verbal interaction; Fillmore is interested in presuppositions or in Searles' [sic] type analysis of speech acts, etc., etc. Only Goffman seems to be very much into attribution—he would do this no matter what the data happened to be. So, I think it might all work out. (Jun 20, 1975, ADG)

Dell and Virginia Hymes stopped in on their way from Pennsylvania to Oregon after filming was completed, and the entire group had a party, joined by Henry Glassie (at that point still teaching at Indiana) as well as Roger Abrahams (at Texas but in Indiana to teach over the summer).

Despite the potential conflicts, Grimshaw did manage to find dates that worked for the majority in July 1975, and so they met in Santa Fe. The initial set of participants was expected to include Bird, Cicourel, Cook-Gumperz, Fillmore, Goffman, Grimshaw, Gumperz, Halliday, Kendon, Sacks, Schegloff, and Wong Fillmore, with Williams and Feld as filmmakers; in the event, all except Gumperz, Cook-Gumperz, and Halliday were able to attend the meeting.[58] Alan Bell, representing NSF, also attended (mentioned in Grimshaw's letter to him, [Aug 6, 1975, ADG]). However, everything fell apart during the meeting due to strong differences of opinion about what should be accomplished and how. Decades later, in discussing the heated exchanges among group members in Santa Fe, Grimshaw, Feld, and Jenness point out: "We have often remarked that we wish we had SIR [sound-image recording] of the Santa Fe interaction!" (1994, 17). That would indeed be fascinating. As Grimshaw wrote Hymes at the time:

> The Santa Fe MAP meeting was a disappointment of major proportions. David and I will tell you (I believe that David and I have congruent, if not identical, perceptions) that we think that we will ultimately have a successful project—though not without additional pain and not without modifying our current proposal. Charles Bird tells people that I'm an idealist (with strong overtones of naivete)—guess he's right, I'm simply unprepared for the intellectual arrogance and self-centeredness of some of our colleagues. (Aug 4, 1975, ADG)

Simultaneously he told Jenness, "I'll have the bruises for some time; I'm also pretty resilient" (Aug 4, 1975, ADG). Jenness responded: "Wow, what things we go through together! Don't be discouraged" (Aug 5, 1975, ADG). Jenness wrote to Bell (at NSF):

> If the Santa Fe Son et Lumière [sound and light] spectacular is still re-playing in your mind the way it is in mine, you will be interested to know what happened after you left. . . .
>
> When we gathered Wednesday morning Aaron Cicourel, Erving Goffman, Charles Fillmore, and Adam Kendon had a proposal. They said that it would be a shame to scrap the project; that we all had learned a lot in the meeting; that the co-operative aspect of the project remained an attractive and unusual opportunity. They proposed that the four of them confer during August (when all will be in California), and if possible come up with a proposal for new film footage, of an interactional event to be decided upon and of a technical nature that would meet the requirements of the group. That proposal would be ready by the end of August, to be discussed then with Allen Grimshaw and me at the ASA meetings in San Francisco.
>
> This was a genuine and constructive suggestion—not just a face-saving gesture—to which Allen and the rest of the group acceded. What it will turn out to mean is impossible to foretell. Probably they will now be able to propose the kind of filming that the participants, or almost all the participants, would work with. Whether that kind of filming is something that our film-makers would want to do is another matter, but it shouldn't be assumed in advance that they wouldn't agree. Whether Allen Grimshaw and the committee would, receiving the recommendation, feel that it was a good risk to proceed (or whether, instead, for example, they would prefer to make use of the data we now have and re-constitute the group somewhat) also remains to be seen. Whether either course would be justifiable and affordable is something your colleagues would probably have to decide. (Aug 6, 1975, ADG)

Goffman played a central role in the difficulties. Jenness wrote to him at length, while trying to sort out his notes and prepare a report for NSF. He decided to edit the draft in such a way "that it would be clear to Allen Grimshaw and the members of the Committee on Sociolinguistics what the differences are between the Grimshaw-Jenness statement and a statement that would be acceptable to Erving Goffman. In other words, I think there are some real and difficult differences, and at this moment I want to highlight rather than conceal them."[59]

Grimshaw responded to that draft: "The kinds of changes that Goffman is demanding, both personally and as a representative of his 'constituency' cannot be met without changing the project from what it was originally intended to be" (Sep 24, 1975, ADG). It becomes clear that "his constituency" refers to Goffman's former students, Sacks and Schegloff. On being told about the disagreements, Hymes said he thought the project was a good idea originally ("It was ambitiously admirable to try to pull together all the 'stars'") and he was upset at the division among members: "I am puzzled and troubled by so much difficulty in agreeing on what to analyze. I would have thought that it was pretty well understood by the time of the Santa Fe conference what one would have, and that people who were not willing to take a stab at it would not have gone so far" (Aug 8, 1975, ADG). A little later Hymes wrote to Goffman that Jenness was going to be in town "to discuss SSRC Committee problems with me; I have a copy of his letter to you. I hope we can work out the MAP project."[60] So he recognized immediately that there were major issues to be resolved. Worth expressed his feelings to Grimshaw with vehemence, presumably because those he had recommended as filmmakers were now involved, and he felt responsible for their best interests: "Your 'geniuses' are behaving like incompetent doctors who feel that they have to treat nurses as dirt in order to increase their own status" (Aug 5, 1975, ADG).

So, what happened? The status report Jenness mentioned to Goffman was circulated to group members in late September 1975. This was the document needed for NSF to release the second half of their grant. That draft has been preserved; since Goffman and Grimshaw both had the opportunity to send revisions to Jenness, it seems likely to be reasonably accurate. The report says Goffman "characterized the footage as relatively useless for the kinds of analyses they do" (apparently because Feld and Williams had not used a stationary camera, but had chosen what to film from what angle, and selected their own focus of interest); also, it was Goffman who wanted to say that they had "reported that they would be unable to carry out naturalistic/interactional analyses" given the film that had been made.[61] The planned meeting of Cicourel, Goffman, Fillmore, and Kendon had gone forward (although without Kendon), and they had prepared a new proposal to maintain the original goals but recommended additional filming to expand the data available for analysis because "several participant-analysts felt that the footage collected by the AFC [Anthropology Film Center] team did not meet the analytic requirements for naturalistic interactional study. A principal purpose of the new proposal is to remedy that problem by providing additional film data tailored specifically to the standards of these participant-analysts."[62] Goffman's initials are indicated next to these comments as well.[63] There is a footnote added, reminding everyone that: "It will be remembered that the identification of subjects and events for the AFC filming was under discussion and negotiation for more than two years," presumably representing Grimshaw's position, as the one who had led that conversation. The subcommittee meeting did not come to a resolution about what new context would be chosen for filming and analysis. They discussed the possibility of inviting Paul Ekman to join the project, perhaps as an additional filmmaker, and Goffman had agreed to invite him. If Ekman were not available, then Kendon would be asked. There was a lengthy list (sixteen items) of what could happen from this point, with Jenness commenting, "Now seems impossible—or very unlikely." As a result of the new schedule, he wrote, "We will have lost somewhere between six and nine months; it is our hope that the time loss will be compensated for by a stronger design and a more valuable final product."[64] In sum, they had completed filming, but the film was deemed inadequate by a group including nearly half of the analysts. That was a huge obstacle.

A few weeks later, Grimshaw wrote the filmmakers (Feld, Williams and Williams), saying:

> When I talked with Steve after the meeting in San Francisco, I thought something had been worked out—even if that something was not maximally satisfactory in terms of our original design. It now appears that there was no real agreement. Consequently, David and I will probably recommend to the Committee on Sociolinguistics that we start again with a new set of analysts—and the AVC [AFC] data. (Sep 25, 1975, ADG)

That is in fact what happened: The committee concluded that "the intended compromise is unfeasible,"[65] in Jenness's words, and the problems "intractable,"[66] in Grimshaw's. Instead, they recommended working with the data already collected, understanding that this would mean some analysts would need to be replaced on the team. Goffman was clearly to be one of those. Grimshaw's response to the conflict was to review all the correspondence over the first two years of the project in order to determine whether the issues brought up were evident earlier; he wrote a lengthy letter to Jenness sharing what he discovered. He did admit that he found several issues clearly stated in letters from Schegloff (doubts about the "edited composite" proposed) and Kendon ("explicitly stating his requirement that the film must be in the LOC [locked-off camera] mode"), and a warning about difficulties in a letter from Jenness (that there were "complaints about Feld and Williams pre-screening data"). That he had lost track of these was attributed to the fact that Grimshaw's daughter died about the same time. However, he also re-read the proposal to NSF, which clearly stated what they intended to do, so he pointed out to Jenness that some others also were guilty of not reading carefully.

> The fact of the matter is, alas, that I didn't heed the early warning signals, and that our colleagues didn't pay attention to our explicit statement as to how the film was to be made (and what it was to include). We have now reached an impasse and the kinds of changes that Goffman is demanding, both personally and as a representative of his "constituency" cannot be met without changing the project from what it was originally intended to be.
>
> ... before we left Austin [where the group had initially met to sort out the project], Goffman was strongly encouraging and insisted that I go ahead with the project in spite of what were already seen as numerous possible difficulties. (In fairness to Erving, he was talking about a much less involved project—simply getting together of something like a G group to mutually examine some tapes or old film—without any intention to publish. (Sep 24, 1975, ADG)

Grimshaw thought it was time to seriously consider who would be leaving the project, and who they might get as replacements. Continuing the letter to Jenness, he wrote:

> It now seems highly unlikely that Goffman or Harvey and Manny will stay with the project. If the rumors we have heard are correct, Gumperz will also be unsatisfied with the AFC film; he is also likely to drop out. Kendon has expressed unhappiness with the data and will probably feel constrained to join those who leave. Of the current set, Bird and Grimshaw, Cicourel, Fillmore, possibly Halliday, and certainly Williams and Feld will stay on if the current data are used and new participant-analysts sought to join with us. If Sacks and Schegloff leave it is almost certain that none of their followers or close associates would participate (e.g., Jefferson, Schenkhein [Jim Schenkein], et al.). There is no one

else who does exactly what Goffman does (I will be reading a dissertation by a new person in our psych department who worked at Penn with Goffman, I'm not particularly sanguine). (Sep 24, 1975, ADG)

In summarizing potential replacements, Grimshaw thought perhaps Edward Hall in lieu of Goffman ("Steve has told us that Edward Hall has expressed strong interest in the data. Hall is certainly one of the very most distinguished scholars in the area of proxemics"); Charles Frake, Anne Salmond, or Joel Sherzer as possible replacements if Gumperz and Cook-Gumperz left; Byers if Kendon left; Peter J. Burke if Sacks and Schegloff left. But he admitted that:

> In making these changes, or similar ones, we will sustain some major losses. Conversational analysis, as practiced by Sacks and Schegloff and their associates, is an extremely promising and exciting activity and may adumbrate a long-awaited grammar of social interaction. Goffman is clearly a major luminary, if he doesn't have an articulated theory of social interaction, he is certainly moving toward one in *Frame Analysis*. Gumperz, who has no articulated theory, is nonetheless one of the most thoughtful students of social interaction and a superb analyst. Kendon is a strong representative of a field moving from empirical taxonomic work toward some kind of integrated kinesic-ethological perspective. (Sep 24, 1975, ADG)

However, despite his regret at losing several participants, he added, "We would, with the new set of participant-analysts, still have figures of major stature in the field. . . . The final product would be different but by no means trivial" (Sep 24, 1975, ADG).

Jenness responded that he was impressed that Grimshaw was willing to take some blame and felt he should share it. "But I wonder whether the outcome, really, would have been different. As you point out, there may have been no way in which that particular group could have agreed on ground-rules acceptable to us and the committee." He recommended Klaus Scherer as another potential replacement, liking the idea of adding a non-American perspective. "[M]oreover, it would be worthwhile in that Scherer and Erving Goffman had together been working on the Royaumont project, so that in effect we'd be involving a Goffman protégé" (Sep 30, 1975, ADG). An explanation is necessary here. The "Royaumont project" refers to the Fondation Royaumont (Goüin-Lang) pour le progrès des Sciences de l'Homme. To briefly provide context for that organization, "In 1972, the Foundation encouraged Europe's first attempt at cross-disciplinary cooperation between biology and anthropology, establishing the Centre Royaumont pour une Science de l'Homme chaired by Jacques Monod."[67] Goffman was one of a large group of scholars gathered together by Royaumont to study animal communication and human communication in 1974.[68] "A preliminary list of specialists to be consulted during the planning phase, or who could take part in some capacity or other in the three-year project was established."[69] Goffman and Birdwhistell were both listed.

There was another attempt to involve Scherer. As the story directly involves Goffman, it is worth a brief sidetrack. Scherer taught at the University of Pennsylvania in 1970,[70] where he sat in on one of Goffman's courses (Fine 2009). In June 1974, Grimshaw had written to Scherer, then back in Germany:

> Professor Erving Goffman, who will be involved in the multiple-analysis project described in the enclosure, has told me that you are planning a similar project in Europe and has suggested that we might profitably exchange information and ideas. I gather from a recent conversation with Goffman that our projects are different enough to warrant independent activity but simultaneously sufficiently similar in goals and in design to assure enhancement of each if we share our problems and resolutions and, on completion of the projects, compare our results. He suggests that on completion we might well want to bring participants from both projects together to mutually review and discuss findings. . . . If Goffman's suggestion makes sense to you I hope you can provide me with some details on your plans and tentative schedule. (Jun 25, 1974, ADG)

Scherer answered, but apparently felt it was far too soon in the process to compare notes, for Grimshaw responded: "I agree with you that we should try to keep in contact; and also agree with you that since both projects are still in a formative state, there is little more we can do at this point than to keep one another informed. . . . I also hope that it may be possible for us, or at least for some participants in the two projects, to get together at a later date" (Oct 21, 1974, ADG). Given that MAP took over twenty years to complete, meeting to compare results became moot.

Interestingly, Zabor learned of Scherer's project a few months later, writing Feld about it. Apparently that letter was forwarded to Grimshaw, for it is in his files. She characterized it as "an international project on the joint analysis and discussion of one particular instance of communication in social interaction" and had heard it might include Bateson, Kendon, Goffman, Guy Cellerier, David Crystal, and others. Duncan had told her about it, and suggested she write Grimshaw, since "the general plan is for many researchers to study one filmed interaction" and it sounded much like what Grimshaw was organizing (Nov 27, 1974, ADG). Of note is that first Goffman and then Duncan and Zabor tried to help Grimshaw connect with a comparable international project, although that effort did not in the end lead to either collaboration or coordination.

To return to the 1975 difficulties with MAP. In October, Grimshaw wrote to Goffman to find out whether he was willing to stay with the project given the committee's decision not to implement the changes he had requested.

> The work you put in to trying to make the project work, in San Francisco and later on with David [Jenness], was a great contribution and we are all grateful for it. Our hope is that you will feel that your participation is still possible. I believe you could do great things with these data, and that the MAP would be poorer for your absence. If you feel you cannot participate, I will of course understand, even though I will regret it. . . .
>
> Erving, I hope you'll decide that you would like to work with the MAP data. Whatever your decision, I'll continue to enjoy what you do with what you use! (Oct 17, 1975, ADG)

Goffman responded to Jenness rather than directly to Grimshaw (asking him to pass on the response to Grimshaw):

> A case, I guess, of the best solution none the less being hard. I do appreciate the very real concern and effort of all parties, and the reasoned and reasonable statement. The course the Committee has decided on assures at least some outcome, which the other did not, and that is a merit. My misgivings about the collected materials arn't [sic] of course altered by your decision nor by the fact that I may well have supported your view were I serving alongside of you, and I withdraw. (Oct 24, 1975, ADG)

Despite letters from Grimshaw encouraging them to stay ("I do think your continued participation in the MAP would be valuable for you, just as I know that it would be valuable for the rest of us" [Oct 17, 1975, ADG]), Schegloff and Sacks likewise withdrew within a few days.[71] Jenness and Grimshaw accepted responsibility rather than attributing blame to others, writing to the entire group:

> It seems, in retrospect, that mistakes were made by the committee and the organizers of the project, such that the knowledge and the intellectual premises of the several participants were not sufficiently understood and taken into account. Collaborative projects are generally at risk in this respect, and this project has been no exception. . . . Goffman undertook to state not only his own requirements but those of the group of conversational analysts [Schegloff and Sacks] represented in MAP, as he understood them. Goffman's efforts were generous indeed; he realized that while trying to represent other analysts was

a risky task, it would be an endless process were each analyst to try to revise or alter the document from his own individual point of view. (Oct 20, 1975, ADG)

While Jenness was particularly gracious about Goffman's role publicly, he was not always so kind. A month earlier, in a letter to Grimshaw, he had mocked Goffman for claiming to have come up with the idea that led to MAP. Specifically, he said: "In fact, Erving now claims that in some sense he 'gave' the basic MAP idea to both you and Scherer, as if he were a football coach trying out two running backs competitively!" (Sep 30, 1975, ADG). But Goffman did, in fact, outline almost exactly what the MAP project attempted in 1970, in a letter to Sebeok. Whether he also explained that design to Grimshaw and Scherer, of course, is a different matter, but if he claimed he did, presumably it is likely. To understand his comment, it may be helpful to realize that he was evaluating the conference he had just co-organized and managed with Sebeok in Amsterdam. The specific idea was this: "I think it might be useful to give thought to a conference methodology suggestion made in the past. If we could videotape or film a five-minute strip of informal spoken interaction and mail each participant or each local team of participants a copy and then spend two days showing off our several efforts at analysis, much, I think, could be gained" (Oct 7, 1970, TS). Unfortunately, Goffman is not explicit about who he thinks previously had made such a suggestion for what purpose, or when in the past. But it is at least clear that he did, in fact, make such a proposal himself as early as October 1970.

Jenness reported to Paul Chapin at NSF in November 1975, to update him as to progress on the grant, and provide documentation as to the logic of the decision:

> Last month, the Committee was finally faced with deciding to proceed with the project as originally intended, thereby losing some highly valued participants, or redesigning the project so as to keep those participants. Because the latter choice would have meant giving up the comparative and collaborative aspects of the project, as originally designed, the Committee chose the first alternative.
>
> Three of the original participants—or two of the nine "teams" of participants—have declined to continue with the project. They are Harvey Sacks and Emanuel Schegloff, and Erving Goffman. We have invited others, appropriately from the interactional and social-science side, rather than from the linguistics side, to take their places. I will be able to let you know shortly who has accepted. (Nov 10, 1975, ADG)

In November 1975, Halliday wrote to Jenness, saying that he would stay with MAP, although he was disappointed in two small issues. The first was that the text to be analyzed was from an academic context, not his favorite. "The second disappointment is over the withdrawal of some of the original participants, with whom I had particularly been hoping to be associated in this project, and whose work on the text I had eagerly looked forward to seeing." At the same time, he understood how much work Grimshaw had already put in, and so he was not ready to withdraw. "I agreed to work with whatever kind of data was generally accepted, and I am sure that I shall get something from it, the more so perhaps because it will force me to look for different things" (Nov 15, 1975, ADG).

Apparently Chapin wrote to Jenness and Grimshaw questioning the viability of MAP at this stage, arguing that "it would not be fruitful to precede with procedural details for the follow-on proposal" because they did not have commitments for participation from a "broad enough spectrum of expertise in the study of interactive behavior"; and based on their apparent inability to provide "the information each participant felt to be necessary."[72] In response, Grimshaw laid out the original teams (Bird/Grimshaw, Cicourel, Fillmore, Goffman, Gumperz/Cook-Gumperz, Halliday, Kendon, Sacks/Schegloff, and C. Williams/Feld) and revised teams of analysts (Bird/Grimshaw, Burke, Cicourel, Fillmore/Lily Wong Fillmore, Gumperz/Cook-Gumperz, Hall, Halliday, Kendon, Williams/Feld), specifying that: "We do *not* consider Burke and Hall to be second-level replacements for those who chose not to continue in the project" (emphasis in original). "Most importantly, these highly qualified analysts all have agreed to work on a common segment of the data. We are now ready to go ahead" (Dec 1, 1975, ADG).

However, Chapin and others at NSF were evidently not impressed by this logic. As Grimshaw mentioned in another letter to Chapin:

> In a letter to me dated 14 January 1976, responding to an earlier letter of mine, you noted that you and your colleagues had reviewed the AP file and our reasons for urging continued support of the project, and that your "unanimous opinion" was that "results of the preliminary phase of the project, despite some reservations, [did] not justify the investment of further research funds." My understanding at that time was that a principal basis for the negative assessment was a shared concern that it was unlikely that the several participant-analysts would either agree on what was to be done, or, if they agreed, do it. (Jun 14, 1975, ADG)

In April 1976, as Grimshaw wrote to Halliday, his feeling at that point was: "We won't be doing the project under the ideal circumstances we had originally hoped; we can still believe that we are engaged in an important activity and that we can carry it through to successful completion" (Apr 7, 1976, ADG).

In June 1976, Grimshaw wrote to all analysts that, while there had been delays, the audio material had by then (finally) been processed, and both still photographs and a transcription were nearly ready; projectors had been purchased and would be sent to Berkeley for the two teams there (Fillmore/ Wong Fillmore; Gumperz/Cook-Gumperz), one to Santa Fe (Hall, Williams/ Williams) and another to Bloomington (Bird, Grimshaw, Burke); Varispeech machines would be available shortly, for Fillmore, Halliday, Hall, and the Bloomington crew. The common data set was a twelve-minute selection. "That period should be long enough to give everyone something to sink their analysic [*sic*] teeth into without being impossibly long for those of you who do very fine-grained work. We decided to use the entire piece because it not only has a variety of kinds of behaviors but also because it includes fragments in which there are, variously, three, four, and all five participants" (Jun 3, 1975, ADG). Grimshaw further requested that everyone begin analysis immediately so there would be initial analyses available by the end of the year; he and Jenness would "draft a proposal for support of the latter phases of the project" at the beginning of 1977 to cover the costs of a conference and preparation of a published volume. "Since one of the reasons we are currently not being supported is reported skepticism that analysts would ever do their several 'shares'—we must be able to show that all of us are sufficiently committed to do the work" (Jun 3, 1976, ADG). At that point, the group he was writing to included: Bird, Burke, Cicourel, Feld, Fillmore and Wong Fillmore, Gumperz and Cook Gumperz, Hall, Halliday, Kendon, Carroll and Joan Williams.

In June 1976, Halliday responded, "I was sorry to learn that NSF were not prepared to go on supporting the project. It has had its ups and downs but no more than any other project of an original nature. Anyway this makes no difference to my own participation; I shall be glad to take part as planned. Ruqaiya and I intend to work on it together" (Jun 16, 1976, ADG). It is a minor note, but an interesting one that none of the spouses (Cook-Gumperz, Hasan, Wong Fillmore, or J. Williams) were ever actually invited to participate. Apparently, it was taken for granted that an invitation to one (the male) spouse included an invitation to the other (the female). In fact, all of them came through when it mattered most, J. Williams in helping with filming, and the other three in writing chapters for the final publication.

In February 1977, Grimshaw wrote everyone again, apologizing for the fact that technical delays meant no one had yet gotten the film segment. He passed on comments from Worth about how they were "part of a long process in which social scientists are going to have to learn how to deal with the mechanics of collecting their data in a much more fundamental fashion . . . unfortunately your experience will give everybody else the necessary knowledge to know precisely what things to be very clear about. . . . being pioneers, we will have undergone an experience from which others can learn" (Feb 1, 1977, ADG). At the same time, he hoped "that each of us will have taken the opportunity to examine some of the data already available (e.g., transcripts, reel-to-reel audio, cassettes)" and that once they had some preliminary analysis, they should send it to him so he and Jenness could prepare the next grant proposal. He included a paragraph summarizing where everyone was physically (several were out of the country at that point, or in transit) and what they were working on (a few working on topics related to MAP, the rest busy with other work).

In April 1978, Grimshaw notified the group that the future of the Committee on Sociolinguistics was in doubt, but that "MAP can continue whatever the fate of the Committee" (Apr 10, 1978, ADG). In fact, the committee ceased existence in 1979 (Heller 2018). He asked whether anyone would object if he added Laurence Wylie to the group, as he was interested in examining the data. "I think that he does very interesting work and that he would be a welcome addition to the analytic team." (Wylie did in fact join.) Grimshaw also shared that Fillmore, Gumperz, and Cicourel had proposed permitting the sharing of data before the project was completed, something that had been agreed should not happen when it was begun. However, given the time elapsed, he was inclined to support them and was asking if anyone objected: "I do hope, however, that we can keep the results of our several analyses from being totally dissipated before we are able to have our post-analysis conference and before we get a finished product together for publication" (Apr 10, 1978, ADG).

In June 1978, Grimshaw wrote to Chapin at NSF, again requesting funding. Picking up with the issues indicated as problems in 1976, he said:

> It now appears that the several analysts *have* agreed on what is to be done and that they *are* doing it. I write, therefore, to ask whether it is reasonable to inquire whether we might again approach the NSF for funds to complete the project. The principal direct costs involved would be for a four-day conference of participant-analysts and commentators, to critically review the completed analyses, and for production of a final report. (Jun 14, 1978, ADG)

Chapin eventually must have agreed to consider a new proposal, because in December 1978, Grimshaw sent "MAP participant-analysts, CSL members, friends and advisors of the Multiple Analysis Project" a draft proposal of a new NSF grant request. The deadline for submission was February 1979. He enclosed a draft proposal with "an appendix on the (checkered) history of the MAP." It would also include his CV, everyone's project summaries, Zabor's transcript of the common data sample, and a budget. He asked that everyone pay particular attention to their own biographies, and longer descriptions of their parts of the project. He requested suggestions of where to host the conference where they would present and compare their analyses. And he added new information about why the second round of funding for the project had been rejected: "When the NSF declined to provide support for continuing the project in 1976, they did so because it didn't appear to people there that the project would succeed. Three original analysts had left the project, many of our colleagues had in mind the failure of the 'natural history of an interview' project and quite frankly didn't believe that we would actually do our several analyses."[73] On the same day, Grimshaw sent his draft proposal for foundation support to Jenness for critique. He had received drafts of several proposals and a few papers from group members, although, despite friendly words in the public announcement, he complained privately about "dilly dallying" by several people and the delays that was causing the group. "I can only hope that I get stuff from delinquents before the final version of the proposal is prepared for submission. . . . I am not very happy about the project, but I suppose that I could write up another version emphasizing the linguistics-humanities implications of MAP for submission to NEH" (Dec 18, 1978, ADG). That letter to Jenness mentioned that there had been a "contretemps" with Hall, and he seemed likely to withdraw from the group as a result. But a letter Grimshaw wrote on the same day to Hall sounds far more positive, mentioning only that it had been several months since Hall had responded; he hoped Hall would stay with the project, but if he would not have time for that, to please return both the documentation and the equipment so they would be available to others.

In March 1979, Grimshaw told Goffman:

> I am making progress on my analysis of the film. I am using a modification of the Labov-Fanshel mode of analysis, adding the visual stuff (I have spent over 300 hours on a run through that) and, of course, more people and a different set of questions. I know that you're not persuaded by some of the things I'll be doing with the materials—but I hope that sometime we can sit down and talk about what it is that I am doing. I am putting the first analysis on the computer

in a format like Bill's—if you're interested I'll be able to send something for
examination in a month or so. (Mar 6, 1979, ADG)

Notice several things here: that Grimshaw, at least, was actively working
on MAP at this point; that he used Labov and Fanshel (1977) as a model
(and wrote a review of that book in 1979); and that he assumed Goffman
would still be happy to talk with him about what he was learning, despite
their disagreement about methodology. In fact, he was right, because the
answer from Goffman was cordial: "Glad to hear that your MAP project is
moving" (Mar 25, 1979, ADG).

In early August 1979, Grimshaw complained to Kendon:

> I wish I could give you some sort of report on MAP funding. The proposal
> has been with NSF for five months now, without any sort of response after
> the original acknowledgment. There are, I understand, some problems about
> funding of the Foundation's social science programs, and apparently there will
> be joint House-Senate conferences before a budget is established. We *will* finish
> the project sometime, I am going ahead with my own analysis, and enjoying it.
> I hope that you and others of our colleagues are also finding tine to work on
> the materials. I am not sure whether I told you that Fred Erickson will be do-
> ing an analysis—he has the data set which Ned Hall had. I will be seeing Aaron
> [Cicourel] shortly and hope to find out what he is doing. (Aug 2, 1979, ADG;
> emphasis in original)

This makes it clear that Hall had left the group, and Erickson had joined in
his place, and that Grimshaw was still assuming the group would be able
to move ahead and complete the project. A few weeks later, Grimshaw told
Kendon: "I am looking forward to reading your contribution, and those of
our colleagues, to the MAP—and to discussing them at a meeting. When
that will be I don't know, I have still not heard from NSF" (Aug 17, 1979,
ADG). The meeting he is referring to here is the one he wanted to hold
where everyone would present their analyses; in fact, that meeting did not
occur for several more years.

In September 1979, Grimshaw circulated the message to group members that the request for NSF funding had been rejected, but that he had
been encouraged to revise the proposal, especially in terms of reducing the
budget, and to resubmit. He was willing, even though the budget reduction
"will come primarily out of my hide—in terms of a reduction of released
time," and expected to have that ready to resubmit within 4–5 weeks (Sep
20, 1979). But in fact, it took far longer to compile the necessary documentation from everyone. In February 1980, Grimshaw was still working on

the proposal for addition funding while writing his own analysis. He wrote Kendon: "I am working on the MAP materials again. . . . My analysis is still a long way from completion (I am about 1/2 to 2/3 of the way through a first draft analysis) but I am satisfied with what I am doing (though I know others won't be). I am still trying to get the last of the materials I need for revision of the MAP proposal" (Feb 7, 1980, ADG).

In April 1980, Grimshaw wrote Kendon that there had been a group meeting on the west coast at which he had met with Gumperz, Cook-Gumperz, Fillmore, Halliday, and Hasan, and then he had met separately with Wylie.

> All were, of course, very busy. All have agreed, however, to send the missing stuff (some is already in hand) and have again expressed interest in working on the project (John and Michael and Ruqaiyah [*sic*] outlined plans [*sic*] specific plans for their work). I am now working on the revision, and trying to find out from NSF if the changes I have projected are those asked for. I'll keep you posted.
>
> May I hear from you soon? It would be nice if we could get this project completed.
>
> I hope you are finding opportunities to work on the MAP materials. I am spending quite a bit of time on the data now, and finding it trying but fascinating. (Apr 22, 1980, ADG)

In May 1980, Grimshaw was still corresponding with Chapin about what they needed to change, and how best to meet the suggestions received to that point. In particular, he was concerned that the budget still came out to about the same, despite cutting reimbursement for his time in half, due to higher expenses for the proposed conference; and the increased length of the proposal, given the request for more information about participants. Even so, he was sure they would be able to make the July 1 deadline (May 19, 1980, ADG). At the same time, he wrote Feld, "I have spent much of my time during the last two weeks working on revision of the NSF proposal (Polly [his wife], I believe, wishes I would just give up the whole business, do my own work, and forget the others. I can't do that—I have too much of an investment—and feel an obligation to those other participants who have continued to be interested and supportive)" (May 16, 1980, ADG). One certainly must admire his stamina and perseverance.

In June 1980, Grimshaw wrote Sankoff that the revised MAP proposal was almost completed, and that "I am going ahead with my own analysis whatever the outcome of the NSF proposal. I think I have some interesting findings; I certainly have ample confirmation of the difficulties (and tentativeness of findings) in working with such materials."[74] At that point, he outlined the complaints from reviewers to an earlier iteration of the proposal. They said the cost was too high, it was unclear that the proposed participants were sufficiently committed, why a conference was needed at the end (instead of a publication), or even why the project was particularly appropriate. He was trying to answer all the concerns and would be sending a draft around to the entire group of MAP researchers. He had worked especially hard to reduce the budget and sent a draft to Feld for comments: "The fact of the matter is that I am not accountant [sic]—and that I find all of this very unpleasant" (May 16, 1980, ADG).

The next month Grimshaw told Chapin that the revised proposal was in the hands of the contract administration office at Indiana and would soon be on its way. At the same time, he thought it might be useful to answer the last set of extended questions from Chapin. The major issue remaining was that one reviewer had "complained about the lack of 'hard-nosed discussants'" at the proposed conference; in response, his new proposal "also includes, I believe, some 'hard-nosed' types and, in the persons of Goffman and Schegloff, two original MAP analysts who withdrew because of dissatisfaction with the data." His willingness to invite Goffman and Schegloff to be discussants of the project from which they had withdrawn is notable. He answered another critique, that of balance between disciplinary approaches, by pointing out that if those he proposed were all able to participate, then "the conference would have quite good disciplinary balance in my view, with five anthropologists, six linguists, three psychologists (including Jenness), seven sociologists, one philosopher and one humanist-social scientist (Wylie)" (Jul 11, 1980, ADG).

In August 1980, Grimshaw told Kendon that he had completed and resubmitted the proposal. "I have no notion of whether we will be funded. . . . But I am confident that we will be able to go ahead and produce some sort of worthwhile volume even if we aren't funded, at least some of us are going ahead with out [sic] analyses, my own reaction is that I find myself more and more intrigued with the data—and more and more disgruntled about some of the detailed work which has to be done" (Aug 4, 1980, ADG). It is perhaps a little odd to be complaining about detail work to Kendon of all people, given that that was his specialty (and the explicit reason Grimshaw wanted him to be part of the project).

In March 1981, Richard Louttit, director of the Division of Behavioral and Neural Sciences at NSF, officially notified Grimshaw that the grant proposal (BNS 80-23112) had been denied. Unfortunately, the same critiques as had been raised earlier had become issues again. A few quotes from the reviews follow:

- I found myself considerably more persuaded by the caliber of the participants in the MAP than by the attempted theoretical rationale. I suspect that interesting and perhaps important results will follow from allowing these people to discuss their work in relation to a common corpus, particularly if first-rate discussants are obtained. However, I'm not inclined to believe that anything like an assessment of the relative explanatory power of the various approaches will happen, nor that any progress will be made toward an integrated theory of sociolinguistic description.
- First, there seem to be serious problems with the data. Three of the initial investigators left the project because of its inadequacy and even the principal investigator now says (p. 15) that it would be shot differently if it were to be redone. . . . Second, while it is quite true that not [sic] single project could bring together everyone working on the analysis of conversation the absence of Goffman and Schegloff (or anyone within the Sacks tradition) as well as some other major researchers (Labov, for example) raises serious questions about whether the project will really be able to do what it is setting out to do.
- . . . there are some important omissions in the review of the relevant previous research. For example, the previous project that the current proposal seems most close to in goals and working procedures is the work of McQuown, Bateson, Birdwhistell, etc. that culminated in *The Natural History of an Interview*. However, no mention is made of this work (and if the first of MAP's objectives is "an [sic] comprehensive an analysis of a single speech event as heretofore been accomplished" it should certainly be assessed).
- . . . the fact that Sacks, Schegloff and Goffman chose to leave after viewing the data and meeting the other investigators raises even more fundamental questions about both the feasability [sic] of the project and that data it is based on.
- This is a fundamentally important, and longstanding project. It is in the best sense of the term "interdisciplinary" (which may be influential in the way NSF chooses to fund the project; to me, it would be appropriate to have funds come from both Linguistics and Sociology). The project is all but completed, and with the funding requested, it should reach fruition. The idea of a joint analysis of a single episode of interaction is, of course, good. It will shed light on the underlying presuppositions, methods of analysis, and kinds of findings. By having the investigators from many fields interacting in a single conference, on a common data base, the specifics of similarities and dif-

ferences will be highlighted. . . . This is the best proposal submitted to NSF Linguistics Program I have read. The organization and thoroughness of the proposal serve as a guide for others to follow. This project is complicated; the conference and publication of these materials has staggering organizational problems. If anyone has the organizational ability, talent, and resourcefulness to "pull this one off" it is Grimshaw. He organized the project while on SSRC Committee on Sociolinguistics, has seen it through all its stages of development, and will see it to its conclusions.

- This project has to make it on (a) the will and drive of the P.I. and (b) sheer inertia. . . . We clearly have a star studded cast. The lack of representation of the conversational analysts is a real gap, though, and I tend to agree with the objections they reportedly (App. C, pp. 4–5) raised at the beginning, i.e. the formality of the material to be analyzed and the lack of a fixed camera. (Mar 10, 1981, ADG)

In terms of ratings, the reviewers gave one "excellent," one "very good," two "good," and one "fair." Obviously, there was no clear agreement that this project should be funded, and it was not.

Grimshaw's response was to write to Chapin, asking, "Would MAP have been funded if the roof had not caved in?" (Mar 24, 1981, ADG). The reference was to political cuts to the NSF budget. Grimshaw told Cicourel a little time later that "both the Sociology and the Linguistics programs at the Foundation had recommended support; the sharply reduced appropriations for social science programs has meant that even continuing programs have either not been funded or have had funding sharply reduced" (May 1, 1981, ADG). Grimshaw was obviously an optimist; the specific comments in the evaluations would not have convinced most applicants that these were strong recommendations for support. Despite the lack of federal funding, he reported to Chapin that he'd been approached with the possibility of private funding, although it seems that also did not work out. However, he had received a sabbatical for the next academic year and planned to spend it "writing up my own analyses of the MAP materials as a monograph" (Mar 24, 1981, ADG). And he did just that (Grimshaw 1989).

MAP at Penn

The majority of MAP had little to do with Penn, but one part of the story did take place there, drawing in a few additional participants. Discussions began in 1981, between Grimshaw and Feld at a conference, continuing via letter and telephone, about an "'Annenberg possibility' for winding up the MAP ... I think that if you and your colleagues are able to work something out we will be able to get a good act together" (Mar 24, 1981, ADG). Feld asked ASC to serve as the setting for what Grimshaw called "a public 'show and tell.'"[75] That initial request was successful, and Grimshaw happily told Cicourel that:

> ... plans for an MAP conference in conjunction with an Annenberg School of Communications Conference on Visual Communication are likely to be approved. A proposal, which includes both the visual communication conference and a separate MAP program has been tentatively approved by Mr. [Walter] Annenberg, and Steve [Feld] and his colleagues at the Annenberg School are working out logistic and financial details. (May 1, 1981, ADG)

The two events were eventually separated, although there was still support forthcoming for MAP. Grimshaw continued:

> It appears likely, then, that after years of delays and disappointments we are going to be in a position to complete our project. . . . Some of us have been using the materials heavily, some in classes and seminars and others in individual analyses. I have, as you know, been heavily engaged in work on the materials. I will still plan on working on my monographic treatment during my sabbatical year in Tucson; I will not want for things to say about the corpus. (May 1, 1981, ADG)

In the end, the Multi-disciplinary Workshop on Analysis of a Naturally Occurring Conversation: The MAP was held November 17–20, 1982, at Penn, with travel, accommodations, and conference facilities all subsidized by Annenberg (Grimshaw 1989). In addition to the major analysts, the group was expanded for this event to include William Corsaro, F. Roger Higgins, Dell Hymes, Teresa Labov, and Elinor Keenan as discussants.[76] Sankoff was also invited to serve as discussant, but turned down the offer as she did not do microsociolinguistic work.[77] And Schegloff was invited to be a discussant; he also declined (Jun 1, 1982, ADG). Grimshaw mentions that Kendon had to withdraw as one of the participant-analysts and might serve as a discussant instead, although that did not happen.[78] That was in April, during the planning stages. By September, Grimshaw was writing to participants asking if they could please complete their papers so the discussants would have them ahead of time; at that point, he only had one paper in hand. According to the draft program included with letter, he was expecting eleven papers (Bird, Burke, Cicourel, Erickson, Fillmore, Wong Fillmore, Feld, Gumperz and Cook-Gumperz, Halliday, Hasan, and Wylie), and these were to be shared with the five discussants mentioned above, with Feld organizing logistics at ASC, supported by Larry Gross and Jay Ruby.[79] Despite the fact that Goffman died November 19, the workshop was in fact held as planned.[80]

A few months after the event, Grimshaw shared with Schegloff that "the Philadelphia conference was a success (though it ended on a somber note because of Erving's death). Everybody had papers, though some were at later stages than others; we are hopeful that we'll have a manuscript completed by late summer" (Feb 7, 1983, ADG). Grimshaw sent Kendon an extensive description since he had been expected yet in the end was unable to attend, so we know what happened.

> I thought you might be interested to learn that we did have our Philadelphia meeting, and that things worked out much better than I had expected as late as the time Polly [his wife] and I boarded our flight to Philadelphia. Almost everyone who finally attended the meeting had a paper; some did send them in advance, a few brought copies with them, one or two had papers which were written but not available for distribution. The discussion sessions generally went very well, the nature of the initial discussant's remarks in each case was, as you would expect, affected by whether or not they had had the paper in advance. Whatever, we now have a schedule (over the next six months) for completion of papers and preparation of final comments, etc., and I am, for the first time in five years or so, fairly confident that the project finally will come to completion. I do wish you had been able to attend and I am very sorry that you were not able to contribute a paper. The fact is that not very many of the contributors have drawn very heavily on the visual record; I suppose that fact is in a way a validation of some of the criticisms of the project. Such problems notwithstanding, I am hopeful that I will have a late draft manuscript by sometime late next summer (or early fall). (Jan 6, 1983, ADG)

Kendon's response was quite positive: "I'm glad your conference was a success. . . . I am also regretful that I had to drop out of your project which, as you know, I've always believed was very worthwhile" (Jan 11, 1983, ADG). Kind words, particularly since Kendon was initially one of those who had strenuously objected to the data collection process.

MAP, Birdwhistell, and NHI

There is a distinct gap in the list of MAP participants overlapping with Penn, and that is Birdwhistell. Szwed is also missing, but there was no reason for him to be involved in a detailed analysis of linguistic data, so his omission seems both obvious and reasonable. Birdwhistell, however, was especially known for this type of work; he was certainly at Penn during the relevant years, and Grimshaw knew of his work, both from correspondence with Kendon, who included both Birdwhistell's and Goffman's publications in his teaching (and research),[81] and from Birdwhistell's involvement with *The Natural History of an Interview* (McQuown 1971), an obvious precursor project. NHI was both less successful (it was never published) and far more so (clearly having influenced all later research on multimodal communication, as documented in Leeds-Hurwitz and Kendon 2021).[82] A large part of the answer may have been that, as Grimshaw told Kendon directly in 1979, "You are the central person among those involved in the kind of microanalysis of video materials which you do" (Oct 29, 1979, ADG), and so he only wanted Kendon. (Kendon had been a late participant in NHI and so had an uncommonly clear sense of what NHI had been about, how participants analyzed data, and whether it would serve as a model.) In addition, it may well have been that Grimshaw thought of Birdwhistell as only being interested in kinesics (body motion communication) and, although early on he explained that MAP would examine kinesic and proxemic behavior as well as language and paralanguage, in fact, the results strongly emphasized verbal over nonverbal behavior. If so, that is a common error; today, Birdwhistell is only known as the person who invented kinesics, while with his own students he emphasized a far broader analysis of communication behavior. He wanted kinesics to be part of it, but studying just that was not his goal; it was rather one piece of a large puzzle. It is also possible that either Hymes's or Sebeok's opinion of Birdwhistell had convinced Grimshaw not to invite Birdwhistell to participate in MAP. Despite having lobbied hard to get Birdwhistell to Penn, Hymes used the phrase "prima donnas such as Birdwhistell" in a letter to Grimshaw in 1975 (Aug 8, 1975, ADG); and Sebeok's opinion, as previously quoted when discussing the Amsterdam conference with Goffman ("sigh, sigh" [Feb 4, 1970, TS]), may have made its way to Grimshaw as well. Perhaps, like many linguists, he really did not think what he wanted to study should include nonverbal behavior. Whatever the logic, Birdwhistell was either not invited into the group or chose not to participate. Given that there is not a single letter to or from Birdwhistell in the Grimshaw papers, the former seems most likely.

The connections with NHI were, however, explicitly discussed, as well as Grimshaw's comments on its use (or rather, its non-use), in Macbeth's review of Grimshaw et al. (1994a).

> But in describing the Natural History of the Interview project (NHI), pursued by Bateson and other fellows at the Center for Advanced Study of the Behavioral

Sciences in the mid-50s, Grimshaw suggests more than a rhetorical interest for it. NHI was the nearest prior approximation of the MAP project, and its failure to come to completion (publication) was cited as grounds for early skepticism about MAP. In Grimshaw's view, "it is difficult to avoid the conclusion that the NHI tropism for completeness proved its downfall...The NHI transcript is more complete than any other in existence. It has not been used because no one knows how to ask questions about it" (p. 34 [of Grimshaw et al., 1994a]). (1995, 710)

I agree with Macbeth that NHI was the obvious precursor to MAP; even if Birdwhistell was not to be asked to participate, that should not have stopped Grimshaw and other MAP analysts from using NHI as a relevant guide. But they did not.

MAP-Related Publications

At the start of MAP, Grimshaw invited Hymes and Labov to participate (though both declined), as well as Goffman (who accepted, was part of the group for several years, but later resigned), and used Worth as a resource. He also invited Sankoff to participate in the conference at Penn where the major analyses were (finally) presented; she also declined. By the end, MAP involved several additional Penn faculty members in some capacity who had not initially been part of the group—specifically, Kendon,[83] Feld, Erickson, and T. Labov—but neither Goffman nor any other Penn faculty prepared major analyses for MAP. As with the project, Grimshaw took the lead on publications, not only publishing several articles of his own on MAP (1982a, 1987a, 1987b) but also editing a special issue for *Sociological Methods & Research* published in 1982, under the title "Sound-Image Records in Social Interaction Research." Grimshaw invited MAP analysts to participate in that issue. For example, he asked Kendon to write about "kinesic and proxemic features and the coding and analysis thereof," despite the fact that "I know that the proxemic part of that isn't really your 'thing'" (Oct 12, 1978, ADG). The tentative publication date was set as May 1980, so Grimshaw requested a manuscript be submitted in June 1979. He enclosed a postcard which Kendon signed, checking the box for "YES, I am interested in submitting the paper you describe."[84] In the end, Kendon had no time to write up an article, but Corsaro (1982) and Erickson (1982) eventually contributed, as did several scholars not otherwise part of MAP: Mark S. Cary (1982), Starkey Duncan Jr. (1982), and Adrian T. Bennett (1982). Grimshaw himself contributed an astonishing three pieces to the special issue (1982b, 1982c, 1982d). In the introduction he argued that "anthropologists, psychologists, and psychiatrists have historically been more receptive to such materials than have been sociologists" (1982b, 116). "Such materials" meant videotapes being used for research. Clearly, he hoped that MAP would change that.

Grimshaw (1982c) names Labov and Fanshel (1977) as a prior, relevant resource (following up on the earlier comment to Goffman that he was using a modification of their method for his own analysis [Mar 6, 1979, ADG]). He outlines the logic of the MAP project which had led to this special issue. In the body of the text, he cites Goffman, Labov, Birdwhistell, Kendon, Feld, Williams, Gumperz, Corsaro, Erickson, Ferguson, Sacks, and Schegloff (thus many of those affiliated with Penn or MAP or both), as well as NHI as an obvious precursor project, like Labov and Fanshel, as well as much of the relevant literature on multimodal communication available at that point. He mentions a few details about the filming for MAP but focuses mostly at a more general theoretical level. He acknowledges help from Condon, Erickson, Feld, Kendon, and Worth (as well as others who were not connected to MAP at any point), for "identification and (at least) partial resolution of the numerous and complex problems of the MAP" (142). Presumably in acknowledgement of the issue that led Goffman to leave MAP, he has a footnote stating that "such requirements vary, of course, and when (as in the MAP) several investigators are analyzing the same record, that record is likely to be less than optimal for any individual researcher" (144n23).

In addition to the journal special issue, Grimshaw began a book during his 1981–1982 sabbatical (eventually published as Grimshaw 1989), was negotiating with publishers for a contract for both the sole authored and the edited books by 1983,[85] and was far enough along to send a draft of his own book for review by Jenness in 1987 (Feb 25, 1987, ADG). Also, Grimshaw had an earlier volume of selected essays (1981) which included one detailed analysis of the MAP data and discussion of the project's goals and methods ("Instrumentality Selection in Naturally Occurring Conversation: A Research Agenda"). As with the major volumes mentioned below, this collection did not attract particularly good reviews. As Murray points out, "How much about the maintenance (let alone 'construction') of vital social structures can be discerned from intensive analysis of the deliberations of one PhD committee planning what to tell the successful candidate remains to be seen" (1982, 744). In addition, Grimshaw presented on MAP at various conferences, such as at the International Conference on Social Psychology and Language held at the University of Bristol in July 1979 (1981, 350), and the Visual Research Conference in 1990 (documented in Grimshaw 1990a; Scherer 2013).

Grimshaw both edited and contributed to a second volume (Grimshaw et al. 1994a), which included a lengthy introduction by Grimshaw, Feld, and Jenness; chapters by Burke, Cicourel, Cook-Gumperz and Gumperz, Fillmore, Grimshaw, Halliday, Hasan, and Wong Fillmore; commentaries by Corsaro, Hymes, and T. Labov; and a substantial epilogue by Grimshaw summarizing what they had learned. Grimshaw and Goffman remained cordial, for as late as 1981 Grimshaw wrote to Goffman, "I can't remember whether I sent you a copy of the first real analysis paper from my work on the MAP materials. . . . I'd much appreciate reactions" (Jul 27, 1981, ADG). Aside from the fact that the 1994 collection is dedicated to Goffman, the very title, *What's Going On Here?*, is an homage to Goffman, who wrote in 1974: "I assume that when individuals attend to any current situation, they face the question: what is going on here?" (8).

One final related publication: Grimshaw's edited collection, *Conflict Talk* (1990b) was an indirect result of the MAP conference held in 1982. As he reports:

> Five years ago this summer several of us whose work appears in this volume had a "show and tell" mini-conference during the course of which we viewed a large number of sound-image records particularly rich in conflict talk. This experience further convinced me of the potential value of more explicit attention to conflict talk. I therefore invited a number of colleagues who seemed to me to have interests or data which would make them valuable contributors to a book on conflict talk to write chapters on the topic. This volume is the result. (1990c, ix)

It seems likely the five years mentioned here should be counted from the conference to the time he was writing the introduction, not when the volume appeared in print, and so probably refers to the MAP at Penn conference in 1982. The overlapping participants between that event and his 1990 book are Teresa Labov and William Corsaro.

MAP's Reception

The reviews of all of Grimshaw books resulting from MAP (Firth 1996; Halkowski 1991; Macbeth 1995; Murray 1982; Schwartzman 1992; Scollon 1995; Stubbs 1991; Zimmerman 1995) were primarily negative, and neither of the major volumes most directly connected (Grimshaw 1989; Grimshaw et al. 1994a) seems to have made much impact on other researchers, as they have hardly been cited. Frequently, reviewers compare MAP to Labov and Fanshel (1977), clearly preferring that book. Scollon's 1995 review, appearing as it did in *Language in Society*, and given that Grimshaw served that journal as associate editor, is the longest and most complimentary, but even it concludes that "a project of such complexity and duration, involving such well-known and busy scholars, is bound to result in a final product of some difficulty" (430). Scollon highlights the gaps remaining from the departure of Goffman, Schegloff, Sacks, Bird, Kendon, and Erickson from the project, and suggests that "the reader is left with tantalizing questions about how those others might have looked upon this body of work" (431). Tantalizing indeed. A different reviewer points out that "Grimshaw asks and answers the question that may occur to many readers of this text: Has it been worth the effort? Not surprisingly, his answer is yes, but he is well aware of the kinds of criticism leveled at this approach (for example, it is work that does not produce reliable findings and cannot be replicated, and it is concerned with trivial, inconsequential and obvious aspects of daily life)" (Schwartzman 1992, 389). Grimshaw sent the first few reviews he read around to all the authors, saying he was "deeply disappointed" not to have reviews published in any major linguistics journal, and "I am also disappointed, of course, that the three reviews we do have essentially disattend the substantive content of our several contributions." He concluded: "Unless, as I think very unlikely, another review appears, the MAP would seem to be completed. I am deeply grateful to each of you for your efforts in our joint project. Things never worked out as I (at least) had hoped, we had problems from the first day. But I think we had to try it and 'I did my damndest!'"[86] In a handwritten note on the copy of this letter to Hymes, he said, "I'm disappointed but not totally devastated," although certainly all the negative reviews had to be a hugely depressing conclusion to twenty years of effort.

MAP lasted from the first planning in 1973 to publication of an edited collection in 1994, and was a major undertaking for Grimshaw, requiring participation by nearly thirty others, including Goffman. The goal was to examine the various approaches used within sociolinguistics, test them against the same data, and in this way learn which worked best. While Grimshaw (1994) outlined some encouraging results (interdisciplinary development, contributing to the theoretical foundations of sociolinguistics, demonstrating how sociolinguistics could contribute to sociology, and pedagogic potential), at the same time, Grimshaw, Feld, and Jenness summarized the problems surprisingly bluntly in their introduction to the 1994 volume:

Even as the Committee endorsed the project, however, there were adumbrations of several of the difficulties which would continue to plague the project over its almost twenty year course. Committee members and interested colleagues argued over such matters as selection of an event for analysis, modes of data collection, definitions of responsibilities of the participating analysts, funding priorities and, most particularly, identification of an optimal "set" of collaborating participant-analysts. Some of the disagreements were based on intellectual biases, some on failures in communication and some, possibly, on clashes of vested interested. Some were resolved, some persisted, and some were exacerbated – and new difficulties emerged throughout the project's course. (10)

As a result, despite the time and effort of so many, for so long, as of 2006 Labov could conclude: "Forty years after the Social Science Research Council set up a Committee on Sociolinguistics, the amount of interaction between linguists and sociologists remains minimal. Despite important work on discourse and conversational analysis, very few sociologists have acquired the basic tools of linguistic analysis, and very few linguists have contributed to the thinking of sociologists" (99). Despite that, as Scollon's 1995 review of the final group report of the MAP findings (Grimshaw et al. 1994a) states, "many of the most important researchers in sociolinguistics" analyzed the data for that book (428). And so, we are left asking: What happened? Why did MAP fail when so many seemingly similar projects succeeded? Scollon points to several possibilities:

(a) it is very difficult to produce a data record which researchers of divergent persuasions will consider to be a suitable body of data; (b) with the exception of Halliday, who analyzed every clause within the agreed 12-minute common segment, this group of analysts selectively attend to only portions of the data, and indeed to very different aspects of the "same" record; and (c) the work of this group of scholars is largely complementary, not competitive. (430)

Further analysis will wait for the conclusion. First, it makes sense to finish discussing Goffman's connections with both Indiana and Texas.

Goffman's Visit to Indiana

Impressively, Goffman and Grimshaw remained friends, getting past their disagreements about MAP. It's worth another detour to examine what it was that Goffman did during his visit to Grimshaw at Indiana University in November 1975. First, it's important to know that Grimshaw had organized the SSRC Committee on Sociolinguistics Conference on Continuing Language Socialization, held November 14–16, 1975, at Indiana, inviting

Goffman as a participant, as well as Gillian Sankoff, Courtney Cazden, and others representing anthropology, linguistics, psycholinguistics, sociology, and English (Grimshaw 1981, 123). Since Goffman already had agreed to visit for that purpose before they conflicted on data collection for MAP, Grimshaw had arranged for him to stay longer to also visit a seminar he was then teaching on Goffman's contributions to sociology. That visit did in fact occur, despite being scheduled for only a short time after Goffman withdrew from MAP. In one of his letters about the logistics of that visit, Goffman wrote he would never think "that such business could strike deep enough to wither affection" (Oct 20, 1975, ADG). The man certainly had a way with words.

The visit to Indiana has nothing to do with MAP, and everything to do with the friendship between these two scholars. In May, Grimshaw wrote Goffman that he had wanted him to give a lecture to his own course but then had discovered that Sebeok wanted Goffman to give a guest lecture to a course Sebeok would be offering on semiotics as well, and that it would make sense if they combined efforts. Sebeok's course was Signaling Behavior in Man and Animals I, which had received funding as a Pilot Program in Semiotics in the Humanities, determining how to use semiotic theory to unify the humanities, and to some extent, also the social, behavioral, and natural sciences. The public announcement of that series states: "Lecturers will include at least ten visiting semioticians of international renown."[87] As the note circulated to relevant faculty includes the comment "I believe Goffman will be one of the visitors," it seems that he was counted as a semiotician, by no less an expert on the topic than Sebeok (see also comments to that effect in Sebeok 1991). Part of what is interesting is that both Sebeok and Grimshaw had met with Goffman on prior occasions to sort out the idea of a visit, Grimshaw while on a visit to Philadelphia, and Sebeok during the conference he co-organized with Goffman and held in Amsterdam. As Grimshaw wrote Goffman: "Tom's goal as outlined to you when the two of you met in Amsterdam is to have you participate in a 'pilot year' class and other activities associated with him [*sic*] projected program on semiotics," and, since that project was funded by a grant, it had multiple additional requirements beyond just a guest lecture in the course: Goffman would need to be available to people in sociology, give a public lecture, and consult on library holdings. Their joint efforts on the 1970 conference makes it clear why Sebeok thought it appropriate to invite Goffman to present lectures within his program, not just to Grimshaw's students, and why he was insulted when that did not work out.

For his own part, Grimshaw wanted Goffman to give a guest lecture in his course Sociology of Erving Goffman. In addition, to qualify for reasonable compensation, Goffman would need to meet with students in the deviant behavior program as well. The combined proposal was therefore for a dense three days, including at least seven major activities: two class lectures, one public lecture, meeting with a library representative, meeting with Sebeok's committee, likely an evening event with "university bigwigs and maybe a couple of outsiders," as well as "some kind of partyish event where you could meet faculty and students." Goffman would stay with Grimshaw, as the Labovs usually did when they visited Indiana. Apparently, they had already discussed what Grimshaw should include in his course, and that there should be no attempt to cover all Goffman's publications, so Grimshaw proposed talking about maybe five books, including *Presentation of Self, Frame Analysis, Asylums*, and whatever else Goffman preferred. Finally, the letter makes clear that Goffman was doing a lot of traveling at this point because Grimshaw hopes it arrives before Goffman leaves for Germany, and says he looks forward to their connecting in both Santa Fe (for MAP) and San Francisco (for the American Sociological Association) (May 12, 1975, ADG).

Goffman's response was cute:

> About my visit. You have set it up in a pattern that prevailed some years ago, where faculty persons spent three days flogging themselves at another university, a change in air providing a contrast to the flogging of themselves at home base. The money, untaxed, was used for a down payment on a summer cottage.
>
> Let's say we skip the University's presentations, library consultations, and ceremonial dinner. If you continue with your foolhardy plan to teach a course on my books, I will come and visit you near the end of the term and spend a session without script answering questions from the students. The same day, if possible, I would like to present something semiotic to Tom's students. For this I would expect tourist air fare and whatever modest honorarium such a double colloquium visit would ordinarily entail. Would this be possible? (May 19, 1975, ADG)

He spent far more time discussing which of his books, and what ideas of his, the students should be exposed to in Grimshaw's course (see Smith 2022c for further analysis of that discussion). However, Sebeok was not impressed by Goffman's response when Grimshaw forwarded it to him and told Grimshaw so: "I am sorry to say that the terms of our grant are quite clear cut in requiring certain specific obligations from all our visiting scholars. . . . Unless Erving is willing to comply with this . . . I just don't see how the expenditure of the honorarium could be authorized" (Jun 3, 1975, ADG). Grimshaw passed that response on to Goffman, saying he didn't think it would be onerous to comply but, if Goffman preferred, they could return to just a lecture to his own course, and a public lecture, for less money (Jun 9, 1975, ADG). That is in fact what happened, much to Sebeok's dismay: "I am greatly disappointed that the arrangements with Erving Goffman haven't worked out in the way we had hoped and planned; the students in semiotics are also immensely disappointed." At the same time, he offered that he and his wife would still like to entertain Goffman at some point during the visit (and copying Goffman on the offer [Aug 29, 1975, ADG]). When Grimshaw followed up that fall, he provided logistical details, and also said "Let me know if there's anyone else you'd like to see" (Oct 7, 1975, ADG). Goffman's response was to say that, "partly in the interests of world harmony I wrote to Tom and volunteered to show his seminar some pictures about pictures; haven't heard from him yet, but if he agrees I propose to take that 2 hours out of whatever else is happening. OK?" (Oct 20, 1975, ADG). The "pictures about pictures" likely means he intended to show students some of the images included in his next book, *Gender Advertisements* (1979a). Sebeok (1977) has documented the visit Goffman did in fact make to his seminar, so the semiotics students were not disappointed in their hopes to hear from the great man himself.

Goffman discussed numerous technical details about the guest lecture for Grimshaw's students ahead of time, such as that they could ask anything they wanted of him and then provided a lengthy response about reviews of his books, which Grimshaw had requested he send.

> By and large I see a biased selection of reviews; some of the favorable ones are sent me by their writers, and often I only see the other ones when publishers send them in. The real issue of course is that favorable ones can easily be as witless as unfavorable ones—perhaps easier. A good review I think should be a piece of literary analysis, touching on themes that no one theretofore had noticed. Only the British seem to be able to do this with social science, perhaps because their journalists have a deeper education than ours, in the main. (Oct 20, 1975, ADG)

In the same folder, there is an undated list of forty-seven questions from Grimshaw's students for Goffman to review and hopefully answer during his visit. These include everything from "How do individuals learn the behaviors you describe in your books?" to "Have you devised any way of testing any of your theories?" and "How much of civil inattention is determined by an individual's socialization and sex?"[88] There is also a list of thirty-eight reviews of Goffman's books, and three general essays on his ideas, all of which were made available for students to read ahead of the class meeting.[89] And, finally, a copy of the course evaluation, mostly about Grimshaw's teaching, a little on the course content ("May be more interesting if the sociologist that was studied had a more diverse field of research. Everyday behavior by Goffman got kind of old after a few weeks"), and a place for students to add comments on Goffman's visit ("Goffman's visit was helpful. At first I found Goffman very hard to follow, but the longer I listened, the more interested and involved I became in what he was saying. It really began to pull together what I had read.").[90] As Grimshaw wrote to Sankoff in 1983, "He had a bad cold, but he sat and talked with the students for several hours—they thought he was great. I have fond memories of his visit" (Oct 21, 1983, ADG).

Overall, it is simply astonishing that such a short time after Goffman left MAP, taking Sacks and Schegloff with him and causing complications for Grimshaw and everyone else involved with that project from that point forward, he and Grimshaw were able to put history behind them and first organize all the details, and then actually manage a visit lasting several days, especially given that Goffman stayed in Grimshaw's home. Perhaps people were simply more polite and considerate in the 1970s, but it seems unlikely that such behavior could be expected today of colleagues who had quarreled professionally to the point of leaving a joint project. It demonstrates an impressive ability to separate the personal from the professional, on the part of both Goffman and Grimshaw. They were personal friends who professionally disagreed.

Grimshaw and Goffman after MAP

As further evidence that Goffman and Grimshaw remained on friendly terms long after their MAP disagreement, in 1981 Grimshaw reported to Hymes that Goffman had invited him "to organize two 'featured' sessions on sociolinguistics for his ASA meetings in San Francisco. Featured sessions differ from 'regular' ones in that they include only invited papers, that those papers can be somewhat longer, that they in some sense are 'showcased' . . . I am delighted that Erving is taking this opportunity to legitimize studies of language in social use."[91] In response, Grimshaw invited Susan Ervin-Tripp, John Gumperz, Susan Philips, Stanley Lieberson, Bud [Hugh] Mehan, and

Deborah Tannen to be panelists. Then he went on to explain why he had not invited Hymes earlier:

> Erv has taken the position that we really couldn't ask you [Hymes] to participate unless we could "offer you" a plenary sessions [*sic*]—something that's not possible within the organizational framework of the ASA meetings. He now tells me that he has approached you informally and that you have said that you would be happy to participate as a discussant. I would like to invite your participation in whichever of several possible capacities seem to you to be most appealing.[92]

These two sessions were in fact held at ASA in 1982. Grimshaw was listed as organizer and presider for both. The first, "Language as a Social Problem," included Tannen and Cynthia Wallat (National Institute of Education), along with Philips, Gumperz, and Mehan as presenters, and Corsaro and a new name, Albert K. Cohen (University of Connecticut), as discussants. The second, "Levels of Analysis in Sociolinguistics," included Ervin-Tripp, Lieberson, and Sherzer as presenters, with Sankoff and Guy E. Swanson (Berkeley) as discussants.[93] Of course, this is the ASA convention that Goffman could not attend at what turned out to be the end of his life. This matters because it demonstrates Goffman's ability to put friendship ahead of disagreement about research methods, and his continuing commitment to the goals that he and Grimshaw had shared until he left the MAP project in 1975.

If evidence of Grimshaw's final feelings about Goffman after MAP is needed, it is easy to document that he chaired the "Hughes-Goffman Memorial Session" at ASA in fall 1983. That they had remained friends despite the substantive disagreement about how to proceed with MAP is manifestly evident in his comments, in addition to the actions of Goffman just mentioned. Specifically, he wanted "to share some experiences—a few—that may help give all of you glimpses of the way he went about the business of being a close friend. Erving did not have an agenda for his friendships. In my case, I think he may have taken me on charitably, a sociology hardship case."[94] Other participants in that panel were Hymes, Howard Becker, and John Lofland.[95] The published ASA schedule shows that the organizer was Robert Habenstein, with Becker, Grimshaw, Arlene Daniels, as well as Charles Edgley and Hans O. Mauksch as participants. Hymes has written up the story of the event: Becker and someone else talking about Hughes (presumably either Mauksch or Edgley) presented their papers, then Lofland began, but collapsed partway through, effectively ending the session.[96] Grimshaw wrote up his memories, describing Goffman's importance, for the readers of *Language in Society* (1983); Hymes did much the same, focusing on Goffman's reviews of submissions to that journal, but published his analysis in *Theory and Society* (1984). Lofland wrote up his comments as well, for a third journal, *Urban Life* (1984). In his oral comments, Hymes pointed out the connections between the two men being honored, saying of Hughes that he served on the SSRC Committee on Sociolinguistics, and so, "I knew him as a father, or better perhaps, an uncle of sociolinguistics."[97] Also in fall 1983, Grimshaw taught his course on Goffman again,[98] and continued teaching it at least as late as 1987, when he invited Kendon to present a guest lecture. The response: "I would certainly like to talk to your Goffman class. It is my hope that I shall be able to work up a piece on 'closings'—which would have a suitably Goffmanian flavor to it."[99]

University of Texas, Austin

Indiana University was not the only campus that can be characterized as "adjacent" to Penn, in the sense of having overlapping people and projects. The other major example is the University of Texas, Austin, and so several stories relating to that university will be explored as well. The three most relevant scholars there were all Penn alumni: Sherzer, Bauman, and Abrahams. Joel Sherzer was a student and then colleague of Goffman and Hymes, attended a class by Labov before Labov even arrived at Penn, and was part of Goffman's conference in Amsterdam. Richard Bauman had a more peripheral connection, given that he was primarily based in American civilization rather than one of the departments where Hymes or Goffman was most active, but he did earn a master's in anthropology before Hymes left, so was also his student, and has been significantly affiliated with the ethnography of communication research tradition ever since. Also, he served as the outside reviewer for Goffman's book *Forms of Talk* (1981). Roger Abrahams started and ended at Penn, knew Szwed particularly well, and was based at Texas with Sherzer and Bauman for some years between. So, it makes perfect sense that they were the next generation of scholars expanding on what they had learned at Penn and sharing it with a larger audience. They had a head start given the connections made at Penn, especially in terms of the role Hymes played in the SSRC Committee on Sociolinguistics, which funded several activities beyond MAP either held in Texas or organized by Texas faculty members.

Working Papers in Sociolinguistics

As Sherzer once explained, "Working papers are a good way to spread stuff around" in order to ensure that potentially interested others could easily learn what people were working on.[100] He initially proposed that Abrahams edit a series of *Working Papers*, but Abrahams declined; and so then Sherzer suggested he, Hymes, someone else from Texas, and someone else from Penn become co-editors.[101] For the first several issues, starting in 1970, the title remained *Penn-Texas Working Papers in Sociolinguistics*.[102] However, with no one at Penn doing editorial work, the title was soon shortened to *Working Papers in Sociolinguistics*. Sherzer and Bauman served as co-editors, and there were many Penn connections among the contributors. The series was officially published by the Southwest Educational Development Laboratory (SEDL), based in Austin, Texas, where they both held affiliations.[103] ("SEDL was established as a regional educational laboratory in 1966, and its work focused primarily on states in the Southwest. . . . SEDL's mission was to strengthen the connections among research, policy, and practice in order to improve outcomes for all learners."[104]) At different times and in different amounts, support was provided by SEDL,[105] by the SSRC Committee on Sociolinguistics (indirectly from NSF),[106] and by NIE.[107]

Sherzer went to the SSRC Committee on Sociolinguistics in 1973 with the concern that he and Bauman were spending so much mailing out copies that they were running out of funds and would have to cease publication. The committee agreed to include the series in the grant proposal they were then preparing for NSF on one condition: "that the series accommodate not only pre-publication versions of papers eventually to be published but also materials that would not be published, for a variety of reasons, but that deserved wide dissemination."[108] Sherzer agreed; the series was included in the grant proposal, funding was granted, and badly needed support was delivered.[109] The committee was happy to contribute because they highly valued turning what members had learned through their research into publications of some sort ("Mr Jenness stressed the importance of having a conference report, or some other means of disseminating what had been learned"[110]). The committee did support research but always asked to have the results presented through a conference and then publication once a project was completed. This could sometimes take the form of just a short notice in the SSRC's own newsletter, *Items* (e.g., Ervin-Tripp 1969; Ferguson 1963, 1964, 1965; Grimshaw 1969b; Hymes 1972b), although they really preferred books (e.g., Hymes 1971; Shuy 1973a).

In 1980, Goffman objected to publishing a submission to *Language in Society* because the author had "already Texas-papered the heart of it,"[111] a wonderful description if you understand it. By this he meant that all the important points had been previously published in the *Working Papers in Sociolinguistics* and so should not appear again in *LiS*. This comment makes it clear that Goffman was not only familiar with, but regularly reading the *Working Papers*, and knew Hymes (as the editor of *LiS*, and the one to whom he submitted his review) could be counted on to be doing the same. It is especially interesting that Goffman apparently viewed it as inappropriate to accept something from the *Working Papers* for *LiS*. As someone who was encouraged by Hymes to publish in the *Working Papers* at that time (Leeds-Hurwitz 1980), my understanding was that it would be a good way to let people know what I had to share, but not the final resting place for a publication. Part of the issue may have been that, also in 1980, Sherzer reported, "success has been causing us to become less and less 'Working Paper' and more and more 'journal'; we have tried to fight this trend. Keeping them free of charge has been a problem, since over 700 people now get them and we're on a fixed grant from NIE."[112] Most publications would love to have such problems. The series continued until 1982—at least the last issue I've seen is Douad (1982)—so it was an enormously successful series, demonstrating that Sherzer and Bauman had learned not just content but strategy from their professors at Penn.

Ethnography of Speaking Conference

In 1970, Hymes, Sherzer, and Abrahams discussed the possibilities of a conference to be held at the University of Texas, Austin, because "it is literally the place where Penn and Berkeley (the two major U.S. centers of sociolinguistics) meet" (that is, students who had earned their degrees either at Penn or Berkeley then took positions at Texas), and because "a movement towards interdisciplinary work seems underway." Sherzer went on to emphasize the role of folklore: "In a sense folklore would be the center or focus of such a conference because it is the place where linguistic and anthropological concerns meet when one takes an ethnographic and interactional point of view,"[113] a view very much in line with how folklore operated at Penn. This conference ended up being organized by Bauman and Sherzer in Austin, April 20–23, 1972 (Bauman and Sherzer 1975, 103), and was co-sponsored by the SSRC Committee and the University of Texas, Austin.[114]

Table 6.3: Ethnography of Speaking Conference, April 21–23, 1972, Austin

Primary organizers:[115] Richard Bauman, Joel Sherzer, Dell Hymes
Committee on Sociolinguistics representatives: Charles Ferguson, Allen Grimshaw, Dell Hymes, Joel Sherzer
Penn participants: Dan Ben-Amos, Erving Goffman, John Szwed
Penn alumni participants: Roger Abrahams, Richard Bauman, Regna Darnell, Michael Foster, Judith Irvine, Elinor Keenan, Susan Philips, Anne Salmond, Peter Seitel, Sheila Seitel, Joel Sherzer
Texas participants: Roger Abrahams, Richard Bauman, Benjamin Blount, David DeCamp, Nicholas Hopkins, Barbara Kirshenblatt-Gimblett,[116] Edgar Polomé, David Roth, Mary Sanches, Harry Selby, Joel Sherzer, Brian Stross, Rudolph Troike
Not-yet-at-Penn participants: Roger Abrahams, Barbara Kirshenblatt-Gimblett, Gillian Sankoff
Berkeley participant: Dale Fitzgerald
Berkeley alumni participants: Benjamin Blount, Michael Foster, Harvey Sacks
Beyond Penn, Texas, Berkeley participants: Keith Basso, Victoria R. Bricker, James J. Fox, Gary Gossen, Karl Reisman
Results: Explorations in the Ethnography of Speaking (Bauman and Sherzer 1974)

The funding for the event came from SSRC's Committee on Sociolinguistics, through their NSF grant. Bauman and Sherzer did the work of organizing, with a lot of advice from Hymes, to the point that, when the draft invitation letter was sent to him, signed by Bauman and identifying Sherzer as co-organizer, Hymes objected: "As to the letter: what happened to Dell Hymes? I thought he was involved in planning the conference?" And later, as a post-script: "In San Diego in November Joel was worried about the conference being squeezed or taken over by Goffman and Sebeok. Little did I expect to get squeezed out, when I reassured him then." [117] Presumably, this was understood to indicate actual annoyance rather than teasing because Bauman sent an immediate apology for the "crossed signals" and an explanation that the intent "was to do you honor, not insult you."[118] This event was viewed by all concerned as a follow-up to the Amsterdam conference organized by

Goffman and Sebeok (as in Goffman's letter to Sebeok [Oct 23, 1970, TS]), which explains why Hymes suggested Goffman and Sebeok might try to take over the event in the quote above.

Labov, Gumperz, Ferguson, and Grimshaw were all invited as representatives of the Committee on Sociolinguistics, but there was no funding available for them as observers rather than participants, and in the end neither Labov nor Gumperz participated. As at other conferences, Goffman served as a respondent, in this case to the panel "Verbal Genres in Social Interaction." As such, he does not appear in the resulting volume. A month after the event was over, Goffman and Szwed were apparently still having difficulty getting reimbursed for expenses, and wrote to Sherzer, who asked Hymes to please sort it out.[119]

This conference resulted in a book, *Explorations in the Ethnography of Speaking*, edited by Bauman and Sherzer (1974) and published by Cambridge University Press through an introduction by Hymes to Elizabeth Case, the editor there who oversaw publication of *Language in Society*.[120] In addition to chapters by Bauman and Sherzer, the book includes multiple scholars previously mentioned in these pages (Hymes, Grimshaw, Sankoff, Philips, Abrahams, Sherzer, Kirshenblatt-Gimblett, Darnell, and Sacks[121]), as well as others who were by then part of the larger network related to the ethnography of speaking (especially Gumperz's students from Berkeley), though not relevant to other projects presented in these pages. Comparing the two years between conference and publication to the fourteen-year gap between the summary conference for MAP in 1982 and the final publication in 1994 highlights just how slow all the parts of MAP were, even when the data collection and analysis are not considered.

Comparative Ethnographic Analysis of Patterns of Speech in the United States Conference

Sherzer was the primary organizer for another conference, despite that one being held in Philadelphia. In 1972, after the successful conclusion of the ethnography of speaking conference, he wrote David Jenness at SSRC about what he initially described as "a working conference on discourse." Designed to "focus on the study of discourse in social life," he wanted to hold it in Philadelphia to ensure participation by Labov, Goffman, and Hymes.[122] The major organizing occurred during a meeting on May 18, 1974, with Sherzer, Hymes, Szwed, Peggy Sanday, and Roger Shuy (in linguistics at Georgetown University, also a member of the SSRC Committee). The date was set for

January 17–19, 1975, and Sugarloaf Conference Center at Temple University was chosen as the location. A title had been agreed upon—Comparative Ethnographic Analysis of Patterns of Speech in the United States—and a tentative list of participants developed.[123]

Table 6.4: Comparative Ethnographic Analysis Conference, January 17–19, 1975, Temple University

Primary organizers: Joel Sherzer, Dell Hymes
Committee on Sociolinguistics representatives: Allen Grimshaw, Dell Hymes, David Jenness, William Labov, Joel Sherzer, Roger Shuy
Penn participants: Renée Fox, Erving Goffman, Dell Hymes, William Labov, Peggy Sanday, John Szwed
Penn alumni participants: Susan Philips, Joel Sherzer
Beyond Penn participants: Aaron Cicourel (sociology, University of California, San Diego), Lucia Elias-Olivares (anthropology, University of Texas, Austin), Peg Griffin (linguistics, Georgetown University), Eduardo Hernandez (linguistics, Stanford), Thomas Kochman (communication, University of Illinois), Ray McDermott (education, Rockefeller University)
Rapporteur: Virginia Hymes
Observers: Lee Ann Draud, Susan Thomas, Nessa Wolfson
Results: Link to Language and Interaction Institute, but no publication

Shuy offered to have the LSA's Committee on Linguistics and the National Interest co-sponsor the event, while admitting they had no budget and could not contribute financially.[124] However, SSRC rejected that, as they had a policy not to co-sponsor activities.[125] After the committee had approved the working conference, Hymes followed up in a letter to Jenness, suggesting they needed to consider what would follow: "I wonder if it should not itself be a step toward a larger activity, perhaps longer conference? From which a useful publication might come? . . . My strongest feeling is the need to get together people who do care about the problem, and want to do something to develop research."[126] Given that he was both based in Philadelphia and on the Committee on Sociolinguistics, Hymes took over organizing much of the event, with Jenness handling logistics. As a working conference, there was no expectation of formal presentations (thus no publication resulted); instead, participants were asked to circulate some of their own prior publications and think about questions of "common problems and interests" and "beginning to block out more clearly and effectively the dimensions of the subject." Hymes at one point summarized the subject as being "What does [*sic*] all our interests in sociolinguistics have in common."[127] Notice that this is exactly the opposite of the MAP project, which could be said to have asked analysts to each do something quite different and then come together to evaluate whose approach worked the best. As it was far more successful, there is obviously something to be said for taking this sort of positive approach, encouraging collaboration rather than competition. The way in which the topics were organized is particularly interesting:

> We believe that all of us share in some respect a sense of there being a range of barely broached problems with regard to the place of language in social life in this country. The source of that sense may be attention to phenomena [supportive and remedial exchanges (Goffman), ritual insults and regional narrative styles (Labov), doctor-patient conversations (Cicourel, Shuy), teacher-student and student-student interactions (McDermott, Philips), etc.]. In the most general terms, the subject could be said to be a serious sociology of language, or ethnography of speaking, of the country.[128]

This letter was sent to those who presented. While not included in this list, Grimshaw was also invited, and also attended.[129] Labov wrote that he was unable to attend,[130] which resulted in a cranky letter from Hymes, pointing out that they had previously discussed the event and the date and Labov had committed to attending.[131] In the end, he did participate, as well as Virginia Hymes (in the role of rapporteur), and Lee Ann Draud, Susan Thomas, and Nessa Wolfson (other Penn affiliates, listed as observers).[132] After it was over, Fox sent Hymes a list of "persons doing valuable work" for the group to know about, which included Elijah Anderson, then being recruited for sociology (and who did in fact take the offer).[133] There was a tentative link between this conference and the Language and Interaction Institute; Hymes wrote Sherzer at one point: "In any case, hope to use January to stimulate more, lay plans for something further. Our Provost is interested in helping to start some sort of institute here; we'll see what happens from an initial meeting."[134]

After the conference was over, Dell Hymes sent Jenness a lengthy report of what had happened, prepared by Virginia Hymes in her role as rapporteur, consisting of thirty-four pages detailing who said what.[135] It includes a number of points made by Goffman, which are highlighted below. In response to Shuy describing interaction between patient and doctor,

> Goffman raises the question of the need to generalize. What he sees is a demand function acting on the interviewee in the interview of this sort which is between a specialist and a lay user of his services. He gives the example of an ordinary customer coming into a hardware store. As a lay person he uses terms for things which a carpenter would not, and the merchant can act as if he does not recognize the term the lay person uses, or he can accept it and then use a question to move to a more technical term, thereby putting the lay person down or holding the distance of roles between specialist and lay person. [This general outline can be seen to apply to a wide range of situations in our society where a "specialist" holds the non-specialist at arm's length by his use of technical language.] (3)

Others join in the conversation: Fox, Shuy, Philips, Hymes. Then Cicourel was asked to talk about his work in medical settings. Goffman questioned him when he finished: "Goffman asks if there is any reason to believe that the kinds of processes physicians go through in making summaries differ from for e.g. what the person taking notes at the conference would do in giving a summary of what happened this morning" (7). Cute! Cicourel said he thought they would be the same, but the notetaker (V. Hymes) disagreed and said so. Further comments from Cicourel, Fox, Sanday, Hymes, Labov, and Grimshaw followed, then a break for lunch. In the afternoon McDermott was asked to talk about educational contexts, with Shuy, Hymes, Philips, and Labov all asking questions. Then Goffman again:

> Goffman suggests that the weakness of McDermott's paper is that all it can do is give an example of the kind of thing you might find if you do this kind of work. In the paper it is not being said that the status the kids come in with is merely validated, reinforced there. A place consists of all these "keepings" (in place); the same kids may be kept in place in the same ways in all kinds of sectors of the society. The paper is saying that in the classroom the places are being re-created in each interaction. But is it really doing more than put meat on the bones of what class discrimination is? The old version that there *is* a social structure may still have some validity. To support the more radical claim the paper must go further. If in fact what happens in fine detail to people of one class is repeated in a wide variety of situations then you have rich documentation for the existence of a class. It would be very dramatic that through complex means the same old lines are drawn. (14; emphasis in original)

Labov and Cicourel chime in, and then "Goffman suggests that on the basis of what happened to the Chinese children in San Francisco classrooms (they achieve) you could argue that the classroom has its own dynamic" (15). Then come remarks from Sanday, McDermott, Hymes, and Fox. Then McDermott shows the group a film. Philips, Griffin, and Hernandez comment. Then it was Labov's turn to present on narratives, with Kochman and Grimshaw responding, and then "Goffman raised the [ethnographic] question of who you can tell a story in front of if he has heard it before. Husbands do it in front of wives, but who else can you do it with?" (18). Sherzer, Labov, Grimshaw, Sanday, Hymes, Fox, and Kochman all chimed in. "Goffman also raised the possibility that working class people are faced with the fact that they are in a world where their words count for nothing; they create in their stories a world in which their words *do* count" (20; emphasis in original). Next to speak are Griffin, Sanday, and Fox, followed by a brief comment from Goffman—"that he didn't see 'structure' in the stories Labov had told" (20). Labov and Sanday discussed this for a bit; then Grimshaw, Fox, Sherzer, and a break for dinner.

In the evening session, Sherzer started the discussion of Chicano socio-linguistics. Hernandez took over, then Oliveras, with Goffman then "ask[ing] how you would distinguish between a situation in which a person had to switch [linguistic codes] and one in which he had the option of switching" (23). Sherzer offered to play an audiotape as an example, but Labov and Grimshaw had further comments, and then Goffman "suggest[ed] that a distinction can be made between licensed instances of code-switching and code-switching situations" (23). Sherzer played the tape; Grimshaw, Labov, and Hernandez talked about it: "Sherzer remarked to Goffman that he (Goffman) makes constant switches in style and that though we can't predict any of them we can *interpret* each of them" (24; emphasis in original). Labov argued that point, then Philips asked to hear Olivares talk about her work with code-switching in children. Labov, Griffin, and Hernandez commented; Philips returned the floor to Oliveras. Hernandez, Philips, Shuy, Cicourel, Labov, and Grimshaw all commented or asked questions.

The next morning the group reconvened with Hymes asking that they try to identify people doing relevant work in this area and specifically asking Grimshaw to talk about a conference he was organizing on language acquisition. Kochman, Philips, Shuy, Fox, and V. Hymes asked questions or made comments, then "Goffman warned against calling lexical accretion socialization" and "Kochman mentioned the problem of how children learn to handle power relationships." Goffman "warned of the need to work in all these areas in ways that are generalizable" (27). Hymes asked Szwed to talk about Black language use, and to compare that to what had been discussed about Chicanos. Szwed gave a summary, with Sanday, Griffin, Hymes, Philips, and Cicourel responding. At that point, Hymes asked the group to consider "the relationship of the training of linguists and social scientists to the ability of the field to contribute to problems of a linguistic nature in society" (29). In response, Griffin asked how the Warm Spring Sahaptin used V. Hymes and Philips as linguistic experts. Kochman had "a modest proposal" that the group should focus on the purpose of ethnography (30).

> In response to Kochman, Goffman asked whether it was in fact the case that there was a consensus among linguists concerned with social policy that there is an answer to problems of bilingualism. Hymes answered that this is not the case; that what we are talking about is that decisions should not be made in ignorance of the *facts* of bilingualism, as they are now being made. Goffman stated that he didn't see how a local community could make these decisions. Local communities don't know what is best for them and we don't know what we're doing. (30–1; emphasis in original)

McDermott, Cicourel, and Philips all discussed, then Goffman argued "that we don't know who the community is—we don't have access to the community, only to representatives of it" (31). As program planner for AAA's next convention, Sanday offered to accept papers on these themes. McDermott, Grimshaw, and Hymes made further comments, and Goffman "returning to the argument about what the community wants, asked if bilingualism as an issue hadn't actually arisen out of the social sciences and not out of the needs of the communities" (32). Hernandez argued with this, Fox provided some general types of studies, and Szwed supported Goffman. Then Goffman "agreed that the functions of literacy should be studied. There is a stigma on its absence because if totally illiterate you can be caught out [as you can't so easily for not being able to read critically]. We mustn't confuse the *need* for literacy with the stigma attached to not having it" (33; emphasis in original). Hymes, Cicourel, Hernandez, Griffin, Grimshaw, Sherzer, and Fox all contributed to the discussion, then Shuy pointed out that they had done more to describe needed work than who was doing that work. And then the conference adjourned.

After the event, Hymes wrote to Jenness (who had participated, representing SSRC), that he was particularly pleased about the way "interaction among participants was good throughout, reinforcing pre-existing links and creating new ones," using further conversations with Sanday, Fox, and Hernandez as examples. In addition, he felt "the conference confirmed our pessimistic appraisal [when they had difficulty in thinking of more people to invite]. There is very little being done." Rather than hold a larger event as originally anticipated, he had discovered that they needed to do more to "change the character of the research that is going on, and the training (and goal orientation) that shape it. Back where we started on the committee ten years ago in a sense: how to get linguistic and social science (I stress here, ethnographic) modes of work together??"[136]

What do the comments reported by Goffman demonstrate about his contributions? He frequently took a step back, trying to move up a level of analysis or generalization; he either made longer comments than others or perhaps was just more memorable. He participated less in the quick back and forth reported for some others. Overall, he was clearly involved, and helping others think through their ideas. Unfortunately, this event did not lead to any publication, although it would be brought up for the next few years in Hymes's letters, mostly in connection with the fact that they had discovered very few people beyond group members who were doing the sort of work they all considered necessary to adequately study the US, so further training was obviously required.

Conclusion

This chapter has covered two major activities (and a visit) at Indiana University linking Goffman to Sebeok and Grimshaw, as well as two conferences and a working papers series organized through the University of Texas, Austin, all with Sherzer as one of the primary organizers; in all cases, others at Penn also played significant roles. The conference Goffman co-organized with Sebeok was a success, with several events occurring afterwards in which Goffman participated; the research project Grimshaw organized was not. It is worth considering in some detail what happened with MAP, since it was the one notable failure despite considerable effort by a large group over several decades.

How to Fail at Interdisciplinarity

Not all projects succeed, whether begun by people within one discipline or across several. No one starts a new project expecting to fail, and failure is not typically a pleasant experience, but failure, especially if time is spent learning why a specific project failed, is heuristic: It will teach us more than just looking at successful projects. While many of the small projects were never implemented, which can be characterized as another sort of failure, MAP is the largest project to be started and then to actively fail, so that serves as an appropriate case study. As with most other activities introduced in these pages, MAP was not only multi- but interdisciplinary: The entire goal was to help move sociolinguistics along in its development, creating something new that neither linguistics nor sociology could adequately investigate alone. So, the question must be asked: Why did MAP fail when so many of these other (especially the Penn-based) interdisciplinary projects succeeded? Presumably not because it was based at Indiana instead of Penn; that seems unlikely and would be contradicted by the success of the Interaction Ethology conference, also managed by someone based at Indiana (in this case, Sebeok).

Grimshaw clearly saw several dangers typical of interdisciplinary work and tried hard to avoid them. He clearly laid them out for others. The first was "that I will be seen as arrogant in a claim of competence I do not have" (since he was a sociologist, and sociolinguistics required equal knowledge of linguistics), which he resolved by admitting what he did not know. The second was "fundamentally misconstruing work in disciplines from which I borrow," which he resolved by consulting experts (especially Hymes and Labov, but also Goffman). The third was "that my treatments of linguistics and sociology, respectively will be too elementary for those familiar with a topic or concept discussed—and too obscure and incomplete for nonfamiliars," which he resolved by walking a fine line (1989, xv). Knowing these dangers, he did his best to resolve them. So, we must look elsewhere for the answer. One obvious difficulty is that MAP was a collaborative research project, when so many of the other efforts examined in these pages were more about sharing information at conferences or describing results in various publications, rather than conducting joint research, which can be far more difficult to manage successfully than it appears. We can return to the comment by Jenness as early as 1975 to MAP participants that "collaborative projects are generally at risk in this respect, and this project has been no exception" (Oct 20, 1975, ADG), but we need more specifics. Multiple potential answers exist, each of which will be briefly considered.

The first possibility is a failure of leadership. MAP resulted in the publication of two—much delayed—volumes (Grimshaw 1989; Grimshaw et al. 1994a), but failed in terms of making a difference to anyone beyond the immediate authors. Perhaps the question to ask is why so many of the other projects in these pages succeeded when this one did not. Murray (1994), who has expanded upon Mullins (1973) and studied just this question across far more topics and decades, attributes most of success or failure to intellectual and/or organizational leadership. As he has demonstrated in detail, both intellectual and organizational leadership are required for any group, but they are especially significant in an interdisciplinary effort. Grimshaw was likely not the strongest leader in either capacity, yet he ended up attempting both. His skill lay in synthesizing large amounts of material and summarizing what he had learned (e.g., Grimshaw 1973a, where he explains sociolinguistics to that point, or any of his review essays, such as 1973c, 1974a), rather than in organizing a diverse group of individuals into a cohesive team ready to work on common materials. There is evidence for this directly from him: Comments in his letters convey his nervousness about the project, such as when he told Goffman, "Feld and Williams are in town now and will be filming tonight and during the week. I am a nervous wreck, I've never been involved in a project whose success or failure is absolutely out of my hands—there's nothing I can do (except, as Williams remarked last night, pray)" (Jun 9, 1975, ADG). Perhaps the most surprising fact is not that MAP ultimately failed, but that it kept going for twenty-one years. Even if he was not the strongest leader, Grimshaw certainly showed dedication and stamina.

A second possibility was changing membership, matched to few meetings where all participants came together to discuss their progress and compare results. MAP involved a particularly large and unwieldy group, which moreover changed membership constantly, as documented in table 6.1, none of which made this an especially easy group to manage. Participants did not live near one another, but were spread across the country, and many left the country for individual research investigations at one or more points. One result was that the entire group almost never met in person, which certainly did not help matters. In fact, they met only three times: once to have an early conversation in Texas, before things got started, to sort out some basics; once in New Mexico, to view the film and agree upon the process; and once at Penn to discuss what they had learned from individual (or team) analyses. But there were no sessions having the goal of sorting out exactly what interaction should be filmed (the largest problem they faced) or for sharing analyses in process (the Penn meeting in 1982 being rather about sharing results of separately completed analyses), and either of those might have helped matters at least a little. These lacks may well have been the cause of the changing membership, for if people do not feel comfortable with a project, they are less likely to prioritize it—especially over their own individual commitments. And everyone in this group was an active scholar, having many other projects demanding attention.

A third possible issue was the question of choosing a goal for a project and then sticking with it until the end. MAP's goals changed several times, rarely a recipe for success. At one point, the goal of the project was to meet in person to compare the results of initial analyses of the same data using different approaches to determine which ones worked best, a goal which was never properly met. Later, the goal was to hold a conference to present findings to a broad audience, which more or less did happen, but with a smaller audience than initially anticipated (not part of a national conference, for example), with only some of the original participants presenting only limited results, and with no effort devoted to comparing what results they had obtained in order to discover which worked "best"—the issue which initially formed the entire objective. (Clearly they needed someone in the role of "carper" that Goffman typically enjoyed, although that was never his intended role in this group.) At a different stage, the goal was to write up what they had learned for a broad audience, which they did, but those results were published a distant fourteen years after the conference at which they were presented, and again, comparison of different approaches completely disappeared, never making it into the final product. It is possible that three different goals might all be accomplished in a single project, but moving the goal posts makes success less likely.

A fourth possible problem was that funding was always in flux. Remember Fishman's comment quoted earlier on the importance of having sufficient available funding. It turned out he was absolutely correct. The Center for Urban Ethnography, to name only one of the major project examples, had significant funding, and so was able to achieve its goals (especially training a new cohort in a new research topic), and so we count it as successful. MAP never had adequate funding. There was some support (especially for Grimshaw's efforts to get things started, with a small but quick grant from the Committee on Sociolinguistics), and they did receive the first portion of a major grant from NSF, but when they requested an early disbursement to film before the semester ended, they unwittingly set themselves up to forfeit the remainder of that support. While the committee gave them additional funds based on the Grant Foundation support, what they received was never enough, and never predictable; they had money to cover the costs of filming, distributing equipment for analysis, and some travel, but that is all. What made matters worse was the tantalizing fact that more money was always potentially forthcoming, which is part of the explanation for the lengthy delays in completing the analyses; since analysts were never paid for their time, this project was always the last to be completed, while individual projects on other topics took priority (especially those that were funded)—a choice which must be acknowledged as perfectly reasonable. This was true even for Grimshaw, who published several other books while waiting for MAP to reach conclusion. The vast majority of the project was completed in hopes of obtaining major grants that never arrived. It is no wonder that goals and participants were constantly in flux.

A fifth possible problem had to do with self-imposed constraints, including an early agreement not to publish until the project was completed. While that made sense when everyone thought it would be a matter of a few years, it made no sense at all when the final book was not to be published until twenty-one years after initial commitments. That is at least part of the explanation for the fact that, as Scollon points out, "Many readers may be surprised to see that some of these analysts ever had contact with others in this project, since their citations rarely make mention of the MAP or of the other participants" (1995, 432).

A sixth possibility has to do with disagreements, and this was probably the most important issue. Goffman withdrew from the project for a reason, and perhaps the failure of MAP to have much impact can be attributed to him being absolutely correct in arguing that the original data set chosen for analysis was not well thought out. One of the few people to have an opportunity to analyze video with Goffman was Charles Goodwin, who tells us: "And he was also wonderful at working in video: we would show video, or he would bring video and it was incredible the way he would look at that" (Goodwin and Salomon 2019, 9). This suggests that Goffman, in fact, was being reasonable to reject the specific video footage made available to the group because he knew something about what would be required for competent analysis. Of course, it was not just Goffman who withdrew before the final analyses were published: Sacks, Schegloff, Kendon, and Erickson did as well; that is, all those who would have wanted to analyze a different type of data in a different way from what was chosen, filmed, and made available for examination. Kendon is particularly important here, as the person involved with the group for a substantial length of time who also had extensive experience analyzing filmed interaction (and focusing on nonverbal behavior); when Grimshaw went back to the comments participants had made early on, he realized that Kendon had argued for a type of recorded visual interaction quite different from what ended up being filmed. The result of these departures from the project meant that no one took on the role of expert in microanalysis of interaction (the role that Birdwhistell should reasonably have been expected to have filled but did not, for reasons never made explicit—perhaps just because he was neither a linguist nor a sociologist and those were the initial groups tapped for the project, perhaps for his reputation by that time of being difficult, or perhaps because he had not succeeded in developing kinesics into a long-term project). Remember that some of the reviews of the second grant proposal to NSF basically argued that since Goffman had left the project, it was obviously unworthy of support.

A seventh possibility is the question of whether members, and especially the leader, have the relevant knowledge to succeed in their efforts. Grimshaw had never filmed interaction nor tried to analyze filmed interaction before this project. That was why he asked Worth who to use as filmmaker and followed his advice faithfully. But there is a substantial difference between what a filmmaker knows how to do technically, and what a more practiced analyst might have known to ask him to do. That gap in knowledge is likely part of what led to the failure of this project. It means that not only did Grimshaw not know how to manage a large, unwieldy group of researchers having little in common in terms of assumptions or methods, but that he did not himself know enough about what they were attempting to set up a potentially successful context. Both the data and the methods to be used were new to him, as well as many of the group participants, which may have been at least one new element too many.

An eighth possibility has to do with the perception of competition between group members (as opposed to cooperation). Hymes may have been right when he told Grimshaw that "it was ambitiously admirable to try to pull together all the 'stars'" (Aug 8, 1975, ADG). Presumably, a project having one star with followers has an easier path to success, and perhaps no one could have managed this project well. But in this case, the various academic stars had quite different assumptions about what needed to happen and how to proceed, and so there was disagreement. That Grimshaw was not the star who shone brightest in the group may have also been a contributing factor. He was always modest, perhaps to a fault, about what he knew compared to the others, presumably part of why he was not the strongest leader, either intellectual or organizational.

Taken together, these possibilities explain why this particular project failed and also provide a list of what needs to happen for other projects to be successful. The mere application of time and effort on the part of the leader and at least some group members, as clearly was evident in MAP, are insufficient for success. Success in research is typically a question of having good ideas and carefully working out their implications rather than choosing a path and sticking to it, even when setbacks occur. The entire goal of the project, remember, was to test several methods of sociolinguistic analysis and compare the results. For this, specialists in different methods needed to come together, analyze the same data in significantly different ways, and then come to an agreement about which method was the most successful. But none of that happened: Given the changes in group membership, the surprisingly few meetings over an absurdly long time, the lack of agreement as to appropriate data or any meeting where different methods of analysis could be compared, the mediocre leadership and lack of relevant knowledge on the part of the group leader, the minimal funding and changing goals, of course this project failed.

In terms of what MAP demonstrated about Goffman, we can say that at least part of the blame for MAP's failure lies with him: He rejected the data and then dropped out of the project altogether. While he was not alone in this, his reputation was greater than that of most others in the project, so his departure was seen as a signal to the grant reviewers of its unworthiness for essential funding. Perhaps he should have simply refused to participate at all, as Hymes, Labov, and Worth all did from the start, claiming they were too busy; he also was busy in those years. It was likely his friendship with Grimshaw that initially convinced him to join. What seems most surprising about the entire story is the fact that his departure from MAP did not damage (let alone destroy) their friendship, as both his explicit comments in letters and their multiple activities after his withdrawal demonstrate.

Endnotes

[1] Minutes, Committee on Sociolinguistics, June 2–3, 1974, DHH, Subcollection 1, Series II: Conferences and Committees, 1955–1987, Subseries D: Social Science Research Council, Committee onw Sociolinguistics, January–June 1974.

[2] Jutant and Vergopoulos (2024) provide an example of treating failure seriously for the lessons we can learn.

[3] https://www.routledge.com/Wenner-Gren-International-Symposium-Series/book-series/BLANTWGISS#.

[4] https://wennergren.org/symposium-seminar/the-use-of-computers-in-anthropology/.

[5] https://wennergren.org/symposium-seminar/revolution-vs-continuity-in-the-study-of-language/.

[6] For a full list of participants in that event, see https://wennergren.org/symposium-seminar/animal-communication/. The resulting publications were Sebeok 1968; Sebeok and Ramsay 1969.

[7] Hymes to Jenness, Jan 25, 1972, DHH, Subcollection 1, Series II: Conferences and Committees, 1955–1987, Subseries D: Social Science Research Council, Committee on Sociolinguistics, January–June 1972.

[8] Conference on Interaction Ethology: Third Circular, Apr 13, 1970, DHH, Subcollection 1, Series I: Correspondence 1951–1987, Sebeok, Thomas, 1955–1982.

[9] "I understand that you and Erving Goffman have discussed your participation" (Sebeok to Hymes, Apr 13, 1970, DHH, Subcollection 1, Series I: Correspondence 1951–1987, Sebeok, Thomas, 1955–1982). "I am very sorry to say that Erv and I, while talking about the desirability of my taking part, didn't check the calendar" (Hymes to Sebeok, Apr 16, 1970, TS).

[10] For Ervin-Tripp, see Goffman to Sebeok, Mar 6, 1970, TS; for Labov, see the list of invitees sent from Sebeok's office to Goffman (Feb 3, 1970, TS).

[11] Ripley has written: "At Berkeley my interests in anthropology have largely been formed in association with Ethel Albert, Theodore McCown, Dell Hymes, Robert Murphy, Clifford Geertz, Lloyd Fallers, May Diaz, George Poster, Gerald Berreman, William Shipley, and Erving Goffman" (1965, 1).

[12] Sommer to Sebeok, Apr 17, 1970, TS.

[13] Adam Kendon knew many of the Penn faculty described in these pages, especially Goffman, Birdwhistell, and Grimshaw. While he never taught full time at Penn, he was an adjunct there from 1988 to 1990, through the Institute for Research in Cognitive Science (Rogow 2013), mentioned in chapter 5.

[14] Goffman to Sebeok, n.d., ca. Feb 1970, TS.

[15] https://annualmeeting.americananthro.org/general-info/future-past/.

[16] The two dates on the letters are in fact the same, so either there was a phone call, or someone made a typo.

[17] Ellen Marks, Conference Director at the New York Academy of Sciences, to Goffman, Feb 27, 1979, TS.

[18] https://www.asanet.org/wp-content/uploads/1972_annual_meeting_program.pdf.

[19] "Adam Kendon: Curriculum Vitae," 1988, ADG.

[20] Hymes participated in another symposium at the Reimers Foundation, this one in 1971, so he may have been the connection for Goffman. Alternatively, Kendon knew at least von Cranach, as von Cranach contributed a chapter to a book he edited (Kendon 1973), so he may have been the connection. Or they may have met at an earlier conference.

[21] https://www.reimers-stiftung.de.

[22] Sherzer to Hymes, Jun 24, 1971, DHH, Subcollection 1, Series I: Correspondence 1951–1987, Sherzer, Joel, 1968–1987.

[23] Sherzer to Hymes, Sep 1, 1971, DHH, Subcollection 1, Series I: Correspondence 1951–1987, Sherzer, Joel, 1968–1987.

[24] Sherzer to Hymes, Jun 11, 1973, DHH, Subcollection 1, Series I: Correspondence 1951–1987, Sherzer, Joel, 1968–1987.

[25] "Minutes, Committee on Sociolinguistics, March 24–25, 1973," DHH, Subcollection 1, Series II: Conferences and Committees, 1955–1987, Subseries D: Social Science Research Council, Committee on Sociolinguistics, January–April 1973.

[26] The funding from the Grant Foundation has an interesting back story. NSF declined the third proposal from SSRC to fund the Committee on Sociolinguistics. (They had funded

the first two, supporting most of the committee's activities to that point—lots of small research projects and conferences across the US.) So Hymes repurposed that proposal and sent it to Philip Sapir, Director of the William T. Grant Foundation (Hymes and Eleanor Sheldon of SSRC to Philip Sapir of Grant Foundation, Jan 21, 1973, DHH, Subcollection 1, Series II: Conferences and Committees, 1955–1987, Subseries D: Social Science Research Council, Committee on Sociolinguistics, May–December 1973). Sapir wrote back to say they had been awarded $95,000 to spend over the next two years, and so they were back on their feet again, remarkably quickly (Philip Sapir to Sheldon, copied to Hymes and Grimshaw, Mar 12, 1974, DHH, Subcollection 1, Series II: Conferences and Committees, 1955–1987, Subseries D: Social Science Research Council, Committee on Sociolinguistics, January–June 1974). It probably helped that Hymes knew Philip Sapir, as he was David Sapir's brother and Edward Sapir's son.

[27] Gumperz explains: "In 1964 at a summer session at the LI [linguistic institute] at Indiana, where the [SSRC] sociolinguistics committee was first formed" (Murray 2013).

[28] Grimshaw vita, n.d., DHH, Subcollection 2, Series I: Correspondence, Grimshaw, 1983–2004.

[29] https://repository.upenn.edu/dissertations/AAI5904624/.

[30] Grimshaw to William Emerson, Director of the Division of Research Grants, National Endowment for the Humanities, Apr 15, 1974, ADG.

[31] Grimshaw to William Emerson, Apr 15, 1974, ADG.

[32] Grimshaw to William Emerson, Apr 15, 1974, ADG. Awkwardly, Grimshaw concludes this letter with a post-script asking for current requirements for NEH applications because, "Who knows, the Social Science Research Council Committee on Sociolinguistics may at some future date come to NEH for support for its joint-analysis project." As a reminder, that was the original name of MAP.

[33] Grimshaw to Hymes, Mar 5, 1973, DHH, Subcollection 1, Series I: Correspondence 1951–1987, Series V: Language in Society, 1968–1992, Subseries A: Early Correspondence, Grimshaw, Allen, 1970–1979.

[34] Grimshaw to Hymes, Feb 26, 1975, DHH, Subcollection 1, Series V: Language in Society, 1968–1992, Subseries A: Early Correspondence, Grimshaw, Allen, 1970–1979.

[35] E.g., Goffman to Grimshaw, Jan 19, 1977, ADG; Goffman to Grimshaw, Jun 29, 1977, ADG.

[36] Grimshaw to Hymes, Apr 29, 1970, DHH, Subcollection 1, Series I: Correspondence 1951–1987, Grimshaw, Allen, 1966–1986, folder 1, 1966–1977.

[37] Hymes to Grimshaw, May 3, 1970, DHH, Subcollection 1, Series I: Correspondence 1951–1987, Grimshaw, Allen, 1966–1986, folder 1, 1966–1977.

[38] Grimshaw to Hymes, Dec 22, 1972, DHH, Subcollection 1, Series I: Correspondence 1951–1987, Grimshaw, Allen, 1966–1986, folder 1, 1966–1977.

[39] Grimshaw to Hymes, Dec 22, 1972, DHH, Subcollection 1, Series I: Correspondence 1951–1987, Grimshaw, Allen, 1966–1986, folder 1, 1966–1977.

[40] Grimshaw to Goffman, Apr 17, 1973, ADG. He took a course on Textual Cohesion, taught by Halliday at the Summer Linguistic Institute of LSA in Ann Arbor in summer 1973 (Grimshaw 1987a).

[41] Jul 10, 1996, ADG. He also mentioned the workshop in Ann Arbor that Schegloff offered with Sacks in an earlier letter (Jan 13, 1976, ADG).

[42] https://openanthroresearch.org/index.php/oarr/preprint/view/40/74.

[43] Grimshaw taught at Berkeley 1968–69 as a visiting faculty member in sociology and South Asian studies, "teaching courses … (with John J. Gumperz) in sociolinguistics, as well as sociology" (Grimshaw 1981, xi); furthermore, he was in India at the same time as Gumperz, and apparently nearby since they connected while there (Grimshaw to Hymes, Mar 5, 1984, DHH, Subcollection 1, Series I: Correspondence, 1951–1987, Grimshaw, Allen, 1966–1986, folder 3).

[44] Grimshaw to Sacks and Schegloff, Apr 17, 1973, ADG. Oddly, he wrote them a single letter, as if they were two parts of a whole, rather than colleagues sharing assumptions. He knew at least Schegloff by 1967, as there is an early letter in the file.

[45] Grimshaw to Hymes and Jenness, May 5, 1973, DHH, Subcollection 1, Series II: Conferences and Committees, 1955–1987, Subseries D: Social Science Research Council, Committee on Sociolinguistics, May–December 1973.

[46] Grimshaw to Hymes and Jenness, May 5, 1973, DHH, Subcollection 1, Series II: Conferences and Committees, 1955–1987, Subseries D: Social Science Research Council, Committee on Sociolinguistics, May–December 1973.

[47] He specifically thanks Kendon for a meeting in fall 1973 (Grimshaw to Kendon, Jun 15, 1974, ADG).

[48] Grimshaw to Madeline Mathiot, May 6, 1975, ADG.

[49] https://items.ssrc.org/from-our-archives/the-scope-of-sociolinguistics/.

[50] Grimshaw to Jenness, Sep 24, 1975, ADG.

[51] Jenness to Grimshaw, Sep 17, 1974, DHH, Subcollection 1, Series II: Conferences and Committees, 1955–1987, Subseries D: Social Science Research Council, Committee on Sociolinguistics, July–December 1974.

[52] Grimshaw and Jenness to Alan Bell, Nation Science Foundation, Feb 26, 1975, ADG.

[53] Jenness to Paul Chapin at NSF, Nov 10, 1975, ADG.

[54] Grimshaw to Chapin, Jun 14, 1978, ADG.

[55] The event in Germany was a seminar organized by Thomas Luckmann and Richard Grathoff at the University of Konstanz; see Winkin (2022a) for details.

[56] Zabor was first a Birdwhistell student at Penn who later earned her PhD at Indiana (Zabor 1978). She prepared the major transcript for the MAP project.

[57] Grimshaw to MAP participants, Feb 1, 1977, ADG.

[58] Grimshaw to Jenness, copied to Hymes, Feld, C. Williams, Sep 24, 1975, ADG.

[59] Jenness to Goffman, Sep 12, 1975, DHH, Subcollection 1, Series II: Conferences and Committees, 1955–1987, Subseries D: Social Science Research Council, Committee on Sociolinguistics, May 1975.

[60] Hymes to Goffman, Sep 28, 1975, DHH, Subcollection 1, Series I: Correspondence 1951–1987, Goodenough, Ward H., 1970–1986. (This letter appears to have been misfiled.)

[61] "The Multiple Analysis Project: A status report (15 September 1975)," Sep 15, 1975, ADG.

[62] "The Multiple Analysis Project: A status report (15 September 1975)," Sep 15, 1975, ADG.

[63] The initials showing who said what were inserted by Jenness (Jenness to Goffman, Sep 12, 1975, DHH, Subcollection 1, Series II: Conferences and Committees, 1955–1987, Subseries D: Social Science Research Council, Committee on Sociolinguistics, May 1975).

[64] "The Multiple Analysis Project: A status report (15 September 1975)," Sep 15, 1975, ADG.

[65] Jenness to MAP participants, Oct 20, 1975, ADG.

[66] Grimshaw to Halliday, Oct 17, 1975, ADG.

[67] https://www.royaumont.com/en/the-foundation/the-cultural-project/.

[68] https://www.normalesup.org/~adanchin/causeries/royaumont.html#chomskypiaget.

[69] https://www.normalesup.org/~adanchin/causeries/royaumont.html#chomskypiaget.

[70] https://www.vox-institute.ch/wp-content/uploads/2020/02/Sherer.pdf.

[71] Schegloff to Grimshaw, Oct 30, 1975, ADG; Sacks to Grimshaw, Oct 28, 1975, ADG.

[72] The letter from Chapin is not in the Grimshaw papers, but Grimshaw quotes from it in his response (Grimshaw to Chapin, copied to Jenness, Dec 1, 1975, ADG).

[73] Grimshaw to MAP participants (Bird, Burke, Cicourel, Feld, C. & L. Fillmore, Gumperz, Cook-Gumperz, Hall, Halliday, Kendon, and Wylie), and CSL (Ferguson, Heath, Hymes, Hugh Mehan, and Sherzer), and Friends (Rolf Kjolseth, Labov, Sankoff, Shuy, and George Bohrnstedt), Dec 18, 1978, ADG.

[74] Grimshaw to Sankoff, Jun 2, 1980, ADG. Grimshaw and Sankoff knew each other at least by 1971 and connected at International Sociological Association meetings while she was still based in Montreal (Sankoff to Grimshaw, Dec 11, 1971, ADG). Also, their terms on the Committee on Sociolinguistics overlapped.

[75] Noted in Grimshaw to Kendon, Jun 1, 1981, ADG.

[76] Grimshaw to Corsaro, Higgins, Hymes, Labov, Keenan, Apr 14, 1982, DHH, Subcollection 1, Series I: Correspondence 1951–1987, Grimshaw, Allen, 1966–1986, folder 1, 1981–1983.

[77] Sankoff to Grimshaw, n.d. [ca. April 1982, based on content], ADG.

[78] Grimshaw to Corsaro, Higgins, Hymes, Labov, Keenan, Apr 14, 1982, DHH, Subcollection 1, Series I: Correspondence 1951–1987, Grimshaw, Allen, 1966-1986, folder 1, 1981–1983.

[79] Grimshaw to all MAP participants, Sep 18, 1982, DHH, Subcollection 1, Series I: Correspondence 1951–1987, Grimshaw, Allen, 1966–1986, folder 3, 1981–1983.

[80] Grimshaw wrote to Goffman (and Sankoff) during his last few weeks, trying to connect while he was going to be in town (Nov 6, 1982, ADG), but clearly that did not work out. Apparently, he did connect with Sankoff just a few days after Goffman died (Grimshaw to Sankoff, Dec 13, 1982, ADG). Between running the conference at Penn and Goffman's death, Grimshaw was so exhausted that he skipped the AAA convention where Hymes gave his presidential address, and he wrote Hymes to apologize: "I was just drained after the Philadelphia experience" (Dec 14, 1982, ADG). Nonetheless, he did manage to write up his thoughts on Goffman for *LiS* and sent that along for review; this was eventually published (Grimshaw 1983). He sent that draft to several others for review, including Glassie (Dec 14, 1982, ADG).

[81] As described in some detail in "Adam Kendon: Curriculum Vitae," 1988, ADG. In fact, much to my surprise, in the attachment to the CV, titled "Synopsis of published work and current and future research," Kendon says: "My work in face-to-face interaction has been largely inspired by Erving Goffman," going on to explain further: "My method has been to use film and video recordings of naturally occurring interactions, analyzing these following methods that were originally developed by such workers as Gregory Bateson (1971), Ray Birdwhistell (1970) and Albert Scheflen (1973). The approach I have followed,

inspired as it has been by both Goffman and the work of those just mentioned, among others, has been termed the 'natural history' approach, because it is non-experimental and entails structural description of specimens of interactions, which are gathered by making audio-visual recordings of naturally occurring interaction episodes." Kendon (1988) provides much more detail about the connections he saw between his own work and Goffman's.

[82] In fact, Grimshaw, Feld, and Jenness stated in print that "If influencing whole traditions of research is considered as a criterion, however, the NHI must be recognized as having succeeded far beyond the modest expectations of its initiators" (1994, 33).

[83] Kendon taught at Penn from 1988 to 1990 (Müller 2007). Because this was after Goffman died, he is not included in chapter 3 with other Penn faculty who connected with Goffman.

[84] The postcard is attached to Grimshaw's original letter (Grimshaw to Kendon, Oct 12, 1978, ADG).

[85] At that point he reported having had interest expressed by four potential publishers: Ablex, Cambridge, Penn, and Texas. Both books were eventually published with Ablex (Grimshaw to MAP analysts, Feb 7, 1983, DHH, Subcollection 2, Series I: Correspondence, Grimshaw, Allen D., 1983–2004).

[86] Grimshaw to MAP analysts, Jun 10, 1996, DHH, Subcollection 2, Series I: Correspondence. Grimshaw, Allen D., 1983–2004.

[87] "Announcement from Acting Graduate Advisor to Faculty and Graduate Students," May 6, 1975, ADG.

[88] "S441 Topics in Social Theory. Special session: Some questions for Goffman," n.d. [fall 1975], ADG.

[89] "S441 The Sociology of Erving Goffman. Supplementary bibliography: The critical response," n.d. [fall 1975], ADG.

[90] "Course and Instructor Evaluation, S441," Dec 1, 1975, ADG.

[91] Grimshaw to Hymes, copied to Goffman, Aug 10, 1981, DHH, Subcollection 1, Series I: Correspondence 1951–1987, Grimshaw, Allen.

[92] Grimshaw to Hymes, copied to Goffman, Aug 10, 1981, DHH, Subcollection 1, Series I: Correspondence 1951–1987, Grimshaw, Allen.

[93] https://www.asanet.org/wp-content/uploads/1982_annual_meeting_program.pdf.

[94] Grimshaw, draft of comments for Erving Goffman/Everett Hughes Memorial Session, American Sociological Association, September 2, 1983, n.d. [fall 1983], ADG.

[95] Grimshaw to Becker, Hymes, Lofland, Jul 25, 1983, ADG. The letter further explains that Arlene Daniels was the original chair but was unable to attend, and asked Grimshaw to take on the role.

[96] Hymes to Pier Paolo Giglioli, copied to Grimshaw, Sep 4, 1983, ADG.

[97] Untitled manuscript [clearly identifiable as Hymes's 1983 paper to the ASA panel on Hughes and Goffman], Hymes to Grimshaw, n.d. [1983], ADG. The vast majority of the comments are about Goffman and are almost verbatim what was published in Hymes (1984).

[98] The description says: "Erving Goffman (1922–1982) was a major figure in the intellectual life of the mid-twentieth century, with an influence which reached well beyond the boundaries of his own discipline of sociology. A thoroughly original thinker, Goffman invented and expounded new ways of discovering the elegant orderliness of what he called

'everyday life'—self presentation and impression management, team performances, talk. The purpose of this course is to introduce sociology majors to the critical foci and central theoretical issues in Goffman's work. A substantial portion of his published work will be reviewed, and attempts made to attend to major critical commentary on his work and to assess his likely lasting influences on social thought" ("S441: Topics in Social Theory: The Sociology of Erving Goffman," fall 1983, ADG).

[99] Kendon to Grimshaw, Dec 15, 1986, ADG. The guest lecture is confirmed in a later letter by Grimshaw to Kendon, naming date and time. With his letter, Kendon included the program of Erving Goffman: An Interdisciplinary Appreciation, held at York, England, July 8–11, 1986 (published as Drew and Wootton 1988), and for which Kendon delivered a plenary (Feb 20, 1987, ADG).

[100] Sherzer to Hymes, Mar 26, 1972, DHH, Subcollection 1, Series II: Conferences and Committees, 1955–1987, Subseries D: Social Science Research Council, Committee on Sociolinguistics, January–June 1972.

[101] Sherzer to Hymes, Sep 11, 1970, DHH, Subcollection 1, Series I: Correspondence 1951–1987, Sherzer, Joel, folder 1, 1968–1972.

[102] Sherzer to Hymes, Jul 20, 1970, DHH, Subcollection 1, Series I: Correspondence 1951–1987, Sherzer, Joel, folder 1, 1968–1972.

[103] Bauman and Sherzer to Jenness, copied to James Perry, Executive Director of Southwest Educational Development Laboratory, Aug 9, 1974, DHH, Subcollection 1, Series II: Conferences and Committees, 1955–1987, Subseries D: Social Science Research Council, Committee on Sociolinguistics, July–December 1974.

[104] https://sedl.org/about/.

[105] James Perry to Jenness, Aug 7, 1974, DHH, Subcollection 1, Series II: Conferences and Committees, 1955–1987, Subseries D: Social Science Research Council, Committee on Sociolinguistics, July–December 1974.

[106] https://eric.ed.gov/?id=ED126692.

[107] Sherzer to Hymes, Aug 31, 1980, DHH, Subcollection 1, Series I: Correspondence 1951–1987, Sherzer, Joel, folder 3, 1980–1987.

[108] Minutes, Committee on Sociolinguistics, March 24–25, 1973, DHH, Subcollection 1, Series II: Conferences and Committees, 1955–1987, Subseries D: Social Science Research Council, Committee on Sociolinguistics, January–April 1973.

[109] Jenness to CSL members, Mar 26, 1974, DHH, Subcollection 1, Series II: Conferences and Committees, 1955–1987, Subseries D: Social Science Research Council, Committee on Sociolinguistics, January–June 1974.

[110] Minutes, Committee on Sociolinguistics, May 15–16, 1975, DHH, Subcollection 1, Series II: Conferences and Committees, 1955–1987: Subseries D, Social Science Research Council, Committee on Sociolinguistics, May 1975.

[111] Goffman to Hymes, Jun 10, 1989, DHH, Subcollection 2, Series I: Correspondence, Goffman, Erving, 1968–1982.

[112] Sherzer to Hymes, Aug 31, 1980, DHH, Subcollection 1, Series I: Correspondence 1951–1987, Sherzer, Joel, folder 3, 1980–1987.

[113] Sherzer to Abrahams, copied to Hymes, May 11, 1970, DHH, Subcollection 1, Series I: Correspondence 1951–1987, Sherzer, Joel.

[114] Hymes to Jenness, Oct 11, 1974, DHH, Subcollection 1, Series II: Conferences and Committees, 1955–1987, Subseries D: Social Science Research Council, Conference on Comparative Ethnographic Analysis of Patterns of Speech in the United States, 1972–

1975.

[115] Conference on the Ethnography of Speaking agenda and participants, n.d. [1972], DHH, Subcollection 1, Series II: Conferences and Committees, 1955–1987, Subseries D: Social Science Research Council, Conference on the Ethnography of Speaking, 1972.

[116] Like Roger Abrahams, at the time, Kirshenblatt-Gimblett was teaching at Texas; she later moved to Penn.

[117] Hymes to Bauman, copied to Sherzer (and apparently Abrahams, given that he also responded), Feb 25, 1971, DHH, Subcollection 1, Series II: Conferences and Committees, 1955–1987, Subseries E: Other Committees, University of Pennsylvania, University of Texas at Austin, Conference on the Ethnography of Speaking, 1970–1972.

[118] Bauman to Hymes, copied to Sherzer, Mar 5, 1971, DHH, Subcollection 1, Series II: Conferences and Committees, 1955–1987, Subseries E: Other Committees, University of Pennsylvania, University of Texas at Austin, Conference on the Ethnography of Speaking, 1970–1972.

[119] Sherzer to Hymes, May 4, 1972, DHH, Subcollection 1, Series II: Conferences and Committees, 1955–1987, Subseries D: Social Science Research Council, Conference on the Ethnography of Speaking, 1972.

[120] Bauman to Case, Oct 8, 1971 and Jan 17, 1972, DHH, Subcollection 1, Series II: Conferences and Committees, 1955–1987, Subseries D: Social Science Research Council, Committee on Sociolinguistics, 1971.

[121] Sacks was not only Goffman's student, but, as Hymes mentions, "Goffman had me serve on Harvey Sacks's dissertation committee" (Hymes 2003, 338), which makes his invitation to this event quite obvious.

[122] Sherzer to Jenness, copied to Hymes, Dec 14, 1972, DHH, Subcollection 1, Series II: Conferences and Committees, 1955–1987, Subseries D: Social Science Research Council, Conference on Comparative Ethnographic Analysis of Patterns of Speech in the United States, 1972–1975.

[123] "Memorandum on small conference on 'Comparative Ethnographic Analysis of Patterns of Speech in the United States,'" prepared by Hymes, May 1974, DHH, Subcollection 1, Series II: Conferences and Committees, 1955–1987, Subseries D: Social Science Research Council, Conference on Comparative Ethnographic Analysis of Patterns of Speech in the United States, 1972–1975.

[124] Shuy to Hymes, copied to John Hammer and Jenness, May 28, 1974, DHH, Subcollection 1, Series II: Conferences and Committees, 1955–1987, Subseries D: Social Science Research Council, Conference on Comparative Ethnographic Analysis of Patterns of Speech in the United States, 1972–1975.

[125] Jenness to Hymes, copied to Shuy and Grimshaw, Oct 8, 1974, DHH, Subcollection 1, Series II: Conferences and Committees, 1955–1987, Subseries D: Social Science Research Council, Conference on Comparative Ethnographic Analysis of Patterns of Speech in the United States, 1972–1975.

[126] Hymes to Jenness, Jun 4, 1974, DHH, Subcollection 1, Series II: Conferences and Committees, 1955–1987, Subseries D: Social Science Research Council, Conference on Comparative Ethnographic Analysis of Patterns of Speech in the United States, 1972–1975.

[127] Hymes to Sherzer, Sep 13, 1974, DHH, Subcollection 1, Series I: Correspondence 1951–1987, Sherzer, Joel.

[128] Hymes to Jenness, draft of letter to participants, Oct 23, 1974, DHH, Subcollection 1, Series II: Conferences and Committees, 1955–1987, Subseries D: Social Science Research Council, Conference on Comparative Ethnographic Analysis of Patterns of Speech in the

United States, 1972–1975.

[129] "When we were at Sugarloaf, Erving said something about all of us getting together for dinner sometime during the meetings—I hope that will be possible.... I hope it will be possible to see you two, the Labovs, and Goffman (I gather it's likely I'll see Sol [Worth] at the Temple meetings)" (Grimshaw to Hymes, Feb 16, 1975, DHH, Subcollection 1, Series V: Language in Society, 1968–1992, Subseries A: Early Correspondence, Grimshaw, Allen, 1970–1979).

[130] Labov to Jenness, Nov 20, 1974, DHH, Subcollection 1, Series II: Conferences and Committees, 1955–1987, Subseries D: Social Science Research Council, Conference on Comparative Ethnographic Analysis of Patterns of Speech in the United States, 1972–1975.

[131] Hymes to Labov, copied to Jenness, Nov 29, 1974, DHH, Subcollection 1, Series II: Conferences and Committees, 1955–1987, Subseries D: Social Science Research Council, Conference on Comparative Ethnographic Analysis of Patterns of Speech in the United States, 1972–1975.

[132] Hymes to Jenness, Report of the conference to SSRC's Committee on Sociolinguistics (presumably prepared by V. Hymes), Jan 24, 1975, DHH, Subcollection 1, Series II: Conferences and Committees, 1955–1987, Subseries D: Social Science Research Council, Committee on Sociolinguistics, January–April 1975.

[133] Fox to Hymes, Jan 22, 1975, DHH, Subcollection 1, Series II: Conferences and Committees, 1955–1987, Subseries D: Social Science Research Council, Conference on Comparative Ethnographic Analysis of Patterns of Speech in the United States, 1972–1975.

[134] Hymes to Sherzer, Sep 13, 1974, DHH, Subcollection 1, Series I: Correspondence 1951–1987, Sherzer, Joel.

[135] Untitled report of the Conference on Comparative Ethnographic Analysis of Patterns of Speech in the United States, prepared by Virginia Hymes, n.d. [February–April 1975], DHH, Subcollection 1, Series II: Conferences and Committees, 1955–1987, Subseries D: Social Science Research Council, Committee on Sociolinguistics, January–April 1975.

[136] Hymes to Jenness, Jan 24, 1975, DHH, Subcollection 1, Series II: Conferences and Committees, 1955–1987, Subseries D: Social Science Research Council, Committee on Sociolinguistics, January–April 1975.

CHAPTER SEVEN

Beyond Penn

The phrase "beyond Penn," used in this chapter, means that no participants in the activities under discussion (aside from Goffman himself) were affiliated with the University of Pennsylvania. There are just two cases in which Goffman participated in multi- or interdisciplinary groups beyond Penn that seem useful to describe, both because they are of intrinsic interest, showing the breadth of his concerns and influence, and because they have not (at least, not yet) been examined in detail elsewhere. Goffman participated in numerous conferences, of course, both in the US and internationally, but many of those have already been well documented (especially in Winkin 2022a). Instead, here are, first, a conference he helped to organize, and then, a national committee established to review incarceration, of which he was a member.

The conference here, as with those emphasized previously, is one he helped to organize. Such examples are rare: While his conference presentations and speaking engagements were legion, Goffman did not typically take the lead on organizing them. What will not be included in this chapter are stories of all the times Goffman went to a conference or was a guest speaker. Even his six-week stay at the University of Manchester in spring 1966 is not a focus of attention.[1]

Nonverbal Dimensions of Social Interaction Conference

Goffman worked with Robert E. Kleck and several others to organize a conference on Nonverbal Dimensions of Social Interaction, held in Glen Cove, NY, June 16–18, 1969.[2] At the time of the conference, Kleck was assistant professor of psychology at Dartmouth College. He had earned his PhD in psychology at Stanford in 1964, where, at different times, he worked with Jack Hildegard, Alex Bavelas, and Albert Hastorf. Since Hastorf had worked with Stephen Richardson, a sociologist affiliated with the Albert Einstein College of Medicine in New York, doing research on disability, that led to a connection between Kleck and Richardson. Kleck had read several of Goffman's books and today describes *Stigma* (Goffman 1963a) as "the book that influenced my subsequent research." While doing early research on physical disability, Kleck told Richardson that it seemed to him that nonverbal communication was an essential element when physically different people interact with physically "normal" individuals, and Richardson thought he was "on to something" and felt "this needed to be pursued—in terms of methodology and what might be discovered," which is what led to the conference. Richardson at that point was Research Director for the Association for the Aid of Crippled Children (AACC),[3] and in that capacity was able to arrange funding for a conference on nonverbal communication and methods for observing social interaction. Kleck explained, "Clearly the agenda for the conference was not to be children with disabilities but what was already known about nonverbal communication, and how to analyze social interaction in order to discover the underlying dynamics.... Persons who were selected resonated with that focus."

Kleck was the chair of the conference, but Richardson, Goffman, and Starkey Duncan all helped with the organization: "Richardson and I carried the burden of pulling together the list of participants—but Goffman clearly had suggestions for additional participants." Most of the organization of the event occurred through correspondence rather than in person. In addition to Goffman, presenters included: Leonard A. Rosenblum (Primate Behavior Laboratory, State University of New York Downstate Medical Center), Paul Ekman (psychology, University of California, San Francisco), George Mahl (psychology and psychiatry, Yale), Robert Sommer (psychology, University of California, Davis), Allen T. Dittmann (psychology, NIMH), Edward T. Hall (anthropology, Northwestern), Robert Rosenthal (psychology, Harvard), Klaus Scherer (psychology, then a doctoral student at Harvard), Sue Milmoe (psychology, Harvard), Starkey Duncan Jr. (psychology, Chicago), John Newson (psychology, Nottingham University), and Howard Rosenfeld (psychology, University of Kansas). Discussants were Gordon Jensen, Michael Argyle (social psychology, University of Oxford), A. Richard Diebold Jr. (linguistics, Stanford), Norman A. McQuown (anthropology, Chicago), and

Nico H. Frijda (psychology, University of Amsterdam). The list is notable both for international participation (Newson and Argyle from England, Frijda from the Netherlands) and for the range of disciplines (psychology, psychiatry, sociology, linguistics, anthropology, and biology). There were several observers, although there was not space for many; one who made a comment and so whose presence was noted in the documentation was Ralph Exline (psychology, University of Delaware). Those who have already been mentioned elsewhere in this book in various capacities in other projects include Duncan, Ekman, Exline, Hall, McQuown, and Scherer, mostly for connections with MAP; in addition, Rosenthal co-edited the proceedings from the Clever Hans conference (Sebeok and Rosenthal 1981). Birdwhistell was not invited to the conference because Kleck was told that he and Ekman had serious theory differences (as in fact they did).

Kleck no longer has a copy of the various conference papers, but he prepared a report of the conference for AACC (1969), which he kept and has been kind enough to share with me. That report reveals that Goffman's paper was entitled "The Analysis of Body Gloss and Remedial Exchanges," which seems likely to have been an early version of content in *Relations in Public* (1971). The description of it in the report begins with a summary by Kleck:

> It is Goffman's contention that most of us (participants at the conference) are really interested in the close-grained structure of social or public order. If we grant that this constitutes the natural focus of our analysis, then the next question concerns the possible unit that one might employ in such an analysis. It is Goffman's initial purpose to suggest a number of possible units of analysis starting with the largest and moving to the smallest. (64)

Goffman's was the final paper of the conference, so it was an appropriate time for such a summary. Among the specific concepts introduced in the rest of the paper were: users vs. stock characters, solos and withs, contacts and service stops, states of talk, a vehicular unit. As Goffman explained, "These then are the initial five sets of units, each of which cut the social order in a slightly different way" (65). The second part of what Goffman presented concerns "how persons 'stand' in relationship to a given rule" (66), with descriptions of body gloss and remedial exchanges, which he said were "a fundamental unit of public order" (67). These concepts should seem familiar to those who know Goffman's work.

In addition to his own paper, the report documents that Goffman frequently commented on the presentations by others at the conference. In fact, he had something to say about nearly everyone's paper, clearly listening carefully and taking what others said seriously. An example comes from discussion of Mahl's presentation on "The Psychological Significance of Posture and Posture Changes within the Therapeutic Relationship," after Ekman's formal response; Sommer and Mahl also commented. In this case, there are quotes around the entire section by Goffman, so presumably this is exactly what he said rather than a paraphrase.

> If we are going to get anywhere, our task is to describe any event in terms of its broadest scope, for therein lies its naturalistic description. We can't talk about an instance of a class when we should be talking about the class. If I can be convinced about anything, it is this. At some level, we have got to forget about the occasion of the act and look at the form and the family from which that form comes. There is a language of those forms in our society and we won't get at the language if we take seriously any particular occasion of its occurrence. (12)

Another example shows the comments Goffman made in response to Hall's paper, simply titled "Proxemics." Here the comments were summarized by Kleck.

> Goffman noted, in response to a series of pictures showing transitions in the use of physical distance from second to third generation foreigners in the United States that one cannot make statements about interaction distances independent of knowledge about the "social frame" which applies to the particular situation in which the photographs or the observations are made. A different set of social rules are invoked when the social frame is modified. He notes for example that when photographs are taken the degree of contact which is permissible is greatly enhanced. (39–40)

A few of the responses by Goffman might have been seen as antagonistic. Asked about this, Kleck suggests:

> Erving had a very critical bent to him obviously and was not shy about saying "I think that's not a good idea," or "that's right on." And he saw it as constructive to give feedback to people and took that as on as his role. . . . Goffman was critical by nature and carefully weighed the substance of an argument and his response to it. The general tenor of the conference was very friendly and people were willing to tolerate different points of view. I don't remember any antagonism. But it was 60 years ago.

Reading the detailed report makes it seem that Goffman adopted the role he took on in other conferences, that of synthesizing at least some of what had been said so everyone would be ready to move on, even though that was not his formal appointed role for this event.

Kleck and Goffman had met in person in August 1967 when they served on the same panel at the American Sociological Association in San Francisco, "The Social Consequences of Stigma." That panel was chaired by Fred Davis, a contemporary of Goffman's in sociology at Chicago, then at the University of California Medical Center; the final panelist was Richardson.[4]

Kleck and Goffman also exchanged at least some unpublished manuscripts: Goffman's files included "Physical Stigma and Nonverbal Cues Emitted in Face to Face Interaction," later published in *Human Relations* (Kleck 1968a).[5] That article cites Goffman several times but does not make substantial use of his work. However, in another 1968 article, "Self-Disclosure Patterns in the Nonobviously Stigmatized," Kleck begins with Goffman's "general categories of persons who are different from others in an 'undesirable way'" and how "in Goffman's analysis of the social-psychological implications of stigma an important aspect of a stigma condition concerns its visibility to others" (1968b, 1239). And he ends with the conclusion that "the results tend to confirm Goffman's observation that information management becomes a strong concern and interpersonal problem area for stigmatized individuals who are permitted the tactic of passing and choose to employ it extensively" (1248).

The 1969 conference did not result in a proceedings volume, partly because Kleck was an assistant professor at the time. But there were other activities and publications influenced by conversations at the conference, and even more by Goffman's ideas and publications. First, Kleck and Richardson studied the Fresh Air Fund's summer camp for children in Fishkill, NY. The site was chosen as "one of the few places where fairly large numbers of physically handicapped kids were integrated with physically normal kids. . . . Goffman stimulated the analysis—we asked what handicapped kids were doing to improve their social status but never discovered anything that seemed to work. The primary finding was that it all depended on how physically attractive the kids were." And that meant the handicapped kids were relegated to the bottom of the social group. The results were published as Richardson, Ronald, and Kleck (1974), and clearly show the influence of Goffman (1959c) on the presentation of self.

Second, Kleck organized a later conference at the Dartmouth Binary Conference Center. This event brought together most of the social psychologists working on stigma issues, another topic for which Goffman is well known (see Goffman 1963a); it resulted in the book *The Social Psychology of Stigma* (Heatherton et al. 2000).

Third, a research project begun by Edward Jones and Albert Hastorf while Jones was a fellow at the Center for Advanced Study in the Behavioral Sciences at Stanford resulted in the book *Social Stigma* (Jones et al. 1984). Overall, Kleck says of these further projects: "I don't know that they were influenced so much by the conference as they were influenced by Goffman." He never saw Goffman after the 1969 conference, but nonetheless acknowledges that Goffman had significant influence: "Oh my goodness, was the influence there—he is one of my mentors who I've had very little contact with."

Committee for the Study of Incarceration

In a completely separate project, having nothing whatsoever to do with Penn or any of the activities or colleagues described to this point, Goffman was invited to be a member of a national group studying incarceration. This story will be told briefly, because it truly had little to do with anything else discussed to this point, but since other Goffman scholars have not yet noted its existence, it merits description. Like all the other stories told to this point, it too involved Goffman collaborating with a variety of colleagues drawn from multiple disciplines, and their connections have remained invisible to those seeking to understand Goffman and his work. Unlike those projects but like the conference just presented, none of the other participants were based at Penn.

As a direct response to the uprising at Attica prison in September 1971, the worst prison riot in US history, resulting in forty-three deaths (Margolis 1971), the Committee for the Study of Incarceration was created in late 1971, funded by grants from the Field Foundation and the New World Foundation (von Hirsch 1976a). The committee's goal was to "study involuntary confinement in mental hospitals and reform schools as well as in prisons and jails" (Lissner 1971). The idea originated with the Field Foundation. Charles E. Goodell, a former US senator and chair of the Presidential Clemency Board, was made chair, and he looked for "leading scholars" who would "examine the validity of all our assumptions about prisons—and about prison reform" (Lissner 1971). Other committee members were: Marshall Cohen (philosophy, City University of New York), Samuel DuBois Cook (political science, Duke), Alan M. Dershowitz (law, Harvard), Willard Gaylin (psychiatry, Columbia), Joseph Goldstein (law, Yale), Jorge Lara-Braud (Commission on Faith and Order, National Council of Churches), Victor Marrero (First

Assistant Council to the Governor of New York), Eleanor Holmes Norton (chair, New York City Commission on Human Rights), David J. Rothman (history, Columbia), Simon Rottenberg (economics, University of Massachusetts), Herman Schwartz (chair, New York Commission of Correction), Stanton Wheeler (law and sociology, Yale), and Leslie T. Wilkins (criminal justice, State University of New York, Albany). The committee was given a staff, several of whom were quite active participants: Andrew von Hirsch (appointed as executive director of the committee; also criminal justice, SUNY Albany; also the former legislative counsel for Goodell), David F. Greenberg (appointed as senior fellow of the committee; also sociology, NYU); as well as Susan Steward (research associate), Patricia Ebener (research assistant), Andrea Shechter (research aide), and Janiska Boudream (secretary) (von Hirsch 1976a). As von Hirsch says in the introduction, "The group was interdisciplinary in the broadest sense" (xxiv), including not only the obvious sociologists, psychiatrists, and lawyers, but also representatives from philosophy, history, economics, and political science. And, as with other multi- or interdisciplinary groups, there were "built-in hazards" (xxiv), largely because each group member was an expert in a limited area, but they came with "different language, different premises, and indeed, often, a different style of reasoning" (xxv). Even so, they all agreed on one thing: "an insistence on not doing harm" (xxxiv). Committee offices were based in Washington, DC. The group was given a budget of $175,000 and asked to "try to devise alternative measures to replace institutions of confinement" (Lissner 1971).

Why was Goffman invited onto this committee? It seems possible, even likely (although unconfirmed) that Louis B. Schwartz, who was a law professor at Penn and one of the Benjamin Franklin Professors with Goffman, as well as director of the National Commission on Reform of Federal Criminal Laws, may have recommended Goffman as a potential member.[6] In addition, Becker has pointed out that *Asylums* "may have, on occasion, helped to instigate attempts at their reform" (2003, 662) because it "made possible a deeper understanding of these phenomena than either denunciation or defense ever had" (669). And so, *Asylums* is an obvious and sufficient reason why Goffman was asked to participate in this committee: That book was both well-known and directly relevant. But was that his only relevant work that the people creating the committee would have known about? Absolutely not. Consideration of Goffman's early activities while at NIMH, both conference presentations and resulting publications through the late 1950s and 1960s, already documented in chapter 2, demonstrates significant activity related to issues of mental health and institutionalization. The result of connections with a wide network of scholars, especially psychologists and psychiatrists, but also anthropologists and sociologists, could easily have brought Goffman to the attention of those choosing members of the committee in 1972. Also, he had just helped Thomas Szasz[7] organize the American Association for the Abolition of Involuntary Mental Hospitalization in 1970 (Szasz 1971; Winkin 2022b), a group having obvious overlaps with prison reform. Adding all those activities to Goffman's status as a Benjamin Franklin Professor at Penn, especially with a possible recommendation from another such, suggests that he must have seemed an obvious choice.

Once membership had been established, the Committee for the Study of Incarceration met for four years, holding over twenty working sessions (Robbins 1977), before issuing its report, the book *Doing Justice* (von Hirsch 1976a). As of March 2025, Google Scholar reports 2,284 citations of the book, so it was certainly noticed. In a short article designed to draw attention to the book, von Hirsch clearly summarizes the committee's major conclusion in that book: It "proposes a system of standardized penalties: for each gradation of seriousness, a definite penalty—the 'presumptive sentence'—would be set" (1976b, 4). This follows a "just deserts" model; the punishment should fit the crime, and so very few people would be imprisoned for more than a few years. Looking back from a distance of several decades, Garland explains the committee's conclusions even more clearly: "*Doing Justice* explicitly endorsed a retributivist philosophy of punishment. It stressed the moral superiority of proportional, backward-looking punishments—'just deserts'—and the immoral, authoritarian dangers of penal measures based upon predictions of future criminality, or upon evaluations of the individual's character and mode of life" (2001, 59).

What was Goffman's role in the committee and the report? The book is made up of brief chapters, with no indication of who said what during meetings except for a few objections provided by a few members in the appendix; none is from Goffman, so presumably he agreed with the book's major conclusions. However, Goffman's name and several quotes from his publications appear in "Chapter 13: Incarceration." Each of these will be listed, because it is interesting to see what von Hirsch chose to highlight out of all Goffman's work, and because this is the only clue found to date as to his role in the group.

- "A free person, Erving Goffman has pointed out, 'tends to sleep, play, and work in different places, with different co-participants, under different authorities.' An incarcerated person must perform most or all of these activities in the same place and under the same authority." (von Hirsch 1976a, 108; quote is from Goffman 1961b, 5–6)
- "In Erving Goffman's words: . . . among inmates in many total institutions there is a strong feeling that time spent in the establishment is time wasted or destroyed or taken from one's life; it is time that must be written off; it is something that must be 'done' or 'marked' or 'put in' or 'pulled.' In prisons and mental hospitals, a general statement of how well one is adapting to the institution may be phrased in terms of how one is doing time, whether easily or hard. This time is something its doers have bracketed off for constant conscious consideration in a way not quite found on the outside. As a result, the inmate tends to feel that for the duration of his required stay—his sentence—he has been totally exiled from living." (von Hirsch 1976a, 110; quote is from Goffman 1961b, 67–68)
- There is a third reference to Goffman, relating to how "time crawls for the incarcerated individual" (von Hirsch 1976a, 114), which cites Goffman (1961b, 67–69), but this time the original words are not quoted in the body of the text.

All of this is relevant because few quotes are provided in the book, and certainly not three for any other committee member, which suggests that Goffman was an active participant in the meetings and, perhaps especially, once they began writing up their report.

A different report produced several decades later, prepared on behalf of the Committee on Causes and Consequences of High Rates of Incarceration and supported by grants from the MacArthur Foundation and the US Department of Justice, names the von Hirsch report as one of three they call "the most influential reform proposals" during the 1970s, because it called for "the abolition of parole release and the creation of enforceable standards to guide judges' decisions in individual cases and provide a basis for appellate review" (Travis et al. 2014, 76). Even more significantly, they found: "Policy makers responded" (76). Interestingly, that later report cites work by both Erving Goffman (although this time for *Stigma*, rather than *Asylums*, as in the earlier report), as well as his daughter, Alice Goffman (2009). And it is common for later analyses of incarceration to cite both the von Hirsch report (1976a) and Goffman's *Asylums* (1961a), as is the case for Garland (2001).

Conclusion

This chapter has been a footnote to the earlier discussions of Goffman's role in multi- or interdisciplinary collaborations and his development of an invisible college. It documents his involvement in a conference on nonverbal behavior and a national commission on incarceration. These are important only insofar as they provide evidence of his connections into areas typically overlooked, two very minor stories to add to his more significant activities, especially those at Penn. In addition, however, they suggest that there remains still more to be learned about his involvement with colleagues across disciplinary boundaries and his involvement in a far wider range of collaborative projects across his career than have been typically even mentioned, let alone documented.

Endnotes

[1] Instead, see Braga 2011; Sharrock 1999; Winkin 2022a, 2022b.

[2] This section is based on a phone interview with Robert Kleck (Mar 14, 2024), and all quotes come either from our conversation or the written materials he provided, unless another source is indicated. I have found no documentation for this conference in any of the archives consulted. What I did find was an incorrect reference to the wrong event, and somehow that led me to Kleck. He was gracious enough to reply and sort things out for me. A good example of the twists and turns of historical research.

[3] For information about the Association for the Aid of Crippled Children, see https://www.fcd-us.org/about-us/history/.

[4] https://www.asanet.org/wp-content/uploads/1967_annual_meeting_program_c.pdf.

[5] This is noted in the list of works in Goffman's files compiled by Winkin (1998).

[6] Schwartz to Benjamin Franklin Professors, n.d. [received Jan 29, 1971], RED. (This letter does not mention Goffman, but it does mention Schwartz's role with the National Commission on Reform of Federal Criminal Laws.)

[7] Goffman and Szasz corresponded from 1957 on, exchanging drafts and publications, and occasionally connecting at conferences (TSz).

CHAPTER EIGHT

Conclusion

It is time to synthesize what has been learned from the abundance of details presented to this point. I have primarily used archival sources rarely discussed in Goffman studies previously. These chronicle many details about who he was talking or working with, when, and on what subject. My emphasis has been on how connections among colleagues led to a series of collaborative projects of various kinds. Some of these are well known while others have vanished without a trace; some were enormously successful; others, entirely without influence. Ideas do not flourish on their own; like plants they require sustenance and support. A complementary group of colleagues, especially within a supportive university, provides just such sustenance and support, as has been abundantly demonstrated in case after case. This book has been all about Goffman, but the lessons to be learned extend far beyond one scholar. Therefore, some generalizations can be made about multi- and interdisciplinarity, invisible colleges, and conducting historical research.

New Understandings About Goffman

Clearly, in a book where Goffman serves as the focus, the first question to be answered concerns what we now know about him that we did not know previously. This leads to discussion of the ways in which Goffman was one of a strong network of colleagues, both at Penn and beyond.

Goffman as Colleague

Was Goffman the loner described by others? The short answer is an equivocal "sometimes." Presumably, his being a loner is part of the story, given that so many others have highlighted it, but it certainly is not the whole story, and most definitely not the story told in these pages. I would not argue that everyone who has called him a loner is wrong, but rather that what has been known to this point has been incomplete. This book has outlined Goffman's development as a scholar from the time he was a graduate student at the University of Chicago, where he and most of his peer group (based in sociology, anthropology, and psychology) first learned to cross disciplinary boundaries, and consider multi- and interdisciplinary research as something to be taken for granted rather than uncommon; to the National Institute of Mental Health, where he worked closely with psychologists and psychiatrists, and began building a national network of connections; to the University of California, Berkeley, where he was an integral part of both a conference and the Saturday group, as well as several briefer affiliations, again all taking for granted that participants would cross disciplinary lines (especially involving linguistics and anthropology, but also psychology and political science, among others); and most importantly, at the University of Pennsylvania, where he was an integral part of a baker's dozen projects involving overlapping groups of others, some major and others minor, some successful while others were stillborn, from an almost impossible number of disciplines (now adding folklore, communication, and education as central, with many more as peripheral). In addition, details have been presented about his work adjacent to Penn, through either Indiana University or the University of Texas, Austin, participating in still more projects, again all either multi- or interdisciplinary, these based in sociology, semiotics, linguistics, folklore, and anthropology, some small and others large, some successful, and one seriously problematic; and finally, beyond Penn, two more activities which were (again) significantly multidisciplinary. And so, it has become obvious that, even though Goffman "rarely described his intersections with other scholars" (Shuman 2013, 348), many such intersections most certainly existed, a fair number of which have been recounted here. Goffman might best be depicted as the soloist in an orchestra; he was part of a group, and when it came time to perform (and when academics perform, they most often write), he would then present a solo performance. He had the support of the entire orchestra, that is, the peers in his invisible college, but what we see and know the most about are his solo performances, that is, his own presentations and publications.

It is time to bring Goffman's various activities with peers into focus through a few tables synthesizing what has been presented. Here information will be arranged chronologically, rather than repeating the arrangements in prior chapters, which focused on organizations and participants and their disciplinary affiliations. First to come is a list of all the projects at Penn, both major and minor.

Table 8.1: Penn Interdisciplinary Projects Involving Goffman, by Date

Years	Project title	Activity	Success?	Goffman's role
1967	Codes in Context	Conference	Yes	Helped organize
1968–1979	Benjamin Franklin Professors	Honor	Yes	Active member
1969–1974	Center for Urban Ethnography	Research center: grants, fellows, events	Yes	Associate director
1969	Urban Ethnography	Conference (CUE)	Yes	Helped organize
1969–1993	Conduct and Communication	Book series	Yes	Initiator; co-leader
1969, 1971	Semiotic Program	Coordinating group	No	Named as likely
1972–	*Language in Society*	Journal	Yes	Active, editorial board; contributor
1974–1979	*Studies in the Anthropology of Visual Communication*	Journal	Yes	Contributor; minor editorial role
1974–1979?	Language and Interaction Institute	Institute	Minimal	Member
1975	Science of Symbolic Behavior	Coordinating group	No	Named as likely
1976–1982?	Cross-cultural Communication Center	Center/grant proposal	Yes, but new focus	Named as likely
1979–1994	Art and Symbolic Behavior	Guest lectures/conference	Yes	Member
1980–1992	Language, Culture, & Society	Coordinating group	Minimal	Member

Arranging the data in this way makes it easy to see several things: First, and most significant, Goffman was engaged in a surprising number of collaborations just at Penn. He was not typically the leader, although it becomes obvious that he gave substantial effort to the major projects; these were both the most significant and the most successful: the early conference, the book series, the journals, and the research center. Unexpectedly, he was involved in activities at Penn even before arriving on campus officially in 1968. As for the minimally successful activities, or those proposed that never actually happened, the main point to stress here is that the organizers wanted him to be involved, and presumably he wanted that as well. He was involved in organizing a conference (Codes in Context) at Penn while still based at Berkeley. He was key to establishing a book series (Conduct and Communication), and an important editorial board member of a major journal (*Language in Society*) still in existence today. He helped to write a substantial grant proposal establishing the Center for Urban Ethnography, which funded research, conferences, publications, and fellowships for five years, and which even today lives on as a phantom, decades after the funding ran out. He published a lengthy article (1976a) in a second journal, *Studies in the Anthropology of Visual Communication*, which then became a major book (1979a). He was included in multiple additional efforts to coordinate courses, presentations, and students across Penn, even though most saw limited success at best. He influenced dozens of students in significant ways they still mention, even though he served as dissertation chair for very few.

Next comes a comparable listing of other interdisciplinary projects highlighted in this book: those with organizers based on other campuses or not attached to a campus at all. In most of these, Goffman was more than just a participant; he was an organizer, or in some other way one of the people responsible for what happened.

Here the most notable events are all conferences, several of which Goffman helped to organize, not an activity typically mentioned for him by others; the one publication was not something he was responsible for getting accepted. But he was part of a national commission which remembered his contributions from twenty years before and clearly attended to his words, evident especially through the quotes from his publications used in the resulting report. And he was part of MAP, a long-term collaborative research project which eventually did result in publications but ultimately failed, in part due to his strong objections to the group's data collection techniques.

Yet he maintained friendly relations with the organizer (Grimshaw) and many other participants despite his withdrawal.

Table 8.2: Other Interdisciplinary Projects Involving Goffman, by Date

Years	Project title	Activity	Success?	EG role
1964	Strategic Interaction and Conflict	Conference	Yes	Helped organize
1968	Interaction Ethology	Conference	Yes	Co-organizer
1969	Nonverbal Dimensions	Conference	Yes	Helped organize
1970–1982	*Working Papers in Sociolinguistics*	Publication	Yes	Peripheral member
1971	Committee for the Study of Incarceration	National commission	Yes	Active member
1972	Ethnography of Speaking	Conference	Yes	Participant
1972	Sociolinguistics: Current Trends & Prospects	Conference	Yes	Plenary
1973–1994	Multiple Analysis Project	Research project	Minimal	Active member; left early
1974	[Goffman/Sacks/Goodwins/Jefferson project]	Grant proposal	No	Participant in proposal
1975	Comparative Ethnographic Analysis	Conference	Yes	Participant
1977	Colloquium on Human Ethology	Conference	Yes	Participant
1980	Clever Hans	Conference	Yes	Participant

These lists show that Goffman met informally with colleagues across multiple disciplines on each of his campuses, helped to organize and coordinate not one but multiple conferences (including one at Berkeley, one at Penn before he arrived, one in New York, and another in Amsterdam), and was included in others, both well-known and rarely mentioned. He also participated in

Table 8.3: Results of Projects at Penn Involving Goffman, by Date

Year	Activity	EG as organizer	EG as presenter	EG as carper	Book	EG as author	EG article	EG as editor
1967	Codes in Context	x		x				
1969	Center for Urban Ethnography	x			x			
1969–1982	Conduct and Communication	x			x	x		x
1972–1982	*Language in Society*						x	x
1974–1982	*Studies in the Anthropology of Visual Communication*						x	x

panels at major international conventions (surprisingly early as chair, but more frequently as discussant, or "carper," as he put it [Feb 27, 1979, TS]), had an article published in a journal special issue (1964a), and published chapters in edited collections (1957b, 1957c, 1958, 1961c, 1961d, 1964b, 1966, 1979c), all demonstrating various levels of collaboration with and connection to colleagues, even though all were sole authored. Goffman was clearly an active player in the many group endeavors examined to this point, even though his role as a team player and valued colleague is hardly what he is known best for today. In fact, quite the opposite. I have tried to expand our understanding of Goffman's contributions to include a well-documented series of positive, productive, and surprisingly frequent interactions with overlapping clusters of colleagues. Overall, taking multiple stories into account should permit a more complex and complete understanding of who Goffman was, and how he interacted with others as he contributed to our understanding of the interaction order that was his focus.

Another way of viewing what has been demonstrated to this point about Goffman's connections with others would be to look at the "productive results" so valued by administrators such as Meyerson.[1] Here the questions to be asked include: Were there conferences where ideas were presented to others beyond the initial group, and, if so, what was Goffman's role? Were there resulting publications (books or articles), since that would again extend the influence? And if there were, was Goffman one of the authors, or did he take an editorial role?

This table includes only major projects at Penn because none of the minor projects had any resulting publications (so far as I have found), and the few conferences from one of them (Art and Symbolic Behavior) did not, in the end, involve Goffman in any role yet documented. Of the more successful projects, Goffman helped to organize two conferences[2] and a book series and played the role of carper at one of the conferences. Two of these projects resulted in the publication of one or more books; Goffman did not have a chapter in the one book resulting from a Center for Urban Ethnography conference, but he did publish several books in the series he proposed and co-edited, Conduct and Communication. In addition, he published an article in each journal, played a significant editorial role in the book series and one journal (*Language in Society*), and a minor editorial role in the other (*Studies in the Anthropology of Visual Communication*). In sum, this table documents a small number of projects resulting in conferences and publications to share what was learned. While there were few such projects, they were remarkably influential far beyond Penn.

Next, to consider the results of activities when the organizer was based somewhere other than Penn (thus combining what was discussed previously as "Penn adjacent" or "beyond Penn"). In addition, many of the conferences briefly mentioned in earlier chapters (especially those "Before Penn") also seem appropriate to include, as they demonstrate his continued willingness to present his work, or to become involved in a working conference designed to further some concept.

When the result of a conference was a book, "EG as author" means he had a chapter in that book; otherwise, "EG article" means he published an article related to what he presented at the event. For conferences, it seems worth noting when he served as organizer, as chair, as presenter, or as carper (discussant or respondent). Goffman was one of the organizers in four of these conferences, and organizer of a panel once; he served as panel chair once, presented a paper sixteen times, and he took the role of carper thirteen times. Obviously, when not presenting himself, being the one to formally respond was his preference. (And others wanted him to do this because he was particularly good at it, often moving far beyond just asking a few

Table 8.4: Results of Projects Outside Penn Involving Goffman, by Date

Year	Activity	EG as organizer	EG as chair	EG as presenter	EG as carper	Results: Book	EG as author	EG article
1956	Macy Conference on Group Processes			x		x	x	
1956	Socio-Environmental Aspects of Patient Care			x		x	x	
1957	American Sociological Association			x				x
1957	Symposium on Preventive and Social Psychiatry			x		x	x	
1960	American Sociological Association		x					
1962	Association for Research in Nervous and Mental Disease			x		x	x	
1962	Conference on Paralinguistics and Kinesics					x		
1963	American Anthropological Association			x		x	x	
1964	Strategic Interaction and Conflict	x		x	x	x	x	
1967	American Anthropological Association			x				
1967	American Sociological Association			x				
1968	Interaction Ethology	x		x	x			

Table 8.4: Results of Projects Outside Penn Involving Goffman, by Date (cont'd)

Year	Activity	EG as organizer	EG as chair	EG as presenter	EG as carper	Results: Book	EG as author	EG article
1969	Nonverbal Dimensions	x		x	x			
1971	American Sociological Association				x			
1971	Committee for the Study of Incarceration					x		
1971	Conference on Visual Anthropology				x			
1972	Ethnography of Speaking				x	x		
1972	Conference on Visual Anthropology	x (session only)						
1972	Sociolinguistics			x		x		
1972	American Sociological Association			x				
1973–1975	Multiple Analysis Project					x		
1974	NWAVE III[3]			x				x
1975	Comparative Ethnographic Analysis[4]							
1976	American Anthropological Association				x			
1977	American Anthropological Association				x			
1977	American Sociological Association			x	x			
Year	Activity	EG as organizer	EG as chair	EG as presenter	EG as carper	Results: Book	EG as author	EG article

Table 8.4: Results of Projects Outside Penn Involving Goffman, by Date (cont'd)

1977	Colloquium on Human Ethology	X				X			
1978	American Anthropological Association					X			
1978	American Sociological Association					X			
1979	Chicago Linguistic Society				X				
1980	Clever Hans					X	X		

questions to drawing broader conclusions.) Books resulted from twelve of these events: Goffman published a total of seven chapters in six of them (and multiple quotes from his publications are included in the group-authored book for the Committee for the Study of Incarceration) and twice published a conference paper from this list as a journal article (and as part of a later book of his own multiple times). He played no editorial role in any of these activities. Thus, in the non-Penn activities, he typically helped organize events, presented his own work, or served as carper. However, as the years went on (especially after arrival at Penn), far less often did he bother to write up a paper for inclusion in the resulting book, presumably as his reputation for writing his own books grew, and it made more sense to publish his ideas in those. In fact, most of his early book chapters or articles were later integrated into one or another of his own books, as has been mentioned when each was first described.

In addition to what has been covered in these pages, it is important to point out that Goffman gave a lot of invited presentations, and was invited to a lot of additional conferences, both in the US and Europe. Those activities already have been covered by others (most clearly in Winkin 2022a, 2022b), and so there is no need for them to be listed here. But they should be understood as background information; they significantly expand the number of conference and other presentations beyond those already listed, making clear that he had international connections, not only domestic connections within the US.

The primary concern in these pages has been with Goffman's time at Penn. Clearly, he was not typically the primary organizer; that was his role only once, for the book series Conduct and Communication. But he was a valued partner in all the major projects at Penn, and an active participant in many of the minor projects, including the Benjamin Franklin Professors, even for political activities, although he is not known for those—quite the opposite. And, of course, Penn was not unique. In other cases presented in these pages, he again took on substantive roles, ranging from co-organizing conferences to speaking up for his "constituency" (Sacks and Schegloff) as Grimshaw put it, as a member of a research team trying to help develop the new field of sociolinguistics. The connection with Sacks (and Schegloff) when they aligned on their assumptions for data collection during MAP provides evidence contradicting another common assumption about Goffman—that "Sacks' relationship with Goffman effectively ended when Goffman refused to sign-off on Sacks' PhD in 1964" (Hoey and Rawls 2022, 371). The connection documented in their joint NEH application (apparently with Goffman as the lead, since Grimshaw refers to it as the Goffman proposal), tying him together with not only Sacks but also Jefferson and both Goodwins, provides further evidence of continued connection. Across the various activities, it is evident that Goffman was rarely someone to be overlooked in a group, that people paid a great deal of attention to what he said, that he was often the one who served as discussant, synthesizing what had been said to that point, and even after an event ended, thinking carefully about next steps (as clearly demonstrated in his letters to Sebeok after the Interaction Ethology conference). At least some of the time, his was the voice of reason when someone was upset, as with Hymes.

Goffman was an uncommonly graceful writer, as has been widely acknowledged in discussions of his books, and the same grace (as well as humor) appears again and again in excerpts from letters he wrote to various friends and colleagues. That is at least one reason why he was valued as a group member. Jacobsen and Kristiansen have critiqued Goffman for being "apparently difficult to work with and to be around" and have suggested that this may be why his work is "exclusively one-author productions" (2015, 25). But sole-authored publications do not mean he never talked about ideas with others, for he clearly did, and often, typically in ways that were cute or funny or gently teasing but always working to build and maintain affiliations with at least some others, if not everyone. Prior chapters have documented repeated efforts to maintain friendships even after disagreements (as with Grimshaw) or inability to accept a manuscript for publication (as with Sherzer) or unwillingness to over-commit himself (as with Sebeok). Long-term friendships and working relationships—primarily with Birdwhistell, Hymes, Labov, Szwed, and Worth at Penn, but also Hughes from Chicago; Schneider, Cicourel, Gumperz, and Ervin-Tripp from Berkeley; Sebeok and Grimshaw from Indiana; and Sherzer from Texas; and many others who have been mentioned more briefly—have all been illustrated in these pages. Each of these people is a major scholar in their own right, and all shared enough basic assumptions with Goffman that they worked hard to maintain connections, whether at conferences, dinners, visits, or through multi- or interdisciplinary projects, both large and small. The fact that so many people show up repeatedly (as when Steiner and Meyer were Benjamin Franklin Professors but also part of minor projects; or when Goodenough had his office in the same building as Goffman and also was part of so many minor projects) makes clear the number of overlapping clusters of which Goffman was part, mostly at Penn, but also elsewhere. And there are undoubtedly more that I have missed.

Goffman and Sociolinguistics

In the context of this analysis of Goffman as part of an invisible college, an obvious question to ask is whether Goffman's network only included Chicago, NIMH, Berkeley, and Penn (and more distantly Indiana and Texas) or whether he belonged to some broader scholarly community, beyond a single campus (where, after all, it is relatively easy to connect with peers, even those based in different departments). The answer is that, in the field of sociolinguistics as it developed through the 1960s and 1970s, Goffman was in on the ground floor, knew all the major players well, and was frequently counted as an important member. The typical descriptions of Goffman do not portray him as a sociolinguist, yet he was part of the small group of scholars (most especially Gumperz, Ervin-Tripp, Hymes, Labov, Grimshaw, and Ferguson) trying to find ways to bring the study of language and society together into a new research area they most often named sociolinguistics. In addition, at least once he referred to himself as an "amateur sociolinguist" (Goffman to McGuigan, Jan 3, 1980, RB). Beyond his own opinion, there is a reasonable argument to be made for including Goffman in this group, given that he was a part of things from the very early days, even to the point that his dissertation can be understood as foreshadowing the move into sociolinguistics, as Winkin (2022e) argues. Specifically, he was included in an early journal special issue in 1964, which was all about establishing sociolinguistics as an approach. He was invited to the 1966 meeting at the home of William Bright, along with many of those from the Saturday group at Berkeley, an event credited with helping to establish sociolinguistics as a distinct approach.[5] And he was a visitor to Ervin-Tripp's SSRC Committee on Sociolinguistics–sponsored summer workshops in sociolinguistics in 1968, participating in analysis of visual data. He presented a plenary and was cited as a relevant source by multiple participants in their own presentations in the 1972 Georgetown University Round Table on Sociolinguistics, another event organized by the Committee on Sociolinguistics, one intended to evaluate the state of the field.[6] By the fact that the organizers wanted him to present a plenary we learn that they must have considered his work not only relevant but central. He served essential editorial roles in managing a book series (Conduct and Communication) and a journal (*Language in Society*) on the topic. As Hymes said at one point in a 1972 letter to Sherzer, "Since 1963 at the very least, that is, a decade, we [Hymes and Gumperz] have considered what he [Goffman] does as integral to what we do."[7] In turn, in *Frame Analysis*, Goffman acknowledged: "Dell Hymes, William Labov, and Joel Sherzer provided a sociolinguistic environment" (1974, vii). Grimshaw provides a definition of sociolinguistics which makes obvious why Goffman would have been interested in sociolinguistics as it was developing: "how talk gets used to accomplish social ends in (primarily) face-to-face interaction" (1998, 444). The overlap with Goffman's research concerns here is substantial.

When Tannen (a Gumperz student) prepared an annotated bibliography of sociolinguistics in 1978, her description of Goffman's 1959 book begins, "Goffman is a giant. His theories of interaction inform everything anyone has written in the last two decades about interaction, whether they know it or not (most know it)" (31). In 1996, discussing what they term "sociological sociolinguistics," Schegloff, Ochs, and Thompson, highlight Goffman as one of the two most important figures (with Garfinkel as the other). Grimshaw, by the way, is barely mentioned—not much of a reward for his twenty years of effort guiding MAP—but the issue was theoretical contribution, not effort. Kendall makes a case that not only is Goffman's influence evident in sociolinguistics, but it "has increased over the decades" (2011, 120). Copland and Creese (2015) add Goffman (as well as Fred Erickson) to their list of metatheorists.[8]

The Saturday group at Berkeley became an important part of the history of sociolinguistics, and Goffman was an integral part of that story as a member nearly from the start (Bucholtz and Hall 2008). Gumperz highlights the significance of the SSRC Committee on Sociolinguistics, on which he,

Hymes, Labov, and Grimshaw all served overlapping terms, along with Bright and Ferguson,[9] writing in 1997 that: "Although our theoretical interests differed, we all shared the premise that sociolinguistic research of all kinds must build on the ethnographer's insights into the everyday life of speech communities" (115). Later, of course, the Committee on Sociolinguistics developed and then supported the MAP project in which Goffman played a significant role, as well as supporting not one but several conferences in which he participated.

Nomenclature Matters: Sociolinguistics vs. Interaction

Part of the reason Goffman is not always considered relevant to the development of sociolinguistics is likely the considerable divergence in the overlapping names for what he and others studied in the 1960s and 1970s. They invented vocabulary as they went along, as happens in the early days of any theoretical approach, and so the names for what they studied kept changing, from sociolinguistics (Labov and Grimshaw) to urban ethnography (Szwed), from the ethnography of speaking (Hymes) to interactional sociolinguistics (Gumperz), from codes in context (Worth) to communication (Birdwhistell). In his turn, Goffman called what he did the interaction order, or communication conduct (both as early as his dissertation [Goffman 1953]), sometimes interaction ethology (as in the conference in Amsterdam in 1970), or a handful of other names (as in his various books), occasionally calling himself an urban ethnographer (as in Verhoeven 1993). Others tried out further terms: semiotics (Sebeok and Hymes), language and interaction (Labov), symbolic behavior (Goodenough), cross-cultural communication (Labov and Gelman), language, culture, and society (Goodenough and Hymes), or ethnolinguistics (Hymes and Sankoff). As Hymes has pointed out, many of these are "bridges" (1983b, 189); that is, they are designed to help connect what otherwise would be viewed as discrete topics or disciplines. Some of his examples at that point were sociolinguistics, ethnography of speaking, and philosophy of language. As Labov referred to it in 1968—this thing, "whatever we're doing"[10]—there was a sense that they were making it up as they went along, and indeed they were, following the work rather than the label, wherever it led, to paraphrase the comment Hymes made to Worth about Goffman in 1969.[11] Worth called what they were doing "this kind of work."[12] Hymes said that "no one name serves."[13] Goffman acknowledged that "the study of face-to-face interaction in natural settings doesn't yet have an adequate name" (1967, 1). Despite the lack of final agreement on a single cover term to refer to everything they were doing, most especially at the point when they were busy inventing it, the point to remember is that they still had no difficulty in thinking the various approaches they were taking should be viewed as having substantial overlaps. Fifty years later, there are almost as many names available, including sociolinguistics, linguistic ethnography, language and social interaction, or communication, describing overlapping areas studied by later generations of researchers. Whatever its name, Goffman was one of those helping outline what needed study and how it could be studied, not just at one university, but nationally (and, to a lesser extent, internationally).

When one idea failed to be taken up, a different proposal was put forward, with a slightly different emphasis, and overlapping membership; when one succeeded on a small scale, a more ambitious effort was deemed justified. Thus do we see how success is achieved: through small steps, repeated connections, and continuous effort. Looking only at these projects involving Goffman, it becomes quite clear: In the 1950s, he conducted his own research, presented at conferences, and began publishing; in the 1960s, he moved from just presenting to helping to organize conferences, he joined first one then several multi- or interdisciplinary groups, and published chapters influenced by discussions with others, as well as much more on his own; in the 1970s and early 1980s, he took a far more active role in a wider range of interdisciplinary projects, continued presenting at and helping to organize some conferences, helped to write a major grant proposal and to coordinate the resulting research center, moved from publishing his own work to having editorial roles with two journals and a book series, and was chosen to join a national committee that closed the circle, having more to do with his research in the 1950s than anything later. Overall, it is the public presentations and resulting publications which make the informal gatherings worthy of attention; these were not just people sitting around chatting, but scholars discussing ideas, influencing one another, and then setting out their ideas on a national stage, publishing as a way to expand the conversation to others who did not have the good luck to be present as they developed approaches that we today take for granted. The Committee on Sociolinguistics made explicit what everyone eventually learned: The goal was not just to conduct research, but to present at conferences, and move from there to publications, so that ideas might be shared with as large a group of potentially interested peers as possible. Hymes provided an early and explicit warning to the committee:

> Sociolinguistics might turn out to have been for the 1960s, what paralinguistics and kinesics were for the 1950s. The focus of attention, even the cynosure, for a few years, of many people and the work of some excellent people—but a field which acquired no steady succession of advances in method and results, and replacement of leaders. Or, sociolinguistics may more resemble psycholinguistics, becoming subject to severe reformulations, but sustained.[14]

As clarification for those unfamiliar with the history of kinesics and paralanguage, they were invented, but never fully developed (Leeds-Hurwitz 1987; Leeds-Hurwitz and Kendon 2021), despite the 1962 conference on that topic organized by Sebeok and attended by Birdwhistell and Goffman (and Bateson and Mead, among others). Largely due to the funding provided by the committee and the support it received from scholars at Penn (and Berkeley, Indiana, and Texas), sociolinguistics did, in fact, fully develop. And Goffman was part of most of the major stages in that development. The terminology one chooses to describe one's research today often depends on disciplinary training and intellectual home; the large pie of potential topics has been divided up again into many smaller pieces.

Multi- and Interdisciplinarity

The key to understanding most of the stories told in this book, but especially what happened at Penn during Goffman's residence there, can be found in the related topics of multi- and interdisciplinarity. The positive result of either approach is the ability to bring together people having shared interests in order to develop new concepts, approaches, methods, etc. As Hymes explained to Worth already in 1969, "It is not possible to develop these lines of work, to meet these needs, within existing departmental alignments. The kinds of training and interest required are distributed across such alignments."[15] He was talking about the need to "succeed in making communicative conduct, verbal and nonverbal, an integrated focus of attention" and "understanding the genesis, meaning, and use of symbolic forms in people's lives." These were certainly interests shared with Goffman as well as all the others in this network. This was not only true at Penn, but also at Berkeley: The Saturday group was largely developed by people finding sympathetic others *outside* their own departmental homes. Hymes at least repeated on multiple occasions that he hated departmental structures; he wanted to focus on ideas, not administration (which makes it even more ironic that he wrote so many letters to department chairs in anthropology, folklore, linguistics, or deans in Arts and Sciences or communication, addressing administrative issues, and especially that he became a dean himself.)

The negative side to working with people having significantly different training and assumptions is the very real possibility of such differences causing misunderstandings, confusions, and conflicts. And, in fact, some of the stories told in these pages report on noteworthy difficulties between scholars both within and across disciplines. Finding or creating a new structure with a different set of people was often the proposed solution. Considering just a few of those at Penn, Fought periodically complained to Hymes about politics in the linguistics department;[16] Szwed complained to him about the folklore department;[17] and, of course, Hymes left anthropology over a tenure decision. Most of the minor projects at Penn were at least partially intended to expand the networks of participants so they would have clear ties to those outside their own departments.

Multidisciplinarity is one obvious solution. As people who share research interests connect across administrative borders, they invent multidisciplinary projects. In addition, there is a strong theoretical reason for introducing interdisciplinarity: There are often gaps in terms of coverage between disciplines, and interdisciplinary work is explicitly intended and designed to fill those gaps. As Hymes points out, "The flourishing of a hybrid term such as sociolinguistics reflects a gap in the disposition of established disciplines with respect to reality" (1972b, 17). In fact, his own phrase, "the ethnography of speaking" (quickly changed to "the ethnography of communication"[18]), pointed to just such a gap in what was then being studied: Anthropologists studied culture, leaving language to linguists, while linguists studied linguistic structure, but not use of language, so no one was studying language in use. It is reasonable to assume that Goffman saw himself as studying the larger topic of social interaction, which included, but was not limited to, the use of language in society.

Obviously, there are multiple barriers to interdisciplinarity, with some disciplines fitting together more easily or gracefully than others. The disciplines most often combined at Penn were anthropology, sociology, linguistics, psychology, folklore, and communication, all of which have substantial overlaps in terms of topics and key concepts, theories and methods. But, depending on the project, faculty members from another dozen disciplines were brought into discussions as it was understood they also would have something relevant to contribute. Just as the role of language in social life was essential to many of the projects in these pages, so was the extension of interaction to include the nonverbal (Birdwhistell) and the visual (Worth); today this larger understanding is typically termed multimodality (and studied by scholars from not one but a range of disciplines). Similarly, certain topics were of concern to numerous scholars across disciplines, such as narrative analysis, cultural identity, or performance, and so collaboration across borders seemed not only possible and reasonable but obvious.

In describing his own involvement in interdisciplinary groups—specifically focusing on that moment in the Berkeley/UCLA meetings in the 1960s involving Garfinkel, Cicourel, Labov, Schegloff, Sacks, and himself—Gumperz points out something rarely noticed: The conversations involved "people . . . who aren't usually grouped together . . . where people would come because they were interested in some of the same things, and we weren't necessarily friends. . . . creating a field is partly a matter of creating social networks of communicating individuals" (in Murray, 2013, 9–10). So, the first essential element is a network of people sharing common theory or research interests; they do not have to be friends, only to talk with one another about ideas. In fact, as has been shown, Goffman did become friends with at least some of the scholars described in these pages, and he valued those friendships, even to the point of putting them above theoretical or methodological disagreements. While friendship is thus not a requirement for interdisciplinary work, it may become a result, as demonstrated over and over here. Hymes told Dean Gregorian in 1974: "As far as I am concerned, the only thing that matters is intellectual growth and vibrancy; I want to be where that is and help it to exist. And that always seems to lead across departmental boundaries." And then he asked whether the new organizational structure just put into place at Penn would be able "to treat research, knowledge, scholars, as wholes, such as they really are," because that was of such importance to him. And it proved to be equally important to the others. He concluded that universities must solve the problem of ensuring their faculty "keep intellectually alive."[19] The projects in these pages, whether major or minor, whether based at Penn or elsewhere, whether successful or not, did exactly that by providing a context within which scholars could meet and discuss ideas with others sharing common interests, crossing traditional (departmental) boundaries. Goffman was one of those who transcended disciplines—in his case, from his PhD all the way through his books and final papers—as has been made clear across all the chapters of this book.

As Birdwhistell once pointed out to me (while discussing the Macy Foundation conferences in the 1950s, but he clearly intending the comment to apply to other contexts as well):

> You have to remember that this was a much smaller world then—many fewer people and most of us knew or knew about one another.... This is part of the ferment out of which Macy was born, bringing together specialists who knew (and were recognized in) their own field and who were interested in ideas coming from other disciplines. *This is important*: People well framed in *particular* disciplines got together as equals [emphasis in original]. It was exciting and productive.[20]

Birdwhistell was not the only one to think this way. Advancing knowledge often works best when we collaborate with those who come from a different starting point yet share some goals and assumptions. Goffman worked far more often and far more closely with multiple peers based in disciplines other than his own academic home of sociology. More scholars should consider doing the same. And more universities should encourage and facilitate opportunities to do just that.

Lessons From a Failed Project

When first envisioned in 1973, the Multiple Analysis Project was intended to bring together linguists and sociologists through the study of the same data using different approaches, as a way of learning which approach would be most useful as they were developing the new area of sociolinguistics. When MAP failed, that larger project of reaching agreement as to methodology failed as well, although certainly it was not the only reason for this. As Shuy noted in 1990:

> The fondly hoped-for coming together of linguistics, sociology and anthropology, a desire which dominated much of the discussion of the leaders in the mid-sixties, can today hardly be seen to have occurred.... It is apparent that today the same general laments that were voiced in the sixties continue to be with us.... It appears that the high hopes that academics have for cross-disciplinary intermingling is somewhat overly optimistic. (204–5)

The question is whether, several decades later, this has changed. It does seem that sociolinguistics is strong and accepted, but mostly it is linguists who view it as an obvious topic, with far fewer sociologists choosing it as their primary focus. I would disagree about the last part of Shuy's comment, however: The lack of success of this one project does not accurately predict the failure of other "cross-disciplinary interminglings"—as demonstrated by the success stories also told in this book. We must learn from this failure, just as we learn from the success of so many of the other projects.

Grimshaw pointed out a truism that has not changed: "Interdisciplinary research has a particular excitement for people like me who as mature scholars suddenly discover that data, theories, and methods from previously unfamiliar disciplines illuminate problems in their own" (1981, 360). So, in addition to appealing to junior scholars looking for a more comfortable intellectual home, it also appeals to senior scholars open to new ideas. Grimshaw proposed the experiment that turned into MAP in good faith, as an interesting way to learn which methods were most likely to prove effective as sociolinguistics was only just being invented. He took Hymes's goal of "a unified theory of sociolinguistic description" seriously and hoped that MAP would help sociolinguistics "to achieve theoretical coherence" (362–63). However, that was not to be, despite his valiant efforts to keep the project on track and bring it to a successful close.

Just as Hymes earlier was quoted pointing out that the Saturday group at Berkeley was made up of marginal department members looking for kindred souls, he also pointed out that the same was true for sociolinguistics more broadly: "An important attraction in the early years of sociolinguistics was that a number of individuals, interested in its use, were marginal to their official affiliations. The idea of there being a field for studying the use—in ways relevant to social life and social problems—brought them together" (1997, 125). Hymes goes on to specifically name Goffman and Labov, as well as Basil Bernstein, William Bright, Susan Ervin-Tripp, John Gumperz, Charles Ferguson, Joshua Fishman, Einar Haugen, Roger Shuy, and Wallace E. Lambert, as examples. At least some members of MAP likely felt a similar marginalization. Hymes has also suggested that "the postwar thrust toward a unified social science, among the relatively much smaller number of social scientists, had not yet faded" (125), yet another reason for working with colleagues beyond a single discipline. The goal of a unified approach documented in Grinker (1956) and Pike ([1954] 1967) had been a topic of discussion during Goffman's years at Chicago and was clearly of interest to many in the 1950s and 1960s, and so it may be credited with some influence over the move to interdisciplinarity especially at Chicago and Penn but occasionally elsewhere as well. As the earlier discussion of MAP shows, however, more care is required to ensure the success of an interdisciplinary project, for all the reasons outlined there. Ideas must reach people at just the right moment, and the stars must align: People must have overlapping interests, and time and funding for their work such that project goals and participation can remain consistent. Leadership must have both the requisite organizational skills and knowledge. These are all essential elements. While it may be easier to fail when reaching across disciplines, whether for multi- or interdisciplinary agendas, this does not mean the attempt is not worth the effort, as demonstrated most clearly by the series of successful major projects at Penn.

Penn and Interdisciplinarity

As a university, Penn has formally highlighted the interdisciplinary nature of the campus and faculty for decades, at least from 1971, when the university officially complained that their American Council on Education evaluation ignored "a number of innovative graduate programs of an interdisciplinary nature for which Pennsylvania is widely known,"[21] up to and including today's Penn Integrates Knowledge (PIK) Professors, who "hold joint appointments in two or more schools and exemplify excellence in multidisciplinary scholarship and learning."[22] (In fact, PIK Professors are a likely descendant of the Benjamin Franklin Professorships; despite no mention of this in official documentation, it would otherwise be an odd coincidence to have two such similar programs at the same university.[23]) In a statement of campus principles released in 2024, Penn has reiterated the significance of interdisciplinarity, starting the list with "Accelerate interdisciplinary pursuits" (Prendergast 2024). Describing how this worked at a personal level, Darnell explains:

> The University of Pennsylvania during my graduate studies from 1965 to 1969 was a disciplinary melting pot, a seething cauldron of ideas in which some faculty from anthropology (Dell Hymes, David Sapir), folklore (Dan Ben-Amos, Ken Goldstein), linguistics (Bill Labov), American studies (Charles Rosenberg), sociology (Erving Goffman), and the Annenberg School of Communication (Sol Worth) came together with graduate students regularly to share ideas. (2021, x)

The fact that Darnell has written a book titled *Invisible Genealogies* (2001a) makes clear that her concern is comparable to mine here—to show connections not yet widely recognized by others.

It is not by chance that Penn was the primary site of Goffman's invisible college. Winkin points out in his discussion of Bourdieu and Goffman that they shared moral values, including "a total commitment to hard work" (2022g, 403), an evaluation which could equally be made of virtually all the scholars mentioned in these pages. Those of us who were present at Penn during any of these projects, who took courses or otherwise connected with any of these scholars, understood well how fantastic our experiences were and, once we moved on to other universities, also came to understand how unique our experience at Penn had been. Because they had first been part of an uncommonly interesting and active and creative group of colleagues at Berkeley, Goffman and Hymes deliberately set out to create another such network at Penn, and they succeeded to an astonishing extent. After all, how many other universities have faculty proposing "a comprehensive and radical reorganization of the whole intellectual map, closer to a geological upheaval in the contours of a continent than a mere re-allocation of national territories"[24] as the Center for the Study of Art and Symbolic Behavior proposed to bring about?

That is not to say that everyone was always happy with all the others. Penn was a paradise compared to many other places, but even in paradise there can be conflicts. With so much going on, and so many people in so many departments involved, despite the enormous number of long—sometimes absurdly long—letters they exchanged (absolutely the opposite of today's emails and texts, but far easier to document after the fact), even central characters occasionally missed telling one another what they were up to. An example is that both Grimshaw and Gumperz gave colloquia in linguistics in 1980, yet Hymes, who probably knew both of them better than anyone else on campus, was not informed of their visits by Labov, who invited them. The result is that Hymes wrote a cranky letter: "I'd very much appreciate whatever can be done to get word to us [GSE] about visitors. . . . It's embarrassing to learn just today that Allen Grimshaw was here last week. As you know, he's an old friend. . . . And I feel badly about learning about John [Gumperz]'s being invited too late to arrange to see him."[25] Labov quickly apologized and blamed the lack of secretarial help.[26] But this sort of inadvertent missed opportunity is exactly what so many of the minor projects were intended to avoid. The network of people sharing common interests had grown so large by the mid-1970s that it became easy to omit notifying someone who would be interested in a visit, a lecture, a course offering, or other activity, and not even realize it.

That so many scholars were willing to move beyond disciplinary borders, when that was no more typical of academia in the 1960s or 1970s than it is today, is noteworthy. (The point here is not to say that other universities never establish campus-wide committees bringing together faculty from several departments, but those are typically about pragmatic matters, such as curriculum design, rather than research investigations resulting in publications.) Near the end of his academic career, Hymes explained the centrality of his own willingness to combine disciplines to his own professional life: "As someone with a degree in linguistics, teaching in anthropology (and with affiliations in folklore), I could not be other than interdisciplinary" (1997, 125), and this was equally true for the other major actors, as well as some of the minor actors, in this story. During his time at Penn from 1968 to 1982, Goffman was surrounded by a group of uncommonly bright, creative, and productive peers interested in collaborating with him. Penn was an interdisciplinary heaven, even if not all the attempts to create something new were successful. Ideas need fertile ground, and Penn certainly provided that for all scholars, central and peripheral, and for students as well. The lesson here is that the institutional structure and assumptions matter, not just ideas; one person with a single good idea cannot hold a candle to a cluster of brilliant people sharing their ideas and helping one another to develop and expand upon them. At Penn, Goffman was surrounded by one small circle, and then a much larger circle beyond that, made up of just such brilliant scholars and their many good ideas. It is probably not surprising that "when Penn alumni left the campus, we discovered that our professors were the scholars everyone else was reading" (Leeds-Hurwitz and Sigman 2010, 261n1); in fact, our professors were frequently several steps ahead of others, and part of that was likely due to their interdisciplinary conversations, where they could work out how to most productively and creatively move ahead.

Everything I saw, experienced, or read at Penn indicated that not only multi- but also interdisciplinarity was integral to the campus, to the point where I took courses in six departments; this was perhaps a bit extreme, but everyone I knew took at least some courses in departments other than the one in which they were officially enrolled. So, it was surprising to discover a study reporting the results of a survey conducted in 1967 which found students complaining of "isolation that existed at Penn between departments and between graduate students of different departments."[27] There are several possible explanations. Perhaps what was an issue in 1967 might have been resolved by the time I entered Penn in 1975, but this does not ring true, given the comments of graduate students in the 1960s, such as Darnell or Sherzer, describing the way students and faculty across several departments spent time together. Or perhaps some of us participated in courses with clusters of Penn faculty who collaborated themselves and brought their students into those collaborations in various ways, but others were not so lucky.

That seems more likely, but it still does not fit with Penn's explicit emphasis on interdisciplinarity, which appears to be campus-wide and decades old. In fact, in 1978, a supplement to the *Almanac*, titled "A Commitment to Interdisciplinarity," summarizes the result of the 1974 creation of a new structure, the Faculty of Arts and Sciences, deliberately intended to bring faculty and students together across disciplinary boundaries, "exploiting the potential that exists at Penn for interdisciplinary research, teaching and discussion."[28] Presumably, that effort was at least in part a response to the 1967 complaint. However, as sorting out when Penn was actually successful in this effort is not my primary concern here, I will leave the final determination to others. I can only say that the 1967 complaint of isolation was certainly not my experience in the 1970s, nor was it the experience of the vast majority of students and faculty in these pages, as evident in a large number of quotes included so far.

Shuy has pointed out that

> in order for the field of sociolinguistics to fully benefit from the combined disciplines upon which it was based, something had to give in the traditional academic structure. The ethnographic insights of anthropologists, the social theory and methods of sociology and the basic information of linguistics had to be merged more comfortably. To this point, they obviously were not. Anthropology students were getting a taste of linguistics, but not enough to do the type of work visualized by Hymes. Sociology departments were even less willing to stretch their traditional curricula to accommodate enough linguistics to further the seminal work of Sacks, Garfinkel, Fishman, and Goffman. . . . Thus the mid sixties revealed great ferment and coming together of social scientists to try to determine how to cooperate across traditional disciplinary lines. (1990, 189–90)

He goes on to say the problem was that "social scientists did not want to give up anything to get linguistics. Nor did linguists want to give up anything to get social science. Each wanted to keep its own field, goals and theory-building foremost while enjoying the most minimal fruits of the other" (190). What was special at Penn is that these fields (and others) did merge, at least more successfully than elsewhere, through coordination between Labov, Hymes, and Goffman, as well as Szwed, Birdwhistell, and Worth, and many of the peripheral actors in this story. Penn provided the context and the support, and then encouraged the resulting collaborations, leading to "clearly the best possible world to be in," as Hymes put it by 1970.[29] Hymes and Goffman spent a great deal of time and effort building the group they wanted to have at Penn, quite successfully. Although Worth preceded them,

Hymes was deliberate about enticing Goffman, and then he and Goffman and Worth jointly attracted first Labov and then Birdwhistell to Penn and helped Szwed find a new academic home in folklore when neither anthropology at Temple nor anthropology at Penn were as impressed by his $1 million grant as they really ought to have been. Given access to so much of Hymes's correspondence, we can see that his efforts were planned (e.g., his letter to Goodenough which refers to "what I came here to build up, and did build up for some years"[30]). That same correspondence makes clear that Goffman was a valued and active partner in building the web of interconnected colleagues. My introduction posed the question: *Who did Goffman deem his own community of like-minded scholars?* That question has now been answered: this team of six central players that Hymes and Goffman wove together, supplemented by the wider community of peers they found and drew in, and the students they trained, at Penn. This community can appropriately be termed an invisible college.

Invisible Colleges

An invisible college is a *college* because those included are scholars conducting research and sharing their conclusions with others in the group, and *invisible* because connections between members remain unacknowledged by many of those outside the group. In common use today, most often an invisible college refers to connections between scholars at different universities who identify as members of the same discipline, even (or especially) when others do not recognize their connections. In these pages, I have turned that concept on its side to examine primarily scholars at the same university drawn from different disciplines. In either case, the affiliations are notably invisible to outsiders—perhaps even more so in the examples described thus far. Like a community of practice (Wenger 1998), members of an invisible college share at least some assumptions, theories, and methods, and discuss ideas in common. It has long been assumed that "each discipline develops as a community of practice," that group members share "assumptions and methods, theories and tools" (Leeds-Hurwitz 2012, 2), and that these differ from those shared by members of other disciplines. That means assumptions, theories, methods, and more were shared among members of this group *despite* their obvious disciplinary differences. It is possible to think of Goffman's connections as one single invisible college or as a set of several overlapping networks; either works. Penn was the center in any case: either the heart of one vast invisible college or the largest of several smaller ones. Maintaining the geographic metaphor used in the title, these would be Chicago, NIMH, Berkeley, Penn, Indiana, and Texas. Obviously, Goffman participated in activities elsewhere, including the conferences in New York and Amsterdam described in detail. But my intent here has not been to describe every activity, every city, every colleague; others have done much of that work already (as in Winkin 2022a). Rather, my intent has been to put some of the puzzle pieces together, focusing on a particular location (Penn) over a specific time period (1968–1982, when Goffman was there).

Hymes proposed another term for the collection of colleagues working together at Penn, calling them a "constellation."[31] Given that, it made sense when he continued the metaphor by later referring to the MAP group's members as all being "stars" (Hymes to Grimshaw, Aug 8, 1975, ADG). (Interestingly, while problems in MAP were said to be due to there being too many stars, the fact that all the core group members at Penn were most certainly all stars did not cause any of the same difficulties.) The important fact was that, at least in the successful projects, group members all helped one another to think through the new ideas they were developing and consider implications; they read one another's drafts and provided detailed critique. As Fine has so gracefully phrased it, "We think as a community: thinking is neither individual nor universal, but is social" (2024, 515). And, as a community, one of the responsibilities was to share their ideas, and talk about what interested them and what they were learning through their individual research projects. Fishman used the phrase "community of like-minded scholars" (1997, 88) in describing what he went looking for in the early stages of developing sociolinguistics. But whether we use the phrase "invisible college" or "constellation of stars" or "community of like-minded scholars," the central concept describes a group whose members share overlapping interests and concerns for a new or developing topic, and who are willing to put in the work needed to contribute to and advance our understanding of it. In any case, meeting, talking, sharing conclusions, presenting at conferences, reviewing drafts, publishing, training the next generation—all of these are activities in which the groups described in these pages engaged. And Goffman was part of it all. Goffman was a valued member of these groups and projects, holding conversations with others and ensuring that publications eventually resulted, even though none of these activities is what he is known for, and his role in these various activities has been obscured and forgotten.

Goffman's ideas were typically published in sole-authored books, articles, or chapters. But, as demonstrated here, those ideas were developed in the context of and with others who held overlapping ideas. This does not mean he was any the less creative, only that original ideas benefit from discussion with others prior to publication, whether in person or on paper, and that creativity begets more creativity. Brilliant ideas by themselves are not really the issue. Goffman had many brilliant and original ideas, without question. But, in order for later generations to respect his accomplishments, we should not require that he have developed them entirely on his own. The fact that he collaborated in various capacities with so many other people demonstrates much of how ideas are formed and shaped and shared, and how they influence others. Goffman was part of group conversations across many contexts and topics. This has not been known only because we have not been looking for evidence, but such evidence has now been uncovered. Conferences, two journals, a book series, and a research center to support junior as well as senior scholars: these are the most substantial contexts in which he developed and shared ideas with others. The large number of unpublished manuscripts Goffman sent out for review by colleagues or reviewed for others sending drafts to him, the conferences he helped to organize, his preference for the role of carper, his thoughtful comments at the end of a conference synthesizing what the group had concluded and consideration of how to move forward, his uncommonly detailed comments on articles (especially those submitted to *Language in Society*, but to some extent also book manuscripts submitted to Communication and Conduct)—all of which have been documented in these pages—together emphasize the ways in which Goffman was clearly engaging with the ideas of others in addition to developing and sharing his own.

Disciplinary History

Finally, there are lessons to be learned from the stories told in these pages relating to disciplinary history. This is partly significant because the value of understanding disciplinary history was taken for granted across departments at Penn where multiple departments offered entire courses in their own discipline's history for new graduate students. (In the 1970s, linguistics alone had two—one offered by Hymes and the other by Labov—with virtually no overlap between these courses, reflecting their quite different emphases; I know this because I took both). But what has been learned about researching disciplinary history as a result of this project? The first and most obvious lesson is to look at archives for records of what was said or what occurred rather than taking received wisdom for granted. Just because all of Goffman's publications were sole authored, that does not mean he did not talk about ideas with colleagues, critique drafts by others and ask others to critique his own, and generally discuss theory, method, and research. As Murray argues, when doing history, correspondence provides a reliable record of who was saying what to whom and when. Goffman did not donate his correspondence, and actively discouraged people from spending time describing him as a person rather than focusing on his ideas. However, that has not stopped later scholars from writing about him as well as his ideas; the incomplete record has simply been misinterpreted. The goal here has not been to attend to what Goffman deemed unworthy of attention, but instead to expand our understanding of the context of his contributions, in addition to those of others with whom he collaborated. More people should read his letters for themselves, now that so many are available in various archives. The majority of my time in preparing this book has been spent discovering previously unknown and/or uncited archival sources and putting the puzzle pieces together into a coherent story. It is when all the pieces are put together—publications and unpublished reports, agendas and meeting minutes, interviews and correspondence—that the full story is most likely to be understood. As Davis says: "The cross-fertilization of ideas and the importance of what were in many cases long collaborations cannot be appreciated from a scan of credits and publications" (2001, 43), so the goal must be to expand the varieties of documentation discovered, consulted, and taken into account.

Another important lesson: New ideas move slowly but with repetition become accepted. Some of the story of sociolinguistics has been told in these pages—how sociologists and anthropologists worked with linguists to emphasize the study of language in use: how people do things with words, and how documenting the context provides essential information about meaning. It took decades, and many, many scholars to move from these separate disciplines to the study of topics otherwise ignored in the gap between disciplines. In the process, Goffman's role in early sociolinguistics has been clarified, as has some of the larger history of that specialization.

However, while we often assume that new ideas are developed by individuals working alone, in fact, much (perhaps most) of the time they arise (or at least are clarified and refined) through discussions held in casual conversations over meals, or more formally in working groups, panels, symposia, and conferences. Successful events lead to publications, and publications influence a still wider set of scholars. That is how knowledge grows. The fact that all of Goffman's publications are sole authored is without question a true statement, yet even so, he was frequently part of larger conversations with an expansive network of overlapping groups of colleagues, a fact which has most often been overlooked or ignored. The implication is that more study of collaborative groups of all sorts would likely repay the effort of documentation. Linked to this is the fact that intellectual history generally, and disciplinary history specifically, most often focus on a few "great men" (and they are nearly always men). Perhaps interdisciplinary history can broaden that to include the study of entire networks instead (and occasionally include women and minorities of various sorts).

Ideas cannot be generated, discussed, or transmitted except through the agency of specific people. Approaching history through the analysis of someone's career ensures that the human element will not be minimized unduly. Disciplinary history is composed of the actions (and interactions) of individuals as they talk and write about their ideas. It is easy to forget this in the process of following ideas through time, but if we forget it, we lose the necessary human perspective. As Gruber explains, "To describe the conflict or growth of ideas without describing the personal medium within which they grew is to deprive them of their human character" (1966, 21).

In addition, we must examine failures as well as successes: MAP and most of the minor projects here might seem irrelevant, since they did not lead to the sort of substantial influence achieved by the more significant major projects. What is the Semiotic Program that Hymes proposed, but which was never created, in comparison to *Language in Society*, when that journal is still viable after more than fifty years? But while there will often be more failures than successes, that is not always a bad thing, for failures can often lead to later successes by building stronger ties between colleagues and revealing what does not work (or even who is not the strongest leader). Past research on theory groups has shed some light on the significance of personal relationships and connections among researchers. Penn provided the context for most of the projects included, brought together the people and their ideas, and offered opportunities for both the intellectual and organizational leadership that Murray (1994) found to be essential to ensure good ideas become accepted rather than only invented and proposed. The successful projects bear out Murray's views of minimum requirements: intellectual leadership (having of good and original ideas) and organizational leadership (facilitating the acceptance of those ideas through the construction of a group as well as public opportunities to share them) are both required (see Mullins 1973 for further details and additional requirements). Others who wish to establish such groups, or simply to have their ideas at least considered seriously if not accepted, would do well to take note.

Building on this case study, other disciplinary historians should look for evidence of other invisible colleges. Those made up of scholars at the same university but organizationally based within different departments can be just as hidden as the more frequently studied type where scholars are aligned disciplinarily but geographically distributed—perhaps even more so, because disciplinary historians have typically been trained within a single discipline themselves and so are more likely to know the story of members of that one field of study rather than others. Perhaps that is why so few people have written more than a sentence or two (and those mostly by Penn alumni) about the incredibly strong interdisciplinary network in which Goffman was embedded. Now that multiple colleagues from his network have deposited their papers in archives (notably Hymes, Grimshaw, Sebeok, and Worth, but also Duncan, Hughes, Wallace, Bauman, and others), there is ample evidence of their connections and of their efforts, and so Goffman's connections to his peers are invisible no more.

Historians should also focus far more often on looking for examples of interdisciplinarity. Darnell has called for "a new paradigm for the histories of anthropology . . . around the concept of interdisciplinarity," since "adequate histories can only exist in their plurality" (2022, 1–2). I would argue that all disciplinary history, not only that of anthropology, requires consideration of interdisciplinarity, since disciplines are made rather than found, and so they are social constructions (Leeds-Hurwitz 2012), with boundaries not set in stone but variable. And, in fact, as I have been writing this, a new book has appeared specifically examining the history of interdisciplinary research projects: Feuerhahn and Mandressi (2025) also highlight the virtual absence of historical studies of interdisciplinary projects. Perhaps one day more universities will find another organizational structure than the currently common divisions of faculty into departments by discipline. Until that occurs, however, historians should not be constrained by such flimsy boundaries.

Finally, it is important for historians to remember that all relevant information is not necessarily included in formal publications. Articles and books are the peaks as it were, but much research and many ideas remain unpublished. These can be discovered through what Gruber (1966) has labeled "fugitive products." He describes them thus: "Dependence upon works written to be published shows us only part of a man; they are the landmarks of an intellectual life. Much more important—and of course, much more difficult to come by—are the informal and fugitive products—letters, journals, and impressions. From these we can glimpse a science in the making" (25–6). In such fugitive products, we can discover the connections between the work of different scholars, as well as their hopes and plans for the future. The use of these fugitive works in conjunction with materials which have been published (for I would not go so far as to argue that the former make sense without the latter) increases the adequacy and depth of our knowledge and understanding of what occurred in the past. One of the sorts of information not generally revealed through publications, but which does become very clear through letters, would be connections between individual researchers such as those documented in these pages; another would be projects that were imagined and designed, but either were never carried out or proved unsuccessful (as with most of the minor projects), which demonstrate interest and intent, as well as interconnections which may otherwise remain undiscovered.

In the end, interdisciplinarity serves as the heart of the story of Goffman's invisible college at Penn, as well as before Penn, adjacent to Penn, and beyond Penn. The scholars included in these pages were willing to ask questions beyond the obvious topics for the disciplines in which they had been trained, and/or into which they had been hired. Long after the fact, peripheral members of the group still comment on how "scholars such as William Labov, Dell Hymes, Erving Goffman and Ray Birdwhistell were pioneers in the social study of social communication" (Appadurai 2016, 5), and notice the continued assumption of connection between these group members decades after the group dispersed and multiple individuals have died. The lesson of this story for other scholars and other universities is simple: It is completely reasonable to look to colleagues with shared interests across departmental and disciplinary boundaries to support one another in research endeavors and, in fact, doing so may result in particularly strong ties as the needs of a research investigation take priority over disciplinary or departmental politics or assumptions. Goffman looked across disciplinary boundaries for the best and the brightest stars to be a part of the constellation he helped to construct at Penn. He participated fully, whether that meant notifying a potential author that their work could not be accepted for publication or helping to design a research center to obtain a major grant. The most important lesson of this story for (inter)disciplinary historians should have become abundantly clear: Do not accept what everyone says; instead, search for relevant documentation, and put together the pieces of your own puzzle. By doing so, I learned that Goffman was a colleague to many, and a good one. He was key to building a particularly strong invisible college, based at Penn yet incorporating additional scholars at Chicago, NIMH, Berkeley, Indiana, and Texas, as well as a few activities extending to New York, and even as far away as Amsterdam.

Endnotes

[1] Myerson to Hymes, Dec 14, 1971, DHH, Subcollection 1, Series I: Correspondence 1951–1987, Meyerson, Martin, 1971, 1979.

[2] I am assuming he helped to organize at least the Urban Ethnography conference sponsored by the Center for Urban Ethnography given that he was the associate director, although I must admit that I have yet to find specific documentation for this. But he clearly was involved in the organization of that event in some ways, as when he checked in early with Hughes about his participation (documented in chapter 4).

[3] NWAVE stands for New Ways of Analyzing Variation in English, a conference organized at Georgetown University. It has not been discussed elsewhere in this book but is included here for the fact that it resulted in one of the few journal articles published by Goffman after a conference presentation (1976b).

[4] There were no formal presentations at this conference, and no resulting publications, but Goffman was an invited and active participant, with others, as described in detail in chapter 6, and shows up frequently in the written (but unpublished) record of the event.

[5] As described in Shuy (1990), others at that meeting included many mentioned in these pages: Ferguson, Fishman, Garfinkel, Goffman, Gumperz, Hymes, Labov, Sacks, and Schegloff.

[6] Minutes, Committee on Sociolinguistics, March 18–19, 1971, DHH, Subcollection 1, Series II: Conferences and Committees, 1955–1987, Subseries D: Social Science Research Council, Committee on Sociolinguistics, 1970.

[7] Hymes to Sherzer, May 24, 1972, DHH, Subcollection 1, Series I: Correspondence 1951–1987, Sherzer, Joel, 1968–87.

[8] For further discussions of Goffman's role in sociolinguistics, see Deckert and Vickers 2011; Duranti 2003; Schiffrin 1996; Weninger and Williams 2022.

[9] Other members of the committee in earlier years included Joseph H. Greenberg, Thomas Sebeok, Everett Hughes, John Useem (Useem 1963), as well as Susan Ervin-Tripp (Heller 2018). Ferguson was chair 1963–70; Hymes moved into the position next (Hymes 1972b). To highlight the connection between the 1964 Committee on Sociolinguistics Conference on Sociolinguistics held at Indiana and the Gumperz and Hymes volume (1972), it is worth noting that the title of Ferguson's report on the former event mirrored their book title: Both were called "Directions in Sociolinguistics" (Ferguson 1965). A related title was used by Grimshaw for an article, "Directions for Research in Sociolinguistics" (1966).

[10] Labov to Hymes, Dec 16, 1968, DHH, Subcollection 1, Series I: Correspondence

1951–1987, Labov, William, folder 1, 1963–1972.

[11] Hymes to Worth, May 25, 1969, DHH, Subcollection 1, Series I: Correspondence 1951–1987, Worth, Sol, 1966–1977.

[12] Worth to Hymes, May 7, 1968, DHH, Subcollection 1, Series I: Correspondence 1951–1987, Worth, Sol, 1966–1977.

[13] Hymes to Glassie, Feb 7, 1970, DHH, Subcollection 1, Series I: Correspondence 1951–1987, Glassie, Henry, 1970–82.

[14] Memorandum on Committee on Sociolinguistics by Hymes to Committee, Apr 11, 1970, DHH, Subcollection 1, Series II: Conferences and Committees, Subseries D: Social Science Research Council, Committee on Sociolinguistics, 1970.

[15] Hymes to Worth, Jun 10, 1969, DHH, Subcollection 1, Series I: Correspondence 1951–1987, Worth, Sol, 1966–1977.

[16] As in Fought to Hymes, Apr 11, 1980, DHH, Subcollection 1, Series II: Conferences and Committees, 1955–1987, Subseries E: Other Committees, Interdisciplinary Committee for a Program in Language, Culture and Society, 1979–1986.

[17] Szwed to Hymes, Aug 7, 1974, DHH, Subcollection 1, Series I: Correspondence 1951–1987, Szwed, John F., 1965–1981.

[18] As explained in Leeds-Hurwitz 1984; see also Winkin 1984b, on Hymes's use of ethnography.

[19] Hymes to Dean Vartan Gregorian, Jul 8, 1974, DHH, Subcollection 1, Series I: Correspondence 1951–1987, Gregorian, Vartan, 1974–1981.

[20] Birdwhistell to Leeds-Hurwitz, n.d. [received August 1991], in the author's files. He was responding to an early draft of Leeds-Hurwitz 1994, when I requested critique because he had been a participant in the project described.

[21] https://almanac.upenn.edu/archive/v17pdf/n03/021271.pdf.

[22] https://web.sas.upenn.edu/endowed-professors/pik/.

[23] https://pikprofessors.upenn.edu/about-pik.

[24] Ben-Amos, Gross, Meyer, G. Prince, Herrnstein Smith to Regular Members, copied to Meyerson and Gregorian, Dec 13, 1978, DHH, Subcollection 1, Series II: Conferences and Committees, 1955–1987, Subseries E: Other Committees, Center for the Study of Art and Symbolic Behavior, 1978, 1986.

[25] Hymes to Labov, Dec 11, 1980, DHH, Subcollection 1, Series I: Correspondence, 1951–1987, Labov, William, folder 2, 1974–1987.

[26] Labov to Hymes, Dec 20, 1980, DHH, Subcollection 1, Series I: Correspondence, 1951–1987, Labov, William, folder 2, 1974–1987.

[27] https://almanac.upenn.edu/archive/v14pdf/n05/021668.pdf.

[28] https://almanac.upenn.edu/archive/v24pdf/n32/052378-insert.pdf.

[29] Hymes to Labov, Jan 21, 1970, DHH, Subcollection 1, Series I: Correspondence 1951–1987, Labov, William, folder 1, 1963–1972.

[30] Hymes to Goodenough, Nov 27, 1971, DHH, Subcollection 1, Series I: Correspondence 1951–1987, Goodenough, Ward H., 1958, 1960, 1970–86.

[31] E.g., Hymes to Goffman, Jan 9, 1968, DHH, Subcollection 1, Series I: Correspondence 1951–1987, Goffman, Erving, 1967–1982; and Hymes to Meyerson, Nov 17, 1971, DHH, Subcollection 1, Series I: Correspondence 1951–1987, Meyerson, Martin, 1971, 1979.

APPENDIX

Peripheral Colleagues at Penn

This appendix includes all the Penn faculty for whom I have found documentation of a connection to Goffman through a collaborative project, major or minor; it is organized by department. As a reminder, summaries of each department and the ways in which Goffman or his small group of peers connected with them appear in chapter 3. What follows are details for each of the individuals, in the same order as these appeared in chapter 3, for consistency.

Anthropology

Anthony F. C. Wallace was born in Canada, like Goffman. He earned a PhD in anthropology from Penn in 1950. He was affiliated with EPPI (as Birdwhistell was, both before and for a time after his arrival at Penn), from 1955 to 1960, simultaneously with a visiting position in anthropology at Penn, until he became a full-time professor and chair in 1961 (Urban 2016). He was department chair at the time Goffman was hired,[1] so he was the one who had the most crucial voice in making a job offer. Wallace published a review in 1962 of Goffman's book *Asylums*, making it clear that he had read not just that book but the body of work well before hiring the author. He concluded: "Goffman's essays are worth reading by any anthropologist, not only for their trenchant ideas on the nature of human organization, but for the good style. He calls a spade a spade. And, be it noted, he is able to present psychologically relevant data without indulging in psychological jargon.

His work thus has a demeanor of intellectual honesty to which we can all gladly defer" (1323). Given this, it should come as no surprise that Wallace was happy to offer Goffman an organizational home in anthropology when his then-colleague Hymes wanted to bring Goffman to Penn. Despite not being part of any of the specific projects, major or minor, successful or unsuccessful, Wallace still merits recognition for his role in that initial move.

Ward H. Goodenough and **William H. Davenport** were additional senior faculty in anthropology whom Hymes mentioned as likely colleagues for Goffman. Goodenough earned a PhD in anthropology at Yale in 1949 and began teaching part-time at Penn in 1949 (Kirch 2015), full-time in 1951.[2] When he was made a University Professor in 1980,[3] Hymes congratulated him, saying it was "an honor long due and well deserved," and then asked: "Am I right in thinking that the position entitles you to teach in any faculty? If so, please consider yourself invited to teach in this faculty, should you wish."[4] "This faculty" meant education, where Hymes was then dean. Hymes acknowledged Goodenough (as well as several others) even before he got to Penn, "for discussion through several years of the nature of ethnography" (1964a, 28n1). Also, remember that Goodenough had specifically recruited Hymes for Penn. Like Wallace, he also clearly appreciated Goffman's work even before Goffman's arrival: He cites several works by Goffman in a 1965 publication, for example, and continued citing him throughout his career (e.g., Goodenough 1997). In addition, Goodenough was one of the members of the Interdisciplinary Committee coordinating the new graduate degrees in folklore once that program was established in 1965 (Miller 2004), so he and Goffman knew people in common across campus. **Davenport** earned a PhD in anthropology from Yale in 1956. He held a dual position at Penn in anthropology and the Penn Museum as a curator, serving as associate director of the museum from 1979 to 1980.[5] In theory, all three of these anthropologists (Wallace, Goodenough, and Davenport) had the potential to become part of the overlapping networks as described in chapters 4 and 5, but in fact, only Goodenough did. Darnell explains at least part of the reason in comments on Goodenough and Davenport: While they shared a "meaning-based perspective" with Goffman and others who did become part of that network, their "interdisciplinary ties were forged in other directions" (2022, x). Despite this, all three of these senior anthropologists were essential to the story simply for the fact that they welcomed Goffman into their department; this could not be taken for granted, given that he was coming from a sociology department, and with a sociology PhD. If they had not welcomed him, Goffman would never have moved from Berkeley to Penn. Wallace then played no further role in terms of projects involving Goffman, and Davenport was a small part of one minor project, the Center for the Study of Art and Symbolic Behavior. However, Goodenough was involved in five of the minor projects to be discussed in chapter 5, taking the lead in two, so he is important on multiple counts.

J. David Sapir was linguist Edward Sapir's son. He earned a PhD from Harvard in 1964,[6] and joined the anthropology department at Penn in 1966, so he was junior faculty, not yet tenured when Goffman moved to Penn. Hymes was largely responsible for Sapir's hiring ("The equivalent of many days has gone into the persuading, shepherding, etc., to work something out for you here") at Sapir's request ("When you first wrote, asking if we could find a place for you . . .").[7] It was the denial of Sapir's tenure in 1971 that led Hymes to leave anthropology and shift his primary affiliation to folklore. Sapir's interests combined linguistics, anthropology, and folklore, like those of Hymes and Szwed. After leaving Penn for the University of Virginia, Sapir submitted a book proposal to the Conduct and Communication series, but Goffman rejected it. While still at Penn, Sapir was part of two projects, one major (the Codes in Context conference) and one minor (the failed attempt to begin a Semiotic Program). Sapir obviously knew Goffman's work, and he cited several Goffman books in a review for *Language in Society* (1979). Sapir and Goffman were colleagues in anthropology for several years and would have seen one another at department meetings if nowhere else, but there is evidence that Sapir, Goffman, and Sherzer had dinner together at least once (Sapir 2014), so they were more than just based in the same department.

Peggy Reeves Sanday earned a PhD in anthropology in 1966 at the University of Pittsburgh, and first took a position at Carnegie-Mellon University before moving to Penn in 1972.[8] She served on the Committee of the Undergraduate Major in Communications as of 1975,[9] was given a secondary appointment in education in 1977,[10] and participated in the NIE grant under the umbrella of the Center for Urban Ethnography once that center had moved to education (Hymes 1981a), so she was a late and peripheral group member. She included Wallace, Goodenough, Erickson, and Gumperz in a book she edited on fieldwork (1976). Goffman is cited multiple times across chapters and clearly was aware of that book prior to its appearance in print because he cited at least the Gumperz chapter ahead of publication (1976b). Sanday served as undergraduate chair of anthropology

(1979–1983, thus across Goffman's years) and later held a named chair (R. Jean Brownlee Endowed Term Chair, 2001–6) at Penn, so her status there was notable.[11] Heath (2011) mentions Sanday as one of the faculty members at Penn who attracted education students, despite being based in another department, and she served on the board of directors of SSRC, and CAE, as well as the executive board of AAA, and reviewed proposals for NIE, so her connections both to education and anthropology, both at and beyond Penn, were substantial.[12]

Arjun Appadurai earned his MA in 1973 and PhD in 1976 at Chicago, both in social thought, and began teaching in anthropology at Penn in the fall of 1976.[13] He held affiliations with the Penn Museum (as consulting curator of the Asian section), and the South Asia regional studies department,[14] as well as ethnohistory (jointly with Wallace and Ben-Amos, among others).[15] He gave at least one guest lecture to folklore, on foodways, in 1978,[16] and folklore students were encouraged to take his courses (which I know because I was and I did). He was part of only one minor project, the Center for the Study of Art and Symbolic Behavior. In addition, writing to his own department members about the problem of anthropology not having a strong program in language and culture in fall 1982, Appadurai highlighted the Interdisciplinary Program in Language, Culture, and Society as "an important first step towards resolving this problem."[17]

Sociology

Philip Rieff earned his PhD in 1954 from Chicago, like Goffman (McFadden 2006). Rieff taught at Chicago from 1947 to 1957, moved to Brandeis University, and then to Berkeley, where he stayed until 1961, when he took a position at Penn.[18] It is unclear whether or how well he and Goffman knew one another at either Chicago or Berkeley, especially given that Rieff was in political science at Chicago (Turner 2011), and education at Berkeley (Bershady 2009). Rieff first became a University Professor, being made Benjamin Franklin Professor along with the other seven University Professors only when Goffman was hired as a Benjamin Franklin Professor in 1968, which meant that two of these scarce and prestigious positions were awarded to a single department.[19] He and Goffman had multiple occasions to connect once Goffman was invited to participate in sociology department activities, but also from the start of Goffman's time as a Benjamin Franklin Professor, since the Benjamin Franklin Professors held not only meetings, but dinners, and a variety of other activities.

In addition to both having been at Chicago and Berkeley prior to Penn, they were the same age, and there were some similarities in their approaches. For example, "Rieff's analysis of culture, like Freud's, paid careful attention to the elements of daily life in which personal and societal character stand revealed" (Eisen 2016) sounds like something Goffman might have appreciated. Rieff was not part of any of the major or minor projects but, as another Benjamin Franklin Professor, he saw Goffman more often than many. However, Fox, who saw them both up close for years, has said that "one was a kind of antithesis of the other" although "they recognized each other as major intellectual figures," clarifying that "though they often disagreed with one another, their relationship was not an antagonistic one" (2009).

Rieff has been credited with attempting to hire Goffman at Penn (Delaney 2014; Heilman 2009), and that presumably is accurate. As mentioned in chapter 3, there was apparently an effort to offer Goffman a position at Penn in 1967, although that went awry, with an actual offer not being made until spring 1968, the point at which Hymes worked hard to convince Goffman to move to Penn. So, this may well have been one more example of a group effort across several departments to attract a good candidate to Penn.

What correspondence between Rieff and Hymes has been preserved shows him to have been quite friendly, at least to Hymes. First, when Hymes left anthropology in 1971 over a tenure decision, Rieff offered a new home in sociology.[20] Interestingly, Hymes jotted notes at the top of this letter, "Call [Henry] Hiz [then chair of linguistics], Renée Fox [chair of sociology]." A few days later there was a brief postscript from Rieff bemoaning the "disease of 'departmentalism,'" and suggesting they talk about establishing some sort of committee to permit a number of people to teach first-rate students in peace.[21] It is unclear whether or how much Rieff knew of the frequent attempts Hymes and others made to coordinate the content offered across departments, since he was not involved in any of them. Of course, Hymes did not move to sociology, and 1971 is not even when he gained a secondary appointment in sociology (that was 1973). But there was another letter from Rieff in 1973, reminding Hymes of his evening phone call in 1971 when Hymes had said he could not remain in anthropology, and stating that Rieff had called President Meyerson the next morning offering that Hymes could move to sociology. Now that Fox had made Hymes and Goffman full voting members of the department, Rieff wanted Hymes to have a title that reflected his new affiliation as well. The logic was that between Hymes and Goffman, the program would take a step toward "world pre-eminence."[22] There is no copy of a response in the file, but Hymes did not take him up on the offer; it seems likely he was finding folklore congenial and did not feel the need to move again so soon. If Rieff truly desired to convince Hymes to move to sociology but failed, and if this example accurately mirrors how he may have managed an early effort to hire Goffman, then it is possible he had the interest but lacked the political skills needed for success.

Renée C. Fox, with a PhD in sociology from Radcliffe College in 1954, took a position in sociology at Penn in 1969, becoming chair in 1972,[23] the first woman department chair ever appointed within the Wharton School (where sociology was based at the time, although Wharton later became a business school), and also the first in the new Faculty of Arts and Sciences (where sociology moved a few years later).[24] She served on the Committee of the Undergraduate Major in Communications,[25] and by 1978, held a secondary appointment in communications.[26] In addition to being one of the few women to play even a peripheral role in these pages, she was just as multidisciplinary as any of the men, having connections to programs across campus, including psychiatry, nursing, medicine, and bio-ethics, as well as communications.[27] Most important, she played a significant role in shaping Goffman's involvement with sociology, as she has explained: "Among my early acts in the office of chairperson was to give Erving voting rights in the sociology department, which he didn't have, and to involve him in departmental affairs to the extent that I could" (2009). At the same time, she gave Hymes a secondary appointment in sociology and offered him voting rights as well.[28] "A felicitous consequence of the legitimacy that I accorded to qualitative methods and teaching was that it motivated the sociologist Erving Goffman and the ethnolinguist-anthropologist Dell Hymes, both of whom had secondary appointments in the sociology department, to become much more actively participant in it" (2011, 271n7). By fall 1974, Fox began assigning both Goffman and Hymes to committees (Personnel for Goffman, and Recruitment for Hymes).[29] She has provided a description of Goffman's integration into the department:

> Erving Goffman was gratified by the steps I had taken to legitimize the teaching of field methods—especially ethnography—in the department. This, in turn, contributed to the fact that he became a really good citizen in the Sociology Department who helped me in various things I tried to do as a chairman, most especially in the recruitment of new faculty members. He almost always came

> to their presentations, agreed to accompany those of us who took the candidates
> out to dinner, and the like. He showed his appreciation for my having introduced
> and institutionalized qualitative methods into the department in this way. (2009)

It makes sense that if Goffman was serving on the Personnel committee, he would need to attend candidate events. It would be interesting to know which new faculty members he met during their interviews. Fox also mentions the informal network surrounding Goffman:

> Erving belonged to a strong and distinguished interdepartmental and interdisciplinary ethnographic and ethnolinguistic subcultural group that existed at Penn at this time. It spanned the Anthropology, Linguistics, and Folklore/Folklife Departments, and the Annenberg School for Communication. Included in it were Dell Hymes, sociolinguist William Labov, and anthropologist Sol Worth (a protégé of Margaret Mead, well known for his research among the Navaho Indians). (2009)

Finally, she worked with Goffman when they were both committee members on Eviatar Zerubavel's dissertation in sociology (Fox 2009; that document is Zerubavel 1979); they also both served on Samuel Heilman's committee (Heilman 2009).

Elijah Anderson earned his MA at Chicago in 1972, and his PhD at Northwestern University in 1976, both in sociology, taking a position in sociology at Penn in 1977.[30] At Northwestern he worked with Howard Becker, who had been a student at Chicago at the same time as Goffman. Anderson is one of the job candidates Goffman took to dinner during his interview at Penn (Bershady 2009; Lidz 2009). Along with Sanday, Anderson participated in a Hymes grant (1981a). Related to this, he was first a fellow and then associate director of the Center for Urban Ethnography in its second iteration, once it was housed within GSE,[31] and Heath (2011) mentions Anderson as another of the faculty members at Penn outside the program to attract education students. In 2007, Anderson moved to Yale, where he started the Urban Ethnography Project "in the tradition of" Goffman and others,[32] and is now presented as "one of the leading urban ethnographers in the United States."[33]

Teresa Labov was Bill Labov's first wife, and moved with him from New York to Penn; like Virginia Hymes, she arrived as an ABD; unlike Virginia Hymes, she eventually earned her PhD, in political science from Penn in 1980, and then took a position in sociology.[34] The degree was awarded for a project having nothing to do with her husband's work in New York, in which she had participated as an interviewer and analyst, and which had earned her an MA at Columbia (1969; her role in the project is documented in W. Labov [1973, 98n14]). She later published in *Language in Society* (1982), was acknowledged and thanked by Goffman for comments on draft manuscripts (e.g., Goffman 1976b, 257), and joined MAP at a late stage, long after Goffman had left it.

Linguistics

John G. Fought was based in linguistics at Penn from his hiring as assistant professor in 1967[35] until his retirement in 1995, with secondary appointments in anthropology as of 1976,[36] in education the same year,[37] and the graduate group in folklore as of 1975.[38] He shows up as part of the story of one major and all of the minor projects, standing just outside the inner circle; for example, he served as a committee member on dissertations with Goffman. These are the sorts of connections that build relationships despite being invisible to those who have no role in a specific project. Fought wrote a review for *Language in Society* of Goffman's *Relations in Public*; in addition to praising the book as one "in a series of extraordinary significance and promise" (1972b, 268), he explains the ways in which Goffman's work overlaps with the concerns of Hymes, Labov, and Gumperz, scholars whose work would undoubtedly have been known to and appreciated by readers of that journal, as well as overlaps with the work of Ervin-Tripp, Sacks, and Schegloff, who were not (yet) publishing in *LiS*. In turn, Goffman acknowledged Fought's helpful comments in some of his own publications (e.g., 1978, 787). Fought was not on the editorial board of *LiS* but did write frequent book reviews (seven, in addition to the one just mentioned). He and Hymes co-authored a book chapter (Hymes and Fought 1975) which they then turned into a book (1981).

When Fought came up for promotion and tenure in 1972, Labov wrote a strong letter of support. Given that Fought was primarily a phonologist specializing in Chorti, a Mayan language, this made him an unlikely colleague for Goffman. Hymes, certainly, for his study of Sahaptin; and Labov, for his attention to small details of linguistic structure. But Goffman? That connection was not so obvious. However, in that letter of support, Labov argued: "The connections that he [Fought] was able to point out with role theory in Goffman's terms have considerable importance for the theory of grammar." Labov also highlighted the difficulties caused by the anthropology department for linguistics: Since they had lost Sapir and Hymes, Fought had become essential as the one person left to train anthropology students in descriptive linguistics.[39] In this way he emphasized Fought's significance for not one but two departments on campus, something presumably taken into account during the tenure decision. Fought was one of the faculty members whose courses students were told to take even when they were formally enrolled in other departments, even when what he most often taught (phonology) and his specialty (Chorti) both might seem narrow. It worked because his interests were far broader than his own research specializations.

Gillian Sankoff earned a PhD in linguistics from McGill University in Canada in 1968,[40] and taught at the University of Montreal from 1968 to 1978. She was visiting professor in linguistics at Penn in fall 1976, hired as associate professor in 1979. By 1981 she was professor, by 1982 she was graduate program chair, and by 1988 she was department chair (Sankoff to Grimshaw, May 15, 1991, ADG). In 1972, Hymes was asked his opinion of Sankoff's research by Elisabeth Case, an editor at Cambridge University Press, and apparently praised her to the skies because, although that letter is not in the files, the response to it is: "There are times when being in publishing offers a special treat. One of these occurred this morning when I got your letter concerning Gillian Sankoff. I think Gillian Sankoff is a very fortunate woman."[41] Like the others here, Sankoff had substantial multi- and interdisciplinary interests. For example, she presented as part of the Language in Education Colloquium Series at Penn in 1979,[42] and was involved with the new cognitive science program started in 1988, along with Labov.[43] Goffman cites Sankoff in some of his publications (e.g., 1978, 787), and she mentions him in some of hers (e.g., 1980, 223). Goffman and Sankoff married in 1981, and, much later, Labov and Sankoff married.

Sankoff was part of two major projects (publishing in the Conduct and Communication series and also serving on the editorial board of *Language in Society*), and one minor project (the Interdisciplinary Program in Language, Culture, and Society). Even before arriving at Penn, she was invited to the 1972 Ethnography of Speaking conference and published in the resulting volume (1974). She was valuable at Penn not only as a linguist in her own right, but also as an obvious addition to their interdisciplinary group, as Labov wrote to Dean Vartan Gregorian in 1977 in support of her hiring, "speaking for the group of scholars who are assembling around the theme of Language and Interaction"[44] (specifically naming Goffman, Hymes, Szwed, Fought, Gleitman, Gelman, and Goodenough). Beyond Penn, Sankoff was one of the younger generation brought into the SSRC's Committee on Sociolinguistics in the mid-1970s, serving with Hymes but after Labov. When it was necessary to find a replacement for Goffman as co-editor of the Conduct and Communication book series, she was one of two chosen (yes, it took two people to replace Goffman).

Henry Hiz earned an MA from the Université libre de Bruxelles in Belgium and a PhD from Harvard, both in philosophy, and so his first appointment at Penn was as visiting lecturer in philosophy in 1951. By 1959 he co-directed a research project with Zellig Harris in linguistics, creating "the first computer program that could analyze the grammar of a human language."[45] He formally moved to linguistics in 1960 as associate professor, was promoted to professor in 1964, and served as chair from 1966 to 1973. Like virtually everyone else in this book, his interests spanned multiple disciplines. (In addition to philosophy and linguistics, he had experience teaching Slavic languages and mathematics before arriving at Penn.)[46] He was a member of just one of the minor projects, the Center for the Study of Art and Symbolic Behavior, but he was also department chair when Labov moved to Penn, and thus helped convince him to leave Columbia.

Ellen Prince earned an MA in 1967 in French from Brooklyn College, then a PhD from Penn in linguistics in 1974, joining linguistics as an associate professor the same year, later being promoted to professor, and serving as department chair in the 1990s. She held a secondary appointment in computer and information science,[47] and was part of the Institute for Research in Cognitive Science once that was established. She also connected with folklore, participating in a conference on "Yiddish in the University" in 1997 with Ben-Amos and a Penn alum having a PhD in folklore, Chava Weissler.[48] Prince was active nationally, and elected president of the Linguistic Society of America for 2008.[49] She was part of two minor projects, the Cross-Cultural Communication Center and the Center for the Study of Art and Symbolic Behavior.

Anthony Kroch received his BA from Harvard in anthropology in 1967, and his PhD in linguistics in 1974 from MIT; he taught in anthropology at the University of Connecticut and Temple University. He held a fellowship in 1978 with Labov for research ("to conduct sociolinguistic interviews and analyze the language of upper-class Philadelphians"), then took a position in linguistics at Penn in 1981, later moving into cognitive science as well.[50]

He was included in one minor project, the Interdisciplinary Program in Language, Culture, and Society.

Folklore

Kenneth Goldstein earned the first PhD in folklore awarded at Penn, in 1963, and began teaching in the department in 1965, serving as department chair on and off for twenty years (Ben-Amos 1996). As of 1975, he also served on the Committee of the Undergraduate Major in Communications.[51] He is particularly important for his role as the one who initially welcomed Szwed, Dell and Virginia Hymes, the Center for Urban Ethnography, and *Language in Society* to the folklore department, but he was also part of a minor project, the Semiotic Program.

Dan Ben-Amos was part of that welcome committee with Goldstein. He earned a PhD in folklore from Indiana in 1967 and was hired in folklore at Penn that same year, just after it had upgraded from a program to a department in need of its own faculty.[52] Thirty years later, when folklore was downgraded from a department back to a program again in 1999, he added an affiliation with Asian and Middle Eastern studies;[53] after that department was divided into sub-specializations, he joined Near Eastern languages and civilizations.[54] In addition, he served on the Ethnohistory Committee, which began in 1978, mostly as a collaboration between anthropology and history, but bringing in faculty based in other programs as well,[55] and had a secondary appointment in communications.[56] Finally, he had at least some contact with education once Hymes moved there, as when he gave a talk for the Language in Education Colloquium series in 1980.[57] He was a small part of one major project, the Center for Urban Ethnography, and two minor projects: the Semiotic Program and the Center for the Study of Art and Symbolic Behavior (and served on the governing board of the latter), as well as participating in the 1972 Ethnography of Speaking conference at Texas.

Barbara Kirshenblatt-Gimblett earned her MA from Berkeley, and her PhD in folklore from Indiana in 1972.[58] She was teaching at the University of Texas, Austin, at the time of the Ethnography of Speaking conference there in 1972, was invited to participate, and published in the resulting volume (1974). She was hired in folklore at Penn in 1973.[59] Like Goffman, she was Canadian.[60] She is most relevant to the story told here for having published a book in the Conduct and Communication series (1976). Goffman had some of her unpublished work in his files, so they obviously talked about research together beyond that book. In addition, she was part of a minor project, the Center for the Study of Art and Symbolic Behavior.

Roger D. Abrahams earned a PhD in English and folklore at Penn in 1961,[61] before these were two separate departments, and there is a wonderful story about how it was his dissertation describing Black folklore in Philadelphia, full of obscenities upsetting to English department faculty members, which helped give MacEdward Leach, his dissertation chair, the excuse to begin a separate folklore program, just so his colleagues would not have to deal with offensive language (Hufford 2020; Miller 2004).[62] Abrahams took a position at the University of Texas, Austin, but several decades later, in 1986, returned to Penn to teach in that new folklore department (Grimes 2017; Hufford 2020; Szwed 2016). He participated in the original discussions about organizing CUE and, as a result, Szwed reports, "I asked Roger to join me in this project, and he was a Fellow of the Center whenever his job at Texas allowed it" (2016, 427). It comes as no surprise that Abrahams often thanks Goffman, Szwed, and Hymes for comments on publications (as in Abrahams and Babcock 1977), or that eleven of his publications are listed in the final record of publications sponsored by the center (Center for Urban Ethnography 1978). Abrahams was also part of the discussions that led to both the *Working Papers in Sociolinguistics*, and the Ethnography of Speaking conference held in Texas (Abrahams 1974); eventually both were managed by Bauman and Sherzer. Like Hymes and Grimshaw, Abrahams wrote up an academic appreciation of Goffman after he died, talking about how he took the roles of "insider and outsider" as an "observing stranger," before concluding that he was a "superbly accurate observer" (1984, 86, 92).

Virginia D. Hymes met Dell Hymes while earning her MA in anthropology at Indiana, which she completed in 1954, and enrolled officially as a PhD student in linguistics at Penn after they left California, but never finished her dissertation.[63] Despite this lack, she served as undergraduate chair of folklore at Penn from 1975 to 1987, teaching courses in that department as well in linguistics, where she had a secondary affiliation.[64] (At Penn, it was not unheard of for students who were ABD to offer the occasional course at the undergraduate or even graduate level, so this does not necessarily imply special dispensation for a faculty spouse.) She served on one minor project, the Interdisciplinary Program in Language, Culture, and Society, and as rapporteur at the Comparative Ethnographic Analysis Conference in

1975. Goffman occasionally cited her work (e.g., 1976b, 25, 273; 1981, 25) and had unpublished copies of some of her work in his files. In addition, she participated in numerous informal dinners with her husband and Goffman, sometimes with others in the extended group as well (especially Grimshaw and Labov), often at conferences, as evident in their correspondence.

Henry H. Glassie earned a PhD from Penn in folklore in 1969, initially taking a position at Indiana, but returning to folklore at Penn as a faculty member in 1976, with a secondary appointment in American civilization.[65] He knew Szwed well—among other things, they co-edited a book, Glassie, Ives and Szwed (1970)—which is likely how he met Goffman. Glassie and Goffman created a business card (email from Yves Winkin, Mar 20, 2022), although so far as I know, they never actually established the antiques business it represented, only enjoyed going antiquing together, including a trip to England in the summer of 1982 (Grimshaw 1983, 148). Glassie mentions that trip as part of his description of how amazing it was to join the ongoing interdisciplinary conversations at Penn:

> I was thrown in among this amazingly exhilarated [*sic*] group of people who were advancing, especially in terms of a sort of anthropology of communication. So then I'm not just reading Dell Hymes, which I'd done; I'm Dell Hymes's friend. I'm not just reading Erving Goffman; I'm Erving Goffman's friend, and Erving and I became ultimately very, very close. He's, I simply loved Erving Goffman, and we, next to my father and Hugh Nolan, I mean he's up in there in the same, some kind of sainthood in my life. When he died it was just horrible for me. I was so fond of Erving. Me and my wife and he and his wife traveled through England. We shared a very great enthusiasm for English furniture. It seems to be off the deep but not. And Erving was just, I'd read his books forever before I met him." (116, HG)

In later comments, describing Goldstein, Abrahams, Hymes, and Goffman, he explained: "I feel emotional about all of those gentlemen. But not only that, all of them great theorists" (117, HG). In addition to being one of the few who traveled with Goffman, Glassie was the second person who filled Goffman's role as co-editor of the Conduct and Communication book series, and was part of one minor project, the Center for the Study of Art and Symbolic Behavior.

Communications

Steven Feld, who earned his PhD at Indiana in 1979 in anthropology, linguistics, and ethnomusicology, took a position at ASC in 1980.[66] He played an essential role in the Multiple Analysis Project on the team filming and recording the event the group analyzed, and facilitated the conference where results were presented. In addition, he published a book in the Conduct and Communication series (1982), published in the journal *Studies in the Anthropology of Visual Communication* (Feld and Williams 1975) and later served on its editorial board, and was a member of one minor project, the Interdisciplinary Program in Language, Culture, and Society. Hymes considered him as one possible replacement for Goffman as a co-editor of the Conduct and Communication series. In addition, he served on the Faculty Grievance Commission with Anderson,[67] thus demonstrating overlaps with others in the larger network.

Larry Gross earned his PhD in social psychology at Columbia in 1968 and immediately started teaching communication at ASC. He was promoted to professor in 1983.[68] Gross was part of two major projects, and one minor. After Worth's unexpected death in 1977, Gross and Jay Ruby (employed at Temple University, and so not described here), took over as editors of *Studies in the Anthropology of Visual Communication* through 1979. In addition, Gross became involved with the Conduct and Communication series by organizing Worth's papers into a book (1981); after Goffman died, Hymes thought of Gross as a possible replacement for him as editor. Gross was also one of the organizers of a minor project, the Interdisciplinary Program in Language, Culture, and Society. Obviously, everyone thought of Gross as particularly competent, which may explain why he ended up first as deputy dean at Annenberg at Penn, and then director of (the other) Annenberg at the University of Southern California.[69]

Percy H. Tannenbaum received his PhD in psychology from the University of Illinois in 1953; he taught at ASC and was named graduate group chair as of spring 1968 when the PhD in communications was first approved.[70] He participated in one major project, the Codes in Context conference (mostly as a courtesy because he approved hosting it at ASC), and was one of those Hymes suggested might help in bringing Labov to Penn, by offering a possible joint appointment.

Paul Messaris was born in South Africa; he earned his PhD in 1975 at ASC, studying under Gross and Worth. He initially took a position at Queens College, but after Worth died, Messaris was invited to teach visual communication courses in his place; he began as assistant professor in 1978,[71] being promoted to professor in 1997.[72] He also helped to create the digital media design major. **Amos Vogel** was born in Austria and earned a BA in economics and political science at the New School for Social Research in 1949. He had an entire career in film before joining Penn in 1973 as Director of Film at the Annenberg Center, and in 1976 became professor of communications.[73] Messaris and Vogel were both part of one minor project, the Center for the Study of Art and Symbolic Behavior.

Education

Brian Sutton-Smith earned a PhD in educational psychology at the University of New Zealand in 1954; he began teaching in education at Penn in 1977, with secondary appointments in folklore[74] and communications.[75] He came strongly recommended by Labov, who knew him from Columbia.[76] Kirshenblatt-Gimblett also apparently expressed interest in having Sutton-Smith at Penn, presumably the reason he was given a secondary appointment in folklore; their research on children's play overlapped significantly.[77] Two of Sutton-Smith's books were published in the Conduct and Communication series in 1981, so he had a role in one of the major projects; he was also a member of the Center for the Study of Art and Symbolic Behavior, one of the minor projects.

Leila Gleitman, who earned a PhD in linguistics in 1967 at Penn, worked first at the Eastern Pennsylvania Psychiatric Institute (1965–1968), where Birdwhistell also worked; once at Penn, she held joint appointments in education, linguistics, and psychology, beginning in 1972 as the William T. Carter Professor at GSE.[78] In that role, she was the first woman at Penn to ever be appointed to a named chair,[79] and served on the search committee for GSE Dean that offered Hymes the position.[80] Apparently, in 1974 she considered leaving Penn; Hymes told Labov he hoped a conversation had helped convince her to stay at Penn because he felt "she would be a great loss."[81] Gleitman played a role in three of the minor projects (the Language and Interaction Institute, Cross-Cultural Communication Center, and Interdisciplinary Program in the Science of Symbolic Behavior) and thus was far more involved than most of the other peripheral group members.

Morton Botel earned a PhD in education at Penn in 1953 and worked in the local school district while teaching part-time at Penn; in 1966, he began a full-time position in what was renamed the Reading and Language Arts Program. By 1980, he was named the William T. Carter Research Chair as Professor of Education and Child Development and started the Penn Literacy Network.[82] With Gleitman, he served on the search committee for GSE Dean that offered Hymes that position.[83] He was part of two minor projects, the Language and Interaction Institute, and the Center for the Study of Art and Symbolic Behavior.

David M. Smith earned a PhD in anthropology from Michigan State University in 1969 and began his career in education at Penn in 1976. He saw linguistics, anthropology, and education as "necessarily intertwined" (Gilmore and McDermott 2006, 199). He directed the second iteration of the Center for Urban Ethnography after it had moved to education (from 1980 to 1985, according to Hornberger 2011), was part of the first Hymes grant from NIE, and was PI for a related grant after those of Hymes (1982). In addition, he was a member of a minor project, the Interdisciplinary Program in Language, Culture, and Society.

Frederick Erickson earned a PhD in the anthropology of education at Northwestern University in 1969; he began a position in education at Penn in 1986,[84] where he also took a turn directing that iteration of CUE (1986–1999), obviously after Goffman's years at Penn. Erickson was at Harvard before Penn, again long after Goffman's time there. However, Erickson also participated in the center's early conference in 1969 and was part of the Multiple Analysis Project. He published a chapter in a book Sanday edited (1976), thus demonstrating his own connections across departmental lines (Wallace, Goodenough, and Gumperz all published chapters in the same book, showing Sanday's own links to others). Goffman had at least one of Erickson's unpublished manuscripts in his files, so they talked about research together.[85] Erickson cites Goffman in many of his publications (at least as early as Erickson and Schultz 1977), and in a review of one of Erickson's books (2004; jointly with another book), Smardon suggests, "The ghost of Goffman lurks behind both of these books" (2005, 20).

Nancy Hornberger received a PhD in education policy studies, with a minor in linguistics, from the University of Wisconsin-Madison in 1985, and immediately joined the education faculty at Penn, later becoming both the Goldie Anna Trustee Term Associate Professor of Education, and acting dean of GSE.[86] Like Smith and Erickson, she served as director of the second iteration of CUE, in her case from 2000 to 2015. She held a secondary appointment in anthropology and served as editor of the *Anthropology and Education Quarterly*.[87] (Hymes was quite active in, and served as president of, the sponsoring organization, the Council on Anthropology and Education (CAE), 1977–1978 [Hornberger 2011].) Despite arriving on campus too late to connect directly with Goffman, she both epitomizes the interdisciplinarity crucial to most of the projects examined here and carried on the CUE legacy.

Michael H. Long earned a PhD in applied linguistics from UCLA with a specialty in second language acquisition. He taught in education at Penn from 1980 to 1982, leaving then for the University of Hawaii.[88] **Nessa Wolfson** earned a PhD in linguistics in 1976 from Penn and began teaching in education at Penn the same year (Hornberger 2001). **Shirley Brice Heath** specialized in anthropology, linguistics, and education while earning her PhD from Columbia in 1970, where she studied with Mead (Heath 2011); she began teaching in education at Penn in 1977, with a secondary appointment in linguistics, leaving in 1980 for Stanford.[89] She briefly participated in Hymes's NIE grant with Sanday and Anderson (Hymes 1981a). **Bambi Schieffelin** earned a PhD at Columbia in anthropology in 1979, held a postdoctoral fellowship at Berkeley for a year, and began teaching in education at Penn in 1980. She was a panelist on "Discourse: Speech Acts and Contextualization" at the American Anthropological Association in 1978, for which Goffman and Hymes served as discussants.[90] All four of these scholars were part of one minor project, the Interdisciplinary Program in Language, Culture, and Society, starting in 1980, but had no other obvious connection to Goffman. Both Wolfson and Heath served a stint on the editorial board of *Language in Society*, but again, after Goffman's term.[91]

Psychology

Rochel Gelman received her PhD in psychology from UCLA in 1967 and began her academic career at Brown University before joining psychology at Penn in 1968.[92] She established an interdisciplinary group around the topic of cognitive science with Gleitman, receiving significant funding from the Sloan Foundation, and then the National Science Foundation.[93] Goffman exchanged at least occasional drafts with her, and she was included in two minor projects: She was part of the group involved with the Language and

Interaction Institute, and co-leader of the proposed Cross-cultural Communication Center (staying with it after the turn to cognitive science).

Leo M. Hurvich earned his graduate degrees from Harvard, in psychology, in the 1930s. He did not arrive at Penn until 1962, having spent time teaching at Harvard and NYU previously,[94] and he began at the rank of professor.[95] His wife, **Dorothea Jameson Hurvich**, initially a research assistant in psychology at Harvard, was without graduate degrees, but had extensive applied experience, having been named "one of the world's foremost theorists of color and vision."[96] Given that Penn had a nepotism rule, once he was hired, she could only be given a position as a research associate in 1962 despite twenty years of research; when the rule was discontinued in 1972, she was immediately moved to the rank of professor.[97] In 1975, she was named University Professor of Psychology and Visual Science.[98] They were both members of the American Academy of Arts and Sciences with Goffman (as were Labov and Hymes),[99] and both were part of a single minor project, the Center for the Study of Art and Symbolic Behavior. In addition, as of 1977, Dorothea Hurvich would have been part of activities with Goffman (as well as Rieff, Steinberg, Meyer, and Goodenough) once Benjamin Franklin University Professors were combined with those who were "merely" University Professors in meetings convened by the provost (then Eliot Stellar) over several years "on matters of academic interest."[100]

David Premack earned a PhD in experimental psychology and philosophy in 1955 at the University of Minnesota; he took a position in psychology at Penn in 1975.[101] **Dan Osherson** earned a PhD at Penn in 1973 and took a position in psychology in 1975; he was "was known for his interdisciplinary research projects."[102] Premack and Osherson were both part of two minor projects, the Language and Interaction Institute and the Cross-Cultural Communication Center; only Premack stayed with the latter after the turn to cognitive science. In addition, Premack was part of one more: the Center for the Study of Art and Symbolic Behavior.

Burton S. Rosner was variously affiliated with psychiatry, psychology, and the School of Medicine at Penn, from 1964 on.[103] He was quite active in faculty committees, including serving on the University Development Commission (with Fox, among others),[104] chairing the Faculty of Arts and Sciences Committee on Graduate Education (with Goldstein, among others),[105] and he chaired the psychology department at least once, which is when he offered a position to Labov.[106] He was a late and peripheral member of three minor projects, the Language and Interaction Institute, the Cross-Cultural Communication Center, and the Center for the Study of Art and Symbolic Behavior. While it is unclear whether he connected with Goffman or not, it seems likely, as they would have had lots to discuss, and he certainly knew many others in these pages. For example, he published jointly with Leonard Meyer in music (e.g., Rosner and Meyer 1982, 1986).

Landscape Architecture

Dan Rose earned a PhD in anthropology from the University of Wisconsin-Madison, in 1973, supported by a grant from the Center for Urban Ethnography.[107] In that capacity, he was invited to attend the center's 1969 and 1971 conferences. Although his book supported by CUE funding was published in the Conduct and Communication series much later (1987), he also had a book published while Goffman was co-editor (1981). Starting in 1974, he took a position in landscape architecture and regional planning at Penn, staying until his retirement in 1998.[108] He was thus a peripheral member in two of the major projects, CUE and Conduct and Communication. In addition, Goffman had some of Rose's unpublished work in his files.

Even once the center had run out of funding, Rose and Szwed obviously maintained connections, because they co-chaired a panel entitled "The Ethnography of the United States: A Meditation" at the American Anthropological Association in 1977. The other panelists were Ben Miller (Columbia), Robert Baron (a doctoral student in folklore at Penn), Theodore Kennedy (State University of New York, Stony Brook), Carol Stack (Duke University), Ray McDermott (Rockefeller University), Shirley Brice Heath (listed as Winston College, but already at Penn), Juliet Flower MacCannell (University of California, Davis), John W. Bennett (Washington University)—and Goffman.[109]

Biology

W. John Smith earned a PhD in biology from Harvard in 1961. He was hired by biology at Penn in 1964,[110] and given secondary appointments in psychology, linguistics, and later the Institute of Neurological Sciences.[111] He was part of three minor projects (the Language and Interaction Institute, the Cross-Cultural Communication Center, and the Interdisciplinary Program in the Science of Symbolic Behavior), and a separate unrelated minor event with Gelman.[112] Most relevant, he was part of the conference that Goffman co-organized on interaction ethology in 1970. Smith published *The Behavior of Communicating: An Ethological Approach* (1977), which not only acknowledged Goffman's help, but discussed his publications repeatedly and at great length, so the link to Goffman is clear. In that book, Smith also discusses the work of many others mentioned in these pages who are known for documenting and analyzing naturally-occurring human interaction: Birdwhistell, Hymes, Labov, Adam Kendon, Gregory Bateson, Albert Scheflen, and Starkey Duncan Jr., among them, so he not only read Goffman's work, but that of relevant others, and he does a particularly nice job of relating animal to human communication. For example:

> In recent years several workers, most notably Goffman, Kendon and Duncan . . . have begun to make detailed analyses of how naturally occurring human interactions are controlled. Goffman particularly is interested in the widest range of interactional behavior and postulates control mechanisms in terms of the sanctioned rights and obligations of participants to maintain "face" and to preserve the flow and structure of encounters. Kendon and Duncan's approaches are more consistently involved with displays, and they do study particular signals in great detail. Their fundamental goal, however, is to understand the rules governing particular kinds of interactions, and they do not attempt to trace single displays through all the diversity of activity in which they occur. (1977, 223)

Goffman had a 1974 draft of that book in his files, so clearly they were exchanging unpublished manuscripts.[113] And one of Smith's articles acknowledges support from CUE (Smith et al. 1974), so he was connected to a major project as well. Interestingly, Gerbner tapped Smith to be a section editor of the *International Encyclopedia of Communications* (Gerbner 1989). Others mentioned in this appendix were also tapped for that project, including Gross as associate editor; Bauman, Feld, Gross, and Kendon as section editors; and Hall and Hymes as editorial advisors. Even when first organized in 1982, that was already past the time Goffman could have contributed, but it is helpful to understand that the collaborations described in detail in this book fostered comparable connections later as well.

English

Barbara Herrnstein Smith earned an MA in 1955 and a PhD in 1964, both in English at Brandeis University, taking a position in English at Penn in 1972,[114] later adding a secondary appointment in communications.[115] She was named University Professor of English and Communications at the same time Goodenough was a University Professor, in 1980,[116] so, like Hurvich and Goodenough, she would have seen Goffman at meetings integrating University Professors with Benjamin Franklin Professors. And in 1982 she was appointed to the Presidential Advisory Council to the University Press, along with Wallace (and others), meaning that she would help to supervise all of the series the press published (including Conduct and Communication).[117] Also, she and Goffman were awarded Guggenheim fellowships the same year, in 1977.[118] She directed one of the minor projects, the Center for the Study of Art and Symbolic Behavior.

Houston Baker Jr. received his PhD in 1968 from UCLA; he taught at Yale and then the University of Virginia, and then joined Penn in 1974 as acting director of the Afro-American studies program.[119] He was quickly appointed professor of English, and director of the Afro-American studies program, and then Faculty Assistant to the President and the Provost in 1976.[120] He was involved in one minor project, the Center for the Study of Art and Symbolic Behavior.

Romance Languages

Gerald Prince joined Penn's Romance languages department in 1967 while still ABD at Brown University; he was awarded the PhD the next year. He was promoted to associate professor in 1973, professor in 1981, and became Lois and Jerry Magnin Family Term Professor in 1993. He was a member of the graduate groups in comparative literature, folklore, and linguistics, and associate faculty at ASC. He served as chair of general literature, comparative literature, French, and Romance languages (in some cases, several times).[121] His research was on narrative, and so his interests overlapped substantially with those of Ben-Amos, Labov, and Hymes; he gave at least one presentation as part of the Language in Education Colloquium (on metanarrative, in 1980),[122] and another to folklore students.[123] He served on the governing board of the Center for the Study of Art and Symbolic Behavior when it began, and later, when it was renamed the Center for Cultural Studies in 1986, was co-convener.

Jean Alter was born in Poland and received his PhD at Chicago. He taught French at several different universities before becoming chair of Romance languages at Penn.[124] Like others described here, he was active on campus in multiple efforts, including presenting at the 1985 conference Ways of Knowing: Comparing World Views and Methodologies, sponsored by the liberal studies graduate group. His presentation was on knowing the future and began with semiotics; one of the other participants was Renée Fox, who talked about matters of life and death.[125] **Lucienne Frappier-Mazur,** born in France, began teaching at Penn in 1962 as assistant professor of French, and was promoted to professor in 1979. She was a member of the graduate group in comparative literature and literary theory, and associate director of the French Institute.[126] She also served on the editorial board at Penn Press and may have had contact with Goffman in that capacity. **Michèle H. Richman** began at Penn as assistant professor of French in 1974.[127] She also joined the comparative literature and literary theory program.[128] Alter, Frappier-Mazur, and Richman were all part of one minor project, the Center for the Study of Art and Symbolic Behavior.

Slavic Languages

Gary Saul Morson earned a PhD at Yale in Russian studies in 1974, immediately joining Penn as assistant professor of Slavic languages, with a specialty in Russian literature. He also was part of the comparative literature program.[129] **Peter Steiner** was hired as assistant professor of Slavic languages and literature in 1979.[130] He gave a colloquium at ASC on "Dual Asymmetry of Cultural Signs" in 1980.[131] Both Morson and Steiner were part of the Center for the Study of Art and Symbolic Behavior.

History of Art

Leo Steinberg, born in Russia, earned a PhD in art history from New York University in 1961, then taught at Hunter College. He joined Penn as Benjamin Franklin Professor of the History of Art in 1975.[132] He overlapped with Goffman and Rieff, as well as Leonard Meyer, in that role, and so would have met with them periodically. **Irene Winter** received her PhD in art history from Columbia; she joined Penn's history of art program in 1976.[133] In 1983, she won a MacArthur prize, the first one for Penn. (Steinberg also won a MacArthur, in 1986.)[134] Both Steinberg and Winter were part of the Center for the Study of Art and Symbolic Behavior.

Music

Leonard B. Meyer studied music and philosophy, earning an MA in music composition at Columbia, and then, while teaching music at Chicago, earned a PhD from the Committee on the History of Culture there in 1956. He continued teaching at Chicago until moving to Penn in 1975 as Benjamin Franklin Professor of Music and the Humanities,[135] so he overlapped in that distinguished group with Goffman, Rieff, and Steinberg. In addition, he served on the governing board of the Center for the Study of Art and Symbolic Behavior.

American Civilization

Janice Radway earned a PhD in English and American studies at Michigan State University in 1977,[136] and began teaching at Penn as assistant professor, being promoted to associate professor in 1984.[137] After leaving Penn in 1988, she taught at Duke, then in communication at Northwestern, thus demonstrating her own ability to move between disciplines.[138] She was part of the Center for the Study of Art and Symbolic Behavior.

Electrical Engineering

Aravind Joshi earned a PhD in engineering from Penn in 1960 and joined the faculty in 1961; he was granted a secondary appointment in linguistics in 1964.[139] (While a graduate student he had worked with Harris and Hiz in linguistics on natural language parsing—the research project that helped to move Hiz into that department full-time.[140]) Joshi also worked with Kroch on formal grammar,[141] and was one of those drawn into the group organized by Gleitman, combining psychology, linguistics, and computer science into the new area of cognitive science.[142] He was part of three minor projects: the Language and Interaction Institute, the Cross-Cultural Communication Center, and the Center for the Study of Art and Symbolic Behavior.

Oriental Studies

Ahmet Evin earned a PhD at Columbia, then taught at NYU, Harvard, and Hacettepe University (in Turkey), before joining Penn as assistant professor of Turkish language and literature in 1977.[143] **Peter Gaeffke** earned a

PhD at the University of Mainz in Germany, worked there as well as India and the Netherlands before joining Penn as visiting professor in 1972. In 1974 he was made professor of modern Indian literature, as part of what was called South Asia regional studies then, and Oriental studies later.[144] **William L. Hanaway Jr.** earned a PhD from Columbia and began teaching Persian language and literature at Penn in 1971. He not only served as chair of Oriental studies in the 1980s but as associate director of the Near East Center in the 1970s.[145] **Barbara Ruch** was hired as assistant professor of Japanese language and literature[146] in the early 1960s and promoted to associate professor in 1969.[147] She founded the Institute for Medieval Japanese Studies in 1970, serving as director.[148] All four were part of the Center for the Study of Art and Symbolic Behavior.

Endnotes

[1] https://almanac.upenn.edu/archive/v08pdf/n02/100161.pdf.

[2] https://findingaids.library.upenn.edu/records/UPENN_MUSEUM_PU-MU.1070.2003.12.

[3] https://almanac.upenn.edu/archive/v27pdf/n01/071080.pdf.

[4] Hymes to Goodenough, Sep 12, 1980, DHH, Subcollection 1, Series II: Conferences and Committees, 1955–1987, Subseries E: Other Committees, Interdisciplinary Committee for a Program in Language, Culture and Society.

[5] http://dla.library.upenn.edu/dla/ead/ead.html?id=EAD_upenn_museum_PUMu1133200520.

[6] https://www.ias.edu/scholars/j-david-sapir.

[7] Hymes to Sapir, Feb 14, 1966, DHH, Subcollection 1, Series I: Correspondence 1951–1987, Sapir, J. David, 1958–1987.

[8] https://web.sas.upenn.edu/psanday/books/cv/.

[9] Worth to Gregorian and Gerbner, Apr 9, 1975, DHH, Subcollection 1, Series I: Correspondence 1951–1987, Worth, Sol, 1966–1977.

[10] https://almanac.upenn.edu/archive/v24pdf/n01/071577.pdf.

[11] https://web.sas.upenn.edu/psanday/books/cv/.

[12] https://web.sas.upenn.edu/psanday/books/cv/.

[13] https://almanac.upenn.edu/archive/v24pdf/n01/071577.pdf; https://www.lai.fu-berlin.de/en/temporalities-of-future/4-members/mercator-fellows/appadurai/index.html.

[14] https://www.lai.fu-berlin.de/en/temporalities-of-future/4-members/mercator-fellows/appadurai/index.html; https://almanac.upenn.edu/archive/v25pdf/n05/092678.pdf.

[15] https://almanac.upenn.edu/archive/v24pdf/n32/052378-insert.pdf.

[16] https://almanac.upenn.edu/archive/v25pdf/n11/110778.pdf.

[17] Arjun Appadurai to Anthropology 5-Year Plan Committee, Nov 30, 1982, DHH, Subcol-

lection 1, Series II: Conferences and Committees, 1955–1987, Subseries E: Other Committees, Interdisciplinary Committee for a Program in Language, Culture and Society.

[18] https://almanac.upenn.edu/archive/v08pdf/n02/100161.pdf.

[19] https://almanac.upenn.edu/archive/v14pdf/n06/031668.pdf.

[20] Rieff to Hymes, Sep 27, 1971, DHH, Subcollection 1, Series I: Correspondence 1951–1987, Rieff, Philip, 1967–1972.

[21] Rieff to Hymes, Sep 30, 1971, DHH, Subcollection 1, Series I: Correspondence 1951–1987, Rieff, Philip, 1967–1972.

[22] Rieff to Hymes, Mar 26, 1973, DHH, Subcollection 1, Series I: Correspondence 1951–1987, University of Pennsylvania, Department of Sociology.

[23] https://almanac.upenn.edu/archive/v16pdf/n01/091969.pdf.

[24] https://almanac.upenn.edu/archive/v22pdf/n28/040676-insert.pdf.

[25] Worth to Gregorian and Gerbner, Apr 9, 1975, DHH, Subcollection 1, Series I: Correspondence 1951–1987, Worth, Sol, 1966–1977.

[26] "Communications #35: The Annenberg School of Communications, University of Pennsylvania,"

[1978,] DHH, Subcollection 1, Series I: Correspondence, 1951–1987, University of Pennsylvania, Annenberg School of Communication, 1978–1984.

[27] Her actual title when hired was professor of sociology in psychiatry (https://almanac.upenn.edu/archive/v16pdf/n01/091969.pdf), and, like others, she ended up with multiple affiliations. In her case, those extended beyond the departments of sociology and psychiatry to medicine, and, in addition, in 1978 she was named the first Annenberg Professor of Social Sciences (https://almanac.upenn.edu/archive/v24pdf/n16/011778.pdf). She gave at least one colloquium at Annenberg, on "Cultural Themes in Medical Innovation: The Case of Organ Transplants" ("Communications Colloquium—Spring 1978," n.d. [1978], DHH, Subcollection 1, Series I: Correspondence 1951–1987, University of Pennsylvania, Annenberg School of Communication, 1978–1984). She held an additional appointment in nursing, and was a senior fellow at the Center for Bioethics (https://provost.upenn.edu/sites/default/files/users/user747/Renee%20Fox%20Obit.pdf). In 1971, before being made a full-time faculty member, she had served as Faculty Assistant to the President and the Provost at Penn (https://almanac.upenn.edu/archive/v18pdf/n05/092871.pdf). Finally, she served on a campus-wide committee jointly with Szwed, the Committee on Minority Recruitment, in 1973 (https://almanac.upenn.edu/archive/v20pdf/n08/101673.pdf), and with Hymes on the Bicentennial Coordinating Committee, that same year (https://almanac.upenn.edu/archive/v19pdf/n22/020673.pdf).

[28] Fox to Hymes, Dec 11, 1972, DHH, Subcollection 1, Series I: Correspondence 1951–1987, Renée Fox, 1972–1977. Within a few months, Fox was asking what courses Hymes wanted cross-listed in sociology (Fox to Hymes, Feb 7, 1973). His answer was The Ethnography of Speaking, and he said he would be glad to include students from sociology as training in linguistics was not required (Hymes to Fox, Feb 16, 1973, same files). Presumably she asked Goffman the same question.

[29] Fox to department of sociology faculty, Sep 30, 1974, DHH, Subcollection 1, Series I: Correspondence 1951–1987, University of Pennsylvania, Department of Sociology. It may have been Hymes's effort six months earlier to recruit Philips for sociology that gave her the idea (Hymes to Philips, Mar 19, 1974, DHH, Subcollection 1, Series I: Correspondence 1951–1987, Philips, Susan, 1967–1984).

[30] https://almanac.upenn.edu/archive/v24pdf/n19/020778.pdf.

[31] https://almanac.upenn.edu/archive/v25pdf/n10/103178.pdf; https://almanac.upenn.edu/archive/v41pdf/n10/110194-insert.pdf.

[32] https://uep.yale.edu.

[33] https://sociology.yale.edu/sites/default/files/elijah_anderson_cv_1.17.24_0_1_0.pdf.

[34] https://works.bepress.com/teresa_labov/1/.

[35] https://almanac.upenn.edu/archive/v14pdf/n02/111667.pdf.

[36] https://almanac.upenn.edu/archive/v23pdf/n12/111676.pdf.

[37] https://almanac.upenn.edu/archive/v24pdf/n01/071577.pdf.

[38] Hymes and Fought to Leigh Lisker, May 20, 1975, DHH, Subcollection 1, Series I: Correspondence 1951–1987, Lisker, Leigh, 1974–1980.

[39] Labov to Leigh Lisker, Feb 29, 1962, DHH, Subcollection 1, Series I: Correspondence 1951–1987, Labov, William, folder 1, 1963–1972. Lisker was chair of linguistics at that point (https://www.ling.upenn.edu/people/in-memoriam).

[40] https://www.ling.upenn.edu/people/sankoff.

[41] Elisabeth Case at Cambridge University Press to Hymes, May 26, 1972, DHH, Subcollection 1, Series V: Language in Society, Subseries A: Early Correspondence, Cambridge University Press.

[42] https://almanac.upenn.edu/archive/v26pdf/n12/110179.pdf.

[43] https://almanac.upenn.edu/archive/v34pdf/n21/020988-insert.pdf.

[44] Labov to Gregorian, Jan 31, 1977, DHH, Subcollection 1, Series I: Correspondence, 1951–1987, Labov, William.

[45] https://almanac.upenn.edu/archive/volumes/v53/n17/obit.html.

[46] https://almanac.upenn.edu/archive/volumes/v53/n17/obit.html.

[47] https://almanac.upenn.edu/archive/volumes/v57/n10/obit.html.

[48] https://almanac.upenn.edu/archive/v43pdf/032597.pdf.

[49] https://www.lsadc.org/content.asp?contentid=161.

[50] https://almanac.upenn.edu/articles/anthony-kroch-linguistics.

[51] Worth to Gregorian and Gerbner, Apr 9, 1975, DHH, Subcollection 1, Series I: Correspondence 1951–1987, Worth, Sol, 1966–1977.

[52] https://almanac.upenn.edu/archive/v14pdf/n01/101667.pdf.

[53] https://almanac.upenn.edu/archive/v46/n16/Apps-Promos2K.html.

[54] https://nelc.sas.upenn.edu/people/dan-ben-amos.

[55] https://almanac.upenn.edu/archive/v24pdf/n32/052378-insert.pdf.

[56] "Communications #35: The Annenberg School of Communications, University of Pennsylvania," 1978, DHH, Subcollection 1, Series I: Correspondence, 1951–1987, University of Pennsylvania, Annenberg School of Communication, 1978–1984.

[57] https://almanac.upenn.edu/archive/v26pdf/n26/030680.pdf.

[58] https://jwa.org/encyclopedia/article/kirshenblatt-gimblett-barbara.

[59] https://archives.upenn.edu/media/2017/10/19730914fac.pdf.

[60] News release, Jun 22, 1973, OP.

61 https://www.english.upenn.edu/people/roger-david-abrahams.

62 The graduate group in folklore was established in 1962 (https://almanac.upenn.edu/archive/v09pdf/n02/100162.pdf), and much (positive) press resulted, although in fact the department was not formally established at that point and, as the provost felt the need to explain, only "a graduate group is permitted to direct students for a doctor's degree, but this is not a University department, nor does it have a chairman, nor does it have a budget" (David R. Goddard, Provost, to Chester E. Tucker, Vice President for Development and Public Relations, Mar 4, 1963, UPF 8.5, News Bureau, Folklore and Folklife, 1962–1985, UR).

63 https://search.amphilsoc.org/collections/view?docId=ead/Mss.Ms.Coll.189-ead.xml.

64 https://search.amphilsoc.org/collections/view?docId=ead/Mss.Ms.Coll.189-ead.xml.

65 https://almanac.upenn.edu/archive/v24pdf/n19/020778.pdf.

66 https://static1.squarespace.com/static/545aad98e4b0f1f9150ad5c3/t/5463d237e4b058 51237ddc72/1516249433057/Steven+Feld+CV.pdf.

67 https://almanac.upenn.edu/archive/v29pdf/n08/101982-insert2.pdf.

68 https://almanac.upenn.edu/archive/v30pdf/n07/101183.pdf.

69 https://annenberg.usc.edu/faculty/larry-p-gross.

70 https://almanac.upenn.edu/archive/v14pdf/n05/021668.pdf.

71 https://almanac.upenn.edu/volume-65-number-18#paul-messaris-annenberg-school.

72 https://almanac.upenn.edu/archive/v44/n20/facultyplus.html.

73 https://almanac.upenn.edu/archive/volumes/v58/n32/pdf_n32/050112.pdf.

74 https://almanac.upenn.edu/articles/brian-sutton-smith-graduate-school-of-education.

75 "Communications #35: The Annenberg School of Communications, University of Pennsylvania," 1978, DHH, Subcollection 1, Series I: Correspondence, 1951–1987, University of Pennsylvania, Annenberg School of Communication, 1978–1984.

76 Labov to Hymes, Dec 17, 1976, DHH, Subcollection 1, Series I: Correspondence 1951–1987, Labov, William, folder 2, 1974–1987.

77 Hymes to Labov, Nov 15, 1976, DHH, Subcollection 1, Series I: Correspondence 1951–1987, Labov, William, folder 2, 1974–1987.

78 https://www.sas.upenn.edu/~gleitman/papers/Lila%20Gleitman's%20Vitae.pdf.

79 https://almanac.upenn.edu/archive/v22pdf/n28/040676-insert.pdf.

80 https://almanac.upenn.edu/archive/v20pdf/n30/041674.pdf.

81 Hymes to Labov, May 15, 1974, DHH, Subcollection 1, Series I: Correspondence, 1951–1987, Labov, William.

82 https://almanac.upenn.edu/articles/morton-botel-gse.

83 https://almanac.upenn.edu/archive/v20pdf/n30/041674.pdf.

84 https://almanac.upenn.edu/archive/v33pdf/n01/071586.pdf.

85 It is included in Winkin's list of Goffman's files from 1998.

86 https://almanac.upenn.edu/archive/v39pdf/n35/052593.pdf.

87 https://www.gse.upenn.edu/academics/faculty-directory/hornberger/.

88 https://arboretum.umd.edu/long-michael-h; https://almanac.upenn.edu/archive/v27pdf/n25/031081.pdf.

[89] https://shirleybriceheath.net/page.php/34.

[90] https://openanthroresearch.org/index.php/oarr/preprint/view/40/74.

[91] At one point, Hymes asked Wolfson to combine her roles as a faculty member in education and an editorial board member for *Language in Society*; he was having problems getting scholars to write book reviews for most of the books sent to the journal, and it had occurred to him that it would be appropriate to ask graduate students in education to write some reviews. They would get free copies of relevant books, and it would create a stronger connection between the journal and its nominal home at GSE (Hymes to Wolfson, Jun 21, 1983, DHH, Subcollection 1, Series V: Language in Society, 1968–1992, Subseries A: Early Correspondence, Editorial Board).

[92] https://fabbs.org/about/in-honor-of/rochel-gelman-phd/.

[93] https://www.psych.upenn.edu/history/history.htm.

[94] https://almanac.upenn.edu/archive/volumes/v55/n32/obit.html.

[95] https://almanac.upenn.edu/archive/v08pdf/n04/120161.pdf.

[96] https://www.psych.upenn.edu/history/jameson.html.

[97] https://almanac.upenn.edu/archive/v44/n30/deaths.html.

[98] https://almanac.upenn.edu/archive/v21pdf/n36/062575.pdf.

[99] https://almanac.upenn.edu/archive/v22pdf/n34/051876.pdf; Goffman was made a member of AAAS in 1969 (https://www.amacad.org/person/erving-manual-goffman).

[100] https://almanac.upenn.edu/archive/v24pdf/n01/071577.pdf.

[101] https://www.sas.upenn.edu/~premack/About.html.

[102] https://www.princeton.edu/news/2022/09/16/legendary-cognitive-scientist-daniel-osherson-scientist-rare-talent-and-excellent.

[103] https://almanac.upenn.edu/archive/v19pdf/n19/012373.pdf; https://almanac.upenn.edu/archive/v36pdf/n11/103189.pdf.

[104] https://almanac.upenn.edu/archive/v19pdf/n20/012373.pdf.

[105] https://almanac.upenn.edu/archive/v22pdf/n09/102175.pdf.

[106] https://almanac.upenn.edu/archive/v19pdf/n20/012373.pdf.

[107] https://danrosespace.wordpress.com/about/.

[108] https://almanac.upenn.edu/archive/volumes/v63/n05/arbitrary-pleasures.html.

[109] https://openanthroresearch.org/index.php/oarr/preprint/view/39/72. Awkwardly, across the same time slot, on the same day, was scheduled a roundtable for the CAE, organized by Hymes, which included Abrahams, Bauman, and Erickson, as well as yet another panel, "Speech Events: Toward a Comparative Framework in the Ethnography of Speaking," organized by Judith Irvine, including Susan Philips and several others, with Michael Silverstein and Hymes as discussants.

[110] https://archives.upenn.edu/collections/finding-aid/upf8_5/.

[111] UPF 8.5B: University Relations, News and Public Affairs Records, Biographical Files, Labov, William, box 149, folder 29, UR.

[112] In 1972 there was an event called "Post Graduate '72," billed as "a one-day seminar program sponsored . . . by the College for Women Alumnae Society for CW alumnae and interested members of the University community," which involved Smith and Gelman holding "a dialogue on 'Communications in Young Children'" (https://almanac.upenn.edu/archive/v19pdf/n08/101772.pdf).

[113] It is included in Winkin's list of Goffman's files from 1998.

[114] https://www.ias.edu/scholars/barbara-herrnstein-smith.

[115] https://almanac.upenn.edu/archive/v23pdf/n29/041977.pdf.

[116] https://almanac.upenn.edu/archive/v27pdf/n01/071080.pdf.

[117] https://almanac.upenn.edu/archive/v28pdf/n30/050482.pdf.

[118] https://almanac.upenn.edu/archive/v23pdf/n29/041977.pdf.

[119] https://almanac.upenn.edu/archive/v21pdf/n03/091074.pdf.

[120] https://almanac.upenn.edu/archive/v23pdf/n07/101276.pdf.

[121] https://french.sas.upenn.edu/sites/default/files/2019%20cv%20prince.pdf.

[122] https://almanac.upenn.edu/archive/v26pdf/n21/013180.pdf.

[123] This would have been between 1975 and 1978; I know because I attended. It may have been presented as a guest lecture in a course by Ben-Amos.

[124] https://www.legacy.com/us/obituaries/dailycamera/name/jean-alter-obituary?id=46853117.

[125] https://almanac.upenn.edu/archive/v31pdf/n31/042385-insert.pdf.

[126] https://www.encyclopedia.com/arts/culture-magazines/frappier-mazur-lucienne.

[127] https://almanac.upenn.edu/archive/v46/n16/benchmarks.html.

[128] https://complit.sas.upenn.edu/people/michele-richman.

[129] https://rprt.northwestern.edu/images/morson-cv.pdf.

[130] https://almanac.upenn.edu/archive/v25pdf/n18/012379.pdf.

[131] https://almanac.upenn.edu/archive/v26pdf/n32/042480.pdf.

[132] https://almanac.upenn.edu/archive/v21pdf/n30/042275.pdf; https://almanac.upenn.edu/archive/volumes/v57/n26/obit.html.

[133] https://haa.fas.harvard.edu/people/irene-j-winter.

[134] https://almanac.upenn.edu/archive/v35pdf/n02/083088.pdf.

[135] https://almanac.upenn.edu/archive/volumes/v54/n17/obit.html.

[136] https://scholars.duke.edu/person/jradway.

[137] https://almanac.upenn.edu/archive/v30pdf/n23/022184.pdf.

[138] https://communication.northwestern.edu/faculty/janice-radway.html.

[139] http://button.provost.upenn.edu/sites/default/files/users/user747/Aravind%20Joshi%20Obit.pdf.

[140] https://archives.upenn.edu/exhibits/penn-history/after-eniac/part-7/.

[141] https://www.ling.upenn.edu/index.php/people/in-memoriam.

[142] https://archives.upenn.edu/exhibits/penn-history/after-eniac/part-7/.

[143] https://almanac.upenn.edu/archive/v24pdf/n01/071577.pdf.

[144] https://almanac.upenn.edu/archive/v21pdf/n01/071974.pdf.

[145] https://almanac.upenn.edu/articles/william-hanaway-asian-and-middle-eastern-studies.

[146] https://almanac.upenn.edu/archive/v14pdf/n07/041668.pdf.

[147] https://almanac.upenn.edu/archive/v16pdf/n01/091969.pdf.

[148] https://almanac.upenn.edu/archive/v16pdf/n10/080770.pdf; https://almanac.upenn.edu/archive/v25pdf/n05/092678-insert.pdf.

References

Abbott, Andrew. 2010. *Chaos of Disciplines*. University of Chicago Press.

Abrahams, Roger D. 1974. "Black Talking on the Streets." In *Explorations in the Ethnography of Speaking*, edited by Richard Bauman and Joel Sherzer. Cambridge University Press.

Abrahams, Roger D. 1984. "Goffman Reconsidered: Pros and Players." *Raritan* 3 (4): 76–94.

Abrahams, Roger D., and Barbara A. Babcock. 1977. "The Literary Use of Proverbs." *Journal of American Folklore* 90 (358): 414–29.

Abrahams, Roger D., and John F. Szwed, eds. 1975. *Discovering Afro-America*. E. J. Brill.

Anthropology News. 1970. "Fellowships Offered in Urban Ethnography." March.

Appadurai, Arjun. 2016. "The Academic Digital Divide and Uneven Global Development." *CARGC [Center for Advanced Research in Global Communication] Papers*, no. 4. https://repository.upenn.edu/cargc_papers/4.

Archibald, Kathleen A., ed. 1966. *Strategic Interaction and Conflict: Original Papers and Discussion*. Institute of International Studies, University of California, Berkeley.

Archibald, Kathleen A. 1968. "The Utilization of Social Research and Policy Analysis." PhD diss., Washington University.

Basso, Ellen B. 1985. *A Musical View of the Universe: Kalapalo Myth and Ritual Performances*. University of Pennsylvania Press.

Bateson, Gregory, and Margaret Mead. 1942. *Balinese Character: A Photographic Analysis*. New York Academy of Sciences.

Baugh, John. 1983. *Black Street Speech: Its History, Structure, and Survival*. University of Texas Press.

Baugh, John, and Joel Sherzer, eds. 1984. *Language in Use: Readings in Sociolinguistics.* Prentice-Hall.

Bauman, Richard. 1975. "Verbal Art as Performance." *American Anthropologist* 77 (2): 290–311.

Bauman, Richard, and Charles L. Briggs. 1990. "Poetics and Performance as Critical Perspectives on Language and Social Life." *Annual Reviews in Anthropology* 19:59–88.

Bauman, Richard, and Joel Sherzer, eds. 1974. *Explorations in the Ethnography of Speaking.* Cambridge University Press.

Bauman, Richard, and Joel Sherzer. 1975. "The Ethnography of Speaking." *Annual Reviews of Anthropology* 5:95–119.

Bazerman, Charles. 2005. "Practically Human: The Pragmatist Project of the Interdisciplinary Journal *Psychiatry.*" *Linguistics & the Human Sciences* 1 (1): 15–38.

Becker, Howard S. 2003. "The Politics of Presentation: Goffman and Total Institutions." *Symbolic Interaction* 26 (4): 659–69.

Becker, Howard S., Blanche Geer, David Reisman, and Robert Weiss, eds. 1968. *Institutions and the Person: Festschrift in Honor of Everett C. Hughes.* Transaction Publishers.

Beeman, William O. 1986. *Language, Status, and Power in Iran.* Indiana University Press.

Belknap, Ivan. 1958. Review of *The Patient and the Mental Hospital*, by Milton Greenblatt, Daniel J. Levinson, and Richard Williams. *Administrative Science Quarterly* 3 (1): 129–34.

Bell, Michael J. 1975. "Running Rabbits and Talking Shit: Folkloric Communication in an Urban Black Bar." PhD diss., University of Pennsylvania.

Bell, Michael J. 1979. "Social Control/Social Order/Social Art." *SubStance 8 (1): 49–65.*

Bell, Michael J. 1982. *The World from Brown's Lounge: An Ethnography of Black Middle-Class Play.* University of Illinois Press.

Ben-Amos, Dan. 1996. "Obituary: Kenneth S. Goldstein (1927–1995)." *Journal of American Folklore* 109 (433): 320–23.

Bennett, Adrian T. 1982. "Melodies Bristling with Change: Prosody and Understanding Conversation." *Sociological Methods & Research* 11 (2): 195–212.

Berger, Mitchell. 1973. "Lobbyist Tells of Bad TV Effects on Children." *Daily Pennsylvanian*, October 23. https://dparchives.library.upenn.edu/.

Bergmann, Jörg R., and Anssi Peräkylä. 2022. "Goffmans Schüler/innen." In *Goffman Handbuch: Leben—Werk—Wirkung*, edited by Karl Lenz and Robert Hettlage. J. B. Metzler.

Bershady, Harold. 2009. "Erving Turned to Me and Said, 'You Know, Elijah Anderson is Really a Professional Sociologist, He is Not a Professional Black.'" In *Bios Sociologicus: The Erving Goffman Archives*, edited by Dmitri N. Shalin. University of Nevada Las Vegas, CDC Publications. https://digitalscholarship.unlv.edu/goffman_archives/45.

Biddle, Steve. 1973. "U. May Host Center for Children's Media." *Daily Pennsylvanian*, April 26. https://dparchives.library.upenn.edu/.

Birdwhistell, Ray L. 1952. *Introduction to Kinesics*. Foreign Service Institute, US Department of State.

Birdwhistell, Ray L. 1970. *Kinesics and Context: Essays in Body Motion Communication*. University of Pennsylvania Press.

Birdwhistell, Ray L. 1972. "A Kinesic-Linguistic Exercise: The Cigarette Scene." In *Directions in Sociolinguistics: The Ethnography of Communication*, edited by John J. Gumperz and Dell H. Hymes. Holt, Rinehart & Winston.

Birdwhistell, Ray L. 1978. Review of *Nonverbal Communication*, by Mary Ritchie Key. *Studies in the Anthropology of Visual Communication* 5 (1): 70. https://repository.upenn.edu/handle/20.500.14332/48315.

Birdwhistell, Ray L. 1980. "In Memoriam: Margaret Mead (1901–1978)." *Studies in Visual Communication* 6 (1): 3. https://repository.upenn.edu/handle/20.500.14332/48346.

Blom, Jan-Petter, and John J. Gumperz. 1972. "Social Meaning in Linguistic Structure: Code-Switching in Norway." In *Directions in Sociolinguistics: The Ethnography of Communication*, edited by John J. Gumperz and Dell H. Hymes. Holt, Rinehart & Winston.

Blumer, Herbert. 1969. *Symbolic Interactionism: Perspective and Method*. Prentice-Hall.

Blumer, Herbert. 1972. "Action Versus Interaction: A Review of *Relations in Public*." *Society* 9 (April): 50–53.

Bott-Spillius, Elizabeth. 2010. "Erving Goffman in Toronto, Chicago and London." In *Bios Sociologicus: The Erving Goffman Archives*, edited by Dmitri N. Shalin. University of Nevada Las Vegas, CDC Publications. https://digitalscholarship. unlv.edu/goffman_archives/8.

Bourdieu, Pierre. 1977. *Outline of a Theory of Practice*. Cambridge University Press.

Braga, Adriana. 2011. "Ethnomethodology and Communication: An Interview with Rod Watson." *E-Compós* 14 (2). https://doi.org/10.30962/ec.710.

Briggs, Charles L. 1988. *Competence in Performance: The Creativity of Tradition in Mexicano Verbal Art*. University of Pennsylvania Press.

Bucholtz, Mary, and Kira Hall. 2008. "All of the Above: New Coalitions in Sociocultural Linguistics." *Journal of Sociolinguistics* 12 (4): 401–31.

Burns, Tom. 1992. *Erving Goffman*. Routledge.

Camic, Charles. 1995. "Three Departments in Search of a Discipline: Localism and Interdisciplinary Interaction in American Sociology, 1890–1940." *Social Research* 62 (4): 1003–33.

Cary, Mark S. 1982. "Data Collection: Film and Videotape." *Sociological Methods & Research* 11 (2): 167–74.

Cavan, Sherri. 2013. "When Erving Goffman Was a Boy: The Formative Years of a Sociological Giant." *Symbolic Interaction* 37 (1): 41–70.

Cazden, Courtney B., Vera P. John, and Dell H. Hymes, eds. 1972. *Functions of Language in the Classroom*. Columbia University Press.

Cefaï, Daniel, and Laurent Perreau, eds. 2012. *Erving Goffman et l'ordre de l'interaction*. Éditions du CURAPP.

Center for Urban Ethnography. 1974. "The Center for Urban Ethnography: A Brief Report on NIMH Grant MH 17216 (1969–1974)." Unpublished manuscript.

Center for Urban Ethnography. 1975. "Outline of the Activities of the Center for Urban Ethnography, University of Pennsylvania." Unpublished manuscript.

Center for Urban Ethnography. 1978. "Publications List." Unpublished manuscript.

Chalfen, Richard. 1979. "Sol Worth (1922–1977)." *American Anthropologist* 81 (1): 91–93.

Chapoulie, Jean-Michel. 1996. "Everett Hughes and the Chicago Tradition." *Sociological Theory* 14 (1): 3–29.

Cicourel, Aaron. 2009. "Remembering Erving Goffman." In *Bios Sociologicus: The Erving Goffman Archives,* edited by Dmitri N. Shalin. University of Nevada Las Vegas, CDC Publications. https://cdclv.unlv.edu/archives/interactionism/goffman/cicourel_09.html.

Ciolek, T. Matthew, Rob H. Elzinga, and Alec W. McHoul. 1979. "Selected References to Coenetics." *Sign Language Studies* 22 (1): 2–6.

Cmejrkova, Svetla, and Carlo L. Prevignano. 2003. "On Conversation Analysis: An Interview with Emanuel A. Schegloff." In *Discussing Conversation Analysis: The Work of Emanuel A. Schegloff,* edited by Carlo L. Prevignano and Paul J. Thibault. John Benjamins.

Cohen, Mabel Blake, ed. 1959. "Introduction." In *Advances in Psychiatry: Recent Developments in Interpersonal Relations,* edited by Mabel Blake Cohen. W. W. Norton.

Collins, Randall. 1986. "The Passing of Intellectual Generations: Reflections on the Death of Erving Goffman." *Sociological Theory* 4 (1): 106–13.

Copland, Fiona, and Angela Creese. 2015. *Linguistic Ethnography: Collecting, Analysing and Presenting Data.* Sage.

Corsaro, William A. 1982. "Something Old and Something New: The Importance of Prior Ethnography in the Collection and Analysis of Audiovisual Data." *Sociological Methods & Research* 11 (2): 145–66.

Corsaro, William A. 1992. Review of *He-said-she-said,* by Marjorie Harness Goodwin. *American Journal of Sociology* 97 (4): 1182–84.

Coser, Lewis A. 1965. *Men of Ideas: A Sociologist's View.* Free Press.

Crane, Diana. 1972. *Invisible Colleges: Diffusion of Knowledge in Scientific Communities.* University of Chicago Press.

Cressey, Donald R., ed. 1961. *The Prison: Studies in Institutional Organization and Change.* Holt, Rinehart & Winston.

Daily Pennsylvanian. 1908. "To Confer Honorary Degrees." February 24. https://dparchives.library.upenn.edu/.

Darnell, Regna. 1974. "Correlates of Cree Narrative Performance." In *Explorations in the Ethnography of Speaking*, edited by Richard Bauman and Joel Sherzer. Cambridge University Press.

Darnell, Regna. 1991. "Ethnographic Genre and Poetic Voice." In *Anthropological Poetics*, edited by Ivan A. Brady. Rowman & Littlefield.

Darnell, Regna. 2001a. *Invisible Genealogies: A History of Americanist Anthropology*. University of Nebraska Press.

Darnell, Regna. 2001b. *History of Theory and Method in Anthropology*. University of Nebraska Press.

Darnell, Regna. 2011. "Dell Hathaway Hymes (1927–2009)." *American Anthropologist* 113 (1): 192–95.

Darnell, Regna. 2021. *History of Anthropology: A Critical Window on the Discipline in North America*. University of Nebraska Press.

Darnell, Regna. 2022. "A Critical Paradigm for the Histories of Anthropology: The Generalization of Transportable Knowledge." *Bérose International Encyclopaedia of the Histories of Anthropology*. https://www.berose.fr/article2718.html.

Davis, Martha. 2001. "Film Projectors as Microscopes: Ray L. Birdwhistell and Microanalysis of Interaction (1955–1975)." *Visual Anthropology Review* 17 (2): 39–49.

Deckert, Sharon K., and Caroline H. Vickers. 2011. *An Introduction to Sociolinguistics: Society and Identity*. Continuum.

Deegan, Mary Jo. 2001. "The Chicago School of Ethnography." In *Handbook of Ethnography*, edited by Paul Atkinson, Amanda Coffey, Sara Delamont, John Lofland, and Lyn Lofland. Sage.

Delaney, Michael. 2014. "Goffman at Penn: Star Presence, Teacher-Mentor, Profaning Jester." *Symbolic Interaction* 37 (1): 87–107.

De Sola Price, Derek J. 1963. *Little Science, Big Science*. Columbia University Press.

Ditton, Jason, ed. 1980. *The View from Goffman*. Macmillan.

Dixon, Keith A. 1983. "The Origin and Development of the Southwestern Anthropological Association: The First Thirty-Four Years (1929–1962)." *SWAA Newsletter* 22 (2/3): 1–5. https://swaa-anthro.org/early-history-of-swaa/.

Douad, Patrick C. 1982. "All Mixed: Canadian Metis Sociolinguistic Patterns." *Working Papers in Sociolinguistics*, no. 101. Southwest Educational Development Laboratory.

Douglas, Mary. 1986. "Lita Osmundsen and the Wenner-Gren Foundation: An Appreciation." *Current Anthropology* 27 (5): 521–25.

Drew, Paul, and Anthony Wootton, eds. 1988. *Erving Goffman: Exploring the Interaction Order*. Northeastern University Press.

Duncan, Hugh D. 1960. *Communication and Social Order*. Oxford University Press.

Duncan, Starkey, Jr. 1981. "Conversational Strategies." In *Conference on the Clever Hans Phenomenon: Communication with Horses, Whales, Apes, and People*, edited by Thomas A. Sebeok and Robert Rosenthal. New York Academy of Sciences.

Duncan, Starkey, Jr. 1982. "Quantitative Studies of Interaction Structure and Strategy." *Sociological Methods & Research* 11 (2): 175–94.

Duranti, Alessandro. 2003. "Language as Culture in U.S. Anthropology: Three Paradigms." *Current Anthropology* 44 (3): 323–35.

Eadie, William F. 2022. *When Communication Became a Discipline*. Lexington.

Ehrlich, Susan, and Tommaso M. Milani. 2021. "*Language in Society*—50 years." *Language in Society* 50 (5): 1–5.

Eisen, Arnold M. 2016. "Remembering a Great 'Jew of Culture.'" *Jewish Theological Seminary*, June 29. https://www.jtsa.edu/remembering-a-great-jew-of-culture/.

Elkind, David. 1975. "Encountering Erving Goffman." *Human Behavior* 4 (3): 25–30.

Emmett, Ross B. 2010. "Specializing in Interdisciplinarity: The Committee on Social Thought as the University of Chicago's Antidote to Compartmentalization in the Social Sciences." *History of Political Economy* 42 (S1): 261–87.

Erickson, Frederick. 1976. "Gatekeeping Encounters: A Social Selection Process." In *Anthropology and the Public Interest: Fieldwork and Theory*, edited by Peggy R. Sanday. Academic.

Erickson, Frederick. 1982. "Audiovisual Records as a Primary Data Source." *Sociological Methods & Research* 11 (2): 213–32.

Erickson, Frederick. 2004. *Talk and Social Theory: Ecologies of Speaking and Listening in Everyday Life*. Polity.

Erickson, Frederick. 2006. "Definition and Analysis of Data from Videotape: Some Research Procedures and Their Rationales." In *Handbook of Complementary Methods in Education Research*, edited by Judith L. Green, Gregory Camilli, and Patricia B. Elmore. Erlbaum.

Erickson, Frederick. 2011. "Uses of Video in Social Research: A Brief History." *International Journal of Social Research Methodology* 14 (3): 179–89.

Erickson, Frederick, and Jeffrey J. Schultz. 1977. "When is a Context? Some Issues and Methods in the Analysis of Social Competence." *The Quarterly Newsletter of the Institute for Comparative Human Development* [Rockefeller University] 1 (2): 5–10.

Errington, J. Joseph. 1988. *Structure and Style in Javanese: A Semiotic View of Linguistic Etiquette.* University of Pennsylvania Press.

Ervin-Tripp, Susan. 1969. "Summer Workshops in Sociolinguistics: Research on Children's Acquisition of Communicative Competence." *Social Science Research Council Items* 23 (2): 23–26.

Ervin-Tripp, Susan. 1997. "The Development of Sociolinguistics." In *The Early Days of Sociolinguistics: Memories and Reflections*, edited by Christina Bratt Paulston and G. Richard Tucker. SIL International.

Faculty Statement. 1970. *Daily Pennsylvanian*, May 4. https://dparchives.library.upenn.edu/.

Farrell, Michael P. 2001. *Collaborative Circles: Friendship Dynamics and Creative Work.* University of Chicago Press.

Feld, Steven. 1974. "Avant Propos: Jean Rouche." *Studies in the Anthropology of Visual Communication* 1 (1): 35–36.

Feld, Steven. 1982. *Sound and Sentiment: Birds, Weeping, Poetics, and Song in Kaluli Expression.* University of Pennsylvania Press.

Feld, Steven, and Carroll Williams. 1975. "Toward a Researchable Film Language." *Studies in the Anthropology of Visual Communication* 2 (1): 25–32.

Ferguson, Charles A. 1963. "Research Seminar on Sociolinguistics at Indiana University." *Social Science Research Council Items* 17 (4): 12.

Ferguson, Charles A. 1964. "Committee Report: Sociolinguistics." *Social Science Research Council Items* 18 (2): 22.

Ferguson, Charles A. 1965. "Directions in Sociolinguistics: Report on an Interdisciplinary Seminar." *Social Science Research Council Items* 19 (4): 1–4.

Feuerhahn, Wolf, and Rafael Mandressi, eds. 2025. *Histoire de l'Interdisciplinarité: Un mot, des pratiques.* Éditions de la Sorbonne.

Fine, Gary Alan, ed. 1995. *A Second Chicago School? The Development of a Postwar American Sociology.* University of Chicago Press.

Fine, Gary Alan. 2009. "Goffman Turns to Me and Says, 'Only a Schmuck Studies his Own Life.'" In *Bios Sociologicus: The Erving Goffman Archives,* edited by Dmitri N. Shalin. University of Nevada Las Vegas, CDC Publications. https://cdclv.unlv. edu/archives/interactionism/goffman/fine_09.html.

Fine, Gary Alan. 2024. "The Frames of Group Culture: Moments and Their Teams." *Symbolic Interaction* 47 (4): 512–24.

Fine, Gary Alan, and Philip Manning. 2003. "Erving Goffman." In *The Blackwell Companion to Major Contemporary Social Theorists,* edited by George Ritzer. Blackwell.

Fine, Gary Alan, and Gregory W. H. Smith, eds. 2000. *Erving Goffman.* Sage.

Firth, Alan. 1996. Review of *Collegial Discourse,* by Allen D. Grimshaw, and *What's Going on Here?,* edited by Allen D. Grimshaw et al. *American Journal of Sociology* 101 (5): 1487–92.

Fishman, Joshua A. 1997. "Bloomington, Summer 1964: The Birth of American Sociolinguistics." In *The Early Days of Sociolinguistics: Memories and Reflections,* edited by Christina Bratt Paulston and G. Richard Tucker. SIL International.

Fought, John G. 1972a. *Chorti Mayan Texts.* University of Pennsylvania Press.

Fought, John G. 1972b. Review of *Relations in Public,* by Erving Goffman. *Language in Society* 1 (2): 266–71.

Fowler, Susan. 1980. "The Clever Hans Phenomenon Conference." *International Journal for the Study of Animal Problems* 1 (6): 355–59.

Fox, Renée C. 2009. "Erving Goffman was a Brilliantly Imaginative, Original Sociologist." In *Bios Sociologicus: The Erving Goffman Archives,* edited by Dmitri N. Shalin. University of Nevada Las Vegas, CDC Publications. https://digitalscholarship. unlv.edu/goffman_archives/22.

Fox, Renée C. 2011. *In the Field: A Sociologist's Journey.* Transaction Publishers.

Galanes, Gloria, and Wendy Leeds-Hurwitz. 2009. "Communication as Social Construction: Catching Ourselves in the Act." In *Socially Constructing Communication*, edited by Gloria Galanes and Wendy Leeds-Hurwitz. Hampton Press.

Gamson, William A. 1975. Review of *Frame Analysis*, by Erving Goffman. *Contemporary Sociology* 4 (6): 603–7.

Gamson, William A. 2009. "A Stranger Determined to Remain One." In *Bios Sociologicus: The Erving Goffman Archives*, edited by Dmitri N. Shalin. University of Nevada Las Vegas, CDC Publications. https://cdclv.unlv.edu/archives/interactionism/goffman/gamson_09.html.

Gardner, Carol Brooks. 1980. "Passing By: Street Remarks, Address Rights, and the Urban Female." *Sociological Inquiry* 50 (3–4): 328–56.

Gardner, Carol Brooks. 1995. *Passing By: Gender and Public Harassment*. University of California Press.

Gardner, Carol Brooks. 2008. "I Don't Have Words Enough to Describe Goffman's Generosity." In *Bios Sociologicus: The Erving Goffman Archives*, edited by Dmitri N. Shalin. University of Nevada Las Vegas, CDC Publications. https://cdclv.unlv.edu/archives/interactionism/goffman/gardner_08.html.

Garland, David. 2001. *The Culture of Control: Crime and Social Order in Contemporary Society*. Oxford University Press.

Gerbner, George, ed. 1989. *International Encyclopedia of Communications*. Oxford University Press.

Gilmore, Perry, and Raymond McDermott. 2006. "'And This is How You Shall Ask': Linguistics, Anthropology, and Education in the Work of David Smith." *Anthropology and Education Quarterly* 37 (2): 199–211.

Glassie, Henry H. 1968. *Pattern in the Material and Folk Culture of the Eastern United States*. University of Pennsylvania Press.

Glassie, Henry H., Edward D. Ives, and John F. Szwed, eds. 1970. *Folksongs and Their Makers*. Bowling Green University Popular Press.

Goffman, Alice. 2009. "On the Run: Wanted Men in a Philadelphia Ghetto." *American Sociological Review* 74 (3): 339–57.

Goffman, Erving. 1949. "Some Characteristics of Response to Depicted Experience." Master's thesis, University of Chicago.

Goffman, Erving. 1951. "Symbols of Class Status." *British Journal of Sociology* 2 (4): 294–304.

Goffman, Erving. 1952. "On Cooling the Mark Out: Some Aspects of Adaptation to Failure." *Psychiatry* 15 (4): 451–63.

Goffman, Erving. 1953. "Communication Conduct in an Island Community." PhD diss., University of Chicago. https://www.mediastudies.press/communication-conduct-in-an-island-community.

Goffman, Erving. 1955a. "On Face-Work: An Analysis of Ritual Elements in Social Interaction." *Psychiatry* 18 (2): 213–31.

Goffman, Erving. 1955b. Review of *Children's Humor: A Psychological Analysis*, by Martha Wolfenstein. *American Journal of Sociology* 61 (3): 283–84.

Goffman, Erving. 1955c. Review of *Tobatí: Paraguayan Town*, by Elman R. Service and Helen S. Service. *American Journal of Sociology* 61 (2): 186–87.

Goffman, Erving. 1956a. "The Nature of Deference and Demeanor." *American Anthropologist* 58 (3): 473–502.

Goffman, Erving. 1956b. "Embarrassment and Social Organization." *American Journal of Sociology* 62 (3): 264–71.

Goffman, Erving. 1957a. "A Sociologist's View (On Some Convergences of Sociology and Psychiatry)." *Psychiatry* 20 (3): 201–3.

Goffman, Erving. 1957b. "Interpersonal Persuasion." In *Group Processes: Transactions of the Third Conference*, edited by Bertram Schaffner, vol. 3. Josiah Macy Jr. Foundation.

Goffman, Erving. 1957c. "The Patient as a 'Normal Deviant': Problems of Stigma and Isolation." In *The Patient and the Mental Hospital: Contributions of Research in the Science of Social Behavior*, edited by Milton Greenblatt, Daniel J. Levinson, and Richard H. Williams. Free Press.

Goffman, Erving. 1957d. Review of *Human Problems of a State Mental Hospital*, by Ivan Belknap. *Administrative Science Quarterly* 2 (1): 120–21.

Goffman, Erving. 1957e. "Alienation from Interaction." *Human Relations* 10 (1): 47–59.

Goffman, Erving. 1957f. Review of *Other People's Money*, by Donald R. Cressey. *Psychiatry* 20 (3): 321–26.

Goffman, Erving. 1958. "Characteristics of Total Institutions." In *Symposium on Preventive and Social Psychiatry*. Walter Reed Army Institute of Research.

Goffman, Erving. 1959a. "On Cooling the Mark Out: Some Aspects of Adaptation to Failure." In *Advances in Psychiatry: Recent Developments in Interpersonal Relations,* edited by Mabel Blake Cohen. W. W. Norton.

Goffman, Erving. 1959b. "The Moral Career of the Mental Patient." *Psychiatry* 22 (2): 123–42.

Goffman, Erving. 1959c. *The Presentation of Self in Everyday Life*. Doubleday Anchor.

Goffman, Erving. 1961a. *Encounters: Two Studies in the Sociology of Interaction*. Bobbs-Merrill.

Goffman, Erving. 1961b. *Asylums: Essays on the Social Situation of Mental Patients and Other Inmates*. Anchor Books.

Goffman, Erving. 1961c. "On the Characteristics of Total Institutions: The Inmate World." In *The Prison: Studies in Institutional Organization and Change*, edited by Donald R. Cressey. Holt, Rinehart & Winston.

Goffman, Erving. 1961d. "On the Characteristics of Total Institutions: Staff-Inmate Relations." In *The Prison: Studies in Institutional Organization and Change*, edited by Donald R. Cressey. Holt, Rinehart & Winston.

Goffman, Erving. 1963a. *Stigma: Notes on the Management of Spoiled Identity*. Prentice Hall.

Goffman, Erving. 1963b. *Behavior in Public Places: Notes on the Social Organization of Gatherings*. Free Press.

Goffman, Erving. 1964a. "The Neglected Situation." *American Anthropologist* 66 (6): 113–36.

Goffman, Erving. 1964b. "Mental Symptoms and Public Order." In *Disorders of Communication*, edited by David M. Rioch and Edwin A. Weinstein. Williams & Wilkins.

Goffman, Erving. 1966. "Communication and Enforcement Systems." In *Strategic Interaction and Conflict: Original Papers and Discussion*, edited by Kathleen Archibald. Institute of International Studies, University of California.

Goffman, Erving. 1967. *Interaction Ritual: Essays in Face-to-Face Behavior*. Aldine.

Goffman, Erving. 1969. "The Insanity of Place." *Psychiatry* 32 (4): 357–88.

Goffman, Erving. 1970. *Strategic Interaction*. University of Pennsylvania Press.

Goffman, Erving. 1971. *Relations in Public: Microstudies of the Public Order*. Basic Books.

Goffman, Erving. 1974. *Frame Analysis: An Essay on the Organization of Experience*. Northeastern University Press.

Goffman, Erving. 1976a. "Gender Advertisements." *Studies in the Anthropology of Visual Communication* 3 (2): 69–154. https://repository.upenn.edu/svc/vol3/iss2/1.

Goffman, Erving. 1976b. "Replies and Responses." *Language in Society* 5 (3): 257–313.

Goffman, Erving. 1978. "Response Cries." *Language* 54 (4): 787–815.

Goffman, Erving. 1979a. *Gender Advertisements*. Harper & Row.

Goffman, Erving. 1979b "Footing." *Semiotica* 25 (1–2): 1–30.

Goffman, Erving. 1979c. "Response Cries." In *Human Ethology: Claims and Limits of a New Discipline*, edited by M. von Cranach, K. Foppa, W. Lepenies, and D. Ploog. Cambridge University Press and Éditions de la Maison des Sciences de l'Homme.

Goffman, Erving. 1981. *Forms of Talk*. University of Pennsylvania Press.

Goffman, Erving. 1983. "Felicity's Condition." *American Journal of Sociology* 89 (1): 1–53.

Goodenough, Ward H. 1965. "Rethinking 'Status' and 'Role': Toward a General Model of the Cultural Organization of Social Relationships." In *The Relevance of Models for Social Anthropology*, edited by Michael Banton. Tavistock Publications.

Goodenough Ward H. 1971. *Culture, Language and Society*. Benjamin Cummings.

Goodenough, Ward H. 1997. "Moral Outrage: Territoriality in Human Guise." *Zygon* 32 (1): 5–27.

Goodwin, Charles, and René Salomon. 2019. "Not Being Bound by What You Can See Now: Charles Goodwin in Conversation with René Salomon." *Forum: Qualitative Social Research* 20 (2). https://www.qualitative-research.net/index.php/fqs/article/view/3271.

Goodwin, Marjorie Harness. 1980. "He-Said-She-Said: Formal Cultural Procedures for the Construction of a Gossip Dispute Activity." *American Ethnologist* 7 (4): 674–95.

Goodwin, Marjorie Harness. 1982. "'Instigating': Storytelling as Social Process." *American Ethnologist* 9 (4): 799–819.

Goodwin, Marjorie Harness. 1990. *He-Said-She-Said: Talk as Social Organization Among Black Children*. Indiana University Press.

Goodwin, Marjorie Harness. 1999. "Participation." *Journal of Linguistic Anthropology* 9 (1/2): 177–80.

Goodwin, Marjorie Harness, and Charles Goodwin. 1987. "Children's Arguing." In *Language, Gender, and Sex in Comparative Perspective*, edited by Susan U. Philips, Susan Steele, and Christine Tanz. Cambridge University Press.

Grimes, William. 2017. "Roger D. Abrahams, Folklorist Who Studied African-American Language, Dies at 84." *New York Times*, June 29. https://www.nytimes.com/2017/06/29/arts/roger-d-abrahams-dead-folklorist.html.

Grimshaw, Allen D. 1966. "Directions for Research in Sociolinguistics: Suggestions of a Non-Linguist Sociologist." *Sociological Inquiry* 36 (2): 319–22.

Grimshaw, Allen D. 1969a. "Sociolinguistics and the Sociologist." *The American Sociologist* 4 (4): 312–21.

Grimshaw, Allen D. 1969b. "Language as Obstacle and as Data in Sociological Research." *Social Science Research Counci Items* 23 (2). https://items.ssrc.org/from-our-archives/language-as-obstacle-and-as-data-in-sociological-research/.

Grimshaw, Allen D. 1973a. "Sociolinguistics." In *Handbook of Communication*, edited by Ithiel de Sola Pool, Fredrick W. Frey, Wilbur Schramm, Nathan Maccoby, and Edwin Parker. Rand McNally College Publishing.

Grimshaw, Allen D. 1973b. "Rules in Linguistic, Social, and Sociolinguistic Systems and Possibilities for a Unified Theory." In *Sociolinguistics: Current Trends and Prospects* [Report of the 23rd Annual Round Table Meeting on Linguistics and Language Studies], edited by Roger W. Shuy. Georgetown University.

Grimshaw, Allen D. 1973c. "Review Essay: On Language in Society, Part 1." *Contemporary Sociology* 2 (6): 575–85.

Grimshaw, Allen D. 1973d. "Rules, Social Interaction, and Language Behavior." *TESOL Quarterly* 7 (2): 99–115.

Grimshaw, Allen D. 1974a. "Review Essay: On Language in Society, Part 2." *Contemporary Sociology* 3 (1): 3–11.

Grimshaw, Allen D. 1974b. Review of *The Sociology of Language*, by Joshua Fishman. *Language in Society* 3 (2): 312–20.

Grimshaw, Allen D. 1978. "Review Essay: Language in Society—Four Texts." *Language* 54 (1): 156–69.

Grimshaw, Allen D. 1979. "What's Been Done—When All's Been Said?" Review of *Therapeutic Discourse*, by William Labov and David Fanshel. *Contemporary Sociology* 8 (2): 170–76.

Grimshaw, Allen D. 1980. "Selection and Labeling of Instrumentalities of Verbal Manipulation." *Discourse Processes* 3 (3): 203–29.

Grimshaw, Allen D. 1981. *Language as Social Resource: Essays by Allen D. Grimshaw*, edited by Anwar S. Dil. Stanford University Press.

Grimshaw, Allen D. 1982a. "Comprehensive Discourse Analysis: An Instance of Professional Peer Interaction." *Language in Society* 11 (1): 15–47.

Grimshaw, Allen D. 1982b. "Foreword: Special Issue on Sound-Image Records in Social Interaction Research." *Sociological Methods & Research* 11 (2): 115–19.

Grimshaw, Allen D. 1982c. "Sound-Image Data Records for Research on Social Interaction: Some Questions and Answers." *Sociological Methods & Research* 11 (2): 121–44.

Grimshaw, Allen D. 1982d. "Whose Privacy? What Harm?" *Sociological Methods & Research* 11 (2): 233–47.

Grimshaw, Allen D. 1983. "Erving Goffman: A Personal Appreciation." *Language in Society* 12 (1): 147–48.

Grimshaw, Allen D. 1987a. "Finishing Others' Talk: Some Structural and Pragmatic Features of Completion Offers." In *Language Topics: Essays in Honour of Michael Halliday*, edited by Ross Steele and Terry Threadgold, vol. 2. John Benjamins.

Grimshaw, Allen D. 1987b. "Disambiguating Discourse: Members' Skill and Analysts' Problem." *Social Psychology Quarterly* 50 (2): 186–204.

Grimshaw, Allen D. 1989. *Collegial Discourse: Professional Conversation Among Peers*. Ablex.

Grimshaw, Allen D. 1990a. "Microanalysis of Sound-Image Records: The Multiple Analysis Project (MAP) and Generals and Admirals International Negotiations (GAIN) Research." Visual Research Conference, New Orleans, LA.

Grimshaw, Allen D., ed. 1990b. *Conflict Talk: Sociolinguistic Investigations of Arguments in Conversations*. Cambridge University Press.

Grimshaw, Allen D. 1990c. "Preface." In *Conflict Talk: Sociolinguistic Investigations of Arguments in Conversations*, edited by Allen D. Grimshaw. Cambridge University Press.

Grimshaw, Allen D. 1991. "Review Essay: Unawareness Without Ignorance: Unexploited Contributions to Sociology." *Contemporary Sociology* 20 (6): 843–48.

Grimshaw, Allen D. 1994. "What We Have Learned: Some Research Conclusions and Some Conclusions about Research." In *What's Going on Here? Complementary Studies of Professional Talk*, edited by Allen D. Grimshaw et al. Ablex.

Grimshaw, Allen D. 1998. "What is a 'Handbook of Sociolinguistics'?" Review of *The Handbook of Sociolinguistics*, by Florian Coulmas. *Journal of Sociolinguistics* 2 (3): 432–45.

Grimshaw, Allen D., Steven Feld, and David Jenness. 1994a. "The Multiple Analysis Project: Background, History, Problems, Data." In *What's Going on Here? Complementary Studies of Professional Talk*, edited by Allen D. Grimshaw et al. Ablex.

Grimshaw, Allen D., et al. 1994b. *What's Going on Here? Complementary Studies of Professional Talk*. Ablex.

Grinker, Roy R., ed. 1956. *Toward a Unified Theory of Human Behavior*. Basic Books.

Gronfein, William. 1999. "Sundered Selves: Mental Illness and the Interaction Order in the Work of Erving Goffman." In *Goffman and Social Organization: Studies in a Sociological Legacy*, edited by Greg Smith. Routledge.

Gross, Larry. 1980. "Sol Worth and the Study of Visual Communication." *Studies in Visual Communication* 6 (3): 2–19. https://repository.upenn.edu/svc/vol6/iss3/2.

Gross, Larry, and Jay Ruby. 1980. "Editorial." *Studies in Visual Communication* 6 (1): 2. https://repository.upenn.edu/handle/20.500.14332/48345.

Gruber, Jacob W. 1966. "In Search of Experience: Biography as an Instrument for the History of Anthropology." In *Pioneers of American Anthropology: The Uses of Biography*, edited by June Helm. University of Washington Press.

Gumperz, John J. 1997. "Some Comments on the Origin and Development of Sociolinguistics." In *The Early Days of Sociolinguistics: Memories and Reflections*, edited by Christina Bratt Paulston and G. Richard Tucker. SIL International.

Gumperz, John J. 2001. "Interactional Sociolinguistics: A Personal Perspective." In *The Handbook of Discourse Analysis*, edited by Deborah Schiffrin, Deborah Tannen, and Heidi E. Hamilton. Blackwell.

Gumperz, John J., and Dell H. Hymes, eds. 1964a. "The Ethnography of Communication." *American Anthropologist* 66 (6): part 2.

Gumperz, John J., and Dell H. Hymes. 1964b. "Preface: The Ethnography of Communication." *American Anthropologist* 66 (6): v.

Gumperz, John J., and Dell H. Hymes, eds. 1972. *Directions in Sociolinguistics: The Ethnography of Communication*. Holt, Rinehart & Winston.

Gusfield, Joseph R. 1995. "Preface: The Second Chicago School?" In *A Second Chicago School? The Development of a Postwar American Sociology*, edited by Gary Alan Fine. University of Chicago Press.

Habermas, Jürgen. 1979. "Comments on Papers by Ekman and Goffman." In *Human Ethology: Claims and Limits of a New Discipline*, edited by M. von Cranach, K. Foppa, W. Lepenies, and D. Ploog. Cambridge University Press and Éditions de la Maison des Sciences de l'Homme.

Halkowski, Timothy. 1991. "Defense and Dissent: Grimshaw's Analysis of Dissertator's Discourse." Review of *Collegial Discourse*, by Allen D. Grimshaw. *Contemporary Sociology* 20 (6): 853–54.

Heath, Shirley Brice. 2011. "New Love, Long Love: Keeping Social Justice and Ethnography of Education in Mind." *Anthropology & Education Quarterly* 42 (4): 397–403.

Heatherton, Todd F., Robert E. Kleck, Michelle R. Hebl, and Jay G. Hull, eds. 2000. *The Social Psychology of Stigma*. Guilford Press.

Heilman, Samuel C. 1975. "The Gift of Alms: Face-to-Face Almsgiving Among Orthodox Jews." *Urban Life and Culture* 3 (4): 371–95.

Heilman, Samuel C. 1976. *Synagogue Life: A Study in Symbolic Interaction*. University of Chicago Press.

Heilman, Samuel C. 2009. "As Goffman was Talking about Remedial Interchanges, He Took a Glass of Water and Spilled it on Rosenberg's Lap." In *Bios Sociologicus: The Erving Goffman Archives*, edited by Dmitri N. Shalin. University of Nevada Las Vegas, CDC Publications. http://cdclv.unlv.edu/archives/interactionism/goffman/heilman_08.html.

Heller, Monica. 2013. "In Memoriam: John Gumperz (1922–2013)." *Journal of Sociolinguistics* 17 (3): 394–99.

Heller, Monica. 2018. "Scholarly Committees as Elite Public Action: The SSRC and the Origins of Sociolinguistics." *Social Science Research Council Items.* https://items. ssrc.org/insights/scholarly-committees-as-elite-public-action-the-ssrc-and-the-origins-of-sociolinguistics/.

Hoey, Elliott, and Anne W. Rawls. 2022. "Harvey Sacks (1935–1975)." In *Goffman Handbuch: Leben—Werk—Wirkung,* edited by Karl Lenz and Robert Hettlage. J. B. Metzler.

Hornberger, Nancy H. 2001. "Educational Linguistics as a Field: A View from Penn's Program on the Occasion of its 25th Anniversary." *Working Papers in Educational Linguistics* 17 (1–2): 6.

Hornberger, Nancy H. 2002. "Introduction." *Penn GSE Perspectives on Urban Education* 1 (2): 1–7. https://urbanedjournal.gse.upenn.edu/archive/volume-1-issue-2-fall-2002/introduction-dr-nancy-h-hornberger-guest-editor.

Hornberger, Nancy H. 2003. Review of *Ethnography and Schools,* by Yali Zou and Enrique (Henry) T. Tureba. *Journal of Anthropological Research* 59 (4): 566–67.

Hornberger, Nancy H. 2011. "Dell H. Hymes: His Scholarship and Legacy in Anthropology and Education." *Anthropology and Education Quarterly* 42 (4): 310–18.

Huber, Joan. 2009. "Erving Goffman's Presentation of Self as ASA President." In *Bios Sociologicus: The Erving Goffman Archives,* edited by Dmitri N. Shalin. University of Nevada Las Vegas, CDC Publications. https://digitalscholarship.unlv.edu/goffman_archives/37.

Hufford, Mary. 2020. "Groundtruthing the Humanities: Penn Folklore and Folklife, 1973–2013." In *Folklore in the United States and Canada: An Institutional History,* edited by Patricia Sawin and Rosemary Lévy Zumwalt. Indiana University Press.

Hymes, Dell H. 1962. "The Ethnography of Speaking." In *Anthropology and Human Behavior,* edited by Thomas Gladwin and William C. Sturtevant. Anthropology Society of Washington.

Hymes, Dell H. 1964a. "Introduction: Toward Ethnographies of Communication." *American Anthropologist* 66 (6): 1–34.

Hymes, Dell H., ed. 1964b. *Language in Culture and Society: A Reader in Linguistics and Anthropology.* Harper and Row.

Hymes, Dell H. 1967. "Why Linguistics Needs the Sociologist." *Social Research* 34 (4): 632–47.

Hymes, Dell H. 1968. "Responsibilities of Dissent." Review of *The Dissenting Academy*, by Theodore Roszak. *Bulletin of the Atomic Scientists* 24 (9): 29–34.

Hymes, Dell H., ed. 1971. *Pidginization and Creolization of Languages: Proceedings of a Conference Held at the University of the West Indies, Mona, Jamaica, April 1968.* Cambridge University Press.

Hymes, Dell H., ed. 1972a. *Reinventing Anthropology*. Pantheon.

Hymes, Dell H. 1972b. "The Scope of Sociolinguistics." *Social Science Research Council Items* 26 (2): 14–18.

Hymes, Dell H. 1974. *Foundations in Sociolinguistics*. University of Pennsylvania Press.

Hymes, Dell H. 1975. "Breakthrough into Performance." In *Folklore: Performance and Communication*, edited by Dan Ben-Amos and Kenneth Goldstein. Mouton.

Hymes, Dell H. 1980. Foreword to *The Social Life of Language*, by Gillian Sankoff. University of Pennsylvania Press.

Hymes, Dell H. 1981a. *Ethnographic Monitoring of Children's Acquisition of Reading/Language Arts Skills In and Out of School.* Final report to National Institute of Education. https://files.eric.ed.gov/fulltext/ED208096.pdf.

Hymes, Dell H. 1981b. *"In Vain I Tried to Tell You": Essays in Native American Ethnopoetics.* University of Pennsylvania Press.

Hymes, Dell H. 1982. *Ethnolinguistic Study of Classroom Discourse.* Final report to National Institute of Education. https://eric.ed.gov/?id=ED217710.

Hymes, Dell H. 1983a. "Introduction." In *Essays in the History of Linguistic Anthropology.* John Benjamins.

Hymes, Dell H. 1983b. "Report from an Underdeveloped Country: Toward Linguistic Competence in the United States." In *The Sociogenesis of Language and Human Conduct,* edited by Bruce Bain. Springer Science + Business Media.

Hymes, Dell H. 1984. "On Erving Goffman." *Theory and Society* 13 (5): 621–31.

Hymes, Dell H. 1992. "Brief Notices." *Language in Society* 21 (4): 711.

Hymes, Dell H. 1997. "History and Development of Sociolinguistics." In *The Early Days of Sociolinguistics: Memories and Reflections*, edited by Christina Bratt Paulston and G. Richard Tucker. SIL International.

Hymes, Dell H. 1999. "Prelude." In *Reinventing Anthropology*, edited by Dell H. Hymes. 2nd ed. University of Michigan Press.

Hymes, Dell H. 2003. "Comment on Duranti." *Current Anthropology* 44 (3): 337–38.

Hymes, Dell H., and John G. Fought. 1975. "American Structuralism." In *Current Trends in Linguistics: Historiography of Linguistics*, edited by Thomas A. Sebeok, vol. 13. Mouton.

Hymes, Dell H., and John G. Fought. 1981. *American Structuralism*. Mouton.

Irvine, Judith T. 1974. "Strategies of Status Manipulation in the Wolof Greeting." In *Explorations in the Ethnography of Speaking*, edited by Richard Bauman and Joel Sherzer. Cambridge University Press.

Irvine, Judith T. 1979. "Formality and Informality in Communicative Events." *American Anthropologist* 81 (4): 773–90.

Jacobsen, Michael Hviid, ed. 2010. *The Contemporary Goffman*. Routledge.

Jacobsen, Michael Hviid. 2017. "Erving Goffman: Exploring the Interaction Order through Everyday Observations and Imaginative Metaphors." In *The Interactionist Imagination: Studying Meaning, Situation and Micro-Social Order*, edited by Michael Hviid Jacobsen. Palgrave Macmillan.

Jacobsen, Michael Hviid, ed. 2023. *The Anthem Companion to Erving Goffman*. Anthem.

Jacobsen, Michael Hviid, and Søren Kristiansen. 2015. *The Social Thought of Erving Goffman*. Sage.

Jacobsen, Michael Hviid, and Greg Smith, eds. 2022. *The Routledge International Handbook of Goffman Studies*. Routledge.

Jansen, Sue Curry. 2008. "Walter Lippmann: Straw Man of Communication Research." In *The History of Media and Communication Research: Contested Memories*, edited by David W. Park and Jefferson Pooley. Peter Lang.

Jaworski, Gary D. 2000. "Erving Goffman: The Reluctant Apprentice." *Symbolic Interaction* 23 (3): 299–308.

Jaworski, Gary D. 2019. "Erving Goffman as Sorcerer's Apprentice: A Reappraisal of the Schelling-Goffman Relationship." *The American Sociologist* 50 (3): 387–401.

Jaworski, Gary D. 2023. *Erving Goffman and the Cold War*. Rowman & Littlefield.

Jaynes, Gerald D., et al. 2009. "The Chicago School and the Roots of Urban Ethnography: An Intergenerational Conversation with Gerald D. Jaynes, David E. Apter, Herbert J. Gans, William Kornblum, Ruth Horowitz, James F. Short, Jr, Gerald D. Suttles and Robert E. Washington." *Ethnography* 10 (4): 375–96.

Jefferson, Gail. 1973. "A Case of Precision Timing in Ordinary Conversation: Overlapped Tag-Positioned Address Terms in Closing Sequences." *Semiotica* 9 (1): 47–96.

Jefferson, Gail. 1974. "Error Correction as an Interactional Resource." *Language in Society* 3 (2): 181–99.

Jerolmack, Colin, Belicia Teo, and Abigail Westberry. 2024. "The Interactional Zoo: Lessons for Sociology from Erving Goffman's Engagement with Animal Ethology." *Sociological Theory* 42 (2): 137–59.

Johnstone, Barbara. 2010. "Remembering Dell." *Language in Society* 39 (3): 307–15.

Jones, Edward E., Amerigo Farina, Albert H. Hastorf, et al. 1984. *Social Stigma: The Psychology of Marked Relationships*. W. H. Freeman.

Joseph, Isaac, Robert Castel, and Jacques Cosnier, eds. 1989. *Le Parler Frais d'Erving Goffman*. Editions de Minuit.

Jutant, Camille, and Hécate Vergopoulos. 2024. "Le ratage: quand l'expérience culturelle est contrariée." *Culture et Musées* 44. https://journals.openedition.org/culturemusees/.

Kendall, Shari. 2011. "Symbolic Interactionism, Erving Goffman, and Sociolinguistics." In *The Sage Handbook of Sociolinguistics*, edited by Ruth Wodak, Barbara Johnstone, and Paul E. Kerswill. Sage.

Kendon, Adam. 1972. Review of *Kinesics and Context: Essays on Body Motion Communication*, by Ray L. Birdwhistell. *American Journal of Psychology* 85 (3): 441–55.

Kendon, Adam. 1973. "The Role of Visible Behavior in the Organization of Face-to-Face Interaction." In *Social Communication and Movement: Studies of Interaction and Expression in Man and Chimpanzee*, edited by Mario von Cranach and Ian Vine. Academic.

Kendon, Adam. 1979. "Some Emerging Features of Face-to-Face Interaction." *Sign Language Studies* 22 (1): 7–22.

Kendon, Adam. 1988. "Goffman's Approach to Face-to-Face Interaction." In *Erving Goffman: Exploring the Interaction Order*, edited by Paul Drew and Anthony Wootton. Polity.

Kendon, Adam. 1990. *Conducting Interaction: Patterns of Behavior in Focused Encounters*. Cambridge University Press.

Kendon, Adam, and Stuart J. Sigman. 1996. "Commemorative Essay: Ray L. Birdwhistell (1918–1994)." *Semiotica* 112 (1–2): 231–61.

Kirch, Patrick V. 2015. "Ward H. Goodenough, 1919–2013." *Biographical Memoirs*. National Academy of Sciences. https://www.nasonline.org/wp-content/uploads/2024/06/goodenough-ward.pdf.

Kirshenblatt-Gimblett, Barbara. 1974. "The Concept and Varieties of Narrative Performance in East European Jewish Culture." In *Explorations in the Ethnography of Speaking*, edited by Richard Bauman and Joel Sherzer. Cambridge University Press.

Kirshenblatt-Gimblett, Barbara, ed. 1976. *Speech Play: Research and Resources for the Study of Linguistic Creativity*. University of Pennsylvania Press.

Kleck, Robert E. 1968a. "Physical Stigma and Nonverbal Cues Emitted in Face-to-Face Interaction." *Human Relations* 21 (1): 19–28.

Kleck, Robert E. 1968b. "Self-Disclosure Patterns of the Nonobviously Stigmatized." *Psychological Reports* 23 (3): 1239–48.

Kleck, Robert E. 1969. "Nonverbal Dimensions of Social Interaction." Unpublished report.

Klein, Julie Thompson. 1990. *Interdisciplinarity: History, Theory, and Practice*. Wayne State University Press.

Knapp, Mark L. 2013. "Establishing a Domain for the Study of Nonverbal Phenomena: *E pluribus unum*." In *Nonverbal Communication*, edited by Judith A. Hall and Mark L. Knapp. De Gruyter Mouton.

Kuipers, Joel C. 1990. *The Power in Performance: The Creation of Textual Authority in Weyewa Ritual Speech*. University of Pennsylvania Press.

Kunze, Elizabeth. 2011. "Amy Shuman Interview." *Minds@UW*. https://minds.wisconsin.edu/handle/1793/52457.

Labov, Teresa. 1969. "When is the Jets? Social Ambiguity in Peer Terminology." Master's thesis, Columbia University.

Labov, Teresa. 1982. "Social Structure and Peer Terminology in a Black Adolescent Gang." *Language in Society* 11 (3): 391–411.

Labov, William. 1964. "Phonological Correlates of Social Stratification." *American Anthropologist* 66 (6): 164–76.

Labov, William. 1972a. "On the Mechanism of Linguistic Change." In *Directions in Sociolinguistics: The Ethnography of Communication,* edited by John J. Gumperz and Dell H. Hymes. Holt, Rinehart & Winston.

Labov, William. 1972b. *Sociolinguistic Patterns.* University of Pennsylvania Press.

Labov, William. 1972c. *Language in the Inner City: Studies in the Black English Vernacular.* University of Pennsylvania Press.

Labov, William. 1972d. "Negative Attraction and Negative Concord in English Grammar." *Language* 48 (4): 773–818.

Labov, William. 1972e. "Some Principles of Linguistic Methodology." *Language in Society 1 (1): 97– 120.*

Labov, William. 1973. "The Linguistic Consequences of Being a Lame." *Language in Society* 2 (1): 81–115.

Labov, William, ed. 1980. *Locating Language in Time and Space.* Academic.

Labov, William. 2006. *The Social Stratification of English in New York City.* 2nd ed. Cambridge University Press.

Labov, William, and David Fanshel. 1977. *Therapeutic Discourse: Psychotherapy as Conversation.* Academic.

Labov, William, Ingrid Rosenfelder, and Josef Fruehwald. 2013. "One Hundred Years of Sound Change in Philadelphia, PA: Linear Incrementation, Reversal, and Reanalysis." *Language 89 (1): 30– 65.*

Labov, William, and Gillian Sankoff. 2023. *Conversations with Strangers.* Cambridge University Press.

Leeds-Hurwitz, Wendy. 1980. "The Use and Analysis of Uncommon Forms of Address: A Business Example." *Working Papers in Sociolinguistics,* no. 80. Southwest Educational Development Laboratory.

Leeds-Hurwitz, Wendy. 1984. "On the Relationship of the 'Ethnography of Speaking' to the 'Ethnography of Communication.'" *Papers in Linguistics* 17 (1): 7–32.

Leeds-Hurwitz, Wendy. 1987. "The Social History of *The Natural History of an Interview*: A Multidisciplinary Investigation of Social Communication." *Research on Language and Social Interaction* 20: 1–51.

Leeds-Hurwitz, Wendy. 1989a. "Frieda Fromm-Reichmann and *The Natural History of an Interview*." In *Psychoanalysis and Psychosis*, edited by Anne-Louise S. Silver. International Universities Press.

Leeds-Hurwitz, Wendy. 1989b. *Communication in Everyday Life: A Social Interpretation*. Ablex.

Leeds-Hurwitz, Wendy. 1990. "Notes in the History of Intercultural Communication: The Foreign Service Institute and the Mandate for Intercultural Training." *Quarterly Journal of Speech* 76 (3): 262–81.

Leeds-Hurwitz, Wendy. 1994. "Crossing Disciplinary Boundaries: The Macy Conferences on Cybernetics as a Case Study in Multidisciplinary Communication." *Cybernetica* 37 (3–4): 349–69.

Leeds-Hurwitz, Wendy. 2000a. Review of *And Then Came Boas: Continuity and Revolution in Americanist Anthropology*, by Regna Darnell. *Language in Society* 29 (4): 612–15.

Leeds-Hurwitz, Wendy. 2000b. Review of *The Early Days of Sociolinguistics: Memories and Reflections*, by Christina Bratt Paulston and G. Richard Tucker. *Language in Society* 29 (3): 413–15.

Leeds-Hurwitz, Wendy. 2009. "Social Construction: Moving from Theory to Research (and Back Again)." In *Socially Constructing Communication*, edited by Gloria Galanes and Wendy Leeds-Hurwitz. Hampton.

Leeds-Hurwitz, Wendy. 2012. "These Fictions We Call Disciplines." *Electronic Journal of Communication/La Revue Électronique de Communication* 22 (3–4). https://www.cios.org/EJCPUBLIC/022/3/022341.html.

Leeds-Hurwitz, Wendy. 2021. "The Role of Theory Groups in the Lives of Ideas." *History of Media Studies* 1. https://doi.org/10.32376/d895a0ea.0b35e36e.

Leeds-Hurwitz, Wendy. 2022. "Gregory Bateson (1904–1980) and Communication Theory." In *Goffman Handbuch: Leben—Werk—Wirkung*, edited by Karl Lenz and Robert Hettlage. J. B. Metzler.

Leeds-Hurwitz, Wendy. 2024. "O 'colégio invisível' de Goffman na Universidade da Pennsylvania." In *Erving Goffman 100 anos: Explorando a ordem da interação*, edited by Carlos B. Martins and Edison Gastaldo. Ateliê das Humanidades.

Leeds-Hurwitz, Wendy. Forthcoming. "The Future of Intercultural Communication is Transdisciplinarity." In *Handbook of Communication and Culture*, edited by Lily Arasaratnam-Smith. Edward Elgar.

Leeds-Hurwitz, Wendy, and Adam Kendon. 2021. *"The Natural History of an Interview* and the Microanalysis of Behavior in Social Interaction: A Critical Moment in Research Practice." In *Holisms of Communication: The Early History of Audio-Visual Sequence Analysis*, edited by James McElvenny and Andrea Ploder. Language Science Press. https://library.oapen.org/handle/20.500.12657/51048.

Leeds-Hurwitz, Wendy, and Stuart J. Sigman. 2010. "The Penn Tradition." In *The Social History of Language and Social Interaction Research: People, Places, Ideas*, edited by Wendy Leeds-Hurwitz. Hampton.

Leeds-Hurwitz, Wendy, and Yves Winkin. 2022. "Goffman and Communication." In *The Interactionist Imagination: Studying Meaning, Situation and Micro-Social Order*, edited by Michael Hviid Jacobsen. Routledge.

Lenz, Karl, and Robert Hettlage, eds. 2022. *Goffman Handbuch: Leben—Werk—Wirkung.* J. B. Metzler.

Levinson, Stephen C. 2003. "Contextualizing 'Contextualization Cues.'" In *Language and Interaction: Discussions with John J. Gumperz*, edited by Susan L. Eerdmans, Carlo L. Prevignano, and Paul J. Thibault. John Benjamins.

Lidz, Victor. 2009. "I Found Goffman Talented, Original, Rewarding to Read, but Basically Problematic." In *Bios Sociologicus: The Erving Goffman Archives*, edited by Dmitri N. Shalin. University of Nevada Las Vegas, CDC Publications. http://cdclv.unlv.edu/ega/comments/lidz_09.html.

Lievrouw, Leah A. 1989. "The Invisible College Reconsidered: Bibliometrics and the Development of Scientific Communication Theory." *Communication Research 16 (5): 615–28.*

Lindee, Susan, and Joanna Radin. 2016. "Patrons of the Human Experience: A History of the Wenner-Gren Foundation for Anthropological Research, 1941–2016." *Current Anthropology* 57 (S14): 211–332.

Lingwood, David Alfred. 1969. "Interpersonal Communication, Research Productivity, and Invisible Colleges." PhD Diss., Stanford University.

Lissner, Will. 1971. "Goodell to Head Scholars' Panel in Examination of Prison Reform." *New York Times,* October 1. https://www.nytimes.com/1971/10/01/archives/goodell-to-head-a-prison-study-panel.html.

Lofland, John. 1984. "Erving Goffman's Sociological Legacies." *Urban Life* 13 (1): 7–34.

Lynch, Barbara Ann. 1984. "Sacred Space: Spatial Communications Patterns in an Irish American and Slovak American Roman Catholic Parish." PhD diss., University of Pennsylvania. https://repository.upenn.edu/dissertations_asc/52.

Macbeth, Douglas. 1995. Review of *What's Going on Here?,* by Allen Grimshaw. *The Journal of Higher Education* 66 (6): 700–11.

Manning, Philip. 1992. *Erving Goffman and Modern Sociology.* Polity.

Margolis, Jon. 1971. "Prison Revolt Upstate: NY Compromising with Inmates in Bid to End Prison Rebellion." *Newsday,* September 10. Nassau edition.

Martins, Carlos Benedito, and Édison Gastaldo, eds. 2024. *Erving Goffman 100 Anos: Explorando a Ordem da Interação.* Ateliê das Humanidades.

Marx, Gary T. 1984. "Role Models and Role Distance: A Remembrance of Erving Goffman." *Theory and Society* 13 (5): 649–62.

Maseda, Ramon Vargas. 2017. *Deciphering Goffman: The Structure of his Sociological Theory Revisited.* Routledge.

McDermott, Raymond P. 1976. "Kids Make Sense: An Ethnographic Account of the Interactional Management of Success and Failure in One First-Grade Classroom." PhD diss., Stanford University.

McFadden, Robert O. 2006. "Philip Rieff, Sociologist and Author on Freud, Dies at 83." *New York Times,* July 4. https://www.nytimes.com/2006/07/04/us/04rieff.html.

McQuown, Norman A., ed. 1971. *The Natural History of an Interview.* Microfilm Collection of Manuscripts on Cultural Anthropology, University of Chicago, Joseph Regenstein Library, Department of Photoduplication.

Meier zu Verl, Christian. 2022. "Dell Hymes (1927–2009)." In *Goffman Handbuch: Leben—Werk—Wirkung,* edited by Karl Lenz and Robert Hettlage. J. B. Metzler.

Mendlovitz, Saul. 2009. "Erving Was a Jew Acting like a Canadian Acting like a Britisher." In *Bios Sociologicus: The Erving Goffman Archives*, edited by Dmitri N. Shalin. University of Nevada Las Vegas, CDC Publications. https://cdclv.unlv. edu/archives/interactionism/goffman/mendlovitz_08.html.

Merritt, Marilyn. 1976a. "Resources for Saying in Service Encounters." Ph.D. diss., University of Pennsylvania.

Merritt, Marilyn. 1976b. "On Questions Following Questions in Service Encounters." *Language in Society* 5 (3): 315–57.

Merritt, Marilyn. 1979. "'Communicative Loading' and Intertwining of Verbal and Non-Verbal Modalities in Service Events." *Research on Language and Social Interaction* 12 (3–4): 365–91.

Merritt, Marilyn. 2018. "An Interdisciplinary Anthropologist at Work: A Focused Intellectual Biography of Erving Goffman." *Bérose International Encyclopaedia of the Histories of Anthropology.* https://www.berose.fr/article1278.html.

Meyer, Christian. 2022. "Harold Garfinkel (1917–2011)." In *Goffman Handbuch: Leben—Werk—Wirkung*, edited by Karl Lenz and Robert Hettlage. J. B. Metzler.

Meyer, Christian. 2024. "Goffman and Garfinkel: Joint Enterprises, Theoretical Differences and Personal Sympathies." In *New Perspectives on Goffman in Language and Interaction: Body, Participation and the Self*, edited by Lorenza Mondada and Anssi Peräkylä. Routledge.

Miller, Raymond C. 2010. "Interdisciplinarity: Its Meaning and Consequences." In *Oxford Research Encyclopedia of International Studies*, edited by Robert A. Denamark, vol. 6. Oxford University Press.

Miller, Rosina S. 2004. "Of Politics, Disciplines, and Scholars: MacEdward Leach and the Founding of the Folklore Program at the University of Pennsylvania." *The Folklore Historian* 21:17–34.

Mills, Margaret A. 2011. "Dell H. Hymes (1927–2009)." *Journal of American Folklore* 124 (491): 88–89.

Moerman, Michael. 1987. *Talking Culture: Ethnography and Conversation Analysis.* University of Pennsylvania Press.

Mokros, Hartmut B. 2010. "Language and Social Interaction at the University of Chicago, 1977–1984." In *The Social History of Language and Social Interaction Research: People, Places, Ideas*, edited by Wendy Leeds-Hurwitz. Hampton.

Mondada, Lorenza. 2016. "Challenges of Multimodality: Language and the Body in Social Interaction." *Journal of Sociolinguistics* 20 (3): 336–66.

Mondada, Lorenza, and Anssi Peräkylä, eds. 2024. *New Perspectives on Goffman in Language and Interaction: Body, Participation and the Self*. Routledge.

Moore, R. Laurence. 1982. "Insiders and Outsiders in American Historical Narrative and American History." *American Historical Review* 87 (2): 390–412.

Müller, Cornelia. 2007. "A Semiotic Profile: Adam Kendon." *Semiotix: A Global Information Bulletin* 9 (May). http://www.semioticon.com/semiotix/semiotix9/sem-9-03.html.

Mullins, Nicholas C. 1973. *Theories and Theory Groups in Contemporary American Sociology*. Harper and Row.

Murphy, John. 1973. "Johnson Urges Change in Broadcast Industry." *Daily Pennsylvanian*, March 26. https://dparchives.library.upenn.edu/.

Murray, Stephen O. 1982. Review of *Language as Social Resource: Essays by Allen D. Grimshaw. American Anthropologist* 84 (3): 743–45.

Murray, Stephen O. 1991. Review of *Edward Sapir*, by Regna Darnell. *Language in Society* 20 (2): 317–22.

Murray, Stephen O. 1994. *Theory Groups and the Study of Language in North America: A Social History*. John Benjamins.

Murray, Stephen O. 1998. *American Sociolinguistics: Theorists and Theory Groups*. John Benjamins.

Murray, Stephen O. 2010. "Interactional Sociolinguistics at Berkeley." In *The Social History of Language and Social Interaction Research: People, Places, Ideas*, edited by Wendy Leeds-Hurwitz. Hampton Press.

Murray, Stephen O. 2013. *John Gumperz in Context: 1977 and 1992 Interviews*. El Instituto Obregón.

Nicholasen, Michelle. 2016. "In Memoriam: Thomas C. Schelling, 1921–2016." Weatherhead Center for International Affairs at Harvard University, December 12. https://wcfia.harvard.edu/in-memoriam/schelling.

Nimura, Janice P. 2016. "History Never Ends, It Just Gets Retold." *Literary Hub*, May 1. https://lithub.com/history-never-ends-it-just-gets-retold/.

Ochs, Elinor. 2022. "Thinking In Between Disciplines." *Annual Review of Anthropology* 51 (1): 1–15.

Oken, Donald. 1960. Review of *Advances in Psychiatry*, edited by Mabel Blake Cohen. *Archives of General Psychiatry* 2 (2): 243–44.

Pallante, Virginia, Lasse Suonperä Liebst, Peter Ejbye-Ernst, Camilla Bank Friis, and Marie Rosenkrantz Lindegaard. 2022. "Putting Actual Behavior Back into the Social Sciences: A Plea for Video-Based Interaction Ethology." Paper presented to the Ernst Strüngmann Forum: "Digital Ethology: From Individuals to Communities and Back."

Paterno, David. 2022. "Rebooting Raymond Birdwhistell." *Communication Research and Practice* 8 (3): 229–42.

Pennsylvania Gazette. 1969. "Moratorium." December. https://cpb-us-w2.wpmucdn.com/web.sas.upenn.edu/dist/0/689/files/2020/04/Moratorium-Day.pdf.

Perry, Stewart E. 1966. *The Human Nature of Science: Researchers at Work in Psychiatry.* Free Press.

Peters, John Durham. 2008. "Institutional Opportunities for Intellectual History in Communication Studies." In *The History of Media and Communication Research: Contested Memories,* edited by David W. Park and Jefferson Pooley. Peter Lang.

Philips, Susan U. 1974. "Warm Springs 'Indian Time': How the Regulation of Participation Affects the Progress of Events." In *Explorations in the Ethnography of Speaking,* edited by Richard Bauman and Joel Sherzer. Cambridge University Press.

Philips, Susan U. 1983. *The Invisible Culture: Communication in Classroom and Community on the Warm Springs Indian Reservation.* Longman.

Pike, Kenneth L. (1954) 1967. *Language in Relation to a Unified Theory of the Structure of Human Behavior.* 2nd ed. Mouton.

Platt, Jennifer. 1995. "Research Methods and the Second Chicago School." In *A Second Chicago School? The Development of a Postwar American Sociology,* edited by Gary Alan Fine. University of Chicago Press.

Pooley, Jefferson, and David W. Park. 2008. "Introduction." In *The History of Media and Communication Research: Contested Memories,* edited by David W. Park and Jefferson Pooley. Peter Lang.

Preda, Alex. 2022. "Strategic Interaction." In *Goffman Handbuch: Leben—Werk—Wirkung*, edited by Karl Lenz and Robert Hettlage. J. B. Metzler.

Prendergast, John. 2024. "(Re)introducing *In Principle and Practice*." *Pennsylvania Gazette*, August 26. https://thepenngazette.com/reintroducing-in-principle-and-practice/.

Prevignano, Carlo L., and Aldo Di Luzio. 2003. "A Discussion with John J. Gumperz." In *Language and Interaction: Discussions with John J. Gumperz*, edited by Susan L. Eerdmans, Carlo L. Prevignano, and Paul J. Thibault. John Benjamins.

Raab, Jürgen. 2019. *Erving Goffman: From the Perspective of the New Sociology of Knowledge*. Routledge.

Rawls, Anne W. 2023. "The Goffman-Garfinkel Correspondence: Planning *On Passing*." *Ethnografia e Ricera Qualitativa* 16 (1): 175–218.

Richardson, Stephen A., Linda Ronald, and Robert E. Kleck. 1974. "The Social Status of Handicapped and Nonhandicapped Boys in a Camp Setting." *The Journal of Special Education* 8 (2): 143–52.

Rickford, John R., and Angela E. Rickford. 1976. "Cut-Eye and Suck-Teeth: African Words and Gestures in a New World Guise." *Journal of American Folklore* 89 (353): 294–309.

Riggins, Stephen Harold, ed. 1990. *Beyond Goffman: Studies on Communication, Institution, and Social Interaction*. Mouton de Gruyter.

Riley, John. 1969. "Price Explains Functions of Open Expression Group." *Daily Pennsylvanian*, December 4. https://dparchives.library.upenn.edu/.

Ripley, Suzanne. 1965. "The Ecology and Social Behavior of the Ceylon Gray Langur." PhD diss., University of California, Berkeley.

Robbins, Ira P. 1977. Review of *Doing Justice*, by Andrew von Hirsch. *Columbia Law Review* 77 (1): 153–59.

Rogow, Pamela. 2013. "Pointing out G'town's Adam Kendon, 'Father of gesture.'" *Chestnut Hill Local*, November 29. https://www.chestnuthilllocal.com/stories/pointing-out-gtowns-adam-kendon-father-of-gesture,4274.

Rose, Dan. 1973. "Social Bonding Practices in an Afro-American Urban Locale." PhD diss., University of Wisconsin.

Rose, Dan. 1981. *Energy Transition and the Local Community*. University of Pennsylvania Press.

Rose, Dan. 1987. *Black American Street Life: South Philadelphia, 1969–1971*. University of Pennsylvania Press.

Rosner, Burton S., and Leonard B. Meyer. 1982. "Melodic Processes and the Perception of Music." In *The Psychology of Music*, edited by Diana Deutsch. Academic.

Rosner, Burton S., and Leonard B. Meyer. 1986. "The Perceptual Roles of Melodic Process, Contour, and Form." *Music Perception* 4 (1): 1–39.

Roszak, Theodore, ed. 1968. *The Dissenting Academy*. Pantheon.

Ruby, Jay. 2005. "The Last 20 Years of Visual Anthropology: A Critical Review." *Visual Studies* 20 (2): 159–70.

Ruby, Jay. 2015. "Remembering Erving Goffman." In *Bios Sociologicus: The Erving Goffman Archives*, edited by Dmitri N. Shalin. University of Nevada Las Vegas, CDC Publications. http://cdclv.unlv.edu/archives/interactionism/goffman/ruby.html.

Ruesch, Jürgen, and Gregory Bateson. 1951. *Communication: The Social Matrix of Psychiatry*. W.W. Norton.

Ruesch, Jürgen, and Weldon Kees. 1956. *Nonverbal Communication: Notes on the Visual Perception of Human Relations*. University of California Press.

Sabetta, Lorenzo, and Eviatar Zerubavel. 2019. "Times of Sociology: Eviatar Zerubavel in Conversation with Lorenzo Sabetta." *Sociologica* 13 (2): 55–74.

Sacks, Harvey, Emanuel Schegloff, and Gail Jefferson. 1974. "A Simplest Systematics for the Organization of Turn-Taking in Conversation." *Language* 50 (4): 696–735.

Sanday, Peggy Reeves, ed. 1976. *Anthropology and the Public Interest: Fieldwork and Theory*. Academic.

Sankoff, Gillian. 1974. "A Quantitative Paradigm for the Study of Communicative Competence." In *Explorations in the Ethnography of Speaking*, edited by Richard Bauman and Joel Sherzer. Cambridge University Press.

Sankoff, Gillian. 1980. *The Social Life of Language*. University of Pennsylvania Press.

Sapir, J. David. 1979. "Speaking of Meaning." A Review of *Meaning in Anthropology*, by Keith H. Basso and Henry A. Selby. *Language in Society* 8 (2): 245–70.

Sapir, J. David. 2014. "Seeing the Photographs Erving Said, 'Do You Think That Those Pictures Say Anything About Reality? Absolutely Not.'" In *Bios Sociologicus: The Erving Goffman Archives*, edited by Dmitri N. Shalin. University of Nevada Las Vegas, CDC Publications. https://cdclv.unlv.edu/archives/interactionism/goffman/sapir_14.html.

Sapir, J. David, and J. Christopher Crocker, eds. 1977. *The Social Use of Metaphor: Essays on the Anthropology of Rhetoric*. University of Pennsylvania Press.

Sarfatti-Larson, Magali. 2009. "Goffman Was One of the Most Memorable People I Have Met in the Academia [*sic*] Because He Was Not an Academic." In *Bios Sociologicus: The Erving Goffman Archives*, edited by Dmitri N. Shalin. University of Nevada Las Vegas, CDC Publications. https://cdclv.unlv.edu/archives/interactionism/goffman/larson_09.html.

Saxton, Calvin. 2002. "Helen Swick Perry (1911–2001)." *Contemporary Psychoanalysis* 38 (1): 153–54.

Scheff, Thomas J. 2006. *Goffman Unbound! A New Paradigm for Social Sciences*. Paradigm.

Schegloff, Emanuel A., Elinor Ochs, and Sandra A. Thompson. 1996. "Introduction." In *Interaction and Grammar*, edited by Elinor Ochs, Emanuel A. Schegloff, and Sandra A. Thompson. Cambridge University Press.

Schelling, Thomas. 2015. "If There Were a Nobel Prize for Sociology and/or Social Psychology Goffman Would Deserve to Be the First One Considered." *Bios Sociologicus: The Erving Goffman Archives*, edited by Dmitri N. Shalin. University of Nevada Las Vegas, CDC Publications. https://cdclv.unlv.edu/archives/interactionism/goffman/schelling_15.html.

Scherer, Joanna Cohan. 2013. "The Society for Visual Anthropology's Visual Research Conference: The First Twenty-Four Years (1985–2008)." *Visual Anthropology Review* 28 (2): 83–119.

Schiffrin, Deborah. 1977. "Opening Encounters." *American Sociological Review* 42 (5): 679–91.

Schiffrin, Deborah. 1980. "Meta-Talk: Organizational and Evaluative Brackets in Discourse." *Sociological Inquiry* 50 (3–4): 199–236.

Schiffrin, Deborah. 1982. "Discourse Markers: Semantic Resource for the Construction of Conversation." PhD diss., University of Pennsylvania.

Schiffrin, Deborah. 1996. "Interactional Sociolinguistics." In *Sociolinguistics and Language Teaching*, edited by Sandra Lee McKay and Nancy H. Hornberger. Cambridge University Press.

Schiffrin, Deborah. 2009. "Erving Said That the Rigor and Formal Nature of Linguistics Could Add Status to the Just-Beginning Study of Social Interaction." In *Bios Sociologicus: The Erving Goffman Archives*, edited by Dmitri N. Shalin. University of Nevada Las Vegas, CDC Publications. https://digitalscholarship. unlv.edu/goffman_archives/59.

Schiffrin, Deborah, Deborah Tannen, and Heidi E. Hamilton. 2015. "Introduction." In *The Handbook of Discourse Analysis*, edited by Deborah Tannen, Heidi E. Hamilton, and Deborah Schiffrin. 2nd ed. Wiley Blackwell.

Scholte, Bob. 1972. "Toward a Reflective and Critical Anthropology." In *Reinventing Anthropology*, edited by Dell H. Hymes. Pantheon.

Schwartzman, Helen B. 1992. Review of *Collegial Discourse*, by Allen D. Grimshaw. *American Ethnologist* 19 (2): 389.

Scollon, Ron. 1995. Review of *Collegial Discourse*, by Allen D. Grimshaw, and *What's Going on Here?*, edited by Allen D. Grimshaw et al. *Language in Society* 24 (3): 428–32.

Scollon, Suzanne Wong. 2004. "Interview of Dell H. Hymes." *Reed College Oral History Project*. https://alumni.reed.edu/oralhistory/pdfs/HymesD1950.pdf.

Sebeok, Thomas A., ed. 1968. *Animal Communication: Techniques of Study and Results of Research*. Indiana University Press.

Sebeok, Thomas A. 1975. "The Semiotic Web: A Chronicle of Prejudices." *Bulletin of Literary Semiotics* 2:1–63.

Sebeok, Thomas A. 1977. "Teaching Semiotics: Report on a Pilot Program." *Semiotic Scene* 1 (2): 23–30.

Sebeok, Thomas A. 1991. *Semiotics in the United States*. Indiana University Press.

Sebeok, Thomas A., Alfred S. Hayes, and Mary Catherine Bateson, eds. 1964. *Approaches to Semiotics: Transactions of the Indiana University Conference on Paralinguistics and Kinesics*. Mouton.

Sebeok, Thomas A., and Alexandra Ramsay, eds. 1969. *Approaches to Animal Communication*. Mouton.

Sebeok, Thomas A., and Robert Rosenthal, eds. 1981. *Conference on the Clever Hans Phenomenon: Communication with Horses, Whales, Apes, and People.* New York Academy of Sciences.

Shalin, Dmitri N. 2023. "Erving Goffman: The Social Science Maverick: Assessing the Interdisciplinary Impact of the Most Cited American Sociologist." *Journal of Contemporary Ethnography* 52 (6): 752–77.

Shalin, Dmitri N. 2025. *Erving Manuel Goffman: Biographical Sources of Sociological Imagination.* Routledge.

Sharrock, Wes. 1999. "The Omnipotence of the Actor: Erving Goffman on the 'Definition of the Situation.'" In *Goffman and Social Organization: Studies of a Sociological Legacy*, edited by Greg Smith. Routledge.

Sherzer, Joel. 1971. "Conference on Interaction Ethology." *Language Sciences* 14:19–21.

Sherzer, Joel. 1973a. "On Linguistic Semantics and Linguistic Subdisciplines: A Review Article." *Language in Society* 2 (2): 269–89.

Sherzer, Joel. 1973b. "Verbal and Nonverbal Deixis: The Pointed Lip Gesture Among the San Blas Cuna." *Language in Society* 2 (1): 117–31.

Sherzer, Joel. 1976. *An Areal-Typological Study of American Indian Languages North of Mexico.* North-Holland Publishing.

Sherzer, Joel. 1978. Review of *The Behavior of Communicating*, by W. John Smith. *Language in Society* 7 (3): 435–38.

Sherzer, Joel. 1983. *Kuna Ways of Speaking: An Ethnographic Perspective.* University of Texas Press.

Sherzer, Joel. 2014. "How I Became a Linguist." *Linguist List*, April 1. https://linguistlist.org/issues/25/25-1539/.

Sherzer, Joel, Barbara Johnstone, and William Marcellino. 2010. "Dell H. Hymes: An Intellectual Sketch." *Language in Society* 39 (3): 301–5.

Shuman, Amy. 1981. "The Rhetoric of Portions." *Western Folklore* 40 (1): 72–80.

Shuman, Amy. 1986. *Storytelling Rights: The Uses of Oral and Written Texts by Urban Adolescents.* Cambridge University Press.

Shuman, Amy. 2006. "Entitlement and Empathy in Personal Narrative." *Narrative Inquiry* 16 (1): 148–55.

Shuman, Amy. 2013. "Goffman, Erving." In *Theory in Social and Cultural Anthropology: An Encyclopedia*, edited by R. Jon McGee and Richard L. Warms. Sage.

Shuman, Amy, and Carol Bohmer. 2012. "The Stigmatized Vernacular: Political Asylum and the Politics of Visibility/Recognition." *Journal of Folklore Research* 49 (2): 199–226.

Shuy, Roger W., ed. 1973a. *Sociolinguistics: Current Trends and Prospects* [Report of the 23rd Annual Round Table Meeting on Linguistics and Language Studies]. Georgetown University Press.

Shuy, Roger W. 1973b. "Introduction." In *Sociolinguistics: Current Trends and Prospects* [Report of the 23rd Annual Round Table Meeting on Linguistics and Language Studies], edited by Roger W. Shuy. Georgetown University Press.

Shuy, Roger W. 1990. "A Brief History of American Sociolinguistics 1949–1989." In *North American Contributions to History of Linguistics*, edited by Francis P. Dineen and E. F. K. Koerner. John Benjamins.

Sidener-Young, Diane. 1994. "Ethnographic Comparison of Four Protestant Congregations." PhD diss., University of Pennsylvania.

Sigman, Stuart J. 1981. "Some Notes on Conversational Fission." *Working Papers in Sociolinguistics*, no. 91. Southwest Educational Development Laboratory.

Sigman, Stuart J. 1987. *A Perspective on Social Communication*. Lexington Books.

Silver, Michael. 1972. "Univ. Announces New Thematic Programs." *Daily Pennsylvanian*, November 6. https://dparchives.library.upenn.edu/.

Silverstein, Michael. 2010. "Dell Hathaway Hymes." *Language* 86 (4): 933–39.

Smardon, Regina. 2005. "Where the Action Is: The Microsociological Turn in Educational Research." *Educational Researcher* 34 (1): 20–25.

Smelser, Neil. 2009. "At the End of That First Year or So I Would Say That I Became as Close to Erving as Anyone Else in the Sociology Department." In *Bios Sociologicus: The Erving Goffman Archives*, edited by Dmitri N. Shalin. University of Nevada Las Vegas, CDC Publications. http://cdclv.unlv.edu/archives/interactionism/goffman/smelser_09.html.

Smith, David M. 1982. *Using Literacy Outside of School: An Ethnographic Investigation*. Final report to National Institute of Education. https://eric.ed.gov/?id=ED225129.

Smith, David M. 2002. "The Challenge of Urban Ethnography." In *Ethnography and Schools: Qualitative Approaches to the Study of Education*, edited by Yali Zou and Henry T. Trueba. Rowman and Littlefield.

Smith, Greg, ed. 1999. *Goffman and Social Organization: Studies in a Sociological Legacy*. Routledge.

Smith, Gregory W. H. 2003. "Chrysalid Goffman: A Note on 'Some Characteristics of Response to Depicted Experience.'" *Symbolic Interaction* 26 (4): 645–48.

Smith, Greg. 2006. *Erving Goffman*. Routledge.

Smith, Gregory W. H. 2022a. "W. Lloyd Warner (1898–1970)." In *Goffman Handbuch: Leben—Werk—Wirkung*, edited by Karl Lenz and Robert Hettlage. J. B. Metzler.

Smith, Gregory W. H. 2022b. "Georg Simmel (1858–1918)." In *Goffman Handbuch: Leben—Werk—Wirkung*, edited by Karl Lenz and Robert Hettlage. J. B. Metzler.

Smith, Greg. 2022c. "Goffman on Goffman: A 1975 Letter." *Przegląd Socjologiczny* 71 (4): 9–22.

Smith, Gregory W. H. 2022d. "Goffman's Empirical Work." In *Goffman Handbuch: Leben—Werk—Wirkung*, edited by Karl Lenz and Robert Hettlage. J. B. Metzler.

Smith, Gregory W. H., and Yves Winkin. 2012. "Comment devenir un chercheur interstitial: W. Lloyd Warner, premier mentor d'Erving Goffman." In *Erving Goffman et l'ordre de l'interaction*, edited by Daniel Cefaï and Laurent Perreau. Éditions du CURAPP.

Smith, Greg, and Yves Winkin. 2013. "Working the Chicago Interstices: Warner and Goffman's Intellectual Formation." In *The Chicago School Diaspora: Epistemology and Substance*, edited by Gary L. Bowden and Jacqueline Low. McGill-Queen's University Press.

Smith, W. John. 1977. *The Behavior of Communicating: An Ethological Approach*. Harvard University Press.

Smith, W. John, Julia Chase, and Anna Katz Lieblich. 1974. "Tongue Showing: A Facial Display of Humans and Other Primate Species." *Semiotica* 11 (3): 201–46.

"Sol Worth (1922–1977)." 1977. *Studies in Visual Communication* 4 (2): 66–77. https://repository.upenn.edu/svc/vol4/iss2/2.

Solomon, Joseph C. 1960. Review of *Advances in Psychiatry*, by Mabel Blake Cohen. *International Journal of Group Psychotherapy* 10 (4): 476–77.

Sommer, Robert, and Humphrey Osmond. 1960. "Symptoms of Institutional Care." *Social Problems* 8 (3): 254–63.

Streeck, Jürgen, and Siri Mehus. 2005. "Microethnography: The Study of Practices." In *Handbook of Language and Social Interaction*, edited by Kristine L. Fitch and Robert E. Sanders. Lawrence Erlbaum.

Stubbs, Michael W. 1991. Review of *Collegial Discourse*, by Allen D. Grimshaw. *Language* 67 (4): 832–35.

Sutton-Smith, Brian. 1981a. *The Folk-Stories of Children*. University of Pennsylvania Press.

Sutton-Smith, Brian. 1981b. *A History of Children's Play*. University of Pennsylvania Press.

Szasz, Thomas S. 1971. "American Association for the Abolition of Involuntary Mental Hospitalization." *American Journal of Psychiatry* 127 (12): 1698.

Szwed, John F. 1966. "Gossip, Drinking, and Social Control: Consensus and Communication in a Newfoundland Parish." *Ethnology* 5 (4): 434–41.

Szwed, John F., ed. 1970. *Black America*. Basic Books.

Szwed, John F. 1972. "An American Anthropological Dilemma: The Politics of Afro-American Culture." In *Reinventing Anthropology*, edited by Dell H. Hymes. Pantheon.

Szwed, John F. 2005. *Crossovers: Essays on Race, Music, and American Culture*. University of Pennsylvania Press.

Szwed, John F. 2016. "Working with Roger: A Memoir." *Western Folklore* 75 (3/4): 421–433.

Szwed, John F., and Roger D. Abrahams. 1978. *Afro-American Folk Culture: An Annotated Bibliography of Materials from North, Central and South America and the West Indies*. Institute for the Study of Human Issues.

Szwed, John F., and Norman E. Witten Jr. 1970. *Afro-American Anthropology: Contemporary Perspectives*. Free Press.

Tagliamonte, Sali A. 2015. *Making Waves: The Story of Variationist Sociolinguistics*. Wiley Blackwell.

Takaragawa, Stephanie. 2020. "History of Society for Visual Anthropology." *Oxford Bibliographies*. https://www.oxfordbibliographies.com/display/document/obo-9780199766567/obo-9780199766567-0232.xml.

Tannen, Deborah. 1978. *An Informally Annotated Bibliography of Sociolinguistics*. Department of Linguistics, University of California, Berkeley. https://files.eric.ed.gov/fulltext/ED166951.pdf.

Taylor, Arthur John. 1972. *Laissez-Faire and State Intervention in Nineteenth-Century Britain*. Palgrave.

Tedlock, Dennis. 1976. "From Prayer to Reprimand." In *Language in Religious Practice*, edited by William J. Samarin. Newbury.

Tedlock, Dennis. 1983. *The Spoken Word and the Work of Interpretation*. University of Pennsylvania Press.

Tedlock, Dennis, and Barbara Tedlock, eds. 1975. *Teachings from the American Earth: Indian Religion and Philosophy*. Liveright.

Toye, Margaret. 2004. "The Interaction Order and the Joint Production of Discourse." *University of Pennsylvania Working Papers in Linguistics* 10 (1). https://repository.upenn.edu/pwpl/vol10/iss1/18.

Travis, Jeremy, Bruce Western, and F. Stevens Redburn, eds. 2014. *The Growth of Incarceration in the United States: Causes and Consequences*. National Academies Press.

Treviño, A. Javier, ed. 2003. *Goffman's Legacy*. Rowman and Littlefield.

Trix, Frances. 1993. *Spiritual Discourse: Learning with an Islamic Master*. University of Pennsylvania Press.

Turner, Charles. 2011. "Sacred Sociology: The Life and Times of Philip Rieff." *Theory, Culture & Society* 28 (3): 80–105.

Urban, Greg. 2016. "Anthony F. C. Wallace, 1923–2015: A Biographical Memoir." *Biographical Memoirs*. National Academy of Sciences. http://www.nasonline.org/publications/biographical-memoirs/memoir-pdfs/wallace-anthony.pdf.

Verhoeven, Jef C. 1993. "An Interview with Erving Goffman, 1980." *Research on Language and Social Interaction* 26 (3): 317–48.

Vienne, Philippe. 2010. "The Enigma of the Total Institution: Rethinking the Hughes-Goffman Intellectual Relationship." *Sociologica* 2:1–30.

Vienne, Philippe. 2022. "Everett C. Hughes (1897–1983)." In *Goffman Handbuch: Leben—Werk—Wirkung*, edited by Karl Lenz and Robert Hettlage. J. B. Metzler.

von Cranach, Mario, Klaus Foppa, Wolf Lepenies, and Detliev Ploog, eds. 1979. *Human Ethology: Claims and Limits of a New Discipline*. Cambridge University Press and Éditions de la Maison des Sciences de l'Homme.

von Hirsch, Andrew. 1976a. *Doing Justice: The Choice of Punishment; The Report of the Committee for the Study of Incarceration*. Hill & Wang.

von Hirsch, Andrew. 1976b. "The Aims of Imprisonment." *Current History* 71 (418): 1–5, 33.

Wahl-Jorgensen, Karin. 2004. "How Not to Found a Field: New Evidence on the Origins of Mass Communication Research." *Journal of Communication* 54 (3): 547–64.

Wallace, Anthony F. C. 1962. Review of *Asylums*, by Erving Goffman. *American Anthropologist* 64 (6): 1323.

Walter Reed Army Institute of Research. 1958. *Symposium on Preventive and Social Psychiatry*. Government Printing Office.

Weigle, Marta. 1988. Review of *A Musical View of the Universe*, by Ellen B. Basso. *Journal of Anthropological Research* 42 (4): 598–99.

Wenger, Etienne. 1998. *Communities of Practice: Learning, Meaning and Identity*. Cambridge University Press.

Weninger, Csilla, and J. Patrick Williams. 2022. "Goffman and Sociolinguistics." In *The Routledge International Handbook of Goffman Studies*, edited by Michael Hviid Jacobsen and Greg Smith. Routledge.

Wenner-Gren Foundation for Anthropological Research. 1967. *Annual Report 1967*. Wenner-Gren Foundation for Anthropological Research.

Wenner-Gren Foundation for Anthropological Research. 1970. *Annual Report 1970*. Wenner-Gren Foundation for Anthropological Research.

Wilder, Carol. 1979. "The Palo Alto Group: Difficulties and Directions of the Interactional View for Human Communication Research." *Human Communication Research* 5 (2): 171–86.

Wilson, Robert N. 1959. Review of *Symposium on Preventive and Social Psychiatry*. *American Sociological Review* 24 (3): 432–33.

Winkin, Yves. 1983. "The French (Re)presentation of Goffman's *Presentation* and Other Books." *Theory, Culture and Society* 2 (1): 47–55.

Winkin, Yves. 1984a. "Elements pour une histoire sociale des sciences sociales Americaines: Une chronique; Entretien avec Erving Goffman." *Actes de la Recherche en Sciences Sociales* 54:85–87.

Winkin, Yves. 1984b. "Hymes' Theory of Ethnography." *Papers in Linguistics 17 (1): 43–51.*

Winkin, Yves. 1988a. *Erving Goffman: Les moments et leurs hommes.* Éditions du Seuil et Éditions de Minuit.

Winkin, Yves. 1988b. *Gregory Bateson: Premier état d'un heritage.* Éditions du Seuil.

Winkin, Yves. 1989. "Goffman, Erving." *International Encyclopedia of Communications,* edited by George Gerbner, vol. 2. Oxford University Press.

Winkin, Yves. 1990. "Goffman et les femmes." *Actes de la Recherche en Sciences Sociales* 83:57–61.

Winkin, Yves. 1993a. "Erving Goffman sur le terrain." *Actes de la Recherche en Sciences Sociales* 100:68–69.

Winkin, Yves. 1993b. "Interaction: Entre Goffman et Bourdieu." In *Dictionnaire encyclopédique et critique de la communication,* edited by Lucien Sfez, vol. 1. Presses Universitaires de France.

Winkin, Yves. 1999. "Erving Goffman: What is a Life? The Uneasy Making of Intellectual Biography." In *Goffman and Social Organization: Studies in a Sociological Legacy,* edited by Greg Smith. Routledge.

Winkin, Yves. 2000. "Baltasound as the Symbolic Capital of Social Interaction." In *Erving Goffman,* edited by Gary Alan Fine and Gregory W. H. Smith, vol. 1. Sage.

Winkin, Yves. 2002. "Erving Goffman: La 'distance au rôle' en salle d'opération." *Actes de la Recherche en Sciences Sociales* 143:80–87.

Winkin, Yves. 2010. "Goffman's Greenings." In *The Contemporary Goffman,* edited by Michael Hviid Jacobsen. Routledge.

Winkin, Yves. 2015. "Goffman, marcheur urbain." In *Actualité d'Erving Goffman: de l'interaction à l'institution,* edited by Pascal Lardellier. L'Harmattan.

Winkin, Yves. 2020. "Goffman, Erving." In *Dictionnaire international Bourdieu*, edited by Gisèle Sapiro. CNRS Editions.

Winkin, Yves. 2022a. *D'Erving à Goffman: Une œuvre performée?* MkF Éditions.

Winkin, Yves. 2022b. "Erving Goffman: The Travelling Hermit." *Etnografia e Ricera Qualitativa* 15 (1): 153–74.

Winkin, Yves. 2022c. "Life and Work of Goffman." In *Goffman Handbuch: Leben—Werk—Wirkung*, edited by Karl Lenz and Robert Hettlage. J. B. Metzler.

Winkin, Yves. 2022d. "Goffman à St. Elizabeths: Comment reconstituer son regard?" In *Penser l'enfermement: Anciens et nouveaux visages de l'institution totale*, edited by Philippe Vienne, Christophe Dargère, and Stéphane Héas. Presses Universitaires de Grenoble.

Winkin, Yves. 2022e. "The Cradle: Introduction to the mediastudies.press Edition." In *Communication Conduct in an Island Community*, by Erving Goffman. mediastudies.press. https://www.mediastudies.press/communication-conduct-in-an-island-community.

Winkin, Yves. 2022f. "Ray Birdwhistell (1918–1994) and Kinesics." In *Goffman Handbuch: Leben—Werk—Wirkung*, edited by Karl Lenz and Robert Hettlage. J. B. Metzler.

Winkin, Yves. 2022g. "Pierre Bourdieu (1930–2002)." In *Goffman Handbuch: Leben—Werk—Wirkung*, edited by Karl Lenz and Robert Hettlage. J. B. Metzler.

Winkin, Yves. 2023. "Goffman, le scopophile qui ne voulait pas être photographié: Propositions pour une biographie construite." In *Actualité d'Erving Goffman: Acte 2; Relations, identités, communautés*, edited by Pascal Lardellier. L'Harmattan.

Winkin, Yves, and Wendy Leeds-Hurwitz. 2013. *Erving Goffman: A Critical Introduction to Media and Communication Theory*. Peter Lang.

Worth, Sol. 1972a. "Toward an Anthropological Politics of Symbolic Forms." In *Reinventing Anthropology*, edited by Dell H. Hymes. Pantheon.

Worth, Sol. 1972b. *Through Navajo Eyes: An Exploration in Film Communication and Anthropology*. Indiana University Press.

Worth, Sol. 1974. "Editor's Introduction." *Studies in the Anthropology of Visual Communication* 1 (1): 1–2. https://repository.upenn.edu/svc/vol1/iss1/1.

Worth, Sol. 1976. "Editor's Introduction." *Studies in the Anthropology of Visual Communication* 3 (2): 65–68. https://repository.upenn.edu/svc/vol3/iss2/1.

Worth, Sol. 1980. "Margaret Mead and the Shift from 'Visual Anthropology' to the 'Anthropology of Visual Communication.'" *Studies in Visual Communication* 6 (1): 3. https://repository.upenn.edu/server/api/core/bitstreams/5dd6193f-7151-4b53-987b-e3abc1df501a/content.

Worth, Sol. 1981. *Studying Visual Communication*, edited by Larry Gross. University of Pennsylvania Press.

Worth, Sol, and John Adair. 1970. "Navajo Filmmakers." *American Anthropologist* 72 (1): 9–34.

Wrong, Dennis. 1990. "Imagining the Real." In *Authors of Their Own Lives: Intellectual Biographies by Twenty American Sociologists*, edited by Bennett M. Berger. University of California Press.

Zabor, Margaret Ruth. 1978. "Essaying Metacommunication: A Survey and Contextualization of Communication Research." PhD diss., Indiana University.

Zerubavel, Eviatar. 1979. *Patterns of Time in Hospital Life: A Sociological Perspective*. University of Chicago Press.

Zerubavel, Eviatar. 2024. "*Frame Analysis*: Erving Goffman and the Sociocognitive Organization of Experience." *Symbolic Interaction* 47 (4): 525–37.

Zimmerman, Don H. 1995. Review of *What's Going on Here?*, by Allen Grimshaw. *Contemporary Sociology* 24 (1): 112–13.

Index

Fernandez, James, 209

Feuerhahn, Wolf, 362

fieldwork, 95, 107, 139, 203, 368; by Goffman, 23; cross–cultural, 95

Fillmore, Charles, 248; and MAP, 258–9, 265–71, 276–81, 285, 290

Fillmore, Lily Wong, 276–7, 285, 290

film, 63, 74, 76, 306, 373, 380; and Goffman, 36, 39–40, 87, 91; and MAP, 249, 257–79, 289, 310–13, 379; and Worth, 52, 77–80, 109. *See also* sound–image–recording

Fine, Gary Alan: profile: 99–100

Finnegan, Ruth, 209

Fishman, Joshua, 5, 160, 311, 352, 356, 358; and IJSL, 171–2

Fitts, Donald D., 213

folklore, as a discipline, 45, 57, 85–6, 130, 209, 214, 300, 334

Folklore and Social Science (conference), 129, 232

Fondation Royaumont, 272–3

Ford Foundation, 6, 43, 104, 215

Foster, Michael, 95

Fought, John G., 62, 72, 83, 87, 251, 349; and CCCC, 204; and Goffman, 91, 149, 164; and LCS, 210, 213; and LII, 197–8, 201–3; and LiS, 164; and Monographs in Folklore, 153, 184n120; and Native American Languages and Verbal Arts Program, 203, 221; and Native American use of language, 154–5, 203, 221; and SP, 195; and SSB, 207–8; and students, 89, 98, 103–4, 109; profile: 373–4

Fowler, Susan, 242

Fox, Renée C., 61, 97, 100, 202, 383, 387, 390n27; and Comparative Ethnographic Analysis conference, 304–7; and Goffman, 5, 83, 89, 200, 370–2; profile: 371–2

Fox, Robin, 243

Frake, Charles, 35–6, 272

Frappier–Mazur, Lucienne, 209; profile: 387

Freeman, Howard E., 44, 47

Friedrich, Paul, 57, 160

Friedson, Eliot, 17

Frijda, Nico H., 325

Fromm–Reichmann, Frieda, 23, 30

Fuller, Lon, 43

Furstenberg, Frank, 252

Gaeffke, Peter, 209; profile: 388–9

Gamson, William A., 44

Gans, Herbert, 17

Gardner, Carol Brooks: profile: 105

Garfinkel, Harold, 28, 60, 128, 345, 350, 356; and Goffman, 42, 45, 55, 181n63; and Saturday group, 34

Garland, David, 330–1

Goffman, 46, 51–5, 60, 65, 115n54, 134, 176, 187n188, 219, 296–8, 343–5, 354, 357, 370, 372–3; and Goodenough, 56–7; and Grimshaw, 247–52; and GSE, 58, 64, 88, 114n38, 380–1; and Harvard, 44; and Interaction Ethology conference, 232–6, 240, 315n9; and Labov, 48n39, 66–73; and LCS, 210–14; and LII, 195–202; and linguistics, 83, 359; and LiS, 160–72; and MAP, 258–69, 285, 288, 290, 313–14; and Native American Languages and Verbal Arts Program, 203; and NIE, 109, 368, 381–2; and Reinventing Anthropology conference, 136–7; and Sacks, 321n120; and Sapir, 113n30, 368; and Saturday group, 33–6; and SAVICOM, 173; and sociolinguistics, 348–9, 356; and SP, 194–5, 361; and SSB; and SSRC, 245–6, 346; and students, 89–109, 298, 353; and *Working Papers in Sociolinguistics*, 299–300; and Worth, 77–8, 87, 121n165; profile: 55–63

Hymes, Virginia D., 83–4, 57, 72, 83, 202; and Comparative Ethnographic Analysis conference, 304–7; and Goffman, 55, 149, 247–8; and LCS, 210–13; and MAP, 267; and Native American Languages and Verbal Arts Program, 203; and Native American use of language, 154; and students, 95, 109; profile: 377–8

Imamura, Ako, 210

Indiana University: Goffman visit, 248, 292–6; Paralinguistics and Kinesics conference, 233–4; Press, 150, 161

institutional: biography, 3; history, 8–9

interaction ethology, 231, 239, 346. *See also* human ethology

Interaction Ethology (conference), 231–40, 343

interaction order, 37, 106, 238, 338

interdisciplinarity, 6–7, 348–51, 362–3, 382; and MAP, 254; and SSRC, 254; at Chicago, 9, 15–16, 18–19, 22; at Penn, 57, 77, 84, 104, 110, 222, 353–7; how to fail at, 308–14, 351–3. *See also* multidisciplinarity

interdisciplinary research, 6–8, 13, 27, 32–3, 40, 127, 198, 222, 334, 356, 361–2. *See also* cross–disciplinary, multidisciplinary, transdisciplinary

International Communication Association (ICA), 108

International Encyclopedia of Communications, 385

International Journal of the Sociology of Language (IJSL), 171–2

interview(s): as research tool, 3, 8–9, 360; by Goffman, 372; Goffman's analysis of, 305; Goffman's opinion of, 14n6; Goffman viewing, 88, 91; of Goffman, 18–19, 103

invisible college(s), 357–9, 362; and interdisciplinarity, 363; and students, 89, 95, 108, 111; definition, 4; Goffman's, 5, 9, 12–13, 31, 38, 44–6, 50–1, 80, 175, 190, 344; Goffman's role in, 334

Irvine, Judith T.: and Goffman, 42, 69, 252; profile: 96

Jackson, Kenneth L., 163

Jacobsen, Michael Hviid, 2, 243

Jakobson, Roman, 60

Jansen, Sue Curry, 8

Jaworski, Gary D., 20, 41

Labov, William, 36, 85, 193, 374; and ASC, 61, 86, 379; and CC, 133, 143, 146, 154, 158, 181n101; and CCC, 127–8; and CCCC, 203–7; and Comparative Ethnographic Analysis conference, 304–6; and CUE, 70, 138, 150; and Ethnography of Speaking conference, 302; and Goffman, 33, 39, 51, 55, 65–7, 71–3, 169, 344–5; and Grimshaw, 247–8, 250–1; and GSE, 87–8; and Hymes, 48n39, 60, 62, 64, 69-72, 354; and Interaction Ethology conference, 235–6; and LCS, 210, 213; and LII, 195–203; 221; and LiS, 163–4, 167, 169; and MAP, 263, 288, 309, 314; and sociolinguistics, 292, 346, 352; and SP, 194–5; and SSB, 207; and SSRC, 246, 253, 375; and students, 89, 91–2, 94, 97–109, 298, 353; profile: 64-73

Labov–Fanshel model, 279–80, 289, 291

Lakoff, Robin, 253, 258, 259

Lamb, Sidney, 35

Lambert, Wallace E., 352

language: and culture, 63, 72, 92, 210–11, 214, 369; and interaction, 222; and social interaction, 203, 347; and society, 83, 143, 149, 246, 344; in context, 195; in social life, 86, 304, 350; in society, 349; in use, 349, 360

Language Change and Variation (book series), 154

Language in Society (LiS), 84, 160–73, 197, 361, 393n91; and CUE, 86, 168; and Goffman, 11, 73, 76, 147, 152, 163–7, 336, 339, 345, 359; and IJSL, 172; and LII, 197–8, 201; and SSRC, 160–2, 177; anthology, 169–70; editorial board, 96, 134, 175; Grimshaw article on Goffman, 297

Lara–Braud, Jorge, 328

Larkin, James, 204

Lasswell, Harold D., 24

Leach, Edmund, 37, 63

Leach, MacEdward, 377

Leeds-Hurwitz, Wendy: profile: 108–10

Lemert, Ed, 38

Lieberson, Stanley, 296–7

Lievrouw, Leah A., 4

Linguistic Society of America (LSA), 61; Committee on Linguistics and the National Interest, 303; Summer Institute, 247, 252

linguistics: as a discipline, 148, 176, 207, 233–4, 246, 260, 325, 334; Goffman's opinion of, 102, 107, 240. *See also* ethnolinguistics; paralinguistics; sociolinguistics

Lipset, Seymour Martin, 40–1, 44

Lofland, John, 101, 297–8

Lomax, Alan, 257

Long, Michael H., 87; profile: 382

Louttit, Richard, 282

Lowie, Robert, 194

Luce, Robert Duncan, 216–17

Lynch, Barbara Ann: profile: 106–7

Meyerson, Martin, 142, 196, 215, 338, 370; and Benjamin Franklin professors, 217, 221; and Goffman 69; and Hymes, 62–3, 174

microanalysis of interaction, 106, 287, 213

micro–behavior, 73

microsociolinguistic work, 285

microsociology, 24, 27, 239

Milani, Tommaso M., 164

Miles, Josephine, 35

Miller, Ben, 384

Miller, George A.,44

Miller, Raymond, 6

Milmoe, Susan, 324

Minuchin, Salvador, 128–9

Moerman, Michael, 159

Monod, Jacques, 272

Moore, R. Laurence, 8

Moratorium, 218–19

Moreno, Jacob, 30–1

Morson, Gary Saul, 209; profile: 387

Mouton Publishers, 162, 172

Mullins, Nicholas C., 2, 133, 309

multidisciplinarity, 7, 9, 61, 68, 349. *See also* interdisciplinarity

multidisciplinary: coordination, 191–215; journal, 164; projects, 10–12, 191, 349; research, 7, 22, 33, 36, 40–1, 58, 63, 164, 216, 222, 334, 353. *See also* cross–disciplinary; interdisciplinary; transdisciplinary

multimodal communication, 287, 289

multimodality, 234, 250

Multiple Analysis Project (MAP): and Birdwhistell, 286–8; and development of sociolinguistics, 12; and Grant Foundation, 246, 311, 315n26; and Goffman, 256–8, 261–2, 266–75, 343; and NSF, 246, 256, 264–71, 275–9, 281-4, 311, 313; and SSRC, 245–7, 254, 259–60, 263, 278; conference at Penn, 285–6; design of, 244–7; goal, 254; lessons, 351–3, 361; original name, 231; publications, 288–90; reception, 290–92; timeline and participants, 254–84

Murray, Stephen O., 2–4, 8, 289, 309, 360–1

Nader, Laura, 136

National Endowment for the Humanities (NEH), 232, 251, 279; Goffman grant proposal to, 248–9, 343

National Film Board (of Canada), 77

National Institute for Child Health and Human Development (NICHD), 205

National Institute of Education (NIE), 368–9, 381–2; and Hymes, 109, 139; and *Working Papers in Sociolinguistics*, 299–300

National Institutes of Health (NIH), 43, 232

www.ingramcontent.com/pod-product-compliance
Lightning Source LLC
Chambersburg PA
CBHW020813270326
41928CB00006B/364